Western Societies

A Documentary History

VOLUME I

Western Societies

A Documentary History

Volume I
SECOND EDITION

Brian Tierney
Cornell University

Joan W. Scott
Institute for Advanced Study

Boston   Burr Ridge, IL   Dubuque, IA   Madison, WI   New York   San Francisco
St. Louis   Bangkok   Bogotá   Caracas   Lisbon   London   Madrid
Mexico City   Milan   New Delhi   Seoul   Singapore   Sydney   Taipei   Toronto

McGraw-Hill Higher Education

*A Division of The **McGraw-Hill** Companies*

WESTERN SOCIETIES: A DOCUMENTARY HISTORY VOLUME I,
SECOND EDITION

3 4 5 6 7 8 9 0 DOC/DOC 0 9 8 7 6 5 4 3 2 1 0

ISBN 0-07-064844-1

Editorial director: *Jane E. Vaicunas*
Senior sponsoring editor: *Lyn Uhl*
Developmental editor: *Donata Dettbarn*
Senior marketing manager: *Suzanne Daghlian*
Project manager: *Mary E. Powers*
Production supervisor: *Enboge Chong*
Designer: *Gino Cieslik*
Compositor: *Carlisle Communications, Ltd.*
Typeface: *10/12 Palatino (display font Optima)*
Printer: *R. R. Donnelley & Sons Company/Crawfordsville, IN*

Cover design: *Gino Cieslik*

Library of Congress Cataloging-in-Publication Data

Western societies : a documentary history / [compiled by] Brian
 Tierney, Joan W. Scott.—2nd ed.
   p.   cm.
  Includes bibliographical references.
  ISBN 0-07-064844-1 (v. 1).—ISBN 0-07-064845-X (v. 2)
  1. Civilization, Western Sources. 2. Europe—Civilization
Sources. I. Tierney, Brian. II. Scott, Joan W.
CB245.W4847   2000
909'.09821—dc21
                                                 99-30725
                                                   CIP

www.mhhe.com

Preface

HISTORIANS are always asking new questions of the past; that is why we need new collections of sources from time to time. This one includes readings drawn from many different types of material—poems, plays, chronicles, government records, letters, diaries, treatises of various kinds. In studying these sources we can enter into the life of past generations on their own terms, so to speak. Such study enhances our own personalities by making us more aware of the whole range of human thought and feeling. Historical study can also help us to understand our present-day society better by learning how its various characteristics—ideas and institutions, achievements and dilemmas—grew out of the life of the past.

Some of the new questions that historians ask arise out of contemporary concerns. Many students nowadays want to know more about women's roles and patterns of family structure in earlier times. Modern interest in ecological problems has led us to ask how people in other ages viewed their relationship to the natural environment. Concern over a possible future era of "diminishing expectations" may stimulate questions about earlier theories of human progress (or regression or cyclical recurrence). Experience of social change in the modern world encourages new forms of writing on social history and especially on the sources of social conflict. The difficulties that many less developed countries encounter in seeking to modernize their economies redirect our attention to the processes of industrialization, urbanization, and demographic expansion that first created a modern society in the Western world. In creating this collection we have tried to bear in mind all these interests of recent historians.

The most evident change in the teaching of history at American colleges during the past decades has been the great growth of courses in the history of women and the family. This interest has proved to be more than a mere passing fashion (if it ever seemed to be that). Scholars in the field have explored new ranges of source material and raised significant new problems for research. It seems important that such work should not remain isolated in courses on Women's History but should be drawn into the mainstream of teaching on the evolution of Western society. One purpose of this book is to make this task easier. We have included many readings that deal with women's roles and family relationships, and every chapter contains material by or about women.

A major problem for makers of anthologies is that new interests do not supplant old ones, but rather supplement them. Historians deal with the whole life of people in society. And to understand the life of any people adequately we need to ask about their religion, their economy, their form of government, their whole world picture. These are subjects of traditional historical disciplines—"history of religions," "economic history," "political history," "history of ideas." Most teachers of Western Civilization courses will not want to neglect such topics. We have aimed therefore to provide a framework of readings illustrating the traditional themes of Western history, but also to include within the framework many readings related to the newer interests of historians.

This new edition of *Western Societies* builds on the strengths of its predecessor. The work retains the basic structure and focus of the original edition. The principal change is that we have included dozens of new readings, including new source materials on women's history. The headnotes to each selection have been rewritten and expanded so as to provide more context for the reader. We have also included in the headnotes questions for students to focus their attention on key points or controversial issues in the source material that follows. Among the many new readings in this edition are selections from Aristophanes, Plato, Aristotle, Plutarch, St. Perpetua, Thomas Aquinas, Dante, Chaucer, Christine de Pisan, Luther, Voltaire, Napoleon Bonaparte, Mary Shelley, Christopher Mayhew, Otto von Bismarck, Vera Brittain, Leon Trotsky, Adolf Hitler, Mikhail Gorbachev, Herbert Marcuse, Pope John Paul II.

The authors wish to thank Saphira Baker for research assistance and Ellen Furlough for her contribution to the organization of material in volume II.

Contents

II
GREEK CIVILIZATION—FROM MYTH TO POLIS
(C. 800–C. 400 B.C.)

III
GREEK CIVILIZATION—PHILOSOPHY, POLITICS, AND SOCIETY (C. 400–C. 330 B.C.)

IV
HELLENISM AND ROME—FROM REPUBLIC TO EMPIRE

V

CHRISTIANITY AND THE FALL OF ROME

Roman Christianity and Northern Europe   172

Charlemagne   178

VII

MEDIEVAL FOUNDATIONS—FEUDALISM, CHURCH REFORM, AND CRUSADE

Feudal Institutions   188

X
AN AGE OF RENAISSANCE—DECLINE AND RENEWAL, 1300–1500

XI
REFORMATIONS—PROTESTANT AND CATHOLIC

XIII
THE SEARCH FOR ORDER—ABSOLUTISM AND ARISTOCRACY

XIV
THE SEARCH FOR ORDER—CONSTITUTIONALISM AND OLIGARCHY

Western Societies

A Documentary History

VOLUME I

PART ONE

THE ANCIENT NEAR EAST— NATURE, GODS, AND HUMANS

The first great civilizations of the Near East grew up in Egypt and Mesopotamia during the fourth and third millennia before Christ. The Hebrew people formed their first kingdom much later, about 1000 B.C. It was a rather petty state, rather trivial in its impact on the great nations of the ancient world. But, for Western culture, the Hebrew experience is all important. For many centuries the beliefs of Western people about the origin and destiny of the human race, their attitudes toward nature, and their views on the proper relationship between men and women were profoundly affected by the books of the Old Testament. The gods of Egypt and Mesopotamia were forgotten for many centuries; the god of Israel has been worshipped continuously. The records of Egypt and Mesopotamia had to be rediscovered by modern archeologists; the sacred writings of the Hebrews were never lost, and they influenced Western civilization during the whole process of its development. This raises an important question for the student of Western origins: In what ways did the Hebrews merely assimilate and transmit elements of earlier Near Eastern cultures? And in what ways did they make a distinctive contribution of their own?

IN THE BEGINNINGS

From the beginning of history humans have tried to understand the origins of the universe. The ancient Near Eastern civilizations recorded several stories of primeval creation. They provide an appropriate first approach to the thought patterns of Egyptian, Mesopotamian, and Hebrew culture.

Egypt

In the third millennium B.C. *the Egyptians conceived of the sun-god as a creator who "spat out" the other gods and the world from his own body. The sun-god, known under various names, is here called Khepri. (The translator points out that there is a play on the name Khepri and the Egyptian word* kheper, *meaning "come into being.")*

From *The Book of Knowing the Creations*

The All-Lord said, after he had come into being:

I am he who came into being as Khepri. When I had come into being, being itself came into being, and all beings came into being after I came into being. Many were the beings which came forth from my mouth, before heaven came into being, before earth came into being, before the ground and creeping things had been created in this place. I put together some of them in Nun [the primordial waters in which creation occurred] before I could find a place in which I might stand. It seemed advantageous to me in my heart; I planned with my face; and I made in concept every form when I was alone, before I had spat out what was Shu, before I had sputtered out what was Tefnut, [1] and before any other had come into being who could act with me.

I planned in my own heart, and there came into being a multitude of forms of beings, the forms of children and the forms of their children. I was the one who copulated with my fist, I masturbated with my hand. Then I spewed with my own mouth:[2] I spat out what was Shu, and I sputtered out what was Tefnut. It was Nun who brought them up, and my Eye followed after them since the ages when they were distant from me.[3]

After I had come into being as the sole god, there were three gods beside me.[4] I came into being in this land, whereas Shu and Tefnut rejoiced in Nun, in

---

[1]The first two children of the creator-god were Shu, the air-god, and Tefnut, the goddess of moisture. The statement of their ejection into being contains plays on the words *ishesh* "spit" and Shu, and *tef* "sputter" and Tefnut.

[2]There is here a fusion of two myths, creation by self-pollution and creation by ejection from the mouth.

From John A. Wilson, trans. in James B. Pritchard, ed., *Ancient Near East Texts: Relating to the Old Testament,* 3rd ed. (Princeton, N.J.: Princeton University Press, 1969), p. 6. Copyright © 1969 by Princeton University Press. Reprinted by permission of Princeton University Press.

[3]The eye of the sun-god was an independent part of himself with a complicated mythological history.

[4]Nun, Shu, and Tefnut.

which they were. They brought to me my Eye with them. After I had joined together my members, I wept over them. That is how men came into being from the tears which came forth from my Eye[5] . . . and I created all creeping things and whatever lives among them. Then Shu and Tefnut brought forth Geb and Nut. Then Geb and Nut brought forth Osiris, Horus Khenti-en-irti, Seth, Isis, and Nephthys from the body, one of them after another; and they brought forth their multitudes in this land.

Mesopotamia

The earliest Babylonian story of creation (from the second millennium) is set in a complex tale about warfare among the gods.

In the beginning two primordial beings existed, Apsu and Tiamat, male and female, identified with fresh water and salt water. These two engendered a whole race of gods. The gods chose Marduk as king and rebelled against the first parents. Finally Marduk killed Tiamat and used her remains to make the universe. (Babylonian concern with astronomy is evident in the detailed account of the arrangements of the heavens.) Why and how did the gods create humankind according to this story?

From *The Creation Epic*

When on high the heaven had not been named,
Firm ground below had not been called by name,
Naught but primordial Apsu, their begetter,
(And) Mummu[6] - Tiamat, she who bore them all,
Their[7] waters commingling as a single body;
No reed hut had been matted, no marsh land had appeared,
When no gods whatever had been brought into being,
Uncalled by name, their destinies undetermined—
Then it was that the gods were formed within them. . . .

Then joined issue Tiamat and Marduk, wisest of gods.
They strove in single combat, locked in battle.
The lord spread out his net to enfold her,
The Evil Wind, which followed behind, he let loose in her face.
When Tiamat opened her mouth to consume him,
He drove in the Evil Wind that she close not her lips.
As the fierce winds charged her belly,
Her body was distended and her mouth was wide open.
He released the arrow, it tore her belly,
It cut through her insides, splitting her heart.

---

[5]The labored point of the context is a play on the words *remit* "tears," and *romet* "mankind," in explanation of human creation.
[6]Perhaps an epithet in the sense of "mother."
[7]I.e., the fresh waters of Apsu and the marine waters of Tiamat "the sea."
From E. A. Speiser, trans. in James B. Pritchard, ed., *Ancient Near East Texts: Relating to the Old Testament*, 3rd ed. (Princeton, N.J.: Princeton University Press, 1969), pp. 60–61, 67–68. Copyright © 1969 by Princeton University Press. Reprinted by permission of Princeton University Press.

Having thus subdued her, he extinguished her life.
He cast down her carcass to stand upon it.
After he had slain Tiamat, the leader,
Her band was shattered, her troupe broken up . . .

When he had vanquished and subdued his adversaries,
Had wholly established Anshar's triumph over the foe,
Nudimmud's desire had achieved, valiant Marduk
Strengthened his hold on the vanquished gods,
And turned back to Tiamat whom he had bound.
The lord trod on the legs of Tiamat,
With his unsparing mace he crushed her skull,
When the arteries of her blood he had severed,
The North Wind bore it to places undisclosed.
On seeing this, his fathers were joyful and jubilant,
They brought gifts of homage, they to him.
Then the lord paused to view her dead body,
That he might divide the monster and do artful works.
He split her like a shellfish into two parts:
Half of her he set up and ceiled it as sky,
Pulled down the bar and posted guards.
He bade them to allow not her waters to escape.
He crossed the heavens and surveyed the regions.
The Great Abode, its likeness, he fixed as Esharra,
The Great Abode, Esharra, which he made as the firmament.
Anu, Enlil, and Ea he made occupy their places.
He constructed stations for the great gods,
Fixing their astral likenesses as the Images.
He determined the year by designating the zones:
He set up three constellations for each of the twelve months.
After defining the days of the year by means of heavenly figures,
He founded the station of Nebiru[8] to determine their heavenly bands,
That none might transgress or fall short.
Alongside it he set up the stations of Enlil and Ea.[9]
Having opened up the gates on both sides,
He strengthened the locks to the left and the right.
In her belly he established the zenith.
The Moon he caused to shine, the night to him entrusting.
He appointed him a creature of the night to signify the days:
"Monthly, without cease, form designs with a crown.
At the month's very start, rising over the land,
Thou shalt have luminous horns to signify six days,
On the seventh day reaching a half-crown.
At full moon stand in opposition in mid-month.[10]
When the sun overtakes thee at the base of heaven,
Diminish thy crown and retrogress in light.

---

[8]The planet Jupiter.
[9]Enlil (wind-god) and Ea (earth- and water-god) were identified with north and south.
[10]I.e., the moon stands in opposition to the sun.

At the time of disappearance approach thou the course of the sun,
And on the thirtieth thou shalt again stand in opposition to the sun."

When Marduk hears the words of the gods,
His heart prompts him to fashion artful works.
Opening his mouth, he addresses Ea
To impart the plan he had conceived in his heart:
"Blood I will mass and cause bones to be.
I will establish a savage, 'man' shall be his name.
Verily, savage-man I will create.
He shall be charged with the service of the gods
That they might be at ease!"

Ea answered him, speaking a word to him,
Giving him another plan for the relief of the gods:
"Let but one of their brothers be handed over;
He alone shall perish that mankind may be fashioned . . .

Let him be handed over who contrived the uprising.
His guilt I will make him bear. You shall dwell in peace!"
The Igigi, the great gods, replied to him,
"It was Kingu who contrived the uprising,
And made Tiamat rebel, and joined battle."
They bound him, holding him before Ea.
They imposed on him his guilt and severed his blood (vessels).
Out of his blood they fashioned mankind.
He imposed the service and let free the gods.
After Ea, the wise, had created mankind,
Had imposed upon it the service of the gods—
That work was beyond comprehension . . .

The Hebrews

*The Hebrew account of creation is based on traditions that go back to the twelfth century
B.C. In its present form it was written down in the fifth century B.C. How does it resemble and differ from the earlier Egyptian and Babylonian accounts?*

From *The Book of Genesis*

In the beginning God created the heavens and the earth. The earth was without
form and void, and darkness was upon the face of the deep; and the Spirit of
God was moving over the face of the waters.

And God said, "Let there be light"; and there was light. And God saw that
the light was good; and God separated the light from the darkness. God called
the light Day, and the darkness he called Night. And there was evening and
there was morning, one day.

And God said, "Let there be a firmament in the midst of the waters, and let it separate the waters from the waters." And God made the firmament and separated the waters which were under the firmament from the waters which were above the firmament. And it was so. And God called the firmament Heaven. And there was evening and there was morning, a second day.

And God said, "Let the waters under the heavens be gathered together into one place, and let the dry land appear." And it was so. God called the dry land Earth, and the waters that were gathered together he called Seas. And God saw that it was good. And God said, "Let the earth put forth vegetation, plants yielding seed, and fruit trees bearing fruit in which is their seed, each according to its kind, upon the earth." And it was so. The earth brought forth vegetation, plants yielding seed according to their own kinds, and trees bearing fruit in which is their seed, each according to its kind. And God saw that it was good. And there was evening and there was morning, a third day.

And God said, "Let there be lights in the firmament of the heavens to separate the day from the night; and let them be for signs and for seasons and for days and years, and let them be lights in the firmament of the heavens to give light upon the earth." And it was so. And God made the two great lights, the greater light to rule the day, and the lesser light to rule the night; he made the stars also. And God set them in the firmament of the heavens to give light upon the earth, to rule over the day and over the night, and to separate the light from the darkness. And God saw that it was good. And there was evening and there was morning, a fourth day.

And God said, "Let the waters bring forth swarms of living creatures, and let birds fly above the earth across the firmament of the heavens."

So God created the great sea monsters and every living creature that moves, with which the waters swarm, according to their kinds, and every winged bird according to its kind. And God saw that it was good. And God blessed them, saying, "Be fruitful and multiply and fill the waters in the seas, and let birds multiply on the earth." And there was evening and there was morning, a fifth day.

And God said, "Let the earth bring forth living creatures according to their kinds: cattle and creeping things and beasts of the earth according to their kinds." And it was so. And God made the beasts of the earth according to their kinds and the cattle according to their kinds, and everything that creeps upon the ground according to its kind. And God saw that it was good.

Then God said, "Let us make man in our image, after our likeness; and let them have dominion over the fish of the sea, and over the birds of the air, and over the cattle, and over all the earth, and over every creeping thing that creeps upon the earth." So God created man in his own image, in the image of God he created him; male and female he created them. And God blessed them, and God said to them, "Be fruitful and multiply, and fill the earth and subdue it; and have dominion over the fish of the sea and over the birds of the air and over every living thing that moves upon the earth." And God said, "Behold, I have given you every plant yielding seed which is upon the face of all the earth, and every tree with seed in its fruit; you shall have them for food. And to every beast of the earth, and to every bird of the air, and to everything that creeps on the earth, everything that has the breath of life, I have given every green plant for food." And it was so. And God saw everything that he had made, and behold, it was very good. And there was evening and there was morning, a sixth day.

Thus the heavens and the earth were finished, and all the host of them. And on the seventh day God finished his work which he had done, and he rested on the seventh day from all his work which he had done. So God blessed the seventh day and hallowed it, because on it God rested from all his work which he had done in creation.

These are the generations of the heavens and earth when they were created.

RELIGION AND NATURE

To people of the ancient world the gods were not merely remote creator figures. They played an important part in day-to-day life. The gods required humans to worship them and obey them. They established divine rulers over kingdoms. How did the ancient writers envisage the relationships that existed among gods, humans, and the natural environment—earth, plants, and animals?

Egypt: The Nile and the Sun

For Egyptians there was no sharp line of distinction between natural and divine. The Nile could be perceived simultaneously as an actual river that watered the crops and as a hidden deity to be worshipped. This hymn probably dates back to the Middle Kingdom (2100–1700 B.C.)

From *Hymn to the Nile*

Hail to thee, O Nile, that issues from the earth and comes to keep Egypt alive! Hidden in his form of appearance,[11] a darkness by day, to whom minstrels have sung. He that waters the meadows which Re created, in order to keep every kid alive. He that makes to drink the desert and the place distant from water: that is his dew coming down from heaven.[12] The beloved of Geb,[13] the one who controls Nepri,[14] and the one who makes the craftsmanship of Ptah to flourish.

The lord of fishes, he who makes the marsh-birds to go upstream. . . . He who makes barley and brings emmer[15] into being, that he may make the temples festive. If he is sluggish, then nostrils are stopped up, and everybody is

---

[11]The Nile had no regular cult or temple in which he might appear in an image.
[12]Regions cut off from the waters of the Nile had his rain to sustain them.
[13]The earth-god.
[14]The grain-god.
[15]A kind of wheat grain used as fodder.

From John A. Wilson, trans. in James B. Pritchard, ed., *Ancient Near Eastern Texts: Relating to the Old Testament,* 3rd ed. (Princeton, N.J.: Princeton University Press, 1969), pp. 372–373 Copyright © 1969 by Princeton University Press. Reprinted by permission of Princeton University Press.

poor. If there be thus a cutting down in the food-offerings of the gods, then a million men perish among mortals, covetousness is practised, the entire land is in a fury, and great and small are on the execution-block. But people are different when he approaches. . . . When he rises, then the land is in jubilation, then every belly is in joy, every backbone takes on laughter, and every tooth is exposed.[16]

The bringer of food, rich in provisions, creator of all good, lord of majesty, sweet of fragrance. What is in him is satisfaction. He who brings grass into being for the cattle and thus gives sacrifice to every god, whether he be in the underworld, heaven, or earth, him who is under his authority. He who takes in possession the Two Lands, fills the magazines, makes the granaries wide, and gives things to the poor.

He Who Makes every beloved Tree to Grow, without lack of them . . . . He cannot be seen; he has no taxes; he has no levies; no one can read of the mystery; no one knows the place where he is; he cannot be found by the power of writing. He has no shrines: he has no portion. He has no service of his desire. But generations of thy children jubilate for thee, and men give thee greeting as a king, stable of laws, coming forth at his season and filling Upper and Lower Egypt. Whenever water is drunk, every eye is in him, who gives an excess of his good.

Besides the Nile, the other great source of fertility was the sun. Around 1370 B.C. the Pharaoh Akhnaton instituted a new cult, the worship of the sun-disc under the name of Aton. This hymn praises Aton as "sole god" and as the source of all life and fruitfulness on earth. (The cult of Aton as sole god was abandoned after Akhnaton's death.)

Hymn to the Aton

Thou appearest beautifully on the horizon of heaven,
Thou living Aton, the beginning of life!
When thou art risen on the eastern horizon,
Thou hast filled every land with thy beauty. . . .

All beasts are content with their pasturage;
Trees and plants are flourishing.
The birds which fly from their nests,
Their wings are stretched out in praise to thy *ka*.
All beasts spring upon their feet.
Whatever flies and alights,
They live when thou hast risen for them.
The ships are sailing north and south as well,
For every way is open at thy appearance.
The fish in the river dart before thy face;
Thy rays are in the midst of the great green sea.

Creator of seed in women,
Thou who makest fluid into man,

---

[16]When the Nile floods, all Egyptians laugh in delight.
From John A. Wilson, trans. in James B. Pritchard, ed., *Ancient Near Eastern Texts: Relating to the Old Testament,* 3rd ed. (Princeton, N.J.: Princeton University Press, 1969), pp. 370–371. Copyright © 1969 by Princeton University Press. Reprinted by permission of Princeton University Press.

Who maintainest the son in the womb of his mother,
Who soothest him with that which stills his weeping,
Thou nurse even in the womb,
Who givest breath to sustain all that he has made! . . .

O sole god, like whom there is no other!
Thou didst create the world according to thy desire,
Whilst thou wert alone:
All men, cattle, and wild beasts.
Whatever is on earth, going upon its feet
And what is on high, flying with its wings. . . .

Thy rays suckle every meadow.
When thou risest, they live, they grow for thee.
Thou makest the seasons in order to rear all that thou hast made,
The winter to cool them,
And the heat that they may taste thee.
Thou hast made the distant sky in order to rise therein,
In order to see all that thou dost make.
Whilst thou wert alone,
Rising in thy form as the living Aton,
Appearing, shining, withdrawing or approaching,
Thou madest millions of forms of thyself alone.
Cities, towns, fields, road, and river—
Every eye beholds thee over against them,
For thou art the Aton of the day over the earth. . . .

Mesopotamia: Fertility and Myth

In Sumerian religion, the sacred matings of the gods, reenacted on earth by kings and priestesses, ensured the continuing fruitfulness of nature. The following verses describe a marriage between Innana, a goddess of fertility, and an unnamed king.

Innana and the King

"May the lord whom you have called to (your) heart,
The king, your beloved husband, enjoy long days at your holy lap, the sweet,
Give him a reign favorable (and) glorious,
Give him the throne of kingship on its enduring foundation. . . .

May he make productive the fields like the farmer,
May he multiply the sheepfolds like a trustworthy shepherd.

Under his reign may there be plants, may there be grain,
At the river, may there be overflow,
In the field may there be late-grain,
In the marshland may the fish (and) birds make much *chatter*,

From S. N. Kramer, trans. in James B. Pritchard, ed., *Ancient Near Eastern Texts: Relating to the Old Testament*, 3rd ed. (Princeton University Press, 1969), p. 645. Copyright © 1969 by Princeton University Press. Reprinted by permission of Princeton University Press.

In the canebrake may the 'old' reeds, the young reeds grow high,
In the steppe may the *mashgur*-trees grow high,
In the forests may the deer and the wild goats multiply,
May the watered garden produce honey (and) wine,
In the trenches may the lettuce and cress grow high,
In the palace may there be long life,

Into the Tigris and Euphrates may flood water be brought,
On their banks may the grass grow high, may the meadows be covered,
May the holy queen of vegetation pile high the grain heaps and mounds,
Oh my queen, queen of the universe, the queen who encompasses the universe,
May he enjoy long days [at your holy] lap.

In Egypt the seasonal rising of the Nile gave a sense of regularity and order to life. Conditions in Mesopotamia were more unstable, with frequent unpredictable floods. This is perhaps reflected in Babylonian religion. The gods of Babylon were arbitrary, inscrutable figures. Sometimes the great mother-goddess Ishtar was asked to intercede for humans with the other gods.

Hymn to Ishtar

How long, O my Lady, shall my adversaries be looking upon me,
In lying and untruth shall they plan evil against me,
Shall my pursuers and those who exult over me rage against me?
How long, O my Lady, shall the crippled and weak seek me out?
One has made for me long sackcloth; thus I have appeared before thee.
The weak have become strong; but I am weak.
I toss about like flood-water, which an evil wind makes violent.
My heart is flying; it keeps fluttering like a bird of heaven.
I mourn like a dove night and day.
I am beaten down, and so I weep bitterly.
With "Oh" and "Alas" my spirit is distressed.
I—what have I done, O my god and my goddess?
Like one who does not fear my god and my goddess I am treated;
While sickness, headache, loss, and destruction are provided for me;
So are fixed upon me terror, disdain, and fullness of wrath,
Anger, choler, and indignation of gods and men.
I have to expect, O my Lady, dark days, gloomy months, and years of trouble.
I have to expect, O my Lady, judgment of confusion and violence.
Death and trouble are bringing me to an end.
Silent is my chapel; silent is my holy place;
Over my house, my gate, and my fields silence is poured out.
As for my god, his face is turned to the sanctuary of another.
My family is scattered; my roof is broken up.
But I have paid heed to thee, my Lady; my attention has been turned to thee.
To thee have I prayed; forgive my debt.

From Ferris J. Stephens, trans. in James B. Pritchard, ed., *Ancient Near Eastern Texts: Relating to the Old Testament,* 3rd ed. (Princeton, N.J.: Princeton University Press, 1969), pp. 384–385. Copyright © 1969 by Princeton University Press. Reprinted by permission of Princeton University Press.

Forgive my sin, my iniquity, my shameful deeds, and my offence.
Overlook my shameful deeds; accept my prayer;
Loosen my fetters; secure my deliverance;
Guide my steps aright; radiantly like a hero let me enter the streets with the
living.
Speak so that at thy command the angry god may be favorable;
And the goddess who has been angry with me may turn again.
Now dark and smoky, may my brazier glow;
Now extinguished, may my torch be lighted.
Let my scattered family be assembled;
May my fold be wide; may my stable be enlarged.
Accept the abasement of my countenance; hear my prayers.
Faithfully look upon me and accept my supplication.

The Babylonian Epic of Gilgamesh *(from the second millennium) presents the first account of man "in a state of nature." The hero, Gilgamesh, is part god, part man. His companion Enkidu grew up as a savage, living in the wilderness with only animals for company. But when Enkidu was seduced by a girl sent by Gilgamesh, the animals turned away from him. The story offers points of comparison with the biblical story of Adam and Eve in the next reading (p. 15).*

From *The Epic of Gilgamesh*

The hunter went forth to Gilgamesh.
He took the road, in Uruk he set his foot:
". . . Gilgamesh . . .,
There is a fellow who has come from the hills,
He is the mightiest in the land; strength he has
Like the essence of Anu, so mighty his strength!
Ever he ranges over the hills,
Ever with the beasts he feeds on grass,
Ever sets he his feet at the watering-place.
I am so frightened that I dare not approach him!
He filled in the pits that I had dug,
He tore up my traps which I had set,
The beasts and creatures of the steppe
He has made slip through my hands.
He does not allow me to engage in fieldcraft!"
Gilgamesh says to him, to the hunter:
"Go, my hunter, take with thee a harlot-lass.
When he waters the beasts at the watering-place,
She shall pull off her clothing, laying bare her ripeness.
As soon as he sees her, he will draw near to her.
Reject him will his beasts that grew up on his steppe!"
Forth went the hunter, taking with him a harlot-lass.
They took the road, going straight on their way.

From E. A. Speiser, trans. in James B. Pritchard, ed., *Ancient Near Eastern Texts: Relating to the Old Testament*, 3rd ed. (Princeton, N.J.: Princeton University Press, 1969), pp. 74–75. Copyright © 1969 by Princeton University Press. Reprinted by permission of Princeton University Press.

On the third day at the appointed spot they arrived.
The hunter and the harlot sat down in their places.
One day, a second day, they sat by the watering-place.
The wild beasts came to the watering-place to drink.

The creeping creatures came, their heart delighting in water.
But as for him, Enkidu, born in the hills—
With the gazelles he feeds on grass,
With the wild beasts he drinks at the watering-place,
With the creeping creatures his heart delights in water—
The lass beheld him, the savage-man,
The barbarous fellow from the depths of the steppe:
"There he is, O lass! Free thy breasts,
Bare thy bosom that he may possess thy ripeness!
Be not bashful! Welcome his ardor!
As soon as he sees thee, he will draw near to thee.
Lay aside thy cloth that he may rest upon thee.
Treat him, the savage, to a woman's task!
Reject him will his wild beasts that grew up on his steppe,
As his love is drawn unto thee."
The lass freed her breasts, bared her bosom,
And he possessed her ripeness.
She was not bashful as she welcomed his ardor.
She laid aside her cloth and he rested upon her.
She treated him, the savage, to a woman's task,
As his love was drawn unto her.
For six days and seven nights Enkidu comes forth,
Mating with the lass.
After he had had his fill of her charms,
He set his face toward his wild beasts.
On seeing him, Enkidu, the gazelles ran off,
The wild beasts of the steppe drew away from his body.
Startled was Enkidu, as his body became taut,
His knees were motionless—for his wild beasts had gone.
Enkidu had to slacken his pace—it was not as before;
But he now had wisdom, broader understanding.
Returning, he sits at the feet of the harlot.
He looks up at the face of the harlot,
His ears attentive, as the harlot speaks;
The harlot says to him, to Enkidu:
"Thou art wise, Enkidu, art become like a god!
Why with the wild creatures dost thou roam over the steppe?
Come, let me lead thee to ramparted Uruk,
To the holy temple, abode of Anu and Ishtar,
Where lives Gilgamesh, accomplished in strength,
And like a wild ox lords it over the folk."
As she speaks to him, her words find favor,
His heart enlightened, he yearns for a friend.
Enkidu says to her, to the harlot:
"Up, lass, escort thou me,

To the pure sacred temple, abode of Anu and Ishtar,
Where lives Gilgamesh, accomplished in strength,
And like a wild ox lords it over the folk.
I will challenge him and will boldly address him. . . ."

The Hebrews: The Garden of Eden

*The story of Adam and Eve follows immediately after the creation narrative given ear-
lier (p. 7). In the first creation story, God gave man "dominion" over all creatures.
Here he gives Adam a garden to "till and keep." Some scholars have seen in such
phrases the source of an "exploitative" approach to the natural world in Western culture. However that may be, this ancient story has certainly exercised a profound and
continuing influence on Western attitudes to God, nature, man, and (especially)
woman. What does the story of Eve suggest about relations between men and women
in ancient Jewish society? How might it influence attitudes to women in later Western
culture? (See, e.g., p. 282)*

From *The Book of Genesis*

In the day that the Lord God made the earth and the heavens, when no plant of
the field was yet in the earth and no herb of the field had yet sprung up—for the
Lord God had not caused it to rain upon the earth, and there was no man to till
the ground; but a mist went up from the earth and watered the whole face of the
ground—then the Lord God formed man of dust from the ground, and breathed
into his nostrils the breath of life; and man became a living being. And the Lord
God planted a garden in Eden, in the east; and there he put the man whom he
had formed. And out of the ground the Lord God made to grow every tree that
is pleasant to the sight and good for food, the tree of life also in the midst of the
garden, and the tree of the knowledge of good and evil. . . .

The Lord God took the man and put him in the garden of Eden to till it and
keep it. And the Lord God commanded the man, saying, "You may freely eat of
every tree of the garden; but of the tree of the knowledge of good and evil you
shall not eat, for in the day that you eat of it you shall die."

Then the Lord God said, "It is not good that the man should be alone; I will
make him a helper fit for him." So out of the ground the Lord God formed every
beast of the field and every bird of the air, and brought them to the man to see
what he would call them; and whatever the man called every living creature,
that was its name. The man gave names to all cattle, and to the birds of the air,
and to every beast of the field; but for the man there was not found a helper fit
for him. So the Lord God caused a deep sleep to fall upon the man, and while
he slept took one of his ribs and closed up its place with flesh; and the rib which
the Lord God had taken from the man he made into a woman and brought her
to the man. Then the man said,

"This at last is bone of my bones and flesh of my flesh;
　　she shall be called Woman,
　　because she was taken out of Man."

Therefore a man leaves his father and his mother and cleaves to his wife, and they become one flesh. And the man and his wife were both naked, and were not ashamed.

Now the serpent was more subtle than any other wild creature that the Lord God had made. He said to the woman, "Did God say, 'You shall not eat of any tree of the garden'?" And the woman said to the serpent, "We may eat of the fruit of the trees of the garden; but God said, 'You shall not eat of the fruit of the tree which is in the midst of the garden, neither shall you touch it, lest you die.'" But the serpent said to the woman, "You will not die. For God knows that when you eat of it your eyes will be opened, and you will be like God, knowing good and evil." So when the woman saw that the tree was good for food, and that it was a delight to the eyes, and that the tree was to be desired to make one wise, she took of its fruit and ate; and she also gave some to her husband, and he ate. Then the eyes of both were opened, and they knew that they were naked; and they sewed fig leaves together and made themselves aprons.

And they heard the sound of the Lord God walking in the garden in the cool of the day, and the man and his wife hid themselves from the presence of the Lord God among the trees of the garden. But the Lord God called to the man, and said to him, "Where are you?" And he said, "I heard the sound of thee in the garden, and I was afraid, because I was naked; and I hid myself." He said, "Who told you that you were naked? Have you eaten of the tree of which I commanded you not to eat?" The man said, "The woman whom thou gavest to be with me, she gave me fruit of the tree, and I ate." Then the Lord God said to the woman, "What is this that you have done?" The woman said, "The serpent beguiled me, and I ate." The Lord God said to the serpent,

"Because you have done this,
　　cursed are you above all cattle,
　　and above all wild animals;
upon your belly you shall go,
　　and dust you shall eat
　　all the days of your life.
I will put enmity between you and the woman,
　　and between your seed and her seed;
he shall bruise your head,
　　and you shall bruise his heel."
To the woman he said,
"I will greatly multiply your pain in childbearing;
　　in pain you shall bring forth children,
yet your desire shall be for your husband,
　　and he shall rule over you."
And to Adam he said,
"Because you have listened to the
　　voice of your wife,
　　and have eaten of the tree

of which I commanded you,
  'You shall not eat of it,'
cursed is the ground because of you;
  in toil you shall eat of it all the
  days of your life;
thorns and thistles it shall bring
  forth to you;
  and you shall eat the plants of the
  field.
In the sweat of your face
  you shall eat bread
  till you return to the ground,
  for out of it you were taken;
  you are dust,
  and to dust you shall return."

The man called his wife's name Eve, because she was the mother of all living. And the Lord God made for Adam and for his wife garments of skins, and clothed them.

Then the Lord God said, "Behold, the man has become like one of us, knowing good and evil; and now, lest he put forth his hand and take also of the tree of life, and eat, and live for ever"—therefore the Lord God sent him forth from the garden of Eden, to till the ground from which he was taken. He drove out the man; and at the east of the garden of Eden he placed the cherubim, and a flaming sword which turned every way, to guard the way to the tree of life.

ETHICS AND LAW

The moral ideals and legal regulations in these texts from Egypt and Babylon may be compared with the later law of Moses.

Egypt: Death and Judgment

In their dealings with the gods Egyptians were especially concerned with a life after death when they would face a divine judgment. This protestation of innocence was written for the chancellor Nu about the middle of the second millennium. What kinds of sins did an Egyptian have to avoid in order to win a favorable judgment after death?

From *The Book of the Dead*

The following shall be said when the overseer of the palace, the chancellor-in-chief, Nu, triumphant, cometh forth into the Hall of Double Maati[17] so that he may be separated from every sin which he hath done and may behold the faces of the gods. Nu, triumphant, saith: . . .

"I have not done evil to mankind. I have not oppressed the members of my family, I have not wrought evil in the place of right and truth. I have had no knowledge

---

[17]Justice or Truth.

of worthless men. I have not wrought evil. I have not made to be the first consideration of each day that excessive labor should be performed for me. I have not brought forward my name for exaltation to honors. I have not ill-treated servants. I have not thought scorn of God. I have not defrauded the oppressed one of his property. I have not done that which is an abomination unto the gods. I have not caused harm to be done to the servant by his chief. I have not caused pain. I have made no one to weep. I have done no murder. I have not given the order for murder to be done for me. I have not inflicted pain upon mankind. I have not defrauded the temples of their oblations. I have not purloined the cakes of the gods. I have not committed fornication. . . . I have not turned back water at the time [when it should flow]. I have not cut a cutting in a canal of running water. . . . I have not repulsed God in his manifestations. I am pure. I am pure. I am pure. I am pure. . . .

"I have given bread to the hungry man, and water to the thirsty man, and clothes to the naked man, and a boat to the marooned mariner. I have made holy offerings to the gods, and funeral offerings to the dead. Be you then my deliverers, be you then my protectors, and make no accusation against me in the presence of the great god. I am pure of mouth and pure of hands; therefore let it be said unto me by those who shall behold me, 'Come in peace; come in peace.' "

Mesopotamia: Law and Justice

The Code of Hammurabi was set down about 1750 B.C. and it incorporates still earlier laws. In substance a stern code of retributive justice, it incidentally provides rich information about many aspects of early Babylonian society. What can you learn from the Code about social gradations, economic activities, family life, and sexual morality in ancient Babylon?

From *The Code of Hammurabi*

　　1. If a man weave a spell and bring a charge of murder against another man and has not justified himself, the accuser shall be put to death.

　　2. If a man has put a spell upon another man, and has not justified himself, the one who is charged with sorcery shall go to the holy river, he shall plunge into the holy river, and if the holy river overcomes him, his accuser shall take his estate. If the holy river shows that man to be innocent and has saved him, he who charged him with sorcery shall be put to death and the man who plunged into the river shall take the estate of him who brought the charge against him.

　　8. If a man has stolen ox or sheep or ass or pig or ship, whether from the temple or from the palace, he shall pay thirtyfold; if he stole from a commoner, he shall render tenfold. If the thief cannot pay, he shall be put to death.

　　14. If a man has stolen the son of a freeman, he shall be put to death.

From E. A. Wallis Budge, trans., *The Book of the Dead According to the Theban Recension* in Epiphanius Wilson, ed., *Egyptian Literature* (London: The Colonial Press, 1901), pp. 102–103.
From C. H. W. Johns, trans. *The Oldest Code of Laws in the World* (Edinburgh: T. and T. Clarke, 1901).

15. If a man has helped a male or female palace slave, or a commoner's male or female slave to escape out of the city gate, he shall be put to death.

21. If a man has broken into a house, he shall be killed before the breach and walled in it.

23. If the robber has not been caught, the man who has been despoiled shall recount before the god what he has lost, and the city and governor in whose territory the robbery took place shall make good to him his loss.

24. If a life was lost, the city and governor shall pay one mina of silver to his people.

27. If a soldier or a constable disappears whilst on military service and they have given his field and his orchard to another and he has carried on his obligations, if he returns and regains his city, they shall restore his field and his orchard and he shall fulfill his obligations himself.

48. If a man has a debt upon him and a thunderstorm ravaged his field or carried away the produce, or the corn has not grown for lack of water, in that year he shall make no return of corn to his creditor; he shall alter his contract-tablet and he shall not pay interest for that year.

53. If a man has neglected to strengthen the dyke of his canal, and a breach has opened in his dyke, and the waters have ravaged the meadow, the man in whose dyke the breach has been opened shall make good the corn that he caused to be lost.

104. If a merchant has lent a trader corn, wool, oil or any sort of goods to traffic with, the trader shall write down the price and pay it back; the trader shall take a sealed receipt of the price which he pays to the merchant.

109. If a wine merchant has collected outlaws in her house and has not seized those outlaws and driven them to the palace, that wine merchant shall be put to death.

110. If a nun, a lady of god, who is not living in a convent, has opened the door of a wine shop or entered the wine shop for a drink, that woman shall be burned.

117. If a debt came due against a man, and he has given his wife, his son, his daughter for the money, or handed himself over to work off the debt, for three years they shall work in the house of their buyer or exploiter, in the fourth year they shall be set free.

128. If a man has married a wife and has not drawn up a contract, that woman is no wife.

129. If the wife of a man has been caught lying with another man, they shall bind them and throw them into the waters.

131. If a wife has been accused by her husband and she has not been caught lying with another male, she shall swear by god and shall return to her house.

132. If a wife has the finger pointed at her on account of another male but has not been caught lying with another male, for the sake of her husband she shall throw herself into the holy river.

133. If a man has been taken captive and in his house there is maintenance, if his wife has gone out from her house and entered into the house of another, because that woman has not guarded her body and has entered the house of another, they shall prove it against that woman and throw her into the waters.

134. If a man has been taken captive and in his house there is no maintenance, and his wife has entered into the house of another, that woman has no blame.

137. If a man has decided to put away his concubine who has borne him children or his wife who has granted him children, to that woman he shall return her marriage portion and shall give her half of the field, orchard and goods, and she shall bring up her children. From the time that her children are grown up, from whatever is given to her children they shall give her a share like that of one son, and she shall marry the husband of her choice.

138. If a man has put away his bride who has not borne him children, he shall return her dowry and pay her the marriage portion which she brought from her father's house, and shall put her away.

141. If the wife of a man who is living in the house of her husband has made up her mind to leave the house to engage in business and has acted the fool, neglecting the house and humiliating the husband, it shall be proved against her; and if her husband has said "I put her away," he shall put her away and she shall go her way, and he shall not give her anything for her divorce.

142. If a woman hates her husband and has said "You shall not possess me," they shall inquire into her record and if she has been economical and has no vice and her husband has gone out and greatly belittled her, that woman has no blame, she will take her marriage portion and go off to her father's house.

143. If she has not been economical, a gadabout, has neglected her house and humiliated her husband, that woman they shall throw into the waters.

153. If a man's wife has caused her husband to be killed on account of another man, they shall impale that woman on a stake.

154. If a man has known his daughter, that man shall be expelled from the city.

157. If a man, after his father, has lain in the bosom of his mother, they shall burn both of them together.

195. If a man has struck his father, his hand shall be cut off.

196. If a man has caused the loss of a gentleman's eye, they shall cause him to lose one eye.

200. If a man has made the tooth of a man that is his equal fall out, they shall make his tooth fall out.

201. If he has made the tooth of a commoner fall out, he shall pay one third of a mina of silver.

202. If a man has struck the cheek of his superior, he shall be struck in the assembly with 60 strokes of a cowhide whip.

203. If a man of gentle birth has struck a man of gentle birth who is his equal, he shall pay one mina of silver.

209. If a man has struck a gentleman's daughter and caused her to have a miscarriage, he shall pay ten shekels of silver for what was in her womb.

210. If that woman has died, they shall put to death his daughter.

211. If by his blows he has caused the daughter of a commoner to have a miscarriage, he shall pay five shekels of silver.

212. If that woman has died, he shall pay half a mina of silver.

213. If he has struck a gentleman's slave and caused a miscarriage, he shall pay two shekels of silver.

214. If that slave has died, he shall pay one third of a mina of silver.

215. If a doctor has treated a gentleman for a severe wound, with a bronze lancet and has cured him, or has opened an abcess of the eye for a gentleman with the bronze lancet and has cured the eye of the gentleman, he shall take ten shekels of silver.

218. If the doctor has treated a gentleman for a severe wound with a lancet of bronze and has caused the gentleman to die or has opened an abcess of the eye of a gentleman with the bronze lancet and has caused the loss of the gentleman's eye, they shall cut off his hands.

229. If a builder has built a house and not made his work strong and the house he built has fallen and so has caused the death of the owner of the house, that builder shall be put to death.

230. If he has caused the son of the owner of the house to die, they shall put to death the son of the builder.

250. If a wild bull in his charge has gored a man, and caused him to die, that case has no remedy.

251. If a man's ox was inclined to gore and it was made known to him that this was so and he took no steps to tie him up or blunt his horns, and that ox has gored a man and caused him to die, he shall pay half a mina of silver for a gentleman, one third of a mina for a slave.

GOD, HUMANS AND HISTORY: THE HEBREW TRADITION

The Hebrew people worshipped the god Yahweh (often transliterated into English as Jehovah). They moved from a belief in Yahweh as their own particular tribal deity to a conviction that he was the one supreme being, the one true God. This God, they believed, had made a convenant with their ancestors as a specially chosen people, the "children of Israel." They could cooperate with God (or fail to cooperate) in working out their historic destiny. Hebrew religious writings thus formed a sacred history, an account of God's dealings with his people down the course of the ages.

The Covenant

The Covenant (originally made with Abraham) was renewed at the time of Moses. (Moses lived c. 1200 B.C. The biblical account is based on traditions going back to that period.) What did God promise to Moses?

From *The Book of Exodus*

In the course of those many days the king of Egypt died. And the people of Israel groaned under their bondage, and cried out for help, and their cry under

From the *Revised Standard Version Bible* (New York: Oxford University Press, 1973). Exodus 2:23–25; 3:7–15. Copyright 1946, 1952 © 1971, 1973 by the Council of the Churches of Christ. Reprinted by permission.

bondage came up to God. And God heard their groaning, and God remembered his covenant with Abraham, with Isaac, and with Jacob. And God saw the people of Israel, and God knew their condition. . . .

Then the Lord said, "I have seen the affliction of my people who are in Egypt, and have heard their cry because of their taskmasters; I know their sufferings, and I have come down to deliver them out of the hand of the Egyptians, and to bring them up out of that land to a good and broad land, a land flowing with milk and honey, to the place of the Canaanites, the Hittites, the Amorites, the Perizzites, the Hivites, and the Jebusites. And now, behold, the cry of the people of Israel has come to me, and I have seen the oppression with which the Egyptians oppress them. Come, I will send you to Pharaoh that you may bring forth my people, the sons of Israel, out of Egypt." But Moses said to God, "Who am I that I should go to Pharaoh, and bring the sons of Israel out of Egypt?" He said, "But I will be with you; and this shall be the sign for you, that I have sent you: when you have brought forth the people out of Egypt, you shall serve God upon this mountain."

Then Moses said to God, "If I come to the people of Israel and say to them, 'The God of your fathers has sent me to you,' and they ask me, 'What is his name?' what shall I say to them?" God said to Moses, "I AM WHO I AM." And he said, "Say this to the people of Israel, 'I AM has sent me to you.' " God also said to Moses, "Say this to the people of Israel, 'The Lord, the God of your fathers, the God of Abraham, the God of Isaac, and the God of Jacob, has sent me to you': this is my name for ever, and thus I am to be remembered throughout all generations."[18]

The Law

How do these commandments given to the Hebrews compare with the laws of Hammurabi?

From *The Book of Exodus*

And God spoke all these words, saying,

"I am the Lord your God, who brought you out of the land of Egypt, out of the house of bondage.

"You shall have no other gods before me.

"You shall not make for yourself a graven image, or any likeness of anything that is in heaven above, or that is in earth beneath, or that is in the water under the earth; you shall not bow down to them or serve them; for I the Lord your God am a jealous God, visiting the iniquity of the fathers upon the children to the third and the fourth generation of those who hate me, but showing steadfast love to thousands of those who love me and keep my commandments.

"You shall not take the name of the Lord your God in vain; for the Lord will not hold him guiltless who takes his name in vain.

---

[18]The Hebrew YHWH, translated above as "The Lord," is a form of the verb "to be." Thus the sentence carries on the thought of the preceding passage. The name of God means "He who is" or "He who causes being."

"Remember the sabbath day, to keep it holy. Six days you shall labor, and do all your work; but the seventh day is a sabbath to the Lord your God; in it you shall not do any work, you, or your son, or your daughter, your manservant, or your maidservant, or your cattle, or the sojourner who is within your gates; for in six days the Lord made heaven and earth, the sea, and all that is in them, and rested the seventh day; therefore the Lord blessed the sabbath day and hallowed it.

"Honor your father and your mother, that your days may be long in the land which the Lord your God gives you.

"You shall not kill.

"You shall not commit adultery.

"You shall not steal.

"You shall not bear false witness against your neighbor.

"You shall not covet your neighbor's house; you shall not covet your neighbor's wife, or his manservant, or his maidservant, or his ox, or his ass, or anything that is your neighbor's. . . .

"Whoever strikes a man so that he dies shall be put to death. But if he did not lie in wait for him, but God let him fall into his hand, then I will appoint for you a place to which he may flee. But if a man willfully attacks another to kill him treacherously, you shall take him from my altar, that he may die.

"Whoever strikes his father or his mother shall be put to death.

"Whoever steals a man, whether he sells him or is found in possession of him, shall be put to death.

"Whoever curses his father or his mother shall be put to death.

"When men quarrel and one strikes the other with a stone or with his fist and the man does not die but keeps his bed, then if the man rises again and walks abroad with his staff, he that struck him shall be clear; only he shall pay for the loss of his time, and shall have him thoroughly healed.

"When a man strikes his slave, male or female, with a rod and the slave dies under his hand, he shall be punished. But if the slave survives a day or two, he is not to be punished; for the slave is his money.

"When men strive together, and hurt a woman with child, so that there is a miscarriage, and yet no harm follows, the one who hurt her shall be fined, according as the woman's husband shall lay upon him; and he shall pay as the judges determine. If any harm follows, then you shall give life for life, eye for eye, tooth for tooth, hand for hand, foot for foot, burn for burn, wound for wound, stripe for stripe.

"When a man strikes the eye of his slave, male or female, and destroys it, he shall let the slave go free for the eye's sake. If he knocks out the tooth of his slave, male or female, he shall let the slave go free for the tooth's sake.

"When an ox gores a man or a woman to death, the ox shall be stoned, and its flesh shall not be eaten; but the owner of the ox shall be clear. But if the ox has been accustomed to gore in the past, and its owner has been warned but has not kept it in, and it kills a man or a woman, the ox shall be stoned, and its owner also shall be put to death. . . .

"When a man causes a field or vineyard to be grazed over, or lets his beast loose and it feeds in another man's field, he shall make restitution from the best in his own field and in his own vineyard.

"When fire breaks out and catches in thorns so that the stacked grain or the standing grain or the field is consumed, he that kindled the fire shall make full restitution.

"If a man seduces a virgin who is not betrothed, and lies with her, he shall give the marriage present for her, and make her his wife. If her father utterly refuses to give her to him, he shall pay money equivalent to the marriage present for virgins.

"You shall not permit a sorceress to live.

"Whoever lies with a beast shall be put to death.

"Whoever sacrifices to any god, save to the Lord only, shall be utterly destroyed.

"You shall not wrong a stranger or oppress him, for you were strangers in the land of Egypt. You shall not afflict any widow or orphan. If you do afflict them, and they cry out to me, I will surely hear their cry; and my wrath will burn, and I will kill you with the sword, and your wives shall become widows and your children fatherless.

"If you lend money to any of my people with you who is poor, you shall not be to him as a creditor, and you shall not exact interest from him.

The Prophets

From time to time prophets arose who rebuked the sins of rulers and people. They warned of God's wrath but also foretold the coming of a Messiah who would finally exalt Israel after all its trials. The early Christians interpreted these prophecies as references to the coming of Jesus. The prophecy of Isaiah is from the eighth century B.C.

From *The Book of Isaiah*

The vision of Isaiah the son of Amoz, which he saw concerning Judah and Jerusalem in the days of Uzziah, Jotham, Ahaz, and Hezekiah, kings of Judah.

Hear, O heavens, and give ear, O earth;
  for the Lord has spoken:
"Sons have I reared and brought up,
  but they have rebelled against me.
The ox knows its owner,
  and the ass its master's crib;

From the *Revised Standard Version Bible* (New York: Oxford University Press, 1973). Isaiah 1:1–9. Copyright 1946, 1952, © 1971, 1973 by the National Council of the Churches of Christ. Reprinted by permission.

but Israel does not know,
   my people does not understand."

Ah, sinful nation,
   a people laden with iniquity,
offspring of evildoers,
   sons who deal corruptly!
They have forsaken the Lord,
   they have despised the Holy One
   of Israel,
   they are utterly estranged.

Why will you still be smitten,
   that you continue to rebel?
The whole head is sick,
   and the whole heart faint.
From the sole of the foot even to the head,
   there is no soundness in it,
but bruises and sores
   and bleeding wounds;
they are not pressed out, or bound
   up,
   or softened with oil.

Your country lies desolate,
   your cities are burned with fire;
in your very presence
   aliens devour your land;
   it is desolate, as overthrown by
   aliens.
And the daughter of Zion is left
   like a booth in a vineyard,
like a lodge in a cucumber field,
   like a besieged city.

If the Lord of hosts
   had not left us a few survivors,
we should have been like Sodom,
   and become like Gomorrah.

After the rebuke comes the promise.

The people who walked in darkness
   have seen a great light;
those who dwelt in a land of deep
   darkness,
   on them has light shined.

Thou hast multiplied the nation,
  thou hast increased its joy;
they rejoice before thee
  as with joy at the harvest,
  as men rejoice when they divide
  the spoil.
For the yoke of his burden,
  and the staff for his shoulder,
  the rod of his oppressor,
  thou hast broken as on the day of
  Midian.
For every boot of the tramping
  warrior in battle tumult
  and every garment rolled in blood
  will be burned as fuel for the fire.
For to us a child is born,
  to us a son is given;
and the government will be upon
  his shoulder,
  and his name will be called
"Wonderful Counselor, Mighty God,
  Everlasting Father, Prince of
  Peace."
Of the increase of his government
  and of peace
  there will be no end,
upon the throne of David, and over
  his kingdom,
  to establish it, and to uphold it
with justice and with righteousness
  from this time forth and for
  evermore.
The zeal of the Lord of hosts will do
  this.

Hebrew Poetry

The following song on the splendor of God's creation was attributed to the hero-king David (ca. 1000 B.C.)

A Psalm

  Praise the Lord!

Praise the Lord from the
   heavens,
      praise him in the heights!
Praise him, all his angels,
      praise him, all his host!

Praise him, sun and moon,
      praise him, all you shining stars!
Praise him, you highest heavens,
      and you waters above the heavens!

Let them praise the name of the
   Lord!
      For he commanded and they were
      created.
And he established them for ever
   and ever;
      he fixed their bounds which
      cannot be passed.

Praise the Lord from the earth,
      you sea monsters and all deeps,
fire and hail, snow and frost,
      stormy wind fulfilling his
      command!

Mountains and all hills,
      fruit trees and all cedars!
Beasts and all cattle,
      creeping things and flying birds!

Kings of the earth and all peoples,
      princes and all rulers of the earth!
Young men and maidens together,
      old men and children!

Let them praise the name of the
   Lord,
      for his name alone is exalted;
      his glory is above earth and
      heaven.
He has raised up a horn for his
   people,
      praise for all his saints,
      for the people of Israel who are
      near to him.
   Praise the Lord!

This love dialogue has affinities both with earlier fertility songs (see p. 11) and with later mystical literature (see p. 256). It was often interpreted as an allegory of the love of God for his people or, later, of Christ for the church.

From *The Song of Solomon*

I am a rose of Sharon,
   a lily of the valleys.
As a lily among brambles,
   so is my love among maidens.
As an apple tree among the trees
   of the wood,
   so is my beloved among young
   men.
With great delight I sat in his shadow,
   and his fruit was sweet to my taste.
He brought me to the banqueting
   house,
   and his banner over me was love.
Sustain me with raisins,
   refresh me with apples;
   for I am sick with love.
O that his left hand were under my
   head,
   and that his right hand embraced
   me!
I adjure you, O daughters of
   Jerusalem,
   by the gazelles or the hinds of the
   field,
that you stir not up nor awaken
   love
   until it please.
The voice of my beloved!
   Behold, he comes,
leaping upon the mountains,
   bounding over the hills.
My beloved is like a gazelle,
   or a young stag.
Behold, there he stands
   behind our wall,
gazing in at the windows,
   looking through the lattice.
My beloved speaks and says to me:
"Arise, my love, my fair one,
   and come away;
for lo, the winter is past,
   the rain is over and gone.

The flowers appear on the earth,
   the time of singing has come,
and the voice of the turtledove
   is heard in our land.
The fig tree puts forth its figs,
   and the vines are in blossom;
   they give forth fragrance.
Arise, my love, my fair one,
   and come away.

O my dove, in the clefts of the rock,
   in the covert of the cliff,
let me see your face,
   let me hear your voice,
for your voice is sweet,
   and your face is comely.
Catch us the foxes,
   the little foxes,
that spoil the vineyards,
   for our vineyards are in blossom."
My beloved is mine and I am his,
   he pastures his flock among the
   lilies.
Until the day breathes
   and the shadows flee,
turn, my beloved, be like a gazelle,
   or a young stag upon rugged
   mountains.

PART TWO

GREEK CIVILIZATION— FROM MYTH TO POLIS (C. 800–C. 400 B.C.)

Historians *often note that Western civilization grew from Greek and Hebrew roots. Like most platitudes this is true. Unlike most, it points to a complex and significant reality. Our culture has always been marked by internal tensions. That is in part because it incorporates elements, often hard to reconcile, from two disparate earlier civilizations.*

The Greek world of the first millennium B.C. *was very different from the contemporary Old Testament world of the Jews. The Greeks lived in scattered communities—first primitive kingdoms, then ordered city-states—separated by mountains and long arms of the sea. They shared a common language and culture but were often in conflict with one another. They worshipped many gods and thought of the gods as very much like themselves, superhuman only in their greater powers. But from the sixth century onward, some Greek philosophers began to find the old mythology unacceptable, both morally and intellectually. Critical thinkers then faced a new problem. How could one explain the intrinsic nature of reality—of the universe and humankind, and ordered society—without an adequate religious myth to give coherence to the whole world picture? Some playwrights learned to use the old myths in fresh ways to express their deepest moral intuitions. A few philosophers embarked on a new enterprise, an attempt to construct, for the first time, a wholly rational picture of the universe. Meanwhile the growth of many self-conscious political communities, exemplifying different lifestyles within a common culture, stimulated new reflections in the field that we would call comparative politics.*

GODS AND HUMANS

Homer's World

*The first great work of Greek literature, Homer's Iliad, was set down in the eighth cen-
tury B.C. It is based on earlier legends about a Greek siege of Troy (which probably took
place about 1200 B.C.). At one point in the story the supreme god, Zeus, forbids the other
gods to join in the fighting. His wife Hera, who wants her brother Poseidon to help the
Greeks, decides to distract his attention. What kind of characteristics did the Greeks attribute to their gods? What does Homer tell us about archaic Greek attitudes toward war,
death, vengeance?*

From *The Iliad*

Now Hera, she of the golden throne, standing on Olympos' horn, looked
out with her eyes, and saw at once how Poseidon, who was her very brother and
her lord's brother, was bustling about the battle where men win glory, and her
heart was happy. Then she saw Zeus, sitting along the loftiest summit on Ida of
the springs, and in her eyes he was hateful. And now the lady ox-eyed Hera was
divided in purpose as to how she could beguile the brain in Zeus of the aegis.
And to her mind this thing appeared to be the best counsel, to array herself in
loveliness, and go down to Ida, and perhaps he might be taken with desire to lie
in love with her next her skin, and she might be able to drift an innocent warm
sleep across his eyelids, and seal his crafty perceptions. . . .

Then Hera light-footed made her way to the peak of Gargaros on towering
Ida. And Zeus who gathers the clouds saw her, and when he saw her desire was
a mist about his close heart as much as on that time they first went to bed together and lay in love, and their dear parents knew nothing of it. He stood before her and called her by name and spoke to her:

'Hera, what is your desire that you come down here from Olympos? And
your horses are not here, nor your chariot, which you would ride in.'

Then with false lying purpose the lady Hera answered him: 'I am going to
the ends of the generous earth, on a visit to Okeanos, whence the gods have
risen, and Tethys our mother, who brought me up kindly in their own house,
and cared for me.

I shall go to visit these, and resolve their division of discord, since now for
a long time they have stayed apart from each other and from the bed of love,
since rancour has entered their feelings.

In the foothills by Ida of the waters are standing my horses, who will carry
me over hard land and water. Only now I have come down here from Olympos
for your sake so you will not be angry with me afterwards, if I have gone silently
to the house of deep-running Okeanos.'

From Richmond Lattimore, trans., *The Illiad of Homer*, pp. 298–299, 302–303, 441–445. Copyright ©
1961 by the University of Chicago Press. Reprinted by permission.

Then in turn Zeus who gathers the clouds answered her: 'Hera, there will be a time afterwards when you can go there as well. But now let us go to bed and turn to love-making. For never before has love for any goddess or woman so melted about the heart inside me, broken it to submission. . . .

Then with false lying purpose the lady Hera answered him: 'Most honoured son of Kronos, what sort of thing have you spoken?

If now your great desire is to lie in love together here on the peaks of Ida, everything can be seen. Then what would happen if some one of the gods everlasting saw us sleeping, and went and told all the other immortals of it? I would not simply rise out of bed and go back again, into your house, and such a thing would be shameful. No, if this is your heart's desire, if this is your wish, then there is my chamber, which my beloved son Hephaistos has built for me, and closed the leaves in the door-posts snugly. We can go back there and lie down, since bed is your pleasure.'

Then in turn Zeus who gathers the clouds answered her: 'Hera, do not fear that any mortal or any god will see, so close shall be the golden cloud that I gather about us. Not even Helios can look at us through it, although beyond all others his light has the sharpest vision.'

So speaking, the son of Kronos caught his wife in his arms.

There underneath them the divine earth broke into young, fresh grass, and into dewy clover, crocus and hyacinth so thick and soft it held the hard ground deep away from them. There they lay down together and drew about them a golden wonderful cloud, and from it the glimmering dew descended.

So the father slept unshaken on the peak of Gargaron with his wife in his arms, when sleep and passion had stilled him; but gently Sleep went on the run to the ships of the Achaians with a message to tell him who circles the earth and shakes it, Poseidon, and stood close to him and addressed him in winged words:

'Poseidon, now with all your heart defend the Danaans [*Greeks*] and give them glory, though only for a little, while Zeus still sleeps; since I have mantled a soft slumber about him and Hera beguiled him into sleeping in love beside her.'

[Toward the end of the poem there is a climactic duel between the Greek hero Achilles and the Trojan prince Hektor. Achilles is enraged because Hektor has killed his friend Patroklos. The goddess Athene appears to Hektor in the guise of his brother Deiphobos and promises to help him in the fight—then she betrays him to Achilles.]

So Athene spoke and led him on by beguilement. Now as the two in their advance were come close together, first of the two to speak was tall helm-glittering Hektor: 'Son of Peleus, I will no longer run from you, as before this I fled three times around the great city of Priam, and dared not stand to your onfall. But now my spirit in turn has driven me to stand and face you. I must take you now, or I must be taken. Come then, shall we swear before the gods? For these are the highest who shall be witnesses and watch over our agreements. Brutal as you are I will not defile you, if Zeus grants to me that I can wear you out, and take the life from you. But after I have stripped your glorious armour, Achilleus, I will give your corpse back to the Achaians. Do you do likewise.'

Then looking darkly at him swift-footed Achilleus answered: 'Hektor, argue me no agreements. I cannot forgive you. As there are no trustworthy oaths between men and lions, nor wolves and lambs have spirit that can be brought to agreement but forever these hold feelings of hate for each other, so there can be no love between you and me, nor shall there be oaths between us, but one or the other must fall before then to glut with his blood Ares the god who fights under the shield's guard.

Remember every valour of yours, for now the need comes hardest upon you to be a spearman and a bold warrior. There shall be no more escape for you, but Pallas Athene will kill you soon by my spear. You will pay in a lump for all those sorrows of my companions you killed in your spear's fury.'

So he spoke, and balanced the spear far shadowed, and threw it; but glorious Hektor kept his eyes on him, and avoided it, for he dropped, watchful, to his knee, and the bronze spear flew over his shoulder and stuck in the ground, but Pallas Athene snatched it, and gave it back to Achilleus, unseen by Hektor shepherd of the people. But now Hektor spoke out to the blameless son of Peleus: 'You missed; and it was not, o Achilleus like the immortals, from Zeus that you knew my destiny; but you thought so; or rather you are someone clever in speech and spoke to swindle me, to make me afraid of you and forget my valour and war strength. You will not stick your spear in my back as I run away from you but drive it into my chest as I storm straight in against you; if the god gives you that; and now look out for my brazen spear. I wish it might be taken full length in your body. And indeed the war would be a lighter thing for the Trojans if you were dead, seeing that you are their greatest affliction.'

So he spoke, and balanced the spear far shadowed, and threw it, and struck the middle of Peleïdes' shield, nor missed it, but the spear was driven far back from the shield, and Hektor was angered because his swift weapon had been loosed from his hand in a vain cast.

He stood discouraged, and had no other ash spear; but lifting his voice he called aloud on Deïphobos of the pale shield, and asked him for a long spear, but Deïphobos was not near him.

And Hektor knew the truth inside his heart, and spoke aloud: 'No use. Here at last the gods have summoned me deathward. I thought Deïphobos the hero was here close beside me, but he is behind the wall and it was Athene cheating me, and now evil death is close to me, and no longer far away, and there is no way out. So it must long since have been pleasing to Zeus, and Zeus' son who strikes from afar, this way; though before this they defended me gladly. But now my death is upon me. Let me at least not die without a struggle, inglorious, but do some big thing first, that men to come shall know of it.'

So he spoke, and pulling out the sharp sword that was slung at the hollow of his side, huge and heavy, and gathering himself together, he made his swoop, like a high-flown eagle who launches himself out of the murk of the clouds on the flat land to catch away a tender lamb or a shivering hare; so Hektor made his swoop, swinging his sharp sword, and Achilleus charged, the heart within him loaded with savage fury. In front of his chest the beautiful elaborate great shield covered him, and with the glittering helm with four horns he nodded; the lovely golden fringes were shaken about it which Hephaistos had driven close along the horn of the helmet. And as a star moves among stars in the night's darkening, Hesper, who is the fairest star who stands in the sky, such was the shining from the pointed spear Achilleus was shaking in his right hand with evil intention toward brilliant Hektor. He was eyeing Hektor's splendid body, to see where it might best give way, but all the rest of the skin was held in the armour, brazen and splendid, he stripped when he cut down the strength of Patroklos; yet showed where the collar-bones hold the neck from the shoulders, the throat, where death of the soul comes most swiftly; in this place brilliant Achilleus drove the spear as he came on in fury, and clean through the soft part of the neck the spearpoint was driven.

Yet the ash spear heavy with bronze did not sever the windpipe, so that Hektor could still make exchange of words spoken. But he dropped in the dust, and brilliant Achilleus vaunted above him:

'Hektor, surely you thought as you killed Patroklos you would be safe, and since I was far away you thought nothing of me, o fool, for an avenger was left, far greater than he was, behind him and away by the hollow ships. And it was I; and I have broken your strength; on you the dogs and the vultures shall feed and foully rip you; the Achaians will bury Patroklos.'

In his weakness Hektor of the shining helm spoke to him: 'I entreat you, by your life, by your knees, by your parents, do not let the dogs feed on me by the ships of the Achaians, but take yourself the bronze and gold that are there in abundance, those gifts that my father and the lady my mother will give you, and give my body to be taken home again, so that the Trojans and the wives of the Trojans may give me in death my rite of burning.'

But looking darkly at him swift-footed Achilleus answered: 'No more entreating of me, you dog, by knees or parents. I wish only that my spirit and fury would drive me to hack your meat away and eat it raw for the things that you have done to me. So there is no one who can hold the dogs off from your head, not if they bring here and set before me ten times and twenty times the ransom, and promise more in addition, not if Priam son of Dardanos should offer to weigh out your bulk in gold; not even so shall the lady your mother who herself bore you lay you on the death-bed and mourn you: no, but the dogs and the birds will have you all for their feasting.'

Then, dying, Hektor of the shining helmet spoke to him: 'I know you well as I look upon you, I know that I could not persuade you, since indeed in your breast is a heart of iron. Be careful now; for I might be made into the gods' curse upon you, on that day when Paris and Phoibos Apollo destroy you in the Skaian gates, for all your valour.'

He spoke, and as he spoke the end of death closed in upon him, and the soul fluttering free of the limbs went down into Death's house mourning her destiny, leaving youth and manhood behind her. Now though he was a dead man brilliant Achilleus spoke to him: 'Die: and I will take my own death at whatever time Zeus and the rest of the immortals choose to accomplish it.'

Golden Age to Iron Age

The farmer-poet Hesiod wrote mostly about everyday country life. But, living in trou-
bled times, he also tried to explain how evil and strife came into the world. Hesiod saw
human history as a degeneration from an original "golden" age to his own "iron" age.

From *Hesiod's Works and Days*

But if you will, another tale will I briefly tell you well and skilfully, and do
you ponder it in your mind, that from the same origin are sprung gods and mortal men. First of all the immortals holding the mansions of Olympus made a
golden race of men. They indeed lived under Kronos what time he ruled in
heaven. And as gods they were wont to live, with a life void of care, apart from,
and without labours and trouble: nor was wretched old age at all impending,
but ever the same in hands and feet, did they delight themselves in festivals out
of the reach of all ills: and they died, as if o'ercome by sleep; all blessings were
theirs; of its own will the fruitful field would bear them fruit, much and ample;
and they gladly used to reap the labours of their hands in quietness along with
many good things, being rich in flocks, and dear to the blessed gods. But after
that Earth had covered this generation by the will of mighty Zeus, they indeed
are Spirits, kindly haunting-earth, guardians of mortal men, who watch both the
decisions of justice and harsh deeds, going to and fro everywhere over the earth,
having wrapt themselves in mist, givers of riches as they are: and this is a kingly
function which they have.

Afterwards again the dwellers in Olympian mansions formed a second race
of silver, far inferior; like unto the golden neither in shape nor mind: but for a
hundred years indeed a boy was reared and grew up beside his wise mother, in
her house, being quite childish: but when they finally came to age and reached
the stature of manhood, but for a brief space used they to live, suffering griefs
through their foolishness: for they could not keep off rash insult one from the
other, nor were they willing to worship the gods, nor to sacrifice at the holy altars of the blessed, as it is right men should in their abodes. Afterwards, Zeus,
son of Kronos, buried these too in his wrath, because they gave not due honours
to the blessed gods, who occupy Olympus. Now when earth had covered this
race also, they too beneath the ground, are called blessed spirits, second in rank;
but still honour attends these also.

And yet a third race of men formed father Zeus of brass, not at all like unto
silver, formidable and mighty by reason of their ashen spears; whose care was
the ghastly deeds of Mars. Nor did they eat bread alone but also flesh. They had
stout-spirited hearts of adamant, unapproachable. Now vast strength and
hands unvanquished grew from their shoulders upon sturdy arms. These had
brazen weapons, and likewise brazen houses, and with brass they wrought; for
there was not yet dark iron. They indeed, destroyed by the hands of one another,

From J. Banks, *The Works of Hesiod, Callimachus, and Theognis* (London: Henry G. Bohn, 1856),
pp. 77–85.

entered the squalid abode of chilling Hades, inglorious: for terrible though they were, black Death seized them and they quitted the bright sunlight.

But when earth had covered this race also, again Zeus, son of Kronos, wrought yet another, a fourth, on the fertile ground, more just and more worthy, a godlike race of hero-men, the race before our own upon the boundless earth. But these too baneful war, as well as the dire battle-din, destroyed, a part fighting before seven-gated Thebes, in the land of Kadmos, for the flocks of Oedipus, and part also in ships beyond the vast depths of the sea, when it had led them to Troy for fair-haired Helen's sake. There indeed the end of death enshrouded them; but to them Zeus, son of Kronos, their sire, having given life and settlements apart from men, made them dwell at the end of earth, afar from the immortals. Among these Kronos rules. And they indeed dwell with careless spirit in the Isles of the Blest, beside deep-eddying Ocean; blest heroes, for whom thrice in a year doth the fertile soil bear blooming fruits as sweet as honey.

Would that I had no part with the fifth race of men, but had either died before, or been born afterward. For now in truth is the iron race. They will never cease by day, nor by night, from toil and wretchedness, corrupt as they are: but the gods will give them severe cares: yet nevertheless even for these shall good be mingled with ill. But Zeus will destroy this race of men too when, soon after being born, they become silvery-templed. Nor will sire agree with sons, nor sons at all with parent, nor guest with host, nor comrade with comrade, nor will brother be dear, as it was aforetime, to brother. But quickly will they dishonour parents growing old, and will blame them, addressing them with harsh words, being impious, and unaware of the vengeance of the gods; nor to aged parents would these pay back the price of their nurture. Using the right of might, one will sack the city of another: nor will there be any favour to the trusty; nor the just, nor the good, but rather they will honour a man that doeth evil and is overbearing; and justice and shame will not be in their hands, and the bad man will injure the better speaking in perverse speeches, and swearing a false oath. But on all wretched mortals envy with its tongues of malice, exulting in ill, will attend with hateful look. Then also indeed shall Shame and Retribution, shrouding their fair skin in white mantles, depart from broad-wayed earth to Olympus, forsaking the whole race of man: but the baneful griefs shall remain behind, and against evil there shall be no recourse.

Human Love

During the transition from the "heroic age" of Greek civilization to the "classical age," new forms of thought and expression arose. Lyric poets produced verses more intimate

From Mary Barnard, *Sappho, A New Translation* (Berkeley and Los Angeles, Calif.: University of California Press, 1958), Nos. 30, 31, 17, 83, 50, 43. Reprinted by permission of the publisher.

and personal than the ancient tales of gods and heroes. The poems of Sappho (active c. 600 B.C.) provide a rare example of a woman's voice speaking to us directly from the world of ancient Greece.

From *Poems of Sappho*

Wedding Song

Lucky bridegroom!
Now the wedding you
asked for is over

and your wife is the
girl you asked for;
she's a bride who is

charming to look at,
with eyes as soft as
honey, and a face

that Love has lighted
with his own beauty.
Aphrodite has surely

outdone herself in
doing honor to you!

BRIDESMAIDS' CAROL

O Bride brimful of
rosy little loves!

O brightest jewel of
the Queen of Paphos!

Come now
to your
bedroom to your
bed
and play there
sweetly gently
with your bridegroom

And may Hesperus
lead you not at all

unwilling
until
you stand wondering
before the silver

Throne of Hera
Queen of Marriage

CLEIS I

I have a small
daughter called
Cleis, who is

like a golden
flower
I wouldn't
take all Croesus'
kingdom with love
thrown in, for her

CLEIS II

I have no embroidered
headband from Sardis to
give you, Cleis, such as
I wore
and my mother
always said that in her
day a purple ribbon
looped in the hair was thought
to be high style indeed

but we were dark:
a girl
whose hair is yellower than
torchlight should wear no
headdress but fresh flowers

ATTHIS I

Atthis, I love you
long ago while you
still seemed to me a
small ungracious child

I was proud of you, too

In skill I think
you need never
bow to any girl

not one who may
see the sunlight
in time to come

After all this

Atthis, you hate
even the thought

of me. You dart
off to Andromeda

ATTHIS II

It was you, Atthis, who said

"Sappho, if you will not get
up and let us look at you
I shall never love you again!

"Get up, unleash your suppleness,
lift off your Chian nightdress
and, like a lily leaning into

"a spring, bathe in the water.
Cleis is bringing your best
purple frock and the yellow

"tunic down from the clothes chest;
you will have a cloak thrown over
you and flowers crowning your hair . . .

"Praxinoa, my child, will you please
roast nuts for our breakfast? One
of the gods is being good to us:

"today we are going at last
into Mitylene, our favorite
city, with Sappho, loveliest

"of its women; she will walk
among us like a mother with
all her daughters around her

"when she comes home from exile . . ."

But you forget everything

FROM MYTHOLOGY TO PHILOSOPHY

Religion

Xenophanes (c. 570–c. 475 B.C.) was the first Greek writer to challenge the accepted mythology about the many gods of Olympus.

From *Xenophanes*

There is one God, supreme among gods and men, not at all like mortals in body or in mind.

It is the whole (of God) that sees, the whole that thinks, and the whole that hears.

From G. S. Kirk and J. E. Raven, *The Presocratic Philosophers*, B. Tierney, trans. (Cambridge: Cambridge University Press, 1969), Nos. 169–175, 189–190. Reprinted by permission of the publisher.

He always remains in the same place, not moving at all; it is not fitting for him to be in different places at different times.

But without effort he sets all things in motion by the thoughts of his mind.

Homer and Hesiod attributed to the gods everything which is shameful and blameworthy among humans—such lawless deeds as stealing, committing adultery and deceiving one another.

Mortals suppose that the gods are born and that they have voices and bodies and clothes like humans.

But if oxen or horses or lions had hands and could draw with their hands and paint pictures as men do, they would portray their gods as having bodies like their own: horses would portray them like horses, and oxen like oxen.

Ethiopians have gods with snub noses and black hair; Thracians have gods with gray eyes and red hair.

Clearly the gods did not reveal everything to mortals at the outset; but, by searching, in the course of time mortals discover for themselves what is better.

There is no man and there will never be one who has plain knowledge about the gods and about all the matters I discuss. For even if one happened by chance to say the complete truth, he still would not know for certain that he did so.

These things have seemed to me resemblances of what is true.

Philosophy

The Greeks, it has been said, invented heresy. They also invented philosophy. If we begin to doubt that everything in the universe is the way it is simply because the gods make it so, then new problems arise. How can the intrinsic order of the universe be explained? Is there anything permanent behind the changing phenomena revealed to us by sense experience?

Parmenides (active c. 475 B.C.) wrestled with the problem of how the world came to exist. Unlike the author of the Hebrew story of creation (p. 7) he maintained that the universe could not have been created at some point in past time. What exists now, he argued, must always have existed. Why did Parmenides believe that the universe had no beginning and would have no end?

From *Parmenides* ⁓ On Time

There remains only one way of inquiry to be discussed: that being *is*. And on this way there are many signs that *What Is* is uncreated and indestructible. It is whole, immovable, without end. It *was* not in the past nor *will* it be since it *is* now, altogether, one, continuous. How can you seek for its creation? How and from what source could it grow? I will not let you say or think that it came from not-being, for it cannot be said or thought that not-being *is*. Besides, what could have stirred it into activity at a later rather than an earlier time if it came from nothingness? Therefore it must exist absolutely or not exist at all. The force of our convictions will not allow anything to emerge from nothingness except nothingness. . . .

Cont'd ↓

From G. S. Kirk and J. E. Raven, *The Presocratic Philosophers*, B. Tierney, trans. (Cambridge: Cambridge University Press, 1969), Nos. 347, 348, 352. Reprinted by permission of the publisher.

How could *What Is* cease to be? And how could it come into being? For if it came into being or is going to come into being there would be a time when it *is* not. So coming-into-being is excluded and destruction is unimaginable.

Nor is it divisible since it is homogeneous. Nor is it more concentrated here than there, which would prevent its cohesion, but it is all full of Being. So the Whole is continuous, for *What Is* is in contact with *What Is.* . . .

To think is the same as thinking that being *is*, for you will not find thought without being which it expresses. Nor is there, nor will there be anything besides *What Is*, for fate has bound it to be whole and immovable. Accordingly all these things that mortals accept as true—coming-into-being and perishing, being and not-being, change of position, and alteration of bright color—these are mere names.

There is a commonsensical persuasiveness in Parmenides' view that nothing can come from nothingness. But his assertion that the eternally existing Whole is unmoving and unchanging seems contrary to sense experience. The first atomic theories were devised to cope with this problem. We know the views of Leucippus (active c. 440 B.C.) and Democritus (active c. 430 B.C.) from surviving fragments of their works and from descriptions by later Greek authors.[1]

Atomism: Leucippus and Democritus

By convention there are sweet and bitter, by convention there are hot and cold, by convention there is color; in reality there are only atoms and the void. (Democritus)

Nothing happens at random; everything for a reason and by necessity. (Leucippus)

The following accounts of early atomic theory are from Aristotle.

Some of the early philosophers thought that *What Is* must necessarily be one and immovable, for empty space is not-being and there could be no motion without empty space beside matter. Likewise there could not be a plurality of things without something to separate them.

But Leucippus believed he had a theory which would be consistent with sense-perception, in that it did not exclude coming-to-be and perishing, nor motion, nor the multiplicity of things. So far he accepted the testimony of appearances. On the other hand he conceded to the monists that there could be no motion without a void, that a void is not-being, and that *What Is* cannot ever be *What Is Not*. Accordingly he agrees that *What Is* must be a complete, continuously full Whole; but he adds that there is not just one such whole; there are many of them; in fact they are infinite in number. Because of their extremely small bulk they are invisible. They move in the void—for there is a void—and by coming together they cause coming-to-be, while by their separation they cause perishing.

According to the theory of Democritus the eternal objects are tiny substances infinite in number. Accordingly he assigns also a place for them that is

[1]From G. S. Kirk and J. E. Raven, *The Presocratic Philosophers*, B. Tierney, trans. (Cambridge: Cambridge University Press, 1969), Nos. 589, 568, 552, 555. Reprinted by permission of the publisher.

infinitesimal in size, which he designates by these names—"the void," "nothing," and "the infinite"; whereas he calls each individual atom "thing," "the compact," and "being." He thinks them so small as to elude our senses, but they have all sorts of forms, shapes, and different sizes. Taking these as elements he thinks of them as combining to produce objects that are visible and otherwise perceptible to the senses. The particles move about and struggle in the void because of their dissimilarity and the other mentioned differences. In their motion they collide or brush against one another, and so they tend to get entangled and interlocked. The process never makes them into a single substance however, for it would be absurd to think that two or more things could ever become one. When these particles remain joined together for some time, it is explained by the fact that they intertwine and so catch hold of one another; for some bodies are angular, others hooked, some concave, others convex, and there are countless other differences. His theory is that they cling together and remain in combination until some stronger outside force separates them and shakes them apart.

For Pythagoras (active c. 530 B.C.) and his followers in the fifth century B.C. mathematical relationships were the basic reality. The Pythagoreans began from the observation that numerical ratios in the physical world are related to musical harmonies. (A lyre string half as long as another produces a note an octave higher.) They proceeded to construct a whole theory of an ordered harmonious universe based on number. Aristotle described their views rather skeptically.

Mathematics: The Pythagoreans

The Pythagoreans, as they are called, devoted themselves to mathematics and were the first to develop this study; and having been brought up in it they thought that its first principles were the first principles of everything. Now since numbers are naturally the first principles of mathematics, they thought they could find in numbers many resemblances to the things that exist and come into being. . . . Since, again, they saw that the properties and ratios of musical scales can be expressed as numbers, and since they considered that everything else, in its intrinsic nature, was modelled after numbers and that numbers were the basic principles of all nature, they concluded that the elements of numbers were the elements of everything, and that the whole heaven consisted of harmony and number.

Accordingly they collected and fitted into their scheme all the properties of numbers and harmonies that they could relate to the properties and parts and the whole arrangement of the heavens; and if any gaps occurred they made additions of their own so as to keep their whole system coherent. For example, since the number ten is considered to be perfect and to contain in itself the whole system of numbers, they say that there must be ten bodies moving through the heavens. But in fact only nine are discernible. Hence they invent a tenth body, called a "counter-earth. . . ."

In all this they are not seeking reasons and causes to explain observed facts but stretching the facts to fit theories and principles of their own.

From G. S. Kirk and J. E. Raven, *The Presocratic Philosophers*, B. Tierney, trans. (Cambridge: Cambridge University Press, 1969), Nos. 289, 329, 306. Reprinted by permission of the publisher.

The Pythagoreans, discerning that things evident to sense experience have many of the attributes of number, supposed that real things are numbers—not just that they are associated with numbers as something separable from themselves but that they really consist of numbers. And why so? Because the properties of numbers inhere in musical harmony, in the movements of the heavens, and in many other things. But for those who hold that number is merely mathematical it is impossible to say such a thing.

SOCIETY AND GOVERNMENT—THE POLIS

Athens

By the fifth century different patterns of civic life had grown up in the various Greek city-states. Athens was the most democratic of them, Sparta more authoritarian. From 431 to 404 B.C. these two rivals fought in a long-drawn-out struggle, the Peloponnesian War, with Sparta finally emerging as the victor. Thucydides, who wrote an extensive history of the war, gave a memorable description of the ideals of Athens in a speech attributed to the Athenian leader Pericles. How did Thuycidides define democracy? How did he characterize Athenian attitudes to wealth and poverty, participation in public affairs, military training?

From Thucydides. *History of the Peloponnesian War*

'Let me say that our system of government does not copy the institutions of our neighbours. It is more the case of our being a model to others, than of our imitating anyone else. Our constitution is called a democracy because power is in the hands not of a minority but of the whole people. When it is a question of settling private disputes, everyone is equal before the law; when it is a question of putting one person before another in positions of public responsibility, what counts is not membership of a particular class, but the actual ability which the man possesses. No one, so long as he has it in him to be of service to the state, is kept in political obscurity because of poverty. And, just as our political life is free and open, so is our day-to-day life in our relations with each other. We do not get into a state with our next-door neighbour if he enjoys himself in his own way, nor do we give him the kind of black looks which, though they do no real harm, still do hurt people's feelings. We are free and tolerant in our private lives; but in public affairs we keep to the law. This is because it commands our deep respect.

'We give our obedience to those whom we put in positions of authority, and we obey the laws themselves, especially those which are for the protection of the oppressed, and those unwritten laws which it is an acknowledged shame to break.

From Thucydides, *History of the Peloponnesian War*, Rex Warner, trans. (Baltimore: Penguin Books, 1954), pp. 117–120.

'And here is another point. When our work is over, we are in a position to enjoy all kinds of recreation for our spirits. There are various kinds of contests and sacrifices regularly throughout the year; in our own homes we find a beauty and a good taste which delight us every day and which drive away our cares. Then the greatness of our city brings it about that all the good things from all over the world flow in to us, so that to us it seems just as natural to enjoy foreign goods as our own local products.

'Then there is a great difference between us and our opponents, in our attitude towards military security. Here are some examples: Our city is open to the world, and we have no periodical deportations in order to prevent people observing or finding out secrets which might be of military advantage to the enemy. This is because we rely, not on secret weapons, but on our own real courage and loyalty. There is a difference, too, in our educational systems. The Spartans, from their earliest boyhood, are submitted to the most laborious training in courage; we pass our lives without all these restrictions, and yet are just as ready to face the same dangers as they are. Here is a proof of this: When the Spartans invade our land, they do not come by themselves, but bring all their allies with them; whereas we, when we launch an attack abroad, do the job by ourselves, and, though fighting on foreign soil, do not often fail to defeat opponents who are fighting for their own hearths and homes. As a matter of fact none of our enemies has ever yet been confronted with our total strength, because we have to divide our attention between our navy and the many missions on which our troops are sent on land. Yet, if our enemies engage a detachment of our forces and defeat it, they give themselves credit for having thrown back our entire army; or, if they lose, they claim that they were beaten by us in full strength. There are certain advantages, I think, in our way of meeting danger voluntarily, with an easy mind, instead of with a laborious training, with natural rather than with state-induced courage. We do not have to spend our time practising to meet sufferings which are still in the future; and when they are actually upon us we show ourselves just as brave as these others who are always in strict training. This is one point in which, I think, our city deserves to be admired. There are also others:

'Our love of what is beautiful does not lead to extravagance; our love of the things of the mind does not make us soft. We regard wealth as something to be properly used, rather than as something to boast about. As for poverty, no one need be ashamed to admit it: the real shame is in not taking practical measures to escape from it. Here each individual is interested not only in his own affairs but in the affairs of the state as well: even those who are mostly occupied with their own business are extremely well-informed on general politics—this is a peculiarity of ours: we do not say that a man who takes no interest in politics is a man who minds his own business; we say that he has no business here at all. We Athenians, in our own persons, take our decisions on policy or submit them to proper discussions: for we do not think that there is an incompatibility between words and deeds; the worst thing is to rush into action before the consequences have been properly debated. And this is another point where we differ from other people. We are capable at the same time of taking risks and of estimating them beforehand. Others are brave out of ignorance; and, when they stop to think, they begin to fear. But the man who can most truly be accounted brave is he who best knows the meaning of what is sweet in life and of what is terrible, and then goes out undeterred to meet what is to come.

'Again, in questions of general good feeling there is a great contrast between us and most other people. We make friends by doing good to others, not by receiving good from them. This makes our friendship all the more reliable, since we want to keep alive the gratitude of those who are in our debt by showing continued goodwill to them: whereas the feelings of one who owes us something lack the same enthusiasm, since he knows that, when he repays our kindness, it will be more like paying back a debt than giving something spontaneously. We are unique in this. When we do kindnesses to others, we do not do them out of any calculations of profit or loss: we do them without afterthought, relying on our free liberality. Taking everything together then, I declare that our city is an education to Greece, and I declare that in my opinion each single one of our citizens, in all the manifold aspects of life, is able to show himself the rightful lord and owner of his own person, and do this, moreover, with exceptional grace and exceptional versatility. And to show that this is no empty boasting for the present occasion, but real tangible fact, you have only to consider the power which our city possesses and which has been won by those very qualities which I have mentioned. Athens, alone of the states we know, comes to her testing time in a greatness that surpasses what was imagined of her. In her case, and in her case alone, no invading enemy is ashamed at being defeated, and no subject can complain of being governed by people unfit for their responsibilities. Mighty indeed are the marks and monuments our empire which we have left. Future ages will wonder at us, as the present age wonders at us now. We do not need the praises of a Homer, or of anyone else whose words may delight us for the moment, but whose estimation of facts will fall short of what is really true. For our adventurous spirit has forced an entry into every sea and into every land; and everywhere we have left behind us everlasting memorials of good done to our friends or suffering inflicted on our enemies.

'This, then, is the kind of city for which these men, who could not bear the thought of losing her, nobly fought and nobly died. It is . . . for you to try to be like them. Make up your minds that happiness depends on being free, and freedom depends on being courageous. Let there be no relaxation in face of the perils of the war.'

Sparta

Plutarch wrote in the first century A.D., *but his* Life of Lycurgus, *based on earlier sources, described Spartan institutions as they had existed several centuries before. (Lycurgus was the legendary founder of Sparta's constitution.) How did attitudes to the individual and the state differ in Athens and Sparta? How did the differences affect political ideals, education, and everyday life?*

From Plutarch. *Life of Lycurgus*

Among the many changes and alterations which Lycurgus made, the first and of greatest importance was the establishment of the senate, which, having a power equal to the kings' in matters of great consequence, and as Plato expresses it, allaying and qualifying the fiery genius of the royal office, gave steadiness and safety to the commonwealth. For the state, which before had no firm basis to stand upon, but leaned one while toward an absolute monarchy, when the kings had the upper hand, and another while toward a pure democracy, when the people had the better, found in this establishment of the senate a central weight, like ballast in a ship, which always kept things in a just equilibrium; the twenty-eight always adhering to the kings so far as to resist democracy, and, on the other hand, supporting the people against the establishment of absolute monarchy. . . .

After the creation of the thirty senators, his next task, and, indeed, the most hazardous he ever undertook, was the making a new division of their lands. For there was an extreme inequality among them, and their state was overloaded with a multitude of indigent and necessitous persons, while its whole wealth had centered upon a very few. To the end, therefore, that he might expel from the state arrogance and envy, luxury and crime, and those yet more inveterate diseases of want and superfluity, he obtained of them to renounce their properties, and to consent to a new division of the land, and that they should live all together on an equal footing; merit to be their only road to eminence, and the disgrace of evil, and credit of worthy acts, the one measure of difference between man and man. . . .

The third and most masterly stroke of this great lawgiver, by which he struck a yet more effectual blow against luxury and the desire of riches, was the ordinance he made, that they should all eat in common, of the same bread, and same meat, and of kinds that were specified, and should not spend their lives at home, laid on costly couches at splendid tables, delivering themselves up into the hands of their tradesmen and cooks, to fatten them in corners, like greedy brutes, and to ruin not their minds only but their very bodies, which, enfeebled by indulgence and excess, would stand in need of long sleep, warm bathing, freedom from work, and, in a word, of as much care and attendance as if they were continually sick. It was certainly an extraordinary thing to have brought about such a result as this, but a greater yet to have taken away from wealth, as Theophrastes observes, not merely the property of being coveted, but its very nature of being wealth. For the rich, being obliged to go to the same table with the poor, could not make use of or enjoy their abundance, nor so much as please their vanity by looking at or displaying it. . . .

In order to promote the good education of their youth (which, as I said before, he thought the most important and noblest work of a lawgiver), he went so far back as to take into consideration their very conception and birth, by regulating

From *Plutarch's Lives,* The Translation Called Dryden's rev. A. H. Clough (Boston: Little, Brown and Co., 1872), pp. 90, 93–96, 100–106, 109, 115, 119–120.

their marriages. For Aristotle is wrong in saying, that, after he had tried all ways to reduce the women to more modesty and sobriety, he was at last forced to leave them as they were, because that in the absence of their husbands, who spent the best parts of their lives in the wars, their wives, whom they were obliged to leave absolute mistresses at home, took great liberties and assumed the superiority; and were treated with overmuch respect and called by the title of lady or queen. The truth is, he took in their case, also, all the care that was possible; he ordered the maidens to exercise themselves with wrestling, running, throwing the quoit, and casting the dart, to the end that the fruit they conceived might, in strong and healthy bodies, take firmer root and find better growth, and withal that they, with this greater vigor, might be the more able to undergo the pains of child-bearing. And to the end he might take away their over-great tenderness and fear of exposure to the air, and all acquired womanishness, he ordered that the young women should go naked in the processions, as well as the young men, and dance, too, in that condition, at certain solemn feasts, singing certain songs, while the young men stood around, seeing and hearing them. On these occasions, they now and then made, by jests, a befitting reflection upon those who had misbehaved themselves in the wars; and again sang encomiums upon those who had done any gallant action, and by these means inspired the younger sort with an emulation of their glory. Those that were thus commended went away proud, elated, and gratified with their honor among the maidens; and those who were rallied were as sensibly touched with it as if they had been formally reprimanded; and so much the more, because the kings and the elders, as well as the rest of the city, saw and heard all that passed. Nor was there any thing shameful in this nakedness of the young women; modesty attended them, and all wantonness was excluded. It taught them simplicity and a care for good health, and gave them some taste of higher feelings, admitted as they thus were to the field of noble action and glory. Hence it was natural for them to think and speak as Gorgo, for example, the wife of Leonidas, is said to have done, when some foreign lady, as it would seem, told her that the women of Lacedaemon were the only women of the world who could rule men; "With good reason," she said, "for we are the only women who bring forth men." . . .

Lycurgus allowed a man who was advanced in years and had a young wife to recommend some virtuous and approved young man, that she might have a child by him, who might inherit the good qualities of the father, and be a son to himself. On the other side, an honest man who had love for a married woman upon account of her modesty and the well-favoredness of her children, might, without formality, beg her company of her husband, that he might raise, as it were, from this plot of good ground, worthy and well-allied children for himself. And indeed, Lycurgus was of a persuasion that children were not so much the property of their parents as of the whole commonwealth, and, therefore, would not have his citizens begot by the first comers, but by the best men that could be found: the laws of other nations seemed to him very absurd and inconsistent, where people would be so solicitous for their dogs and horses as to exert interest and pay money to procure fine breeding, and yet kept their wives shut up, to be made mothers only by themselves, who might be foolish, infirm, or diseased; as if it were not apparent that children of a bad breed would prove their bad qualities first upon those who kept and were rearing them, and well-born children, in like manner, their good qualities. . . .

Nor was it lawful, indeed, for the father himself to breed up the children after his own fancy; but as soon as they were seven years old they were to be enrolled in certain companies and classes, where they all lived under the same order and discipline, doing their exercises and taking their play together. Of these, he who showed the most conduct and courage was made captain; they had their eyes always upon him, obeyed his orders, and underwent patiently whatsoever punishment he inflicted; so that the whole course of their education was one continued exercise of a ready and perfect obedience. The old men, too, were spectators of their performances, and often raised quarrels and disputes among them, to have a good opportunity of finding out their different characters, and of seeing which would be valiant, which a coward, when they should come to more dangerous encounters. Reading and writing they gave them, just enough to serve their turn; their chief care was to make them good subjects, and to teach them to endure pain and conquer in battle. To this end, as they grew in years, their discipline was proportionably increased; their heads were close-clipped, they were accustomed to go barefoot, and for the most part to play naked. . . . Their lovers and favorers, too, had a share in the young boy's honor or disgrace; and there goes a story that one of them was fined by the magistrate, because the lad whom he loved cried out effeminately as he was fighting. And though this sort of love was so approved among them, that the most virtuous matrons would make professions of it to young girls, yet rivalry did not exist, and if several men's fancies met in one person, it was rather the beginning of an intimate friendship, while they all jointly conspired to render the object of their affection as accomplished as possible. . . . Their discipline continued still after they were full-grown men. No one was allowed to live after his own fancy; but the city was a sort of camp, in which every man had his share of provisions and business set out, and looked upon himself not so much born to serve his own ends as the interest of his country.

One of the greatest and highest blessings Lycurgus procured his people was the abundance of leisure which proceeded from his forbidding to them the exercise of any mean and mechanical trade. Of the money-making that depends on troublesome going about and seeing people and doing business they had no need at all in a state where wealth obtained no honor or respect. The Helots tilled their ground for them, and paid them yearly in kind the appointed quantity, without any trouble of theirs. . . .

And this was the reason why he forbade them to travel abroad, and go about acquainting themselves with foreign rules of morality, the habits of ill-educated people, and different views of government. Withal he banished from Lacedaemon all strangers who could not give a very good reason for their coming thither; not because he was afraid lest they should inform themselves of and imitate his manner of government (as Thucydides says), or learn any thing to their good; but rather lest they should introduce something contrary to good manners. With strange people, strange words must be admitted; these novelties produce novelties in thought; and on these follow views and feelings whose discordant character destroys the harmony of the state. He was as careful to save his city from the infection of foreign bad habits, as men usually are to prevent the introduction of a pestilence.

The Peloponnesian War

After the Peloponnesian War between Athens and Sparta had dragged on for nearly twenty years, Aristophanes, the greatest Greek comic playwright, protested against the war in his play Lysistrata. *Led by Lysistrata, the women of Athens first refused to sleep with their husbands, then seized the Athenian treasury to cut off funds for the war. In the following reading Lysistrata speaks with a magistrate sent to quell the women's rebellion. How did Lysistrata think that women could bring the war to an end?*

From *Lysistrata*

Lysistrata. Thank you.
All through the war—and what a long war—
By controlling ourselves we managed to endure
Somehow what you men did. We never once
Let ourselves grumble—not that we approved
What you did do. Simply, we understood you.
Oh, how often at home one would hear you spouting
Hot air about something serious!—and masking
Our misery with a smile we'd ask you gently,
'Dear, in the Assembly today, did you decide
Anything about peace?' And, 'what's that to do with *you*'
You'd growl, 'Shut up!' And I did.

Stratyllis. *I never did!*

Magistrate. You'd have been sorry if you hadn't! —Well . . .

Lysistrata. I held my tongue. And immediately you'd make
Some even more crazy decision, and I'd sigh and say,
'But how *can* you have passed this lunatic thing?'
And you'd frown and mutter 'Stick to your spinning,
'Or you *will* have something to complain of.
'War is men's business.'

Magistrate. And quite right too!

Lysistrata. Shouldn't we try to save you from your follies?—
When we see you mooning about the streets moaning
'Isn't there a *man* left in this country?' 'Not one,'
Says the old blimp with you. So we called a rally
Of all the women and planned: *we* would save Greece.
Why wait any longer? Now you must listen to *us*—

From *Lysistrata*, P. Dickinson, trans. in *Aristophanes Against War* (London: Oxford University Press, 1957), pp. 126–130.

It's our turn to talk, and *yours* to be quiet as we've been,
While *we're* busy, putting things right again.

Magistrate.   You do that for *us!* Intolerab—

Lysistrata.   Silence!

Magistrate.   Told to be quiet by a woman in a veil,

I'd rather die—

Lysistrata.   Oh if *that's* all it is—
You put my veil on *your* head and be QUIET!
[*She puts it on him*]

Kalonike.   And here's a spindle—[*forces it into his hand*]

Myrrhine.   And a *dear* little wool-basket—

Lysistrata.   Now bundle up your skirt, card wool, and
chew beans—
War is women's work! . . .

Magistrate.   And how do you propose
To disentangle all this and settle everybody?

Lysistrata.   Easily.

Magistrate.   How?

Lysistrata.   Just as when wool is tangled
We untangle it, working it through
This way and that—so we'll settle the war,
Sending embassies this way and that.

Magistrate.   Threads, skeins, spindles, you little fool:
What's this to do with *war?*

Lysistrata.   If you had any sense you could handle
Politics as we do wool!

Magistrate.   Well . . .?

Lysistrata.   Like the raw fleece in the wash tub, first
You must cleanse the city of dirt:
As *we* beat out the muck and pick out the burrs,
You must pluck out the place-seekers, sack the spongers
Out of their sinecure offices, rip off their heads—
Then the common skein of good sense:—
Blend the good aliens, the allies, the strangers,
Even the debtors, into one ball;
Consider the colonies scattered threads,
Pick up their ends and gather them quick;
Make one magnificent bobbin and weave
A garment of government fit for the people!

Magistrate.   It's all very well this carding and winding—
women!
You haven't any idea what a war *means.*

Lysistrata   [*very deliberate and serious*]. We know just twice
as well.
We bore the sons
You took for soldiers.

Thucydides presented an idealized picture of democratic Athens in his Funeral Oration (p. 52). But Athenian democrats could be far from generous in dealing with other cities. In one minor incident of the Peloponnesian War, Athens attacked the island of Melos, an ally of Sparta. The ensuing "Melian Dialogue" was recorded by Thucydides in his history of the war. What does it tell us about Athenian foreign policy?

From *The Melian Dialogue*

Melians: It is natural and understandable that people who are placed as we are should have recourse to all kinds of arguments and different points of view. However, you are right in saying that we are met together here to discuss the safety of our country and, if you will have it so, the discussion shall proceed on the lines that you have laid down.

Athenians: Then we on our side will use no fine phrases saying, for example, that we have a right to our empire because we defeated the Persians, or that we have come against you now because of the injuries you have done us—a great mass of words that nobody would believe. And we ask you on your side not to imagine that you will influence us by saying that you, though a colony of Sparta, have not joined Sparta in the war, or that you have never done us any harm. Instead we recommend that you should try to get what it is possible for you to get, taking into consideration what we both really do think; since you know as well as we do that, when these matters are discussed by practical people, the standard of justice depends on the equality of power to compel and that in fact the strong do what they have the power to do and the weak accept what they have to accept.

Melians: Then in our view (since you force us to leave justice out of account and to confine ourselves to self-interest)—in our view it is at any rate useful that you should not destroy a principle that is to the general good of all men— namely, that in the case of all who fall into danger there should be such a thing as fair play and just dealing, and that such people should be allowed to use and to profit by arguments that fall short of a mathematical accuracy. And this is a principle which affects you as much as anybody, since your own fall would be visited by the most terrible vengeance and would be an example to the world.

Athenians: As for us, even assuming that our empire does come to an end, we are not despondent about what would happen next. One is not so much

From Thucydides, *History of the Peloponnesian War,* Rex Warner, trans. (Baltimore, Penguin Books, 1954), pp. 360–362, 365.

frightened of being conquered by a power which rules over others, as Sparta does (not that we are concerned with Sparta now), as of what would happen if a ruling power is attacked and defeated by its own subjects. So far as this point is concerned, you can leave it to us to face the risks involved. What we shall do now is to show you that it is for the good of our own empire that we are here and that it is for the preservation of your city that we shall say what we are going to say. We do not want any trouble in bringing you into our empire, and we want you to be spared for the good both of yourselves and of ourselves:

Melians: And how could it be just as good for us to be the slaves as for you to be the masters?

Athenians: You, by giving in, would save yourselves from disaster; we, by not destroying you, would be able to profit from you.

Melians: So you would not agree to our being neutral, friends instead of enemies, but allies of neither side?

Athenians: No, because it is not so much your hostility that injures us; it is rather the case that, if we were on friendly terms with you, our subjects would regard that as a sign of weakness in us, whereas your hatred is evidence of our power.

Melians: Is that your subjects' idea of fair play—that no distinction should be made between people who are quite unconnected with you and people who are mostly your own colonists or else rebels whom you have conquered?

Athenians: So far as right and wrong are concerned they think that there is no difference between the two, that those who still preserve their independence do so because they are strong, and that if we fail to attack them it is because we are afraid. So that by conquering you we shall increase not only the size but the security of our empire. We rule the sea and you are islanders, and weaker islanders too than the others; it is therefore particularly important that you should not escape.

Melians: But do you think there is no security for you in what we suggest? For here again, since you will not let us mention justice, but tell us to give in to your interests, we, too, must tell you what our interests are and, if yours and ours happen to coincide, we must try to persuade you of the fact. Is it not certain that you will make enemies of all states who are at present neutral, when they see what is happening here and naturally conclude that in course of time you will attack them too? Does not this mean that you are strengthening the enemies you have already and are forcing others to become your enemies even against their intentions and their inclinations?

Athenians: As a matter of fact we are not so much frightened of states on the continent. They have their liberty, and this means that it will be a long time before they begin to take precautions against us. We are more concerned about islanders like yourselves, who are still unsubdued, or subjects who have already become embittered by the constraint which our empire imposes on them. These are the people who are most likely to act in a reckless manner and to bring themselves and us, too, into the most obvious danger.

Melians: Then surely, if such hazards are taken by you to keep your empire and by your subjects to escape from it, we who are still free would show ourselves great cowards and weaklings if we failed to face everything that comes rather than submit to slavery.

Athenians: No, not if you are sensible. This is no fair fight, with honour on one side and shame on the other. It is rather a question of saving your lives and not resisting those who are far too strong for you.

Melians: Yet we know that in war fortune sometimes makes the odds more level than could be expected from the difference in numbers of the two sides. And if we surrender, then all our hope is lost at once, whereas, so long as we remain in action, there is still a hope that we may yet stand upright.

The Athenian representatives then went back to the army, and the Athenian generals, finding that the Melians would not submit, immediately commenced hostilities and built a wall completely round the city of Melos, dividing the work out among the various states. [*The Melians still refused to submit and attacked their besiegers.*] Siege operations were now carried on vigorously and, as there was also some treachery from inside, the Melians surrendered unconditionally to the Athenians, who put to death all the men of military age whom they took, and sold the women and children as slaves. Melos itself they took over for themselves, sending out later a colony of 500 men.

DIVINE AND HUMAN LAW

Sophocles

In his play Antigone, *Sophocles (c. 495–c. 406 B.C.) raised moral problems that have persisted in Western culture down to modern times.*

For Sophocles the will of the gods is no longer mere divine caprice (as in Homer) but "unwritten and unfailing" law. Also Sophocles sees loyalty to the state as a necessary safeguard against anarchy in all normal circumstances. But what if the law of the state conflicts with divine law?

Antigone and Polineices are children of Oedipus, the king of Thebes who offended the gods by unknowingly marrying his own mother. A new king of Thebes, Creon, commands that the body of Polineices be left unburied as a penalty for treason. Antigone, defying the royal edict, sprinkles dust on her brother's corpse.

Why did Antigone disobey King Creon? Did she protest against injustice in general? Or maintain that family loyalties were more important than obligations to the state? How did Creon defend his treatment of Antigone? Was his condemnation of her justified?

From *Antigone*

Creon (to Antigone)	You—tell me not at length but in a word.
	You knew the order not to do this thing?

From Sophocles, *Antigone,* Elizabeth Wyckoff, trans. in *The Complete Greek Tragedies,* David Grene and Richmond Lattimore, eds., pp. 174–175, 180–187, 203. Copyright © 1954 by University of Chicago Press. Reprinted by permission of the publisher.

Antigone	I knew, of course I knew. The word was plain.
Creon	And still you dared to overstep these laws?
Antigone	For me it was not Zeus who made that order.
	Nor did that Justice who lives with the gods below
	mark out such laws to hold among mankind.
	Nor did I think your orders were so strong
	that you, a mortal man, could over-run
	the gods' unwritten and unfailing laws.
	Not now, nor yesterday's, they always live,
	and no one knows their origin in time.
	So not through fear of any man's proud spirit
	would I be likely to neglect these laws,
	draw on myself the gods' sure punishment.
	I knew that I must die; how could I not?
	even without your warning. If I die
	before my time, I say it is a gain.
	Who lives in sorrows many as are mine
	how shall he not be glad to gain his death?
	And so, for me to meet this fate, no grief.
	But if I left that corpse, my mother's son,
	dead and unburied I'd have cause to grieve
	as now I grieve not.
	And if you think my acts are foolishness
	the foolishness may be in a fool's eye.
Chorus	The girl is bitter. She's her father's child.
	She cannot yield to trouble; nor could he.
Creon	These rigid spirits are the first to fall.
	The strongest iron, hardened in the fire,
	most often ends in scraps and shatterings.
	Small curbs bring raging horses back to terms.
	Slave to his neighbor, who can think of pride?
	This girl was expert in her insolence
	when she broke bounds beyond established law.
	Once she had done it, insolence the second,
	to boast her doing, and to laugh in it.
	I am no man and she the man instead
	if she can have this conquest without pain . . .
Chorus	Fortunate they whose lives have no taste of pain.
	For those whose house is shaken by the gods
	escape no kind of doom. It extends to all the kin
	like the wave that comes when the winds of Thrace
	run over the dark of the sea.
	The black sand of the bottom is brought from the depth;
	the beaten capes sound back with a hollow cry.
	Ancient the sorrow of Labdacus' house, I know.
	Dead men's grief comes back, and falls on grief.
	No generation can free the next.
	One of the gods will strike. There is no escape.

So now the light goes out
for the house of Oedipus, while the bloody knife
cuts the remaining root. Folly and Fury have done this . . .
(*Haemon enters from the side.*)

Here is your one surviving son.
Does he come in grief at the fate of his bride,
in pain that he's tricked of his wedding?

Creon

Soon we shall know more than a seer could tell us.
Son, have you heard the vote condemned your bride?
And are you here, maddened against your father,
or are we friends, whatever I may do?

Haemon

My father, I am yours. You keep me straight
with your good judgment, which I shall ever follow.
Nor shall a marriage count for more with me
than your kind leading.

Creon

There's my good boy. So should you hold at heart
and stand behind your father all the way.
It is for this men pray they may beget
households of dutiful obedient sons,
who share alike in punishing enemies,
and give due honor to their father's friends.
Whoever breeds a child that will not help
what has he sown but trouble for himself,
and for his enemies laughter full and free?
Son, do not let your lust mislead your mind,
all for a woman's sake, for well you know
how cold the thing he takes into his arms
who has a wicked woman for his wife.
What deeper wounding than a friend no friend?
Oh spit her forth forever, as your foe.
Let the girl marry somebody in Hades.
Since I have caught her in the open act,
the only one in town who disobeyed,
I shall not now proclaim myself a liar,
but kill her. Let her sing her song of Zeus
who guards the kindred.
If I allow disorder in my house
I'd surely have to license it abroad.
A man who deals in fairness with his own,
he can make manifest justice in the state.
But he who crosses law, or forces it,
or hopes to bring the rulers under him,
shall never have a word of praise from me.
The man the state has put in place must have
obedient hearing to his least command
when it is right, and even when it's not.
He who accepts this teaching I can trust,

ruler, or ruled, to function in his place,
to stand his ground even in the storm of spears,
a mate to trust in battle at one's side.
There is no greater wrong than disobedience.
This ruins cities, this tears down our homes,
this breaks the battle-front in panic-rout.
If men live decently it is because
discipline saves their very lives for them.
So I must guard the men who yield to order,
not let myself be beaten by a woman.
Better, if it must happen, that a man
should overset me.
I won't be called weaker than womankind.

Chorus

We think—unless our age is cheating us—
that what you say is sensible and right.

Haemon

Father, the gods have given men good sense,
the only sure possession that we have.
I couldn't find the words in which to claim
that there was error in your late remarks.
Yet someone else might bring some further light.
Because I am your son I must keep watch
on all men's doing where it touches you,
their speech, and most of all, their discontents.
Your presence frightens any common man
from saying things you would not care to hear.
But in dark corners I have heard them say
how the whole town is grieving for this girl,
unjustly doomed, if ever woman was,
to die in shame for glorious action done.
She would not leave her fallen, slaughtered brother
there, as he lay, unburied, for the birds
and hungry dogs to make an end of him.
Isn't her real desert a golden prize?
This is the undercover speech in town.
Father, your welfare is my greatest good.
What loveliness in life for any child
outweighs a father's fortune and good fame?
And so a father feels his children's faring.
Then, do not have one mind, and one alone
that only your opinion can be right.
Whoever thinks that he alone is wise,
his eloquence, his mind, above the rest,
come the unfolding, shows his emptiness.
A man, though wise, should never be ashamed
of learning more, and must unbend his mind.
Have you not seen the trees beside the torrent,
the ones that bend them saving every leaf,
while the resistant perish root and branch?

And so the ship that will not slacken sail,
the sheet drawn tight, unyielding, overturns.
She ends the voyage with her keel on top.
No, yield your wrath, allow a change of stand.
Young as I am, if I may give advice,
I'd say it would be best if men were born
perfect in wisdom, but that failing this
(which often fails) it can be no dishonor
to learn from others when they speak good sense.

Chorus	Lord, if your son has spoken to the point you should take his lesson. He should do the same. Both sides have spoken well.
Creon	At my age I'm to school my mind by his? This boy instructor is my master, then?
Haemon	I urge no wrong. I'm young, but you should watch my actions, not my years, to judge of me.
Creon	A loyal action, to respect disorder?
Haemon	I wouldn't urge respect for wickedness.
Creon	You don't think she is sick with that disease?
Haemon	Your fellow-citizens maintain she's not.
Creon	Is the town to tell me how I ought to rule?
Haemon	Now there you speak just like a boy yourself.
Creon	Am I to rule by other mind than mine?
Haemon	No city is property of a single man.
Creon	But custom gives possession to the ruler.
Haemon	You'd rule a desert beautifully alone.
Creon *(to the Chorus)*	It seems he's firmly on the woman's side.
Haemon	If you're a woman. It is you I care for.
Creon	Wicked, to try conclusions with your father.
Haemon	When you conclude unjustly, so I must.
Creon	Am I unjust, when I respect my office?
Haemon	You tread down the gods' due. Respect is gone.
Creon	Your mind is poisoned. Weaker than a woman!
Haemon	At least you'll never see me yield to shame.
Creon	Your whole long argument is but for her.

Haemon	And you, and me, and for the gods below.
Creon	You shall not marry her while she's alive.
Haemon	Then she shall die. Her death will bring another . . . (*Haemon leaves, by one of the side entrances.*)
Chorus	And what death have you chosen for the other?
Creon	To take her where the foot of man comes not. There shall I hide her in a hollowed cave living, and leave her just so much to eat as clears the city from the guilt of death. There, if she prays to Death, the only god of her respect, she may manage not to die. Or she may learn at last and even then how much too much her labor for the dead. (*Creon returns to the palace.*)
Chorus	Love unconquered in fight, love who falls on our havings. You rest in the bloom of a girl's unwithered face. You cross the sea, you are known in the wildest lairs. Not the immortal gods can fly, nor men of a day. Who has you within him is mad. You twist the minds of the just. Wrong they pursue and are ruined. You made this quarrel of kindred before us now. Desire looks clear from the eyes of a lovely bride: power as strong as the founded world. For there is a goddess at play with whom no man can fight.

(*Creon is finally persuaded to relent. But by then Antigone has committed suicide in her prison-tomb. Haemon in turn kills himself. At the end of the play Creon is left in despair.*)

Creon	Take me away at once, the frantic man who killed my son, against my meaning. I cannot rest. My life is warped past cure. My fate has struck me down. (*Creon and his attendants enter the house.*)
Chorus	Our happiness depends on wisdom all the way. The gods must have their due. Great words by men of pride bring greater blows upon them. So wisdom comes to the old.

PART THREE

GREEK CIVILIZATION—
PHILOSOPHY,
POLITICS, AND SOCIETY
(c. 400–c. 330 B.C.)

The three greatest thinkers of the ancient world—Socrates, Plato, and Aristotle—lived and worked in Athens during the century after the outbreak of the Peloponnesian War.

Socrates (469–399 B.C.) reoriented the whole tradition of Greek philosophy by turning away from speculation about the external universe to consider the inner nature of human life itself. (He held that "the unexamined life is not worth living.") Socrates questioned all the everyday assumptions of respectable Athenian citizens. But the Athenians, especially after their defeat in the Peloponnesian War, were in no mood to accept such probing criticism. In the end they put Socrates to death for "worshipping false gods and corrupting the youth."

Socrates' disciple, Plato (428–347 B.C.), believed that the world revealed to us by sense experience was only a shadowy world of half-truths. The pure intellect of the philosopher could rise above these mere appearances to contemplate a world of absolute forms or archetypes—absolute beauty, absolute justice, and, at the furthest reach of the human mind, absolute good.

Aristotle (384–322 B.C.) was a more down-to-earth philosopher. He did not despise sense experience but rather collected great masses of information in fields that we would call "natural sciences" and "social sciences" and organized it all in accordance with his own scientific methodology. (Typically, when he wanted to write on politics, he had his students collect for study the constitutions of 158 Greek city-states.)

To complement the abstract teachings of the philosophers we have included some comments of a hard-headed country gentleman, Xenophon (c. 434–c. 355 B.C.), on Athenian family life and political affairs.

THE IDEA OF THE GOOD

Socrates: Critics and Friends

In The Apology *Plato described how Socrates defended himself at his trial in 399. How did Socrates seek wisdom? Why did the Athenians resent him?*

From *The Apology*

I will begin at the beginning, and ask what is the accusation which has given rise to the slander of me, and in fact has encouraged Meletus to prefer this charge against me. Well, what do the slanderers say? They shall be my prosecutors, and I will sum up their words in an affidavit: 'Socrates is an evil-doer, and a curious person, who searches into things under the earth and in heaven, and he makes the worse appear the better cause; and he teaches the aforesaid doctrines to others.' Such is the nature of the accusation: it is just what you have yourselves seen in the comedy of Aristophanes,[1] who has introduced a man whom he calls Socrates, going about and saying that he walks in air, and talking a deal of nonsense concerning matters of which I do not pretend to know either much or little—not that I mean to speak disparagingly of any one who is a student of natural philosophy. . . .

I will refer you to a witness who is worthy of credit; that witness shall be the God of Delphi—he will tell you about my wisdom, if I have any, and of what sort it is. You must have known Chaerephon; he was early a friend of mine, and also a friend of yours. . . . Well, Chaerephon, as you know, was very impetuous in all his doings, and he went to Delphi and boldly asked the oracle to tell him whether—as I was saying, I must beg you not to interrupt—he asked the oracle to tell him whether any one was wiser than I was, and the Pythian prophetess answered, that there was no man wiser. . . .

Why do I mention this? Because I am going to explain to you why I have such an evil name. When I heard the answer, I said to myself, What can the god mean? and what is the interpretation of his riddle? for I know that I have no wisdom, small or great. What then can he mean when he says that I am the wisest of men? And yet he is a god, and cannot lie; that would be against his nature. After long consideration, I thought of a method of trying the question. I reflected that if I could only find a man wiser than myself, then I might go to the god with a refutation in my hand. I should say to him, 'Here is a man who is wiser than I am; but you said that I was the wisest.' Accordingly I went to one who had the reputation of wisdom, and observed him—his name I need not mention; he was a politician whom I selected for examination—and the result was as follows: When I began to talk with him, I could not help thinking that he was not really wise, although he was thought wise by many, and still wiser by himself; and thereupon

[1]See p. 64.

From Plato, *Apology,* B. Jowett, trans. in *The Dialogues of Plato,* 3rd ed. (Oxford: Oxford University Press, 1892, reprinted 1924), Vol. 2, pp. 111, 113–116, 123.

I tried to explain to him that he thought himself wise, but was not really wise; and the consequence was that he hated me, and his enmity was shared by several who were present and heard me. So I left him, saying to myself, as I went away: Well, although I do not suppose that either of us knows anything really beautiful and good, I am better off than he is,—for he knows nothing, and thinks that he knows; I neither know nor think that I know. In this latter particular, then, I seem to have slightly the advantage of him. Then I went to another who had still higher pretensions to wisdom, and my conclusion was exactly the same. Whereupon I made another enemy of him, and of many others besides him. . . .

And so I go about the world, obedient to the god, and search and make enquiry into the wisdom of any one, whether citizen or stranger, who appears to be wise; and if he is not wise, then in vindication of the oracle I show him that he is not wise; and my occupation quite absorbs me, and I have no time to give either to any public matter of interest or to any concern of my own, but I am in utter poverty by reason of my devotion to the god.

There is another thing:—young men of the richer classes, who have not much to do, come about me of their own accord; they like to hear the pretenders examined, and they often imitate me, and proceed to examine others; there are plenty of persons, as they quickly discover, who think that they know something, but really know little or nothing; and then those who are examined by them instead of being angry with themselves are angry with me: This confounded Socrates, they say; this villainous misleader of youth!—and then if somebody asks them, Why, what evil does he practise or teach? they do not know, and cannot tell; but in order that they may not appear to be at a loss, they repeat the ready-made charges which are used against all philosophers about teaching things up in the clouds and under the earth, and having no gods, and making the worse appear the better cause; for they do not like to confess that their pretence of knowledge has been detected—which is the truth; and as they are numerous and ambitious and energetic, and are drawn up in battle array and have persuasive tongues, they have filled your ears with their loud and inveterate calumnies. . . .

For I do nothing but go about persuading you all, old and young alike, not to take thought for your persons or your properties, but first and chiefly to care about the greatest improvement of the soul. I tell you that virtue is not given by money, but that from virtue comes money and every other good of man, public as well as private. This is my teaching, and if this is the doctrine which corrupts the youth, I am a mischievous person. But if any one says that this is not my teaching, he is speaking an untruth. Wherefore, O men of Athens, I say to you, do as Anytus bids or not as Anytus bids, and either acquit me or not; but whichever you do, understand that I shall never alter my ways, not even if I have to die many times.

Aristophanes presented a derisive caricature of Socrates in The Clouds. *The play, a good specimen of Athenian comedy, may tell us nothing about the real Socrates, but it does convey the exasperation aroused in many ordinary Athenians by Socrates' questioning of their traditional beliefs.*

Strepsiades is a foolish old farmer who has accumulated huge debts through his son's passion for horse racing. He decides to enter the school of Socrates. Does he learn anything useful there?

From *The Clouds*

Strepsiades.
Throw open the Thinkery! Unbolt the door
and let me see this wizard Sokrates in person.
Open up! I'm MAD for education! . . .

He catches sight of Sokrates
dangling in a basket overhead. . . .

Sokrates.

From a vast philosophical height.

Well, creature of a day?

Strepsiades.
What in the world are you doing up there?

Sokrates.

Ah, sir,
I walk upon the air and look down upon the sun
from a superior standpoint.

Strepsiades.

Well, I suppose it's better
that you sneer at the gods from a basket up in the air
than do it down here on the ground.

Sokrates.

Precisely. You see,
only by being suspended aloft, by dangling
my mind in the heavens and mingling my rare thought
with the ethereal air, could I ever achieve strict
scientific accuracy in my survey of the vast empyrean.
Had I pursued my inquiries from down there on the ground,
my data would be worthless. The earth, you see, pulls down
the delicate essence of thought to its own gross level.

As an afterthought.

Much the same thing happens with watercress.

Strepsiades.

Ecstatically bewildered.

You don't say?
Thought draws down . . . delicate essence . . . into watercress.
O dear little Sokrates, please come down.
Lower away, and teach me what I need to know!

From Aristophanes, *The Clouds*, in *Three comedies,* William Arrowsmith, trans. (Ann Arbor, Mich.: The University of Michigan Press, P.O. Box 1104, Ann Arbor, MI 48106. Reprinted by permission.

Sokrates is slowly lowered earthwards.

Sokrates.

What subject?

Strepsiades.
Your course on public speaking and debating techniques.
You see, my creditors have become absolutely ferocious.
You should see how they're hounding me. What's more, Sokrates,
they're about to seize my belongings.

Sokrates.

How in the world
could you fall so deeply in debt without realizing it?

Strepsiades.

How?

A great, greedy horse-pox ate me up, that's how.
But that's why I want instruction in your second Logic,
you know the one—the get-away-without-paying argument.
I'll pay you *any* price you ask. I swear it.
By the gods.

Sokrates.

By the gods? The gods, my dear simple fellow,
are a mere expression coined by vulgar superstition.
We frown upon such coinage here.

Strepsiades.

Holy name of Earth! Olympian Zeus is a figment?

Sokrates.

Zeus?
What Zeus?
Nonsense.
There is no Zeus.

Strepsiades.

No Zeus?

Then *who* makes it rain? Answer me that.

Sokrates.

Why, the Clouds,
of course.
What's more, the proof is incontrovertible.
For instance,
have you ever yet seen rain when you didn't see a cloud?
But if your hypothesis were correct, Zeus could drizzle from an empty
sky
while the clouds were on vacation.

Strepsiades.

                             By Apollo, you're right. A pretty
proof.
And to think I always used to believe the rain was just Zeus
pissing through a sieve.

                      All right, *who* makes it thunder?
Brrr. I get goosebumps just saying it.

Sokrates.

                           The Clouds again,
of course. A simple process of Convection.

Strepsiades.

                           I admire you,
but I don't follow you.

Sokrates.

                 Listen. The Clouds are a saturate water-solution.
Tumescence in motion, of necessity, produces precipitation.
When those distended masses collide—*boom!*

                         Fulmination.

Strepsiades.
But who makes them move before they collide? Isn't that Zeus?

Sokrates.
Not Zeus, idiot. The Convection-principle!

Strepsiades.

                        Convection? That's a
new one.
Just think. So Zeus is out and convection-principle's in.
Tch, tch.

                But wait: you haven't told me who makes it thunder.

Sokrates.
But I just *finished* telling you! The Clouds are water-packed;
they collide with each other and explode because of the pressure.

Strepsiades.
And what's your proof for *that*?

Sokrates.

                    Why, take yourself as example.
You know that meat-stew the vendors sell at the Panathenaia?
How it gives you the cramps and your stomach starts to rumble?

Strepsiades.

                                     Yes
by Apollo! I remember. What an awful feeling! You feel sick
and your belly churns and the fart rips loose like thunder.
First just a gurgle, *pappapax;* then louder, *pappaPAPAXapaX,*
and finally like thunder, *PAPAPAPAXAPAXAPPAPAXapap!*

Sokrates.
Precisely.
First think of the tiny fart that your intestines make.
Then consider the heavens: their infinite farting is thunder.
For thunder and farting are, in principle, one and the same. . . .

Chorus.
—Ah, how he hungers after learning!

To Strepsiades.
                                    —Sir, if you can pass our test,
        we guarantee that you shall be
                                    —the cynosure of Hellas.
        —Our requirements are these:
                                    —First, is your memory keen?
        —Do you hanker for researching?
                                    —Are you subject to fatigue
        from standing up or walking?
                                    —Does winter weather daunt you?
        —Can you go without a meal?
                                    —Abstain from wine and exercise?
        —And keep away from girls?
                                    —Last, do you solemnly swear
        adherence to our code?
                        —*To wrangle*
                                —niggle
                                        —haggle
                                                —battle

—a loyal soldier of the Tongue, conducting yourself always
like a true philosopher.

Strepsiades.
                        Ladies, if all you require
        is hard work, insomnia, worry, endurance, and a stomach
        that eats anything, why, have no fear. For I'm your man
        and as hard as nails.

Sokrates.
                        And you promise to follow faithfully in my path
        acknowledging no other gods but mine, to wit, the Trinity—
        GREAT CHAOS, THE CLOUDS, and BAMBOOZLE?

Strepsiades.
                                                        If I met
            another god,
        I'd cut him dead, so help me. Here and now I swear off sacrifice and
        prayer forever.

At the opposite extreme from Aristophanes' mockery is the grave and reverent account by Plato of
Socrates' last conversation with his friends and his death. Plato and Aristophanes were writing
about the same person, Socrates. How could they see him so differently?

From *Phaedo*

But do you mean to take away your thoughts with you, Socrates? said Simmias. Will you not impart them to us?—for they are a benefit in which we too are entitled to share. Moreover, if you succeed in convincing us, that will be an answer to the charge against yourself.

I will do my best, replied Socrates. But you must first let me hear what Crito wants; he has long been wishing to say something to me.

Only this, Socrates, replied Crito:—the attendant who is to give you the poison has been telling me, and he wants me to tell you, that you are not to talk much; talking, he says, increases heat, and this is apt to interfere with the action of the poison; persons who excite themselves are sometimes obliged to take a second or even a third dose.

Then, said Socrates, let him mind his business and be prepared to give the poison twice or even thrice if necessary; that is all.

I knew quite well what you would say, replied Crito; but I was obliged to satisfy him.

Never mind him, he said.

And now, O my judges, I desire to prove to you that the real philosopher has reason to be of good cheer when he is about to die, and that after death he may hope to obtain the greatest good in the other world . . . let us discuss the matter among ourselves. Do we believe that there is such a thing as death?

To be sure, replied Simmias.

Is it not the separation of soul and body? And to be dead is the completion of this; when the soul exists in herself, and is released from the body and the body is released from the soul, what is this but death?

Just so, he replied.

There is another question, which will probably throw light on our present enquiry if you and I can agree about it:—Ought the philosopher to care about the pleasures—if they are to be called pleasures—of eating and drinking?

Certainly not, answered Simmias.

And what about the pleasures of love—should he care for them?

By no means.

And will he think much of the other ways of indulging the body, for example, the acquisition of costly raiment, or sandals, or other adornments of the body? Instead of caring about them, does he not rather despise anything more than nature needs? What do you say?

I should say that the true philosopher would despise them.

Would you not say that he is entirely concerned with the soul and not with the body? He would like, as far as he can, to get away from the body and to turn to the soul.

Quite true.

In matters of this sort philosophers, above all other men, may be observed in every sort of way to dissever the soul from the communion of the body.

From Plato, *Phaedo*, B. Jowett, trans. in *The Dialogues of Plato*, 3rd ed. (Oxford: Oxford University Press, 1892, reprinted 1924), Vol. 2, pp. 202–206, 264–266.

Very true.

Whereas, Simmias, the rest of the world are of opinion that to him who has no sense of pleasure and no part in bodily pleasure, life is not worth having; and that he who is indifferent about them is as good as dead.

That is also true.

What again shall we say of the actual acquirement of knowledge?—is the body, if invited to share in the enquiry, a hinderer or a helper? I mean to say, have sight and hearing any truth in them? Are they not, as the poets are always telling us, inaccurate witnesses? and yet, if even they are inaccurate and indistinct, what is to be said of the other senses?—for you will allow that they are the best of them?

Certainly, he replied.

Then when does the soul attain truth?—for in attempting to consider anything in company with the body she is obviously deceived.

True.

Then must not true existence be revealed to her in thought, if at all?

Yes.

And thought is best when the mind is gathered into herself and none of these things trouble her—neither sounds nor sights nor pain nor any pleasure,—when she takes leave of the body, and has as little as possible to do with it, when she has no bodily sense or desire, but is aspiring after true being?

Certainly.

And in this the philosopher dishonours the body; his soul runs away from his body and desires to be alone and by herself?

That is true.

Well, but there is another thing, Simmias: Is there or is there not an absolute justice?

Assuredly there is.

And an absolute beauty and absolute good?

Of course.

But did you ever behold any of them with your eyes?

Certainly not.

Or did you ever reach them with any other bodily sense?—and I speak not of these alone, but of absolute greatness, and health, and strength, and of the essence or true nature of everything. Has the reality of them ever been perceived by you through the bodily organs? or rather, is not the nearest approach to the knowledge of their several natures made by him who so orders his intellectual vision as to have the most exact conception of the essence of each thing which he considers?

Certainly.

And he attains to the purest knowledge of them who goes to each with the mind alone, not introducing or intruding in the act of thought sight or any other sense together with reason, but with the very light of the mind in her own clearness searches into the very truth of each; he who has got rid, as far as he can, of eyes and ears and, so to speak, of the whole body, these being in his opinion distracting elements which when they infect the soul hinder her from acquiring truth and knowledge—who, if not he, is likely to attain to the knowledge of true being?

What you say has a wonderful truth in it, Socrates, replied Simmias.

And when real philosophers consider all these things, will they not be led to make a reflection which they will express in words something like the following? 'Have we not found,' they will say, 'a path of thought which seems to bring us and our argument to the conclusion, that while we are in the body, and while the soul is infected with the evils of the body, our desire will not be satisfied? and our desire is of the truth. For the body is a source of endless trouble to us by reason of the mere requirement of food; and is liable also to diseases which overtake and impede us in the search after true being: it fills us full of loves, and lusts, and fears, and fancies of all kinds, and endless foolery, and in fact, as men say, takes away from us the power of thinking at all. Whence come wars, and fightings, and factions? whence but from the body and the lusts of the body? Wars are occasioned by the love of money, and money has to be acquired for the sake and in the service of the body; and by reason of all these impediments we have no time to give to philosophy; and, last and worst of all, even if we are at leisure and betake ourselves to some speculation, the body is always breaking in upon us, causing turmoil and confusion in our enquiries, and so amazing us that we are prevented from seeing the truth. It has been proved to us by experience that if we would have pure knowledge of anything we must be quit of the body—the soul in herself must behold things in themselves: and then we shall attain the wisdom which we desire, and of which we say that we are lovers; not while we live, but after death; for if while in company with the body, the soul cannot have pure knowledge, one of two things follows—either knowledge is not to be attained at all, or, if at all, after death. For then, and not till then, the soul will be parted from the body and exist in herself alone. In this present life, I reckon that we make the nearest approach to knowledge when we have the least possible intercourse or communion with the body, and are not surfeited with the bodily nature, but keep ourselves pure until the hour when God himself is pleased to release us. And thus having got rid of the foolishness of the body we shall be pure and hold converse with the pure, and know of ourselves the clear light everywhere, which is no other than the light of truth.' For the impure are not permitted to approach the pure. These are the sort of words, Simmias, which the true lovers of knowledge cannot help saying to one another, and thinking. You would agree; would you not?

Undoubtedly, Socrates.

But, O my friend, if this be true, there is great reason to hope that, going whither I go, when I have come to the end of my journey, I shall attain that which has been the pursuit of my life. And therefore I go on my way rejoicing, and not I only, but every other man who believes that his mind has been made ready and that he is in a manner purified. . . .

When he had spoken these words, he arose and went into a chamber to bathe; Crito followed him and told us to wait. So we remained behind, talking and thinking of the subject of discourse, and also of the greatness of our sorrow; he was like a father of whom we were being bereaved, and we were about to pass the rest of our lives as orphans. When he had taken the bath his children were brought to him—(he had two young sons and an elder one); and the women of his family also came, and he talked to them and gave them a few directions in the presence of Crito; then he dismissed them and returned to us.

Now the hour of sunset was near, for a good deal of time had passed while he was within. When he came out, he sat down with us again after his bath, but not much was said. Soon the jailer, who was the servant of the Eleven, entered and stood by him, saying:—To you, Socrates, whom I know to be the noblest and gentlest and best of all who ever came to this place, I will not impute the angry feelings of other men, who rage and swear at me, when, in obedience to the authorities, I bid them drink the poison—indeed, I am sure that you will not be angry with me; for others, as you are aware, and not I, are to blame. And so fare you well, and try to bear lightly what must needs be—you know my errand. Then bursting into tears he turned away and went out.

Socrates looked at him and said: I return your good wishes, and will do as you bid. Then turning to us, he said, How charming the man is: since I have been in prison he has always been coming to see me, and at times he would talk to me, and was as good to me as could be, and now see how generously he sorrows on my account. We must do as he says, Crito; and therefore let the cup be brought, if the poison is prepared: if not, let the attendant prepare some.

Yet, said Crito, the sun is still upon the hill-tops, and I know that many a one has taken the draught late, and after the announcement has been made to him, he has eaten and drunk, and enjoyed the society of his beloved; do not hurry—there is time enough.

Socrates said: Yes, Crito, and they of whom you speak are right in so acting, for they think that they will be gainers by the delay; but I am right in not following their example, for I do not think that I should gain anything by drinking the poison a little later; I should only be ridiculous in my own eyes for sparing and saving a life which is already forfeit. Please then to do as I say, and not to refuse me.

Crito made a sign to the servant, who was standing by; and he went out, and having been absent for some time, returned with the jailer carrying the cup of poison. Socrates said: You, my good friend, who are experienced in these matters, shall give me directions how I am to proceed. The man answered: You have only to walk about until your legs are heavy, and then to lie down, and the poison will act. At the same time he handed the cup to Socrates, who in the easiest and gentlest manner, without the least fear or change of colour or feature, looking at the man with all his eyes, Echecrates, as his manner was, took the cup and said: What do you say about making a libation out of this cup to any god? May I, or not? The man answered: We only prepare, Socrates, just so much as we deem enough. I understand, he said: but I may and must ask the gods to prosper my journey from this to the other world—even so—and so be it according to my prayer. Then raising the cup to his lips, quite readily and cheerfully he drank off the poison. And hitherto most of us had been able to control our sorrow; but now when we saw him drinking, and saw too that he had finished the draught, we could no longer forbear, and in spite of myself my own tears were flowing fast; so that I covered my face and wept, not for him, but at the thought of my own calamity in having to part from such a friend. Nor was I the first; for Crito, when he found himself unable to restrain his tears, had got up, and I followed; and at that moment, Apollodorus, who had been weeping all the time, broke out in a loud and passionate cry which made cowards of us all. Socrates alone retained his calmness: What is this strange outcry? he said. I sent away the women mainly in order that they might not misbehave in this way, for I have been told that a man should die in peace. Be quiet then, and have patience. When we heard his words we were ashamed, and refrained our tears; and he walked about until, as he said, his legs began to fail, and then he lay on his back, according to the directions, and the man who gave him the poison now and then looked at his feet and legs; and after a while he pressed his foot hard, and asked him if he could feel; and he said, No; and then his leg, and so upwards and upwards, and showed us that he was cold and stiff. And he felt them himself, and said: When the poison reaches the heart, that will be the end. He was beginning to grow cold about the groin, when he uncovered his face, for he had covered himself up, and said—they were his last words—he said: Crito, I owe a cock to Asclepius; will you remember to pay the debt? The debt shall be paid, said Crito; is there anything else? There was no answer to this question; but in a minute or two a movement was heard, and the attendants uncovered him; his eyes were set, and Crito closed his eyes and mouth.

Such was the end, Echecrates, of our friend; concerning whom I may truly say, that of all the men of his time whom I have known, he was the wisest and justest and best.

Plato's Cave

Socrates affirmed the existence of "absolute beauty and absolute good." In his famous allegory of the cave, Plato explained how a philosopher could ascend from the world of sense experience to a contemplation of these ultimate realities.

From *The Republic*

And now, I said, let me show in a figure how far our nature is enlightened or unenlightened:—Behold! human beings living in an underground den, which has a mouth open towards the light and reaching all along the den; here they have been from their childhood, and have their legs and necks chained so that they cannot move, and can only see before them [facing inward], being prevented by the chains from turning round their heads. Above and behind them a fire is blazing at a distance, and between the fire and the prisoners there is a raised way; and you will see, if you look, a low wall built along the way, like the screen which marionette players have in front of them, over which they show the puppets.

I see.

And do you see, I said, men passing along the wall carrying all sorts of vessels, and statues and figures of animals made of wood and stone and various materials, which appear over the wall? Some of them are talking, others silent.

You have shown me a strange image, and they are strange prisoners.

From Plato, *The Republic*, B. Jowett, trans. in *The Dialogues of Plato*, 3rd ed. (Oxford: Oxford University Press, 1895, reprinted 1924), Vol. 3, pp. 214–217.

Like ourselves, I replied; and they see only their own shadows, or the shadows of one another, which the fire throws on the opposite wall of the cave?

True, he said; how could they see anything but the shadows if they were never allowed to move their heads?

And of the objects which are being carried in like manner they would only see the shadows?

Yes, he said.

And if they were able to converse with one another, would they not suppose that they were naming what was actually before them?

Very true.

And suppose further that the prison had an echo which came from the other side, would they not be sure to fancy when one of the passers-by spoke that the voice which they heard came from the passing shadow?

No question, he replied.

To them, I said, the truth would be literally nothing but the shadows of the images.

That is certain.

And now look again, and see what will naturally follow if the prisoners are released and disabused of their error. At first, when any of them is liberated and compelled suddenly to stand up and turn his neck round and walk and look towards the light, he will suffer sharp pains; the glare will distress him, and he will be unable to see the realities of which in his former state he had seen the shadows; and then conceive some one saying to him, that what he saw before was an illusion, but that now, when he is approaching nearer to being and his eye is turned towards more real existence, he has a clearer vision,—what will be his reply? And you may further imagine that his instructor is pointing to the objects as they pass and requiring him to name them,—will he not be perplexed? Will he not fancy that the shadows which he formerly saw are truer than the objects which are now shown to him?

Far truer.

And if he is compelled to look straight at the light, will he not have a pain in his eyes which will make him turn away to take refuge in the objects of vision which he can see, and which he will conceive to be in reality clearer than the things which are now being shown to him?

True, he said.

And suppose once more, that he is reluctantly dragged up a steep and rugged ascent, and held fast until he is forced into the presence of the sun himself, is he not likely to be pained and irritated? When he approaches the light his eyes will be dazzled, and he will not be able to see anything at all of what are now called realities.

Not all in a moment, he said.

He will require to grow accustomed to the sight of the upper world. And first he will see the shadows best, next the reflections of men and other objects in the water, and then the objects themselves; then he will gaze upon the light of the moon and the stars and the spangled heaven; and he will see the sky and the stars by night better than the sun or the light of the sun by day?

Certainly.

Last of all he will be able to see the sun, and not mere reflections of him in the water, but he will see him in his own proper place, and not in another; and he will contemplate him as he is.

Certainly.

He will then proceed to argue that this is he who gives the season and the years, and is the guardian of all that is in the visible world, and in a certain way the cause of all things which he and his fellows have been accustomed to behold?

Clearly, he said, he would first see the sun and then reason about him.

And when he remembered his old habitation, and the wisdom of the den and his fellow-prisoners, do you not suppose that he would felicitate himself on the change, and pity them?

Certainly, he would.

And if they were in the habit of conferring honours among themselves on those who were quickest to observe the passing shadows and to remark which of them went before, and which followed after, and which were together; and who were therefore best able to draw conclusions as to the future, do you think that he would care for such honours and glories, or envy the possessors of them? Would he not say with Homer,

'Better to be the poor servant of a poor master,'

and to endure anything, rather than think as they do and live after their manner?

Yes, he said, I think that he would rather suffer anything than entertain these false notions and live in this miserable manner.

Imagine once more, I said, such an one coming suddenly out of the sun to be replaced in his old situation; would he not be certain to have his eyes full of darkness?

To be sure, he said.

And if there were a contest, and he had to compete in measuring the shadows with the prisoners who had never moved out of the den, while his sight was still weak, and before his eyes had become steady (and the time which would be needed to acquire this new habit of sight might be very considerable), would he not be ridiculous? Men would say of him that up he went and down he came without his eyes; and that it was better not even to think of ascending; and if any one tried to loose another and lead him up to the light, let them only catch the offender, and they would put him to death.

No question, he said.

This entire allegory, I said, you may now append, dear Glaucon, to the previous argument; the prison-house is the world of sight, the light of the fire is the sun, and you will not misapprehend me if you interpret the journey upwards to be the ascent of the soul into the intellectual world according to my poor belief, which, at your desire, I have expressed—whether rightly or wrongly God knows. But, whether true or false, my opinion is that in the world of knowledge the idea of good appears last of all, and is seen only with an effort; and, when seen, is also inferred to be the universal author of all things beautiful and right, parent of light and of the lord of light in this visible world, and the immediate source of reason and truth in the intellectual; and that this is the power upon which he who would act rationally either in public or private life must have his eye fixed.

FAMILY AND STATE—IDEALISM

Platonic Utopianism

Plato's Republic *deals with the ideal of justice as embodied in the individual and the state. In the course of his argument Plato expressed some radical views on community of property and roles of women.*

From *The Republic*

Is not the love of learning the love of wisdom, which is philosophy?

They are the same, he replied.

And may we not say confidently of man also, that he who is likely to be gentle to his friends and acquaintances, must by nature be a lover of wisdom and knowledge?

That we may safely affirm.

Then he who is to be a really good and noble guardian of the State will require to unite in himself philosophy and spirit and swiftness and strength?

Undoubtedly.

Then we have found the desired natures; and now that we have found them, how are they to be reared and educated? Is not this an enquiry which may be expected to throw light on the greater enquiry which is our final end—How do justice and injustice grow up in States?

Adeimantus thought that the enquiry would be of great service to us. . . .

Come then, and let us pass a leisure hour in story-telling, and our story shall be the education of our heroes.

By all means.

And what shall be their education? Can we find a better than the traditional sort?—and this has two divisions, gymnastic for the body, and music for the soul.

True. . . .

Very good, I said; then what is the next question? Must we not ask who are to be rulers and who subjects?

Certainly.

There can be no doubt that the elder must rule the younger.

Clearly.

And that the best of these must rule.

That is also clear.

Now, are not the best husbandmen those who are most devoted to husbandry?

From Plato, *The Republic*, B. Jowett, trans. in *The Dialogues of Plato*, 3rd ed. (Oxford: Oxford University Press, 1895, reprinted 1924), Vol. 3, pp. 58, 100–101, 103, 106, 142–144, 147–149, 150–151, 159, 170–171, 270–272.

Yes.

And as we are to have the best of guardians for our city, must they not be those who have most the character of guardians?

Yes. . . .

Then there must be a selection. Let us note among the guardians those who in their whole life show the greatest eagerness to do what is for the good of their country, and the greatest repugnance to do what is against her interests.

Those are the right men.

And they will have to be watched at every age, in order that we may see whether they preserve their resolution, and never, under the influence either of force or enchantment, forget or cast off their sense of duty to the State. . . . And he who at every age, as boy and youth and in mature life, has come out of the trial victorious and pure, shall be appointed a ruler and guardian of the State; he shall be honoured in life and death, and shall receive sepulture and other memorials of honour, the greatest that we have to give. But him who fails, we must reject. I am inclined to think that this is the sort of way in which our rulers and guardians should be chosen and appointed. I speak generally, and not with any pretension to exactness.

And, speaking generally, I agree with you, he said. . . .

Then let us consider what will be their way of life, if they are to realize our idea of them. In the first place, none of them should have any property of his own beyond what is absolutely necessary; neither should they have a private house or store closed against any one who has a mind to enter; their provisions should be only such as are required by trained warriors, who are men of temperance and courage; they should agree to receive from the citizens a fixed rate of pay, enough to meet the expenses of the year and no more; and they will go to mess and live together like soldiers in a camp. Gold and silver we will tell them that they have from God; the diviner metal is within them, and they have therefore no need of the dross which is current among men, and ought not to pollute the divine by any such earthly admixture; for that commoner metal has been the source of many unholy deeds, but their own is undefiled. And they alone of all the citizens may not touch or handle silver or gold, or be under the same roof with them, or wear them, or drink from them. And this will be their salvation, and they will be the saviours of the State. But should they ever acquire homes or lands or moneys of their own, they will become housekeepers and husbandmen instead of guardians, enemies and tyrants instead of allies of the other citizens; hating and being hated, plotting and being plotted against, they will pass their whole life in much greater terror of internal than of external enemies, and the hour of ruin, both to themselves and to the rest of the State, will be at hand. For all which reasons may we not say that thus shall our State be ordered, and that these shall be the regulations appointed by us for our guardians concerning their houses and all other matters?

Yes, said Glaucon. . . .

The part of the men has been played out, and now properly enough comes the turn of the women. Of them I will proceed to speak, and the more readily since I am invited by you.

For men born and educated like our citizens, the only way, in my opinion, of arriving at a right conclusion about the possession and use of women and children is to follow the path on which we originally started, when we said that the men were to be the guardians and watchdogs of the herd.

True.

Let us further suppose the birth and education of our women to be subject to similar or nearly similar regulations; then we shall see whether the result accords with our design.

What do you mean?

What I mean may be put into the form of a question, I said: Are dogs divided into hes and shes, or do they both share equally in hunting and in keeping watch and in the other duties of dogs? or do we entrust to the males the entire and exclusive care of the flocks, while we leave the females at home, under the idea that the bearing and suckling their puppies is labour enough for them?

No, he said, they share alike; the only difference between them is that the males are stronger and the females weaker.

But can you use different animals for the same purpose, unless they are bred and fed in the same way?

You cannot.

Then, if women are to have the same duties as men, they must have the same nurture and education?

Yes.

The education which was assigned to the men was music and gymnastic.

Yes.

Then women must be taught music and gymnastic and also the art of war, which they must practise like the men?

That is the inference, I suppose.

I should rather expect, I said, that several of our proposals, if they are carried out, being unusual, may appear ridiculous.

No doubt of it.

Yes, and the most ridiculous thing of all will be the sight of women naked in the palaestra, exercising with the men, especially when they are no longer young; they certainly will not be a vision of beauty, any more than the enthusiastic old men who in spite of wrinkles and ugliness continue to frequent the gymnasia.

Yes, indeed, he said: according to present notions the proposal would be thought ridiculous.

But then, I said, as we have determined to speak our minds, we must not fear the jests of the wits which will be directed against this sort of innovation; how they will talk of women's attainments both in music and gymnastic, and above all about their wearing armour and riding upon horseback!

Very true, he replied. . . .

My friend, I said, there is no special faculty of administration in a state which a woman has because she is a woman, or which a man has by virtue of his sex, but the gifts of nature are alike diffused in both; all the pursuits of men are the pursuits of women also, but in all of them a woman is inferior to a man.

Very true.

Then are we to impose all our enactments on men and none of them on women?

That will never do.

One woman has a gift of healing, another not; one is a musician, and another has no music in her nature?

Very true.

And one woman has a turn for gymnastic and military exercises, and another is unwarlike and hates gymnastics?

Certainly.

And one woman is a philosopher, and another is an enemy of philosophy; one has spirit, and another is without spirit?

That is also true.

Then one woman will have the temper of a guardian, and another not. Was not the selection of the male guardians determined by differences of this sort?

Yes.

Men and women alike possess the qualities which make a guardian; they differ only in their comparative strength or weakness.

Obviously.

And those women who have such qualities are to be selected as the companions and colleagues of men who have similar qualities and whom they resemble in capacity and in character?

Very true.

And ought not the same natures to have the same pursuits?

They ought.

Then, as we were saying before, there is nothing unnatural in assigning music and gymnastic to the wives of the guardians—to that point we come round again.

Certainly not.

The law which we then enacted was agreeable to nature, and therefore not an impossibility or mere aspiration; and the contrary practice, which prevails at present, is in reality a violation of nature.

That appears to be true. . . .

Then let the wives of our guardians strip, for their virtue will be their robe, and let them share in the toils of war and the defence of their country; only in the distribution of labours the lighter are to be assigned to the women, who are the weaker natures, but in other respects their duties are to be the same. . . .

Very true.

Here, then, is one difficulty in our law about women, which we may say that we have now escaped; the wave has not swallowed us up alive for enacting that the guardians of either sex should have all their pursuits in common; to the utility and also to the possibility of this arrangement the consistency of the argument with itself bears witness.

Yes, that was a mighty wave which you have escaped.

Yes, I said, but a greater is coming; you will not think much of this when you see the next.

Go on; let me see.

The law, I said, which is the sequel of this and of all that has preceded, is to the following effect,—'that the wives of our guardians are to be common, and their children are to be common, and no parent is to know his own child, nor any child his parent.'

Yes, he said, that is a much greater wave than the other; and the possibility as well as the utility of such a law are far more questionable. . . .

Both the community of property and the community of families, as I am saying, tend to make them more truly guardians; they will not tear the city in pieces by differing about 'mine' and 'not mine;' each man dragging any acquisition which he has made into a separate house of his own, where he has a separate wife and children and private pleasures and pains; but all will be affected as far as may be by the same pleasures and pains because they are all of one opinion about what is near and dear to them, and therefore they all tend towards a common end.

Certainly, he replied. . . .

Let me next endeavour to show what is that fault in States which is the cause of their present maladministration, and what is the least change which will enable a State to pass into the truer form; and let the change, if possible, be of one thing only, or, if not, of two; at any rate, let the changes be as few and slight as possible.

Certainly, he replied.

I think, I said, that there might be a reform of the State if only one change were made, which is not a slight or easy though still a possible one.

What is it? he said.

Now then, I said, I go to meet that which I liken to the greatest of the waves; yet shall the word be spoken, even though the wave break and drown me in laughter and dishonour; and do you mark my words.

Proceed.

I said: *Until philosophers are kings, or the kings and princes of this world have the spirit and power of philosophy, and political greatness and wisdom meet in one, and those commoner natures who pursue either to the exclusion of the other are compelled to stand aside, cities will never have rest from their evils,—no, nor the human race, as I believe,— and then only will this our State have a possibility of life and behold the light of day.*

Against Democracy

In another part of the Republic *Plato presented a critique of democratic government. How would an ideal state be ruled according to Plato? Why did he dislike democracy?*

From *The Republic*

Say then, my friend, In what manner does tyranny arise?—that it has a democratic origin is evident.

~~Clearly.~~ not so

And does not tyranny spring from democracy in the same manner as democracy from oligarchy—I mean, after a sort?

How?

The good which oligarchy proposed to itself and the means by which it was maintained was excess of wealth—am I not right?

Yes.

And the insatiable desire of wealth and the neglect of all other things for the sake of money-getting was also the ruin of oligarchy?

True.

And democracy has her own good, of which the insatiable desire brings her to dissolution?

What good?

Freedom, I replied; which, as they tell you in a democracy, is the glory of the State—and that therefore in a democracy alone will the freeman of nature deign to dwell.

Yes; the saying is in every body's mouth.

I was going to observe, that the insatiable desire of this and the neglect of other things introduces the change in democracy, which occasions a demand for tyranny.

How so?

When a democracy which is thirsting for freedom has evil cup-bearers presiding over the feast, and has drunk too deeply of the strong wine of freedom, then, unless her rulers are very amenable and give a plentiful draught, she calls them to account and punishes them, and says that they are cursed oligarchs.

Yes, he replied, a very common occurrence.

Yes, I said; and loyal citizens are insultingly termed by her slaves who hug their chains and men of naught; she would have subjects who are like rulers, and rulers who are like subjects: these are men after her own heart, whom she praises and honours both in private and public. Now, in such a State, can liberty have any limit?

Certainly not.

By degrees the anarchy finds a way into private houses, and ends by getting among the animals and infecting them.

How do you mean?

I mean that the father grows accustomed to descend to the level of his sons and to fear them, and the son is on a level with his father, he having no respect or reverence for either of his parents; and this is his freedom, and the metic is equal with the citizen and the citizen with the metic, and the stranger is quite as good as either.

Yes, he said, that is the way.

And these are not the only evils, I said—there are several lesser ones: In such a state of society the master fears and flatters his scholars, and the scholars despise their masters and tutors; young and old are all alike; and the young man is on a level with the old, and is ready to compete with him in word or deed; and old men condescend to the young and are full of pleasantry and gaiety; they are loth to be thought morose and authoritative, and therefore they adopt the manners of the young.

Quite true, he said. . . .

And above all, I said, and as the result of all, see how sensitive the citizens become; they chafe impatiently at the least touch of authority, and at length, as you know, they cease to care even for the laws, written or unwritten; they will have no one over them.

Yes, he said, I know it too well.

Such, my friend, I said, is the fair and glorious beginning out of which springs tyranny.

FAMILY AND STATE—REALISM

An Athenian Household

The everyday life of an upper-class Athenian housewife was very different from that of Plato's imaginary female guardians. In his treatise on household management Xenophon gives a more realistic picture. What are the presuppositions of Ischomachus about women's roles? Does he seem to love and respect his wife?

From Xenophon. *Household Management*

"Ischomachus," said I, "I would like to ask you whether you instructed your wife yourself, so that she might be qualified as she ought to be, or whether, when you received her from her father and mother, she was possessed of sufficient knowledge to manage what belongs to her." "And how," said he, "could she have had sufficient knowledge when I took her, since she came to my house when she was not fifteen years old, and had spent the preceding part of her life under the strictest restraint, in order that she might see as little, hear as little, and ask as few questions as possible? Does it not appear to you to be quite sufficient, if she did but know, when she came, how to take wool and make a garment, and had seen how to apportion the tasks of spinning among the maid-servants? for as to what concerns the appetite,"[2] added he, "which seems to me a most important part of instruction both for a man and for a woman, she came to me extremely well instructed." "But as to other things, Ischomachus," said I, "did you yourself instruct your wife, so that she should be qualified to attend to the affairs belonging to her?" . . .

"Well," returned Ischomachus, "when she grew familiarized and domesticated with me, so that we conversed freely together, I began to question her in some such way as this: 'Tell, me, my dear wife, have you ever considered with what view I married you, and with what object your parents gave you to me? For that there was no want of other persons with whom we might have shared our respective beds must, I am sure, be evident to you as well as to me. But when I considered for myself, and your parents for you, whom we might select as the best partner for a house and children, I preferred you, and your parents, as it appears, preferred me, out of those who were possible objects of choice. If, then,

From Xenophon, *Oeconomicus*, translation based on J. S. Watson, *Xenophon's Minor Works* (London: George Bell and Sons, 1882), pp. 97–103, 113–114.
[2]I.e., as regards temperance.

the gods should ever grant children to be born to us, we shall then consult together, with regard to them, how we may bring them up as well as possible; for
it will be a common advantage to both of us to find them of the utmost service
as supporters and maintainers of our old age. At present, however, this is our
common household; for I deposit all that I have as in common between us, and
you put everything that you have brought into our common stock. Nor is it necessary to consider which of the two has contributed the greater share, but we
ought to feel assured that whichsoever of us is the better manager of our common fortune will give the more valuable service.' To these remarks, my wife
replied, 'In what respect could I coöperate with you? What power have I?
Everything lies with you. My duty, my mother told me, was to conduct myself
discreetly.' 'Yes, by Jupiter, my dear wife,' replied I, 'and my father told me the
same. But it is the part of discreet people, as well husbands as wives, to act in
such a manner that their property may be in the best possible condition, and that
as large additions as possible may be made to it by honourable and just means.'
'And, what do you see,' said my wife, 'that I can do to assist in increasing our
property?'

" 'The gods, as it seems to me,' said I, 'have plainly adapted the nature of
the woman for works and duties within doors, and that of the man for works
and duties without doors. For the divinity has fitted the body and mind of the
man to be better able to bear cold, and heat, and travelling, and military exercises, so that he has imposed upon him the work without doors; and by having
formed the body of the woman to be less able to bear such exertions, he appears
to me to have laid upon her,' said I, 'the duties within doors. But knowing that
he had given the woman by nature, and laid upon her, the office of rearing
young children, he has also bestowed upon her a greater portion of love for her
newly-born offspring than on the man. Since, too, the divinity has laid upon the
woman the duty of guarding what is brought into the house, he, knowing that
the mind, by being timid, is not less adapted for guarding, has given a larger
share of timidity to the woman than to the man; and knowing also that if any
one injures him who is engaged in the occupations without, he must defend
himself, he has on that account given a greater portion of boldness to the man.
But as it is necessary for both alike to give and to receive, he has bestowed memory and the power of attention upon both impartially, so that you cannot distinguish whether the female or the male has the larger portion of them. The
power of being temperate also in what is necessary he has conferred in equal
measure upon both, and has allowed that whichsoever of the two is superior in
this virtue, whether the man or the woman, shall receive a greater portion of the
benefit arising from it. But as the nature of both is not fully adapted for all these
requirements, they in consequence stand in greater need of aid from one another, and the pair are of greater service to each other, when the one is able to do
those things in which the other is deficient. As we know, then, my dear wife,'
continued I, 'what is appointed to each of us by Providence, it is incumbent on
us to discharge as well as we can that which each of us has to do.' . . .

" 'Will it then be necessary for me,' said my wife, 'to do such things?' 'It will
certainly be necessary for you,' said I, 'to remain at home, and to send out such

of the labourers as have to work abroad, to their duties; and over such as have business to do in the house you must exercise a watchful superintendence. Whatever is brought into the house, you must take charge of it; whatever portion of it is required for use you must give out; and whatever should be laid by, you must take account of it and keep it safe, so that the provision stored up for a year, for example, may not be expended in a month. Whenever wool is brought home to you, you must take care that garments be made for those who want them. You must also be careful that the dried provisions may be in a proper condition for eating. One of your duties, however,' I added, 'will perhaps appear somewhat disagreeable, namely that whoever of all the servants may fall sick, you must take charge of him, that he may be recovered.' 'Nay, assuredly,' returned my wife, 'that will be a most agreeable office, if such as receive good treatment are likely to make a grateful return, and to become more attached to me than before.' . . .

" 'Some other of your occupations, my dear wife,' continued I, 'will be pleasing to you. For instance, when you take a young woman who does not know how to spin, and make her skilful at it, and she thus becomes of twice as much value to you. Or when you take one who is ignorant of the duties of a housekeeper or servant, and, having made her accomplished, trustworthy, and handy, render her of the highest value. Or when it is in your power to do services to such of your attendants as are steady and useful, while, if any one is found transgressing, you can inflict punishment. But you will experience the greatest of pleasures, if you show yourself superior to me, and render me your servant, and have no cause to fear that, as life advances, you may become less respected in your household. . . .

At another point Ischomachus chided his young wife for using cosmetics. He told her that putting on make-up ("white lead and vermilion") did not make her more sexually attractive. The following passage gives further insight into the affairs of an Athenian household.

'And what in the name of the gods,' said I, 'did she answer to these remarks?' 'Her only answer was,' said he, 'that she never afterwards practised any such art, but took care to appear in a natural and becoming manner. She even asked me if I could recommend her any course by which she might render herself really good looking, and not merely make herself be thought so. I then, my dear Socrates,' continued he, 'advised her not to sit about like a slave, but to take upon herself, with the help of the gods, to preside at the loom like a mistress, and to teach others what she knew better than they, and to learn what she did not know so well; I recommended her also to overlook the bread-maker, to attend to the housekeeper as she was measuring out her stores, and to go about and examine whether everything was in the place in which it ought to be; for such occupations, it appeared to me, would be at once a discharge of her duties and a means of exercise. I told her, too, that it would be good exercise to wet and knead the bread, and to shake out and put up the clothes and bed-coverings. I assured her that if she thus exercised herself she would take her food with a better appetite, would enjoy better health, and would assume a more truly pleasing complexion. A wife's looks are really attractive to a husband when, compared to a slave girl, she seems more pure and healthy, and is dressed more becomingly, and especially because she gratifies her husband willingly and not because she is compelled to do so.

State Finances

Another work of Xenophon shows how the institution of slavery was completely taken for granted in Athenian society. Can you see any flaws in his plan to enhance the revenues of the state?

From Xenophon. *On the Revenues*

I come to a new topic. I am persuaded that the establishment of the silver mines on the proper footing would be followed by a large increase of wealth apart from the other sources of revenue. And I would like, for the benefit of those who may be ignorant, to point out what the capacity of these mines really is. You will then be in a position to decide how to turn them to better account. It is clear, I presume, to every one that these mines have for a very long time been in active operation; at any rate no one will venture to fix the date at which they first began to be worked. Now in spite of the fact that the silver ore has been dug and carried out for so long a time, I would ask you to note that the mounds of rubbish so shovelled out are but a fractional portion of the series of hillocks containing veins of silver, and as yet unquarried. Nor is the silver-bearing region gradually becoming circumscribed. On the contrary it is evidently extending in wider area from year to year. That is to say, during the period in which thousands of workers have been employed within the mines no hand was ever stopped for want of work to do. Rather, at any given moment, the work to be done was more than enough for the hands employed. And so it is to-day with the owners of slaves working in the mines: no one dreams of reducing the number of his hands. On the contrary, the object is perpetually to acquire as many additional hands as the owner possibly can. The fact is that with few hands to dig and search, the find of treasure will be small, but with an increase of labour the discovery of the ore itself is more than proportionally increased. So much so, that of all operations with which I am acquainted, this is the only one in which no sort of jealousy is felt at a further development of the industry. . . .

It is an old story, trite enough to those of us who have cared to attend to it, how once on a time Nicias, the son of Niceratus, owned a thousand men in the silver mines, whom he let out to Sosias, a Thracian, on the following terms. Sosias was to pay him a net obol a day, without charge or deduction, for every slave of the thousand, and be responsible for keeping up the number perpetually at that figure. So again Hipponicus had six hundred slaves let out on the same principle, which brought him in a net mina a day without charge or deduction. Then there was Philemonides, with three hundred, bringing him in half a mina, and others, I make no doubt there were, making profits in proportion to their respective resources and capital. But there is no need to revert to ancient

From Xenophon, *On the Revenues*, in H. G. Dakyns, trans., *The Works of Xenophon* (London: Macmillan, 1892), Vol. 2, pp. 334–341.

history. At the present moment there are hundreds of human beings in the mines let out on the same principle. And given that my proposal were carried into effect, the only novelty in it is that, just as the individual in acquiring the ownership of a gang of slaves finds himself at once provided with a permanent source of income, so the state, in like fashion should possess herself of a body of public slaves, to the number, say, of three for every Athenian citizen. As to the feasibility of our proposals, I challenge any one whom it may concern to test the scheme point by point and to give his verdict. . . .

Let it be granted, however, that at first a nucleus of twelve hundred slaves is formed. It is hardly too sanguine a supposition that out of the profits alone, within five or six years this number may be increased to at least six thousand. Again, out of that number of six thousand—supposing each slave to bring in an obol a day clear of all expenses—we get a revenue of sixty talents a year. And supposing twenty talents out of this sum laid out on the purchase of more slaves, there will be forty talents left for the state to apply to any other purpose it may find advisable. By the time the round number of ten thousand is reached the yearly income will amount to a hundred talents. . . .

The citizens of Athens are divided, as we all know, into ten tribes. Let the state then assign to each of these ten tribes an equal number of slaves, and let the tribes agree to associate their fortunes and proceed to open new cuttings. What will happen? Any single tribe hitting upon a productive lode will be the means of discovering what is advantageous to all. Or, supposing two or three, or possibly the half of them, hit upon a lode, clearly these several operations will proportionately be more remunerative still. That the whole ten will fail is not at all in accordance with what we should expect from the history of the past. It is possible, of course, for private persons to combine in the same way, and share their fortunes and minimise their risks. Nor need you apprehend, sirs, that a state mining company, established on this principle, will prove a thorn in the side of the private owner, or the private owner prove injurious to the state. But rather like allies who render each other stronger the more they combine, so in these silver mines, the greater number of companies at work the larger the riches they will discover and disinter.

This then is a statement, as far as I can make it clear, of the method by which, with the proper state organisation, every Athenian may be supplied with ample maintenance at the public expense.

ARISTOTLE—NATURAL SCIENCE AND SOCIAL SCIENCE

Scientific Method

Plato hoped to arrive at truth by pure thought. Aristotle emphasized also the value of practical experience as a guide to action and as a starting point for the further reflections that could lead to real wisdom. (Aristotle uses the term "art" to refer to any branch of knowledge—here he mentions the art of medicine. "Art" also means the skill by which we derive general conclusions from particular experiences.)

From *Metaphysics*

All men by nature desire to know. An indication of this is the delight we take in our senses; for even apart from their usefulness they are loved for themselves; and above all others the sense of sight. For not only with a view to action, but even when we are not going to do anything, we prefer sight to almost everything else. The reason is that this, most of all the senses, makes us know and brings to light many differences between things.

The animals other than man live by appearances and memories, and have but little of connected experience; but the human race lives also by art and reasonings. And from memory experience is produced in men; for many memories of the same thing produce finally the capacity for a single experience. Experience seems to be very similar to science and art, but really science and art come to men *through* experience; for 'experience made art', as Polus says, 'but inexperience luck'. And art arises, when from many notions gained by experience one universal judgement about similar objects is produced. For to have a judgement that when Callias was ill of this disease this did him good, and similarly in the case of Socrates and in many individual cases, is a matter of experience; but to judge that it has done good to all persons of a certain constitution, marked off in one class, when they were ill of this disease, e.g. to phlegmatic or bilious people when burning with fever,—this is a matter of art.

With a view to action experience seems in no respect inferior to art, and we even see men of experience succeeding more than those who have theory without experience. The reason is that experience is knowledge of individuals, art of universals, and actions and productions are all concerned with the individual; for the physician does not cure a man, except in an incidental way, but Callias or Socrates or some other called by some such individual name, who happens to be a man. If, then, a man has theory without experience, and knows the universal but does not know the individual included in this, he will often fail to cure; for it is the individual that is to be cured. But yet we think that *knowledge* and *understanding* belong to art rather than to experience, and we suppose the masters of an art to be wiser than men of mere experience (which implies that wisdom depends in all cases rather on knowledge); and this because the former know the cause, but the latter do not. For men of experience know that the thing is so, but do not know why, while the others know the 'why' and the cause . . . thus we view them as being wiser not in virtue of being able to act, but of having the theory for themselves and knowing the causes. And in general it is a sign of the man who knows, that he can teach, and therefore we think art more truly knowledge than experience is; for artists can teach, and men of mere experience cannot.

Ethics and Politics

Aristotle believed that everything in the universe pursued an end or purpose by functioning in a manner consistent with its own nature. In his Ethics *he applied the idea to*

From Aristotle, *Metaphysica*, W. D. Ross trans. in *The Works of Aristotle Translated into English*, J. A. Smith and W. D. Ross eds. (Oxford: Clarendon Press, 1908), Vol. 8, pp. 1–2.

human personality. What was the final end of humanity according to Aristotle? And how could it be achieved?

From *The Nichomachean Ethics*

Every art and every scientific inquiry, and similarly every action and purpose, may be said to aim at some good. Hence the good has been well defined as that at which all things aim. . . . As there are various actions, arts, and sciences, it follows that the ends are also various. Thus health is the end of medicine, a vessel of shipbuilding, victory of strategy, and wealth of domestic economy.

As it appears that there are more ends than one and some of these, e.g. wealth, flutes, and instruments generally we desire as means to something else, it is evident that they are not all final ends. But the highest good is clearly something final. Hence if there is only one final end, this will be the object of which we are in search, and if there are more than one, it will be the most final of them. We speak of that which is sought after for its own sake as more final than that which is sought after as a means to something else; we speak of that which is never desired as a means to something else as more final than the things which are desired both in themselves and as means to something else; and we speak of a thing as absolutely final, if it is always desired in itself and never as a means to something else.

It seems that happiness preeminently answers to this description, as we always desire happiness for its own sake and never as a means to something else, whereas we desire honour, pleasure, intellect, and every virtue, partly for their own sakes (for we should desire them independently of what might result from them) but partly also as being means to happiness, because we suppose they will prove the instruments of happiness. Happiness, on the other hand, nobody desires for the sake of these things, nor indeed as a means to anything else at all. . . .

Perhaps, however, it seems a truth which is generally admitted, that happiness is the supreme good; what is wanted is to define its nature a little more clearly. The best way of arriving at such a definition will probably be to ascertain the function of Man. For, as with a flute-player, a sculptor, or any artisan, or in fact anybody who has a definite function and action, his goodness, or excellence seems to lie in his function, so it would seem to be with Man, if indeed he has a definite function. Can it be said then that, while a carpenter and a cobbler have definite functions and actions, Man, unlike them, is naturally functionless? The reasonable view is that, as the eye, the hand, the foot, and similarly each several part of the body has a definite function, so Man may be regarded as having a definite function apart from all these. What then, can this function be? It is not life; for life is apparently something which man shares with the plants; and it is something peculiar to him that we are looking for. We must exclude therefore the life of nutrition and increase. There is next what may be called the life of sensation. But this too, is apparently shared by Man with horses, cattle, and all other animals. There remains what I may call the practical life of the reason, part of Man's very being.

From Aristotle, *The Nichomachean Ethics*, J. E. C. Welldon, trans. (London: Macmillan, 1897), pp. 1, 13–14, 15–16.

The function of Man then is an activity of soul in accordance with reason, or not independently of reason. Again the functions of a person of a certain kind, and of such a person who is good of his kind e.g. of a harpist and a good harpist, are in our view generically the same, and this view is true of people of all kinds without exception, the superior excellence being only an addition to the function; for it is the function of a harpist to play the harp, and of a good harpist to play the harp well. This being so, if we define the function of Man as a kind of life, and this life as an activity of soul, or a course of action in conformity with reason, if the function of a good man is such activity or action of a good and noble kind, and if everything is successfully performed when it is performed in accordance with its proper excellence, it follows that the good of Man is an activity of soul in accordance with virtue or, if there are more virtues than one, in accordance with the best and most complete virtue. But it is necessary to add the words "in a complete life." For as one swallow or one day does not make a spring, so one day or a short time does not make a fortunate or happy man.

Aristotle began his Politics *with an account of the origin of the state, a common theme in many later works of Western political theory. Why did he think the state was "natural to mankind?"*

From *The Politics*

Every state is a community of some kind, and every community is established with a view to some good; for mankind always act in order to obtain that which they think good. But, if all communities aim at some good, the state or political community, which is the highest of all, and which embraces all the rest, aims at good in a greater degree than any other, and at the highest good. . . . He who thus considers things in their first growth and origin, whether a state or anything else, will obtain the clearest view of them. In the first place there must be a union of those who cannot exist without each other; namely, of male and female, that the race may continue (and this is a union which is formed, not of deliberate purpose, but because, in common with other animals and with plants, mankind have a natural desire to leave behind them an image of themselves), and of natural ruler and subject, that both may be preserved. For that which can foresee by the exercise of mind is by nature intended to be lord and master, and that which can with its body give effect to such foresight is a subject, and by nature a slave; hence master and slave have the same interest. Now nature has distinguished between the female and the slave. For she is not niggardly, like the smith who fashions the Delphian knife for many uses; she makes each thing for a single use, and every instrument is best made when intended for one and not for many uses. But among barbarians no distinction is made between women and slaves, because there is no natural ruler among them: they are a community of slaves, male and female. Wherefore the poets say,—

'It is meet that Hellenes should rule over barbarians';

as if they thought that the barbarian and the slave were by nature one.

From Aristotle, *The Politics*, in B. Jowett, trans., *The Works of Aristotle*, X, rev. ed. (Oxford: Clarendon Press, 1921), I. 1–2; III. 7; IV. 1; II. 4; III. 11; IV. 11.

Out of these two relationships between man and woman, master and slave, the first thing to arise is the family, and Hesiod is right when he says,—

'First house and wife and an ox for the plough',

for the ox is the poor man's slave. The family is the association established by nature for the supply of men's everyday wants, and the members of it are called by Charondas 'companions of the cupboard', and by Epimenides the Cretan, 'companions of the manger'. But when several families are united, and the association aims at something more than the supply of daily needs, the first society to be formed is the village. And the most natural form of the village appears to be that of a colony from the family, composed of the children and grandchildren, who are said to be 'suckled with the same milk'. And this is the reason why Hellenic states were originally governed by kings; because the Hellenes were under royal rule before they came together, as the barbarians still are. Every family is ruled by the eldest, and therefore in the colonies of the family the kingly form of government prevailed because they were of the same blood. As Homer says:

'Each one gives law to his children and to his wives.'

For they lived dispersedly, as was the manner in ancient times. Wherefore men say that the Gods have a king, because they themselves either are or were in ancient times under the rule of a king. For they imagine, not only the forms of the Gods, but their ways of life to be like their own.

When several villages are united in a single complete community, large enough to be nearly or quite self-sufficing, the state comes into existence, originating in the bare needs of life, and continuing in existence for the sake of a good life. And therefore, if the earlier forms of society are natural, so is the state, for it is the end of them, and the nature of a thing is its end. For what each thing is when fully developed, we call its nature, whether we are speaking of a man, a horse, or a family. Besides, the final cause and end of a thing is the best, and to be self-sufficing is the end and the best.

Hence it is evident that the state is a creation of nature, and that man is by nature a political animal. And he who by nature and not by mere accident is without a state, is either a bad man or above humanity; he is like the

'Tribeless, lawless, heartless one,'

whom Homer denounces—the natural outcast is forthwith a lover of war; he may be compared to an isolated piece at draughts.

Now, that man is more of a political animal than bees or any other gregarious animals is evident. Nature, as we often say, makes nothing in vain, and man is the only animal whom she has endowed with the gift of speech. And whereas mere voice is but an indication of pleasure or pain, and is therefore found in other animals (for their nature attains to the perception of pleasure and pain and the intimation of them to one another, and no further), the power of speech is intended to set forth the expedient and inexpedient, and therefore likewise the just and the unjust. And it is a characteristic of man that he alone has any sense of good and evil, of just and unjust, and the like, and the association of living beings who have this sense makes a family and a state.

Further, the state is by nature clearly prior to the family and to the individual, since the whole is of necessity prior to the part; for example, if the whole body be destroyed, there will be no foot or hand, except in an equivocal sense, as we might speak of a stone hand; for when destroyed the hand will be no better than that. But things are defined by their working and power; and we ought not to say that they are the same when they no longer have their proper quality, but only that they have the same name. The proof that the state is a creation of nature and prior to the individual is that the individual, when isolated, is not self-sufficing; and therefore he is like a part in relation to the whole. But he who is unable to live in society, or who has no need because he is sufficient for himself, must be either a beast or a god: he is no part of a state. A social instinct is implanted in all men by nature, and yet he who first founded the state was the greatest of benefactors. For man, when perfected, is the best of animals, but, when separated from law and justice, he is the worst of all. . . . But justice is the bond of men in states, for the administration of justice, which is the determination of what is just, is the principle of order in political society.

Aristotle also discussed the disadvantages of various forms of government and a possible way of overcoming them. Do you agree with his judgments?

There is also a doubt as to what is to be the supreme power in the state:—Is it the multitude? Or the wealthy? Or the good? Or the one best man? Or a tyrant? Any of these alternatives seems to involve disagreeable consequences. If the poor, for example, because they are more in number, divide among themselves the property of the rich,—is not this unjust? No, by heaven (will be the reply), for the supreme authority justly willed it. But if this is not injustice, pray what is? Again, when in the first division all has been taken, and the majority divide anew the property of the minority, is it not evident, if this goes on, that they will ruin the state? Yet surely, virtue is not the ruin of those who possess her, nor is justice destructive of a state; and therefore this law of confiscation clearly cannot be just. If it were, all the acts of a tyrant must of necessity be just; for he only coerces other men by superior power, just as the multitude coerce the rich. But is it just then that the few and the wealthy should be the rulers? And what if they, in like manner, rob and plunder the people,—is this just? If so, the other case will likewise be just. But there can be no doubt that all these things are wrong and unjust.

Then ought the good to rule and have supreme power? But in that case everybody else, being excluded from power, will be dishonoured. For the offices of a state are posts of honour; and if one set of men always hold them, the rest must be deprived of them. Then will it be well that the one best man should rule? Nay, that is still more oligarchical, for the number of those who are dishonoured is thereby increased. Some one may say that it is bad in any case for a man, subject as he is to all the accidents of human passion, to have the supreme power, rather than the law. But what if the law itself be democratical or oligarchical, how will that help us out of our difficulties? Not at all; the same consequences will follow.

Thus it is manifest that the best political community is formed by citizens of the middle class, and that those states are likely to be well-administered, in which the middle class is large, and stronger if possible than both the other classes, or at any rate than either singly; for the addition of the middle class turns the scale, and prevents either of the extremes from being dominant. Great then is the good fortune of a state in which the citizens have a moderate and sufficient property; for where some possess much, and the others nothing, there may arise an extreme democracy, or a pure oligarchy; or a tyranny may grow out of either extreme,—either out of the most rampant democracy, or out of an oligarchy; but it is not so likely to arise out of the middle constitutions and those akin to them. . . . And democracies are safer and more permanent than oligarchies, because they have a middle class which is more numerous and has a greater share in the government; for when there is no middle class, and the poor greatly exceed in number, troubles arise, and the state soon comes to an end. A proof of the superiority of the middle class is that the best legislators have been of a middle condition; for example, Solon, as his own verses testify; and Lycurgus, for he was not a king; and Charondas, and almost all legislators.

PART FOUR

HELLENISTIC CULTURE

The Empire of Alexander

From Plutarch. *Moralia*

Hellenism and Judaism

From *The First Book of Maccabees*

Epicureanism

From Lucretius. *On the Nature of the Universe*

Stoicism

From *Works of Epictetus*

ROME—REPUBLIC TO EMPIRE

Republican Institutions

From *The Histories of Polybius*
From *The Roman History of Appian*

The Roman Revolution

From *The Roman History of Appian*
From Cicero. *On the Laws*

From Sallust. *The Conspiracy of Catiline*
From Cicero. *On Moral Duties*
From Suetonius. *The Twelve Caesars*
From *The Annals of Tacitus*

Imperial Administration

From *Letters of Pliny*

ROMAN FAMILIES

Patriarchal Tradition

From *Roman Antiquities*
From *The Histories of Polybius*
From Plutarch. *Life of Cato*

Legislation of Augustus

From *Dio's Roman History*
From *The Institutes of Gaius*
From *Opinions of Julius Paulus*

Roman Wives

From *Juvenal's Sixth Satire*
From *Praise of Turia*

HELLENISM AND ROME—
FROM REPUBLIC
TO EMPIRE

Alexander the Great (356–323 B.C.) absorbed the world of Greek city-states into the vast empire that he conquered, stretching from Egypt to Afghanistan. But he left no successor and when he died the Mediterranean region again divided into independent kingdoms and city-states. In spite of the political fragmentation a common "Hellenistic" culture permeated the life of the Greek-speaking upper classes. In this changed world some thinkers carried on the tradition of Greek philosophy and built up new systems of thought; at the same time various oriental cults, the religions of the peoples that Alexander had conquered, spread westward. The two major new philosophical systems, Epicurianism and Stoicism, both tried in different ways to explain the whole nature of the universe and also to show how individual persons could live satisfying lives in the new cosmopolitan multi-ethnic world order.

The rise of Roman power created a new political unity in the Mediterranean world. The Romans were a practical people. They built good roads; they deployed disciplined armies; they made enduring laws. By the end of the first century B.C., the Romans dominated the whole Mediterranean basin and their conquests had extended northward to the Rhine and the Danube. This was a most formidable aggregation of power and territory; but tensions existed even at the height of Roman power. Class disputes arose between aristocratic and "middle-class" Romans; major problems were encountered in adapting the institutions of the original Roman city-state to the rule of a great empire; and the old ideal of a stable family ruled by a stern patriarch—the traditional foundation of Roman morality—was more and more seen to conflict with the practical realities of Roman social life.

HELLENISTIC CULTURE

The Empire of Alexander

Historians have never agreed about the personality of Alexander; there are just no ade-quate contemporary sources on which to base a judgment. Alexander was certainly a great conqueror, but he died before he was thirty-three and we cannot know how he would have ruled his empire if he had lived. The Greek historian Plutarch (c.A.D. 46–126), writing centuries later, gave a very favorable account of Alexander's achieve-ments. What motives and ideals did this author attribute to Alexander?

From Plutarch. *Moralia*

The much-admired *Republic* of Zeno, the founder of the Stoic sect, may be summed up in this one main principle: that all the inhabitants of this world of ours should not live differentiated by their respective rules of justice into sepa-rate cities and communities, but that we should consider all men to be of one community and one polity, and that we should have a common life and an or-der common to us all, even as a herd that feeds together and shares the pas-turage of a common field. This Zeno wrote, giving shape to a dream or, as it were, shadowy picture of a well-ordered and philosophic commonwealth; but it was Alexander who gave effect to the idea. For Alexander did not follow Aristotle's advice to treat the Greeks as if he were their leader, and other peoples as if he were their master; to have regard for the Greeks as for friends and kin-dred, but to conduct himself toward other peoples as though they were plants or animals; for to do so would have been to cumber his leadership with numer-ous battles and banishments and festering seditions. But, as he believed that he came as a heaven-sent governor to all, and as a mediator for the whole world, those whom he could not persuade to unite with him, he conquered by force of arms, and he brought together into one body all men everywhere, uniting and mixing in one great loving-cup, as it were, men's lives, their characters, their marriages, their very habits of life. He bade them all consider as their fatherland the whole inhabited earth, as their stronghold and protection his camp, as akin to them all good men, and as foreigners only the wicked. . . . clothing and food, marriage and manner of life they should regard as common to all, being blended into one by ties of blood and children. . . .

For he did not overrun Asia like a robber nor was he minded to tear and rend it, as if it were booty and plunder bestowed by unexpected good fortune. . . . But Alexander desired to render all upon earth subject to one law of reason and one form of government and to reveal all men as one people, and to this purpose he made himself conform. But if the deity that sent down Alexander's soul into this world of ours had not recalled him quickly, one law would govern all mankind, and they all would look toward one rule of justice as though toward a common source of light.

From *Plutarch's Moralia*, trans. F. C. Babbitt in *The Loeb Classical Library* (Cambridge, Mass., Harvard University Press, 1972), Vol. 4, pp. 397, 399, 405.

Hellenism and Judaism

Plutarch regarded the imposition of a common culture on disparate peoples as a noble ideal. But things did not always go smoothly in practice. The Jews, like other Near Eastern peoples were influenced by Hellenism. The Hebrew scriptures were translated into Greek and some upper-class Jews began to adopt Greek customs. But a crisis arose in 167 B.C. A Syrian king ruling over Judea tried to suppress the Jewish religion and impose Hellenistic forms of worship. (He set up an altar to Zeus in the Temple court at Jerusalem.) How did the Jews respond according to the Book of Maccabees?

From *The First Book of Maccabees*

Then the king wrote to his whole kingdom that all should be one people, and that each should give up his customs. All the Gentiles accepted the command of the king. Many even from Israel gladly adopted his religion; they sacrificed to idols and profaned the sabbath. And the king sent letters by messengers to Jerusalem and the cities of Judah; he directed them to follow customs strange to the land, to forbid burnt offerings and sacrifices and drink offerings in the sanctuary, to profane sabbaths and feasts, to defile the sanctuary and the priests, to build altars and sacred precincts and shrines for idols, to sacrifice swine and unclean animals, and to leave their sons uncircumcised. They were to make themselves abominable by everything unclean and profane, so that they should forget the law and change all the ordinances. "And whoever does not obey the command of the king shall die."

In such words he wrote to his whole kingdom. And he appointed inspectors over all the people and commanded the cities of Judah to offer sacrifice, city by city. Many of the people, every one who forsook the law, joined them, and they did evil in the land; they drove Israel into hiding in every place of refuge they had.

Now on the fifteenth day of Chislev, in the one hundred and forty-fifth year [167 B.C.] they erected a desolating sacrilege upon the altar of burnt offering. They also built altars in the surrounding cities of Judah, and burned incense at the doors of the houses and in the streets. The books of the law which they found they tore to pieces and burned with fire. Where the book of the covenant was found in the possession of any one, or if any one adhered to the law, the decree of the king condemned him to death. They kept using violence against Israel, against those found month after month in the cities. And on the twenty-fifth day of the month they offered sacrifice on the altar which was upon the altar of burnt offering. According to the decree, they put to death the women who had their children circumcised, and their families and those who circumcised them; and they hung the infants from their mothers' necks.

But many in Israel stood firm and were resolved in their hearts not to eat unclean food. They chose to die rather than to be defiled by food or to profane the holy covenant; and they did die. And very great wrath came upon Israel.

From *The Revised Standard Version Bible* (New York: Oxford University Press, 1973). The First Book of the Maccabees 1:41–64; 4:36–51.

An uprising led by Judas Maccabeus defeated the king and restored traditional Judaism. (The modern festival of Hanukkah celebrates this event.)

Then said Judas and his brothers, "Behold, our enemies are crushed; let us go up to cleanse the sanctuary and dedicate it." So all the army assembled and they went up to Mount Zion. And they saw the sanctuary desolate, the altar profaned, and the gates burned. In the courts they saw bushes sprung up as in a thicket, or as on one of the mountains. They saw also the chambers of the priests in ruins. Then they rent their clothes, and mourned with great lamentation, and sprinkled themselves with ashes. They fell face down on the ground, and sounded the signal on the trumpets, and cried out to Heaven. Then Judas detailed men to fight against those in the citadel until he had cleansed the sanctuary.

He chose blameless priests devoted to the law, and they cleansed the sanctuary and removed the defiled stones to an unclean place. They deliberated what to do about the altar of burnt offering, which had been profaned. And they thought it best to tear it down, lest it bring reproach upon them, for the Gentiles had defiled it. So they tore down the altar, and stored the stones in a convenient place on the temple hill until there should come a prophet to tell what to do with them. Then they took unhewn stones, as the law directs, and built a new altar like the former one. They also rebuilt the sanctuary and the interior of the temple, and consecrated the courts. They made new holy vessels, and brought the lampstand, the altar of incense, and the table into the temple. Then they burned incense on the altar and lighted the lamps on the lampstand, and these gave light in the temple. They placed the bread on the table and hung up the curtains. Thus they finished all the work they had undertaken.

Epicureanism

Two major philosophies of the Hellenistic world, Epicureanism and Stoicism, were founded by the Greek thinkers Epicurus (c. 340–c. 270 B.C.) and Zeno (c. 340–c. 265 B.C.). Their ideas were taken up and developed by later authors working at Rome, among them Lucretius (94–55 B.C.) and Epictetus (c.A.D. 60–120). The Epicureans derived a skeptical view of the universe from earlier Greek atomism. They recommended a life of quiet enjoyment, spent away from the troubles of the world.

From Lucretius. On the Nature of the Universe

What joy it is, when out at sea the stormwinds are lashing the waters, to gaze from the shore at the heavy stress some other man is enduring! Not that anyone's afflictions are in themselves a source of delight; but to realize from what troubles you yourself are free is joy indeed. What joy, again, to watch opposing hosts marshalled on the field of battle when you have yourself no part in

From Lucretius, *On the Nature of the Universe*, R. E. Latham, trans. (Harmondsworth: Penguin Classics, 1951), pp. 60, 62–63, 175–177, 183–184, 195, 199–200, 205–206, 215. Copyright © 1951 by R. E. Latham. Reprinted by permission of Penguin Books Ltd.

their peril! But this is the greatest joy of all: to stand aloof in a quiet citadel, stoutly fortified by the teaching of the wise, and to gaze down from that elevation on others wandering aimlessly in a vain search for the way of life, pitting their wits one against another, disputing for precedence, struggling night and day with unstinted effort to scale the pinnacles of wealth and power. O joyless hearts of men! O minds without vision! How dark and dangerous the life in which this tiny span is lived away! Do you not see that nature is clamouring for two things only, a body free from pain, a mind released from worry and fear for the enjoyment of pleasurable sensations?

And now to business. I will explain *the motion by which the generative bodies of matter give birth to various things*, and, after they are born, dissolve them once more; the force that compels them to do this; and the power of movement through the boundless void with which they are endowed. . . . Since the atoms are moving freely through the void, they must all be kept in motion either by their own weight or on occasion by the impact of another atom. For it must often happen that two of them in their course knock together and immediately bounce apart in opposite directions, a natural consequence of their hardness and solidity and the absence of anything behind to stop them.

As a further indication that all particles of matter are on the move, remember that the universe is bottomless: there is no place where the atoms could come to rest. As I have already shown by various arguments and proved conclusively, space is without end or limit and spreads out immeasurably in all directions alike.

It clearly follows that no rest is given to the atoms in their course through the depths of space. Driven along in an incessant but variable movement, some of them bounce far apart after a collision while others recoil only a short distance from the impact. From those that do not recoil far, being driven into a closer union and held there by the entanglement of their own interlocking shapes, are composed firmly rooted rock, the stubborn strength of steel and the like. Those others that move freely through larger tracts of space, springing far apart and carried far by the rebound—these provide for us thin air and blazing sunlight. Besides these, there are many other atoms at large in empty space which have been thrown out of compound bodies and have nowhere even been granted admittance so as to bring their motions into harmony.

Next, the theory that the gods deliberately created the world in all its natural splendour for the sake of man, so that we ought to praise this eminently praiseworthy piece of divine workmanship and believe it eternal and immortal and think it a sin to unsettle by violence the everlasting abode established for mankind by the ancient purpose of the gods and to worry it with words and turn it topsy-turvy—this theory, Memmius, with all its attendant fictions is sheer nonsense. For what benefit could immortal and blessed beings reap from our gratitude, that they should undertake any task on our behalf? Or what could tempt those who had been at peace so long to change their old life for a new? The revolutionary is one who is dissatisfied with the old order. But one who has known no trouble in the past, but spent his days joyfully—what could prick such a being with the itch for novelty? Or again, what harm would it have done us to have remained uncreated? Are we to suppose that our life was sunk in gloom and grief till the light of creation blazed forth? True that, once a man is born, he must will to remain alive so long as beguiling pleasure holds him. But one who has never tasted the love of life, or been enrolled among the living, what odds is it to him if he is never created?

Even if I knew nothing of the atoms, I would venture to assert on the evidence of the celestial phenomena themselves, supported by many other arguments, that the universe was certainly not created for us by divine power: it is so full of imperfections. In the first place, of all that is covered by the wide sweep of the sky, part has been greedily seized by mountains and the woodland haunts of wild beasts. Part is usurped by crags and desolate bogs and the sea that holds far asunder the shores of the lands. Almost two-thirds are withheld from mankind by torrid heat and perennial deposits of frost. The little that is left of cultivable soil, if the force of nature had its way, would be choked with briars, did not the force of man oppose it. It is man's way, for the sake of life, to groan over the stout mattock and cleave the earth with downpressed plough. Unless we turn the fruitful clods with the coulter and break up the soil to stimulate the growth of the crops, they cannot emerge of their own accord into the open air. Even so, when by dint of hard work all the fields at last burst forth into leaf and flower, then either the fiery sun withers them with intemperate heat, or sudden showers and icy frosts destroy them and gales of wind batter them with hurricane force. Again, why does nature feed and breed the fearsome brood of wild beasts, a menace to the human race by land and sea? Why do the changing seasons bring pestilence in their train? Why does untimely death roam abroad?

Certainly the atoms did not post themselves purposefully in due order by an act of intelligence, nor did they stipulate what movements each should perform. But multitudinous atoms, swept along in multitudinous courses through infinite time by mutual clashes and their own weight, have come together in every possible way and realized everything that could be formed by their combinations. So it comes about that a voyage of immense duration, in which they have experienced every variety of movement and conjunction, has at length brought together those whose sudden encounter normally forms the starting-point of substantial fabrics—earth and sea and sky and the races of living creatures.

First of all, the earth girdled its hills with a green glow of herbage, and over every plain the meadows gleamed with verdure and with bloom. Then trees of every sort were given free rein to join in an eager race for growth into the gusty air. As feathers, fur and bristles are generated at the outset from the bodies of winged and four-footed creatures, so then *the new-born earth first flung up herbs and shrubs. Next in order it engendered the various breeds of mortal creatures,* manifold in mode of origin as in form. The animals cannot have fallen from the sky, and those that live on land cannot have emerged from the briny gulfs. We are left with the conclusion that the name of mother has rightly been bestowed on the earth, since out of the earth everything is born.

Stoicism

As a young man, Epictetus lived in Rome as the slave of a rich freedman. While still a slave he attended the lectures of an eminent Stoic philosopher, C. Musonius Rufus. Later Epictetus was freed and taught at Nicopolis in Greece. How does the world view of Epictetus differ from that of Lucretius? Is either view persuasive?

From *Works of Epictetus*

. . . What else can I do, a lame old man, but sing hymns to God? Were I a nightingale, I would act the part of a nightingale; were I a swan, the part of a swan. But since I am a reasonable creature, it is my duty to praise God. This is my business. I do it. Nor will I ever desert this post, so long as it is permitted me; and I call on you to join in the same song.

From every event that happens in the world it is easy to celebrate Providence, if a person hath but these two qualities in himself; a faculty of considering what happens to each individual, and a grateful temper. Without the first, he will not perceive the usefulness of things which happen; and without the other, he will not be thankful for them. If God had made colors, and had not made the faculty of seeing them, what would have been their use? None. On the other hand, if he had made the faculty of observation, without objects to observe, what would have been the use of that? None. Again; if he had formed both the faculty and the objects, but had not made light? Neither in that case would they have been of any use.

Who is it then that hath fitted each of these to the other? Who is it that hath fitted the sword to the scabbard, and the scabbard to the sword? Is there no such Being? From the very construction of a complete work, we are used to declare positively, that it must be the operation of some artificer, and not the effect of mere chance. Doth every such work, then, demonstrate an artificer; and do not visible objects, and the sense of seeing, and light, demonstrate one? Do not the difference of the sexes, and their inclination to each other, and the use of their several powers; do not these things demonstrate an artificer? Most certainly they do.

All things serve and obey the laws of the universe; the earth, the sea, the sun, the stars, and the plants and animals of the earth. Our body likewise obeys the same laws, in being sick and well, young and old, and passing through the other changes they decree. It is therefore reasonable that what depends on ourselves, that is, our own understanding, should not be the only rebel against natural law. For the universe is powerful and superior, and consults the best for us by governing us in conjunction with the whole. And further; opposition, besides that it is unreasonable, and produces nothing except a vain struggle, throws us into pain and sorrows.

If what philosophers say of the kinship between God and men be true, what has any one to do, but, like Socrates, when he is asked what countryman he is,

From T. W. Higginson, *The Works of Epictetus* (Boston, Mass.: Little, Brown and Co., 1886).

never to say that he is a citizen of Athens, or of Corinth, but of the universe? . . . Men alone are qualified to partake of a communication with the Deity, being connected with him by reason; why may not such a one call himself a citizen of the universe? Why not a son of God?

You, O man are God's principal work. You are a distinct portion of the essence of God; and contain a certain part of him in yourself. Why then are you ignorant of your noble birth? Why do not you consider whence you came? You carry a God about with you, poor wretch, and know nothing of it. Do you suppose I mean some god without you of gold or silver? It is within yourself that you carry him; and you do not observe that you profane him by impure thoughts and unclean actions. If the mere external image of God were present, you would not dare to act as you do; and when God himself is within you, and hears and sees all, are not you ashamed to think and act thus; insensible of your own nature, and at enmity with God?

When we are children, our parents deliver us to the care of a tutor; who is continually to watch over us that we get no hurt. When we are become men, God delivers us to the guardianship of an implanted conscience. We ought by no means, then, to despise this guardian; for it will both displease God, and we shall be enemies to our own conscience.

Why should any one person envy another? Why should he be impressed with awe by those who have great possessions, or are placed in high rank? especially, if they are powerful and passionate? For what will they do to us? The things which they can do, we do not regard: the things about which we are concerned, they cannot reach. Who then, after all, shall hold sway over a person thus disposed?

Women from fourteen years old are flattered by men with the title of mistresses. Therefore, perceiving that they are regarded only as qualified to give men pleasure, they begin to adorn themselves, and in that to place all their hopes. It is worth while, therefore, to take care that they may perceive themselves honored only so far as they appear beautiful in their demeanor, and modestly virtuous.

Sickness is an impediment to the body, but not to the will, unless itself pleases. Lameness is an impediment to the leg, but not to the will[1]; and say this to yourself with regard to everything that happens. For you will find it to be an impediment to something else, but not truly to yourself.

I must die: if instantly, I will die instantly; if in a short time, I will dine first; and when the hour comes, then I will die. How? As becomes one who restores what is not his own.

Do not you know that both sickness and death must overtake us? At what employment? The husbandman at his plough; the sailor on his voyage. At what employment would you be taken? For my own part, I would be found engaged

---

[1]The Christian author Origen handed down a story that Epictetus was lamed by his master. The master tortured Epictetus by twisting his leg. Epictetus remarked calmly, "You are going to break it." When the leg broke he added in the same tone, "There, I told you so."

in nothing but in the regulation of my own Will; how to render it undisturbed, unrestrained, uncompelled, free. I would be found studying this, that I may be able to say to God, "Have I transgressed Thy commands? Have I perverted the powers, the senses, the instincts, which Thou hast given me? Have I ever accused Thee, or censured Thy dispensations? I have been sick, because it was Thy pleasure, like others; but I willingly. I have been poor, it being Thy will; but with joy. I have not been in power, because it was not Thy will; and power I have never desired. Hast Thou ever seen me saddened because of this? Have I not always approached Thee with a cheerful countenance; prepared to execute Thy commands and the indications of Thy will? Is it Thy pleasure that I should depart from this assembly? I depart. I give Thee all thanks that Thou hast thought me worthy to have a share in it with Thee; to behold Thy works, and to join with Thee in comprehending Thy administration." Let death overtake me while I am thinking, while I am writing, while I am reading such things as these.

ROME—REPUBLIC TO EMPIRE

Republican Institutions

The Greek historian Polybius (205–125 B.C.) believed that most state constitutions followed a cyclical pattern. He held that royal government would commonly lead to tyranny and so provoke an aristocratic reaction. The aristocracy would in turn become corrupt and be replaced by a democracy. But then democracy would degenerate into anarchy and mob rule. The people would set up a king to restore order. And so the cycle would begin again. But Polybius thought that the Roman constitution was an exception. Why could this constitution remain stable according to Polybius?

From *The Histories of Polybius*

As for the Roman constitution, it had three elements, each of them possessing sovereign powers: and their respective share of power in the whole state had been regulated with such a scrupulous regard to equality and equilibrium, that no one could say for certain, not even a native, whether the constitution as a whole were an aristocracy or democracy or despotism. And no wonder: for if we confine our observation to the power of the Consuls we should be inclined to regard it as despotic; if on that of the Senate, as aristocratic; and if finally one looks at the power possessed by the people it would seem a clear case of a democracy. What the exact powers of these several parts were, and still, with slight modifications, are, I will now state.

The Consuls,[2] before leading out the legions, remain in Rome and are supreme masters of the administration. All other magistrates, except the Tribunes, are under them and take their orders. They introduce foreign ambassadors to the

[2]The Consuls were elected for a two-year term in an assembly of the Roman people.
From E. S. Shuckburgh, trans., *The Histories of Polybius* (London: Macmillan, 1889), pp. 468–474.

Senate; bring matters requiring deliberation before it; and see to the execution of its decrees. If, again, there are any matters of state which require the authorisation of the people, it is their business to see to them, to summon the popular meetings, to bring the proposals before them, and to carry out the decrees of the majority. In the preparations for war also, and in a word in the entire administration of a campaign, they have all but absolute power. It is competent to them to impose on the allies such levies as they think good, to appoint the Military Tribunes, to make up the roll for soldiers and select those that are suitable. Besides they have absolute power of inflicting punishment on all who are under their command while on active service: and they have authority to expend as much of the public money as they choose, being accompanied by a quaestor[3] who is entirely at their orders. A survey of these powers would in fact justify our describing the constitution as despotic,—a clear case of royal government. Nor will it affect the truth of my description, if any of the institutions I have described are changed in our time, or in that of our posterity: and the same remarks apply to what follows.

The Senate has first of all the control of the treasury, and regulates the receipts and disbursements alike. For the Quaestors cannot issue any public money for the various departments of the state without a decree of the Senate, except for the service of the Consuls. The Senate controls also what is by far the largest and most important expenditure, that, namely, which is made by the censors every *lustrum* for the repair or construction of public buildings; this money cannot be obtained by the censors except by the grant of the Senate. Similarly all crimes committed in Italy requiring a public investigation, such as treason, conspiracy, poisoning, or wilful murder, are in the hands of the Senate. Besides, if any individual or state among the Italian allies requires a controversy to be settled, a penalty to be assessed, help or protection to be afforded,—all this is the province of the Senate. Or again, outside Italy, if it is necessary to send an embassy to reconcile warring communities, or to remind them of their duty, or sometimes to impose requisitions upon them, or to receive their submission, or finally to proclaim war against them,—this too is the business of the Senate. In like manner the reception to be given to foreign ambassadors in Rome, and the answers to be returned to them, are decided by the Senate. With such business the people have nothing to do. Consequently, if one were staying at Rome when the Consuls were not in town, one would imagine the constitution to be a complete aristocracy: and this has been the idea entertained by many Greeks, and by many kings as well, from the fact that nearly all the business they had with Rome was settled by the Senate.

After this one would naturally be inclined to ask what part is left for the people in the constitution, when the Senate has these various functions, especially the control of the receipts and expenditure of the exchequer; and when the Consuls, again, have absolute power over the details of military preparation, and an absolute authority in the field? There is, however, a part left the people, and it is a most important one. For the people is the sole fountain of honour and

---

[3]A financial official.

of punishment; and it is by these two things and these alone that dynasties and constitutions and, in a word, human society are held together: for where the distinction between them is not sharply drawn both in theory and practice, there no undertaking can be properly administered,—as indeed we might expect when good and bad are held in exactly the same honour. The people then are the only court to decide matters of life and death; and even in cases where the penalty is money, if the sum to be assessed is sufficiently serious, and especially when the accused have held the higher magistracies. And in regard to this arrangement there is one point deserving especial commendation and record. Men who are on trial for their lives at Rome, while sentence is in process of being voted,—if even only one of the tribes whose votes are needed to ratify the sentence has not voted,—have the privilege at Rome of openly departing and condemning themselves to a voluntary exile. Such men are safe at Naples or Praeneste or at Tibur, and at other towns with which this arrangement has been duly ratified on oath.

Again, it is the people who bestow offices on the deserving, which are the most honourable rewards of virtue. It has also the absolute power of passing or repealing laws; and, most important of all, it is the people who deliberate on the question of peace or war. And when provisional terms are made for alliance, suspension of hostilities, or treaties, it is the people who ratify them or the reverse.

These considerations again would lead one to say that the chief power in the state was the people's, and that the constitution was a democracy.

Such, then, is the distribution of power between the several parts of the state. . . .

The result of this power of the several estates for mutual help or harm is a union sufficiently firm for all emergencies, and a constitution than which it is impossible to find a better. For whenever any danger from without compels them to unite and work together, the strength which is developed by the State is so extraordinary, that everything required is unfailingly carried out by the eager rivalry shown by all classes to devote their whole minds to the need of the hour, and to secure that any determination come to should not fail for want of promptitude; while each individual works, privately and publicly alike, for the accomplishment of the business in hand. Accordingly, the peculiar constitution of the State makes it irresistible, and certain of obtaining whatever it determines to attempt. Nay, even when these external alarms are past, and the people are enjoying their good fortune and the fruits of their victories, and, as usually happens, growing corrupted by flattery and idleness, show a tendency to violence and arrogance,—it is in these circumstances, more than ever, that the constitution is seen to possess within itself the power of correcting abuses. For when any one of the three classes becomes puffed up, and manifests an inclination to be contentious and unduly encroaching, the mutual interdependency of all the three, and the possibility of the pretensions of any one being checked and thwarted by the others, must plainly check this tendency: and so the proper equilibrium is maintained by the impulsiveness of the one part being checked by its fear of the other.

Polybius's idealized version of the constitution masked real social stresses. The underlying ten-sions—between rich and poor and between freemen and slaves—gave rise to open conflict in the time of Tiberius Gracchus, who became a tribune of the plebs in 133 B.C. What abuses did Tiberius Gracchus complain of? How did he try to remedy them? The author of the following account, the historian Appian of Alexandria, lived from A.D. 96 to 165.

From *The Roman History of Appian*

The Romans, as they subdued the Italian nations successively in war, seized a part of their lands and built towns there, or established their own colonies in those already existing, and used them in place of garrisons. Of the land acquired by war they assigned the cultivated part forthwith to settlers, or leased or sold it. Since they had no leisure as yet to allot the part which then lay desolated by war (this was generally the greater part), they made proclamation that in the mean-time those who were willing to work it might do so for a share of the yearly crops—a tenth of the grain and a fifth of the fruit. From those who kept flocks was required a share of the animals, both oxen and small cattle. They did these things in order to multiply the Italian race, which they considered the most la-borious of peoples, so that they might have plenty of allies at home. But the very opposite thing happened; for the rich, getting possession of the greater part of the undistributed lands, and being emboldened by the lapse of time to believe that they would never be dispossessed, and adding to their holdings the small farms of their poor neighbors, partly by purchase and partly by force, came to cultivate vast tracts instead of single estates, using for this purpose slaves as laborers and herdsmen, lest free laborers should be drawn from agriculture into the army. The ownership of slaves itself brought them great gain from the multitude of their progeny, who increased because they were exempt from military service. Thus the powerful ones became enormously rich and the race of slaves multiplied throughout the country, while the Italian people dwindled in numbers and strength, being oppressed by penury, taxes, and military service. If they had any respite from these evils they passed their time in idleness, because the land was held by the rich, who employed slaves instead of freemen as cultivators.

For these reasons the people became troubled lest they should no longer have sufficient allies of the Italian stock, and lest the government itself should be endangered by such a vast number of slaves. Not perceiving any remedy, as it was not easy, nor exactly just, to deprive men of so many possessions they had held so long, including their own trees, buildings, and fixtures, a law was once passed with difficulty at the instance of the tribunes, that nobody should hold more than 500 jugera of this land, or pasture on it more than 100 cattle or 500 sheep. To ensure the observance of this law it was provided also that there should be a certain number of freemen employed on the farms, whose business it should be to watch and report what was going on. Those who held possession of lands under the law were required to take an oath to obey the law, and penal-ties were fixed for violating it, and it was supposed that the remaining land would soon be divided among the poor in small parcels. But there was not the

From H. White, trans., *The Roman History of Appian* (New York: Macmillan, 1899), Vol. 2, pp. 5–14.

smallest consideration shown for the law or the oaths. The few who seemed to pay some respect to them conveyed their lands to their relations fraudulently, but the greater part disregarded it altogether.

At length Tiberius Sempronius Gracchus, an illustrious man, eager for glory, a most powerful speaker, and for these reasons well known to all, delivered an eloquent discourse, while serving as tribune, concerning the Italian race, lamenting that a people so valiant in war, and blood relations to the Romans, were declining little by little in pauperism and paucity of numbers without any hope of remedy. He inveighed against the multitude of slaves as useless in war and never faithful to their masters, and adduced the recent calamity brought upon the masters by their slaves in Sicily, where the demands of agriculture had greatly increased the number of the latter; recalling also the war waged against them by the Romans, which was neither easy nor short, but long-protracted and full of vicissitudes and dangers. After speaking thus he again brought forward the law, providing that nobody should hold more than 500 jugera of the public domain. But he added a provision to the former law, that the sons of the present occupiers might each hold one-half of that amount, and that the remainder should be divided among the poor by triumvirs, who should be changed annually.

This was extremely disturbing to the rich because, on account of the triumvirs, they could no longer disregard the law as they had done before; nor could they buy the allotments of others, because Gracchus had provided against this by forbidding sales. They collected together in groups, and made lamentation, and accused the poor of appropriating the results of their tillage, their vineyards, and their dwellings. Some said that they had paid the price of the land to their neighbors. Were they to lose the money with the land? Others said that the graves of their ancestors were in the ground, which had been allotted to them in the division of their fathers' estates. Others said that their wives' dowries had been expended on the estates, or that the land had been given to their own daughters as dowry. Money-lenders could show loans made on this security. All kinds of wailing and expressions of indignation were heard at once. On the other side were heard the lamentations of the poor—that they had been reduced from competence to extreme penury, and from that to childlessness, because they were unable to rear their offspring. They recounted the military services they had rendered, by which this very land had been acquired, and were angry that they should be robbed of their share of the common property. They reproached the rich for employing slaves, who were always faithless and ill-tempered and for that reason unserviceable in war, instead of freemen, citizens, and soldiers. While these classes were lamenting and indulging in mutual accusations, a great number of others, composed of colonists, or inhabitants of the free towns, or persons otherwise interested in the lands and who were under like apprehensions, flocked in and took sides with their respective factions. Emboldened by numbers and exasperated against each other they attached themselves to turbulent crowds, and waited for the voting on the new law, some trying to prevent its enactment by all means, and others supporting it in every possible way. In addition to personal interest the spirit of rivalry spurred both sides in the preparations they were making against each other for the day of the comitia.

What Gracchus had in his mind in proposing the measure was not wealth, but an increase of efficient population. Inspired greatly by the usefulness of the work, and believing that nothing more advantageous or admirable could ever happen to Italy, he took no account of the difficulties surrounding it. When the time for voting came he advanced many other arguments at considerable length and also asked them whether it was not just to divide among the common people what belonged to them in common; whether a citizen was not worthy of more consideration at all times than a slave; whether a man who served in the army was not more useful than one who did not; and whether one who had a share in the country was not more likely to be devoted to the public interests. He did not dwell long on this comparison between freemen and slaves, which he considered degrading, but proceeded at once to a review of their hopes and fears for the country, saying that the Romans had acquired most of their territory by conquest, and that they had hopes of occupying the rest of the habitable world, but now the question of greatest hazard was, whether they should gain the rest by having plenty of brave men, or whether, through their weakness and mutual jealousy, their enemies should take away what they already possessed. After exaggerating the glory and riches on the one side and the danger and fear on the other, he admonished the rich to take heed, and said that for the realization of these hopes they ought to bestow this very land as a free gift, if necessary, on men who would rear children, and not, by contending about small things, overlook larger ones; especially since they were receiving an ample compensation for labor expended in the undisputed title to 500 jugera each of free land, in a high state of cultivation, without cost, and half as much more for each son of those who had sons. After saying much more to the same purport and exciting the poor, as well as others who were moved by reason rather than by the desire for gain, he ordered the scribe to read the proposed law.

Gracchus succeeded in having his law passed but only by persuading the people to depose (unconstitutionally) another tribune who opposed it. The following year Gracchus was assassinated by partisans of the wealthy senatorial class.

The Roman Revolution

During the first century B.C. faction fighting among the ruling classes at Rome weakened the republican government and created opportunities for ambitious generals to seize absolute power. The sequence of events leading to the "Roman revolution" was succinctly described by Appian of Alexandria.

From *The Roman History of Appian*

No unseemly deed was wanting until, about fifty years after the death of Gracchus, Cornelius Sulla, one of these chiefs of factions, doctoring one evil with another, made himself the absolute master of the state for an indefinite period. Such officials were formerly called dictators—an office created in the most

From H. White, trans., *The Roman History of Appian* (New York: Macmillan, 1899), Vol. 2, pp. 2–4.

perilous emergencies for six months only, and long since fallen into disuse. Sulla, although nominally elected, became dictator for life by force and compulsion. Nevertheless, he became satiated with power and was the first man, so far as I know, holding supreme power, who had the courage to lay it down voluntarily and to declare that he would render an account of his stewardship to any who were dissatisfied with it. And so, for a considerable period, he walked to the forum as a private citizen in the sight of all and returned home unmolested, so great was the awe of his government still remaining in the minds of the onlookers, or their amazement at his laying it down. Perhaps they were ashamed to call for an accounting, or entertained other good feeling toward him, or a belief that his despotism had been beneficial to the state. Thus there was a cessation of factions for a short time while Sulla lived, and a compensation for the evils which Sulla had wrought.

After his death the troubles broke out afresh and continued until Gaius Caesar, who had held the command in Gaul by election for some years, was ordered by the Senate to lay down his command. He charged that it was not the wish of the Senate, but of Pompey, his enemy, who had command of an army in Italy, and was scheming to depose him. So he sent a proposal that both should retain their armies, so that neither need fear the other's enmity, or that Pompey should dismiss his forces also and live as a private citizen under the laws in like manner with himself. Both requests being refused, he marched from Gaul against Pompey in the Roman territory, entered it, put him to flight, pursued him into Thessaly, won a brilliant victory over him in a great battle, and followed him to Egypt. After Pompey had been slain by the Egyptians Caesar set to work on the affairs of Egypt and remained there until he had settled the dynasty of that country. Then he returned to Rome. Having overpowered by war his principal rival, who had been surnamed the Great on account of his brilliant military exploits, he now ruled without disguise, nobody daring any longer to dispute him about anything, and was chosen, next after Sulla, dictator for life. Again all civil dissensions ceased until Brutus and Cassius, envious of his great power and desiring to restore the government of their fathers, slew in the Senate this most popular man, who was also the one most experienced in the art of government. The people mourned for him greatly. They scoured the city in pursuit of his murderers. They buried him in the middle of the forum and built a temple on the place of his funeral pile, and offered sacrifice to him as a god.

And now civil discord broke out again worse than ever and increased enormously. Massacres, banishments, and proscriptions of both senators and the so-called knights took place straightway, including great numbers of both classes, the chief of factions surrendering their enemies to each other, and for this purpose not sparing even their friends and brothers; so much does animosity toward rivals overpower the love of kindred. So in the course of events the Roman empire was partitioned, as though it had been their private property, by these three men: Antony, Lepidus, and the one who was first called Octavius, but afterward Caesar from his relationship to the other Caesar and adoption in his will. Shortly after this division they fell to quarrelling among themselves, as was natural, and Octavius, who was the superior in understanding and skill, first

deprived Lepidus of Africa, which had fallen to his lot, and afterward, as the result of the battle of Actium, took from Antony all the provinces lying between
Syria and the Adriatic gulf. Thereupon, while all the world was filled with astonishment at these wonderful displays of power, he sailed to Egypt and took
that country, which was the oldest and at that time the strongest possession of
the successors of Alexander, and the only one wanting to complete the Roman
empire as it now stands. In consequence of these exploits he was at once ele-
vated to the rank of a deity while still living, and was the first to be thus distinguished by the Romans, and was called by them Augustus. He assumed to himself an authority like Caesar's over the country and the subject nations, and even
greater than Caesar's, not needing any form of election, or authorization, or
even the pretence of it. His government being strengthened by time and mas-
tery, and himself successful in all things and revered by all, he left a lineage and
succession that held the supreme power in like manner after him.

Thus, out of multifarious civil commotions, the Roman state passed into sol-
idarity and monarchy.

*Marcus Tullius Cicero (104–43 B.C.), a great master of Latin eloquence, was a Roman senator and
an outstanding defender of the republic in its last days. Among his works was a treatise,* On the
Laws, *influenced by Stoic teachings. How did Cicero define law? How did he think law was exemplified in the institutions of the Roman republic?*

From Cicero. *On the Laws*

It has been the opinion of the wisest men that Law is not a product of human thought, nor is it any enactment of peoples, but something eternal which
rules the whole universe by its wisdom in command and prohibition. Thus
they have been accustomed to say that Law is the primal and ultimate mind of
God, whose reason directs all things either by compulsion or restraint.
Wherefore that Law which the gods have given to the human race has been
justly praised; for it is the reason and mind of a wise lawgiver applied to command and prohibition. . . .

As the laws govern the magistrate, so the magistrate governs the people,
and it can truly be said that the magistrate is a speaking law, and the law a silent
magistrate. Nothing, moreover, is so completely in accordance with the principles of justice and the demands of Nature (and when I use these expressions, I
wish it understood that I mean Law) as is government, without which existence
is impossible for a household, a city, a nation, the human race, physical nature,
and the universe itself. For the universe obeys God; seas and lands obey the universe, and human life is subject to the decrees of supreme Law. . . . Accordingly
we must have magistrates, for without their prudence and watchful care a State
cannot exist. In fact the whole character of a republic is determined by its
arrangements in regard to magistrates. Not only must we inform them of the
limits of their administrative authority; we must also instruct the citizens as to

Reprinted by permission of the publishers and the Loeb Classical Library from CICERO: ON THE
LAWS, VOLUME XVI, translated by C. W. Keyes, Cambridge, Mass., Harvard University Press, 1928).

the extent of their obligation to obey them. For the man who rules efficiently must have obeyed others in the past, and the man who obeys dutifully appears fit at some later time to be a ruler. Thus he who obeys ought to expect to be a ruler in the future, and he who rules should remember that in a short time he will have to obey. . . .

For this is the balanced type of State which Scipio praises and most highly approves in the treatise to which I have referred, and such a State could not have been constituted without such provisions as these in regard to its magistrates. For you must understand that a government consists of its magistrates and those who direct its affairs, and that different types of States are recognized by their constitution of these magistracies. And since the wisest and most evenly balanced system has been devised by our own ancestors, I had no innovations, or at least only a few, which I thought ought to be introduced into the constitution.

A younger contemporary of Cicero, the historian Sallust (86–35 B.C.), who was a supporter of Julius Caesar, gave a less idealistic account of how the Roman constitution functioned. In the following passage he referred to popular support for an attempted coup d'etat staged by the Roman noble Catiline in 63 B.C. What was wrong with the conduct of Roman government according to Sallust?

From Sallust. *The Conspiracy of Catiline*

The city populace were especially eager to fling themselves into a revolutionary adventure. There were several reasons for this. To begin with, those who had made themselves conspicuous anywhere by vice and shameless audacity, those who had wasted their substance by disgraceful excesses, and those whom scandalous or criminal conduct had exiled from their homes—all these had poured into Rome till it was like a sewer. Many, remembering Sulla's victory, and seeing men who had served under him as common soldiers now risen to be senators, or so rich that they lived as luxuriously as kings, began to hope that they too, if they took up arms, might find victory a source of profit. Young men from the country, whose labour on the farms had barely kept them from starvation, had been attracted by the private and public doles available at Rome, and preferred an idle city life to such thankless toil. These, like all the rest, stood to gain by public calamities. It is no wonder, therefore, that these paupers, devoid of moral scruple and incited by ambitious hopes, should have held their country as cheap as they held themselves. Those also to whom Sulla's victory had brought disaster by the proscription of their parents, the confiscation of their property, and the curtailment of their civil rights, looked forward with no less sanguine expectations to what might result from the coming struggle. Moreover, all the factions opposed to the Senate would rather see the state embroiled than accept their own exclusion from political power.

From Sallust, *The Conspiracy of Catiline*, trans. S. A. Handford (Baltimore: Penguin Books Inc., 1963), pp. 203–205.

Such was the evil condition by which, after an interval of some years, Rome was once more afflicted. After the restoration of the power of the tribunes in the consulship of Pompey and Crassus,[4] this very important office was obtained by certain men whose youth intensified their natural aggressiveness. These tribunes began to rouse the mob by inveighing against the Senate, and then inflamed popular passion still further by handing out bribes and promises, whereby they won renown and influence for themselves. They were strenuously opposed by most of the nobility, who posed as defenders of the Senate but were really concerned to maintain their own privileged position. The whole truth—to put it in a word—is that although all disturbers of the peace in this period put forward specious pretexts, claiming either to be protecting the rights of the people or to be strengthening the authority of the Senate, this was mere pretence: in reality, every one of them was fighting for his personal aggrandizement. Lacking all self-restraint, they stuck at nothing to gain their ends, and both sides made ruthless use of any successes they won.

In 49 B.C. the Roman senate, dominated by enemies of Julius Caesar, tried to deprive Caesar of his army command in Gaul. In response Caesar led his army from Gaul into Italy and seized power in Rome. After defeating his enemies in the ensuing civil war, Caesar ruled as dictator until 44 B.C., when he was assassinated. Cicero defended the assassination. Why did he consider it justified?

From Cicero. *On Moral Duties*

[Caesar] used to have constantly upon his lips the Greek verses from the *Phoenissae*, which I will reproduce as well as I can—awkwardly, it may be, but still so that the meaning can be understood:

"If wrong may e'er be right, for a throne's sake
Were wrong most right—be God in all else feared!"

Our tyrant deserved his death for having made an exception of the one thing that was the blackest crime of all. Why do we gather instances of petty crime—legacies criminally obtained and fraudulent buying and selling? Behold, here you have a man who was ambitious to be king of the Roman people and master of the whole world; and he achieved it! The man who maintains that such an ambition is morally right is a madman, for he justifies the destruction of law and liberty and thinks their hideous and detestable suppression glorious. But if anyone agrees that it is not morally right to be king in a state that once was free and that ought to be free now, and yet imagines that it is advantageous for him who can reach that position, with what remonstrance or rather with what appeal should I try to tear him away from so strange a delusion? For, O ye immortal gods! can the most horrible and hideous of all murders—that of fatherland—bring advantage to anybody, even though he who has committed such a crime receives from his enslaved fellow citizens the title of "Father of his Country"?

[4] 70 B.C.

From Cicero, *On Moral Duties*, trans. W. Miller in *The Loeb Classical Library* (Cambridge, Mass.: Harvard University Press, 1928), p. 357.

The Roman historian Suetonius (c.A.D. 69–140) gave a rather different account of Caesar. According to this author Caesar was on the whole a benevolent dictator. He gave lavish games for the people, initiated major public works in Rome, reformed the calendar, began a codification of Roman law, and administered justice in a manner that was "conscientious and severe." But Suetonius also explained Caesar's downfall. How did Caesar come to make so many enemies?

From Suetonius. *The Twelve Caesars*

One of the Consuls died suddenly on New Year's Eve and, when someone asked to hold office for the remaining few hours, Caesar granted his request. He showed equal scorn of constitutional precedent by choosing magistrates several years ahead, decorating ten former praetors with the emblems of consular rank, and admitting to the Senate men of foreign birth, including semi-civilized Gauls who had been granted Roman citizenship. He placed his own slaves in charge of the Mint and the public revenues, and sent one of his favourites, a freedman's son, to command the three legions stationed at Alexandria.

Titus Ampius has recorded some of Caesar's public statements which reveal a similar presumption: that the Republic was nothing—a mere name without form or substance; that Sulla had proved himself a dunce by resigning his dictatorship; and that, now his own word was law, people ought to be more careful how they approached him. Once, when a soothsayer reported that a sacrificial beast had been found to have no heart—an unlucky omen indeed—Caesar told him arrogantly: 'The omens will be as favourable as I wish them to be; meanwhile I am not at all surprised that a beast should lack the organ which inspires our finer feelings.'

What made the Romans hate him so bitterly was that when, one day, the entire Senate, armed with an imposing list of honours that they had just voted him, came to where he sat in front of the Temple of Mother Venus, he did not rise to greet them. According to some accounts he would have risen had not Cornelius Balbus prevented him; according to others, he made no such move and grimaced angrily at Gaius Trebatius who suggested this courtesy. . . .

This open insult to the Senate was emphasized by an even worse example of his scorn for the Constitution. As he returned to Rome from the Alban Hill, where the Latin Festival had been celebrated, a member of the crowd set a laurel wreath bound with a royal white fillet on the head of his statue. Two tribunes of the people, Epidius Marullus and Caesetius Flavus, ordered the fillet to be removed at once and the offender imprisoned. But Caesar reprimanded and summarily degraded them both: either because the suggestion that he should be crowned King had been so rudely rejected, or else because—this was his own version—they had given him no chance to reject it himself and so earn deserved credit. From that day forward, however, he lay under the odious suspicion of having tried to revive the title of King; though, indeed, when the commons greeted him with 'Long live the King!' he now protested: 'No, I am Caesar, not King'; and though, again, when he was addressing the crowd from the Rostra at

From Suetonius, *The Twelve Caesars*, R. Graves trans. (Baltimore, Penguin Books, 1957), pp. 42–43.

the Lupercalian Festival, and Mark Antony, the Consul, made several attempts to crown him, he refused the offer each time and at last sent the crown away for dedication to Capitoline Juppiter. What made matters worse was a persistent rumour that Caesar intended to move the seat of government to Troy or Alexandria, carrying off all the national resources, drafting every available man in Italy for military service, and letting his friends govern what was left of the City. At the next meeting of the House (it was further whispered), Lucius Cotta would announce a decision of the Fifteen who had charge of the Sibylline Books, that since these prophetic writings stated clearly: 'Only a king can conquer the Parthians,' the title of King must be conferred on Caesar.

After Julius Caesar's assassination and a period of civil wars, Augustus, Caesar's great-nephew and adopted son, emerged as sole ruler. He maintained a facade of republican institutions, but really established a new system of monarchical power, often called "the principate." Tacitus, a contemporary writer, described his way of ruling.

From *The Annals of Tacitus*

When the last army of the Republic had fallen with Brutus and Cassius on the field; when Sextus Pompeius had been crushed in Sicily; and when the deposition of Lepidus, followed by the death of Antonius, had left Augustus sole leader of the Julian party, he laid aside the title of Triumvir, assumed the Consulship, and professed himself content with the Tribunitian Power for the protection of the plebs. But when he had won the soldiery by bounties, the populace by cheap corn, and all classes alike by the sweets of peace, he rose higher and higher by degrees, and drew into his own hands all the functions of the Senate, the magistrates and the laws. And there was no one to oppose; for the most ardent patriots had fallen on the field, or in the proscriptions; and the rest of the nobles, advanced in wealth and place in proportion to their servility, and drawing profit out of the new order of affairs, preferred the security of the present to the hazards of the past.

Nor did the provinces resent the change; for the rule of the Senate and the People had become odious to them from the contests between great leaders, and the greed of magistrates, against whom the law, upset by force, by favour, and, in fine, by bribery, were powerless to protect them. . . .

Thus a revolution had been accomplished. The old order had passed away; everything had suffered change. The days of equality were gone: men looked to the Prince for his commands, having no anxiety for the present, so long as Augustus was of the age, and had the strength, to keep himself, his house and the public peace secure. But when he advanced in years, when his health and strength failed, and his approaching end gave birth to new hopes, some few discoursed idly on the blessings of liberty; many dreaded war; some longed for it.

From G. G. Ramsey, trans., *The Annals of Tacitus* (London: John Murray, 1904), pp. 3–5, 8.

Imperial Administration

Under the successors of Augustine the Roman empire reached the height of its power. The following letters were exchanged between the emperor Trajan and Pliny the Younger (c.A.D. 61–c.112), who served as governor of the Roman province of Bythinia (in modern Turkey). What do the letters tell us about the duties of a Roman governor and about the relations between central and local government?

From *Letters of Pliny*

Letter XXX. To the Emperor Trajan

I beg your determination, Sir, in a point wherein I am greatly doubtful: it is, whether I should place the public slaves as sentinels round the prisons of the several cities in this province (as has been hitherto the practice) or employ a party of soldiers for that purpose? On the one hand, I am afraid the public slaves will not attend this duty with the fidelity they ought; and on the other, that it will engage too large a body of the soldiery: in the mean while I have joined a few of the latter with the former. I suspect however, there may be some danger that this method will occasion a general neglect of duty, as it will afford them a mutual pretence of throwing the blame upon each other.

Letter XXXI. Trajan to Pliny

There is no occasion, my dear Pliny, to draw off any soldiers in order to guard the prisons. Let us rather persevere in the ancient customs observed by this province, of employing the public slaves for that purpose: and the fidelity with which they shall execute their duty will depend much upon your care and strict discipline. It is greatly to be feared, as you observe, if the soldiers should be mixed with the public slaves, they will mutually trust to each other, and by that means grow so much the more negligent. But the principal objection I have, is, that as few soldiers as possible should be called off from their colors.

Letter XXXIV. To the Emperor Trajan

The Prusenses, Sir, have an ancient and ruinous bath, which they desire your leave to repair. Upon examining into the condition of it, I find it ought to be rebuilt. I think therefore you may indulge them in this request, as there will be a sufficient fund for that purpose, partly from those debts which are due from private persons to the public, which I am now calling in; and partly from what they raise among themselves towards furnishing the bath with oil, which they are willing to apply to the carrying on of this building: a work which the dignity of the city, and the splendor of your times seems to demand.

Letter XXXV. Trajan to Pliny

If the erecting a public bath will not be too great a charge upon the Prusenses, we may comply with their request: provided, however, that no new

From W. Melmoth, trans., *The Letters of Pliny the Consul* (London: J. Dodsley, 1770), Vol. 2, pp. 595–598, 610–614, 620–624.

tax be levied for this purpose, nor any of those taken off which are applied for necessary services.

Letter XLII. To the Emperor Trajan

While I was making a progress in a different part of the province, a prodigious fire broke out at Nicomedia, which not only consumed several private houses, but also two public buildings; the town-house and the temple of Isis, tho' they stood on contrary sides of the street. The occasion of its spreading thus far, was partly owing to the violence of the wind, and partly to the indolence of the people, who I am well assured, stood fixed and idle spectators of this terrible calamity. The truth is, the city was not provided either with engines, buckets, or any one single instrument proper to extinguish fires; which I have now however given directions to have prepared. You will consider, Sir, whether it may not be advisable to institute a company of fire-men, consisting only of one hundred and fifty members. I will take care none but those of that business shall be admitted into it; and that the privileges granted them shall not be extended to any other purpose. As this incorporated body will consist of so small a number, it will be easy enough to keep them under proper regulation.

Letter XLIII. Trajan to Pliny

You are of opinion it would be proper to constitute a company of fire-men in Nicomedia, agreeably to what has been practised in several other cities. But it is to be remember'd, that this sort of societies have greatly disturb'd the peace of that province in general, and of those cities in particular. Whatever name we give them, and for whatever purposes they may be founded, they will not fail to form themselves into assemblies, however short their meetings may be. It will therefore be safer, to provide such machines as are of service in extinguishing fires, enjoining the owners of houses to assist upon such occasions; and if it shall be necessary, to call in the help of the populace.

Letter XLVI. To the Emperor Trajan

The city of Nicomedia, Sir, have expended three millions three hundred and twenty nine sesterces building an aquaeduct; but, not being able to finish it, the works are entirely falling to ruin. They made a second attempt in another place, where they laid out two millions. But this likewise is discontinued; so that after having been at an immense charge to no purpose, they must still be at a farther expence, in order to be accommodated with water. I have examined a fine spring from whence the water may be conveyed over arches (as was done in their first design) in such a manner that the higher, as well as level and low parts of the city may be supplied. There are but very few of the old arches remaining; the square stones, however, employed in the former building, may be used in turning the new ones. I am of opinion part should be raised with brick, as that will be the easier and cheaper method. But that this work may not be carried on with the same ill success as the former, it will be necessary to send here an architect and an engineer. And I will venture to say, from the beauty and usefulness of the design, it will be a work worthy the splendor of your times.

Letter XLVII. Trajan to Pliny

Care must be taken to supply the city of Nicomedia with water; and you will do so, I am well persuaded, with all the diligence you ought. But it is most certainly no less incumbent upon you to examine, by whose misconduct it has happened, that such large sums have been thrown away upon this work, lest by applying the money to private purposes, this aquaeduct should likewise be left unfinished. You will let me know the result of your enquiry.

ROMAN FAMILIES

The readings in this section present a variety of views on Roman family life. How do the different authors portray the role of women in Roman society? What were the rights and responsibilities of fathers? What abuses did Augustus legislate against?

Patriarchal Tradition

Early Roman society was strictly patriarchal in structure. The Greek historian Dionysius of Halicarnassus, who wrote c. 20 B.C., preserved a tradition of the first laws established by Romulus, legendary founder of Rome.

From *Roman Antiquities*

The law was to this effect, that a woman joined to her husband by a holy marriage should share in all his possessions and sacred rites. . . . This law obliged both the married women, as having no other refuge, to conform themselves entirely to the temper of their husbands, and the husbands to rule their wives as necessary and inseparable possessions. Accordingly, if a wife was virtuous and in all things obedient to her husband, she was mistress of the house to the same degree as her husband was master of it, and after the death of her husband she was heir to his property in the same manner as a daughter was to that of her father; that is, if he died without children and intestate, she was mistress of all that he left, and if he had children, she shared equally with them. But if she did any wrong, the injured party was her judge and determined the degree of her punishment. Other offences, however, were judged by her relations together with her husband; among them was adultery, or where it was found she had drunk wine—a thing which the Greeks would look upon as the least of all faults. For Romulus permitted them to punish both these acts with death, as being the gravest offences women could be guilty of, since he looked upon adultery as the source of reckless folly, and drunkenness as the source of adultery.

From E. Cary, *The Roman Antiquities of Dionysius of Halicarnassus* (Cambridge, Mass.: Harvard University Press, 1937), Vol. 1, pp. 381, 383, 385, 387, 389.

And both these offences continued for a long time to be punished by the Romans with merciless severity. . . .

Mild punishments are not sufficient to restrain the folly of youth and its stubborn ways or to give self-control to those who have been heedless of all that is honourable; and accordingly among the Greeks many unseemly deeds are committed by children against their parents. But the lawgiver of the Romans gave virtually full power to the father over his son, even during his whole life, whether he thought proper to imprison him, to scourge him, to put him in chains and keep him at work in the fields, or to put him to death, and this even though the son were already engaged in public affairs, though he were numbered among the highest magistrates, and though he were celebrated for his zeal for the commonwealth. Indeed, in virtue of this law men of distinction, while delivering speeches from the rostra hostile to the senate and pleasing to the people, and enjoying great popularity on that account, have been dragged down from thence and carried away by their fathers to undergo such punishment as these thought fit; and while they were being led away through the Forum, none present, neither consul, tribune, nor the very populace, which was flattered by them and thought all power inferior to its own, could rescue them.

Upper-class Romans cherished intense family loyalties. One way of expressing them was to cultivate the memory of ancestors.

From *The Histories of Polybius*

Whenever one of their illustrious men dies, in the course of his funeral, the body with all its paraphernalia is carried into the forum to the Rostra, as a raised platform there is called, and sometimes is propped upright upon it so as to be conspicuous, or, more rarely, is laid upon it. Then with all the people standing round, his son, if he has left one of full age and he is there, or, failing him, one of his relations, mounts the Rostra and delivers a speech concerning the virtues of the deceased, and the successful exploits performed by him in his lifetime. By these means the people are reminded of what has been done, and made to see it with their own eyes,—not only such as were engaged in the actual transactions but those also who were not;—and their sympathies are so deeply moved, that the loss appears not to be confined to the actual mourners, but to be a public one affecting the whole people. After the burial and all the usual ceremonies have been performed, they place the likeness of the deceased in the most conspicuous spot in his house, surmounted by a wooden canopy or shrine. This likeness consists of a mask made to represent the deceased with extraordinary fidelity both in shape and colour. These likenesses they display at public sacrifices adorned with much care. And when any illustrious member of the family dies, they carry these masks to the funeral, putting them on men whom they thought as like the originals as possible in height and other personal peculiarities. And

From E. S. Shuckburgh, *The Histories of Polybius* (London: Macmillan, 1889), pp. 503–504.

these substitutes assume clothes according to the rank of the person represented: if he was a consul or praetor, a toga with purple stripes; if a censor, whole purple; if he had also celebrated a triumph or performed any exploit of that kind, a toga embroidered with gold. These representatives also ride themselves in chariots, while the fasces and axes, and all the other customary insignia of the particular offices, lead the way, according to the dignity of the rank in the state enjoyed by the deceased in his lifetime; and on arriving at the Rostra they all take their seats on ivory chairs in their order. There could not easily be a more inspiring spectacle than this for a young man of noble ambitions and virtuous aspirations. For can we conceive any one to be unmoved at the sight of all the likenesses collected together of the men who have earned glory, all as it were living and breathing? Or what could be a more glorious spectacle?

The elder Cato (239–149 B.C.) was remembered as a paragon of stern republican virtue. This is how he managed his household.

From Plutarch. *Life of Cato*

He married a wife more noble than rich; being of opinion, that the rich and the high-born are equally haughty and proud; but that those of noble blood, would be more ashamed of base things, and consequently more obedient to their husbands in all that was fit and right. A man who beat his wife or child, laid violent hands, he said, on what was most sacred; and a good husband he reckoned worthy of more praise than a great senator; and he admired the ancient Socrates for nothing so much, as for having lived a temperate and contented life with a wife who was a scold, and children who were half-witted.

As soon as he had a son born, though he had never such urgent business upon his hands, unless it were some public matter, he would be by when his wife washed it, and dressed it in its swaddling clothes. For she herself suckled it, nay, she often too gave her breast to her servants' children, to produce, by sucking the same milk, a kind of natural love in them to her son. When he began to come to years of discretion, Cato himself would teach him to read, although he had a servant, a very good grammarian, called Chilo, who taught many others; but he thought not fit, as he himself said, to have his son reprimanded by a slave, or pulled, it may be, by the ears when found tardy in his lesson: nor would he have him owe to a servant the obligation of so great a thing as his learning; he himself, therefore, (as we were saying,) taught him his grammar, law, and his gymnastic exercises. Nor did he only show him, too, how to throw a spear, to fight in armor, and to ride, but to box also and to endure both heat and cold, and to swim over the most rapid and rough rivers. He says, likewise, that he wrote histories, in large characters, with his own hand, that so his son, without stirring out of the house, might learn to know about his countrymen and forefathers: nor did he less abstain from speaking any thing obscene

From *Plutarch's Lives*, The Translation Called Dryden's, rev. A. H. Clough (Boston, Mass.: Little, Brown and Co., 1872), Vol. 2, pp. 341–344.

before his son, than if it had been in the presence of the sacred virgins, called vestals. Nor would he ever go into the bath with him; which seems indeed to have been the common custom of the Romans. Sons-in-law used to avoid bathing with fathers-in-law, disliking to see one another naked: but having, in time, learned of the Greeks to strip before men, they have since taught the Greeks to do it even with the women themselves.

Thus, like an excellent work, Cato formed and fashioned his son to virtue. . . .

He purchased a great many slaves out of the captives taken in war, but chiefly bought up the young ones, who were capable to be, as it were, broken and taught like whelps and colts. None of these ever entered another man's house, except sent either by Cato himself or his wife. If any one of them were asked what Cato did, they answered merely, that they did not know. When a servant was at home, he was obliged either to do some work or sleep; for indeed Cato loved those most who used to lie down often to sleep, accounting them more docile than those who were wakeful, and more fit for any thing when they were refreshed with a little slumber. Being also of opinion, that the great cause of the laziness and misbehavior of slaves was their running after their pleasures, he fixed a certain price for them to pay for permission amongst themselves, but would suffer no connections out of the house. At first, when he was but a poor soldier, he would not be difficult in any thing which related to his eating, but looked upon it as a pitiful thing to quarrel with a servant for the belly's sake; but afterwards, when he grew richer, and made any feasts for his friends and colleagues in office, as soon as supper was over he used to go with a leathern thong and scourge those who had waited or dressed the meat carelessly. He always contrived, too, that his servants should have some difference one among another, always suspecting and fearing a good understanding between them. Those who had committed any thing worthy of death, he punished, if they were found guilty by the verdict of their fellow-servants. But being after all much given to the desire of gain, he looked upon agriculture rather as a pleasure than profit; resolving, therefore, to lay out his money in safe and solid things, he purchased ponds, hot baths, grounds full of fuller's earth, remunerative lands, pastures, and woods; from all which he drew large returns, nor could Jupiter himself, he used to say, do him much damage.

Legislation of Augustus

The emperor Augustus was concerned about a growing instability of marriages and a low birth rate among the free Roman population. Because the old death penalty for adultery was hard to enforce in practice, he devised a new one. He also introduced incentives to increase the size of families, including one providing that a woman with three children could be freed from guardianship. (Normally every Roman woman was under the care of some man—father, husband, or legally appointed guardian.)

In the following reading the emperor is addressing Roman fathers of the equestrian class.

From *Dio's Roman History*

Surely the best of all things is a woman who is temperate, domestic, a good housekeeper, a rearer of children; one to gladden you when in health, to tend you when sick; to be your partner in good fortune, to console you in misfortune; to restrain the frenzied nature of the youth and to temper the superannuated severity of the old man. Is it not a delight to acknowledge a child bearing the nature of both, to nurture and educate it, a physical image and a spiritual image, so that in its growth you yourself live again? Is it not most blessed on departing from life to leave behind a successor to and inheritor of one's substance and family, something that is one's own, sprung from one's self? . . . These are the private advantages that accrue to those who marry and beget children: but for the State, for whose sake we ought to do many things that are even distasteful to us, how excellent and how necessary it is, if cities and peoples are to exist, if you are to rule others and others are to obey you, that there should be a multitude of men to till the earth in peace and quiet, to make voyages, practice arts, follow handicrafts, men who in war will protect what we already have with the greater zeal because of family ties and will replace those that fall by others. Therefore, men,—for you alone may properly be called men,—and fathers,—for you are worthy to hold this title like myself,—I love you and I praise you for this, I am glad of the prizes I have already offered and I will glorify you still more besides by honors and offices. Thus you may yourselves reap great benefits and leave them to your children undiminished.

The texts of Augustus's marriage laws (known as the Julian and Pappian laws) have not survived. But later jurists described their content and commented on them. The following texts date from the second century A.D.

From *The Institutes of Gaius*

Parents are permitted to appoint guardians . . . for male children under the age of puberty and for females who are beyond it, even if they are married; for the ancients thought it right that women should be under guardianship, even when of full age, because of their fickleness of mind.

Therefore, if anyone appoints a guardian for his son and daughter and both reach the age of puberty, the son will cease to have a guardian but the daughter will still be under guardianship; for according to the Julian and Pappian Laws women are freed from guardianship only by the birth of children.

Moreover, a freeborn woman is freed from guardianship by the birth of three children, a freedwoman by the birth of four. . . .

There does not seem to be any good reason though why women of full age should be under guardianship. The one commonly assigned—that owing to their fickleness of mind they are easily misled and so it is only just that they be

From H. B. Foster, trans., *Dio's Roman History* (Troy: Pafraets Book Co., 1905), Vol. 4, pp. 206–207. From T. Muirhead, ed., *Institutes of Gaius* (Edinburgh: T. and T. Clark, 1880), Vol. 1, pp. 144–145, 190, 194.

under the authority of guardians—seems more specious than real. For women of full age manage their own business affairs. In some cases the guardian interposes his authority merely as a matter of form; and not infrequently he is compelled to do so by the praetor even though he may be unwilling.

From *Opinions of Julius Paulus*

It was enacted (under Augustus) that women convicted of adultery should be punished by the confiscation of half of their dowry and a third of their property and by relegation to an island. Also that male adulterers be punished by confiscation of half of their property and relegation to an island—provided that the parties were relegated to different islands.

Roman Wives

Toward the end of the first century A.D. the satirist Juvenal was still complaining about the faults of Roman women. What did he accuse them of? How did he explain their behavior?

From *Juvenal's Sixth Satire*

> The bed holds more than a bride; you lie with bicker and
>   quarrel
> Always, all night long, and sleep is the last thing you get there.
> There she can really throw her weight around, like a tigress
> Robbed of her young; or else, to atone for her own bad
>   conscience,
> She fakes the outraged sigh, and hates the boys whom her
>   husband
> Has, or she says he has, or sheds tears over a mistress
> Purely fictitious, of course. Her tears come down like the
>   raindrops,
> With plenty more where they came from, ready to flow at her
>   bidding.
> Abject slug that you are, you think this proves that she loves you.
> Aren't you pleased with yourself, as your lips go seeking those
>   lashes
> Wet with her pitiful tears? But what if you happened to open
> The drawers of her desk, and found those notes, those fervent
>   epistles,
>
> Saved by your green-eyed wife, the hypocritical cheater?
> You may catch her in bed with a slave or a knight. What
>   happens?
> All she can do in that case is invoke the art of Quintilian,
> "Master of Rhetoric, help! Come to my aid, I implore you."

From R. Gniest, ed., *Opinions of Julius Paulus* (Leipzig: B. G. Teubner, 1880), II.26.4.
From Rolfe Humphries, trans., *The Satires of Juvenal* (Bloomington, IN: Indiana University Press, 1958), pp. 73, 74, 87. Copyright © 1958. Reprinted by permission of the publisher.

"Sorry," Quintilian replies, "I'm stuck; get yourself out of this
  one."
This does not bother her much; her explanation is ready.
"Long ago," she says, "it was understood between us
Perfectly well, you could do what you pleased, and no double
  standard
Kept me from having my fun. So howl as much as you want to,
I am human, too." Can you beat their nerve when you catch
  them?
That's when their very guilt supplies them anger and spirit.

Where, you ask, do they come from, such monsters as these? In
  the old days
Latin women were chaste by dint of their lowly fortunes.
Toil and short hours for sleep kept cottages free from contagion,
Hands were hard from working the wool, and husbands were
  watching,
Standing to arms at the Colline Gate, and the shadow of
  Hannibal's looming.
Now we suffer the evils of long peace. Luxury hatches
Terrors worse than the wars, avenging a world beaten down.
Every crime is here, and every lust, as they have been
Since the day, long since, when Roman poverty perished. . . .
(Poor) women at least endure the perils of childbirth,
Suffer the nuisance of nursing—but when did you ever discover
Labor pains in a golden bed? There are potent prescriptions,
Fine professional skill, to be hired for inducing abortions,
Killing mankind in the womb. Rejoice, unfortunate husband,
Give her the dose yourself, whatever it is; never let her
Carry till quickening time, or go on to full term and deliver
Something whose hue would seem to prove you a blackamoor
  father,
Sire of an off-color heir you'd prefer not to meet in the daylight.

A funeral oration from the time of Augustus describes a different sort of wife. (Her husband, who delivered the eulogy, was proscribed in the political troubles of 43 B.C.)

From *Praise of Turia*

Marriages of such long duration, not dissolved by divorce, but terminated by death alone, are indeed rare. For our union was prolonged in unclouded happiness for forty-one years. Would that our long marriage had come to its final end by *my* death, and that *I* as the older—which was more just—had yielded to fate.

Why recall your natural qualities, your modesty, deference, affability, your amiable disposition, your faithful attendance to household duties, your enlightened religion, your unassuming elegance, the modest simplicity of your attire? Need I speak of your attachment to your kindred, your affection

From Naphtali Lewis and Meyer Reinhold, eds., *Roman Civilization* (New York: Columbia University Press, 1951), Vol. 1, pp. 485–487. Reprinted courtesy of the publisher.

for your family—when you cherished my mother as you did your own parents—you who share countless other virtues with Roman matrons who cherish their fair name? These qualities which I claim for you are your own; few have possessed the like and been able to hold on to and maintain them; the experience of men teaches us how rare they are.

With joint zeal we have preserved all the patrimony which you received from your parents. Entrusting it all to me, you were not troubled with the care of increasing it; thus did we share the task of administering it, that I undertook to protect your fortune, and you to guard mine. On this point I pass by many things in silence, for fear of attributing to myself a portion of your desserts. . . .

You helped my escape by selling your jewels and turning over to me all your gold and the pearls removed from your person; and thereupon the household furnished money; and deceiving the guards of our opponents, you made my absence comfortable. . . . Why should I now conjure up the memory of the hidden counsels, concealed plans, and secret talks? How, aroused by the sudden arrival of messages from you to a realization of the present and imminent perils, I was saved by your counsel. How you did not allow me recklessly through excessively bold plans to face danger, and how, bent on more discreet plans, you provided for me a safe retreat, choosing as sharers in your plans for my safety—fraught with danger as they were for you all—your sister and her husband, Gaius Cluvius. Were I to attempt to touch on all these matters, it would be an endless task. Suffice it for me and for you that the retreat provided by you ensured my safety.

I should confess, however, that on this occasion I suffered one of the bitterest experiences of my life, in the fate that befell you. When the favor and decision of Caesar Augustus, then absent [from Rome], had restored me to my country, still a useful citizen perhaps, Marcus Lepidus, his colleague, then present in the city, interposed objections to my pardon. Then, when you prostrated yourself at his feet, he not only did not raise you up—but, dragged along and abused, as though a common slave, your body all covered with bruises, yet with unflinching steadfastness of purpose you recalled to him Caesar's edict and the letter of felicitation on my pardon. Braving his taunts and suffering the most brutal insults and wounds, you denounced these cruelties publicly so that he became known as the author of all my perils. And his punishment for this was not long delayed.

When all the world was again at peace and the Republic reestablished, peaceful and happy days followed for us. We longed for children, which an envious fate denied us for some time. Had Fortune permitted herself to smile on us in the ordinary fashion, what had been lacking to complete our happiness? But advancing age put an end to our hopes. . . . Despairing of your fertility and disconsolate to see me without children . . . you spoke of divorce because of my unhappiness on this account, offering to yield our home to another spouse more fertile, with no other intention than that of yourself searching for and providing for me a spouse worthy of our well-known mutual affection, whose children you assured me you would have treated as though your own. . . . Nothing would have been changed, only that you would have rendered to me henceforth the services and devotion of a sister or mother-in-law.

I must admit that I was so angry that I was deprived of my mind, and that I was so horrified at your proposal that I scarcely regained control of myself. That you should have spoken of divorce between us before the decree of fate had been given; that you should have conceived of any reason why you, while you were still alive, should cease to be my wife, you who when I was almost an exile from life remained most faithful. . . .

Would that our time of life had permitted our union to endure until I, the older, had passed away—which was more just—and that you might perform for me the last rites, and that I might have departed, leaving you behind, with a daughter to replace me in your widowhood.

By fate's decree your course was run before mine. You left me the grief, the longing for you, the sad fate to live alone. . . .

PART FIVE

THE ORIGIN OF CHRISTIANITY

The Coming of Jesus

From *The Gospel According to Luke*
From *The Gospel According to John*

Life and Teaching

From *The Gospel According to Matthew*
From *The Gospel According to Matthew*
From *The Gospel According to Mark*

Jesus and Women

From *The Gospel According to Luke*
From *The Gospel According to Mark*
From *The Gospel According to John*

THE EARLY CHURCH

Christian and Pagan

From *Paul's First Epistle to the Corinthians*
From Minucius Felix. *Octavius*
From Hippolytus. *Apostolic Tradition*
From *Clement of Alexandria*
The Nicene Creed

Church and State

From *The Annals of Tacitus*

From *Letters of Pliny*
From *The "Edict of Milan"*
From Eusebius. *Life of Constantine*
From *The Theodosian Code*

Christian Women: Marriage and Celibacy

From *Paul's Epistle to the Ephesians*
From *Paul's First Epistle to the Corinthians*
From Jerome. *Against Helvidius*
From *The Acts of the Christian Martyrs*
From *Letter of Pope Damasus on Celibacy*

DECLINE AND FALL

Imperial Centralization

From *The Death of the Persecutors*
From *The Theodosian Code*

Christian Reactions

Salvianus. *The Burden of Taxation*
Jerome. *The Barbarian Invasions*
Augustine. *The Two Cities*

Eastern Survival

From *The Institutes of Justinian*

CHRISTIANITY AND THE FALL OF ROME

As the Roman state approached the height of its power in the second century, a new religion was spreading from the eastern Mediterranean through the provinces of the empire. Christianity resembled various other Eastern mystery religions in offering secret ceremonies, redemption from sin, and a promise of life after death. But its founder was not just a mythical figure. He was a real person who had taught on earth and commissioned disciples to carry his message to all nations. Christians believed in the resurrection of Jesus as an actual historical event that justified their hope of everlasting life. Their teachings appealed mainly to humble and illiterate people at first, but eventually they came to fascinate the most subtle minds of the late classical world. The new religion influenced every level of life and thought—philosophy, politics, morality, attitudes towards marriage and sexuality.

Christianity preserved the Judaic tradition of monotheism. A Christian could not worship any other god or even join in the state ceremonies honoring the emperor as a divine being. The imperial authorities responded with fierce persecutions of the Christians, but the persecutions were never sustained long enough to wipe out the whole church and the martyrs they created inspired new generations of Christians by their heroic examples. The last great persecution was launched by Diocletian in 303. A dramatic change came under Constantine, the next emperor. Constantine first proclaimed tolerance for Christianity in 313, then himself embraced the Christian faith. Under his successors Christianity became the official religion of the empire.

Between 400 and 500 the empire experienced repeated invasions by barbarian peoples who had been settled along its borders. Under these attacks the institutions of the Roman state crumbled away, but the Christian church survived and helped to shape the new world of early medieval Europe.

THE ORIGIN OF CHRISTIANITY

The Coming of Jesus

Jesus did not set down his teachings in writing. At first they were handed down by oral tradition, then recorded in the four Gospels (written c. 60–c. 100). The early Christians believed that Jesus was not an ordinary man but a divine being. This belief was reflected in different ways in the Gospel accounts of how Jesus came into the world. The Gospel of Luke recorded a tradition of a miraculous virgin birth.

From *The Gospel According to Luke*

In the sixth month the angel Gabriel was sent from God to a city of Galilee named Nazareth, to a virgin betrothed to a man whose name was Joseph, of the house of David; and the virgin's name was Mary. And he came to her and said, "Hail, O favored one, the Lord is with you!" But she was greatly troubled at the saying, and considered in her mind what sort of greeting this might be. And the angel said to her, "Do not be afraid, Mary, for you have found favor with God. And behold, you will conceive in your womb and bear a son, and you shall call his name Jesus.

He will be great, and will be called
   the Son of the Most High;
and the Lord God will give to him
   the throne of his father David,
and he will reign over the house of
   Jacob for ever;
and of his kingdom there will be no
   end."

And Mary said to the angel, "How shall this be, since I have no husband?" And the angel said to her,

"The Holy Spirit will come upon
   you,
and the power of the Most High
   will overshadow you;
therefore the child to be born
   will be called holy,
the Son of God. . . ."

And Mary said, "Behold, I am the handmaid of the Lord; let it be done to me according to your word." And the angel departed from her.

John's later account is more abstract and philosophical. The idea of a divine creative "Word" (logos) existed in early Hellenistic philosophy.

From *The Gospel According to John*

In the beginning was the Word, and the Word was with God, and the Word was God. He was in the beginning with God; all things were made through him, and without him was not anything made that was made. In him was life, and the life was the light of men. The light shines in the darkness, and the darkness has not overcome it.

There was a man sent from God, whose name was John. He came for testimony, to bear witness to the light, that all might believe through him. He was not the light, but came to bear witness to the light.

The true light that enlightens every man was coming into the world. He was in the world, and the world was made through him, yet the world knew him not. He came to his own home, and his own people received him not. But to all who received him, who believed in his name, he gave power to become children of God; who were born, not of blood nor of the will of the flesh nor of the will of man, but of God.

And the Word became flesh and dwelt among us, full of grace and truth; we have beheld his glory, glory as of the only Son from the Father. (John bore witness to him, and cried, "This was he of whom I said, 'He who comes after me ranks before me, for he was before me.' ") And from his fulness have we all received, grace upon grace. For the law was given through Moses; grace and truth came through Jesus Christ. No one has ever seen God; the only Son, who is in the bosom of the Father, he has made him known.

Life and Teaching

Jesus' moral teaching is summarized in this collection of his sayings known as the Sermon on the Mount. How did Jesus extend the moral teachings of Jewish law?

From *The Gospel According to Matthew*

Seeing the crowds, he went up on the mountain, and when he sat down his disciples came to him. And he opened his mouth and taught them, saying:

"Blessed are the poor in spirit, for theirs is the kingdom of heaven.

"Blessed are those who mourn, for they shall be comforted.

"Blessed are the meek, for they shall inherit the earth.

"Blessed are those who hunger and thirst for righteousness, for they shall be satisfied.

"Blessed are the merciful, for they shall obtain mercy.

"Blessed are the pure in heart, for they shall see God.

"Blessed are the peacemakers, for they shall be called sons of God.

From the *Revised Standard Version Bible* (New York: Oxford University Press, 1973). The Gospel According to John 1:1–18. Copyright 1946, 1952, © 1971, 1973 by the National Council of the Churches of Christ. Reprinted by permission.
From the *Revised Standard Version Bible* (New York: Oxford University Press, 1973). The Gospel According to Matthew 5:1–18, 38–48; 6:1, 7–14, 24–33. Copyright 1946, 1952, © 1971, 1973 by the National Council of the Churches of Christ. Reprinted by permission.

"Blessed are those who are persecuted for righteousness' sake, for theirs is the kingdom of heaven.

"Blessed are you when men revile you and persecute you and utter all kinds of evil against you falsely on my account. Rejoice and be glad, for your reward is great in heaven, for so men persecuted the prophets who were before you.

"You are the salt of the earth; but if salt has lost its taste, how shall its saltness be restored? It is no longer good for anything except to be thrown out and trodden under foot by men.

"You are the light of the world. A city set on a hill cannot be hid. Nor do men light a lamp and put it under a bushel, but on a stand, and it gives light to all in the house. Let your light so shine before men, that they may see your good works and give glory to your Father who is in heaven.

"Think not that I have come to abolish the law and the prophets; I have come not to abolish them but to fulfill them. For truly, I say to you, till heaven and earth pass away, not an iota, not a dot, will pass from the law until all is accomplished. . . .

"You have heard that it was said, 'An eye for an eye and a tooth for a tooth.' But I say to you, Do not resist one who is evil. But if any one strikes you on the right cheek, turn to him the other also; and if any one would sue you and take your coat, let him have your cloak as well; and if any one forces you to go one mile, go with him two miles. Give to him who begs from you, and do not refuse him who would borrow from you.

"You have heard that it was said, 'You shall love your neighbor and hate your enemy.' But I say to you, Love your enemies and pray for those who persecute you, so that you may be sons of your Father who is in heaven; for he makes the sun rise on the evil and on the good, and sends rain on the just and on the unjust. For if you love those who love you, what reward have you? Do not even the tax collectors do the same? And if you salute only your brethren, what more are you doing than others? Do not even the Gentiles do the same? You, therefore, must be perfect, as your heavenly Father is perfect.

"Beware of practicing your piety before men in order to be seen by them; for then you will have no reward from your Father who is in heaven. . . .

"And in praying do not heap up empty phrases as the Gentiles do; for they think that they will be heard for their many words. Do not be like them, for your Father knows what you need before you ask him. Pray then like this:

Our Father who art in heaven,
Hallowed be thy name.
Thy kingdom come.
Thy will be done,
    On earth as it is in heaven.
Give us this day our daily bread;
And forgive us our debts,
As we also have forgiven our
    debtors;
And lead us not into temptation,
    But deliver us from evil.

For if you forgive men their trespasses, your heavenly Father also will forgive you; but if you do not forgive men their trespasses, neither will your Father forgive your trespasses. . . .

"No one can serve two masters; for either he will hate the one and love the other, or he will be devoted to the one and despise the other. You cannot serve God and mammon.

"Therefore I tell you, do not be anxious about your life, what you shall eat or what you shall drink, nor about your body, what you shall put on. Is not life more than food, and the body more than clothing? Look at the birds of the air: they neither sow nor reap nor gather into barns, and yet your heavenly Father feeds them. Are you not of more value than they? And which of you by being anxious can add one cubit to his span of life? And why are you anxious about clothing? Consider the lilies of the field, how they grow; they neither toil nor spin; yet I tell you, even Solomon in all his glory was not arrayed like one of these. But if God so clothes the grass of the field, which today is alive and tomorrow is thrown into the oven, will he not much more clothe you, O men of little faith? Therefore do not be anxious, saying, 'What shall we eat?' or 'What shall we drink?' or 'What shall we wear?' For the Gentiles seek all these things; and your heavenly Father knows that you need them all. But seek first his kingdom and his righteousness, and all these things shall be yours as well."

The words of Jesus to Peter in the following passage have given rise to endless debates among different groups of Christians about Peter's position in the early church and about the role of the popes who claimed to be Peter's successors.

From *The Gospel According to Matthew*

Now when Jesus came into the district of Caesarea Philippi, he asked his disciples, "Who do men say that the Son of man is?" And they said, "Some say John the Baptist, others say Elijah, and others Jeremiah or one of the prophets." He said to them, "But who do you say that I am?" Simon Peter replied, "You are the Christ, the Son of the living God." And Jesus answered him, "Blessed are you, Simon Bar-Jona! For flesh and blood has not revealed this to you, but my Father who is in heaven. And I tell you, you are Peter, and on this rock I will build my church, and the powers of death shall not prevail against it. I will give you the keys to the kingdom of heaven, and whatever you bind on earth shall be bound in heaven, and whatever you loose on earth shall be loosed in heaven." Then he strictly charged the disciples to tell no one that he was the Christ.

From that time Jesus began to show his disciples that he must go to Jerusalem and suffer many things from the elders and chief priests and scribes, and be killed, and on the third day be raised.

Each of the four Gospels tells of Jesus's death and resurrection. The earliest account is from Mark.

From *The Gospel According to Mark*

And on the first day of Unleavened Bread, when they sacrificed the passover lamb, his disciples said to him, "Where will you have us go and prepare for you to eat the passover?" And he sent two of his disciples, and said to them, "Go into the city, and a man carrying a jar of water will meet you; follow him, and wherever he enters, say to the householder, 'The Teacher says, Where is my guest room, where I am to eat the passover with my disciples?' And he will show you a large upper room furnished and ready; there prepare for us." And the disciples set out and went to the city, and found it as he had told them; and they prepared the passover.

And when it was evening he came with the twelve. And as they were at table eating, Jesus said, "Truly, I say to you, one of you will betray me, one who is eating with me." They began to be sorrowful, and to say to him one after another, "Is it I?" He said to them, "It is one of the twelve, one who is dipping bread into the dish with me. For the Son of man goes as it is written of him, but woe to that man by whom the Son of man is betrayed! It would have been better for that man if he had not been born."

And as they were eating, he took bread, and blessed, and broke it, and gave it to them, and said, "Take; this is my body." And he took a cup, and when he had given thanks he gave it to them, and they all drank of it. And he said to them, "This is my blood of the covenant, which is poured out for many. Truly, I say to you, I shall not drink again of the fruit of the vine until that day when I drink it new in the kingdom of God." . . .

And as soon as it was morning the chief priests, with the elders and scribes, and the whole council held a consultation; and they bound Jesus and led him away and delivered him to Pilate. And Pilate asked him, "Are you the King of the Jews?" And he answered him, "You have said so." And the chief priests accused him of many things. And Pilate again asked him, "Have you no answer to make? See how many charges they bring against you." But Jesus made no further answer, so that Pilate wondered.

Now at the feast he used to release for them one prisoner for whom they asked. And among the rebels in prison, who had committed murder in the insurrection, there was a man called Barabbas. And the crowd came up and began to ask Pilate to do as he was wont to do for them. And he answered them, "Do you want me to release for you the King of the Jews?" For he perceived that it was out of envy that the chief priests had delivered him up. But the chief priests stirred up the crowd to have him release for them Barabbas instead. And Pilate

From the *Revised Standard Version Bible* (New York: Oxford University Press, 1973). The Gospel According to Mark 14:12–25; 15:1–15, 33–47; 16:1–20. Copyright 1946, 1952, © 1971, 1973 by the National Council of the Churches of Christ. Reprinted by permission.

again said to them, "Then what shall I do with the man whom you call the King of the Jews?" And they cried out again, "Crucify him." And Pilate said to them, "Why, what evil has he done?" But they shouted all the more, "Crucify him." So Pilate, wishing to satisfy the crowd, released for them Barabbas; and having scourged Jesus, he delivered him to be crucified. . . .

And when the sixth hour had come, there was darkness over the whole land until the ninth hour. And at the ninth hour Jesus cried with a loud voice, "Elo-i, Elo-i, lama sabach-thani?" which means, "My God, my God, why hast thou forsaken me?" And some of the bystanders hearing it said, "Behold, he is calling Elijah." And one ran and, filling a sponge full of vinegar, put it on a reed and gave it to him to drink, saying, "Wait, let us see whether Elijah will come to take him down." And Jesus uttered a loud cry, and breathed his last. And the curtain of the temple was torn in two, from top to bottom. And when the centurion, who stood facing him, saw that he thus breathed his last, he said, "Truly this man was the Son of God!"

There were also women looking on from afar, among whom were Mary Magdalene, and Mary, the mother of James the younger and of Joses, and Salome, who, when he was in Galilee, followed him and ministered to him; and also many other women who came up with him to Jerusalem.

And when evening had come, since it was the day of Preparation, that is, the day before the sabbath, Joseph of Arimathea, a respected member of the council, who was also himself looking for the kingdom of God, took courage and went to Pilate, and asked for the body of Jesus. And Pilate wondered if he were already dead; and summoning the centurion, he asked him whether he was already dead. And when he learned from the centurion that he was dead, he granted the body to Joseph. And he bought a linen shroud, and taking him down, wrapped him in the linen shroud, and laid him in a tomb which had been hewn out of the rock; and he rolled a stone against the door of the tomb. Mary Magdalene and Mary the mother of Joseph saw where he was laid.

And when the sabbath was past, Mary Magdalene, and Mary the mother of James, and Salome, bought spices, so that they might go and anoint him. And very early on the first day of the week they went to the tomb when the sun had risen. And they were saying to one another, "Who will roll away the stone for us from the door of the tomb?" And looking up, they saw that the stone was rolled back—it was very large. And entering the tomb, they saw a young man sitting on the right side, dressed in a white robe; and they were amazed. And he said to them, "Do not be amazed; you seek Jesus of Nazareth, who was crucified. He has risen, he is not here; see the place where they laid him. But go, tell his disciples and Peter that he is going before you to Galilee; there you will see him, as he told you." And they went out and fled from the tomb; for trembling and astonishment had come upon them; and they said nothing to any one, for they were afraid.

Now when he rose early on the first day of the week, he appeared first to Mary Magdalene, from whom he had cast out seven demons. She went and told those who had been with him, as they mourned and wept. But when they heard that he was alive and had been seen by her, they would not believe it.

After this he appeared in another form to two of them, as they were walking into the country. And they went back and told the rest, but they did not believe them.

Afterward he appeared to the eleven themselves as they sat at the table; and he upbraided them for their unbelief and hardness of heart, because they had not believed those who saw him after he had risen. And he said to them, "Go into all the world and preach the gospel to the whole creation. He who believes and is baptized will be saved; but he who does not believe will be condemned." ...

So then the Lord Jesus, after he had spoken to them, was taken up into heaven, and sat down at the right hand of God. And they went forth and preached everywhere, while the Lord worked with them and confirmed the message by the signs that attended it. Amen.

Jesus and Women

In Mark's resurrection story two women friends of Jesus were the first to find the empty tomb. And in fact, in a way unusual for his time, Jesus included women among his close friends and followers. He did not think their role should be limited to domestic service.

From *The Gospel According to Luke*

Now as they went on their way, he entered a village; and a woman named Martha received him into her house. And she had a sister called Mary, who sat at the Lord's feet and listened to his teaching. But Martha was distracted with much serving; and she went to him and said, "Lord, do you not care that my sister has left me to serve alone? Tell her then to help me." But the Lord answered her, "Martha, Martha, you are anxious and troubled about many things; one thing is needful. Mary has chosen the good portion, which shall not be taken away from her."

What can you gather about Jesus' attitude toward women and family from the following passages?

From *The Gospel According to Mark*

And Pharisees came up and in order to test him asked, "Is it lawful for a man to divorce his wife?" He answered them, "What did Moses command you?" They said, "Moses allowed a man to write a certificate of divorce, and to put her away." But Jesus said to them, "For your hardness of heart he wrote you this commandment. But from the beginning of creation, 'God made them male and female.' 'For this reason a man shall leave his father and mother and be

From the *Revised Standard Version Bible* (New York: Oxford University Press, 1973). The Gospel According to Luke 10:38–42.
From the *Revised Standard Version Bible* (New York: Oxford University Press, 1973). The Gospel According to Mark 10:2–16; The Gospel According to John 8:3–11.

joined to his wife, and the two shall become one flesh.' So they are no longer two but one flesh. What therefore God has joined together, let not man put asunder."

And in the house the disciples asked him again about this matter. And he said to them, "Whoever divorces his wife and marries another, commits adultery against her; and if she divorces her husband and marries another, she commits adultery."

And they were bringing children to him, that he might touch them; and the disciples rebuked them. But when Jesus saw it he was indignant, and said to them, "Let the children come to me, do not hinder them; for to such belongs the kingdom of God. Truly, I say to you, whoever does not receive the kingdom of God like a child shall not enter it." And he took them in his arms and blessed them, laying his hands upon them.

From *The Gospel According to John*

The scribes and the Pharisees brought a woman who had been caught in adultery, and placing her in the midst they said to him, "Teacher, this woman has been caught in the act of adultery. Now in the law Moses commanded us to stone such. What do you say about her?" This they said to test him, that they might have some charge to bring against him. Jesus bent down and wrote with his finger on the ground. And as they continued to ask him, he stood up and said to them, "Let him who is without sin among you be the first to throw a stone at her." And once more he bent down and wrote with his finger on the ground. But when they heard it, they went away, one by one, beginning with the eldest, and Jesus was left alone with the woman standing before him. Jesus looked up and said to her, "Woman, where are they? Has no one condemned you?" She said, "No one, Lord." And Jesus said, "Neither do I condemn you; go, and do not sin again."

THE EARLY CHURCH

Christian and Pagan

One of the early converts to Christianity was Paul of Tarsus, a learned Jew who became the first great Christian theologian. Paul at first persecuted the followers of Jesus, but then became convinced through a visionary experience that Jesus really was the Messiah. In letters to the scattered Christian communities he expounded his own very influential understanding of Jesus' teachings.

Do you think the emphasis on love as against all other virtues in Paul's letter to the Corinthians is unduly one-sided?

From *Paul's First Epistle to the Corinthians*

If I speak in the tongues of men and of angels, but have not love, I am a noisy gong or a clanging cymbal. And if I have prophetic powers, and understand all mysteries and all knowledge, and if I have all faith, so as to remove mountains, but have not love, I am nothing. If I give away all I have, and if I deliver my body to be burned, but have not love, I gain nothing.

Love is patient and kind; love is not jealous or boastful; it is not arrogant or rude. Love does not insist on its own way; it is not irritable or resentful; it does not rejoice at wrong, but rejoices in the right. Love bears all things, believes all things, hopes all things, endures all things.

Love never ends; as for prophecies, they will pass away; as for tongues, they will cease; as for knowledge, it will pass away. For our knowledge is imperfect and our prophecy is imperfect; but when the perfect comes, the imperfect will pass away. When I was a child, I spoke like a child, I thought like a child, I reasoned like a child; when I became a man, I gave up childish ways. For now we see in a mirror dimly, but then face to face. Now I know in part; then I shall understand fully, even as I have been fully understood. So faith, hope, love abide, these three; but the greatest of these is love.

To many educated pagans the new religion seemed a vicious, superstitious cult. Minucius Felix (c. 200), a Christian himself, attributed the following views to a pagan, Caecilius. What did Caecilius object to in Christian practices?

From Minucius Felix. *Octavius*

"Evil weeds grow apace and so, day by day, this depraved way of life now creeps further over all the face of the globe and the foul religious shrines of this abominable congregation are getting a stronger hold. This confederacy must be torn out, it must be sworn to perdition.

"They recognize each other by secret marks and signs; hardly have they met when they love each other, throughout the world uniting in the practice of a veritable religion of lusts. Indiscriminately they call each other brother and sister, thus turning even ordinary fornication into incest by the intervention of these hallowed names. Such a pride does this foolish, deranged superstition take in its wickedness.

"Unless there were some underlying truth, such a wide variety of charges, and very serious ones, would not be made about them; they can hardly be repeated in polite company. Rumor is a shrewd informant. I hear, for example, that they do reverence to the head of that most degraded of beasts, an ass; I cannot imagine what absurdity has persuaded them to consecrate it, but it is indeed a cult born of such morals and well suited for them. It is also reported that they worship the genitals of their pontiff and priest, adoring, it appears, the sex of their 'father.' Perhaps this is incorrect but it certainly is a suspicion that befits their clandestine and nocturnal ceremonies. There are also stories about the objects of their veneration: they are said to be a man who was punished with death as a criminal and the fell wood of his cross, thus providing suitable liturgy for the depraved fiends: they worship what they deserve.

Felix, *Octavius*, G. W. Clarke, trans. in *Ancient Christian Writers* (Newman Press:), Vol. 39, pp. 64–65.

"To turn to another point. The notoriety of the stories told of the initiation of new recruits is matched by their ghastly horror. A young baby is covered over with flour, the object being to deceive the unwary. It is then served before the person to be admitted into their rites. The recruit is urged to inflict blows onto it—they appear to be harmless because of the covering of flour. Thus the baby is killed with wounds that remain unseen and concealed. It is the blood of this infant—I shudder to mention it—it is this blood that they lick with thirsty lips; these are the limbs they distribute eagerly; this is the victim by which they seal their covenant; it is by complicity in this crime that they are pledged to mutual silence; these are their rites, more foul than all sacrileges combined."

The charge of ritual cannibalism was probably based on confused accounts of the Christian eucharist. Hippolytus of Rome tells us what actually went on at a Christian service. This early eucharistic prayer—still used in some churches—dates from the beginning of the third century.

From Hippolytus. *Apostolic Tradition*

When one has been consecrated bishop all give him the kiss of peace . . . and the deacons bring him the offering . . . he lays hands upon it with all the priests and gives thanks, saying, "The Lord be with you." And all answer, "And with your spirit." "Lift up your hearts." "We have lifted them up to the Lord." "Let us give thanks to the Lord." "It is right and just."

And he thus continues, "We give thanks to you O God through your beloved son Jesus Christ whom in these last times you have sent to us as the redeemer and saviour and messenger of your will. He is your inseparable Word, through whom you created all things and who was acceptable to you. You sent him from heaven into the Virgin's womb and in her womb he was made man and was manifested your son, born of the Holy Spirit and of the Virgin. Fulfilling your will and buying for you a holy people, he stretched forth his hands when he suffered, that by his Passion he might deliver those who believed in you. When he was delivered over to his Passion of his own will, to destroy death, to break the bonds of the devil, to trample upon Hell, to enlighten the just, and to manifest his resurrection, taking bread and giving thanks to you, he said: *Take and eat, this is my body which shall be broken for you.* And taking likewise the cup, he said: *This is my blood which shall be shed for you; when you do this, do it in memory of me.*

"Mindful therefore of his death and resurrection, we offer you this bread and cup, giving thanks to you because you have found us worthy to stand before you and serve you. And we beg you to send the Holy Spirit upon the offering of the holy church and gather into one all who have received it . . . that we may praise and glorify you through your son Jesus Christ, through whom is glory and honor to the Father and the Son and the Holy Spirit, in your holy church both now and forever. Amen."

Some of the early church Fathers held that Christians should reject all pagan philosophy and rely only on the revealed word of God. Tertullian (c. 160–c. 240) wrote, in a famous phrase, "What has

From H. Achelis, *Die Canones Hippolyti* (Leipzig, 1881), pp. 48–55.

Athens to do with Jerusalem?" But Clement of Alexandria (c. 150–c. 215) expressed a different point of view. The argument about whether religious faith can coexist harmoniously with a rational understanding of the universe has continued down to the present day. Why did Clement value Greek philosophy?

From *Clement of Alexandria*

I am well aware of the repeated comments of certain people who suffer from ignorant fears. They say that we ought to concentrate on essentials involving the faith, and ignore external superfluities which cause us useless worries and confine us to matters totally irrelevant to our destiny. These people think that philosophy comes from an evil source, that it drifted into our life at the hands of some evil deviser to do damage to human beings. . . . I shall suggest that philosophy too is in some manner a work of divine providence.

Before the Lord's coming, philosophy was an essential guide to righteousness for the Greeks. At the present time, it is a useful guide towards reverence for God. It is a kind of preliminary education for those who are trying to gather faith through demonstration. "Your foot will not stumble," says Scripture, if you attribute good things, whether Greek or Christian, to Providence. God is responsible for all good things: of some, like the blessings of the Old and New Covenants, directly; of others, like the riches of philosophy, indirectly. Perhaps philosophy too was a direct gift of God to the Greeks before the Lord extended his appeal to the Greeks. For philosophy was to the Greek world what the Law was to the Hebrews, a tutor escorting them to Christ. So philosophy is a preparatory process; it opens the road for the person whom Christ brings to his final goal. . . . There is only one way of truth, but different paths from different places join it, just like tributaries flowing into a perennial river.

So if people say that it was by accident that the Greeks delivered a slice of true philosophy, the accident was a part of the divine dispensation; but if it was by coincidence, the coincidence was governed by Providence. Again, if anyone were to say that the Greeks have grasped an innate notion of nature, nature is the work of a single creator, as we know, just as we have declared righteousness natural. If it is said that they possess only the common human mind, let us consider who is the father of that common human mind and of the righteousness that accords with its widespread existence. If anyone speaks of a gift of prediction or lays the responsibility on telepathy, he is talking about forms of prophecy. Yes, and others claim that the philosophers made some statements to reflect the truth. The divine Apostle writes of us: "At present we see as in a mirror." We know ourselves by reflection from it. We contemplate, so far as we may, the creative cause on the basis of the divine element in us. . . . Those among the Greeks with the most precise grasp of philosophy discern God through a reflection or through a transparent medium. Such are the images of truth our weakness admits, like an image perceived in water or seen through transparent or translucent bodies.

From J. Ferguson, trans. *Clement of Alexandria. Stromateis. Books One to Three*, pp 35, 41–42, 94–95, 98. Copyright © 1991. Reprinted by permission of Catholic University of America Press.

And yet philosophy on its own did bring the Greeks to righ
though not to perfect righteousness (we have seen it as a contribu
rather as the first two steps make a contribution to a prospective ascent to u
loft or the elementary teacher to the prospective philosopher). . . . The contribu-
tory causes vary in their efficacity. Clarity contributes to the transmission of
truth, dialectic to escaping from the attacks of the heresies.

The Savior's teaching is sufficient without additional help, for it is "the
power and wisdom of God." The addition of Greek philosophy does not add
more power to the truth; it reduces the power of the sophistic attack on it. It
turns aside the treacherous assaults on truth, and is rightly called the wall of defense for the vine.

*Around A.D. 300, the Egyptian priest Arius raised new problems concerning the divinity of
Christ. He denied that Christ was "eternally begotten" of the Father. The first general council of
the church, meeting at Nicea in 325, rejected his doctrine. The Nicene Creed became a touchstone
of orthodoxy in later disputes.*

The Nicene Creed

We believe in one God the Father All-sovereign, maker of heaven and earth,
and of all things visible and invisible;

And in one Lord Jesus Christ, the only-begotten Son of God, Begotten of the
Father before all ages, Light of Light, true God of true God, begotten not made,
of one substance with the Father, through whom all things were made; who for
us men and for our salvation came down from the heavens, and was made flesh
of the Holy Spirit and the Virgin Mary, and became man, and was crucified for
us under Pontius Pilate, and suffered and was buried, and rose again on the
third day according to the Scriptures, and ascended into the heavens, and sitteth
on the right hand of the Father, and cometh again with glory to judge living and
dead, of whose kingdom there shall be no end:

And in the Holy Spirit, the Lord and the Life-giver, that proceedeth from the
Father, who with Father and Son is worshipped together and glorified together,
who spake through the prophets:

In one holy Catholic and Apostolic Church:

We acknowledge one baptism unto remission of sins. We look for a resurrection of the dead, and the life of the age to come.

Church and State

*Roman rulers often regarded the Christian church as a dangerous, subversive organiza-
tion—and a convenient scapegoat in times of trouble. A major persecution was launched
by the emperor Nero after the great fire of Rome in A.D. 64.*

From *The Annals of Tacitus*

Neither human aid, nor imperial bounty, nor atoning-offerings to the Gods, could remove the sinister suspicion that the fire had been brought about by Nero's order. To put an end therefore to this rumour, he shifted the charge on to others, and inflicted the most cruel tortures upon a body of men detested for their abominations, and popularly known by the name of Christians. This name came from one Christus, who was put to death in the reign of Tiberius by the Procurator Pontius Pilate; but though checked for the time, the detestable superstition broke out again, not in Judaea only, where the mischief began, but even in Rome, where every horrible and shameful iniquity, from every quarter of the world, pours in and finds a welcome.

First those who acknowledged themselves of this persuasion were arrested; and upon their testimony a vast number were condemned, not so much on the charge of incendiarism as for their hatred of the human race. Their death was turned into a diversion. They were clothed in the skins of wild beasts, and torn to pieces by dogs; they were fastened to crosses, or set up to be burned, so as to serve the purpose of lamps when daylight failed. Nero gave up his own gardens for this spectacle; he provided also Circensian games, during which he mingled with the populace, or took his stand upon a chariot, in the garb of a charioteer. But guilty as these men were and worthy of direst punishment, the fact that they were being sacrificed for no public good, but only to glut the cruelty of one man, aroused a feeling of pity on their behalf.

The emperor Trajan (98–117) advised a more temperate approach to the Christian problem. How did Pliny deal with Christians? How could someone accused of the "crime" of Christianity prove his or her innocence?

From *Letters of Pliny*

Letter XCVII. To the Emperor Trajan

It is a rule, Sir, which I inviolably observe, to refer myself to you in all my doubts; for who is more capable of removing my scruples, or informing my ignorance? Having never been present at any trials concerning those who profess Christianity, I am unacquainted not only with the nature of their crimes, or the measure of their punishment, but how far it is proper to enter into an examination concerning them. Whether therefore any difference is usually made with respect to the ages of the guilty, or no distinction is to be observed between the young and the adult; whether repentance intitles them to a pardon; or if a man has been once a Christian, it avails nothing to desist from his error; whether the very profession of Christianity, unattended with any criminal act, or only the crimes themselves inherent in the profession are punishable; in all these points I am greatly doubtful. In the mean while the

From G. G. Ramsay, trans., *The Annals of Tacitus* (London: J. Murray, 1904), Vol. 2, pp. 280–282.
From W. Melmoth, trans., *The Letters of Pliny the Consul* (London: J. Dodsley, 1770), Vol. 2, pp. 671–677.

method I have observed towards those who have been brought before me as Christians, is this: I interrogated them whether they were Christians; if they confessed I repeated the question twice again, adding threats at the same time; when, if they still persevered, I ordered them to be immediately punished: for I was persuaded, whatever the nature of their opinions might be, a contumacious and inflexible obstinacy certainly deserved correction. There were others also brought before me possessed with the same infatuation, but being citizens of Rome, I directed them to be carried thither. But this crime spreading (as is usually the case) while it was actually under prosecution, several instances of the same nature occurred. An information was presented to me without any name subscribed, containing a charge against several persons, who upon examination denied they were Christians, or had ever been so. They repeated after me an invocation to the gods, and offered religious rites with wine and frankincense before your statue; (which for the purpose I had ordered to be brought together with those of the gods) and even reviled the name of Christ: whereas there is no forcing, it is said, those who are really Christians, into a compliance with any of these articles: I thought proper therefore to discharge them. Some among those who were accused by a witness in person, at first confessed themselves Christians, but immediately after denied it; while the rest own'd indeed that they had been of that number formerly, but had now (some above three, others more, and a few above twenty years ago) forsaken that error. They all worshipped your statue and the images of the gods, throwing out imprecations at the same time against the name of Christ. They affirmed, the whole of their guilt, or their error, was, that they met on a certain stated day before it was light, and addressed themselves in a form of prayer to Christ, as to some God, binding themselves by a solemn oath, not for the purposes of any wicked design, but never to commit any fraud, theft, or adultery, never to falsify their word, nor deny a trust when they should be called upon to deliver it up; after which, it was their custom to separate, and then reassemble, to eat in common a harmless meal. From this custom, however, they desisted after the publication of my edict, by which, according to your orders, I forbade the meeting of any assemblies. After receiving this account, I judged it so much the more necessary to endeavor to extort the real truth, by putting two female salves to the torture, who were said to administer in their religious functions: but I could discover nothing more than an absurd and excessive superstition. I thought proper therefore to adjourn all farther proceedings in this affair, in order to consult with you. For it appears to be a matter highly deserving your consideration; more especially as great numbers must be involved in the danger of these prosecutions, this enquiry having already extended, and being still likely to extend, to persons of all ranks and ages, and even of both sexes. For this contagious superstition is not confined to the cities only, but has spread its infection among the country villages. Nevertheless, it still seems possible to remedy this evil and restrain its progress. The temples, at least, which were once almost deserted, begin now to be frequented; and the sacred solemnities, after a long intermission, are again revived; while there is a general demand for the victims, which for some time past have met with but few purchasers. From hence it is easy to imagine, what numbers might be reclaimed from this error, if a pardon were granted to those who shall repent.

Letter XCVIII. Trajan to Pliny

The method you have pursued, my dear Pliny, in the proceedings against those Christians which were brought before you, is extremely proper; as it is not possible to lay down any fixed plan by which to act in all cases of this nature. But I would not have you officiously enter into any enquiries concerning them. If indeed they should be brought before you, and the crime is proved, they must be punished; with the restriction however that where the party denies himself to be a Christian, and shall make it evident that he is not, by invoking our Gods, let him (notwithstanding any former suspicion) be pardoned upon his repentance. Information without the accuser's name subscribed, ought not to be received in prosecutions of any sort, as it is introducing a very dangerous precedent, and by no means agreeable to the equity of my government.

The emperor Constantine (306–337) instituted a radical change of policy. Supposedly influenced by a dream or vision, he had Christian symbols painted on his soldiers' shields before a crucial battle and then won a decisive victory. In 313 The "Edict of Milan" granted toleration to the Christians. Later Constantine himself became a Christian and took an active part in directing the affairs of the church. Do you think that Constantine's role as "general bishop" could possibly harm the church?

From *The "Edict of Milan"*

When we, Constantine and Licinius, Emperors, met at Milan in conference concerning the welfare and security of the realm, we decided that of the things that are of profit to all mankind, the worship of God ought rightly to be our first and chiefest care, and that it was right that Christians and all others should have freedom to follow the kind of religion they favoured; so that the God who dwells in heaven might be propitious to us and to all under our rule. We therefore announce that, notwithstanding any provisions concerning the Christians in our former instructions, all who choose that religion are to be permitted to continue therein, without any let or hindrance, and are not to be in any way troubled or molested. Note that at the same time all others are to be allowed the free and unrestricted practice of their religions; for it accords with the good order of the realm and the peacefulness of our times that each should have freedom to worship God after his own choice; and we do not intend to detract from the honour due to any religion or its followers. Moreover, concerning the Christians, we before gave orders with respect to the places set apart for their worship. It is now our pleasure that all who have bought such places should restore them to the Christians, without any demand for payment.

From Henry Bettenson, ed., *Documents of the Christian Church,* 2nd ed. (London: Oxford University Press, 1963), pp. 22–23. Copyright © 1963 by Oxford University Press. Reprinted by permission of Oxford University Press.

From Eusebius. *Life of Constantine*

He [Constantine] exercised a peculiar care over the church of God: and whereas, in the several provinces there were some who differed from each other in judgment, he, like some general bishop constituted by God, convened synods of his ministers. Nor did he disdain to be present and sit with them in their assembly, but bore a share in their deliberations, ministering to all that pertained to the peace of God. He took his seat, too, in the midst of them, as an individual amongst many, dismissing his guards and soldiers, and all whose duty it was to defend his person; but protected by the fear of God, and surrounded by the guardianship of his faithful friends. Those whom he saw inclined to a sound judgment, and exhibiting a calm and conciliatory temper, received his high approbation, for he evidently delighted in a general harmony of sentiment; while he regarded the unyielding with aversion.

In 380 the emperor Theodosius established orthodox Christianity as the official religion of the empire.

From *The Theodosian Code*

It is our desire that all the various nations which are subject to our Clemency and Moderation, should continue in the profession of that religion which was delivered to the Romans by the divine Apostle Peter, as it hath been preserved by faithful tradition; and which is now professed by the Pontiff Damasus and by Peter, Bishop of Alexandria, a man of apostolic holiness. According to the apostolic teaching and the doctrine of the Gospel, let us believe the one deity of the Father, the Son and the Holy Spirit, in equal majesty and in a holy Trinity. We authorize the followers of this law to assume the title of Catholic Christians; but as for the others, since, in our judgment, they are foolish madmen, we decree that they shall be branded with the ignominious name of heretics, and shall not presume to give to their conventicles the name of churches. They will suffer in the first place the chastisement of the divine condemnation, and in the second the punishment which our authority, in accordance with the will of Heaven, shall decree.

Christian Women: Marriage and Celibacy

From the beginning, the Christian church displayed an ambivalent attitude toward human sexuality. In some contexts, the love between husband and wife was praised as a symbol of the love between Christ and the church. In others, virginity was presented as a higher state than marriage. Both attitudes appear in Paul's writings.

From Eusebius, *The Life of Constantine*, E. C. Richardson, trans. in *A Select Library of Nicene and Post–Nicene Fathers,* Second Series (New York: The Christian Literature Co., 1890), Vol. 1, pp. 494–495.
From Henry Bettenson, ed., *Documents of the Christian Church,* 2nd ed. (London: Oxford University Press, 1963), p. 31. Copyright © 1963 by Oxford University Press. Reprinted by permission of Oxford University Press.

From *Paul's Epistle to the Ephesians*

Be subject to one another out of reverence for Christ. Wives, be subject to your husbands, as to the Lord. For the husband is the head of the wife as Christ is the head of the church, his body, and is himself its Savior. As the church is subject to Christ, so let wives also be subject in everything to their husbands. Husbands, love your wives, as Christ loved the church and gave himself up for her, that he might sanctify her, having cleansed her by the washing of water with the word, that he might present the church to himself in splendor, without spot or wrinkle or any such thing, that she might be holy and without blemish. Even so husbands should love their wives as their own bodies. He who loves his wife loves himself. For no man ever hates his own flesh, but nourishes and cherishes it, as Christ does the church, because we are members of his body. "For this reason a man shall leave his father and mother and be joined to his wife, and the two shall become one flesh." This mystery is a profound one, and I am saying that it refers to Christ and the church; however, let each one of you love his wife as himself, and let the wife see that she respects her husband.

From *Paul's First Epistle to the Corinthians*

Now concerning the matters about which you wrote. It is well for a man not to touch a woman. But because of the temptation to immorality, each man should have his own wife and each woman her own husband. The husband should give to his wife her conjugal rights, and likewise the wife to her husband. For the wife does not rule over her own body, but the husband does; likewise the husband does not rule over his own body, but the wife does. Do not refuse one another except perhaps by agreement for a season, that you may devote yourselves to prayer; but then come together again, lest Satan tempt you through lack of self-control. I say this by way of concession, not of command. I wish that all were as I myself am. But each has his own special gift from God, one of one kind and one of another.

To the unmarried and the widows I say that it is well for them to remain single as I do. But if they cannot exercise self-control, they should marry. For it is better to marry than to be aflame with passion. . . .

I think that in view of the present distress it is well for a person to remain as he is. Are you bound to a wife? Do not seek to be free. Are you free from a wife? Do not seek marriage. But if you marry, you do not sin, and if a girl marries she does not sin. Yet those who marry will have worldly troubles, and I would spare you that. I mean, brethren, the appointed time has grown very short; from now on, let those who have wives live as though they had none, and those who mourn as though they were not mourning, and those who rejoice as though they were not rejoicing, and those who buy as though they had no goods, and those who deal with the world as though they had no dealings with it. For the form of this world is passing away.

I want you to be free from anxieties. The unmarried man is anxious about the affairs of the Lord, how to please the Lord; but the married man is anxious about worldly affairs, how to please his wife, and his interests are divided. And the unmarried woman or girl is anxious about the affairs of the Lord, how to be holy in body and spirit; but the married woman is anxious about worldly affairs, how to please her husband. I say this for your own benefit, not to lay any restraint upon you, but to promote good order and to secure your undivided devotion to the Lord.

If any one thinks that he is not behaving properly toward his betrothed, if his passions are strong, and it has to be, let him do as he wishes: let them marry—it is no sin. But whoever is firmly established in his heart, being under no necessity but having his desire under control, and has determined this in his heart, to keep her as his betrothed, he will do well. So that he who marries his betrothed does well; and he who refrains from marriage will do better.

The early church Fathers often extolled virginity as a higher state of life than marriage. This passage from St. Jerome (c. 340–c. 420) is typical. Does he give any persuasive arguments against marriage from a wife's point of view?

From Jerome. *Against Helvidius*

A virgin is defined as she that is holy in body and in spirit, for it is no good to have virgin flesh if a woman be married in mind.

"But she that is married is careful for the things of the world, how she may please her husband."[1] Do you think there is no difference between one who spends her time in prayer and fasting, and one who must, at her husband's approach, make up her countenance, walk with mincing gait, and feign a shew of endearment? The virgin's aim is to appear less comely; she will wrong herself so as to hide her natural attractions. The married woman has the paint laid on before her mirror, and, to the insult of her Maker, strives to acquire something more than her natural beauty. Then come the prattling of infants, the noisy household, children watching for her word and waiting for her kiss, the reckoning up of expenses, the preparation to meet the outlay. On one side you will see a company of cooks, girded for the onslaught and attacking the meat: there you may hear the hum of a multitude of weavers. Meanwhile a message is delivered that the husband and friends have arrived. The wife, like a swallow, flies all over the house. She has to see to everything. Is the sofa smooth? Is the pavement swept? Are the flowers in the cups? Is dinner ready? Tell me, pray, where amid all this is there room for the thought of God? Are these happy homes? Where there is the beating of drums, the noise and clatter of pipe and lute, the clanging of cymbals, can any fear of God be found? Enter next the half-naked

From Jerome, *Against Helvidius*, W. H. Fremantle, trans. in *A Select Library of Nicene and Post–Nicene Fathers*, Second Series (New York: The Christian Literature Co., 1893), Vol. 6, pp. 344–345.
[1] I Corinthians 7:34.

victims of the passions, a mark for every lustful eye. The unhappy wife must either take pleasure in them, and perish, or be displeased, and provoke her husband. Hence arises discord, the seed-plot of divorce. Or suppose you find me a
house where these things are unknown, which is rare indeed! yet even there the
very management of the household, the education of the children, the wants of
the husband, the correction of the servants, cannot fail to call away the mind
from the thought of God. "It had ceased to be with Sarah after the manner of
women"[2]: so the Scripture says, and afterwards Abraham received the command, "In all that Sarah saith unto thee, hearken unto her voice."[3] She who is
not subject to the anxiety and pain of child-bearing and having passed the
change of life has ceased to perform the functions of a woman, is freed from the
curse of God: nor is her desire to her husband, but on the contrary her husband
becomes subject to her, and the voice of the Lord commands him, "In all that
Sarah saith unto thee, hearken unto her voice." Thus they begin to have time for
prayer. For so long as conjugal rights are used, earnest prayer is neglected.

*In spite of such views, some of the most admired martyrs of the early church were married women.
The young mother, Perpetua, was put to death in the arena at Carthage in 202. Her story is unusual in that it is written in the first person, supposedly by Perpetua herself.*

From *The Acts of the Christian Martyrs*

A number of young catechumens were arrested, Revocatus and his fellow
slave Felicitas, Saturninus and Secundulus, and with them Vibia Perpetua, a
newly married woman of good family and upbringing. Her mother and father
were still alive and one of her two brothers was a catechumen like herself. She
was about twenty-two years old and had an infant son at the breast. (Now from
this point on the entire account of her ordeal is her own, according to her own
ideas and in the way that she herself wrote it down.)

A few days later we were lodged in the prison; and I was terrified, as I had
never before been in such a dark hole. What a difficult time it was! With the
crowd the heat was stifling; then there was the extortion of the soldiers; and to
crown all, I was tortured with worry for my baby there.

Then Tertius and Pomponius, those blessed deacons who tried to take care
of us, bribed the soldiers to allow us to go to a better part of the prison to refresh
ourselves for a few hours. Everyone then left that dungeon and shifted for himself. I nursed my baby, who was faint from hunger. In my anxiety I spoke to my
mother about the child, I tried to comfort my brother, and I gave the child in
their charge. I was in pain because I saw them suffering out of pity for me. These
were the trials I had to endure for many days. Then I got permission for my baby
to stay with me in prison. At once I recovered my health, relieved as I was of my

[2]Genesis 18:11.
[3]Genesis 21:12.
From Herbert Musurillo, trans., *The Acts of the Christian Martyrs* (Oxford: Clarendon Press, 1972),
pp. 109–119. Copyright © 1972 by Oxford University Press. Reprinted by permission of Oxford
University Press.

worry and anxiety over the child. My prison had suddenly become a palace, so that I wanted to be there rather than anywhere else.

One day while we were eating breakfast we were suddenly hurried off for a hearing. We arrived at the forum, and straight away the story went about the neighbourhood near the forum and a huge crowd gathered. We walked up to the prisoner's dock. All the others when questioned admitted their guilt. Then, when it came my turn, my father appeared with my son, dragged me from the step, and said: 'Perform the sacrifice—have pity on your baby!'

Hilarianus the governor, who had received his judicial powers as the successor of the late proconsul Minucius Timinianus, said to me: 'Have pity on your father's grey head; have pity on your infant son. Offer the sacrifice for the welfare of the emperors.'

'I will not', I retorted.

'Are you a Christian?' said Hilarianus.

And I said: 'Yes, I am.'

When my father persisted in trying to dissuade me, Hilarianus ordered him to be thrown to the ground and beaten with a rod. I felt sorry for father, just as if I myself had been beaten. I felt sorry for his pathetic old age.

Then Hilarianus passed sentence on all of us: we were condemned to the beasts, and we returned to prison in high spirits. But my baby had got used to being nursed at the breast and to staying with me in prison. So I sent the deacon Pomponius straight away to my father to ask for the baby. But father refused to give him over. But as God willed, the baby had no further desire for the breast, nor did I suffer any inflammation; and so I was relieved of any anxiety for my child and of any discomfort in my breasts.

The day before we were to fight with the beasts I saw the following vision. Pomponius the deacon came to the prison gates and began to knock violently. I went out and opened the gate for him. He was dressed in an unbelted white tunic, wearing elaborate sandals. And he said to me: "Perpetua, come; we are waiting for you.'

Then he took my hand and we began to walk through rough and broken country. At last we came to the amphitheatre out of breath, and he led me into the centre of the arena.

Then he told me: 'Do not be afraid. I am here, struggling with you.' Then he left.

I looked at the enormous crowd who watched in astonishment. I was surprised that no beasts were let loose on me; for I knew that I was condemned to die by the beasts. Then out came an Egyptian against me, of vicious appearance, together with his seconds, to fight with me. There also came up to me some handsome young men to be my seconds and assistants.

My clothes were stripped off, and suddenly I was a man. My seconds began to rub me down with oil (as they are wont to do before a contest). Then I saw the Egyptian on the other side rolling in the dust. Next there came forth a man of marvellous stature, such that he rose above the top of the amphitheatre. He was clad in a beltless purple tunic with two stripes (one on either side) running down the middle of his chest. He wore sandals that were wondrously made of gold and silver, and he carried a wand like an athletic trainer and a green branch on which there were golden apples.

And he asked for silence and said: 'If this Egyptian defeats her he will slay her with the sword. But if she defeats him, she will receive this branch.' Then he withdrew.

We drew close to one another and began to let our fists fly. My opponent tried to get hold of my feet, but I kept striking him in the face with the heels of my feet. Then I was raised up into the air and I began to pummel him without as it were touching the ground. Then when I noticed there was a lull, I put my two hands together linking the fingers of one hand with those of the other and thus I got hold of his head. He fell flat on his face and I stepped on his head.

The crowd began to shout and my assistants started to sing psalms. Then I walked up to the trainer and took the branch. He kissed me and said to me: 'Peace be with you, my daughter!' I began to walk in triumph towards the Gate of Life. Then I awoke. I realized that it was not with wild animals that I would fight but with the Devil, but I knew that I would win the victory. So much for what I did up until the eve of the contest. About what happened at the contest itself, let him write of it who will.

Toward the end of the fourth century a Roman synod required celibacy of all higher clergy. Its decision was announced in this letter, probably written by Pope Damasus in 384.

From *Letter of Pope Damasus on Celibacy*

This is what has been decided, about bishops in the first place, but also about priests and deacons, whose duty it is to take part in the divine sacrifice (of the Eucharist) and whose hands confer the grace of baptism and make present the body of Christ. It is not only us but divine Scripture that binds them to be perfectly chaste. . . . How could a bishop or priest dare to preach continence to a widow or virgin, or urge anyone to keep his bed pure, if he himself were more concerned to have children for this world than for God? Why did Paul say "You are not in the flesh but in the spirit" and "Let those who have wives live as though they had none"? Would he, who so exhorted the people, complaisantly allow carnal activity to priests?—he who also said "Make no provision for the flesh, to gratify its desires" and "I wish that all were as I myself am." One who is in the service of Christ, who sits in the chair of the master, can he not observe the rule of service. . . . Those who offered sacrifices in the Temple remained the whole year in the Temple so that they should be pure and did not enter their own homes. . . . Even idolaters, in order to celebrate their impious cult and sacrifice to demons, imposed continence on themselves as regards women and abstained from certain foods so as to remain pure. And you ask me if the priest of the living God, who is to offer spiritual sacrifices, should live always in a state of purity or if, wholly involved in the flesh he should give himself to the cares of the flesh. If intercourse is defilement . . . that is why the mystery of God may not be entrusted to men of that sort, defiled and faithless. . . . They doubtless know that "flesh and blood cannot inherit the kingdom of God, nor does the corrupt inherit the incorruptible"; shall a priest or deacon dare then to lower himself to act as the animals do?

From H. T. Bruns, *Canones apostolorum et conciliorum saeculorum IV–VII* (Berlin, 1839), Vol. 2, p. 276. Translated by B. Tierney.

DECLINE AND FALL

Imperial Centralization

During the third century, new civil wars threatened to tear apart the Roman world. The emperor Diocletian (284–305) succeeded in restoring order but only by imposing a more absolutist form of government on the empire. This criticism of Diocletian's policies is from a contemporary Christian author, Lactantius.

From *The Death of the Persecutors*

While Diocletian, that author of ill, and deviser of misery, was ruining all things, he could not withhold his insults, not even against God. This man, by avarice partly, and partly by timid counsels, overturned the Roman empire: for he made choice of three persons to share the government with him; and thus, the empire having been quartered, armies were multiplied, and each of the four princes strove to maintain a much more considerable military force than any sole emperor had done in times past. There began to be fewer men who paid taxes than there were who received wages from the state; so that the means of the husbandmen being exhausted by enormous impositions, the farms were abandoned, cultivated grounds became woodland, and universal dismay prevailed. Besides, the provinces were divided into minute portions, and many presidents and a multitude of inferior officers lay heavy on each territory, and almost on each city. There were also many stewards of different degrees, and deputies of presidents. Very few civil causes came before them: but there were condemnations daily, and forfeitures frequently inflicted; taxes on numberless commodities, and those not only often repeated, but perpetual, and, in exacting them, intolerable wrongs.

Whatever was laid on for the maintenance of the soldiery might have been endured; but Diocletian, through his insatiable avarice, would never allow the sums of money in his treasury to be diminished: he was constantly heaping together extraordinary aids and free gifts, that his original hoards might remain untouched and inviolable. He also, when by various extortions he had made all things exceedingly dear, attempted by an ordinance to limit their prices.[4] Then much blood was shed for the veriest trifles; men were afraid to expose aught to sale, and the scarcity became more excessive and grievous than ever, until, in the end, the ordinance, after having proved destructive to multitudes, was from mere necessity abrogated.

Under Diocletian's successors many occupations considered useful to the state were made compulsory and hereditary. (Coloni were dependent peasants forbidden to leave the land they cultivated. Decurions were members of municipal councils, responsible for local government and tax collection; in earlier centuries the position had been much sought after as one of high honor.) What does the following legislation tell us about imperial tax policies?

---

[4]Lactantius refers to a price control edict issued in 301.
From Lactantius, *On the Manner in Which the Persecutors Died*, W. Fletcher, trans. in *The Ante–Nicene Fathers VII* (New York: The Christian Literature Co., 1888), p. 303.

From *The Theodosian Code*

I, 5, 11. All persons who govern provinces shall exact payment of the delinquent taxes for their term of office when they have laid aside their administration. Those landholders whom no sense of shame can move to fulfill their public obligations shall be notified three times within a year, and if they do not complete all such public obligations, they shall pay double the amount of the debt through the office of Your Magnificence.

V, 17, 1. Any person in whose possession a colonus that belongs to another is found not only shall restore the aforesaid colonus to his birth status but also shall assume the capitation tax for this man for the time that he was with him.

1. Coloni also who meditate flight must be bound with chains and reduced to a servile condition, so that by virtue of their condemnation to slavery, they shall be compelled to fulfill the duties that befit freemen.

VI, 2, 14. We order that exemption from the payment of the glebal tax shall be granted to all those persons from Macedonia . . . who have been added to the Most August Order of the City of Constantinople [the Senate], according to the precedent of the Senators who were chosen from Thrace.

XI, 2, 4. Whenever, in accordance with custom, payment is demanded in the case of regular taxes or of taxes due, not the prices of natural products demanded shall be paid, but the natural products themselves. . . .

XII, 1, 13. Since we have learned that the municipal councils are being left desolate by those persons who are obligated to them through birth status and who are requesting imperial service for themselves through supplications to the Emperor and are running away to the legions and various governmental offices, We order all municipal councils to be admonished that if they should apprehend any persons with less than twenty terms of service in governmental offices . . . they shall drag such persons back to the municipal councils. . . .

XII, 1, 18. It is our will, indeed, that the sons of military men, according to the former regulation, either shall pursue the aforesaid service of their fathers, or, if they refuse to perform military service and had reached the age of thirty-five years, they shall be assigned to the municipal councils.

XII, 1, 62. If a decurion should steal into a guild of artisans for the purpose of evading other duties, he shall be restored to his pristine status, and in the future no person who derives his birth status from decurions shall dare to aspire to the duties of such a guild.

XIV, 2, 4. If any guild members of the City of Rome have illegally passed into foreign parts, they shall be forced to return by the administrative action of the governors of the provinces, in order that they may perform the compulsory public services which ancient custom has imposed upon them.

XIV, 3, 8. The office of Your Sincerity shall be on guard that if any man should once and for all be assigned to the guild of breadmakers, he shall not be granted the opportunity and power in any way to withdraw, even if the assent of all the bread-makers should strive to obtain his release and their assembly should appear to have agreed. Not even this privilege shall be granted to any breadmaker, namely, that he may pass from one breadmaking establishment to another.

XIV, 3, 14. If a daughter of a breadmaker should marry any man and after-ward, when her fortune had been squandered, he should suppose that she may be released from the guild, We command that he shall be bound to the compul-sory duties and guild of breadmaking by the same law and reason as if he were held by the bond of birth service to such compulsory status.

Christian Reactions

According to Salvianus (c. 400–480) the oppressive burden of taxation had undermined loyalty to the Roman state at the time of the barbarian invasions.

Salvianus. *The Burden of Taxation*

But what else can these wretched people wish for, they who suffer the inces-sant and even continuous destruction of public tax levies. To them there is always imminent a heavy and relentless proscription. They desert their homes, lest they be tortured in their very homes. They seek exile, lest they suffer torture. The enemy is more lenient to them than the tax collectors. This is proved by this very fact, that they flee to the enemy in order to avoid the full force of the heavy tax levy. This very tax levying, although hard and inhuman, would nevertheless be less heavy and harsh if all would bear it equally and in common. Taxation is made more shameful and burdensome because all do not bear the burden of all. They extort tribute from the poor man for the taxes of the rich, and the weaker carry the load for the stronger. There is no other reason that they cannot bear all the taxation ex-cept that the burden imposed on the wretched is greater than their resources.

They suffer from envy and want, which are misfortunes most diverse and unlike. Envy is bound up with payment of the tax; need, with the ability to pay. If you look at what they pay, you will think them abundant in riches, but if you look at what they actually possess, you will find them poverty stricken. Who can judge an affair of this wretchedness? They bear the payment of the rich and en-dure the poverty of beggars.

Do we think we are unworthy of the punishment of divine severity when we thus constantly punish the poor? Do we think, when we are constantly wicked, that God should not exercise His justice against all of us? Where or in whom are evils so great, except among the Romans? Whose injustice so great ex-cept our own? The Franks are ignorant of this crime of injustice. The Huns are immune to these crimes. There are no wrongs among the Vandals and none among the Goths. So far are the barbarians from tolerating these injustices among the Goths, that not even the Romans who live among them suffer them.

From J. F. O'Sullivan, trans., *The Writings of Salvian the Presbyter,* Fathers of the Church Series (Washington, D.C.: The Catholic University of America Press, 1947), Vol. 3, pp. 138, 141. Reprinted by permission of the publisher.

Therefore, in the districts taken over by the barbarians, there is one desire among all the Romans, that they should never again find it necessary to pass under Roman jurisdiction. In those regions, it is the one and general prayer of the Roman people that they be allowed to carry on the life they lead with the barbarians. And we wonder why the Goths are not conquered by our portion of the population, when the Romans prefer to live among them rather than with us. Our brothers, therefore, are not only altogether unwilling to flee to us from them, but they even cast us aside in order to flee to them.

During the fifth century all the provinces of the Western empire were occupied by barbarians. Jerome, living far away in Bethlehem, heard the news with dismay.

Jerome. *The Barbarian Invasions*

Innumerable and most ferocious people have overrun the whole of Gaul. The entire area bounded by the Alps, the Pyrenees, the ocean and the Rhine is occupied by the Quadi, Vandals, Sarmatians, Alanni, Gepides, Saxons, Burgundians, Alammani—oh weep for the empire—and the hostile Pannonians. . . . Mainz, once a noble city, is captured and razed, and thousands have been massacred in the church. Worms has succumbed to a long siege. Rheims, the impregnable, Amiens, Artois . . Tours, Nimes and Strasburg are in the hands of the Germans. The provinces of Aquitaine, of the land of the nine peoples, of Lyons and Narbonne are completely occupied and devastated either by the sword from without or famine within. I cannot mention Toulouse without tears, for until now it has been spared, due to the merits of its saintly bishop Exuperus. The Spaniards tremble, expecting daily the invasion and recalling the horrors of the incursion of the Cimbri. What others are going through the Spaniards suffer in continual anticipation.

Who would believe that Rome, victor over all the world, would fall, that she would be to her people both the womb and the tomb. Once all the East, Egypt and Africa acknowledged her sway and were counted among her men servants and her maid servants. Who would believe that holy Bethlehem would receive as beggars nobles, both men and women, once abounding in riches? Where we cannot help we mourn and mingle with theirs our tears. . . . There is not an hour, not even a moment, when we are not occupied with crowds of refugees, when the peace of the monastery is not invaded by a horde of guests so that we shall either have to shut the gates or neglect the Scriptures for which the gates were opened. Consequently I have to snatch furtively the hours of the night, which now with winter approaching are growing longer, and try to dictate by candle light and thus through the labor of exegesis relieve a mind distraught. I am not boasting of our hospitality, as some may suspect, but simply explaining to you the delay.

The most profound Christian reflections on the fall of Rome came from St. Augustine (354–430). In his City of God, Augustine saw the whole human race divided into two "cities"—those who loved God and those who valued only worldly goods. Christians could accept the rule of a temporal power devoted only to material ends for the sake of the peace and order that it imposed; but their

From R. H. Bainton, *The Medieval Church* (Princeton, N.J.: D. Van Nostrand, 1962), pp. 89–90.

true, permanent allegiance was only to the City of God, the community of faithful Christians. Augustine was arguing, in effect, that the Christian church could endure whatever happened to the Roman state. As it turned out, this was a prophetic insight.

Augustine. *The Two Cities*

We see then that the two cities spring from two different kinds of love, the earthly from love of self leading to contempt of God, and the heavenly from love of God leading to contempt of self. The one glories in itself, the other in the Lord. The one seeks glory from men, to the other the greatest glory is the witness of God in the conscience. The one raises its proud head in self-glory, the other says to its God, 'My glory, and the lifter up of my head.' The one is dominated by the passion for dominance either in the person of its leaders or in respect of those nations which it subdues. In the other each citizen serves his neighbour in love, the rulers in giving counsel and the subjects in humble duty. The former loves its own strength as represented in its leaders; the latter says to God, 'I will love *thee*, O Lord, my strength.'

In the former the intelligentsia, living after the fashion of men, pursued pleasures of body or mind or both. . . . But in the Heavenly City there is none of man's wisdom, but only religion in accordance with which the true God is rightly worshipped, with expectation of due reward in the fellowship, not only of saints but of angels, that God may be all in all.

The household of those who do not live by faith tries to secure a worldly peace out of the business and profit of this temporal life. The household of those who live by faith looks forward to the fulfilment of the promise of eternal bliss in the future. . . .

The earthly city, which does not live by faith, seeks an earthly peace, and therein contrives a civic harmony of command and obedience, so that there is among the citizens a sort of coherence of human wills in matters belonging to this mortal life. The heavenly City, on the other hand, or rather that part of it that is a stranger on earth and lives by faith, also uses that peace because it must, until the mortality that makes it necessary shall itself pass away. And so, while the heavenly City spends the time of its sojourning as a captive in the earthly city, it holds the promise of redemption and has received the gift of the Spirit as a pledge. Therefore it has no hesitation in conforming to the laws of the earthly city by which the administration of mortal affairs is maintained. So, as mortality is common to both, in matters pertaining to it harmony is preserved between the two cities. . . .

This heavenly City, while it is a pilgrim on earth, gathers citizens out of every nation. It builds up a pilgrim community of every language. It has no particular concern about differences of customs, laws, institutions by which earthly peace is sought or maintained. Although they differ in different nations they all tend to one and the same end in earthly peace. Therefore it does not rescind them or break them: rather it preserves and follows them, so long as they do not hinder that religion, which teaches that only the one true God is to be worshipped.

Augustine, *The City of God*, J. W. C. Wand, trans. (London: Oxford University Press, 1963), pp. 240, 347–349, 406.

Thus the heavenly City in the course of its pilgrimage uses the peace of this world. In matters pertaining to the nature of mortal man it protects and cultivates the harmony of human wills, as far as religion and piety allow. And it relates the earthly to the heavenly peace, which is peace indeed, and is the only peace worth calling such for a rational creature, namely an orderly and harmonious fellowship in the enjoyment of God and of one another in God. When it arrives at that point, life will be no longer mortal, but life indeed; the body will not be merely animal, weighing down the soul by its corruptibility, but spiritual, free from all need, and in every particular subject to the will.

This peace the heavenly City enjoys while it is a pilgrim in faith, and by this faith of the just it lives. In the meantime it does what good it can for God and its neighbour (for the life of the City is a social existence) and relates it all to the obtaining of that other peace which is eternal.

Augustine's emphasis on the afterlife did not make him insensitive to the natural beauties of the earthly environment. He regarded them as gifts of God to human life.

Then how can tongue describe all the beauty and use of the creation, which the divine bounty has poured out for man to see and take, although he is condemned to such toils and miseries? The diverse and varied beauty of sky and earth and sea, the abundance and loveliness of light in sun and moon and stars, the shady woods, the colours and perfumes of flowers, the many species of bright and chattering birds, the vast variety of living creatures, the smallest of which move us to the greatest wonder (for we are more surprised by the accomplishments of ants and bees than by the size of whales)! The grand spectacle of the sea, dressing itself in its different garments, now green, now blue, now purple. . . . How pleasant the alternation of day and night! How soothing the coolness of the breeze! How much material for clothings in trees and beasts! All such blessings who can enumerate?

Eastern Survival

After the Roman empire in the West collapsed, the eastern capital of Constantinople survived for centuries as the center of a great east Roman civilization. In the sixth century the emperor Justinian organized a codification of the Roman law that had been accumulating in a haphazard fashion for centuries. His work exercised a great influence on European jurisprudence when it became known in the West from the eleventh century onward. What sources of law did Justinian recognize?

From *The Institutes of Justinian*

Justice is the set and constant purpose which gives to every man his due. Jurisprudence is the knowledge of things divine and human, the science of the just and the unjust. . . .

From *The Institutes of Justinian*, J. B. Moyle, trans. 3rd ed. (Oxford: Oxford University Press, 1896), pp. 3–5.

The precepts of the law are these: to live honestly, to injure no one, and to give every man his due. The study of law consists of two branches, law public and law private. The former relates to the welfare of the Roman State; the latter to the advantage of the individual citizen. Of private law then we may say that it is of threefold origin, being collected from the precepts of nature, from those of the law of nations, or from those of the civil law of Rome.

The law of nature is that which she has taught all animals; a law not peculiar to the human race, but shared by all living creatures, whether denizens of the air, the dry land, or the sea. Hence comes the union of male and female, which we call marriage; hence the procreation and rearing of children, for this is a law by the knowledge of which we see even the lower animals are distinguished. The civil law of Rome, and the law of all nations, differ from each other thus. The laws of every people governed by statutes and customs are partly peculiar to itself, partly common to all mankind. Those rules which a state enacts for its own members are peculiar to itself, and are called civil law: those rules prescribed by natural reason for all men are observed by all people alike, and are called the law of nations. Thus the laws of the Roman people are partly peculiar to itself, partly common to all nations; a distinction of which we shall take notice as occasion offers. . . .

Our law is partly written, partly unwritten, as among the Greeks. The written law consists of statutes, plebiscites, senatusconsults, enactments of the Emperors, edicts of the magistrates, and answers of those learned in the law. A statute is an enactment of the Roman people, which it used to make on the motion of a senatorial magistrate, as for instance a consul. A plebiscite is an enactment of the commonalty, such as was made on the motion of one of their own magistrates, as a tribune. . . . A senatusconsult is a command and ordinance of the senate, for when the Roman people had been so increased that it was difficult to assemble it together for the purpose of enacting statutes, it seemed right that the senate should be consulted instead of the people. Again, what the Emperor determines has the force of a statute, the people having conferred on him all their authority and power by the *lex regia*, which was passed concerning his office and authority. Consequently, whatever the Emperor settles by rescript, or decides in his judicial capacity, or ordains by edicts, is clearly a statute: and these are what are called constitutions.

PART SIX

A NEW EUROPE—
BARBARIANS AND
CHRISTIANS

Edward Gibbon, author of the classic work, The Decline and Fall of the Roman Empire, saw the fall of Rome as a "triumph of barbarism and superstition." But, from another point of view, the settlement of the western provinces of the empire by barbarian invaders and their conversion to Christianity can be seen as the beginning of a new European civilization.

The barbarians brought their own values—ideas about honor and law and family structure—that helped to shape the growth of Western society in the following centuries. The Christian church, surviving the fall of the empire, had enough vitality to assimilate these new peoples. For a time the genius for government that had characterized the Roman state in its best days seemed to pass to the Roman church. Great pontiffs like Leo I (440–461) and Gregory I (590–604) played major roles in civil as well as religious affairs. Christian monasteries, standing as islands of peaceful life through all the violence and disorders of the age, preserved in their libraries not only the writings of the Christian church Fathers, but also much of the classical literature of ancient Rome.

The Anglo-Saxon peoples were converted to Christianity during the seventh century. Subsequently they sent out missionaries who carried their new religion to regions of central and eastern Germany that had never formed part of the old Roman empire. A new cultural entity was being formed that would later be called "Western Christendom." Its emergence was symbolized by the coronation of a great Germanic warrior king, Charlemagne, as head of a new Western empire in St. Peter's church, Rome, on Christmas Day in the year 800.

THE EARLY GERMANS—SOCIETY AND CULTURE

A Roman Account

The first detailed account of the German peoples was written by Tacitus in A.D. 98. How were the Germans governed? What were their favorite occupations? Modern critics often suggest that Tacitus emphasized certain qualities of the Germans in order to call attention to corresponding defects in his own Roman society. Can you see any evidence of this?

From Tacitus. *On Germany*

Physical Characteristics. For my own part, I agree with those who think that the tribes of Germany are free from all taint of intermarriages with foreign nations, and that they appear as a distinct, unmixed race, like none but themselves. Hence, too, the same physical peculiarities throughout so vast a population. All have fierce blue eyes, red hair, huge frames, fit only for a sudden exertion. They are less able to bear laborious work. Heat and thirst they cannot in the least endure; to cold and hunger their climate and their soil inure them. . . .

Government. Influence of Women. They choose their kings by birth, their generals for merit. These kings have not unlimited or arbitrary power, and the generals do more by example than by authority. If they are energetic, if they are conspicuous, if they fight in the front, they lead because they are admired. But to reprimand, to imprison, even to flog, is permitted to the priests alone, and that not as a punishment, or at the general's bidding, but, as it were, by the mandate of the god whom they believe to inspire the warrior. They also carry with them into battle certain figures and images taken from their sacred groves. And what most stimulates their courage is, that their squadrons or battalions, instead of being formed by chance or by a fortuitous gathering, are composed of families and clans. Close by them, too, are those dearest to them, so that they hear the shrieks of women, the cries of infants. *They* are to every man the most sacred witnesses of his *bravery—they* are his most generous applauders. The soldier brings his wounds to mother and wife, who shrink not from counting or even demanding them and who administer both food and encouragement to the combatants.

Councils. About minor matters the chiefs deliberate, about the more important the whole tribe. Yet even when the final decision rests with the people, the affair is always thoroughly discussed by the chiefs. They assemble,

From Tacitus, *The Agricola and Germany*, A. J. Church and W. J. Brodribb, trans. (London: Macmillan, 1877), pp. 87–107.

except in the case of a sudden emergency, on certain fixed days, either at new or at full moon. . . . Then the king or the chief, according to age, birth, distinction in war, or eloquence, is heard, more because he has influence to persuade than because he has power to command. If his sentiments displease them, they reject them with murmurs; if they are satisfied, they **bran**dish their spears. The most complimentary form of assent is to express approbation with their weapons. . . .

Punishments. Administration of Justice. In their councils an accusation may be preferred or a capital crime prosecuted. Penalties are distinguished according to the offence. Traitors and deserters are hanged on trees; the coward, the unwarlike, the man stained with abominable vices, is plunged into the mire of the morass with a hurdle put over him. This distinction in punishment means that crime, they think, ought, in being punished, to be exposed, while infamy ought to be buried out of sight. Lighter offences, too, have penalties proportioned to them; he who is convicted, is fined in a certain number of horses or of cattle. Half of the fine is paid to the king or to the state, half to the person whose wrongs are avenged and to his relatives. In these same councils they also elect the chief magistrates, who administer law in the cantons and the towns. Each of these has a hundred associates chosen from the people, who support him with their advice and influence. . . .

Warlike Ardour of the People. When they go into battle, it is a disgrace for the chief to be surpassed in valour, a disgrace for his followers not to equal the valour of the chief. And it is an infamy and a reproach for life to have survived the chief, and returned from the field. To defend, to protect him, to ascribe one's own brave deeds to his renown, is the height of loyalty. The chief fights for victory; his vassals fight for their chief. If their native state sinks into the sloth of prolonged peace and repose, many of its noble youths voluntarily seek those tribes which are waging some war, both because inaction is odious to their race, and because they win renown more readily in the midst of peril, and cannot maintain a numerous following except by violence and war. Indeed, men look to the liberality of their chief for their war-horse and their bloodstained and victorious lance. Feasts and entertainments, which, though inelegant, are plentifully furnished, are their only pay. The means of this bounty come from war and rapine. Nor are they as easily persuaded to plough the earth and to wait for the year's produce as to challenge an enemy and earn the honour of wounds. Nay, they actually think it tame and stupid to acquire by the sweat of toil what they might win by their blood.

Habits in Time of Peace. Whenever they are not fighting, they pass much of their time in the chase, and still more in idleness, giving themselves up to sleep and to feasting, the bravest and the most warlike doing nothing, and surrendering the management of the household, of the home, and of the land, to the woman, the old men, and all the weakest members of the family. They themselves lie buried in sloth, a strange combination in their nature that the same men should be so fond of idleness, so averse to peace. . . .

Marriage Laws. Their marriage code, however, is strict, and indeed no part of their manners is more praiseworthy. Almost alone among barbarians they are content with one wife, except a very few among them, and these not from sensuality, but because their noble birth procures for them many offers of alliance. The wife does not bring a dower to the husband, but the husband to the wife. The parents and relatives are present, and pass judgment on the marriage-gifts, gifts not meant to suit a woman's taste, nor such as a bride would deck herself with, but oxen, a caparisoned steed, a shield, a lance, and a sword. With these presents the wife is espoused, and she herself in her turn brings her husband a gift of arms. This they count their strongest bond of union, these their sacred mysteries, these their gods of marriage. Lest the woman should think herself to stand apart from aspirations after noble deeds and from the perils of war, she is reminded by the ceremony which inaugurates marriage that she is her husband's partner in toil and danger, destined to suffer and to dare with him alike both in peace and in war. The yoked oxen, the harnessed steed, the gift of arms, proclaim this fact. She must live and die with the feeling that she is receiving what she must hand down to her children neither tarnished nor depreciated, what future daughters-in-law may receive, and may be so passed on to her grandchildren.

Thus with their virtue protected they live uncorrupted by the allurements of public shows or the stimulant of feastings. Clandestine correspondence is equally unknown to men and women. Very rare for so numerous a population is adultery, the punishment for which is prompt, and in the husband's power. Having cut off the hair of the adulteress and stripped her naked, he expels her from the house in the presence of her kinsfolk, and then flogs her through the whole village. The loss of chastity meets with no indulgence; neither beauty, youth, nor wealth will procure the culprit a husband. No one in Germany laughs at vice, nor do they call it the fashion to corrupt and to be corrupted. . . .

Hereditary Feuds. Fines for Homicide. Hospitality. It is a duty among them to adopt the feuds as well as the friendships of a father or a kinsman. These feuds are not implacable; even homicide is expiated by the payment of a certain number of cattle and of sheep, and the satisfaction is accepted by the entire family, greatly to the advantage of the state, since feuds are dangerous in proportion to a people's freedom.

No nation indulges more profusely in entertainments and hospitality. To exclude any human being from their roof is thought impious; every German, according to his means, receives his guest with a well-furnished table. . . .

Of lending money on interest and increasing it by compound interest they know nothing—a more effectual safeguard than if it were prohibited.

Laws and Customs

Tacitus wrote about the Germans as an outsider. The various Germanic codes of customary law provide more direct evidence about their ways of living. In Germanic law every person had a wergeld *("man-price"), the fine for his or her murder that had to be paid to the victim's family. Other fines were scaled according to the gravity of the offense and the status of the person involved. How do these laws compare in form and content with the Roman laws (pp. 125, 152)? What do the laws tell us about social classes in Germanic society and about the status of women? How serious a crime was rape? What were the grounds for divorce?*

From *Laws of the Salian Franks*

Title I. Concerning Summonses.

1. If any one be summoned before the "Thing"[1] by the king's law, and do not come, he shall be sentenced to 600 denars, which make 15 shillings (solidi).

Title XI. Concerning Thefts or Housebreakings of Freemen.

1. If any freeman steal, outside of the house, something worth 2 denars, he shall be sentenced to 600 denars, which make 15 shillings.

2. But if he steal, outside of the house, something worth 40 denars, and it be proved on him, he shall be sentenced, besides the amount and the fines for delay, to 1400 denars, which make 35 shillings.

Title XII. Concerning Thefts or Housebreakings on the Part of Slaves.

1. If a slave steal, outside of the house, something worth two denars, he shall, besides paying the worth of the object and the fines for delay, be stretched out and receive 120 blows.

2. But if he steal something worth 40 denars, he shall either be castrated or pay 6 shillings. But the lord of the slave who committed the theft shall restore to the plaintiff the worth of the object and the fines for delay.

Title XIII. Concerning Rape Committed by Freemen.

1. If three men carry off a free born girl, they shall be compelled to pay 30 shillings.

2. If there are more than three, each one shall pay 5 shillings.

3. Those who shall have been present with boats shall be sentenced to three shillings.

4. But those who commit rape shall be compelled to pay 2500 denars, which make 63 shillings.

---

[1]The folk assembly.
From E. F. Henderson, trans. in *Select Historical Documents of the Middle Ages* (London: George Bell and Sons, 1892), pp. 176–189.

Title XVII. Concerning Wounds.

1. If any one have wished to kill another person, and the blow have missed, he on whom it was proved shall be sentenced to 2500 denars, which make 63 shillings.

2. If any person have wished to strike another with a poisoned arrow, and the arrow have glanced aside, and it shall be proved on him: he shall be sentenced to 2500 denars, which make 63 shillings.

3. If any person strike another on the head so that the brain appears, and the three bones which lie above the brain shall project, he shall be sentenced to 1200 denars, which make 30 shillings.

4. But if it shall have been between the ribs or in the stomach, so that the wound appears and reaches to the entrails, he shall be sentenced to 1200 denars—which make 30 shillings—besides five shillings for the physician's pay.

Title XXIV. Concerning the Killing of Little Children and Women.

1. If any one have slain a boy under 10 years—up to the end of the tenth—and it shall have been proved on him, he shall be sentenced to 24000 denars, which make 600 shillings.

3. If any one have hit a free woman who is pregnant, and she dies, he shall be sentenced to 28000 denars, which make 700 shillings.

6. If any one have killed a free woman after she has begun bearing children, he shall be sentenced to 24000 denars, which make 600 shillings.

7. After she can have no more children, he who kills her shall be sentenced to 8000 denars, which make 200 shillings.

Title XXX. Concerning Insults.

3. If any one, man or woman, shall have called a woman harlot, and shall not have been able to prove it, he shall be sentenced to 1800 denars, which make 45 shillings.

4. If any person shall have called another "fox," he shall be sentenced to 3 shillings.

5. If any man shall have called another "hare," he shall be sentenced to 3 shillings.

Title XLI. Concerning the Murder of Freemen.

1. If any one shall have killed a free Frank, or a barbarian living under the Salic law, and it have been proved on him, he shall be sentenced to 8000 denars.

2. But if he shall have thrown him into a well or into the water, or shall have covered him with branches or anything else, to conceal him, he shall be sentenced to 24000 denars, which make 600 shillings.

3. But if any one has slain a man who is in the service of the king, he shall be sentenced to 24000 denars, which make 600 shillings.

4. But if he have put him in the water or in a well, and covered him with anything to conceal him, he shall be sentenced to 72000 denars, which make 1800 shillings.

5. If any one have slain a Roman who eats in the king's palace, and it have been proved on him, he shall be sentenced to 12000 denars, which make 300 shillings.

6. But if the Roman shall not have been a landed proprietor and table companion of the king, he who killed him shall be sentenced to 4000 denars, which make 100 shillings.

Title LIX. Concerning Private Property.

1. If any man die and leave no sons, if the father and mother survive, they shall inherit.

2. If the father and mother do not survive, and he leave brothers or sisters, they shall inherit.

3. But if there are none, the sisters of the father shall inherit.

4. But if there are no sisters of the father, the sisters of the mother shall claim that inheritance.

5. If there are none of these, the nearest relatives on the father's side shall succeed to that inheritance.

6. But of Salic land no portion of the inheritance shall come to a woman: but the whole inheritance of the land shall come to the male sex.

Title LXII. Concerning Wergeld.

1. If any one's father have been killed, the sons shall have half the compounding money (wergeld); and the other half the nearest relatives, as well on the mother's as on the father's side, shall divide among themselves.

2. But if there are no relatives, paternal or maternal, that portion shall go to the fisc.

The laws of other German peoples contain parallel provisions regulating family affairs and inheritances, with variations of detail from people to people.

From *Laws of the Burgundians*

Of the Stealing of Girls.

1. If anyone shall steal a girl, let him be compelled to pay the price set for such a girl ninefold, and let him pay a fine to the amount of twelve solidi.

2. If a girl who has been seized returns uncorrupted to her parents, let the abductor compound six times the wergeld of the girl; moreover, let the fine be set at twelve solidi.

3. But if the abductor does not have the means to make the above-mentioned payment, let him be given over to the parents of the girl that they may have the power of doing to him whatever they choose.

From *The Burgundian Code*, Katherine Fischer, trans. (Philadelphia, Pa.: University of Pennsylvania Press, 1949), pp. 31, 32, 40, 45, 46, 85. Reprinted by permission of the publisher.

Of Succession.

1. Among Burgundians we wish it to be observed that if anyone does not leave a son, let a daughter succeed to the inheritance of the father and mother in place of the son.

Of Burgundian Women Entering a Second or Third Marriage.

1. If any Burgundian woman, as is the custom, enters a second or third marriage after the death of her husband, and she has children by each husband, let her possess the marriage gift (*donatio nuptialis*) in usufruct while she lives; after her death, let what his father gave her be given to each son, with the further provision that the mother has the power neither of giving, selling, or transferring any of the things which she received in the marriage gift.

2. If by chance the woman has no children, after her death let her relatives receive half of whatever has come to her by way of marriage gift, and let the relatives of the dead husband who was the donor receive half.

3. But if perchance children shall have been born and they shall have died after the death of their father, we command that the inheritance of the husband or children belong wholly to the mother.

Of Women Violated.

1. Whatever native freeman does violence to a maidservant, and force can be proved, let him pay twelve solidi to him to whom the maidservant belongs.

2. If a slave does this, let him receive a hundred fifty blows.

Of Divorces.

1. If any woman leaves (puts aside) her husband to whom she is legally married, let her be smothered in mire.

2. If anyone wishes to put away his wife without cause, let him give her another payment such as he gave for her marriage price, and let the amount of the fine be twelve solidi.

3. If by chance a man wishes to put away his wife, and is able to prove one of these three crimes against her, that is, adultery, witchcraft, or violation of graves, let him have full right to put her away: and let the judge pronounce the sentence of the law against her, just as should be done against criminals.

4. But if she admits none of these three crimes, let no man be permitted to put away his wife for any other crime. But if he chooses, he may go away from the home, leaving all household property behind, and his wife with their children may possess the property of her husband.

Of Women Who Go to Their Husbands Voluntarily.

If any woman, Burgundian or Roman, gives herself voluntarily in marriage to a husband, we order that the husband have the property of that woman; just as he has power over her, so also over her property and all her possessions.

A Germanic Hero-King

At the end of the Anglo-Saxon epic Beowulf, *the hero ("lord of the Geats") fights to the death with a monstrous fire-breathing dragon who guards a great treasure-hoard. The story of* Beowulf *illustrates early Germanic ideals with vivid force. What conduct was most admired in a hero-king?*

From *Beowulf*

It was not long until they came together again, dreadful foes. The hoard-guard took heart, once more his breast swelled with his breathing. Encircled with flames, he who before had ruled a folk felt harsh pain. Nor did his companions, sons of nobles, take up their stand in a troop about him with the courage of fighting men, but they crept to the wood, protected their lives. In only one of them the heart surged with sorrows: nothing can ever set aside kinship in him who means well.

He was called Wiglaf, son of Weohstan, a rare shield-warrior, a man of the Scylfings, kinsman of Aelfhere. He saw his liege lord under his war-mask suffer the heat. Then he was mindful of the honors he had given him before, the rich dwelling-place of the Waegmundings, every folk-right such as his father possessed. He might not then hold back, his hand seized his shield, the yellow linden-wood; he drew his ancient sword. . . .

Wiglaf spoke, said many fit words to his companions—his mind was mournful: "I remember that time we drank mead, when we promised our lord in the beer-hall—him who gave us these rings—that we would repay him for the war-arms if a need like this befell him—the helmets and the hard swords. Of his own will he chose us among the host for this venture, thought us worthy of fame—and gave me these treasures—because he counted us good war-makers, brave helm-bearers, though our lord intended to do this work of courage alone, as keeper of the folk, because among men he had performed the greatest deeds of glory, daring actions. Now the day has come that our liege lord has need of the strength of good fighters. Let us go to him, help our war-chief while the grim terrible fire persists. God knows of me that I should rather that the flame enfold my body with my gold-giver. It does not seem right to me for us to bear our shields home again unless we can first fell the foe, defend the life of the prince of the Weather-Geats. I know well that it would be no recompense for past deeds that he alone of the company of the Geats should suffer pain, fall in the fight. For us both shall there be a part in the work of sword and helmet, of battle-shirt and war-clothing."

Then he waded through the deadly smoke, bore his war-helmet to the aid of his king, spoke in few words: "Beloved Beowulf, do all well, for, long since in your youth, you said that you would not let your glory fail while you lived.

Now, great-spirited noble, brave of deeds, you must protect your life with all your might. I shall help you."

After these words, the worm came on, angry, the terrible malice-filled foe, shining with surging flames, to seek for the second time his enemies, hated men. Fire advanced in waves; shield burned to the boss; mail-shirt might give no help to the young spear-warrior; but the young man went quickly under his kins-man's shield when his own was consumed with flames. Then the war-king was again mindful of fame, struck with his war-sword with great strength so that it stuck in the head-bone, driven with force: Naegling broke, the sword of Beowulf failed in the fight, old and steel-gray. It was not ordained for him that iron edges might help in the combat. Too strong was the hand that I have heard strained every sword with its stroke, when he bore wound-hardened weapon to battle: he was none the better for it.

Then for the third time the folk-harmer, the fearful fire-dragon, was mind-ful of feuds, set upon the brave one when the chance came, hot and battle-grim seized all his neck with his sharp fangs: he was smeared with life-blood, gore welled out in waves. . . .

Then the wound that that earth-dragon had caused began to burn and to swell; at once he felt dire evil boil in his breast, poison within him. Then the prince, wise of thought, went to where he might sit on a seat near the wall. He looked on the work of giants, how the timeless earth-hall held within it stone-arches fast on pillars. Then with his hands the thane, good without limit, washed him with water, blood-besmeared, the famous prince, his beloved lord, sated with battle; and he unfastened his helmet.

Beowulf spoke—despite his wounds spoke, his mortal hurts. He knew well he had lived out his days' time, joy on earth; all passed was the number of his days, death very near. "Now I would wish to give my son my war-clothing, if any heir after me, part of my flesh, were granted. I held this people fifty winters. There was no folk-king of those dwelling about who dared approach me with swords, threaten me with fears. In my land I awaited what fate brought me, held my own well, sought no treacherous quarrels, nor did I swear many oaths un-rightfully. Sick with life-wounds, I may have joy of all this, for the Ruler of Men need not blame me for the slaughter of kinsmen when life goes from my body. Now quickly go to look at the hoard under the gray stone, beloved Wiglaf, now that the worm lies sleeping from sore wounds, bereft of his treasure. Be quick now, so that I may see the ancient wealth, the golden things, may clearly look on the bright curious gems, so that for that, because of the treasure's richness, I may the more easily leave life and nation I have long held."

Then sorrow came to the young man that he saw him whom he most loved on the earth, at the end of his life, suffering piteously. His slayer likewise lay dead, the awful earth-dragon bereft of life, overtaken by evil. No longer should the coiled worm rule the ring-hoard, for iron edges had taken him, hard and battle-sharp work of the hammers, so that the wide-flier, stilled by wounds, had fallen on the earth near the treasure-house. He did not go flying through the air at midnight, proud of his property, showing his aspect, but he fell to earth through the work of the chief's hands. Yet I have heard of no man of might on land, though he was bold of every deed, whom it should prosper to rush against the breath of the venomous foe or disturb with hands the ring-hall, if he found the guard awake who lived in the barrow. The share of the rich treasures became Beowulf's, paid for by death: each of the two had journeyed to the end of life's loan.

Then it was not long before the battle-slack ones left the woods, ten weak troth-breakers together, who had not dared fight with their spears in their liege lord's great need. But they bore their shields, ashamed, their war-clothes, to where the old man lay, looked on Wiglaf. He sat wearied, the foot-soldier near the shoulders of his lord, would waken him with water: it gained him nothing. He might not, though he much wished it, hold life in his chieftain on earth nor change anything of the Ruler's: the judgment of God would control the deeds of every man, just as it still does now. Then it was easy to get from the young man a grim answer to him who before had lost courage. Wiglaf spoke, the son of Weohstan, a man sad at heart, looked on the unloved ones:

"Yes, he who will speak truth may say that the liege lord who gave you treasure, the war-gear that you stand in there, when he used often to hand out to hall-sitters on the ale-benches, a prince to his thanes, helmets and war-shirts such as he could find mightiest anywhere, both far and near—that he quite threw away the war-gear, to his distress when war came upon him. The folk-king had no need to boast of his war-comrades. Yet God, Ruler of Victories, granted him that he might avenge himself, alone with his sword, when there was need for his courage. I was able to give him little life-protection in the fight, and yet beyond my power I did begin to help my kinsman. The deadly foe was ever the weaker after I struck him with my sword, fire poured less strongly from his head. Too few defenders thronged about the prince when the hard time came upon him. Now there shall cease for your race the receiving of treasure and the giving of swords, all enjoyment of pleasant homes, comfort. Each man of your kindred must go deprived of his land-right when nobles from afar learn of your flight, your inglorious deed. Death is better for any earl than a life of blame."

Then the people of the Geats made ready for him a funeral pyre on the earth, no small one, hung with helmets, battle-shields, bright mail-shirts, just as he had asked. Then in the midst they laid the great prince, lamenting their hero, their beloved lord. Then warriors began to awaken on the barrow the greatest of funeral-fires; the wood-smoke climbed, black over the fire; the roaring flame mixed with weeping—the wind-surge died down—until it had broken the bone-house, hot at its heart. Sad in spirit they lamented their heart-care, the death of their liege lord. And the Geatish woman, wavy-haired, sang a sorrowful song about Beowulf, said again and again that she sorely feared for herself invasions of armies, many slaughters, terror of troops, humiliation, and captivity. Heaven swallowed the smoke.

Then the people of the Weather-Geats built a mound on the promontory, one that was high and broad, wide-seen by seafarers, and in ten days completed a monument for the bold in battle, surrounded the remains of the fire with a wall, the most splendid that men most skilled might devise. In the barrow they placed rings and jewels, all such ornaments as troubled men had earlier taken from the hoard. They let the earth hold the wealth of earls, gold in the ground, where now it still dwells, as useless to men as it was before. Then the brave in battle rode round the mound, children of nobles, twelve in all, would bewail their sorrow and mourn their king, recite dirges and speak of the man. They praised his great deeds and his acts of courage, judged well of his powers. So it is fitting that man honor his liege lord with words, love him in heart when he must be led forth from the body. Thus the people of the Geats, his hearth-companions, lamented the death of their lord. They said that he was of world-kings the mildest of men and the gentlest, kindest to his people, and most eager for fame.

CHRISTIAN INSTITUTIONS

The Papacy

In the centuries of turmoil that followed the barbarian invasions of Europe two institutions—the Roman papacy and Benedictine monasticism—were especially important in preserving the tradition of Christianity in the West. Pope Leo I (440–461) strongly reasserted the doctrine of papal primacy in the church. How did he justify this claim?

From Sermon of Leo I

For the solidity of that faith which was praised in the chief of the Apostles is perpetual: and as that remains which Peter believed in Christ, so that remains which Christ instituted in Peter. For when, as has been read in the Gospel lesson, the Lord had asked the disciples whom they believed Him to be amid the various opinions that were held, and the blessed Peter had replied, saying, "Thou art the Christ, the Son of the living God," the Lord says, "Blessed art thou, Simon Bar-Jona, because flesh and blood hath not revealed it to thee, but My Father, which is in heaven. And I say to thee, that thou art Peter, and upon this rock will I build My church, and the gates of Hades shall not prevail against it. And I will give unto thee the keys of the kingdom of heaven. And whatsoever thou shalt bind on earth, shall be bound in heaven; and whatsoever thou shalt loose on earth, shall be loosed also in heaven."

The dispensation of Truth therefore abides, and the blessed Peter persevering in the strength of the Rock, which he has received, has not abandoned the helm of the Church, which he undertook. For he was ordained before the rest in such a way that from his being called the Rock, from his being pronounced the Foundation, from his being constituted the Doorkeeper on the kingdom of heaven, from his being set as the Umpire to bind and to loose, whose judgments shall retain their validity in heaven, from all these mystical titles we might know the nature of his association with Christ. And still to-day

From *Sermon of Leo the Great*, C. L. Feltoe, trans. in *Library of Nicene and Post–Nicene Fathers*, Second Series (New York: Christian Literature Co., 1895), Vol. 12, p. 117.

he more fully and effectually performs what is entrusted to him, and carries out every part of his duty and charge in Him and with Him, through Whom he has been glorified. And so if anything is rightly done and rightly decreed by us, if anything is won from the mercy of God by our daily supplications, it is of his work and merits whose power lives and whose authority prevails in his See.

Pope Gelasius (492–496) made an important declaration on the right relationship between papal and imperial power. His words were later assimilated into the canon law of the medieval church and they were often quoted in later arguments about church and state. What authority did Gelasius claim for the priesthood?

From Gelasius I. *Letter to Emperor Anastasius*

. . . Two there are, august emperor, by which this world is chiefly ruled, the sacred authority [*auctoritas*] of the priesthood and the royal power [*potestas*]. Of these the responsibility of the priests is more weighty in so far as they will answer for the kings of men themselves at the divine judgement. You know, most clement son, that, although you take precedence over all mankind in dignity, nevertheless you piously bow the neck to those who have charge of divine affairs and seek from them the means of your salvation, and hence you realize that, in the order of religion, in matters concerning the reception and right administration of the heavenly sacraments, you ought to submit yourself rather than rule, and that in these matters you should depend on their judgement rather than seek to bend them to your will. For if the bishops themselves, recognizing that the imperial office was conferred on you by divine disposition, obey your laws so far as the sphere of public order is concerned lest they seem to obstruct your decrees in mundane matters, with what zeal, I ask you, ought you to obey those who have been charged with administering the sacred mysteries? Moreover, just as no light risk attends pontiffs who keep silent in matters concerning the service of God, so too no little danger threatens those who show scorn—which God forbid—when they ought to obey. And if the hearts of the faithful should be submitted to all priests in general who rightly administer divine things, how much more should assent be given to the bishop of that see which the Most High wished to be preeminent over all priests, and which the devotion of the whole church has honored ever since. As Your Piety is certainly well aware, no one can ever raise himself by purely human means to the privilege and place of him whom the voice of Christ has set before all, whom the church has always venerated and held in devotion as its primate. The things which are established by divine judgement can be assailed by human presumption; they cannot be overthrown by anyone's power.

Monasticism

*Various different forms of monasticism grew up in the early church. The pattern that be-
came dominant in the West was defined in* The Rule of St. Benedict *(c. 480–543).
Benedict prescribed for his monks a stable life of prayer and hard work. Although it is
not specified in* The Rule, *the "work" of the monks became primarily the copying of
manuscripts. In this way the monks preserved a whole heritage of early Christian and
classical literature. How was a Benedictine monastery governed? What were the daily
tasks of the monks? What virtues did Benedict especially emphasize?*

From *The Rule of St. Benedict*

What the Abbot Should Be Like. An abbot who is worthy to preside
over a monastery ought always to remember what he is called, and carry out
with his deeds the name of a Superior. For he is believed to be Christ's representative, since he is called by His name, the apostle saying: "Ye have received the spirit of adoption of sons, whereby we call Abba, Father." And so
the abbot should not—grant that he may not—teach, or decree, or order, any
thing apart from the precept of the Lord; but his order or teaching should be
sprinkled with the ferment of divine justice in the minds of his disciples. Let
the abbot always be mindful that, at the tremendous judgment of God, both
things will be weighed in the balance: his teaching and the obedience of his
disciples. And let the abbot know that whatever the father of the family finds
of less utility among the sheep is laid to the fault of the shepherd. . . . Therefore, when any one receives the name of abbot, he ought to rule over his disciples with a double teaching; that is, let him show forth all good and holy
things by deeds more than by words. . . . He shall make no distinction of persons in the monastery. One shall not be more cherished than another, unless
it be the one whom he finds excelling in good works or in obedience. A free-
born man shall not be preferred to one coming from servitude, unless there
be some other reasonable cause . . . for whether we be bond or free we are one
in Christ; and, under one God, we perform an equal service of subjection; for
God is no respecter of persons . . . In his teaching indeed the abbot ought always to observe that form laid down by the apostle when he says: "reprove,
rebuke, exhort." That is, mixing seasons with seasons, blandishments with
terrors, let him display the feeling of a severe yet devoted master. He should,
namely, rebuke more severely the unruly and the turbulent. The obedient,
moreover, and the gentle and the patient, he should exhort, that they may
progress to higher things. But the negligent and scorners, we warn him to admonish and reprove. . . .

From E. F. Henderson, trans. in *Select Historical Documents of the Middle Ages* (London: George Bell
and Sons, 1892), pp. 176–189.

About Calling in the Brethren to Take Council As often as anything especial is to be done in the monastery, the abbot shall call together the whole congregation, and shall himself explain the question at issue. And, having heard the advice of the brethren, he shall think it over by himself, and shall do what he considers most advantageous.

Concerning Obedience. The first grade of humility is obedience without delay. This becomes those who, on account of the holy service which they have professed, or on account of the fear of hell or the glory of eternal life, consider nothing dearer to them than Christ: so that, so soon as anything is commanded by their superior, they may not know how to suffer delay in doing it, even as if it were a divine command. Concerning whom the Lord said: "As soon as he heard of me he obeyed me."

Concerning Humility . . . The sixth grade of humility is, that a monk be contented with all lowliness or extremity, and consider himself, with regard to everything which is enjoined on him, as a poor and unworthy workman; saying to himself with the prophet: "I was reduced to nothing and was ignorant; I was made as the cattle before thee, and I am always with thee." The seventh grade of humility is, not only that he, with his tongue, pronounce himself viler and more worthless than all; but that he also believe it in the innermost workings of his heart; humbling himself and saying with the prophet, etc. . . . The eighth degree of humility is that a monk do nothing except what the common rule of the monastery, or the example of his elders, urges him to do. . . .

How Divine Service Shall Be Held Through the Day. As the prophet says: "Seven times in the day do I praise Thee." Which sacred number of seven will thus be fulfilled by us if, at matins, at the first, third, sixth, ninth hours, at vesper time and at "completorium" we perform the duties of our service; for it is of these hours of the day that he said: "Seven times in the day do I praise Thee."[1] For, concerning nocturnal vigils, the same prophet says: "At midnight I arose to confess unto thee." Therefore, at these times, let us give thanks to our Creator concerning the judgments of his righteousness; that is, at matins, etc. . . ., and at night we will rise and confess to him. . . .

How the Monks Shall Sleep They shall sleep separately in separate beds. They shall receive positions for their beds, after the manner of their characters, according to the dispensation of their abbot. If it can be done, they shall all sleep in one place. If, however, their number do not permit it, they shall rest by tens or twenties, with elders who will concern themselves about them. A candle shall always be burning in that same cell until early in the morning. They shall sleep

[1]"Completorium" or "compline" was the last prayer of the evening before the monks went to bed. Then they rose during the night for "Vigils."

clothed, and girt with belts or with ropes; and they shall not have their knives at their sides while they sleep, lest perchance in a dream they should wound the sleepers. And let the monks be always on the alert; and, when the signal is given, rising without delay, let them hasten to mutually prepare themselves for the service of God—with all gravity and modesty, however. The younger brothers shall not have beds by themselves, but interspersed among those of the elder ones. And when they rise for the service of God, they shall exhort each other mutually with moderation on account of the excuses that those who are sleepy are inclined to make.

Whether the Monks Should Have Anything of Their Own. More than anything else is this special vice to be cut off root and branch from the monastery, that one should presume to give or receive anything without the order of the abbot, or should have anything of his own. He should have absolutely not anything: neither a book, nor tablets, nor a pen—nothing at all.—For indeed it is not allowed to the monks to have their own bodies or wills in their own power. But all things necessary they must expect from the Father of the monastery; nor is it allowable to have anything which the abbot did not give or permit. All things shall be common to all, as it is written: "Let not any man presume or call anything his own." But if any one shall have been discovered delighting in this most evil vice: being warned once and again, if he do not amend, let him be subjected to punishment. . . .

Concerning Old Age and Infancy . . . Although human nature itself is prone to have pity for these ages—that is, old age and infancy—nevertheless the authority of the Rule also has regard for them. Their weakness shall always be considered, and in the matter of food, the strict tenor of the Rule shall by no means be observed, as far as they are concerned; but they shall be treated with pious consideration, and may anticipate the canonical hours. . . .

Concerning the Amount of Food . . . We believe, moreover, that, for the daily refection of the sixth as well as of the ninth hour, two cooked dishes, on account of the infirmities of the different ones, are enough for all tables: so that whoever, perchance, can not eat of one may partake of the other. Therefore let two cooked dishes suffice for all the brothers: and, if it is possible to obtain apples or growing vegetables, a third may be added. One full pound of bread shall suffice for a day, whether there be one refection, or a breakfast and a supper. . . . But to younger boys the same quantity shall not be served, but less than that to the older ones; moderation being observed in all things. But the eating of the flesh of quadrupeds shall be abstained from altogether by every one, excepting alone the weak and the sick.

Concerning the Amount of Drink. Each one has his own gift from God, the one in this way, the other in that. Therefore it is with some hesitation that the amount of daily sustenance for others is fixed by us. Nevertheless, in view of the weakness of the infirm we believe that a hemina of wine a day is enough for each one. Those moreover to whom God gives the ability of bearing abstinence shall know that they will have their own reward. But the prior shall judge if either the needs of the place, or labour or the heat of summer, requires more; considering in all things lest satiety or drunkenness creep in. Indeed we read that wine is not suitable for monks at all. But because, in our day, it is not possible to persuade the monks of this, let us agree at least as to the fact that we should not drink till we are sated, but sparingly. For wine can make even the wise to go astray. Where, moreover, the necessities of the place are such that the amount written above can not be found—but much less or nothing at all—those who live there shall bless God and shall not murmur. And we admonish them to this above all: that they be without murmuring. . . .

Concerning the Daily Manual Labour. Idleness is the enemy of the soul. And therefore, at fixed times, the brothers ought to be occupied in manual labour; and again, at fixed times, in sacred reading. . . . Above all there shall certainly be appointed one or two elders, who shall go round the monastery at the hours in which the brothers are engaged in reading, and see to it that no troublesome brother chance to be found who is open to idleness and trifling, and is not intent on his reading; being not only of no use to himself, but also stirring up others.

Concerning Clothes and Shoes . . . Vestments shall be given to the brothers according to the quality of the places where they dwell, or the temperature of the air. For in cold regions more is required; but in warm, less. This, therefore, is a matter for the abbot to decide. We nevertheless consider that for ordinary places there suffices for the monks a cowl and gown apiece—the cowl, in winter hairy, in summer plain or old—and a working garment, on account of their labours. As clothing for the feet, shoes and boots. . . .

Concerning the Manner of Receiving Brothers. When any new comer applies for conversion, an easy entrance shall not be granted him: but, as the apostle says, "Try the spirits if they be of God." Therefore, if he who comes perseveres in knocking, and is seen after four or five days to patiently endure the insults inflicted upon him, and the difficulty of ingress, and to persist in his demand: entrance shall be allowed him, and he shall remain for a few days in the cell of the guests. After this, moreover, he shall be in the cell of the novices, where he shall meditate and eat and sleep. . . . If he promise perseverance in his steadfastness, after the lapse of two months this Rule shall be read to him in order, and it shall be said to him: Behold the law under which thou dost wish to serve; if thou canst observe it, enter; but if thou canst not, depart freely. And, after the lapse of six months, the Rule shall be read to him; that he may know upon what he is entering. And, if he stand firm thus far, after four months the same Rule shall again be reread to him. And if, having deliberated with himself, he shall promise to keep everything, and to obey all the commands that are laid upon him: then he shall be received in the congregation; knowing that it is decreed, by the law of the Rule, that from that day he shall not be allowed to depart from the monastery, nor to shake free his neck from the yoke of the Rule, which, after such tardy deliberation, he was at liberty either to refuse or receive. . . .

Concerning the Ordination of An Abbot. In ordaining an abbot this consideration shall always be observed: that such a one shall be put into office as the whole congregation, according to the fear of God, with one heart—or even a part, however small, of the congregation with more prudent counsel—shall have chosen. He who is to be ordained, moreover, shall be elected for merit of life and learnedness in wisdom; even though he be the lowest in rank in the congregation. But even if the whole congregation with one consent shall have elected a person consenting to their vices—which God forbid;—and those vices shall in any way come clearly to the knowledge of the bishop to whose diocese that place pertains, or to the neighbouring abbots or Christians: the latter shall not allow the consent of the wicked to prevail, but shall set up a dispenser worthy of the house of God; knowing that they will receive a good reward for this, if they do it chastely and with zeal for God. Just so they shall know, on the contrary, that they have sinned if they neglect it.

ROMAN CHRISTIANITY AND NORTHERN EUROPE

Gregory the Great and England

Gregory I (590–604), the greatest of the early medieval popes, lived in a city ruined by the wars that followed the Germanic invasions of Italy. In one of his sermons he spoke of "the loss of citizens, the assaults of enemies, the frequent fall of ruined buildings." Gregory thought that the world would soon come to an end, but he labored to bring as many people as possible to Christianity in the time that remained, and in doing so he greatly influenced the future of the Western church.

In 596 Gregory sent a group of monks led by Augustine—the first archbishop of Canterbury—to convert the pagan English. Later (601) he sent instructions about the conduct of the mission. How were the Roman missionaries to treat the established pagan practices of the English?

From Gregory I. *Letter to Mellitus*

When Almighty God shall have brought you to our most reverend brother the bishop Augustine, tell him that I have long been considering with myself about the case of the Angli; to wit, that the temples of idols in that nation should not be destroyed, but that the idols themselves that are in them should

From *Selected Epistles of Gregory the Great*, J. Barmby, trans. in *Library of Nicene and Post–Nicene Fathers*, Second Series (New York: Christian Literature Co., 1895), Vol. 13, pp. 84–85.

be. Let blessed water be prepared, and sprinkled in these temples, and altars constructed, and relics deposited, since, if these same temples are well built, it is needful that they should be transferred from the worship of idols to the service of the true God; that, when the people themselves see that these temples are not destroyed, they may put away error from their heart and, knowing and adoring the true God, may have recourse with the more familiarity to the places they have been accustomed to. And, since they are wont to kill many oxen in sacrifice to demons, they should have also some solemnity of this kind in a changed form, so that on the day of dedication, or on the anniversaries of the holy martyrs whose relics are deposited there, they may make for themselves tents of the branches of trees around these temples that have been changed into churches, and celebrate the solemnity with religious feasts. Nor let them any longer sacrifice animals to the devil, but slay animals to the praise of God for their own eating, and return thanks to the Giver of all for their fulness, so that, while some joys are reserved to them outwardly, they may be able the more easily to incline their minds to inward joys. For it is undoubtedly impossible to cut away everything at once from hard hearts, since one who strives to ascend to the highest place must needs rise by steps or paces, and not by leaps.

The Roman missionary Paulinus preached before King Edwin of Northumbria in 627. This story suggests something of the appeal of the new religion.

From Bede. *Ecclesiastical History*

Paulinus consenting, the king did as he said; for, holding a council with the wise men, he asked of every one in particular what he thought of this doctrine hitherto unknown to them, and the new worship of God that was preached?... [One of the chief men replied] "The present life of man upon earth, O king, seems to me, in comparison with that time which is unknown to us, like to the swift flight of a sparrow through the house wherein you sit at supper in winter, with your ealdormen and thegns, while the fire blazes in the midst, and the hall is warmed, but the wintry storms of rain or snow are raging abroad. The sparrow, flying in at one door and immediately out of another, whilst he is within, is safe from the wintry tempest; but after a short space of fair weather, he immediately vanishes out of your sight, passing from winter into winter again. So this life of man appears for a little while, but of what is to follow or what went before we know nothing at all. If, therefore, this new doctrine tells us something more certain, it seems justly to deserve to be followed." The other elders and king's counsellors, by Divine prompting, spoke to the same effect.

But Coifi added, that he wished more attentively to hear Paulinus discourse concerning the God Whom he preached. When he did so, at the king's command,

From *Bede's Ecclesiastical History of England*, A. M. Sellar, trans. (London: George Bell and Sons, 1907), pp. 116–117.

Coifi, hearing his words, cried out, "This long time I have perceived that what we worshipped was naught; because the more diligently I sought after truth in that worship, the less I found it. But now I freely confess, that such truth evidently appears in this preaching as can confer on us the gifts of life, of salvation, and of eternal happiness. For which reason my counsel is, O king, that we instantly give up to ban and fire those temples and altars which we have consecrated without reaping any benefit from them." In brief, the king openly assented to the preaching of the Gospel by Paulinus, and renouncing idolatry, declared that he received the faith of Christ.

In the north of England Roman missionaries encountered Irish monks who had begun to preach there. In 664 King Oswy of Northumbria had to choose between the two groups. (They disagreed about the date of Easter and other points of church usage.) Why did King Oswy agree to accept the Roman form of Christianity?

From Bede. *Ecclesiastical History*

Then Colman said, "The Easter which I keep, I received from my elders, who sent me hither as bishop; all our forefathers, men beloved of God, are known to have celebrated it after the same manner; and that it may not seem to any contemptible and worthy to be rejected, it is the same which the blessed John the Evangelist, the disciple specially beloved of our Lord, with all the churches over which he presided, is recorded to have celebrated."

Then Wilfrid, being ordered by the king to speak, began thus:—"The Easter which we keep, we saw celebrated by all at Rome, where the blessed Apostles, Peter and Paul, lived, taught, suffered, and were buried; we saw the same done by all in Italy and in Gaul, when we travelled through those countries for the purpose of study and prayer. We found it observed in Africa, Asia, Egypt, Greece, and all the world, wherever the Church of Christ is spread abroad, among divers nations and tongues, at one and the same time; save only among these and their accomplices in obstinacy, I mean the Picts and the Britons, who foolishly, in these two remote islands of the ocean, and only in part even of them, strive to oppose all the rest of the world.

"But as for you and your companions, you certainly sin, if, having heard the decrees of the Apostolic see, nay, of the universal Church, confirmed, as they are, by Holy Scripture, you scorn to follow them; for, though your fathers were holy, do you think that those few men, in a corner of the remotest island, are to be preferred before the universal Church of Christ throughout the world? And if that Columba of yours (and, I may say, ours also, if he was Christ's servant) was a holy man and powerful in miracles, yet could he be preferred before the most blessed chief of the Apostles, to whom our Lord said, 'Thou art Peter, and upon this rock I will build my Church, and the gates of hell shall not prevail against it, and I will give unto thee the keys of the kingdom of Heaven?' "

From *Bede's Ecclesiastical History of England,* A. M. Sellar, trans. (London: George Bell and Sons, 1907), pp. 195–196, 200–201.

When Wilfrid had ended thus, the king said, "Is it true, Colman, that these words were spoken to Peter by our Lord?" He answered, "It is true, O king!" Then said he, "Can you show any such power given to your Columba?" Colman answered, "None." Then again the king asked, "Do you both agree in this, without any controversy, that these words were said above all to Peter, and that the keys of the kingdom of Heaven were given to him by our Lord?" They both answered, "Yes." Then the king concluded, "And I also say unto you, that he is the door-keeper, and I will not gainsay him, but I desire, as far as I know and am able, in all things to obey his laws, lest haply when I come to the gates of the kingdom of Heaven, there should be none to open them, he being my adversary who is proved to have the keys." The king having said this, all who were seated there or standing by, both great and small, gave their assent, and renouncing the less perfect custom, hastened to conform to that which they had found to be better.

Mission to Germany

In the eighth century the English church sent out missionaries to Germany. The greatest of them, St. Boniface, worked in close contact with the papacy. His missionary work extended the influence of the Roman church to large areas of Germany that had never been part of the Roman empire.

Oath of Boniface

I, Boniface, bishop by the grace of God, promise to you, the blessed Peter, chief of the apostles, and to thy vicar, the blessed Pope Gregory, and to his successors, by the Father and the Son and the Holy Ghost, the indivisible Trinity, and by this thy most holy body, that, God helping me, I will maintain all the belief and the purity of the holy Catholic faith, and I will remain steadfast in the unity of this faith in which the whole salvation of Christians lies, as is established without doubt.

I will in no wise oppose the unity of the one universal Church, no matter who may seek to persuade me. But as I have said, I will maintain my faith and purity and union with thee and the benefits of thy Church, to whom God has given the power to loose and to bind, and with thy vicar and his successors, in all things. And if it comes to my knowledge that priests have turned from the ancient practices of the holy fathers, I will have no intercourse nor connection with them; but rather, if I can restrain them, I will. If I cannot, I will at once faithfully make known the whole matter to my apostolic lord.

To convert the heathen Germans Boniface first had to overcome the old pagan gods that were thought to inhabit sacred trees and springs. According to his first biographer he was helped by an occasional miracle.

From J. H. Robinson, trans. in *Readings in European History* (Boston, Mass.: Ginn and Co., 1904), Vol. 1, p. 106.

From *Life of Boniface*

Many of the people of Hesse were converted [by Boniface] to the Catholic faith and confirmed by the grace of the spirit: and they received the laying on of hands. But some there were, not yet strong of soul, who refused to accept wholly the teachings of the true faith. Some men sacrificed secretly, some even openly, to trees and springs. Some secretly practiced divining, soothsaying, and incantations, and some openly. But others, who were of sounder mind, cast aside all heathen profanation and did none of these things; and it was with the advice and consent of these men that Boniface sought to fell a certain tree of great size, at Geismar, and called, in the ancient speech of the region, the oak of Thor.

The man of God was surrounded by the servants of God. When he would cut down the tree, behold a great throng of pagans who were there cursed him bitterly among themselves because he was the enemy of their gods. And when he had cut into the trunk a little way, a breeze sent by God stirred overhead, and suddenly the branching top of the tree was broken off, and the oak in all its huge bulk fell to the ground. And it was broken into four parts, as if by the divine will, so that the trunk was divided into four huge sections without any effort of the brethren who stood by. When the pagans who had cursed did see this, they left off cursing and, believing, blessed God. Then the most holy priest took counsel with the brethren: and he built from the wood of the tree an oratory, and dedicated it to the holy apostle Peter.

Boniface established monasteries following the Benedictine Rule to provide centers for the conversion of the surrounding countryside. He invited women as well as men to come from England in order to help him with this work. One of them was Leoba, a nun from a noble English family. What qualities made Leoba such an outstanding abbess? And how did she impress the local German people?

From *Life of Leoba*

[Boniface] appointed persons in authority over the monasteries and established the observance of the Rule: he placed Sturm as abbot over the monks and Leoba as abbess over the nuns. He gave her the monastery at a place called Bischofsheim, where there was a large community of nuns. These were trained according to her principles in the discipline of monastic life and made such progress in her teaching that many of them afterwards became superiors of others, so that there was hardly a convent of nuns in that part which had not one of her disciples as abbess. She was a woman of great virtue and was so strongly attached to the way of life she had vowed that she never gave thought to her native country or her relatives. She expended all her energies on the work she had undertaken in order to appear blameless before God and to become a pattern of perfection to those who obeyed her in word and action. She was ever on her

From *Willibald's Life of Boniface*, J. H. Robinson, trans. in *Readings in European History* (Boston, Mass.: Ginn and Co., 1904), Vol. 1, pp. 106–107.
From *Anglo-Saxon Missionaries in Germany*, C. H. Talbot, trans. (London: Sheed and Ward Ltd., 1954), pp. 214–216, 219–221.

guard not to teach others what she did not carry out herself. In her conduct there was no arrogance or pride; she was no distinguisher of persons, but showed herself affable and kindly to all. In appearance she was angelic, in word pleasant, clear in mind, great in prudence, Catholic in faith, most patient in hope, universal in her charity. But though she was always cheerful, she never broke out into laughter through excessive hilarity. No one ever heard a bad word from her lips; the sun never went down upon her anger. In the matter of food and drink she always showed the utmost understanding for others but was most sparing in her own use of them. She had a small cup from which she used to drink and which, because of the meagre quantity it would hold, was called by the sisters "the Beloved's little one". So great was her zeal for reading that she discontinued it only for prayer or for the refreshment of her body with food or sleep: the Scriptures were never out of her hands. For, since she had been trained from infancy in the rudiments of grammar and the study of the other liberal arts, she tried by constant reflection to attain a perfect knowledge of divine things so that through the combination of her reading with her quick intelligence, by natural gifts and hard work, she became extremely learned. She read with attention all the books of the Old and New Testaments and learned by heart all the commandments of God. To these she added by way of completion the writings of the church Fathers, the decrees of the Councils and the whole of ecclesiastical law. She observed great moderation in all her acts and arrangements and always kept the practical end in view, so that she would never have to repent of her actions through having been guided by impulse. She was deeply aware of the necessity for concentration of mind in prayer and study, and for this reason took care not to go to excess either in watching or in other spiritual exercises. Throughout the summer both she and all the sisters under her rule went to rest after the midday meal, and she would never give permission to any of them to stay up late, for she said that lack of sleep dulled the mind, especially for study. . . .

She preserved the virtue of humility with such care that, though she had been appointed to govern others because of her holiness and wisdom, she believed in her heart that she was the least of all. This she showed both in her speech and behaviour. She was extremely hospitable. She kept open house for all without exception, and even when she was fasting gave banquets and washed the feet of the guests with her own hands, at once the guardian and the minister of the practice instituted by our Lord. . . .

I think it should be counted amongst her virtues also that one day, when a wild storm arose and the whole sky was obscured by such dark clouds that day seemed turned into night, terrible lightning and falling thunderbolts struck terror into the stoutest hearts and everyone was shaking with fear. At first the people drove their flocks into the houses for shelter so that they should not perish; then, when the danger increased and threatened them all with death, they took refuge with their wives and children in the church, despairing of their lives. They locked all the doors and waited there trembling, thinking that the last judgment was at hand. In this state of panic they filled the air with the din of their mingled cries. Then the holy virgin went out to them and urged them all to have patience. She promised them that no harm would come to them; and after exhorting them to join with her in prayer, she fell prostrate at the foot of the altar. In the meantime the storm raged, the roofs of the houses were torn off by the violence of the wind, the ground shook with the repeated shocks of the thunderbolts, and the thick darkness, intensified by the incessant flicker of lightning which flashed through the windows, redoubled their terror. Then the mob, unable to endure the suspense any longer, rushed to the altar to rouse her from prayer and seek her protection. Thecla, her kinswoman, spoke to her first, saying: "Beloved, all the hopes of these people lie in you: you are their only support. Arise, then, and pray to the Mother of God, your mistress, for us, that by her intercession we may be delivered from this fearful storm." At these words Leoba rose up from prayer and, as if she had been challenged to a contest, flung off the cloak which she was wearing and boldly opened the doors of the church. Standing on the threshold, she made a sign of the cross, opposing to the fury of the storm the name of the High God. Then she stretched out her hands towards heaven and three times invoked the mercy of Christ, praying that through the intercession of Holy Mary, the Virgin, He would quickly come to the help of His people. Suddenly God came to their aid. The sound of thunder died away, the winds changed direction and dispersed the heavy clouds, the darkness rolled back and the sun shone, bringing calm and peace. Thus did divine power make manifest the merits of His handmaid. Unexpected peace came to His people and fear was banished. . . .

The people's faith was stimulated by such tokens of holiness, and as religious feeling increased so did contempt of the world. Many nobles and influential men gave their daughters to God to live in the monastery in perpetual chastity; many widows also forsook their homes, made vows of chastity and took the veil in the cloister. To all of these the holy virgin pointed out both by word and example how to reach the heights of perfection.

CHARLEMAGNE

The Frankish King Charles (772–814), a great conqueror, made himself ruler of nearly all Western Europe. In a long series of campaigns he conquered Saxony and compelled the inhabitants to accept Christianity. In 773 he invaded north Italy, defeated the Lombard king who ruled there and had himself declared King of the Lombards. In 787 he extended his power over Bavaria. Finally, in association with the pope, he created a new Roman empire in the West—later known as the Holy Roman Empire.

Charlemagne and His Family

Charlemagne's biographer Einhard (c. 770–840) knew the emperor personally. He borrowed from the Lives of the Caesars *by the Roman historian Suetonius in constructing his own work, but still he gives us a lively and persuasive portrait of a great ruler. Charlemagne evidently had a large family. How did he bring up his children?*

From Einhard. *Life of Charlemagne*

Charles was large and strong, and of lofty stature, though not disproportionately tall (his height is well known to have been seven times the length of his foot); the upper part of his head was round, his eyes very large and animated, nose a little long, hair fair, and face laughing and merry. Thus his appearance was always stately and dignified, whether he was standing or sitting; although his neck was thick and somewhat short, and his belly rather prominent; but the symmetry of the rest of his body concealed these defects. His gait was firm, his whole carriage manly, and his voice clear, but not so strong as his size led one to expect. His health was excellent, except during the four years preceding his death, when he was subject to frequent fevers; at the last he even limped a little with one foot. . . .

Charles was temperate in eating, and particularly so in drinking, for he abominated drunkenness in anybody, much more in himself and those of his household; but he could not easily abstain from food, and often complained that fasts injured his health. He very rarely gave entertainments, only on great feast-days, and then to large numbers of people. His meals ordinarily consisted of four courses, not counting the roast, which his huntsmen used to bring in on the spit; he was more fond of this than of any other dish. While at table, he listened to reading or music. The subjects of the readings were the stories and deeds of olden time: he was fond, too, of St. Augustine's books, and especially of the one entitled "The City of God." He was so moderate in the use of wine and all sorts of drink that he rarely allowed himself more than three cups in the course of a meal. In summer, after the midday meal, he would eat some fruit, drain a single cup, put off his clothes and shoes, just as he did for the night, and rest for two or three hours. He was in the habit of awaking and rising from bed four or five times during the night. While he was dressing and putting on his shoes, he not only gave audience to his friends, but if the Count of the Palace told him of any suit in which his judgment was necessary, he had the parties brought before him forthwith, took cognizance of the case, and gave his decision, just as if he were sitting on the judgment-seat. This was not the only business that he transacted at this time, but he performed any duty of the day whatever, whether he had to attend to the matter himself, or to give commands concerning it to his officers.

Charles had the gift of ready and fluent speech, and could express whatever he had to say with the utmost clearness. He was not satisfied with command of his native language merely, but gave attention to the study of foreign ones, and in particular was such a master of Latin that he could speak it as well as his native tongue; but he could understand Greek better than he could speak it. He was so eloquent, indeed, that he might have passed for a teacher of eloquence. . . . He also tried to write, and used to keep tablets and blanks in bed

From Einhard, *The Life of Charlemagne*, S. E. Turner, trans. (New York: American Book Co., 1880), pp. 47–62. Foreword copyright © 1960 by The University of Michigan. Reprinted by permission of University of Michigan Press.

under his pillow, that at leisure hours he might accustom his hand to form the letters; however, as he did not begin his efforts in due season, but late in life, they met with ill success.

He married a daughter of Desiderius, King of the Lombards, at the instance of his mother; but he repudiated her at the end of a year for some reason unknown, and married Hildegard, a woman of high birth, of Suabian origin. He had three sons by her—Charles, Pepin, and Lewis—and as many daughters—Hruodrud, Bertha, and Gisela. He had three other daughters besides these—Theoderada, Hiltrud, and Ruodhaid—two by his third wife, Fastrada, a woman of East Frankish (that is to say, of German) origin, and the third by a concubine, whose name for the moment escapes me. At the death of Fastrada, he married Liutgard, an Alemannic woman, who bore him no children. After her death he had three concubines—Gersuinda, a Saxon, by whom he had Adaltrud; Regina, who was the mother of Drogo and Hugh; and Ethelind, by whom he had Theodoric. Charles's mother, Berthrada, passed her old age with him in great honour; he entertained the greatest veneration for her; and there was never any disagreement between them except when he divorced the daughter of King Desiderius, whom he had married to please her. She died soon after Hildegard, after living to see three grandsons and as many granddaughters in her son's house, and he buried her with great pomp in the Basilica of St. Denis, where his father lay. He had an only sister, Gisela, who had consecrated herself to a religious life from girlhood, and he cherished as much affection for her as for his mother. She also died a few years before him in the nunnery where she had passed her life.

The plan that he adopted for his children's education was, first of all, to have both boys and girls instructed in the liberal arts, to which he also turned his own attention. As soon as their years admitted, in accordance with the custom of the Franks, the boys had to learn horsemanship, and to practise war and the chase, and the girls to familiarize themselves with cloth-making, and to handle distaff and spindle, that they might not grow indolent through idleness, and he fostered in them every virtuous sentiment. He only lost three of all his children before his death, two sons and one daughter, Charles, who was the eldest, Pepin, whom he had made King of Italy, and Hruodrud, his oldest daughter, whom he had betrothed to Constantine, Emperor of the Greeks. . . . When his sons and his daughter died, he was not so calm as might have been expected from his remarkably strong mind, for his affections were no less strong, and moved him to tears. Again, when he was told of the death of Hadrian, the Roman Pontiff, whom he had loved most of all of his friends, he wept as much as if he had lost a brother, or a very dear son. He was by nature most ready to contract friendships, and not only made friends easily, but clung to them persistently, and cherished most fondly those with whom he had formed such ties. He was so careful of the training of his sons and daughters that he never took his meals without them when he was at home, and never made a journey without them; his sons would ride at this side, and his daughters follow him, while a number of his body-guard, detailed for their protection, brought up the rear. Strange to say, although they were very handsome women, and he loved them very dearly, he was never willing to marry any of them to a man of their own nation or to a foreigner, but kept them all at home until his death, saying that he could not dispense with their society. Hence, though otherwise happy, he experienced the malignity of fortune as far as they were concerned: yet he concealed his knowledge of the rumours current in regard to them, and of the suspicions entertained of their honour.[2]

Economic Foundations

Charlemagne's revenues came mainly from great agricultural estates scattered throughout his domains. This letter illustrates the material basis of early medieval society. In the absence of any extensive network of commerce each estate had to be almost entirely self-supporting. How did Charlemagne's instructions ensure this?

From *Capitulary De Villis*

We desire that each steward shall make an annual statement of all our income, giving an account of our lands cultivated by the oxen which our own plowmen drive and of our lands which the tenants of farms ought to plow; of the pigs, of the rents, of the obligations and fines; of the game taken in our forests without our permission; of the various compositions; of the mills, of the forest, of the fields, of the bridges and ships; of the free men and the districts under obligations to our treasury; of markets, vineyards, and those who owe wine to us; of the hay, firewood, torches, planks, and other kinds of lumber; of the waste lands; of the vegetables, millet, panic; of the wool, flax, and hemp; of the fruits of the trees; of the nut trees, larger and smaller; of the grafted trees of all kinds; of the gardens; of the turnips; of the fish ponds; of the hides, skins, and horns; of the honey and wax; of the fat, tallow, and soap; of the mulberry wine, cooked wine, mead, vinegar, beer, and wine, new and old; of the new grain and the old; of the hens and eggs; of the geese; of the number of fishermen, workers in metal, sword makers, and shoemakers; of the bins and boxes; of the turners and saddlers; of the forges and mines—that is, of iron, lead, or other substances; of the colts and fillies. They shall make all these known to us, set forth separately and in order, at Christmas, so that we may know what and how much of each thing we have.

The greatest care must be taken that whatever is prepared or made with the hands—that is, bacon, smoked meat, sausage, partially salted meat, wine, vinegar, mulberry wine, cooked wine, garum, mustard, cheese, butter, malt, beer, mead, honey, wax, flour—all should be prepared and made with the greatest cleanliness.

Each steward on each of our domains shall always have, for the sake of ornament, peacocks, pheasants, ducks, pigeons, partridges, and turtle-doves.

---

[2]Bertha had a notorious affair with a Frankish noble, Angilbert, and had two children by him.
From J. H. Robinson, trans. in *Readings in European History* (Boston, Mass., Ginn and Co., 1904), Vol. 1, pp. 137–139.

In each of our estates the chambers shall be provided with counterpanes, cushions, pillows, bedclothes, coverings for the tables and benches; vessels of brass, lead, iron, and wood; andirons, chains, pothooks, adzes, axes, augers, cutlasses, and all other kinds of tools, so that it shall never be necessary to go elsewhere for them, or to borrow them. And the weapons which are carried against the enemy shall be well cared for, so as to keep them in good condition; and when they are brought back they shall be placed in the chamber.

For our women's work they are to give at the proper time, as has been ordered, the materials—that is, the linen, wool, woad, vermilion, madder, wool combs, teasels, soap, grease, vessels, and the other objects which are necessary.

Of the kinds of food not forbidden on fast days, two thirds shall be sent each year for our own use—that is, of the vegetables, fish, cheese, butter, honey, mustard, vinegar, millet, panic, dried and green herbs, radishes, and, in addition, of the wax, soap, and other small products; and let it be reported to us, by a statement, how much is left, as we have said above; and this statement must not be omitted as in the past, because after those two thirds we wish to know how much remains.

Each steward shall have in his district good workmen, namely, blacksmiths, a goldsmith, a silversmith, shoemakers, turners, carpenters, sword makers, fishermen, foilers, soap makers, men who know how to make beer, cider, perry, or other kind of liquor good to drink, bakers to make pastry for our table, net makers who know how to make nets for hunting, fishing, and fowling, and other sorts of workmen too numerous to be designated.

Carolingian Government

Charlemagne imposed on his empire an unusual degree of peace and order (for those days). This capitulary of 802 described the aims of his government. The missi were traveling emissaries sent out by Charlemagne to supervise local administration.

From *General Capitulary for the Missi*

Concerning the embassy sent out by the lord emperor. Therefore, the most serene and most Christian lord emperor Charles has chosen from his nobles the wisest and most prudent men, both archbishops and some of the other bishops also, and venerable abbots and pious laymen, and has sent them throughout his whole kingdom, and through them by all the following chapters has allowed men to live in accordance with the correct law. Moreover, where anything which is not right and just has been enacted in the law, he has ordered them to inquire into this most diligently and to inform him of it; he desires, God granting, to reform it. And let no one, through his cleverness or astuteness, dare to oppose or thwart the written law, as many are wont to do, or the judicial sentence passed upon him, or to do injury to the churches of God or the poor or

From D. C. Munro, trans. in *University of Pennsylvania Translations and Reprints* (Philadelphia, Pa.: University of Pennsylvania, 1900), Vol. 4, No. 5, pp. 16.

the widows or the wards or any Christian. But all shall live entirely in accordance with God's precept, justly and under a just rule, and each one shall be admonished to live in harmony with his fellows in his business or profession; the canonical clergy ought to observe in every respect a canonical life without heeding base gain, nuns ought to keep diligent watch over their lives, laymen and the secular clergy ought rightly to observe their laws without malicious fraud and all ought to live in mutual charity and perfect peace. And let the *missi* themselves make a diligent investigation whenever any man claims that an injustice has been done to him by any one, just as they desire to deserve the grace of omnipotent God and to keep their fidelity promised to Him, so that entirely in all cases everywhere, in accordance with the will and fear of God, they shall administer the law fully and justly in the case of the holy churches of God and of the poor, of wards and widows and of the whole people. And if there shall be anything of such a nature that they, together with the provincial counts, are not able of themselves to correct it and to do justice concerning it, they shall, without any ambiguity, refer this, together with their reports, to the judgment of the emperor; and the straight path of justice shall not be impeded by any one on account of flattery or gifts from any one, or on account of any relationship, or from fear of the powerful. . . .

The Imperial Coronation

In 800 Charlemagne traveled to Rome to support Pope Leo III who had been driven from the city by his enemies. On Christmas Day, in St. Peter's Church, the pope placed a crown on Charlemagne's head and he was acclaimed as emperor. There are several ninth-century accounts of the coronation. How do they differ from one another?

From Einhard. *Life of Charlemagne*

The Romans had inflicted many injuries upon the Pontiff Leo, tearing out his eyes and cutting out his tongue, so that he had been compelled to call upon the King for help. Charles accordingly went to Rome, to set in order the affairs of the Church, which were in great confusion, and passed the whole winter there. It was then that he received the titles of Emperor and Augustus, to which he at first had such an aversion that he declared that he would not have set foot in the Church the day that they were conferred, although it was a great feast-day, if he could have foreseen the design of the Pope. He bore very patiently with the jealousy which the [East] Roman emperors showed upon his assuming these titles, for they took this step very ill; and by dint of frequent embassies and letters, in which he addressed them as brothers, he made their haughtiness yield to his magnanimity, a quality in which he was unquestionably much their superior.

From Einhard, *The Life of Charlemagne*, S. E. Turner, trans. (New York: American Book Co.), pp. 65–66. Foreword copyright © 1960 by The University of Michigan. Reprinted by permission of University of Michigan Press.

From *Annals of Lorsch*

Now since the title of emperor had become extinct among the Greeks and a woman claimed the imperial authority it seemed to the apostle Leo and to all the holy fathers who were present at the council and to the rest of the Christian people that Charles, king of the Franks, ought to be named emperor, for he held Rome itself where the Caesars were always wont to reside and also other cities in Italy, Gaul, and Germany. Since almighty God had put all these places in his power it seemed to them that, with the help of God, and in accordance with the request of all the Christian people, he should hold this title. King Charles did not wish to refuse their petition, and, humbly submitting himself to God and to the petition of all the Christian priests and people, he accepted the title of emperor on the day of the nativity of our Lord Jesus Christ and was consecrated by the lord Pope Leo.

From *Frankish Royal Annals*

On the most holy day of the nativity of the Lord, as the king rose from praying at Mass before the tomb of the blessed apostle Peter, pope Leo placed a crown on his head and all the Roman people cried out, "To Charles Augustus, crowned by God, great and peace-giving emperor of the Romans, life and victory." And after the laudation he was adored by the pope in the manner of the ancient princes and, the title of patrician being set aside, he was called emperor and Augustus. A few days later he commanded the men who had deposed the pope the year before to be brought before him. They were examined according to Roman law on a charge of treason and condemned to death. However, the pope interceded for them with the emperor and they were spared in life and limb. Subsequently they were sent into exile for so great a crime.

From *Annals of Lorsch*, G. H. Pertz, *Monumenta Germaniae Historica, Scriptores I* (Hanover, 1826), p. 38, Brian Tierney, trans. in *Great Issues in Western Civilization*, 3rd ed., Brian Tierney, Donald Kagan, and L. Pearce Williams, eds. (New York: Random House, 1976), p. 337. Copyright © 1967, 1972, 1976 by Random House, Inc. Reprinted by permission of the publisher.
From *Frankish Royal Annals*, G. H. Pertz, *Monumenta Germaniae Historica, Scriptores I* (Hanover, 1826), p. 188, Brian Tierney, trans. in *Great Issues in Western Civilization*, 3rd ed., Brian Tierney, Donald Kagan, and L. Pearce Williams, eds. (New York: Random House, 1976), p. 338. Copyright © 1967, 1972, 1976 by Random House, Inc. Reprinted by permission of the publisher.

PART SEVEN

MEDIEVAL FOUNDATIONS— FEUDALISM, CHURCH REFORM, AND CRUSADE

Charlemange's empire soon disintegrated. His descendants established separate kingdoms and waged frequent wars against one another. At the same time Europe was invaded by Vikings from the north and Magyars from the east. The forces of Islam, which had occupied Spain during the eighth century, took Sicily and attacked southern Italy. The very survival of Christian Europe seemed threatened for a time.

But slowly the foundations for a new growth of civilization in the West were established. Most important were the development of feudal institutions and the emergence of a revitalized church. Feudalism, based on a relationship of personal loyalty between a vassal and a lord, evolved as a response to the near-anarchy of the times. In the difficult conditions of the ninth century, kings were often unable to govern effectively all their territories. Sometimes they would grant a whole province as a fief to a great lord. Such a lord would usually divide his lands into lesser fiefs, each held by a vassal who owed him military service. Europe came to be dominated by a warrior aristocracy. Government was decentralized. Such order as existed was provided by personal bonds of loyalty, not by the allegiance of citizens to a state. Marriages were commonly arranged to serve feudal ends—to create family alliances or consolidate existing fiefs.

The church suffered in the general disorder of the times. Great monasteries and cathedral churches fell under the control of lay lords. The old discipline of celibacy for clergy was forgotten and priests commonly married or lived with concubines. From the early tenth century, movements of reform grew up, at first in monastic centers. Then, from the mid-eleventh century onward, a revitalized papacy began to carry through a general reform of the whole Western church. The claims of the popes, and especially their attempts to free churches from lay control, led on to the first great conflict of empire and papacy. After fifty years of strife, it was ended by a compromise agreement in 1122.

By that time the combination of feudal force and religious enthusiasm had made possible a new movement of expansion. Crusading armies first pushed back the Saracens in Spain, then launched an attack on Palestine to establish a Christian kingdom in the Holy Land.

FEUDAL INSTITUTIONS

Lords and Vassals

Nowadays historians often point out that "the feudal system" was not really an organized system at all. Feudal practices grew up in a haphazard fashion as individuals struggled for power or security in the violent world of the ninth and tenth centuries. The following records are from the German abbey of Xanten. What do they tell us about the circumstances in which early feudal society emerged?

From *Annals of Xanten*

846

According to their custom the Northmen plundered Eastern and Western Frisia and burned the town of Dordrecht, with two other villages, before the eyes of Lothaire, who was then in the castle of Nimwegen, but could not punish the crime. The Northmen, with their boats filled with immense booty, including both men and goods, returned to their own country.

In the same year Louis sent an expedition from Saxony against the Wends across the Elbe. He personally, however, went with his army against the Bohemians, whom we called Beu-winitha, but with great risk. . . . Charles advanced against the Britons, but accomplished nothing.

At this same time, as no one can mention or hear without great sadness, the mother of all churches, the basilica of the apostle Peter, was taken and plundered by the Moors, or Saracens, who had already occupied the region of Beneventum. The Saracens, moreover, slaughtered all the Christians whom they found outside the walls of Rome, either within or without this church. They also carried men and women away prisoners. They tore down, among many others, the altar of the blessed Peter, and their crimes from day to day bring sorrow to Christians. Pope Sergius departed life this year.

847

After the death of Sergius no mention of the apostolic see has come in any way to our ears. Rabanus [Maurus], master and abbot of Fulda, was solemnly chosen archbishop as the successor of Bishop Otger, who had died. Moreover the Northmen here and there plundered the Christians and engaged in a battle with the counts Sigir and Liuthar. They continued up the Rhine as far as Dordrecht, and nine miles farther to Meginhard, when they turned back, having taken their booty.

849

While King Louis was ill his army of Bavaria took its way against the Bohemians. Many of these were killed and the remainder withdrew, much humiliated, into their own country. The heathen from the North wrought havoc in

From *Annals of Xanten, 845–854,* J. H. Robinson, trans. In *Readings in European History* (Boston, Mass.: Ginn and Co., 1904), Vol. 1, pp. 158–162.

Christendom as usual and grew greater in strength; but it is revolting to say more of this matter.

850

On January 1st of that season, in the octave of the Lord, towards evening, a great deal of thunder was heard and a mighty flash of lightning seen; and an overflow of water afflicted the human race during this winter. In the following summer an all too great heat of the sun burned the earth. Leo, pope of the apostolic see, an extraordinary man, built a fortification round the church of St. Peter the apostle. The Moors, however, devastated here and there the coast towns in Italy. The Norman Rorik, brother of the above-mentioned younger Heriold, who earlier had fled dishonored from Lothaire, again took Dordrecht and did much evil treacherously to the Christians. In the same year so great a peace existed between the two brothers—Emperor Lothaire and King Louis—that they spent many days together in Osning [Westphalia] and there hunted, so that many were astonished thereat; and they went each his way in peace.

851

The bodies of certain saints were sent from Rome to Saxony,—that of Alexander, one of seven brethren, and those of Romanus and Emerentiana. In the same year the very noble empress, Irmingard by name, wife of the emperor Lothaire, departed this world. The Normans inflicted much harm in Frisia and about the Rhine. A mighty army of them collected by the river Elbe against the Saxons, and some of the Saxon towns were besieged, others burned, and most terribly did they oppress the Christians. A meeting of our kings took place on the Maas.

852

The steel of the heathen glistened; excessive heat; a famine followed. There was not fodder enough for the animals. The pasturage for the swine was more than sufficient.

In these difficult times the protection of a local lord often seemed to offer the best chance of survival.

Capitulary of Mersen (Kings Lothar, Lewis, and Charles, 847)

We will moreover that each free man in our kingdom shall choose a lord, from us or our faithful, such a one as he wishes.

We command moreover that no man shall leave his lord without just cause, nor should any one receive him, except in such a way as was customary in the time of our predecessors.

And we wish you to know that we want to grant right to our faithful subjects and we do not wish to do anything to them against reason. Similarly we

From E. P. Cheyney, trans. In *University of Pennsylvania Translations and Reprints* (Philadelphia, Pa.: University of Pennsylvania Press, 1898), Vol. 4, No. 3, pp. 3–15, 18.

admonish you and the rest of our faithful subjects that you grant right to your men and do not act against reason toward them.

And we will that the man of each one of us in whosoever kingdom he is, shall go with his lord against the enemy, or in his other needs unless there shall have been (as may there not be) such an invasion of the kingdom as is called a *landwer*, so that the whole people of that kingdom shall go together to repel it.

The relationship of loyalty between a warrior and his chosen lord goes back to early Teutonic practices. From the seventh century onward we have set formulas of commendation. These early examples are from England and France respectively.

Oaths of Allegiance

Thus shall one take the oath of fidelity:

By the Lord before whom this sanctuary is holy, I will to N. be true and faithful, and love all which he loves and shun all which he shuns, according to the laws of God and the order of the world. Nor will I ever with will or action, through word or deed, do anything which is unpleasing to him, on condition that he will hold to me as I shall deserve it, and that he will perform everything as it was in our agreement when I submitted myself to him and chose his will.

It is right that those who offer to us unbroken fidelity should be protected by our aid. And since *such and such* a faithful one of ours, by the favor of God, coming here in our palace with his arms, has seen fit to swear trust and fidelity to us in our hand, therefore we decree and command by the present precept that for the future *such and such* above mentioned be counted with the number of antrustions. And if anyone perchance should presume to kill him, let him know that he will be judged guilty of his wergild of 600 shillings.

The following ceremony took place in Flanders in 1127.

From *Chronicle of Galbert of Bruges*

Through the whole remaining part of the day those who had been previously enfeoffed by the most pious count Charles, did homage to the count, taking up now again their fiefs and offices and whatever they had before rightfully and legitimately obtained. On Thursday the seventh of April, homages were again made to the count being completed in the following order of faith and security.

First they did their homage thus, the count asked if he was willing to become completely his man, and the other replied, "I am willing"; and with clasped hands, surrounded by the hands of the count, they were bound together by a kiss. Secondly, he who had done homage gave his fealty to the representative of the count in these words, "I promise on my faith that I will in future be faithful to count William, and will observe my homage to him completely against all persons in good faith and without deceit," and thirdly, he took his

From O. J. Thatcher and E. H. McNeal, trans., *A Source Book for Mediaeval History* (New York: Charles Scribner's, 1905), pp. 364–365.

oath to this upon the relics of the saints. Afterward, with a little rod which the count held in his hand, he gave investitures to all who by this agreement had given their security and homage and accompanying oath.

It could often happen that a vassal came to hold fiefs from several different lords. How was the problem of conflicting loyalties resolved?

Liege Homage

I, John of Toul, make known that I am the liege man of the lady Beatrice, countess of Troyes, and of her son, Theobald, count of Champagne, against every creature, living or dead, saving my allegiance to lord Enjorand of Coucy, lord John of Arcis, and the count of Grandpré. If it should happen that the count of Grandpré should be at war with the countess and count of Champagne on his own quarrel, I will aid the count of Grandpré in my own person, and will send to the count and the countess of Champagne the knights whose service I owe to them for the fief which I hold of them. But if the count of Grandpré shall make war on the countess and the count of Champagne on behalf of his friends and not in his own quarrel, I will aid in my own person the countess and count of Champagne, and will send one knight to the count of Grandpré for the service which I owe him for the fief which I hold of him, but I will not go myself into the territory of the count of Grandpré to make war on him.

The Fief

A form of land tenure (precarium) *similar to the later fief existed already in the eighth century. In 747, churches were required to grant out lands as* precaria *to support Frankish warriors. How did the king justify this use of church lands??*

Capitulary of Lestinnes (747)

Because of the threats of war and the attacks of certain tribes on our borders, we have determined, with the consent of God and by the advice of our clergy and people, to appropriate for a time part of the ecclesiastical property for the support of our army. The lands are to be held as *precaria* for a fixed rent; one solidus, or twelve denarii, shall be paid annually to the church or monastery for each *casata* [farm]. When the holder dies the whole possession shall return to the church. If, however, the exigency of the time makes it necessary, the prince may require the *precarium* to be renewed and given out again. Care shall be taken, however, that the churches and monasteries do not incur suffering or poverty through the granting of *precaria*. If the poverty of the church makes it necessary, the whole possession shall be restored to the church.

The grant of a fief often included immunity from royal jurisdiction, leaving the lord free to govern his own lands.

From O. J. Thatcher and E. H. McNeal, trans., *A Source Book for Mediaeval History* (New York: Charles Scribner's, 1905), pp. 357, 353.

Grant of Fief with Immunity (815)

In the name of our Lord and Savior Jesus Christ. Louis, by divine providence emperor, Augustus. Be it known to all our subjects, present and future, that our faithful subject, John, has come to us and commended himself to us, and has besought us to confirm to him the possession of lands [described] which he and his sons and their men have cleared and occupied. He has shown us the charter which he received from our father Charles the Great. We have consented to do this and have done even more; we have given him certain villas [named] with their extent and dependencies . . . granting that he and his sons and his posterity may hold them in peace and security. No count, *vicarius*, or their subordinates, or any other public official shall presume to judge or constrain any persons living on those lands, but John and his sons and their posterity shall judge and constrain them. . . .

Sometimes the "gift" of a fief merely recognized a seizure of lands that the king could not defend. Thus King Charles of France founded the Duchy of Normandy by conferring on a Viking, Rollo, territories that Rollo had already conquered. Why did Rollo object to the ceremony of homage?

Foundation of the Duchy of Normandy (911)

At the agreed time Charles and Rollo came together at the place that had been decided on. . . . Looking on Rollo, the invader of France, the Franks said to one another, "This duke who has fought such battles against the warriors of this realm is a man of great power and great courage and prowess and good counsel and of great energy too." Then, persuaded by the words of the Franks, Rollo put his hands between the hands of the king, a thing which his father and grandfather and great-grandfather had never done; and so the king gave his daughter Gisela in marriage to the duke and conferred on him the agreed lands from the River Epte to the sea as his property in hereditary right, together with all Brittany from which he could live.

Rollo was not willing to kiss the foot of the king. The bishops said, "Anyone who receives such a gift ought to be eager to kiss the king's foot." He replied, "I have never bent my knees at anyone's knees, nor will I kiss anyone's foot." But, urged by the entreaties of the Franks, he commanded one of his warriors to kiss the foot of the king. The warrior promptly seized the king's foot, carried it to his mouth and kissed it standing up while the king was thrown flat on his back. At that there was a great outburst of laughter and great excitement among the people. Nevertheless King Charles, Duke Robert, the counts and nobles, the bishops and abbots swore by the Catholic faith and by their lives, limbs and the honor of the whole kingdom to the noble Rollo that he should hold and possess the land described above and pass it on to his heirs.

From *De Moribus et Actis Primorum Normanniae Ducum, Mémoires de la Société des Antiquaires de Normandie,* 3e Série, III (1858), pp. 165–169, trans. Brian Tierney in *Great Issues in Western Civilization,* 3rd ed., Brian Tierney, Donald Kagan, and L. Pearce Williams, eds. (New York: Random House, 1976). Copyright © 1967, 1972, 1976 by Random House, Inc. Reprinted by permission of the publisher.

Feudal Obligations

Bishop Fulbert of Chartres gave a somewhat idealized description of feudal relationships. What were the duties of lord and vassal to one another?

From *Fulbert of Chartres*

To William most glorious duke of the Aquitanians, bishop Fulbert the favor of his prayers.

Asked to write something concerning the form of fealty, I have noted briefly for you on the authority of the books the things which follow. He who swears fealty to his lord ought always to have these six things in memory; what is harmless, safe, honorable, useful, easy, practicable. Harmless, that is to say that he should not be injurious to his lord in his body; safe, that he should not be injurious to him in his secrets or in the defenses through which he is able to be secure; honorable, that he should not be injurious to him in his justice or in other matters that pertain to his honor; useful, that he should not be injurious to him in his possessions; easy or practicable, that that good which his lord is able to do easily, he make not difficult, nor that which is practicable he make impossible to him.

However, that the faithful vassal should avoid these injuries is proper, but not for this does he deserve his holding; for it is not sufficient to abstain from evil, unless what is good is done also. It remains, therefore, that in the same six things mentioned above he should faithfully counsel and aid his lord, if he wishes to be looked upon as worthy of his benefice and to be safe concerning the fealty which he has sworn.

The lord also ought to act toward his faithful vassal reciprocally in all these things. And if he does not do this he will be justly considered guilty of bad faith, just as the former, if he should be detected in the avoidance of or the doing of or the consenting to them, would be perfidious and perjured.

I would have written to you at greater length, if I had not been occupied with many other things, including the rebuilding of our city and church which was lately entirely consumed in a great fire; from which loss though we could not for a while be diverted, yet by the hope of the comfort of God and of you we breathe again.

The next three readings define feudal obligations more specifically.

Feudal Aids

Next it is proper to see the chief aids of Normandy, which are called chief because they should be paid to the chief lords.

In Normandy there are three chief aids. One is to make the oldest son of his lord a knight; the second, to marry his oldest daughter; the third to ransom the body of his lord from prison when he is taken in the Duke's war.

From E. P. Cheyney, *University of Pennsylvania Translations and Reprints* (Philadelphia, Pa.: University of Pennsylvania Press, 1898), Vol. 4, No. 3, pp. 23–24.

Knight Service

The baron and all vassals of the king are bound to appear before him when he shall summon them, and to serve him at their own expense for forty days and forty nights, with as many knights as each one owes; and he is able to exact from them these services when he wishes and when he has need of them. And if the king wishes to keep them more than forty days at their own expense, they are not bound to remain if they do not wish it. And if the king wishes to keep them at his expense for the defence of the realm, they are bound to remain. And if the king wishes to lead them outside of the kingdom, they need not go unless they wish to, for they have already served their forty days and forty nights.

Court Service

To every lord it is allowed to summon his man that he may be at right to him in his court; and even if he is resident at the most distant manor of that honor from which he holds, he shall go to the plea if his lord summons him. If his lord holds different fiefs the man of one honor is not compelled by law to go to another plea, unless the cause belongs to the other to which his lord has summoned him.

When a vassal died leaving a widow with dependent children they fell under the lord's control. A king might hold many such wardships at a given time as indicated in the following excerpts recording payments to the English exchequer. How did the king profit from these wardships? What evidence do the records provide about marriage practices in medieval society?

Wardship and Marriage

Alice, countess of Warwick, renders account of £1000 and 10 palfreys to be allowed to remain a widow as long as she pleases, and not to be forced to marry by the king. And if perchance she should wish to marry, she shall not marry except with the assent and on the grant of the king, where the king shall be satisfied; and to have the custody of her sons whom she has from the earl of Warwick her late husband.

Hawisa, who was wife of William Fitz Robert renders account of 130 marks and 4 palfreys that she may have peace from Peter of Borough to whom the king has given permission to marry her; and that she may not be compelled to marry.

Geoffrey de Mandeville owes 20,000 marks to have as his wife Isabella, countess of Gloucester, with all the lands and tenements and fiefs which fall to her.

Thomas de Colville renders an account of 100 marks for having the custody of the sons of Roger Torpel and their land until they come of age.

From *Le Grand Coutumier de Normandie, Les Etablissements de St. Louis, Leges Henrici Primi*, E. P. Cheyney, trans. in *University of Pennsylvania Translations and Reprints* (Philadelphia, Pa.: University of Pennsylvania Press, 1898), Vol. 4, No. 3, pp. 28–33.
From *English Exchequer Rolls*, E. P. Cheyney, trans. In *University of Pennsylvania Translations and Reprints* (Philadelphia, Pa.: University of Pennsylvania Press, 1898), Vol. 4, No. 3, p. 27.

William, bishop of Ely, owes 220 marks for having the custody of Stephen de Beauchamp with his inheritance and for marrying him where he wishes.

William of St. Mary's church, renders an account of 500 marks for having the custody of the heir of Robert Young, son of Robert Fitzharding, with all his inheritance and all its appurtenances and franchises; that is to say with the services of knights and gifts of churches and marriages of women, and to be allowed to marry him to whatever one of his relatives he wishes; and that all his land is to revert to him freely when he comes of age.

Bartholomew de Muleton renders an account of 100 marks for having the custody of the land and the heiress of Lambert of Ibtoft, and for marrying the wife of the same Lambert to whomsoever he wishes where she shall not be disparaged and that he may be able to confer her (the heiress) upon whom he wishes.

Violence and Restraint

From around the year 1000, bishops sought to restrain random violence by persuading feudal lords to observe a "Peace of God." The following peace oath was proposed by Bishop Warin of Beavais in 1023. What does it suggest about everyday conditions in early feudal society?

Peace Oath of Bishop Warin, 1023

I will not invade a church for any reason. . . . I will not assault an unarmed cleric or monk, nor anyone walking with him who is not carrying a spear or a shield, nor will I seize their horse unless they are committing a crime or unless it is in recompense for a crime for which they would not make amends, fifteen days after my warning. I will not seize bulls, cows, pigs, sheep, lambs, goats, asses or the burden they bear, mares, or their untamed colts.

I will not seize villeins of either sex, or sergeants or merchants, or their coins, or hold them for ransom, or ruin them with exactions on account of their lord's war, or whip them for their possessions. I will not exact by extortion mules and horses, male and female, and colts pasturing in the fields from the first of March to All Souls' Day unless I should find them doing damage to me. I will not burn or destroy houses unless I find an enemy horseman or thief within, and unless they are joined to a real castle. I will not cut down or uproot the vineyards of another, or harvest them for reasons of war, unless it is on my land, or what, to my knowledge, ought to be my land. I will not destroy a mill, or seize the grain that is in it, unless I am on a cavalcade, or with the host, or it is on my land.

I will not, to my knowledge, harbor or assist an admitted and notorious public robber. And that man who will break this peace knowingly, I will not protect him after I learn of it, and if he did it unknowingly and came to me for protection, either I will make amends for him, or I will make him make amends within fifteen days after I have been informed, or I will deny him my protection.

From "Peace Oath of Bishop Warin," R. Landes trans. in T. Head and R. Landes, *The Peace of God* (Ithaca, N.Y.: Cornell University Press, 1992), pp. 332–333.

I will not attack merchants or pilgrims or take their possessions unless they commit crimes. I will not kill the animals of villeins except for my consumption or that of my men. I will not plunder a villein or take his property at the perfidious instigation of his lord. I will not assault noble women in the absence of their husbands, or those who travel with them, unless I should find them committing misdeeds against me; and the same holds for widows and nuns. I will not take wine from those who carry it in carts or take their oxen. I will not capture hunters or take their horses or dogs, unless, as it is said, I find them doing me damage. And from those who will have sworn this [oath] and keep it in my regard—with the exception of lands that are mine by freehold or benefice or by delegation, and except when building or besieging a castle, or when I am in the host of the king or our bishops, or on cavalcade—I will accept only what I need for subsistence, and I will take nothing home with me except horseshoes, and I will not break into the protected areas of churches while on the aforementioned military expeditions, unless they refuse to sell me what I need to live.

From the beginning of Lent until the end of Easter, I will not assault unarmed horsemen or take their possessions, and if a villein should do damage to another villein or horseman, before I seize him, first I will make complaints about him and await fifteen days for satisfaction before punishing him, but no more than the law allows.

The spiritual penalties imposed by bishops were more effective when they were backed by the power of a king. Louis VI (1108–1131) waged frequent campaigns against the "robber barons" in the region of Paris. How did king and church cooperate in this work?

From *Suger's Life of Louis VI*

A king, when he takes the royal power, vows to put down with his strong right arm insolent tyrants whensoever he sees them vex the state with endless wars, rejoice in rapine, oppress the poor, destroy the churches, give themselves over to lawlessness which, and it be not checked, would flame out into ever greater madness; for the evil spirits who instigate them are wont cruelly to strike down those whom they fear to lose, but give free rein to those whom they hope to hold, while they add fuel to the flames which are to devour their victims to all eternity.

Such an utterly abandoned man was Thomas of Marle. While King Louis was busied with many wars, he laid waste the territories of Laon, Rheims, and Amiens, devouring like a raging wolf. He spared not the clergy—fearing not the vengeance of the Church—nor the people for humanity's sake. And the devil aided him, for the success of the foolish does ever lead them to perdition. Slaying all men, spoiling all things, he seized two manors, exceeding rich, from the abbey of the nuns of St. John of Laon. He fortified the two exceeding strong castles, Crécy and Nogent, with a marvelous wall and very high towers, as if they had been his own; and made them like to a den of dragons and a cave of

From J. H. Robinson, trans. in *Readings in European History* (Boston, Mass.: Ginn and Co., 1904), Vol. 1, pp. 202–204.

robbers, whence he did waste almost the whole country with fire and pillage; and he had no pity.

The Church of France could no longer bear this great evil; wherefore the clergy, who had met together in a general synod at Beauvais, proceeded to pass sentence of condemnation upon the enemy of the Church's true spouse, Jesus Christ. The venerable Cono, bishop of Praeneste and legate of the holy Roman Church, troubled past endurance by the plaints of churches, of the orphans, of the poor, did smite this ruthless tyrant with the sword of the blessed Peter, which is general anathema. He did also ungird the knightly sword belt from him, though he was absent, and by the judgment of all declared him infamous, a scoundrel, unworthy the name of Christian.

And the king was moved by the plaints of this great council and led an army against him right quickly. He had the clergy, to whom he was ever humbly devoted, in his company, and marched straight against the castle of Crécy. Well fortified was it; yet he took it unprepared because his soldiers smote with an exceeding strong hand; or rather, because the hand of the Lord fought for him. He stormed the strongest tower as if it were the hut of a peasant, and put to confusion the wicked men and piously destroyed the impious. Because they had no pity upon other men, he cut them down without mercy. None could behold the castle tower flaming like the fires of hell and not exclaim, "The whole universe will fight for him against these madmen."

After he had won this victory, the king, who was ever swift to follow up his advantage, pushed forward toward the other castle, called Nogent. There came to him a man who said: "Oh, my lord king, it should be known to thy Serenity that in that wicked castle dwell exceeding wicked men who are worthy to lie in hell, and there only. Those are they who, when thou didst issue commands to destroy the commune of Laon, did burn with fire not only the city of Laon, but the noble church of the Mother of God, and many others beside. And well-nigh all the noble men of the city suffered martyrdom because they were true to their faith and defended their lord the bishop. And these evil men feared not to raise their hands against thy venerable Bishop Gaudin, the anointed of the Lord, defender of the church, but did him most cruelly to death, and exposed his naked body on the open road for beasts and birds of prey to feed upon; but first they cut off his finger with the pontifical ring. And they have agreed together, persuaded by the wicked Thomas, to attack and hold your tower."

The king was doubly animated by these words, and he attacked the wicked castle, broke open the abominable places of confinement, like prisons of hell, and set free the innocent; the guilty he punished with very heavy punishment. He alone avenged the injuries of many. Athirst for justice, he ordained that whatsoever murderous wretches he came upon should be fastened to a gibbet, and left as common food for the greed of kites, crows, and vultures. And this they deserved who had not feared to raise their hand against the Lord's anointed.

When he had taken these two adulterine castles and given back to the monastery of St. John the domains that had been seized, he returned to the city of Amiens and laid siege to a tower of that city which was held by a certain

Adam, a cruel tyrant who was laying waste the churches and all the regions round about. He held the place besieged for hard upon two years, and at last forced those who defended it to give themselves up. When he had taken it he destroyed it utterly, and thus brought peace to the realm. He fulfilled most worthily the duty of a king who beareth not the sword in vain, and he deprived the wicked Thomas and his heirs forever of the lordship over that city.

REFORM OF THE CHURCH

Abuses, Theocracy, and Reform

The influence of the church on early feudal society was limited because the churches themselves often fell under the control of kings or local nobles. Often churches were bought and sold like pieces of private property. The plaintiff in the following case, Count Berengar of Narbonne, was addressing a church council in 1056. What did he complain about?

Complaint of Berengar of Narbonne, 1056

The archbishopric of Narbonne used to belong to my uncle, Archbishop Ermengaud, and in his day it was one of the best bishoprics between Rome and Spain, richly endowed with manors and castles, with estates and allodial lands. The church, filled with books and adorned with gilded pictures, caskets and crucifixes, was resplendent with golden crowns and precious stones. The voices of many canons were heard at regular hours, prayers were offered, and all good works increased. . . .

But, when the aforementioned archbishop of holy memory died, Count Wifred of Cerdana, to whom my wife was a kinswoman, came to Narbonne and approached both my parents and myself to obtain the archbishopric for his son, who was only ten years old at the time; and he offered a great gift of a hundred thousand *solidi* to my father and the count of Rodez. But my father and mother would not agree. I, however, moved by regard for his kinship and deceived by his pretence of friendship, broke with my parents over this matter and declared that I would destroy them if they did not give way to me. My father, seeing me so moved and so hostile to him acceded to my wishes and to the requests of Wifred, and, having received a hundred thousand *solidi* for ourselves and the count of Rodez as the price of the bishopric, we gave it to Wifred's son, our bishop. Calling God to witness and swearing an oath, he gave his firm word and pledged his faith that if he was to be our bishop, as he was and is, no injury would be done to us or ours or to the bishopric. I was confident that when he was enthroned in the cathedral and grew in years and honor he would be a pro-

From Brian Tierney, trans., *The Crisis of Church and State, 1050–1300* (New York: Prentice-Hall, 1964), pp. 29–30. Copyright © 1964 by Prentice-Hall, Inc. Reprinted courtesy of the publisher.

tection to me and a shield against the spears of all my enemies, that he would remember his kinship to my wife and how I had helped to place him in a position of such honor, and that, as he had declared, he would help me to have and to hold my honor. But then, arrogant as a devil, he unexpectedly provoked me to anger and harassed me and built castles against me and made cruel war on me with a vast army, so that on account of him almost a thousand men were slaughtered on both sides. Then he snatched away from God and his ministers the castles and manors, estates and possessions of the aforesaid church, together with the revenues and possessions of the canons and what they held in common, and gave them to the devil and his servants. . . .

Before the late eleventh century the church generally supported the claim of kings to rule by divine right. Kings were called vicars of God. They regularly appointed bishops in the territories they ruled. They were crowned in a solemn ecclesiastical ceremony.

Coronation of Otto I, 936

Going to the altar and taking from it the sword with swordbelt and turning to the king, [Archbishop Hildibert] said:

"Accept this sword, with which you may chase out all the adversaries of Christ, barbarians and bad Christians, by the divine authority handed down to you and by the power of all the empire of the Franks, for the most lasting peace of all Christians."

Then taking the bracelets and cloak, he clothed him saying, "These points [of the cloak] falling to ground will remind you with what zeal of faith you should burn and how you ought to endure in preserving peace to the end."

Then taking the scepter and staff, he said: "With these symbols you may be reminded that you should reproach your subjects with paternal castigation, but first of all you should extend the hand of mercy to ministers of God, widows, and orphans. And never let the oil of compassion be absent from your head in order that you may be crowned with eternal reward in the present and in the future."

After having been sprinkled with holy oil and crowned with a golden diadem by the bishops Hildibert and Wikfried [of Cologne, 924–953] and all legal consecration having been completed, the king was led to the throne, to which he ascended by means of a spiral staircase. The throne of marvelous beauty had been constructed between two marble pillars, and from there the king could see and be seen by all.

After the divine praise was intoned and the mass was solemnly celebrated, the king descended from the throne and walked to the palace. Going up to a marble table decorated with regal utensils, he sat down with the bishops and all the people while the dukes waited on them.

From Widukind of Corvey, *Res gestae Saxonicae*, Boyd R. Hill trans. in *The Rise of the First Reich* (New York: John Wiley and Sons, 1969), p. 14.

In 1046 King Henry established a line of reforming popes at Rome. The reformers at first attacked two widespread abuses of the time—simony (the buying and selling of spiritual offices) and clerical marriage (priests were supposed to be celibate according to the discipline of the early church). But the more extreme reformers came to believe that the root cause of all the abuses was lay control of church offices. They objected especially to lay rulers investing their bishops with the ring and staff that were the symbols of sacred authority. Under Pope Gregory VII (1073–1085) the reform movement took a radical turn.

Papal Reform Decrees (1074–1075)

Those who have been advanced to any grade of holy orders, or to any office, through simony, that is, by the payment of money, shall hereafter have no right to officiate in the holy church. Those also who have secured churches by giving money shall certainly be deprived of them.

If there are any priests, deacons, or subdeacons who are married, by the power of omnipotent God and the authority of St. Peter we forbid them to enter a church until they repent and mend their ways. But if any remain with their wives, no one shall dare hear them [when they officiate in the church], because their benediction is turned into a curse, and their prayer into a sin. For the Lord says through the prophet, "I will curse your blessings" [Mal. 2:2]. Whoever shall refuse to obey this most salutary command shall be guilty of the sin of idolatry. For Samuel says: "For rebellion is as the sin of witchcraft, and stubbornness is as iniquity and idolatry" [1 Sam. 15:23]. Whoever therefore asserts that he is a Christian but refuses to obey the apostolic see, is guilty of paganism.

Since we know that investitures have been made by laymen in many places, contrary to the decrees of the holy fathers, and that very many disturbances injurious to the Christian religion have thereby arisen in the church, we therefore decree: that no clergyman shall receive investiture of a bishopric, monastery, or church from the hand of the emperor, or the king, or any lay person, man or woman. And if anyone has ventured to receive such investiture, let him know that it is annulled by apostolic authority, and that he is subject to excommunication until he has made due reparation.

In prohibiting lay investiture Gregory was challenging King Henry IV of Germany who was seeking to install his own candidate as archbishop of Milan. Anticipating an open conflict with Henry, Gregory set down his conception of the papal office in the Dictatus Papae, *"Assertions of the Pope." This document has been called "revolutionary." What might be considered revolutionary about it? How does it compare with earlier assertions of papal power (see pp. 166, 167)?*

Dictatus Papae (1075)

1. That the Roman church was founded by God alone.

2. That the Roman pontiff alone can with right be called universal.

From O. J. Thatcher and E. H. McNeal, trans., *A Source Book for Mediaeval History* (New York: Charles Scribner's, 1905), pp. 135–136.

3. That he alone can depose or reinstate bishops.

4. That, in a council, his legate, even if a lower grade, is above all bishops, and can pass sentence of deposition against them.

5. That the pope may depose the absent.

6. That, among other things, we ought not to remain in the same house with those excommunicated by him.

7. That for him alone is it lawful, according to the needs of the time, to make new laws, to assemble together new congregations, to make an abbey of a canonry; and, on the other hand, to divide a rich bishopric and unite the poor ones.

8. That he alone may use the imperial insignia.

9. That of the pope alone all princes shall kiss the feet.

10. That his name alone shall be spoken in the churches.

11. That this is the only name in the world.

12. That it may be permitted to him to depose emperors.

13. That he may be permitted to transfer bishops if need be.

14. That he has power to ordain a clerk of any church he may wish.

15. That he who is ordained by him may *preside* over another church, but may not hold a subordinate position; and that such a one may not receive a higher grade from any bishop.

16. That no synod shall be called a general one without his order.

17. That no chapter and no book shall be considered canonical without his authority.

18. That a sentence passed by him may be retracted by no one; and that he himself, alone of all, may retract it.

19. That he himself may be judged by no one.

20. That no one shall dare to condemn one who appeals to the apostolic chair.

21. That to the latter should be referred the more important cases of every church.

22. That the Roman church has never erred; nor will it err to all eternity, the Scripture bearing witness.

From E. F. Henderson, ed., *Select Historical Documents of the Middle Ages* (London: Sons, 1892), pp. 366–367.

23. That the Roman pontiff, if he have been canonically ordained, is undoubtedly made a saint by the merits of St. Peter; St. Ennodius, bishop of Pavia, bearing witness, and many holy fathers agreeing with him. As is contained in the decrees of St. Symmachus the pope.

24. That, by his command and consent, it may be lawful for subordinates to bring accusations.

25. That he may depose and reinstate bishops without assembling a synod.

26. That he who is not at peace with the Roman church shall not be considered catholic.

27. That he may absolve subjects from their fealty to wicked men.

Empire and Papacy

Henry IV refused to obey the pope's decrees. When Gregory threatened to depose him the king denounced Gregory as a usurper.

Henry IV to Gregory VII (January 24, 1076)

Henry, king not through usurpation but through the holy ordination of God, to Hildebrand, at present not pope but false monk. Such greeting as this hast thou merited through thy disturbances, inasmuch as there is no grade in the church which thou hast omitted to make a partaker not of honour but of confusion, not of benediction but of malediction. For, to mention few and especial cases out of many, not only hast thou not feared to lay hands upon the rulers of the holy church, the anointed of the Lord—the archbishops, namely, bishops and priests—but thou hast trodden them under foot like slaves ignorant of what their master is doing. Thou hast won favour from the common herd by crushing them; thou hast looked upon all of them as knowing nothing, upon thy sole self, moreover, as knowing all things. This knowledge, however, thou hast used not for edification but for destruction; so that with reason we believe that St. Gregory, whose name thou hast usurped for thyself, was prophesying concerning thee when he said: "The pride of him who is in power increases the more, the greater the number of those subject to him; and he thinks that he himself can do more than all." And we, indeed, have endured all this, being eager to guard the honour of the apostolic see; thou, however, hast understood our humility to be fear, and hast not, accordingly, shunned to rise up against the royal power conferred upon us by God, daring to threaten to divest us of it. As if we had received our kingdom from thee! As if the kingdom and the empire were in thine and not in God's hand! And this although our Lord Jesus Christ did call us to the kingdom, did not, however, call thee to the priesthood. For thou has ascended by the following steps. By wiles, namely, which the profession of monk

From E. F. Henderson, ed., *Select Historical Documents of the Middle Ages* (London: George Bell and ⁀ons, 1892), pp. 372–373.

abhors, thou hast achieved money; by money, favour; by the sword, the throne of peace. And from the throne of peace thou hast disturbed peace, inasmuch as thou hast armed subjects against those in authority over them; inasmuch as thou, who were not called, hast taught that our bishops called of God are to be despised; inasmuch as thou hast usurped for laymen the ministry over their priests, allowing them to depose or condemn those whom they themselves had received as teachers from the hand of God through the laying on of hands of the bishops. On me also who, although unworthy to be among the anointed, have nevertheless been anointed to the kingdom, thou hast lain thy hand; me who— as the tradition of the holy Fathers teaches, declaring that I am not to be deposed for any crime unless, which God forbid, I should have strayed from the faith— am subject to the judgment of God alone. For the wisdom of the holy fathers committed even Julian the apostate not to themselves, but to God alone, to be judged and to be deposed. For himself the true pope, Peter, also exclaims: "Fear God, honour the king." But thou who dost not fear God, dost dishonour in me his appointed one. Wherefore St. Paul, when he has not spared an angel of Heaven if he shall have preached otherwise, has not excepted thee also who dost teach otherwise upon earth. For he says: "If any one, either I or an angel from Heaven, should preach a gospel other than that which has been preached to you, he shall be damned." Thou, therefore, damned by this curse and by the judgment of all our bishops and by our own, descend and relinquish the apostolic chair which thou hast usurped. Let another ascend the throne of St. Peter, who shall not practise violence under the cloak of religion, but shall teach the sound doctrine of St. Peter. I Henry, king by the grace of God, do say unto thee, together with all our bishops: Descend, descend, to be damned throughout the ages.

Gregory responded with a sentence of deposition. On what grounds did he claim the power to depose a king?

Deposition of Henry IV (February 22, 1076)

O St. Peter, chief of the apostles, incline to us, I beg, thy holy ears, and hear me thy servant whom thou hast nourished from infancy, and whom, until this day, thou hast freed from the hand of the wicked, who have hated and do hate me for my faithfulness to thee. Thou, and my mistress the mother of God, and thy brother St. Paul are witnesses for me among all the saints that thy holy Roman church drew me to its helm against my will; that I had no thought of ascending thy chair through force, and that I would rather have ended my life as a pilgrim than, by secular means, to have seized thy throne for the sake of earthly glory. And therefore I believe it to be through thy grace and not through my own deeds that it has pleased and does please thee that the Christian people, who have been especially committed to thee, should obey me. And especially to me, as thy representative and by thy favour, has the power been granted by God of binding and loosing in Heaven and on earth. On the strength of this

From E. F. Henderson, ed., *Select Historical Documents of the Middle Ages* (London: George Bell and Sons, 1892), pp. 376–377.

belief therefore, for the honour and security of thy church, in the name of Almighty God, Father, Son and Holy Ghost, I withdraw, through thy power and authority, from Henry the king, son of Henry the emperor, who has risen against thy church with unheard of insolence, the rule over the whole kingdom of the Germans and over Italy. And I absolve all Christians from the bonds of the oath which they have made or shall make to him; and I forbid any one to serve him as king. For it is fitting that he who strives to lessen the honour of thy church should himself lose the honour which belongs to him. And since he has scorned to obey as a Christian, and has not returned to God whom he had deserted— holding intercourse with the excommunicated; practising manifold iniquities; spurning my commands which, as thou dost bear witness, I issued to him for his own salvation; separating himself from thy church and striving to rend it— I bind him in thy stead with the chain of the anathema. And, leaning on thee, I so bind him that the people may know and have proof that thou art Peter, and above thy rock the Son of the living God hath built His church, and the gates of Hell shall not prevail against it.

These two depositions called into question the whole leadership of Christian society. When the two powers conflicted, who was supreme—pope or king? Gregory's condemnation of Henry provoked a rebellion in Germany and in 1077 Henry had to seek absolution from the pope. Gregory sent this account of Henry's submission to his allies, the German princes.

Gregory VII to the Princes of Germany (1077)

Bishop Gregory, servant of the servants of God, to all the archbishops, bishops, dukes, counts and other princes of the realm of the Germans who defend the Christian faith, greeting and apostolic benediction.

Inasmuch as for love of justice ye assumed common cause and danger with us in the struggle of Christian warfare, we have taken care to indicate to you, beloved, with sincere affection, how the king, humbled to penance, obtained the pardon of absolution and how the whole affair has progressed since his entry into Italy up to the present time. . . .

He also, before entering Italy, sent on to us suppliant legates, offering in all things to render satisfaction to God, to St. Peter and to us. And he renewed his promise that, besides amending his life, he would observe all obedience if only he might merit to obtain from us the favour of absolution and the apostolic benediction. When, after long deferring this and holding frequent consultations, we had, through all the envoys who passed, severely taken him to task for his excesses: he came at length of his own accord, with a few followers, showing nothing of hostility or boldness, to the town of Canossa where we were tarrying. And there, having laid aside all the belongings of royalty, wretchedly, with bare feet and clad in wool, he continued for three days to stand before the gate of the castle. Nor did he desist from imploring with many tears the aid and con-

From E. F. Henderson, ed., *Select Historical Documents of the Middle Ages* (London: George Bell and Sons, 1892), pp. 385–387.

solation of the apostolic mercy until he had moved all of those who were present there, and whom the report of it reached, to such pity and depth of compassion that, interceding for him with many prayers and tears, all wondered indeed at the unaccustomed hardness of our heart, while some actually cried out that we were exercising, not the gravity of apostolic severity, but the cruelty, as it were, of a tyrannical ferocity.

Finally, conquered by the persistency of his compunction and by the constant supplications of all those who were present, we loosed the chain of the anathema and at length received him into the favour of communion and into the lap of the holy mother church, those being accepted as sponsors for him whose names are written below. And of this transaction we also received a confirmation at the hands of the abbot of Cluny, of our daughters Matilda and the countess Adelaide, and of such princes, episcopal and lay, as seemed to us useful for this purpose.

Having thus accomplished these matters, we desire at the first opportunity to cross over to your parts in order that, by God's aid, we may more fully arrange all things for the peace of the church and the concord of the kingdom, as has long been our wish. For we desire, beloved, that ye should know beyond a doubt that the whole question at issue is as yet so little cleared up—as ye can learn from the sponsors mentioned—that both our coming and the unanimity of your counsels are extremely necessary. Wherefore strive ye all to continue in the faith in which ye have begun and in the love of justice; and know that we are not otherwise bound to the king save that, by word alone as is our custom, we have said that he might have hopes from us in those matters in which, without danger to his soul or to our own, we might be able to help him to his salvation and honour either through justice or through mercy.

In 1080 Henry defied Gregory again and Gregory deposed him for a second time. When Bishop Hermann of Metz questioned the pope's right to depose a king Gregory sent him a detailed explanation of the papal claim. How did Gregory's attitude to royal power differ from that of Pope Gelasius or of Archbishop Hildebert (see pp. 167, 197)?

Gregory VII to Hermann of Metz (1081)

Thy demand to be aided, as it were, by our writings and fortified against the madness of those who babble forth with unhallowed mouth that the authority of the holy and apostolic see had no right to excommunicate Henry—a man who despises the Christian law; a destroyer, namely, of the churches and of the empire; a favourer of heretics and a partaker with them—or to absolve any one from the oath of fealty to him, does not seem to us to be altogether necessary when so many and such absolutely certain proofs are to be found in the pages of Holy Scripture. . . .

For, to cite a few passages from among many, who does not know the words of our Lord and Saviour Jesus Christ who says in the gospel: "Thou art Peter and

From E. F. Henderson, ed., *Select Historical Documents of the Middle Ages* (London: George Bell and Sons, 1892), pp. 394–395.

upon this rock will I build my church, and the gates of hell shall not prevail against it; and I will give unto thee the keys of the kingdom of Heaven; and whatsoever thou shalt bind upon earth shall be bound also in Heaven, and whatsoever thou shalt loose upon earth shall be loosed also in Heaven"? Are kings excepted here, or do they not belong to the sheep which the Son of God committed to St. Peter? Who, I ask, in this universal concession of the power of binding and loosing, can think that he is withdrawn from the authority of St. Peter, unless, perhaps, that unfortunate man who is unwilling to bear the yoke of the Lord and subjects himself to the burden of the devil, refusing to be among the number of Christ's sheep? It will help him little to his wretched liberty, indeed, that he shake from his proud neck the divinely granted power of Peter. For the more any one, through pride, refuses to bear it, the more heavily shall it press upon him unto damnation at the judgment. . . .

Who does not know that kings and leaders are sprung from those who—ignorant of God—by pride, plunder, perfidy, murders—in a word by almost every crime, the devil, who is the prince of this world, urging them on as it were—have striven with blind cupidity and intolerable presumption to dominate over their equals; namely, over men? To whom, indeed, can we better compare them, when they seek to make the priests of God bend to their footprints, than to him who is head over all the sons of pride and who, tempting the Highest Pontiff Himself, the Head of priests, the Son of the Most High, and promising to Him all the kingdoms of the world, said: "All these I will give unto Thee if Thou wilt fall down and worship me"? Who can doubt but that the priests of Christ are to be considered the fathers and masters of kings and princes and of all the faithful? . . .

In the different kingdoms of the earth, from the beginning of the world, very few of the innumerable multitude of kings are found to have been holy: whereas in one see alone—the Roman one, namely—almost a hundred of the successive pontiffs since the time of St. Peter the apostle are counted among the most holy. Why, then, is this—except that the kings and princes of the earth, enticed by vain glory, prefer, as has been said, the things that are their own to the things that are spiritual; but the pontiffs of the church, despising vain glory, prefer to carnal things the things that are of God? The former readily punish those who sin against themselves and are indifferent to those who sin against God; the latter quickly pardon those who sin against themselves and do not lightly spare those who sin against God. The former, too much bent on earthly deeds, think slightingly of spiritual ones; the latter, sedulously meditating on heavenly things, despise the things which are of earth.

Therefore all Christians who desire to reign with Christ should be warned not to strive to rule through ambition of worldly power. . . . Let them always prefer the honour of God to their own; let them cherish and guard justice by observing the rights of every man; let them not walk in the counsel of the ungodly but, with an assenting heart, always consort with good men. Let them not seek to subject to themselves or to subjugate the holy church as a handmaid; but chiefly let them strive, by recognizing the teachers and fathers, to honour in due form her eyes—namely the priests of God. For if we are ordered to honour our carnal fathers and mothers—how much more our spiritual ones!

The dispute over lay investiture was never settled in the lifetimes of Gregory VII and Henry IV. A compromise was finally reached in 1122. What did the king concede? What did the pope concede?

Concordat of Worms

Privilege of Pope Calixtus II

I, bishop Calixtus, servant of the servants of God, do grant to thee beloved son, Henry—by the grace of God august emperor of the Romans—that the elections of the bishops and abbots of the German kingdom, who belong to the kingdom, shall take place in thy presence, without simony and without any violence; so that if any discord shall arise between the parties concerned, thou, by the counsel or judgment of the metropolitan and the co-provincials, may'st give consent and aid to the party which has the more right. The one elected, moreover, without any exaction may receive the regalia from thee through the lance, and shall do unto thee for these what he rightfully should. But he who is consecrated in the other parts of thy empire (*i.e.* Burgundy and Italy) shall, within six months, and without any exaction, receive the regalia from thee through the lance, and shall do unto thee for these what he rightfully should. Excepting all things which are known to belong to the Roman church. Concerning matters, however, in which thou dost make complaint to me, and dost demand aid,—I, according to the duty of my office, will furnish aid to thee. I give unto thee true peace.

Edict of the Emperor Henry V

In the name of the holy and indivisible Trinity, I, Henry, by the grace of God august emperor of the Romans, for the love of God and of the holy Roman church and of our master pope Calixtus, and for the healing of my soul, do remit to God, and to the holy apostles of God, Peter and Paul, and to the holy catholic church, all investiture through ring and staff; and do grant that in all the churches that are in my kingdom or empire there may be canonical election and free consecration. All the possessions and regalia of St. Peter which, from the beginning of this discord unto his day, whether in the time of my father or also in mine, have been abstracted, and which I hold: I restore to that same holy Roman church. As to those things, moreover, which I do not hold, I will faithfully aid in their restoration. As to the possessions also of all other churches and princes, and of all others lay and clerical persons which have been lost in that war: according to the counsel of the princes, or according to justice, I will restore the things that I hold; and of those things which I do not hold I will faithfully aid in the restoration. And I grant true peace to our master pope Calixtus, and to the holy Roman church, and to all those who are or have been on its side. And in matters where the holy Roman church shall demand aid I will grant it; and in matters concerning which it shall make complaint to me I will duly grant to it justice.

From E. F. Henderson, ed., *Select Historical Documents of the Middle Ages* (London: George Bell and Sons, 1892), pp. 397–398, 403–404.

THE FIRST CRUSADERS

Western Views

The mixture of feudal warrior ethics and religious enthusiasm that inspired the crusades is captured perfectly in The Song of Roland *(written toward 1100). The story is set in the days of Charlemagne but it reflects the ideals of the eleventh-century crusaders against the Saracens of Spain. (The hero, Roland, commanding Charlemagne's rear guard, refuses out of pride to sound his horn in order to recall the main army when he is attacked by a host of Saracens.) What kind of audiences would most enjoy this kind of story? What would they find to admire in Roland and Oliver? What do you think of the attempt to unite Christian zeal and warrior violence that characterized the whole crusading movement?*

From *The Song of Roland*

> The pagans put Saracen hauberks on,
> Most of them reinforced with triple mail;
> They lace the splendid Saragossan helms,
> Gird on their swords wrought of Viana steel,
> Take their fine shields and their spears from Valence
> With gonfalons of crimson, blue and white.
> Then they forsake their palfreys and their mules,
> Mount on their steeds, and ride in close array.
> Bright was the day and radiant the sun;
> All their equipment glitters in its rays.
> A thousand bugles sound a flourish forth:
> Great is the clamour, and the Frenchmen hear.
> Said Oliver: 'Sir comrade, I believe
> We may do battle with the Saracens.'
> Roland replies: 'And may God grant it so!
> Our duty bids us stand firm for our king:
> A man should suffer hardship for his lord,
> Endure great heat and bear with bitter cold,
> And be prepared to lose both hair and skin.
> Now let each man take care to deal great blows,
> So that no song of shame be sung of us!
> Pagans are wrong and Christians in the right;
> No bad example shall be set by me.'
>
> Said Oliver: 'The pagans have vast strength,
> And our Frenchmen beside them seem so few.
> Friend Roland, I beseech you, sound your horn!
> Then Charles will hear; the army will turn back.'
> Roland replies: 'Should I act like a fool
> And lose my fame and honour in fair France?
> No! I shall strike great blows with Durendal,

From *The Song of Roland*, D. D. R. Owen, trans. (London: George Allen and Unwin, 1972), pp. 51–55 (*ll.* 994–1016, 1049–1069, 1082–1109, 1124–1138). Reprinted by permission of D. D. R. Owen.

Stain it with gore up to its golden hilt.
The pagan knaves shall rue their coming here,
For this I pledge: each one is doomed to die.'

'Companion Roland, sound your oliphant!
The king will hear, and turn the army back;
Charles and his barons will come to our aid.'
Roland replies: 'May it never please God
That blame should fall on my kinsfolk through me,
Or fair France ever lapse in infamy!
Rather I'll strike amain with Durendal
My trusty sword that hangs here at my side;
And you will see its blade all stained with gore.
Those pagan knaves shall rue their gathering.
I pledge you this: they are all marked for death.'

Said Oliver: 'I see no blame in it;
For I have seen the Saracens from Spain:
They cover both the mountains and the vales,
Swarming on hillsides and throughout the plains.
Huge are the armies of the foreign folk,
While we have but a puny company,'
Roland replies: 'I like it better so.
May God Himself and His angels forbid
That through me France's worth should ever wane!
I'd rather die than suffer such a shame.
Stout blows endear us to the emperor.'

Roland is valiant, Oliver is wise,
And both are matchless in their chivalry.
When they are armed and mounted on their steeds,
For fear of death neither will shun the fray.
Excellent are the counts, lofty their speech.
The wicked pagans wrathfully ride on.
Oliver said: 'Roland, just see them all!

How close they are, with Charles so far away!
You did not deign to sound your oliphant,
Yet if the king were here, we'd have no harm.
Look up towards the passes into Spain!
Now you can see what plight the rearguard's in:
Its men will never form another one.'
Roland replies: 'Tell no such tale to me!
Cursed be the heart that quakes within the breast!
We shall stand fast and firm to hold our ground,
Hewing and hacking there as best we may.'

Archbishop Turpin is not far away.
Spurring his horse, he gallops up a hill,
Summons the French, and speaks these solemn words:
'My lords and barons, Charles has left us here,

And for our king we should in duty die.
Lend aid now to maintain the Christian faith!
You'll join in battle, as you know full well:
Before your eyes you see the Saracens.
Say your confessions, for God's mercy pray!
I will absolve you to secure your souls.
If you die, blessed martyrs you will be
And have your place on high in Paradise.'
The French dismount and to the ground they fall,
And God's archbishop gives the benison.
As penance he commands that they strike hard.

During the eleventh century Seljuk Turks conquered much of the eastern Mediterranean region, including substantial territories of the Christian Byzantine empire. In response, Pope Urban II proclaimed the first crusade in 1096. What did the pope hope to achieve? What incentives did he offer to the crusaders?

Pope Urban's Speech at Clermont

Now that you, O sons of God, have consecrated yourselves to God to maintain peace among yourselves more vigorously and to uphold the laws of the Church faithfully, there is work to do, for you must turn the strength of your sincerity, now that you are aroused by divine correction, to another affair that concerns you and God. Hastening to the way, you must help your brothers living in the Orient, who need your aid for which they have already cried out many times.

For, as most of you have been told, the Turks, a race of Persians, who have penetrated within the boundaries of Romania even to the Mediterranean to that point which they call the Arm of Saint George, in occupying more and more of the lands of the Christians, have overcome them, already victims of seven battles, and have killed and captured them, have overthrown churches, and have laid waste God's kingdom. If you permit this supinely for very long, God's faithful ones will be still further subjected.

Concerning this affair, I, with suppliant prayer—not I, but the Lord—exhort you, heralds of Christ, to persuade all of whatever class, both knights and footmen, both rich and poor, in numerous edicts, to strive to help expel that wicked race from our Christian lands before it is too late.

I speak to those present, I send word to those not here; moreover, Christ commands it. Remission of sins will be granted for those going thither, if they end a shackled life either on land or in crossing the sea, or in struggling against the heathen. I, being vested with that gift from God, grant this to those who go.

O what a shame, if a people, so despised, degenerate, and enslaved by demons would thus overcome a people endowed with the trust of almighty God, and shining in the name of Christ! O how many evils will be imputed to you by the Lord Himself, if you do not help those who, like you, profess Christianity!

From Fulcher of Chartres, *Chronicle of the First Crusade*, M. E. McGinty, trans. (Philadelphia, Pa.: University of Pennsylvania Press, 1941), pp. 15–17.

Let those who are accustomed to wage private wars wastefully even against Believers, go forth against the Infidels in a battle worthy to be undertaken now and to be finished in victory. Now, let those, who until recently existed as plunderers, be soldiers of Christ; now, let those, who formerly contended against brothers and relations, rightly fight barbarians; now, let those, who recently were hired for a few pieces of silver, win their eternal reward. Let those, who wearied themselves to the detriment of body and soul, labor for a twofold honor. Nay, more, the sorrowful here will be glad there, the poor here will be rich there, and the enemies of the Lord here will be His friends there.

Let no delay postpone the journey of those about to go, but when they have collected the money owed to them and the expenses for the journey, and when winter has ended and spring has come, let them enter the crossroads courageously with the Lord going on before.

Crusaders and Jews

Pope Urban's launching of a crusade had an unintended result. As the crusaders moved into Germany they perpetrated savage massacres of Jews in several Rhineland cities. What was their motive?

From *Chronicle of Alan of Aix*

At the beginning of summer in the same year in which Peter and Gottschalk, after collecting an army, had set out, there assembled in like fashion a large and innumerable host of Christians from diverse kingdoms and lands; namely, from the realms of France, England, Flanders, and Lorraine. . . . I know not whether by a judgment of the Lord, or by some error of mind, they rose in a spirit of cruelty against the Jewish people scattered throughout these cities and slaughtered them without mercy, especially in the Kingdom of Lorraine, asserting it to be the beginning of their expedition and their duty against the enemies of the Christian faith. This slaughter of Jews was done first by citizens of Cologne. These suddenly fell upon a small band of Jews and severely wounded and killed many; they destroyed the houses and synagogues of the Jews and divided among themselves a very large amount of money. When the Jews saw this cruelty, about two hundred in the silence of the night began flight by boat to Neuss. The pilgrims and crusaders discovered them, and after taking away all their possessions, inflicted on them similar slaughter, leaving not even one alive.

An Arab View

Ousama Ibn Mounkidh, an Arab chieftain, left an account of the Frankish settlers in the Levant. From his Muslim viewpoint they seemed coarse and uncivilized and their women oddly liberated.

From A. C. Krey, trans., *The First Crusade: The Accounts of Eyewitnesses and Participants* (Princeton, N.J.: Princeton University Press, 1921), p. 54.

From *Autobiography of Ousama*

It is always those who have recently come to live in Frankish territory who show themselves more inhuman than their predecessors who have been established amongst us and become familiarised with the Mohammedans.

A proof of the harshness of the Franks (the scourge of Allah upon them!) is to be seen in what happened to me when I visited Jerusalem. I went into the mosque Al-Aksa. By the side of this was a little mosque which the Franks had converted into a church. When I went into the mosque Al-Aksa, which was occupied by the Templars, who were my friends, they assigned me this little mosque in which to say my prayers. One day I went into it and glorified Allah. I was engrossed in my praying when one of the Franks rushed at me, seized me and turned my face to the East, saying, "That is how to pray!" A party of Templars made for him, seized his person and ejected him. I returned to my prayers. The same man, escaping their attention, made for me again and turned my face round to the East, repeating, "That is how to pray!" The Templars again made for him and ejected him, then they apologised to me and said to me, "He is a stranger who has only recently arrived from Frankish lands. He has never seen anyone praying without turning to the East." I answered, "I have prayed sufficiently for to-day."

The Franks understand neither the feeling of honour nor the nature of jealousy. If one of them is walking with his wife and he meets another man, the latter takes the woman's hand and goes and talks to her while the husband stands aside waiting for the end of the interview. If the woman prolongs it unreasonably, the husband leaves her alone with her companion and goes back.

Here is a fact of the same nature of which I was witness. When I was in Neapolis, I lived at the house of a man named Mou'izz at whose house Mohammedans used to stay. Our windows opened on to the street. Opposite, on the other side, there lived a Frank who sold wine to merchants. . . . One day, going to his bedroom, the wine-merchant found a man in bed with his wife. "What has induced you to come in to my wife?" he asked. "I was tired," the other said, "and I came in to rest myself." "But how," said the Frank, "did you dare to go in to my bed?" "I found a couch smoothed over like a rug and I went to sleep on it." "But my wife was sleeping by your side." "The bed belonged to her, could I turn her away from it?" "By the truth of my religion," the husband answered, "I swear to you that if you do it again we shall see an estrangement between us." That is what discontent is with a Frank and that is the measure of his jealousy.

Another fact of the same nature: We had with us a bath-attendant named Salim, who came from Ma'arrat an-No'man, and who was employed in my father's service (may Allah have mercy upon him!). Salim told us one day, "I set up some baths at Ma'arrat an-No'man to make a living by them. A Frankish knight came to them. Now they dislike our custom of bathing with a costume. My customer reached out his hand and pulled my costume off. He then saw that I had a little previously shaved my body. He called to me, 'Salim!' I came to him. He

From *The Autobiography of Ousama* (1095–1188), G. R. Potter, trans. (London: George Routledge, 1929), pp. 176–179, 181–182. Reprinted by permission of Routledge & Kegan Paul Ltd.

touched me and said, 'Salim is magnificent (*salim*)! By the truth of my religion, do to me likewise.' He lay on his back and I shaved the hair from his body. He passed his hand over his skin and felt how smooth it was. He then said to me, 'Salim, by your religion, I conjure you, do likewise to madame (*dama*).' Now in their language, 'madame' (*dama*) is the wife. He was thinking of his wife. He sent one of his servants to tell his wife to come. The servant went to her and brought her. At his orders a similar operation was performed on her, while her husband sat by her and watched it done. He then thanked me and gave me my fee for my pains."

Consider this absolute contradiction. Here are men without jealousy and without a feeling of honour. On the other hand they are endowed with great courage. Generally speaking, courage originates solely in feelings of honour and the care people take to avoid any slur on their reputation.

At Neapolis, I was once present at a curious sight. They brought in two men for trial by battle, the cause being the following. Some Mohammedan brigands had raided some property in the neighbourhood of Neapolis. A farmer was suspected of having guided the brigands to this spot. The farmer took flight but soon returned, the king having had his children imprisoned. "Treat me with equity," said the accused, " and allow me to fight with him who has named me as the person who brought the brigands into the village." The king then said to the lord who had received the village as a fief: "Send for his opponent." The lord returned to his village, picked out a blacksmith who was working there, and said to him, "You must go and fight a duel." For the owner of the fief was primarily anxious to see that none of his labourers got himself killed, for fear his crops should suffer.

I saw this blacksmith. He was a strong young man, but one who, walking or sitting, was always wanting something to drink. As for the other, the challenger to single combat, he was an old man of great courage, who snapped his fingers as a token of defiance and prepared for the fight without perturbation. The sheiff (*al-biskound*), governor (*schihna*) of the town, appeared, gave each of the two fighters a cudgel and shield and made the crowd form a ring round them.

The fight started. The old man forced the blacksmith backwards, throwing him on to the edge of the crowd, and then returned to the middle of the ring. The exchange of blows was so violent that the rivals, who remained standing, seemed to make up one pillar of blood.

The fight continued, while the sheriff urged them to force a conclusion. "Quicker," he shouted to them. The blacksmith profited by his experience at wielding a hammer. When the old man was exhausted, the blacksmith aimed a blow at him which overthrew him, making the cudgel, which he was holding in his hand, fall behind him. The blacksmith crouched over the old man so as to put his fingers into his eyes, but he could not reach them because of the streams of blood which were flowing from them; he got up and struck his head so violently with his cudgel that he finished him off.

PART EIGHT

THE MEDIEVAL WORLD—
ECONOMY AND
GOVERNMENT

Medieval civilization was built on an agrarian foundation—rural manors worked by peasant labor. Then, from the eleventh century onward, an increasing volume of international commerce stimulated the growth of trading cities, which came to play a major role in economic and political life. In the cities new guilds of craft workers and merchants grew up. They sought to regulate production and exchange while providing fellowship and mutual support for the members.

The slowly expanding medieval economy made possible a growth of more sophisticated institutions of government. National monarchies were consolidated in England and France and in other regions of Europe. Important experiments in constitutional government occurred. The kings of Germany, who also claimed the title emperor, tried to extend their rule over Italy, but they were defeated by the combined opposition of the northern Italian cities and the papacy.

Throughout the thirteenth century the papacy was the greatest center of organized government in western Europe. While dominating Rome and central Italy as temporal princes, the popes controlled the ecclesiastical affairs of all Europe as heads of the church. Under Innocent III (1198–1217) they claimed a kind of universal jurisdiction over all the kings of Europe, and under Boniface VIII (1298–1303) such claims were put forward in an extreme form. Boniface, however, was defeated in a struggle with the king of France. At the beginning of the fourteenth century various political philosophers were seeking to discriminate between the proper spheres of action of the church and the state.

RURAL LIFE

The Medieval Manor

From records of landholding and peasant obligations like this survey of the manor of Alwalton, we can construct a rough sociology of village life. What kind of rents and services did the peasants owe? Can you distinguish different economic classes among them? Which family held most land? How many women held land in their own name?

From *A Manor of the Hundred Rolls (1279)*

The abbot of Peterborough holds the manor of Alwalton and vill from the lord king directly; which manor and vill with its appurtenances the lord Edward, formerly king of England gave to the said abbot and convent of that place in free, pure, and perpetual alms. And the court of the said manor with its garden contains one half an acre. And to the whole of the said vill of Alwalton belong 5 hides and a half and 1 virgate of land and a half; of which each hide contains 5 virgates of land and each virgate contains 25 acres. Of these hides the said abbot has in demesne 1 hide and a half of land and half a virgate, which contain as above. Likewise he has there 8 acres of meadow. Also he has there separable pasture which contains 1 acre. Likewise he has there three water mills. Likewise he has there a common fish pond with a fish-weir on the bank of the Nene, which begins at Wildlake and extends to the mill of Newton and contains in length 2 leagues. Likewise he has there a ferry with a boat.

Free Tenants Thomas le Boteler holds a messuage with a court yard which contains 1 rood, and 3 acres of land, by charter, paying thence yearly to the said abbot 14s.

Likewise the rector of the church of Alwalton holds 1 virgate of land with its appurtenances, with which the said church was anciently endowed. Likewise the said rector has a holding the tenant of which holds 1 rood of ground by paying to the said rector yearly 12d.

And the abbot of Peterboro is patron of the church.

Villeins Hugh Miller holds 1 virgate of land in villenage by paying thence to the said abbot 3s. 1d. Likewise the same Hugh works through the whole year except 1 week at Christmas, 1 week at Easter, and 1 at Whitsuntide, that is in each week 3 days, each day with 1 man, and in autumn each day with 2 men, performing the said works at the will of the said abbot as in plowing and other work. Likewise he gives 1 bushel of wheat for benseed and 18 sheaves of oats

From "A Manor of the Hundred Rolls: Alwalton," in J. H. Robinson, *University of Pennsylvania Translations and Reprints* (Philadelphia, Pa.: University of Pennsylvania Press, 1897), Vol. 3, No. 5, pp. 4–8.

for fodder-corn. Likewise he gives 3 hens and 1 cock yearly and 5 eggs at Easter. Likewise he does carrying to Peterborough and to Jakele and no where else, at the will of the said abbot. Likewise if he sells a brood mare in his court yard for 10s. or more, he shall give to the said abbot 4d., and if for less he shall give nothing to the aforesaid. He gives also merchet and heriot,[1] and is tallaged at the feast of St. Michael, at the will of the said abbot. There are also there 17 other villeins, viz. John of Ganesoupe, Robert son of Walter, Ralph son of the reeve, Emma ate Pertre, William son of Reginald, Thomas son of Gunnilda, Eda widow of Ralph, Ralph Reeve, William Reeve, William son of William Reeve, Thomas Flegg, Henry Abbott, William Hereward, Serle son of William Reeve, Walter Palmer, William Abbot, Henry Serle; each of whom holds 1 virgate of land in villenage, paying and doing in all things, each for himself, to the said abbot yearly just as the said Hugh Miller. There are also 5 other villeins, viz. Simon Mariot, Robert of Hastone, Thomas Smith, John Mustard, and William Carter, each of whom holds half a virgate of land by paying and doing in all things half of the whole service which Hugh Miller pays and does.

Cotters[2] Henry, son of the miller, holds a cottage with a croft which contains 1 rood, paying thence yearly to the said abbot 2s. Likewise he works for 3 days in carrying hay and in other works at the will of the said abbot, each day with 1 man and in autumn 1 day in cutting grain with 1 man.

Likewise Ralph Miller holds a cottage with a croft which contains a rood, paying to the said abbot 2s.; and he works just as the said Henry.

Likewise William Arnold holds a cottage with a croft which contains half a rood, paying to the abbot 2d.; and he works just as the said Henry.

Likewise Hugh Day holds a cottage with a croft which contains 1 rood, paying to the abbot 8d.; and he works just as the said Henry.

Likewise Sara, widow of Matthew Miller, holds a cottage and a croft which contains half a rood, paying to the said abbot 4d.; and she works just as the said Henry.

Likewise William Drake holds a cottage with a croft which contains half a rood, paying to the abbot 6d.; and he works just as the said Henry.

There are there also 6 other cotters, viz. William Drake Jr., Amycia the widow, Alice the widow, Robert son of Eda, William Pepper, William Coleman, each of whom holds a cottage with a croft which contains half a rood, paying and doing in all things, each for himself, just as the said William Drake.

Likewise William Russel holds a cottage with a croft which contains half a rood, paying to the abbot 8d.; and he works in all things just as the said Henry Miller.

There are moreover there 5 other cotters, viz. Walter Pestel, Ralph Shepherd, Henry Abbot, Matilda Tut, Jordan Mustard, each of whom holds a cottage with

---

[1]Merchet was a tax for permission to marry, heriot an inheritance tax.
[2]The cotters evidently did not have enough land to support a family. They probably worked as laborers for the lord or for a richer peasant.

a croft which contains half a rood, paying thence and doing in all things to the said abbot just as the said William Russel.

Likewise Beatrice of Hampton holds a cottage and croft which contains 1 rood, paying to the abbot 12d.; and she works in all things just as the said Henry.

Likewise Hugh Miller holds 3 acres of land paying to the abbot 42d.

Likewise Thomas, son of Richard, holds a cottage with a croft which contains half a rood, and 3 acres of land, paying to the abbot 4s. and he works just as the said Henry.

Likewise Ralph Reeve holds a cottage with a croft which contains 1 rood, and 1 acre of land, paying to the abbot 2s.; and he works just as the said Henry.

Likewise each of the said cottagers, except the widows, gives yearly after Christmas a penny which is called head-penny.

Many details of day-to-day village life survive in the records of manorial courts. These examples are from the years 1246 to 1249. How do the cases resemble and differ from those that might come before a modern police court?

From *Select Pleas in Manorial Courts*

John Sperling complains that Richard of Newmere on the Sunday next before S. Bartholomew's day last past with his cattle, horses, and pigs wrongfully destroyed the corn on his [John's] land to his damage to the extent of one thrave of wheat, and to his dishonour to the extent of two shillings; and of this he produces suit. And Richard comes and defends all of it. Therefore let him go to the law six handed.[3] His pledges, Simon Combe and Hugh Frith.

Hugh Free in mercy for his beast caught in the lord's garden. Pledges, Walter Hill and William Slipper. Fine 6d.

[The] twelve jurors say that Hugh Cross has right in the bank and hedge about which there was a dispute between him and William White. Therefore let him hold in peace and let William be distrained for his many trespasses. (Afterwards he made fine for 12d.)

From the whole township of Little Ogbourne, except seven, for not coming to wash the lord's sheep, 6s. 8d.

Gilbert Richard's son gives 5s. for licence to marry a wife. Pledge, Seaman. Term [for payment,] the Purification.

William Jordan in mercy for bad ploughing on the lord's land. Pledge, Arthur. Fine, 6d.

The parson of the Church is in mercy for his cow caught in the lord's meadow. Pledges, Thomas Ymer and William Coke.

From Martin Shepherd 6d. for the wound that he gave Pekin.

Ragenhilda of Bec gives 2s. for having married without licence. Pledge, William of Primer.

---

[3]i.e., he must appear with six companions who will swear to his innocence.
From F. W. Maitland, ed., "Select Pleas in Manorial Courts," in G. G. Coulton, ed., *Social Life in Britain from the Conquest to the Reformation* (London: Cambridge University Press, 1918), pp. 306–308.

The Court presented that William Noah's son is the born bondman of the lord and a fugitive and dwells at Dodford. Therefore he must be sought. They say also that William Askil, John Parsons and Godfrey Green have furtively carried off four geese from the vill of Horepoll.

It was presented that Robert Carter's son by night invaded the house of Peter Burgess and in felony threw stones at his door so that the said Peter raised the hue. Therefore let the said Robert be committed to prison. Afterwards he made fine with 2s.

All the ploughmen of Great Ogbourne are convicted by the oath of twelve men ... because by reason of their default [the land] of the lord was ill-ploughed whereby the lord is damaged to the amount of 9s. .... And Walter Reaper is in mercy for concealing [i.e. not giving information as to] the said bad ploughing. Afterwards he made fine with the lord with 1 mark.

Peasant Daily Fare

A medieval peasant's diet was barely adequate at best. The poorest ones often went hungry.

From *Piers Plowman*

> The needy are our neighbours, if we note rightly;
> As prisoners in cells, or poor folk in hovels,
> Charged with children and overcharged by landlords.
> What they may spare in spinning they spend on rental,
> On milk, or on meal to make porridge
> To still the sobbing of the children at meal time.
> Also they themselves suffer much hunger.
> They have woe in winter time, and wake at midnight
> To rise and to rock the cradle at the bedside,
> To card and to comb, to darn clouts and to wash them,
> To rub and to reel and to put rushes on the paving.
> The woe of these women who dwell in hovels
> Is too sad to speak of or to say in rhyme.
> And many other men have much to suffer
> From hunger and from thirst; they turn the fair side outward,
> For they are abashed to beg, lest it should be acknowledged
> At their neighbours what they need at noon and even.
> I know all this well; for the world has taught me
> What befalls another who has many children,
> With no claim but his craft to clothe and feed them,
> When the mouths are many and the money scarce.
> They have bread and penny ale in place of a pittance,
> And cold flesh and cold fish for venison from the butcher.
> On Fridays and fast days a farthing worth of mussels

Would be a feast for such folk, with a few cockles.
It were an alms to help all with such burdens,
And to comfort such cottagers and crooked men and blind folk.

TOWNS AND TRADE

City Life

William FitzStephen, a citizen of London, wrote this description of the city in the late twelfth century. Evidently he was not lacking in civic pride. What features of London life did he consider especially admirable? How did the sports of the young people resemble and differ from modern ones?

From *A Description of London*

Amongst the noble and celebrated cities of the world, that of London, the capital of the kingdom of England, is one of the most renowned, possessing above all others abundant wealth, extensive commerce, great grandeur and magnificence. It is happy in the salubrity of its climate, in the profession of the Christian religion, in the strength of its fortresses, the nature of its situation, the honour of its citizens, and the chastity of its matrons; in its sports too it is most pleasant, and in the production of illustrous men most fortunate. All which things I wish separately to consider.

There then

"Men's minds are soft'ned by a temp'rate clime,"

not so however that they are addicted to licentiousness, but so that they are not savage and brutal, but rather kind and generous.

There is in St. Paul's church an episcopal see. . . . As regards divine worship, there are also in London and in the suburbs thirteen larger conventional churches, besides one hundred and thirty-six parochial ones.

On the east stands the Palatine tower, a fortress of great size and strength, the court and walls of which are erected upon a very deep foundation, the mortar used in the building being tempered with the blood of beasts. On the west are two castles strongly fortified; the wall of the city is high and thick, with seven double gates, having on the north side towers placed at proper intervals. London formerly had walls and towers in like manner on the south, but that most excellent river the Thames, which abounds with fish, and in which the tide ebbs and flows, runs on that side, and has in a long space of time washed down, undermined, and subverted the walls in that part. On the west also, higher up on the bank of the river, the royal palace rears its head, an incomparable struc-

From William FitzStephen, "A Description of the Most Noble City of London," *The Survey of London by John Stow* (London: Everyman's Library, 1912), pp. 504–509. Reprinted courtesy of J. M. Dent & Sons Ltd.

ture, furnished with a breastwork and bastions, situated in a populous suburb, at a distance of two miles from the city.

Adjoining to the houses on all sides lie the gardens of those citizens that dwell in the suburbs, which are well furnished with trees, spacious and beautiful.

On the north side too are fields for pasture, and a delightful plain of meadow land, interspersed with flowing streams, on which stand mills, whose clack is very pleasing to the ear. Close by lies an immense forest, in which are densely wooded thickets, the coverts of game, stags, fallow-deer, boars, and wild bulls. The tillage lands of the city are not barren gravelly soils, but like the fertile plains of Asia, which produce abundant crops, and fill the barns of their cultivators with

"Ceres' plenteous sheaf."

There are also round London, on the northern side, in the suburbs, excellent springs; the water of which is sweet, clear, and salubrious,

"Mid glistening pebbles gliding playfully:"

amongst which, Holywell, Clerkenwell, and St. Clement's well, are of most note, and most frequently visited, as well by the scholars from the schools, as by the youth of the city when they go out to take the air in the summer evenings. The city is delightful indeed, when it has a good governor. . . .

The artizans of the several crafts, the vendors of the various commodities, and the labourers of every kind, have each their separate station, which they take every morning. There is also in London, on the bank of the river, amongst the wine-shops which are kept in ships and cellars, a public eating-house: there every day, according to the season, may be found viands of all kinds, roast, fried, and boiled, fish large and small, coarser meat for the poor, and more delicate for the rich, such as venison, fowls, and small birds. . . . There is, without one of the gates, immediately in the suburb, a certain smooth field in name and in reality [Smithfield]. There every Friday, unless it be one of the more solemn festivals, is a noted show of well-bred horses exposed for sale. . . . To this city, from every nation under heaven, merchants bring their commodities by sea,

"Arabia's gold, Sabaea's spice and incense,
Scythia's keen weapons, and the oil of palms
From Babylon's rich soil, Nile's precious gems,
Norway's warm peltries, Russia's costly sables,
Sera's rich vestures, and the wines of Gaul,
Hither are sent."

The only inconveniences of London are, the immoderate drinking of foolish persons, and the frequent fires. Moreover, almost all the bishops, abbots, and great men of England, are, in a manner, citizens and freemen of London; as they have magnificent houses there, to which they resort, spending large sums of money, whenever they are summoned thither to councils and assemblies by the king or their metropolitan, or are compelled to go there by their own business.

OF THE SPORTS

Let us now proceed to the sports of the city; since it is expedient that a city be not only an object of utility and importance, but also a source of pleasure and diversion. . . . To begin with the sports of the boys (for we have all been boys), annually on the day which is called Shrovetide, the boys of the respective schools bring each a fighting cock to their master, and the whole of that forenoon is spent by the boys in seeing their cocks fight in the school-room. After dinner, all the young men of the city go out into the fields to play at the well-known game of foot-ball. The scholars belonging to the several schools have each their ball; and the city tradesmen, according to their respective crafts, have theirs. . . . Every Sunday in Lent, after dinner, a company of young men enter the fields, mounted on warlike horses—

"On coursers always foremost in the race;"

of which

"Each steed's well-train'd to gallop in a ring."

The lay-sons of the citizens rush out of the gates in crowds, equipped with lances and shields, the younger sort with pikes from which the iron head has been taken off, and there they get up sham fights, and exercise themselves in military combat.

During the holydays in summer the young men exercise themselves in the sports of leaping, archery, wrestling, stone-throwing, slinging javelins beyond a mark, and also fighting with bucklers. Cytherea leads the dances of the maidens, who merrily trip along the ground beneath the uprisen moon. Almost on every holyday in winter, before dinner, foaming boars, and huge-tusked hogs, intended for bacon, fight for their lives, or fat bulls or immense boars are baited with dogs. When that great marsh which washes the walls of the city on the north side is frozen over, the young men go out in crowds to divert themselves upon the ice. Some, having increased their velocity by a run, placing their feet apart, and turning their bodies sideways, slide a great way. . . . Others are more expert in their sports upon the ice; for fitting to, and binding under their feet the shinbones of some animal, and taking in their hands poles shod with iron, which at times they strike against the ice, they are carried along with as great rapidity as a bird flying or a bolt discharged from a cross-bow. Sometimes two of the skaters having placed themselves a great distance apart by mutual agreement, come together from opposite sides; they meet, raise their poles, and strike each other; either one or both of them fall, not without some bodily hurt. . . . But youth is an age eager for glory and desirous of victory, and so young men engage in counterfeit battles, that they may conduct themselves more valiantly in real ones. Most of the citizens amuse themselves in sporting with merlins, hawks, and other birds of a like kind, and also with dogs that hunt in the woods. The citizens have the right of hunting in Middlesex, Hertfordshire, all the Chilterns, and Kent, as far as the river Cray.

As trading cities grew up in the feudal world of the twelfth century, merchants were particularly eager to obtain freedom from arbitrary taxation by the local lord, the right to travel and trade freely without burdensome tolls, and the right to settle disputes in their own town court. How did these provisions from the Charter of St. Omer, *granted by Count William of Flanders in 1137, respond to these demands?*

From *Charter of St. Omer*

I, William, by God's grace Count of the Flemings, not wishing to oppose the petition of the burghers of Saint-Omer, especially because they gladly accepted my petition concerning the consulate of Flanders and always behaved more honorably and faithfully towards me than the other Flemings, concede the underwritten laws or customs in perpetuity to them and order them to remain permanently valid.

1. First of all, I shall make peace with every one of them, maintain and defend them without malice like my own men, and agree to have the right judgment of the aldermen enforced against anyone, myself included. I also grant to the aldermen liberties as extensive as any which other aldermen in my land may have.

3. If someone has been sued in canon law by someone, he shall not leave the town of Saint-Omer to seek justice elsewhere. What is right shall be determined by the judgment of clerics and aldermen in St. Omer instead, before the bishop, his archdeacon, or his priest. Nor does he have to answer someone except for three reasons, namely breaking into a church or its vestibule, wounding a cleric, or overpowering and violating a woman. If the complaint regards other matters, it shall be settled before the judges and my provost. For this is what was established before Count Charles and Bishop John.

4. I also grant to them the liberty which they enjoyed at the time of my predecessors, namely that they need never do military service outside their own land, except if a hostile army invades Flanders. Then they must defend me and my land.

5. I completely release all of those who have their guild, are its members, and reside within the limits of their town from paying tolls at the ports of Dixmuiden and Gravelines.

8. If anyone raises a complaint against them in any market of Flanders, they shall, without a duel, undergo judgment by the aldermen about every complaint. From duels, however, they shall henceforth be exempt.

9. I exempt all of those who live within the walls of Saint-Omer, and those who are going to live there in future, from *cavagium*, that is, the poll-tax, and from the rights of the advocate.

11. They have, furthermore, asked the King of France and Raoul of Péronnes to be free from all tolls, crossing, and passing dues wherever in their land they may go. I, too, wish them to be so free.

12. I order their commune to continue as they have sworn it, will not permit it to be dissolved by anyone, and grant to them everything that is right, and right justice, as best it exists in my land, that is, in Flanders.

13. And just as I wish the better and freer burghers of Flanders to be freed from all customs henceforth, so shall I demand no scot and tallage from them, and make no petition for their money.

From *Charter of St. Omer*, C. Fasolt: trans. in J. Kirshner and K. F. Morrison (eds.), *Medieval Europe*, pp. 90–94. University of Chicago Press. Copyright © 1986. Reprinted by permission.

14. My mint in Saint-Omer, from which I have annually derived 30 pounds, and whatever I ought to have in it, I order to be used to repair their losses and maintain their guild. The burghers, however, shall keep the coinage stable and good throughout my life, which will redound to the advantage of their town.

15. The guards who are on duty every night throughout the year, watching over the castle of Saint-Omer, who are accustomed unjustly and violently to exact a loaf of bread and one or two pennies at Christmas from every house in this town, namely in Saint-Omer and Saint Bertin, or who have taken money pledged to the poor instead, beyond their fief and livelihood, which of old has been allotted them in oats, cheeses, and sheepskins, shall not dare to exact anything at all henceforth beyond their fief and livelihood.

20. If any foreigner attacks a burgher of Saint-Omer and inflicts insult or injury on him or violently robs him, avoids arrest, and gets away with his transgression, and afterwards he is summoned by the Castellan or his wife, or by his standard-bearer, and refuses or neglects to appear within three days to do satisfaction, the community of the citizens shall avenge their brother's injury. If, as a result of taking vengeance, a house is demolished or burned, or if anyone is wounded or killed, the avenger shall not be held liable in his body or his goods, nor shall he come to experience, or stand in fear of, my displeasure in this respect. But if the person who committed the injury is immediately arrested, he shall be promptly judged according to the laws and customs of the town and punished according to the magnitude of his deed, which is to say that he shall give an eye for an eye, a tooth for a tooth, and a head for a head.

Economic Activities

Each major city had a merchant guild and numerous craft guilds. They combined economic, religious, and charitable functions. What services did the guild provide for its members? How did it protect their economic interests?

Rules of a Merchant Guild (Southampton)

In the first place, there shall be elected from the gild merchant, and established, an alderman, a steward, a chaplain, four skevins, and an usher. And it is to be known that whosoever shall be alderman shall receive from each one entering into the gild fourpence; the steward, twopence; the chaplain, twopence; and the usher, one penny. And the gild shall meet twice a year: that is to say, on the Sunday next after St. John the Baptist's day, and on the Sunday next after St. Mary's day.

And when the gild shall be sitting no one of the gild is to bring in any stranger, except when required by the alderman or steward. And the alderman

From E. P. Cheyney, trans., *University of Pennsylvania Translations and Reprints* (Philadelphia, Pa.: University of Pennsylvania Press, 1897), Vol. 2, No. 1, pp. 12–17.

shall have a sergeant to serve before him, the steward another sergeant, ai
chaplain shall have his clerk.

And when the gild shall sit, the alderman is to have, each night, so long as
the gild sits, two gallons of wine and two candles, and the steward the same; and
the four skevins and the chaplain, each of them one gallon of wine and one candle, and the usher one gallon of wine.

And when the gild shall sit, the lepers of La Madeleine shall have of the alms
of the gild, two sesters (approximately eight gallons) of ale, and the sick of God's
House and of St. Julian shall have two sesters of ale. And the Friars Minors shall
have two sesters of ale and one sester of wine. And four sesters of ale shall be
given to the poor wherever the gild shall meet.

And when the gild is sitting, no one who is of the gild shall go outside the
town for any business, without the permission of the steward. And if any does
so, let him be fined two shillings, and pay them.

And when the gild sits, and any gildsman is outside of the city so that he
does not know when it will happen, he shall have a gallon of wine, if his servants come to get it. And if a gildsman is ill and is in the city, wine shall be
sent to him, two loaves of bread and a gallon of wine and a dish from the
kitchen; and two approved men of the gild shall go to visit him and look after his condition.

And when a gildsman dies, all those who are of the gild and are in the city
shall attend the service of the dead, and the gildsmen shall bear the body and
bring it to the place of burial. And whoever will not do this shall pay according to his oath, two pence, to be given to the poor. And those of the ward
where the dead man shall be ought to find a man to watch over the body the
night that the dead shall lie in his house. And so long as the service of the
dead shall last, that is to say the vigil and the mass, there ought to burn four
candles of the gild, each candle of two pounds weight or more, until the body
is buried. And these four candles shall remain in the keeping of the steward
of the gild.

And when a gildsman dies, his eldest son or his next heir shall have the seat
of his father, or of his uncle, if his father was not a gildsman, and of no other one;
and he shall give nothing for his seat. No husband can have a seat in the gild by
right of his wife, nor demand a seat by right of his wife's ancestors.

And no one of the city of Southampton shall buy anything to sell again in
the same city, unless he is of the gild merchant or of the franchise. And if anyone shall do so and is convicted of it, all which he has so bought shall be forfeited to the king; and no one shall be quit of custom unless he proves that he is
in the gild or in the franchise, and this from year to year.

And no one shall buy honey, fat, salt herrings, or any kind of oil, or mill-
stones, or fresh hides, or any kind of fresh skins, unless he is a gildsman: nor
keep a tavern for wine, nor sell cloth at retail, except in market or fair days; nor
keep grain in his granary beyond five quarters, to sell at retail, if he is not a gildsman; and whoever shall do this and be convicted, shall forfeit all to the king.

If any gildsman falls into poverty and has not the wherewithal to live, and
is not able to work or to provide for himself, he shall have one mark from the

gild to relieve his condition when the gild shall sit. No one of the gild nor of the franchise shall avow another's goods for his by which the custom of the city shall be injured. And if any one does so and is convicted, he shall lose the gild and the franchise; and the merchandise so avowed shall be forfeited to the king.

And no private man nor stranger shall bargain for or buy any kind of merchandise coming into the city before a burgess of the gild merchant, so long as the gildsman is present and wishes to bargain for and buy this merchandise; and if anyone does so and is convicted, that which he buys shall be forfeited to the king.

The common chest shall be in the house of the chief alderman or of the steward, and the three keys of it shall be lodged with three discreet men of the aforesaid twelve sworn men, or with three of the skevins, who shall loyally take care of the common seal, and the charters and of the treasure of the town, and the standards, and other muniments of the town; and no letter shall be sealed with the common seal, nor any charter taken out of the common-chest but in the presence of six or twelve sworn men, and of the alderman or steward; and nobody shall sell by any kind of measure or weight that is not sealed, under forfeiture of two shillings.

No one shall go out to meet a ship bringing wine or other merchandise coming to the town, in order to buy anything, before the ship be arrived and come to anchor for unlading; and if any one does so and is convicted, the merchandise which he shall have bought shall be forfeited to the king.

Some medieval crafts were dominated by women. The spinners' guild of Paris provides an example.

Silk Spinners at Paris

Any woman who wishes to be a silk spinster on large spindles in the city of Paris—i.e., reeling, spinning, doubling and retwisting—may freely do so, provided she observe the following customs and usages of the craft:

No spinster on large spindles may have more than three apprentices, unless they be her own or her husband's children born in true wedlock; nor may she contract with them for an apprenticeship of less than seven years or for a fee of less than 20 Parisian sols to be paid to her, their mistress. The apprenticeship shall be for eight years if there is no fee, but she may accept more years and money if she can get them. . . .

No woman of the said craft may hire an apprentice or workgirl who has not completed her years of service with the mistress to whom she was apprenticed. If a spinster has assumed an apprentice, she may not take on another before the first has completed her seven years unless the apprentice die or forswear the craft forever. If an apprentice spinster buy her freedom before serving the said seven years, she may not herself take on an apprentice until she has practiced the craft for seven years. If any spinster sell her apprentice, she shall owe six de-

From Etienne Boileau, *Livres des Métiers* in J. D. O'Faolain and L. Martines, *Not in God's Image* (New York: Harper & Row, 1973), pp. 155–156. Reprinted courtesy of the publisher.

niers to the guardians appointed in the King's name to guard the [standards of the] craft. The buyer shall also owe six deniers. . . .

If a working woman comes from outside Paris and wishes to practice the said craft in the city, she must swear before two guardians of the craft that she will practice it well and loyally and conform to its customs and usages.

If anyone give a woman of the said craft silk to be spun and the woman pawn it and the owner complain, the fine shall be 5 sols.

No workwoman shall farm out another's silk to be worked upon outside her own house.

The said craft has as guardians two men of integrity sworn in the King's name but appointed and changed at the will of the provost of Paris. Taking an oath in the provost's presence, they shall swear to guard the craft truly, loyally, and to their utmost, and to inform him or his agents of all malpractices discovered therein.

During the twelfth century new networks of commerce grew up stretching from Scandinavia to the eastern Mediterranean. This is the advice of a Norwegian merchant to his son. What did a merchant need to study? How should he treat his customers? Compare a merchant's way of life with that of a feudal lord or a peasant.

Advice to Merchants

The man who is to be a trader will have to brave many perils, sometimes at sea and sometimes in heathen lands, but nearly always among alien peoples; and it must be his constant purpose to act discreetly wherever he happens to be. On the sea he must be alert and fearless.

When you are in the market town, or wherever you are, be polite and agreeable; then you will secure the friendship of all good men. Make it a habit to rise early in the morning, and go first and immediately to church wherever it seems most convenient to hear the canonical hours, and hear all the hours and mass from matins on. Join in the worship, repeating such psalms and prayers as you have learned. When the services are over, go out to look after your business affairs. If you are unacquainted with the traffic of the town, observe carefully how those who are reputed the best and most prominent merchants conduct their business. You must also be careful to examine the wares that you buy before the purchase is finally made to make sure that they are sound and flawless. And whenever you make a purchase, call in a few trusty men to serve as witnesses as to how the bargain was made.

You should keep occupied with your business till breakfast or, if necessity demands it, till midday; after that you should eat your meal. Keep your table well provided and set with a white cloth, clean victuals, and good drinks. Serve enjoyable meals, if you can afford it. After the meal you may either take a nap or stroll about a little while for pastime and to see what other good merchants

From *The King's Mirror*, L. M. Larson, trans. (New York: The American-Scandinavian Foundation, 1917), pp. 79–81, 83–86. Reprinted courtesy of the American-Scandinavian Foundation.

are employed with, or whether any new wares have come to the borough which you ought to buy. On returning to your lodgings examine your wares, lest they suffer damage after coming into your hands. If they are found to be injured and you are about to dispose of them, do not conceal the flaws from the purchaser: show him what the defects are and make such a bargain as you can; then you cannot be called a deceiver. Also put a good price on your wares, though not too high, and yet very near what you see can be obtained; then you cannot be called a foister.

Finally, remember this, that whenever you have an hour to spare you should give thought to your studies, especially to the law books. . . . But although I have most to say about laws, I regard no man perfect in knowledge unless he has thoroughly learned and mastered the customs of the place where he is sojourning. And if you wish to become perfect in knowledge, you must learn all the languages, first of all Latin and French, for these idioms are most widely used; and yet do not neglect your native tongue or speech. . . .

And further, there are certain things which you must beware of and shun like the devil himself: these are drinking, chess, harlots, quarrelling, and throwing dice for stakes. For upon such foundations the greatest calamities are built; and unless they strive to avoid these things, few only are able to live long without blame or sin.

Observe carefully how the sky is lighted, the course of the heavenly bodies, the grouping of the hours, and the points of the horizon. Learn also how to mark the movements of the ocean and to discern how its turmoil ebbs and swells; for that is knowledge which all must possess who wish to trade abroad. Learn arithmetic thoroughly, for merchants have great need of that.

If you come to a place where the king or some other chief who is in authority has his officials, seek to win their friendship; and if they demand any necessary fees on the ruler's behalf, be prompt to render all such payments, lest by holding too tightly to little things you lose the greater. Also beware lest the king's belongings find their way into your purse; for you cannot know but that he may be covetous who has those things in charge, and it is easier to be cautious beforehand than to crave pardon afterwards. If you can dispose of your wares at suitable prices, do not hold them long; for it is the wont of merchants to buy constantly and to sell rapidly.

If you are preparing to carry on trade beyond the seas and you sail your own ship, have it thoroughly coated with tar in the autumn and, if possible, keep it tarred all winter. But if the ship is placed on timbers too late to be coated in the fall, tar it when spring opens and let it dry thoroughly afterwards. Always buy shares in good vessels or in none at all. Keep your ship attractive, for then capable men will join you and it will be well manned. Be sure to have your ship ready when summer begins and do your traveling while the season is best. Keep reliable tackle on shipboard at all times, and never remain out at sea in late autumn, if you can avoid it. If you attend carefully to all these things, with God's mercy you may hope for success. This, too, you must keep constantly in mind, if you wish to be counted a wise man, that you ought never to let a day pass without learning something that will profit you. . . .

If your wealth takes on rapid growth, divide it and invest it in a partnership trade in fields where you do not yourself travel; but be cautious in selecting partners. Always let Almighty God, the holy Virgin Mary, and the saint whom you have most frequently called upon to intercede for you be counted among your partners. Watch with care over the property which the saints are to share with you and always bring it faithfully to the place to which it was originally promised.

If you have much capital invested in trade, divide it into three parts: put one-third into partnerships with men who are permanently located in market boroughs, are trustworthy, and are experienced in business. Place the other two parts in various business ventures; for if your capital is invested in different places, it is not likely that you will suffer losses in all your wealth at one time; more likely it will be secure in some localities, though frequent losses be suffered. But if you find that the profits of trade bring a decided increase to your funds, draw out the two-thirds and invest them in good farm land, for such property is generally thought the most secure, whether the enjoyment of it falls to one's self or to one's kinsmen. With the remaining third you may do as seems best—continue to keep it in business or place it all in land. However, though you decide to keep your funds invested in trade, discontinue your own journeys at sea or as a trader in foreign fields, as soon as your means have attained sufficient growth and you have studied foreign customs as much as you like. Keep all that you see in careful memory, the evil with the good; remember evil practices as a warning, and the good customs as useful to yourself and to others who may wish to learn from you.

MEDIEVAL MONARCHIES

England

A baronial rebellion compelled King John (1199–1216) to issue Magna Carta *in 1215. In later times the document was seen as a classic statement of English liberties; but its actual content was determined by specific abuses of John's government that had angered his subjects. Which clauses refer to specifically feudal grievances? Which have a more general application? Who stood to gain from the provisions of the charter? How was it to be enforced?*

From *Magna Carta*

John, by the grace of God, king of England, lord of Ireland, duke of Normandy and Aquitaine, count of Anjou, to the archbishops, bishops, abbots, earls, barons, justiciars, foresters, sheriffs, reeves, servants, and all bailiffs and his faithful people greeting.

From "Magna Carta," in E. P. Cheyney, trans., *University of Pennsylvania Translations and Reprints* (Philadelphia, Pa.: University of Pennsylvania Press, 1897), Vol. 1, No. 6, pp. 6–16.

1. In the first place we have granted to God, and by this our present charter confirmed, for us and our heirs forever, that the English church shall be free, and shall hold its rights entire and its liberties uninjured; and we will that it thus be observed; which is shown by this, that the freedom of elections, which is considered to be most important and especially necessary to the English church, we, of our pure and spontaneous will, granted, and by our charter confirmed, before the contest between us and our barons had arisen; and obtained a confirmation of it by the lord Pope Innocent III.; which we will observe and which we will shall be observed in good faith by our heirs forever.

We have granted moreover to all free men of our kingdom for us and our heirs forever all the liberties written below, to be had and holden by themselves and their heirs from us and our heirs.

2. If any of our earls or barons, or others holding from us in chief by military service shall have died, and when he has died his heir shall be of full age and owe relief, he shall have his inheritance by the ancient relief; that is to say, the heir or heirs of an earl for the whole barony of an earl a hundred pounds; the heir or heirs of a baron for a whole barony a hundred pounds; the heir or heirs of a knight, for a whole knight's fee, a hundred shillings at most; and who owes less let him give less according to the ancient custom of fiefs.

3. If moreover the heir of any one of such shall be under age, and shall be in wardship, when he comes of age he shall have his inheritance without relief and without a fine.

4. The custodian of the land of such a minor heir shall not take from the land of the heir any except reasonable products, reasonable customary payments, and reasonable services, and this without destruction or waste of men or of property. . . .

6. Heirs shall be married without disparity, so nevertheless that before the marriage is contracted, it shall be announced to the relatives by blood of the heir himself.

7. A widow, after the death of her husband, shall have her marriage portion and her inheritance immediately. . . .

8. No widow shall be compelled to marry so long as she prefers to live without a husband, provided she gives security that she will not marry without our consent, if she holds from us, or without the consent of her lord from whom she holds, if she holds from another.

12. No scutage or aid shall be imposed in our kingdom except by the common council of our kingdom, except for the ransoming of our body, for the making of our oldest son a knight, and for once marrying our oldest daughter, and for these purposes it shall be only a reasonable aid; in the same way it shall be done concerning the aids of the city of London.

13. And the city of London shall have all its ancient liberties and free customs, as well by land as by water. Moreover, we will and grant that all other cities and boroughs and villages and ports shall have all their liberties and free customs.

14. And for holding a common council of the kingdom concerning the assessment of an aid otherwise than in the three cases mentioned above, or concerning the assessment of a scutage we shall cause to be summoned the archbishops, bishops, abbots, earls, and greater barons by our letters under seal; and besides we shall cause to be summoned generally, by our sheriffs and bailiffs all those who hold from us in chief, for a certain day, that is at the end of forty days at least, and for a certain place; and in all the letters of that summons, we will express the cause of the summons, and when the summons has thus been given the business shall proceed on the appointed day, on the advice of those who shall be present, even if not all of those who were summoned have come.

15. We will not grant to any one, moreover, that he shall take an aid from his free men, except for ransoming his body, for making his oldest son a knight, and for once marrying his oldest daughter; and for these purposes only a reasonable aid shall be taken.

16. No one shall be compelled to perform any greater service for a knight's fee, or for any other free tenement than is owed from it.

17. The common pleas shall not follow our court, but shall be held in some certain place.

20. A free man shall not be fined for a small offence, except in proportion to the measure of the offence; and for a great offence he shall be fined in proportion to the magnitude of the offence, saving his freehold; and a merchant in the same way, saving his merchandise; and the villain shall be fined in the same way, saving his wainage, if he shall be at our mercy; and none of the above fines shall be imposed except by the oaths of honest men of the neighborhood.

21. Earls and barons shall only be fined by their peers, and only in proportion to their offence.

28. No constable or other bailiff of ours shall take anyone's grain or other chattels, without immediately paying for them in money, unless he is able to obtain a postponement at the good-will of the seller.

39. No free man shall be taken or imprisoned or dispossessed, or outlawed, or banished, or in any way destroyed, nor will we go upon him, nor send upon him, except by the legal judgment of his peers or by the law of the land.

40. To no one will we sell, to no one will we deny, or delay right or justice.

41. All merchants shall be safe and secure in going out from England and coming into England and in remaining and going through England, as well by land as by water, for buying and selling, free from all evil tolls, by the ancient and rightful customs, except in time of war, and if they are of a land at war with us; and if such are found in our land at the beginning of war, they shall be attached without injury to their bodies or goods, until it shall be known from us or from our principal justiciar in what way the merchants of our land are treated who shall be then found in the country which is at war with us; and if ours are safe there, the others shall be safe in our land.

60. Moreover, all those customs and franchises mentioned above which we have conceded in our kingdom, and which are to be fulfilled, as far as pertains to us, in respect to our men; all men of our kingdom as well clergy as laymen, shall observe as far as pertains to them, in respect to their men.

61. Since, moreover, for the sake of God, and for the improvement of our kingdom, and for the better quieting of the hostility sprung up lately between us and our barons, we have made all these concessions; wishing them to enjoy these in a complete and firm stability forever, we make and concede to them the security described below; that is to say, that they shall elect twenty-five barons of the kingdom, whom they will, who ought with all their power to observe, hold, and cause to be observed, the peace and liberties which we have conceded to them, and by this our present charter confirmed to them; in this manner, that if we or our justiciar, or our bailiffs, or any one of our servants shall have done wrong in any way toward any one, or shall have transgressed any of the articles of peace or security; and the wrong shall have been shown to four barons of the aforesaid twenty-five barons, let those four barons come to us or to our justiciar, if we are out of the kingdom, laying before us the transgression, and let them ask that we cause that transgression to be corrected without delay. And if we shall not have corrected the transgression or, if we shall be out of the kingdom, if our justiciar shall not have corrected it within a period of forty days, counting from the time in which it has been shown to us or to our justiciar, if we are out of the kingdom; the aforesaid four barons shall refer the matter to the remainder of the twenty-five barons, and let these twenty-five barons with the whole community of the country distress and injure us in every way they can; that is to say by the seizure of our castles, lands, possessions, and in such other ways as they can until it shall have been corrected according to their judgment, saving our person and that of our queen, and those of our children; and when the correction has been made, let them devote themselves to us as they did before.

Around 1300 the English parliament began to develop as a representative assembly. Along with the great prelates and barons who traditionally advised the king, elected representatives of towns and counties were often summoned to its meetings.

Summons of Representatives to Parliament (1295)

The king to the sheriff of Northamptonshire. Since we intend to have a consultation and meeting with the earls, barons and other principal men of our kingdom with regard to providing remedies against the dangers which are in these days threatening the same kingdom; and on that account have commanded them to be with us on the Lord's day next after the feast of St. Martin in the approaching winter, at Westminster, to consider, ordain, and do as may be necessary for the avoidance of these dangers; we strictly require you to cause two knights from the aforesaid county, two citizens from each city in the same county, and two burgesses from each borough, of those who are especially discreet and capable of laboring, to be elected without delay, and to cause them to come to us at the aforesaid time and place.

Moreover, the said knights are to have full and sufficient power for themselves and for the community of the aforesaid county, and the said citizens and burgesses for themselves and the communities of the aforesaid cities and boroughs separately, then and there for doing what shall then be ordained according to the common counsel in the premises; so that the aforesaid business shall not remain unfinished in any way for defect of this power. And you shall have there the names of the knights, citizens and burgesses and this writ.

Witness the king at Canterbury on the third day of October.

The principal reason why the king summoned representatives to parliament was to obtain grants of taxes from them. From the representatives' point of view, attendance at parliament provided a valuable opportunity to present petitions to the king on behalf of individuals and communities. These examples illustrate the wide varieties of issues that could be raised at a medieval parliament.

From *Rolls of Parliament*

Community of the Realm, 1301

Bill of the prelates and lords delivered to the lord King on behalf of the whole community at the Parliament of Lincoln in the year aforesaid:

... Thus, if it please our lord the King, the said community is of the opinion that the two charters of liberties and of the forest[4] should henceforth be completely observed in all particulars. [Answer] It expressly pleases the lord King.

And the statutes contrary to the said charters should be annulled and voided. [Answer] It expressly pleases.

County of Hertford, 1290

The men of the county of Hertford beg that they may build a prison in the town of Hertford, from doing which William of Valence [Earl of Pembroke] hinders them, as it is said, to the King's loss and the county's vexation.

[Answer] The King granted it.

County of Cumberland, 1305

To the petition of the community of Cumberland, seeking redress for that when the lord King by his writ commanded the sheriff of the county to provide the King's larder against the King's arrival in Scotland in the twenty-second

From E. P. Cheney, trans., *University of Pennsylvania Translations and Reprints* (Philadelphia, Pa.: University of Pennsylvania Press, 1897), Vol. 1, No. 6, p. 35.
[4]i.e., Magna Carta and a supplementary Charter of the Forest issued in 1217.
From F. Palgrave, ed., *Parliamentary Writs* (London: Record Commission, 1827) in B. D. Henning, A. S. Foord, and B. L. Mathias, *Crises in English History* (New York: Holt, Rinehart and Winston, 1949), pp. 62–64. Copyright © 1949 by Holt, Rinehart and Winston, CBS College Publishing. Reprinted courtesy of the publisher.

year of his reign, the sheriff on pretext of the order took from the community a certain number of oats, and though he had an appropriation for them in his account, he paid nothing to the community:—

It is answered thus: Let suit be brought at the Exchequer, and if the sheriff has received an appropriation but has not paid, let him be punished by the established penalty and let him pay. But if otherwise let the treasurer ordain what is proper.

Merchants of England, 1290

The merchants of England sought £2000 damages from the Count of Flanders, by virtue of the convention made with the king at Mustrel, which damages they suffered by the seizure and detention in Flanders of their chattels valued at £10,000.

[Answer] The King can do nothing except to ask him [the Count] by a letter (which he granted) to satisfy them and cause them to be indemnified; because it is not recorded that any convention was made or discussed for paying damages, and because the Count can seek his damages from the English in the same way.

Hospital of St. Katherine, 1290

The brothers and sisters of the hospital of St. Katherine petition that the King grant them the fifty shillings which King Henry, father of the present lord King, gave them annually, which they received for the soul of Sanchia, formerly Queen of Germany, that they might maintain a chapel in the Tower of London where they celebrate [masses] for her soul; and the arrears of the same for ten years back.

[Answer] It is not found at the Exchequer that they received any of the said fifty shillings either in the time of King Henry or in the time of the present King, . . . and nothing is to be done in the matter.

Countess of Cornwall, 1298

Touching the lands of the Countess of Cornwall, which were assigned to her for her sustenance by her lord, and from which she claims that she was ejected: it seemed to the council that the *Curia Regis* can not interfere in any arrangement made between the Countess and her husband the Earl.

Poor Alice, 1302

Alice de la Chapele of the Isle of Guernsey begs the magnanimity, grace, and compassion of our lord the King: for that she has taken thirty-five sheaves of various kinds of grain from the sharecrop of our lord the King, which sheaves were of little value, . . . so she begs in charity and compassion that grace be granted her upon her oath that she took them because of her poverty and to nourish her child.

[Answer] Let her have grace. Let the bailiffs certify the King concerning the cause and manner [of the theft], and if they find it as stated, the King concedes that it be done as is petitioned.

France

King Louis IX (1226–1270), later canonized as Saint Louis, seemed to many of his friends and his biographer, Joinville, an ideal king. What qualities made Louis so popular? What abuses of government did he seek to remedy?

From Joinville. *Life of St. Louis*

The Virtues of St. Louis

St. Louis loved God with his whole heart and it was on Him that he modelled his actions. This could be seen in that, as God died for the love of His people, so did the King more than once put his own body in danger of death for the love he bore his people; and this although, had he wished it, he might well have been excused. Of this I will tell you more later.

The great love that he had for his people was shown by what he said, when he lay very sick at Fontainebleau, to his eldest son, my Lord Louis. "Dear son," he said, "I pray you to win the love of the people of your Kingdom. In truth, I would rather that a Scotsman came from Scotland and governed them, so long as his rule was good and fair, than that you should be seen by the world to govern it ill." The holy King so loved truth that not even to the Saracens would he break his word when he had once made an agreement with them, as I shall tell you later.

In eating he was so temperate that never once in my life did I hear him order any dish for his table, as many rich men do. He was content to eat what his cook prepared for him and what was set before him. In his speech he was restrained. Never in my life did I hear him speak ill of any man, nor name the devil—whose name is much heard in the Kingdom now, a thing which I think can hardly be pleasing to God.

He mixed his wine with water, measuring the water according to the amount that he saw the wine could stand. Once in Cyprus he asked me why I put no water in my wine. I told him that the doctors were responsible for this; they told me that I had a large head and a cold stomach and that it was impossible for me to get drunk. The King told me that they were deluding me, for if I did not learn to water my wine in my youth and tried to do so when I was old, I should be attacked by gout and diseases of the stomach, so that I should never enjoy my health; and if I drank my wine neat when I was an old man I should be drunk every evening; and it was a mighty ugly thing for a good man to get drunk.

St. Louis' Justice

Often in the summer he went after Mass to the wood of Vincennes and sat down with his back against an oak tree, and made us sit all around him.

From John of Joinville, *The Life of St. Louis*, Rene Hague, trans. from the text edited by Natalis De Wailly (New York: Sheed & Ward, 1955), pp. 26–27, 37–38, 203–207. Copyright 1955 by Sheed & Ward, Inc. Reprinted by permission of Andrews and McMeel, Inc.

Everyone who had an affair to settle could come and speak to him without the interference of any usher or other official. The King would speak himself and ask, "Is there any one here who has a case to settle?" All those who had would then stand up and he would say, "Quiet, all of you, and your cases shall be dealt with in turn." Then he would call my Lord Peter of Fontaines and my Lord Geoffrey of Villette and say to one of them, "Now give me your judgment in this case."

St. Louis' Charity
From his childhood the King was very compassionate to the poor and suffering. It was always the custom, wherever he went, every day for six score poor persons to be fed in his house with bread and wine and meat or fish. In Lent and Advent a larger number were fed; and it sometimes happened that the King served them himself and set their meat before them, carving it for them, and when they left giving them money with his own hand.

Decree for the Reform of the Realm, 1256
We, Louis, by the grace of God King of France, do ordain that all our judges, viscounts, provosts, mayors, and all other officers, in whatever matter it may be, and whatever office they may hold, shall take oath that so long as they hold their office or judgeship, they shall do justice to all men, without exception of person, to poor as well as to rich, to strangers as well as to natives, and shall keep the usages and customs that are good and proved.

And should it happen that the judges or viscounts or others, as officers or forest rangers, should violate their oaths, and should so be convicted, it is our wish that they be punished in their goods, or in their persons should the misdeed require it; the judges shall be punished by us, and the others by the judges.

Again, the other provosts, judges and officers, shall swear that they will loyally guard our revenues and our rights, and that they will not allow our rights to be stolen or taken away or diminished; with this they shall swear that they will not take or receive, either themselves or through others, gold nor silver nor any indirect benefits, nor anything else, other than fruit, or bread, or wine, or other such present up to the value of ten *sous*, which sum shall not be exceeded. . . .

We will and ordain that all our provosts and judges shall refrain from any speech which is disrespectful to God, Our Lady or any of the saints, and that they shall abstain from dicing and taverns. We will that the manufacture of dice be forbidden throughout our Kingdom and that loose women be expelled from their houses, and that whoever lets a house to a loose woman, shall pay to the provost or judge one year's rent of the house. . . .

We order that neither judges nor provosts nor any others shall maintain too many sergeants or beadles, so that the people may not be over-burdened. . . .

We order that neither judge nor provost in our service shall oppress honest folk in his jurisdiction by excessive sentences, beyond what is right; and that no subjects of ours shall be imprisoned for debt, except the debt be owed to us.

We ordain that none of our judges shall impose any fine for a debt owed by our subjects, nor for any misdemeanour, except in open court, where the fine can be judged and assessed, and with the advice of honest men. . . .

We forbid our judges and provosts to burden our subjects who have brought cases before them by moving from one place to another; they are to hear the business brought to them in the place where they have customarily sat, so that our subjects may not be forced by trouble and expense to abandon their search for justice.

Again, we order that they shall not dispossess any man of seisin he holds, without a full examination of the matter or without our special order; nor shall they burden our people with new impositions or taxes or new tolls; nor shall they summon them to ride to arms in order to obtain money from them; for it is our wish that no man from whom military service is due be summoned to the army without necessary cause, and those who are willing to join the army in person shall not be obliged to compound in money for their service. . . .

Again, it is our wish that all former judges, viscounts, provosts, and mayors, shall, after they are out of office, remain for forty days either in person or by proxy in the district in which they held office, that they may answer to the new judges for any injustice they may have done against those who wish to bring complaints against them.

In all these things which we have ordained for the well-being of our subjects and our Kingdom, we reserve to ourselves the power to explain, amend, add, or diminish, as we shall be advised.

The Empire

The German king Frederick Barbarossa (1153–1190) spent much of his reign in striving to impose his imperial authority on the cities of north Italy. This description of the Italian cities was written by a German bishop who accompanied Frederick in an invasion of Italy in 1154.

From *Otto of Freising's Chronicle*

In the governing of their cities and in the conduct of public affairs, [the Lombards] still imitate the wisdom of the ancient Romans. Finally, they are so desirous of liberty that, avoiding the insolence of power, they are governed by the will of consuls rather than rulers. There are known to be three orders among them: captains, vavasors, and commoners. And in order to suppress arrogance, the aforesaid consuls are chosen not from one but from each of the classes. And lest they should exceed bounds by lust for power, they are changed almost every year. The consequence is that, as practically that entire land is divided among the cities, each of them requires its bishops to live in the cities, and scarcely any noble or great man can be found in all the surrounding territory who does not acknowledge the authority of his city. And from this power to force all elements

From Otto of Freising and his continuator, Rahewin, *The Deeds of Frederick Barbarossa*, C. C. Mierow, trans. (New York: Columbia University Press, 1953), pp. 127–128. Reprinted courtesy of Columbia University Press.

together they are wont to call the several lands of each [noble, or magnate] their contado (*comitatus*). . . .

Also, that they may not lack the means of subduing their neighbors, they do not disdain to give the girdle of knighthood or the grades of distinction to young men of inferior station and even some workers of the vile mechanical arts, whom other peoples bar like the pest from the more respected and honorable pursuits. From this it has resulted that they far surpass all other states of the world in riches and in power. They are aided in this not only, as has been said, by their characteristic industry, but also by the absence of their princes, who are accustomed to remain on the far side of the Alps. In this, however, forgetful of their ancient nobility, they retain traces of their barbaric imperfection, because while boasting that they live in accordance with law, they are not obedient to the laws. For they scarcely if ever respect the prince to whom they should display the voluntary deference of obedience or willingly perform that which they have sworn by the integrity of their laws, unless they sense his authority in the power of his great army. Therefore it often happens that although a citizen must be humbled by the laws and an adversary subdued by arms in accordance with the laws, yet they very frequently receive in hostile fashion him whom they ought to accept as their own gentle prince, when he demands what is rightfully his own.

Frederick Barbarossa expressed his imperial claims vigorously in this address to the representatives of the commune of Rome (1155). The representatives offered to confer the imperial dignity on him in return for a huge bribe. How did Frederick answer them? How did he defend his claim to be emperor?

From *Otto of Freising's Chronicle*

We have heard much heretofore concerning the wisdom and the valor of the Romans, yet more concerning their wisdom. Wherefore we cannot wonder enough at finding your words insipid with swollen pride rather than seasoned with the salt of wisdom. You set forth the ancient renown of your city. You extoll to the very stars the ancient status of your sacred republic. Granted, granted! To use the words of your own writer, "There was, *there was once* virtue in this republic." "Once," I say. And O that we might truthfully and freely say "now"! Your Rome—nay, ours also—has experienced the vicissitudes of time. She could not be the only one to escape a fate ordained by the Author of all things for all that dwell beneath the orb of the moon. What shall I say? It is clear how first the strength of your nobility was transferred from this city of ours to the royal city of the East, and how for the course of many years the thirsty Greekling sucked the breasts of your delight. Then came the Frank, truly noble, in deed as in name, and forcibly possessed himself of whatever freedom was still left to you. Do you wish to know the ancient glory of your Rome? The worth of the senatorial dig-

From Otto of Freising and his continuator, Rahewin, *The Deeds of Frederick Barbarossa*, C. C. Mierow, trans. (New York: Columbia University Press, 1953), pp. 146–148. Reprinted courtesy of Columbia University Press.

nity? The impregnable disposition of the camp? The virtue and the disc
the equestrian order, its unmarred and unconquerable boldness when a
ing to a conflict? Behold our state. All these things are to be found with us. All
these have descended to us, together with the empire. Not in utter nakedness
did the empire come to us. It came clad in its virtue. It brought its adornments
with it. With us are your consuls. With us is your senate. With us is your soldiery.
These very leaders of the Franks must rule you by their counsel, these very
knights of the Franks must avert harm from you with the sword. You boastfully
declare that by you I have been summoned, that by you I have been made first
a citizen and then the prince, that from you I have received what was yours.
How lacking in reason, how void of truth this novel utterance is, may be left to
your own judgment and to the decision of men of wisdom! Let us ponder over
the exploits of modern emperors, to see whether it was not our divine princes
Charles [Charlemagne] and Otto [I] who, by their valor and not by anyone's
bounty, wrested the City along with Italy from the Greeks and the Lombards
and added it to the realms of the Franks. Desiderius and Berengar teach you this,
your tyrants, of whom you boasted, on whom you relied as your princes. We
have learned from reliable accounts that they were not only subjugated and
taken captive by our Franks, but grew old and ended their lives in their servitude. Their ashes, buried among us, constitute the clearest evidence of this fact.
But, you say: "You came on my invitation," I admit it; I was invited. Give me the
reason why I was invited! You were being assailed by enemies and could not be
freed by your own hand or by the effeminate Greeks. The power of the Franks
was invoked by invitation. I would call it entreaty rather than invitation. In your
misery you besought the happy, in your frailty the valiant, in your weakness the
strong, in your anxiety the carefree. Invited after that fashion—if it may be called
an invitation—I have come. I have made your prince my vassal and from that
time until the present have transferred you to my jurisdiction. I am the lawful
possessor. Let him who can, snatch the club from the hand of Hercules. . . .

CHURCH AND STATE

Innocent III—Papal Power at Its Zenith

*Innocent III (1198–1216) claimed a role of leadership for the papacy in all the spiritual
and temporal affairs of Christendom. Were there any limits to his claims?*

From *Letters of Innocent III*

To the Nobles of Tuscany
Just as the founder of the universe established two great lights in the firmament of heaven, a greater one to preside over the day and a lesser to preside over
the night, so too in the firmament of the universal church, which is signified by
the word heaven, he instituted two great dignities, a greater one to preside over
souls as if over day and a lesser one to preside over bodies as if over night. These
are the pontifical authority and the royal power. Now just as the moon derives

its light from the sun and is indeed lower than it in quantity and quality, in position and in power, so too the royal power derives the spendor of its dignity from the pontifical authority. . . .

In 1202 Innocent intervened to support his own candidate in the election of a German king. On what ground did he claim this right?

To the Princes of Germany
. . . Just as we do not want our justice to be usurped by others, so too we do not want to claim for ourselves the rights of the princes. We do indeed acknowledge, as we should, that the princes, to whom this belongs by right and ancient custom, have the right and power to elect a king who is afterwards to be promoted emperor; and especially so since this right and power came to them from the apostolic see which transferred the Roman empire from the Greeks to the Germans in the person of the great Charles. But the princes should acknowledge, and indeed they do acknowledge, that right and authority to examine the person elected as king, who is to be promoted to the imperial dignity, belong to us who anoint, consecrate and crown him; for it is regularly and generally observed that the examination of a person pertains to the one to whom the laying-on of hands belongs. If the princes elected as king a sacrilegious man or an excommunicate, a tyrant, a fool or a heretic, and that not just by a divided vote but unanimously, ought we to anoint, consecrate and crown such a man? Of course not.

It is clear from law and precedent that, if the votes of the princes are divided in an election, we can favor one of the parties after due warning and a reasonable delay, especially after the unction, consecration and coronation are demanded of us, for it has often happened that both parties demanded them. For if the princes after due warning and delay cannot or will not agree, shall the apostolic see then lack an advocate and defender and be penalized for their fault? . . .

In 1204 Innocent tried to judge a feudal dispute between Richard I of England and Philip II of France. (Richard claimed that Philip had broken an oath establishing peace between the two monarchs.) What was the basis of Innocent's claim this time?

To the Bishops of France
. . . Let no one suppose that we wish to diminish or disturb the jurisdiction and power of the king when he ought not to impede or restrict our jurisdiction and power. Since we are insufficient to exercise all our own jurisdiction why should we want to usurp another's? . . . For we do not intend to judge concerning a fief, judgement on which belongs to him—except when some special privilege or contrary custom detracts from the common law—but to decide concerning a sin, of which the judgement undoubtedly belongs to us, and we can

From *Letters of Innocent III,* Brian Tierney, trans. in *The Crisis of Church and State 1050–1300* (New York: Prentice-Hall, 1964), pp. 132–137. Copyright © 1964 by Prentice-Hall, Inc. Reprinted courtesy of Prentice-Hall, Inc., Englewood Cliffs, N.J.

and should exercise it against any-one. . . . But it may be said that kings are to be treated differently from others. We, however, know that it is written in the divine law, "You shall judge the great as well as the little and there shall be no difference of persons" (*cf.* Deuteronomy 1:17). . . . Although we are empowered to proceed in this fashion against any criminal sin in order to recall the sinner from error to truth and from vice to virtue, this is especially so when it is a sin against peace, peace which is the bond of love. . . . Finally, when a treaty of peace was made between the kings and confirmed on both sides by oaths which, however, were not kept for the agreed period, can we not take cognizance of such a sworn oath, which certainly belongs to the judgement of the church, in order to re-establish the broken treaty of peace? . . .

Innocent IV and Frederick II

Emperor Frederick II (1215–1250) aimed to unite all Italy under his rule. This led to frequent conflicts with the papacy. The somewhat colorful personality of the emperor was described by a thirteenth-century Franciscan, Salimbene. His account is paraphrased below.

Frederick II According to Salimbene

To Salimbene, as to Dante, Frederick was a man of heroic proportions in his very sins. "Of faith in God he had none; he was crafty, wily, avaricious, lustful, malicious, wrathful; and yet a gallant man at times, when he would show his kindness or courtesy; full of solace, jocund, delightful, fertile in devices. He knew to read, write, and sing, and to make songs and music. He was a comely man, and well-formed, but of middle stature. I have seen him, and once I loved him, for on my behalf he wrote to Bro. Elias, Minister-General of the Friars Minor, to send me back to my father. Moreover, he knew to speak with many and varied tongues, and, to be brief, if he had been rightly Catholic, and had loved God and His Church, he would have had few emperors his equals in the world." [Salimbene] goes on to enumerate several specimens of the Emperor's "curiosities" or "excesses," though for sheer weariness he will not tell them all. Frederick cut off a notary's thumb who had spelt his name *Fredericus* instead of *Fridericus*. Like Psammetichus in Herodotus, he made linguistic experiments on the vile bodies of hapless infants, "bidding foster-mothers and nurses to suckle and bathe and wash the children, but in no wise to prattle or speak with them; for he would have learnt whether they would speak the Hebrew language (which had been the first), or Greek, or Latin, or Arabic, or perchance the tongue of their parents of whom they had been born. But he laboured in vain, for the children could not live without clappings of the hands, and gestures, and gladness of countenance, and blandishments." Again, "when he saw the Holy Land, (which God had so oft-times commended as a land flowing with milk and honey and most excellent above all lands,) it pleased him not, and he said that

From G. G. Coulton, *St. Francis to Dante* (London: David Nutt, 1906), pp. 242–243.

if the God of the Jews had seen *his* lands of Terra di Lavoro, Calabria, Sicily, and Apulia, then He would not so have commended the land which He promised to the Jews." Again, he compelled "Nicholas the Fish," whom his mother's curse had condemned to an amphibious life, to dive and fetch his golden cup a second time from the very bottom of Charybdis: in which repeated attempt the poor man knew that he must perish. Fifthly, "he enclosed a living man in a cask that he might die there, wishing thereby to show that the soul perished utterly, as if he might say the word of Isaiah 'Let us eat and drink, for to-morrow we die.' For he was an Epicurean; wherefore, partly of himself and partly through his wise men, he sought out all that he could find in Holy Scripture which might make for the proof that there was no other life after death, as for instance 'Thou shalt destroy them, and not build them up': and again 'Their sepulchres shall be their houses for ever.' "

Pope Innocent IV (1243–1254) struggled for several years—in the end successfully—against Frederick's plans to dominate Italy.

Deposition of Frederick II (1245)

[Frederick] has committed four very grave offences, which can not be covered up by any subterfuge (we say nothing for the moment about his other crimes); he has abjured God on many occasions; he has wantonly broken the peace which had been re-established between the Church and the Empire; he has also committed sacrilege by causing to be imprisoned the Cardinals of the holy Roman Church and the prelates and clerics, regular and secular, of other churches, coming to the Council which our predecessor had summoned; he is also accused of heresy not by doubtful and flimsy but by formidable and clear proofs. . . .

We therefore, who are the vicar, though unworthy, of Jesus Christ on earth and to whom it was said in the person of blessed Peter the Apostle: "Whatsoever thou shalt bind on earth," etc., show and declare an account of the above-mentioned shameful crimes and of many others, having held careful consultation with our brethren and the holy Council, that the aforesaid prince—who has rendered himself so unworthy of all the honor and dignity of the Empire and the kingdom and who, because of his wickedness, has been rejected by God from acting as king or Emperor—is bound by his sins and cast out and deprived of all honor and dignity by God, to which we add our sentence of deprivation also. We absolve for ever all who owe him allegiance in virtue of an oath of fealty from any oath of this kind; and we strictly forbid by Apostolic authority that any one should obey him or look upon him henceforth as king or Emperor, and we decree that whoever shall in the future afford him advice, help or goodwill as if he were Emperor or king, shall fall "ipso facto" under the binding force of excommunication. But let those in the same Empire whose duty it is to look to the election of an Emperor, elect a successor freely. We shall make it our business to

From Innocent IV, in S. Z. Ehler and J. B. Morrall, eds. and trans., *Church and State Through the Centuries* (Westminster, Md.: Newman Press, 1954), pp. 80, 86.

provide for the aforesaid kingdom of Sicily as seems best to us with the advice of our brethren.

Boniface VIII—The Crisis of Papal Power

In the years around 1300 a new conflict arose. This time the pope's adversary was not an emperor but a powerful national king, Philip IV of France. The dispute concerned the king's claim to tax the clergy of his realm and to exercise jurisdiction over them. In the course of the conflict Pope Boniface VIII promulgated the bull Unam Sanctam, *often seen as the high-water mark of papal claims to temporal power. Does it go beyond previous assertions of papal power?*

Unam Sanctam

That there is one holy, Catholic and apostolic church we are bound to believe and to hold, our faith urging us, and this we do firmly believe and simply confess; and that outside this church there is no salvation or remission of sins, as her spouse proclaims in the Canticles, "One is my dove, my perfect one. She is the only one of her mother, the chosen of her that bore her" (Canticles 6:8); which represents one mystical body whose head is Christ, while the head of Christ is God. In this church there is our Lord, one faith, one baptism. At the time of the Flood there was one ark, symbolizing the one church. It was finished in one cubit and had one helmsman and captain, namely Noah, and we read that all things on earth outside of it were destroyed. This church we venerate and this alone, the Lord saying through his prophet, "Deliver, O God, my soul from the sword, my only one from the power of the dog" (Psalm 21:21). He prayed for the soul, that is himself, the head, and at the same time for the body, which he called the one church on account of the promised unity of faith, sacraments and charity of the church. This is that seamless garment of the Lord which was not cut but fell by lot. Therefore there is one body and one head of this one and only church, not two heads as though it were a monster, namely Christ and Christ's vicar, Peter and Peter's successor, for the Lord said to this Peter, "Feed my sheep" (John 21:17). He said "My sheep" in general, not these or those, whence he is understood to have committed them all to Peter. Hence, if the Greeks or any others say that they were not committed to Peter and his successors, they necessarily admit that they are not of Christ's flock, for the Lord says in John that there is one sheepfold and one shepherd.

We are taught by the words of the Gospel that in this church and in her power there are two swords, a spiritual one and a temporal one. For when the apostles said "Here are two swords" (Luke 22:38), meaning in the church since it was the apostles who spoke, the Lord did not reply that it was too many but enough. Certainly anyone who denies that the temporal sword is in the power of Peter has not paid heed to the words of the Lord when he said, "Put up thy

From Brian Tierney, *The Crisis of Church and State 1050–1300* (New York: Prentice-Hall, 1964), pp. 188–189. Copyright © 1964 by Prentice-Hall, Inc. Reprinted courtesy of Prentice-Hall, Inc., Englewood Cliffs, N.J.

sword into its sheath" (Matthew 26:52). Both then are in the power of the church, the material sword and the spiritual. But the one is exercised for the church, the other by the church, the one by the hand of the priest, the other by the hand of the kings and soldiers, though at the will and suffrance of the priest. One sword ought to be under the other and the temporal authority subject to the spiritual power. For, while the apostle says, "There is no power but from God and those that are ordained of God" (Romans 13:1), they would not be ordained unless one sword was under the other and, being inferior, was led by the other to the highest things. For, according to the blessed Dionysius, it is the law of divinity for the lowest to be led to the highest through intermediaries. In the order of the universe all things are not kept in order in the same fashion and immediately but the lowest are ordered by the intermediate and inferiors by superiors. But that the spiritual power excels any earthly one in dignity and nobility we ought the more openly to confess in proportion as spiritual things excel temporal ones. Moreover we clearly perceive this from the giving of tithes, from benediction and sanctification, from the acceptance of this power and from the very government of things. For, the truth bearing witness, the spiritual power has to institute the earthly power and to judge it if it has not been good. So is verified the prophecy of Jeremias [1.10] concerning the church and the power of the church, "Lo, I have set thee this day over the nations and over kingdoms" etc.

Therefore, if the earthly power errs, it shall be judged by the spiritual power, if a lesser spiritual power errs it shall be judged by its superior, but if the supreme spiritual power errs it can be judged only by God not by man, as the apostle witnesses, "The spiritual man judgeth all things and he himself is judged of no man" (1 Corinthians 2:15). Although this authority was given to a man and is exercised by a man it is not human but rather divine, being given to Peter at God's mouth, and confirmed to him and to his successors in him, the rock whom the Lord acknowledged when he said to Peter himself "Whatsoever thou shalt bind" etc. (Matthew 16:19). Whoever therefore resists this power so ordained by God resists the ordinance of God unless, like the Manicheans, he imagines that there are two beginnings, which we judge to be false and heretical, as Moses witnesses, for not "in the beginnings" but "in the beginning" God created heaven and earth (Genesis 1:1). Therefore we declare, state, define and pronounce that it is altogether necessary to salvation for every human creature to be subject to the Roman Pontiff.

In June 1303, King Philip launched an extraordinary series of charges against Boniface. The accusations were presented by the king's minister, Guillaume de Plaisans, to a royal council in Paris.

Accusations Against Boniface VIII

He does not believe in the immortality or incorruptibility of the rational soul but believes that the rational soul undergoes corruption with the body. He does not believe in an eternal life to come . . . and he was not ashamed to declare that he would rather be a dog or an ass or any brute animal than a Frenchman, which he would not have said if he believed that a Frenchman had an immortal soul. . . . He does not faithfully believe that, through the words instituted by

Christ, spoken by a faithful and properly ordained priest in the manner prescribed by the church over a Host, it becomes the true body of Christ. . . . He is reported to say that fornication is not a sin any more than rubbing the hands together is . . . He has often said that he would ruin himself and the whole world and the whole church to lay low the king and the French people if he could not do it otherwise. . . . He has had silver images of himself erected in churches to perpetuate his damnable memory, so leading men into idolatry. . . . He has a private demon whose advice he takes in all matters. . . . He has publicly preached that the Roman pope cannot commit simony, which is heresy. . . . He is guilty of the crime of sodomy. . . . He has caused many clerics to be murdered in his presence, rejoicing in their deaths. . . . He has compelled certain priests to reveal men's confessions and then, without the consent of those who confessed, has made them public to their shame and confusion. . . . He does not fast on fast days or in Lent. . . . He has depressed and debased the rank and status of the cardinals. . . . He is openly called a simonist or rather the fount and origin of simony. . . . He is publicly accused of treating inhumanly his predecessor Celestine—a man of holy memory and holy life who perhaps did not know that he could not resign and that accordingly Boniface could not legitimately enter upon his see—imprisoning him in a dungeon and causing him to die there swiftly and secretly, and this is notorious throughout the whole world. . . . He does not seek the salvation of souls but their perdition.

Philip succeeded in rallying French support against the claims of Boniface. A later pope, Clement V (1305–1314), put forward a conciliatory explanation of Unam Sanctam *and commended the actions of the French king. For the first time a medieval pope was thoroughly defeated in a struggle with a temporal monarch.*

Decree of Clement V (1306)

The full and sincere affection that our son Philip, illustrious king of the French, bears toward us and the Roman church has merited—and the outstanding merits of his forefathers, together with the sincerity and purity of the devotion of the people of his kingdom have also merited—that we show benevolent favor to both king and kingdom. Hence it is that we do not wish or intend that anything prejudicial to that king or kingdom should arise from the declaration of our predecessor of happy memory Pope Boniface VIII, which began with the words "Unam sanctam"; nor that the aforementioned king, kingdom and people should be any more subject to the Roman church on account of it than they were before. But everything is understood to be in the same state as it was before the said definition, both as regards the church and as regards the aforementioned king, kingdom and people.

From P. Dupony, *Histoire du différend d'entre le pape Boniface VIII et Philippe le Bel* (Paris, 1655), Brian Tierney, trans. in *The Crisis of Church and State 1050–1300* (New York: Prentice-Hall, 1964), p. 190. Copyright © 1964 by Prentice-Hall, Inc. Reprinted courtesy of Prentice-Hall, Inc., Englewood Cliffs, N.J.

Decree of Clement V (1311)

... Finally, having inquired diligently into the matter we find that the said assertors, objectors and denouncers [of Boniface] ... and the said king ... were not impelled by any preconceived malice but were actuated by an estimable, just and sincere zeal ... and by apostolic authority we pronounce and with the council of our brothers we decree and by these presents declare that they were and are guiltless of malicious accusation and that they acted out of an estimable, just and sincere zeal and from the fervor of their Catholic faith.

Reflections on Government

Innocent IV was not only a pope but also a great jurist. This canonistic text from his Commentary on the Decretals *was often cited in the sixteenth-century Spanish debates about the rights of American Indians. What did Innocent concede to the infidels? What did he claim for the pope?*

From Innocent IV. *Commentary on the Decretals*

Is it licit to invade the lands of infidels? ... In truth the earth belongs to God ... for God is the creator of all things, and he subjected everything to the rational creature for whom he had made all these things as in Genesis, 1.

... I maintain, therefore, that lordship, possession and jurisdiction can belong to infidels licitly and without sin, for these things were made not only for the faithful but for every rational creature as has been said. For he makes his sun to rise on the just and the wicked and he feeds the birds of the air, Matthew c.5, c.6. Accordingly we say that it is not licit for the pope or the faithful to take away from infidels their belongings or their lordships or jurisdictions because they possess them without sin. Nevertheless we do certainly believe that the pope, who is vicar of Jesus Christ, has power not only over Christians but also over all infidels, for Christ had power over all, whence it is said in the psalm, "Give to the king thy judgment O God" (Psalm 71:2), and he would not seem to have been a careful father unless he had committed full power over all to his vicar whom he left on earth. Again he gave the keys of the kingdom of heaven to Peter and his successors and said, "Whatsoever you shall bind, etc." (Matthew 16:19). And again, elsewhere, "Feed my sheep, etc." (John 21:17). ... But all men, faithful and infidels, are Christ's sheep by creation even though they are not of the fold of the church and thus from the foregoing it is clear that the pope has jurisdiction and power over all *de iure* though not *de facto*.

The conflict Between Boniface VIII and Philip IV stimulated much new writing on the right re-
lationship between spiritual and temporal power. The Dominican theologian John of Paris tried to
distinguish carefully between the two spheres. How could a king or pope be deposed according to
this author?

From John of Paris. *On Royal and Papal Power (1303)*

First it should be known that kingship, properly understood, can be defined
as the rule of one man over a perfect multitude so ordered as to promote the
public good. . . .

Next it must be borne in mind that man is not ordered only to such a good
as can be acquired by nature, which is to live virtuously, but is further ordered
to a supernatural end which is eternal life, and the whole multitude of men living virtuously is ordered to this. . . . and because Christ was to withdraw his corporal presence from the church it was necessary for him to institute others as
ministers who would administer the sacraments to men, and these are called
priests. . . . Hence priesthood may be defined in this fashion. Priesthood is a spiritual power of administering sacraments to the faithful conferred by Christ on
ministers of the church.

The royal power both existed and was exercised before the papal, and there
were kings in France before there were Christians. Therefore neither the royal
power nor its exercise is from the pope but from God and from the people, who
elect a king by choosing either a person or a royal house. . . . It would seem that the
power of inferior pontiffs and ministers is derived from the pope more than
the royal power, for ecclesiastical prelates are more immediately dependent on the
pope than secular princes. But the power of prelates is not from God through the
pope but immediately from God and from the people who elect or consent.

Concerning the ecclesiastical power of censure or correction it should be
known that, directly, it is only spiritual, for it can impose no penalty in the external court but a spiritual one, except conditionally and incidentally. For
though the ecclesiastical judge has to lead men back to God and draw them
away from sin and correct them, he has to do this only in the way laid down for
him by God, which is to say by cutting them off from the sacraments and from
the company of the faithful and by similar measures which are proper to ecclesiastical censure. I said "conditionally" in reference to one who is willing to repent and accept a pecuniary penalty, for the ecclesiastical judge cannot impose
any corporal or pecuniary penalty for a crime as a secular judge can, except only
on one who is willing to accept it. . . . I said "incidentally" because if a prince
was a heretic and incorrigible and contemptuous of ecclesiastical censures, the
pope might so move the people that he would be deprived of his secular dignity
and deposed by the people. The pope might do this in the case of an ecclesiastical crime, of which cognizance belonged to him, by excommunicating all who

From *De potestate regia et papali*, J. Leclereq, ed. in *Jean de Paris et l'ecclsiologie du XIII siècle* (Paris: J.
Vrin, 1942), pp. 176–178, 199, 214, 236.

obeyed such a man as a lord, and thus the people would depose him, and the pope "incidentally." So too, if the pope on the other hand behaved criminally and brought scandal on the church and was incorrigible, the prince might indirectly excommunicate him and "incidentally" bring about his deposition by warning him personally or through the cardinals. And if the pope were unwilling to yield the emperor might so move the people as to compel him to resign or be deposed by the people, for the emperor could, by taking securities or imposing corporal penalties, prevent each and everyone from obeying him or serving him as pope. So each can act toward the other, for both pope and emperor have jurisdiction universally and everywhere, but the one has spiritual jurisdiction, the other temporal.

. . . Although a form of government in which one man simply rules according to virtue is better than any other simple government, as the Philosopher proves in Book III of the *Politics*, nevertheless if it is mixed with aristocracy and democracy it is better than a simple form in that, in a mixed constitution, all have some part in the government. Through this the peace of the people is maintained and all of them love such a government and preserve it.

PART NINE

THE MEDIEVAL WORLD— RELIGION AND CULTURE

The twelfth century was a time of vivid new life in many areas of human conduct and intellectual activity. The people of the age often reveal themselves to us as living personalities—for instance, a Peter Abelard, Heloise, or Bernard of Clairvaux. A fresh, more confident attitude to nature inspired poets, religious mystics, and philosophers. Francis of Assisi especially combined deep religious devotion with a delight in the natural beauty of the created world. Devotion to the Virgin Mary led to an emphasis on the "feminine" virtues of tenderness and compassion in medieval religion. At the same time the cult of courtly love provided for the lay aristocracy a new conception of the ideal relationship between women and men.

In the sphere of thought, the rediscovery of Aristotle's philosophy and science opened up a new world to medieval intellectuals. The great problem that emerged for them was to fit all the new knowledge into a framework of generally accepted religion. Peter Abelard pointed to the need for using critical reason in interpreting old texts. The outstanding philosophers of the next century, like Thomas Aquinas, sought to combine Aristotle's philosophy with biblical revelation in great syntheses of universal knowledge. Their efforts did not satisfy everyone. During the later Middle Ages heretical sects grew up that rejected the teachings of the established church. They were often harshly persecuted. Unhappily, as medieval civilization grew more mature, it also grew more intolerant.

In this chapter we shall consider first an outstanding intellectual of the twelfth century, Peter Abelard; then the rise of the university of Paris and the work of one of its great masters, Thomas Aquinas. Francis of Assisi's different approach to religion is considered next, and then the dissident sects and the Jews who lived on the margin of medieval society. A final section illustrates the many different attitudes toward women that grew up in this complex civilization.

REASON, FAITH, AND LOVE

Abelard and Bernard: Reason and Faith

Peter Abelard (1079–1142), a brilliant teacher in the schools of Paris at the beginning of the twelfth century, was renowned for his critical approach to sacred authorities. In his Sic et Non (Yes and No) *he showed that, superficially at least, they often seemed to contradict one another. Part of the Introduction and the first Question follow. How did Abelard justify his treatment of the great church Fathers?*

From Abelard. *Sic et Non*

In order that the way be not blocked and posterity deprived of the healthy labor of treating and debating difficult questions of language and style, a distinction must be drawn between the work of later authors and the supreme canonical authority of the Old and New Testaments. If, in Scripture, anything seems absurd you are not permitted to say, "The author of this book did not hold to the truth"—but rather that the codex is defective or that the interpreter erred or that you do not understand. But if anything seems contrary to truth in the works of later authors, which are contained in innumerable books, the reader or auditor is free to judge, so that he may approve what is pleasing and reject what gives offense, unless the matter is established by certain reason or by canonical authority (of the Scriptures). . . .

In view of these considerations we have undertaken to collect various sayings of the Fathers that give rise to questioning because of their apparent contradictions as they occur to our memory. This questioning excites young readers to the maximum of effort in inquiring into the truth, and such inquiry sharpens their minds. Assiduous and frequent questioning is indeed the first key to wisdom. Aristotle, that most perspicacious of all philosophers, exhorted the studious to practice it eagerly, saying, "Perhaps it is difficult to express oneself with confidence on such matters if they have not been much discussed. To entertain doubts on particular points will not be unprofitable." For by doubting we come to inquiry; through inquiring we perceive the truth, according to the Truth Himself. "Seek and you shall find," He says, "Knock and it shall be opened to you."

QUESTION I

That Faith Should Be Based on Human Reason—And the Contrary

Gregory in Homily XXVI.

We know that the works of the Lord would not excite wonder if they were understood by reason; nor is there any merit in faith where human reason offers proof.

From Brian Tierney, trans. in *Great Issues in Western Civilization*, Brian Tierney, Donald Kagan, and L. Pearce Williams, eds. (New York: Random House, 1976), pp. 397–400. Copyright © 1967, 1972, 1976 by Random House, Inc. Reprinted by permission of the publisher.

Idem in Homily V.

At one word of command Peter and Andrew left their nets and followed the Redeemer. They had seen him work no miracles; they had heard nothing from him about eternal retribution; and nevertheless, at one command of the Lord, they forgot what they had seemed to possess. . . .

From the First Book of Augustine against Faustus.

Faustus: It is a weak profession of faith if one does not believe in Christ without evidence and argument.

From the Life of St. Sylvester,

where, disputing with the Jews, he said to the Rabbi Roasus, "Faith is not submitted to human reason, and faith teaches us that this God, whom you confess to be one God, is Father, Son, and Holy Spirit."

Augustine, on the Morals of the Church Against the Manicheans.

The order of nature is such that, when we state anything, authority precedes reason for a reason might seem weak if, after it has been presented, authority is cited to confirm it. . . .

Ambrose.

If I am convinced by reason I give up faith. . . .

Gregory to Bishop Dominicus.

Although these things are so I wish that all heretics be held in check by Catholic priests vigorously and always by reasoning.

Idem in Pastoral Care.

The wise of this world and the dull are to be admonished differently. The former are for the most part converted by the arguments of reason, the latter sometimes better by examples. . . .

Hilary, on the Trinity, Book XII.

It is fitting that those who preach Christ to the world should refute the irreligious and unsound doctrines of the world through their knowledge of omnipotent wisdom, according as the Apostle says. . . .

Augustine to Count Valerian.

The Apostle Peter commanded us to be always ready to give satisfaction to anyone asking us the reason for our faith and hope. . . . We should give an account of our faith and hope to enquirers in a two-fold fashion. We should always explain the just grounds of our faith and hope to questioners, whether they ask honestly or dishonestly, and we should hold fast to the pure profession of our faith and hope even amid the pressures of our adversaries.

(Abelard then considered in the same fashion, giving authorities for and against each proposition, some of the central teachings of the church—e.g., "That there is one God—and the contrary"; "That the Son is without beginning—and the contrary"; "That God can do all things—and the contrary"; "That without baptism of water no one can be saved—and the contrary"; "That saintly works do not justify man—and the contrary.")

Bernard of Clairvaux, a great spiritual teacher and a leader of the Cistercian Order of monks, was outraged by Abelard's approach to sacred learning. Why did he object to it?

From Bernard. *Letter to Pope Innocent II*

To his most loving Father and Lord, Innocent, Supreme Pontiff Brother Bernard, called Abbot of Clairvaux, sends humble greeting. . . .

We have in France an old teacher turned into a new theologian, who in his early days amused himself with dialectics, and now gives utterance to wild imaginations upon the Holy Scriptures. He is endeavoring again to quicken false opinions, long ago condemned and put to rest, not only his own, but those of others; and is adding fresh ones as well. I know not what there is in heaven above and in the earth beneath which he deigns to confess ignorance of: he raises his eyes to Heaven, and searches the deep things of God, and then returning to us, he brings back unspeakable words which it is not lawful for a man to utter, while he is presumptuously prepared to give a reason for everything, even of those things which are above reason; he presumes against reason and against faith. For what is more against reason than by reason to attempt to transcend reason? And what is more against faith than to be unwilling to believe what reason cannot attain?

But on the other hand our theologian says: "What is the use of speaking of doctrine unless what we wish to teach can be explained so as to be intelligible?" And so he promises understanding to his hearers, even on those most sublime and sacred truths which are hidden in the very bosom of our holy faith. . . . It is no wonder if a man who is careless of what he says should, when rushing into the mysteries of the Faith, so irreverently assail and tear asunder the hidden treasures of godliness, since he has neither piety nor faith in his notions about the piety of faith. For instance, on the very threshold of his theology (I should rather say his stultology) he defines faith as private judgment; as though in these mysteries it is to be allowed to each person to think and speak as he pleases, or as though the mysteries of our faith are to hang in uncertainty amongst shifting and varying opinions, when on the contrary they rest on the solid and unshakable foundation of truth. Is not our hope baseless if our faith is subject to change? Fools then were our martyrs for bearing so cruel tortures for an uncertainty, and for entering, without hesitation, on an everlasting exile, through a bitter death, when there was a doubt as to the recompense of their reward. But far be it from us to think that in our faith or hope anything, as he supposes, depends on the fluctuating judgment of the individual, and that the whole of it does not rest on sure and solid truth, having been commended by miracles and revelations from above, founded and consecrated by the Son of the Virgin, by the Blood of the Redeemer, by the glory of the risen Christ. These infallible proofs have been given us in superabundance. But if not, the Spirit it-

From S. J. Eales, trans., *Life and Works of St. Bernard* (London: John Hodges, 1889), Vol. 2, pp. 565, 574–575.

self, lastly, bears witness with our spirit that we are the sons of God. How, then, can any one dare to call faith opinion, unless it be that he has not yet received that Spirit, or unless he either knows not the Gospel or thinks it to be a fable? *I know in whom I have believed, and I am confident* (2 Tim. i. 12), cries the Apostle, and you mutter in my ears that faith is only an opinion. . . . Faith is not an opinion, but a certitude.

Abelard insisted in his Dialectica, *a treatise on logic, that a Christian philosopher should pursue all available knowledge.*

From Abelard. *Dialectica*

A new calumny against me, have my rivals lately devised, because I write upon the dialectic art; affirming that it is not lawful for a Christian to treat of things which do not pertain to the Faith. Not only they say that this science does not prepare us for the Faith, but that it destroys faith by the implications of its arguments. But it is wonderful if I must not discuss what is permitted them to read. If they allow that the art militates against faith, surely they deem it not to be science *(scientia)*. For the science of truth is the comprehension of things, whose *species* is the wisdom in which faith consists. Truth is not opposed to truth. For not as falsehood may be opposed to falsity, or evil to evil, can the true be opposed to the true, or the good to the good; but rather all good things are in accord. All knowledge is good, even that which relates to evil, because a righteous man must have it. Since he may guard against evil, it is necessary that he should know it beforehand: otherwise he could not shun it. Though an act be evil, knowledge regarding it is good; though it be evil to sin, it is good to know the sin, which otherwise we could not shun. Nor is the science *mathematica* to be deemed evil, whose practice (astrology) is evil. Nor is it a crime to know with what services and immolations the demons may be compelled to do our will, but to use such knowledge. For if it were evil to know this, how could God be absolved, who knows the desires and cogitations of all His creatures, and how the concurrence of demons may be obtained? If therefore it is not wrong to know, but to do, the evil is to be referred to the act and not to the knowledge. Hence we are convinced that all knowledge, which indeed comes from God alone and from His bounty, is good. Wherefore the study of every science should be conceded to be good, because that which is good comes from it; and especially one must insist upon the study of that *doctrina* by which the greater truth is known. This is dialectic, whose function is to distinguish between every truth and falsity; as leader in all knowledge, it holds the primary and rule of all philosophy. The same also is shown to be needful to the Catholic Faith, which cannot without its aid resist the sophistries of schismatics.

From H. O. Taylor, trans., *The Mediaeval Mind,* 4th ed. (Cambridge, Mass.: Harvard University Press, 1962), Vol. 2, p. 379. Reprinted by permission of the publisher.

For Bernard the way to approach God was not through logical argumentation but through love, expressed in an intense personal devotion to Jesus. In writing of this love, Bernard turned to the passionate language of the biblical Song of Solomon *(p. 28).*

From Bernard. *The Love of God*

The faithful surely know how utterly they need Jesus and him crucified whilst wondering at and embracing the love in Him which passeth knowledge. . . . The Pagan is in no wise stirred by such prickings of love as the Church feels, who says: *I am wounded with charity;* and again: *Stay me with flowers, comfort me with apples; for I am sick of love.* She beholds the Only Begotten of the Father, bearing His cross; she beholds the Lord of Majesty buffeted and spat upon; she beholds the Author of life and of glory fastened by nails, pierced by the lance, overwhelmed with reproaches, and at last laying down that dear life of His for His friends. She beholds these things, and the more the sword of love pierces her own soul, and she says: *Stay me with flowers, comfort me with apples; for I am sick of love.* . . . [S]he desires to wax strong on the apples of the Passion, which she has plucked from the tree of the Cross, and on the flowers of the Resurrection, whose fragrance especially invites the Bridegroom to visit her more often. . . . *Now,* He saith, *the winter is past, the rain is over and gone, the flowers have appeared on the earth;* meaning that the time of summer is come with Him who was loosed from the cold of death into a spring mildness of new life. *Behold,* He saith, *I make all things new;* whose flesh was sown in death, and flowered again in the Resurrection, at the fragrance whereof straightway in the field of our valley the dry becomes green, the cold grows warm, the dead return to life.

. . . Lo, I remember what I said in the beginning, that the manner of loving God is to love without measure. And since the object of the love of God is immeasurable and infinite (for God is infinite and immeasurable), what, I ask, should be the limit or measure of our love? Our very love is not rendered as a free gift, but repaid as a debt. Immeasurableness loves, eternity loves, *charity which passeth knowledge* loves; God loves, whose greatness is unsearchable, whose wisdom is infinite, whose peace passeth all understanding; and do we pay back again with measure? *I will love thee, O Lord, my strength, my rock, my refuge, and my deliverer;* and my sum of all that is desirable and worthy of love. My God, my helper, I love thee according to Thy gift, and in my measure, less indeed than just, but surely not less than my power; I, who cannot as much as I ought, and yet cannot beyond what I can. I shall, indeed, be able to love more, when Thou shalt deign to give more; though never in proportion to Thy worth. *Thine eyes did see my imperfect being;* but, nevertheless, *in thy book all shall be written,* they who do what they can, albeit they cannot what they should. It is clear enough, methinks, both in what measure God is to be loved, and by what desert of His own. By what desert of His, I say; for the greatness of it, who may fully see? Who may tell? Who may know?

From Bernard of Clairvaux, *On the Love of God*, E. G. Gardner, trans. (London: J. M. Dent, 1916), pp. 27, 39, 71. Reprinted by permission of J. M. Dent & Sons Ltd.

Abelard and Heloise: Learning and Love

Abelard was remembered at Paris not only for his teachings but also for his role in one of the most famous love stories of the Middle Ages. Each of the lovers, Abelard and Heloise, wrote an account of their relationship and, fortunately, both accounts have survived. Abelard told the story in an autobiography called A Story of Calamities.

From Abelard. *A Story of Calamities*

How having fallen in love with Heloise he was thereby wounded as well in body as in mind.

Now there was in this city of Paris a certain young maiden by the name of Heloise, the niece of a certain Canon who was called Fulbert, who, so great was his love for her, was all the more diligent in his zeal to instruct her, so far as was in his power, in the knowledge of letters. Who, while in face she was not inferior to other women, in the abundance of her learning was supreme. For inasmuch as this advantage, namely literary knowledge, is rare in women, so much the more did it commend the girl and had won her the greatest renown throughout the realm. Seeing in her, therefore, all those things which are wont to attract lovers, I thought it suitable to join her with myself in love, and believed that I could effect this most easily. For such renown had I then, and so excelled in grace of youth and form, that I feared no refusal from whatever woman I might deem worthy of my love.

So, being wholly inflamed with love for this girl, I sought an opportunity whereby I might make her familiar with me in intimate and daily conversation, and so the more easily lead her to consent. With which object in view, I came to terms with the aforesaid uncle of the girl, certain of his friends intervening, that he should take me into his house, which was hard by our school, at whatever price he might ask. . . .

What more need I say? First in one house we are united, then in one mind. So, under the pretext of discipline, we abandoned ourselves utterly to love, and those secret retreats which love demands, the study of our texts afforded us. And so, our books lying open before us, more words of love rose to our lips than of literature, kisses were more frequent than speech. Oftener went our hands to each other's bosom than to the pages; love turned our eyes more frequently to itself than it directed them to the study of the texts. That we might be the less suspected, blows were given at times, by love, not by anger, affection, not indignation, which surpassed all ointments in their sweetness. What more shall I say? No stage of love was omitted by us in our cupidity, and, if love could elaborate anything new, that we took in addition. The less experienced we were in these joys, the more ardently we persisted in them and the less satiety did they bring us. And the more this pleasure occupied me the less leisure could I find for my philosophy and to attend to my school. Most tedious was it for me to go to the school or to stay there; laborious likewise when I was keeping nightly vigils of love and daily of study. Which also so negligently and tepidly I now performed that I produced nothing from my mind but everything from memory; nor was I anything now save a reciter of things learned in the past, and if I found time to compose a few verses, they were amorous, and not secret hymns of philosophy. Of which songs the greater part are to this day, as thou knowest, repeated and sung in many parts, principally by those to whom a like manner of life appeals. . . .

[Heloise had a child and Abelard married her. He tried, however, to keep the marriage secret and sent Heloise to stay at the convent of Argenteuil, where she had been brought up as a young girl.]

Hearing which, the uncle and his kinsmen and associates were of the opinion that I had played a trick on them, and had taken an easy way to rid myself of Heloise, making her a nun. Whereat vehemently indignant, and conspiring together against me, on a certain night while I slumbered and slept in an inner room of my lodging, having corrupted a servant of mine with money, they punished me with a most cruel and shameful vengeance, and one that the world received with the utmost amazement: amputating, to wit, those parts of my body wherewith I had committed that of which they complained. Who presently taking flight, two of them who could be caught were deprived of their eyes and genitals. One of whom was the servant aforementioned, who while he remained with me in my service was by cupidity led to my betrayal.

After his mutilation Abelard entered the monastery of St. Denis as a monk and Heloise became a nun. This was in 1118. Abelard was thirty-nine, Heloise nineteen. When Heloise read the Story of Calamities, *written in 1132, she sent a letter to Abelard asking him to write to her. Heloise was now a respected abbess. How does she write about love and desire and marriage? Compare her account of the love affair with Abelard's.*

From Heloise. *Letter to Abelard*

To her master, rather to a father, to her husband, rather to a brother, his maid or rather daughter, his wife or rather sister, to Abaelard, Heloise.

Dearest, thou knowest—who knows not?—how much I lost in thee, and that an infamous act of treachery robbed me of thee and of myself at once. The greater my grief, the greater need of consolation, not from another but from thee, that thou who art alone my cause of grief may be alone my consolation. It is thou alone that canst sadden me or gladden me or comfort me. And thou alone owest this to me, especially since I have done thy will so utterly that, unable to offend thee, I endured to wreck myself at thy command. Nay, more than this, love turned to madness and cut itself off from hope of that which alone it sought, when I obediently changed my garb and my heart too in order that I might prove thee sole owner of my body as well as of my spirit. God knows, I

From H. O. Taylor, trans. *The Mediaeval Mind*, 4th ed. (Cambridge, Mass.: Harvard University Press, 1962), Vol. 2, pp. 38–40. Reprinted by permission of the publisher.

have ever sought in thee only thyself, desiring simply thee and not what was thine. I asked no matrimonial contract, I looked for no dowry; not my pleasure, not my will, but thine have I striven to fulfil. And if the name of wife seemed holier or more potent, the word mistress (*amica*) was always sweeter to me, or even—be not angry!—concubine or harlot; for the more I lowered myself before thee, the more I hoped to gain thy favour, and the less I should hurt the glory of thy renown. This thou didst graciously remember, when condescending to point out in that letter to a friend some of the reasons (but not all!) why I preferred love to wedlock and liberty to a chain. I call God to witness that if Augustus, the master of the world, would honour me with marriage and invest me with equal rule, it would still seem to me dearer and more honourable to be called thy strumpet than his empress. . . .

What country, what city does not thirst to see you? Who, I ask, did not hurry to see you appearing in public and crane his neck to catch a last glimpse as you departed? What wife, what maid did not yearn for you absent, and burn when you were present? What queen did not envy me my joys and couch? There were in you two qualities by which you could draw the soul of any woman, the gift of poetry and the gift of singing, gifts which other philosophers have lacked. As a distraction from labour, you composed love-songs both in metre and in rhyme, which for their sweet sentiment and music have been sung and resung and have kept your name in every mouth. Your sweet melodies do not permit even the illiterate to forget you. Because of these gifts women sighed for your love. And, as these songs sung of our loves, they quickly spread my name in many lands, and made me the envy of my sex. What excellence of mind or body did not adorn your youth? No woman, then envious, but now would pity me bereft of such delights. What enemy even would not now be softened by the compassion due me? . . .

God knows, at your command I would have followed or preceded you to fiery places. For my heart is not with me, but with thee; and now more than ever, if not with thee it is nowhere, for it cannot exist without thee. That my heart may be well with thee, see to it, I beg; and it will be well if it finds thee kind, rendering grace for grace—a little for much. Beloved, would that thy love were less sure of me so that it might be more solicitous; I have made you so secure that you are negligent. Remember all I have done and think what you owe. While I enjoyed carnal joy with you, many people were uncertain whether I acted from love or lust. Now the end makes clear the beginning; I have cut myself off from pleasure to obey thy will. I have kept nothing, save to be more than ever thine. Think how wicked it were in thee where all the more is due to render less, nothing almost; especially when little is asked, and that so easy for you. In the name of God to whom you have vowed yourself, give me that of thee which is possible, the consolation of a letter. I promise, thus refreshed, to serve God more readily. When of old you would call me to pleasures, you sought me with frequent letters, and never failed with thy songs to keep thy Heloise on every tongue; the streets, the houses re-echoed me. How much fitter that you should now incite me to God than then to lust? Bethink thee what thou owest; heed what I ask; and a long letter I will conclude with a brief ending: farewell only one!

After Bernard's attack, Abelard's theology was condemned by a church council in France. Abelard set off for Rome to appeal the sentence but fell ill on the way and spent the last months of his life in a priory of the great abbey of Cluny. When he died, the abbot of Cluny, Peter the Venerable, one of the greatest prelates of the Christian world, wrote to Heloise about Abelard's last days. How did Peter the Venerable regard Heloise?

From Peter the Venerable. *Letter to Heloise*

To his venerable and dearly loved sister in Christ, the abbess Heloise.

. . . I rejoice in your renowned learning; your piety, of which many have spoken to me, is still more attractive. Would that our order of Cluny had you! Would that our convent of Marcigny held you . . . I would prefer your gifts of learning and religion to the greatest treasures of any kings. . . .

But although God's providence denied us this, it was granted us to enjoy the presence of him—who was yours—Master Peter Abaelard, a man always to be spoken of with honour as a true servant of Christ and a philosopher. The divine dispensation placed him in Cluny for his last years, and through him enriched our monastery with treasure richer than gold. No brief writing could do justice to his holy, humble, and devoted life among us. I have not seen his equal in humility of garb and manner. When in the crowd of our brethren I forced him to take a first place, in meanness of clothing he appeared as the last of all. Often I marvelled, as the monks walked past me, to see a man so great and famous thus despise and abase himself. He was abstemious in food and drink, refusing and condemning everything beyond the bare necessities. He was assiduous in study, frequent in prayer, always silent unless compelled to answer the question of some brother or expound sacred themes before us. He partook of the sacrament as often as possible. Truly his mind, his tongue, his act, taught and exemplified religion, philosophy, and learning. So he dwelt with us, a man simple and righteous, fearing God, turning from evil, consecrating to God the latter days of his life. At last, because of his bodily infirmities, I sent him to a quiet and salubrious retreat on the banks of the Saone. There he bent over his books, as long as his strength lasted, always praying, reading, writing, or dictating. . . . When he came to pay humanity's last debt, his illness was brief. With holy devotion he made confession of the Catholic Faith, then of his sins. The brothers who were with him can testify how devoutly he received the viaticum of that last journey, and with what fervent faith he commended his body and soul to his Redeemer. Thus this master, Peter, completed his days. He who was known throughout the world by the fame of his teaching, entered the school of Him who said, "Learn of me, for I am meek and lowly of heart"; and continuing meek and lowly he passed to Him, as we may believe.

Venerable and dearest sister in the Lord, the man who was once joined to you in the flesh, and then by the stronger chain of divine love, him in your place,

From H. O. Taylor, trans., *The Mediaeval Mind*, 4th ed. (Cambridge, Mass.: Harvard University Press, 1962), Vol. 2, pp. 52–53. Reprinted by permission of the publisher.

or as another you, the Lord holds in His bosom; and at the day of His coming, His grace will restore him to you.

THE WORLD OF THOUGHT

The fame of teachers like Peter Abelard attracted crowds of students to Paris. Toward the end of the twelfth century, the masters of the schools there combined to form a guild—in Latin universitas. *This was the beginning of the University of Paris.*

University Life: Masters and Students

The first statutes of the university that survive were promulgated by a papal legate, Robert de Courçon, in 1215. What were the qualifications for teaching? What subjects were emphasized in the curriculum?

From *University Statutes, 1215*

No one shall lecture in the arts[1] at Paris before he is twenty-one years of age, and he shall have heard lectures for at least six years before he begins to lecture, and he shall promise to lecture for at least two years, unless a reasonable cause prevents, which he ought to prove publicly or before examiners. He shall not be stained by any infamy, and when he is ready to lecture, he shall be examined according to the form which is contained in the writing of the lord bishop of Paris, where is contained the peace confirmed between the chancellor and scholars by judges delegated by the pope. . . . And they shall lecture on the books of Aristotle on dialectic old and new in the schools ordinarily and not cursorily. They shall also lecture on both Priscians ordinarily,[2] or at least on one. They shall not lecture on feast days except on philosophers and rhetoric and the quadrivium and *Barbarismus*[3] and ethics,[4] if it please them, and the fourth book of the *Topics*. They shall not lecture on the books of Aristotle on metaphysics and natural philosophy[5] or on summaries of them or concerning the doctrine of master David of Dinant or the heretic Amaury or Mauritius of Spain. . . .

No one shall receive the licentiate from the chancellor or another for money given or promise made or other condition agreed upon. Also, the masters and scholars can make both between themselves and with other persons obligations

[1]"Arts" means the seven liberal arts, divided into the *trivium* (grammar, rhetoric, and logic) and the *quadrivium* (arithmetic, geometry, music, and astronomy).
[2]Two works on grammar by the classical author Priscian.
[3]Another classical grammatical work, by Donatus.
[4]Aristotle's *Nichomachean Ethics.*
[5]This prohibition was later rescinded. All Aristotle's known works on philosophy and natural science were regularly taught at Paris by the mid-thirteenth century.
From Lynn Thorndike, ed., *University Records and Life in the Middle Ages* (New York: Columbia University Press, 1944), pp. 28–30, 78–80, 237.

and constitutions supported by faith or penalty or oath in these cases: namely, the murder or mutilation of a scholar or atrocious injury done a scholar, if justice should not be forthcoming, arranging the prices of lodging, costume, burial, lectures and disputations, so, however, that the university be not thereby dissolved or destroyed.

As to the status of the theologians, we decree that no one shall lecture at Paris before his thirty-fifth year and unless he has studied for eight years at least, and has heard the books faithfully and in classrooms, and has attended lectures in theology for five years before he gives lectures himself publicly. And none of these shall lecture before the third hour on days when masters lecture. No one shall be admitted at Paris to formal lectures or to preachings unless he shall be of approved life and science. No one shall be a scholar at Paris who has no definite master.

During the thirteenth century a dispute arose about the proper method of lecturing. Do you think the professors made a right decision?

Method of Lecturing

IN THE NAME of the Lord, amen. Two methods of lecturing on books in the liberal arts having been tried, the former masters of philosophy uttering their words rapidly so that the mind of the hearer can take them in but the hand cannot keep up with them, the latter speaking slowly until their listeners can catch up with them with the pen; having compared these by diligent examination, the former method is found the better. Wherefore, the consensus of opinion warns us that we imitate it in our lectures. We, therefore, all and each, masters of the faculty of arts, teaching and not teaching, convoked for this specially by the venerable man, master Albert of Bohemia, then rector of the university, at St. Julien le Pauvre, have decreed in this wise, that all lecturers, whether masters or scholars of the same faculty, whenever and wherever they chance to lecture on any text ordinarily or cursorily in the same faculty, or to dispute any question concerning it, or anything else by way of exposition, shall observe the former method of lecturing to the best of their ability, so speaking forsooth as if no one was taking notes before them, in the way that sermons and recommendations are made in the university and which the lectures in other faculties follow. Moreover, transgressors of this statute, if the lecturers are masters or scholars, we now deprive henceforth for a year from lecturing, honors, offices and other advantages of our faculty. Which if anyone violates, for the first relapse we double the penalty, for the second we quadruple it, and so on. Moreover, listeners who oppose the execution of this our statute by clamor, hissing, noise, throwing stones by themselves or by their servants and accomplices, or in any other way, we deprive of and cut off from our society for a year, and for each relapse we increase the penalty double and quadruple as above.

From the early days of universities unruly students created problems for local authorities.

Proclamation Against Criminal Students

Proclamation of the Official of the Episcopal Court of Paris Against Clerks and Scholars Who Go About Paris Armed by Day and Night and Commit Crimes

THE OFFICIAL OF THE COURT OF PARIS to all the rectors of churches, masters and scholars residing in the city and suburb of Paris, to whom the present letters may come, greeting in the Lord. A frequent and continual complaint has gone the rounds that there are in Paris some clerks and scholars, likewise their servants, trusting in the folly of the same clerks, unmindful of their salvation, not having God before their eyes, who, under pretense of leading the scholastic life, more and more often perpetrate unlawful and criminal acts, relying on their arms: namely, that by day and night they atrociously wound or kill many persons, rape women, oppress virgins, break into inns, also repeatedly committing robberies and many other enormities hateful to God. And since they attempt these and other crimes relying on their arms, we . . . do excommunicate in writing clerks and scholars and their servants who go about Paris by day or night armed, unless by permission of the reverend bishop of Paris or ourselves. We also excommunicate in writing those who rape women, break into inns, oppress virgins, likewise all those who have banded together for this purpose. . . .

Geoffrey Chaucer (c. 1340–1400) described a better kind of student in his Canterbury Tales.

> There was an *Oxford Cleric* too, a student,
> Long given to Logic, longer than was prudent;
> The horse he had was leaner than a rake,
> And he was not too fat, I undertake,
> But had a hollow look, a sober air;
> The thread upon his overcoat was bare.
> He had found no preferment in the church
> And he was too unworldly to make search.
> He thought far more of having by his bed
> His twenty books all bound in black and red,
> Of Aristotle and philosophy
> Than of gay music, fiddles or finery.
> Though a philosopher, as I have told,
> He had not found the stone for making gold.
> Whatever money from his friends he took
> He spent on learning or another book
> And prayed for them most earnestly, returning
> Thanks to them thus for paying for his learning.
> His only care was study, and indeed
> He never spoke a word more than was need,

From Geoffrey Chaucer, *The Canterbury Tales*, N. Coghill trans. (London: Penguin Books Ltd., 1951), p. 33.

Formal at that, respectful in the extreme,
Short, to the point, and lofty in his theme.
The thought of moral virtue filled his speech
And he would gladly learn, and gladly teach.

Religion, Philosophy, and Law

The Dominican friar Thomas Aquinas (1225–1274) was one of the greatest of the masters who taught at Paris during the thirteenth century. The next reading illustrates both Aquinas's method of argumentation and his approach to the old problem of reason and faith that had been raised in the early church by Clement of Alexandria (p. 136) and then again by Peter Abelard (p. 252). (Although Abelard was condemned in his lifetime, his "dialectical" method of citing conflicting authorities was commonly adopted by later authors. The difference was that they offered solutions to the apparent conflicts.) Why did Aquinas think that religious faith was necessary as well as rational inquiry?

From Aquinas. *Summa Theologiae*

Whether, Besides the Philosophical Sciences, Any Further Doctrine Is Required?

We proceed thus to the First Article:—

Objection 1. It seems that, besides the philosophical sciences, we have no need of any further knowledge. For man should not seek to know what is above reason: *Seek not the things that are too high for thee (Ecclus.* iii. 22). But whatever is not above reason is sufficiently considered in the philosophical sciences. Therefore any other knowledge besides the philosophical sciences is superfluous.

Obj. 2. Further, knowledge can be concerned only with being, for nothing can be known, save the true, which is convertible with being. But everything that is, is considered in the philosophical sciences—even God Himself; so that there is a part of philosophy called theology, or the divine science, as is clear from Aristotle. Therefore, besides the philosophical sciences, there is no need of any further knowledge.

On the contrary, It is written (2 *Tim.* iii. 16): *All Scripture inspired of God is profitable to teach, to reprove, to correct, to instruct in justice.* Now Scripture, inspired of God, is not a part of the philosophical sciences discovered by human reason. Therefore it is useful that besides the philosophical sciences there should be another science—*i.e.,* inspired of God.

I answer that, It was necessary for man's salvation that there should be a knowledge revealed by God, besides the philosophical sciences investigated by human reason. First, because man is directed to God as to an end that surpasses the grasp of his reason: *The eye hath not seen, O God, besides Thee, what things Thou*

From Aquinas, *Summa Theologiae* in Anton C. Pegis, ed., *Basic Writings of Saint Thomas Aquinas* (New York: Random House, 1945), pp. 5–6.

hast prepared for them that wait for Thee (Isa. lxiv. 4). But the end must first be known by men who are to direct their thoughts and actions to the end. Hence it was necessary for the salvation of man that certain truths which exceed human reason should be made known to him by divine revelation. Even as regards those truths about God which human reason can investigate, it was necessary that man be taught by a divine revelation. For the truth about God, such as reason can know it, would only be known by a few, and that after a long time, and with the admixture of many errors; whereas man's whole salvation, which is in God, depends upon the knowledge of this truth. Therefore, in order that the salvation of men might be brought about more fitly and more surely, it was necessary that they be taught divine truths by divine revelation. It was therefore necessary that, besides the philosophical sciences investigated by reason, there should be a sacred science by way of revelation.

Reply Obj. 1. Although those things which are beyond man's knowledge may not be sought for by man through his reason, nevertheless, what is revealed by God must be accepted through faith. Hence the sacred text continues, *For many things are shown to thee above the understanding of man (Ecclus.* iii. 25). And in such things sacred science consists.

Reply Obj. 2. Sciences are diversified according to the diverse nature of their knowable objects. For the astronomer and the physicist both prove the same conclusion—that the earth, for instance, is round: the astronomer by means of mathematics (*i.e.*, abstracting from matter), but the physicist by means of matter itself. Hence there is no reason why those things which are treated by the philosophical sciences, so far as they can be known by the light of natural reason, may not also be treated by another science so far as they are known by the light of the divine revelation. Hence the theology included in sacred doctrine differs in genus from that theology which is part of philosophy.

Aquinas included in his Summa Theologiae *an influential treatise on law. How did natural law differ from the other kinds that he described?*

From Aquinas. *Summa Theologiae*

Whether There Is an Eternal Law?
Law is nothing other than a decree of practical reason from a sovereign who governs a perfect community. But it is evident, granted that the world is governed by divine providence (as we have shown in the *First Book*), that the whole community of the universe is governed by divine reason. Moreover, this reason that rules all things exists in God as the sovereign of the universe; hence it has the nature of law. And since the divine reason conceives nothing in time but has

an eternal concept as is said in *Proverbs 8.23 (I was set up from eternity and of old before the earth was made)*, it follows that this law should be called eternal.

Whether There Is in Us a Natural Law?

Since all things subject to divine providence are regulated and measured by eternal law as we have seen, it is evident that all things participate in some way in eternal law, in that they have from its impress their tendencies toward their own proper acts and ends.

But, among all the rest, intelligent creatures are subject to divine Providence in a more noble way in that they participate in Providence by taking thought for themselves and others. Thus they share in the eternal reason through which they have a natural inclination to their proper acts and ends. And such a sharing in the eternal law by an intelligent creature is called natural law.

Whether There Is a Human Law?

Just as speculative reason draws the conclusions of various sciences from first principles that are indemonstrable but naturally recognized . . . so too it is necessary for the human reason to make more detailed arrangements, derived from the principles of natural law as indemonstrable and commonly-held principles. And these detailed arrangements made by human reason are called human law.

Whether There Was Any Need for a Divine Law?

The direction of human life requires a divine law besides natural law and human law . . . because law directs man to the acts proper for the achievement of his final end. If man was destined for an end that did not exceed the measure of his natural abilities he would not need any directive of reason apart from natural law and the human law derived from it. But since man is destined to achieve an eternal happiness which is beyond the measure of natural human ability, it is necessary that he be directed to this end by a divinely given law above natural law and human law.

Aquinas also asked about unjust laws. Could his argument be applied to any modern law that you consider unjust?

Whether Human Law Binds a Man in Conscience?

Laws framed by man are either just or unjust. If they be just, they have the power of binding in conscience, from the eternal law whence they are derived. . . .

On the other hand laws may be unjust in two ways: first, by being contrary to human good, through being opposed to the things mentioned above:—either in respect of the end, as when an authority imposes on his subjects burdensome laws, conducive, not to the common good, but rather to his own cupidity or vainglory;—or in respect of the author, as when a man makes a law that goes beyond the power committed to him;—or in respect of the form, as when burdens are imposed unequally on the community, although with a view to the common good. The like are acts of violence rather than laws; because, as Augustine says *(De Lib. Arb.i.), a law that is not just, seems to be no law at all.* Wherefore such laws do not bind in conscience, except perhaps in order to avoid scandal or disturbance, for which cause a man should even yield his right, according to Matth. v. 40, 41: *If a man . . . take away thy coat, let go thy cloak also unto him; and whosoever will force thee one mile, go with him another two.*

Secondly, laws may be unjust through being opposed to the Divine good: such are the laws of tyrants inducing to idolatry, or to anything else contrary to the Divine law: and laws of this kind must nowise be observed, because, as stated in Acts v. 29, *we ought to obey God rather than men.*

THE FRANCISCAN VISION

Franciscan Ideals

Francis of Assisi (1182–1226) inspired a great new religious order by striving to follow simply and literally the teachings of Jesus. What virtues did he especially emphasize?

From *The Rule of St. Francis*

1. This is the rule and life of the Minor Brothers, namely, to observe the holy gospel of our Lord Jesus Christ by living in obedience, in poverty, and in chastity. Brother Francis promises obedience and reverence to pope Honorius and to his successors who shall be canonically elected, and to the Roman Church. The other brothers are bound to obey brother Francis, and his successors.

2. . . . And after they have promised obedience, those who wish may have one robe with a hood and one without a hood. Those who must may wear shoes, and all the brothers shall wear common clothes, and they shall have God's blessing if they patch them with coarse cloth and pieces of other kinds of cloth. But I warn and exhort them not to despise nor judge other men who wear fine and gay clothing, and have delicious foods and drinks. But rather let each one judge and despise himself.

3. The clerical brothers shall perform the divine office according to the rite of the holy Roman church, except the psalter, and so they may have breviaries. The lay brothers shall say 24 Paternosters at matins, 5 at lauds, 7 each at primes, terces, sexts, and nones, 12 at vespers, 7 at completorium, and prayers for the dead. And they shall fast from All Saints' day [November 1] to Christmas. . . . But I counsel, warn, and exhort my brothers in the Lord Jesus Christ that when they go out into the world they shall not be quarrelsome

From *The Rule of St. Francis*, trans. O. J. Thatcher and E. H. McNeal in *A Source Book for Mediaeval History* (New York: Charles Scribner's Sons, 1905), pp. 499–503.

or contentious, nor judge others. But they shall be gentle, peaceable, and kind, mild and humble, and virtuous in speech, as is becoming to all. They shall not ride on horseback unless compelled by manifest necessity or infirmity to do so. When they enter a house they shall say, "Peace be to this house." According to the holy gospel, they may eat of whatever food is set before them.

4. I strictly forbid all the brothers to accept money or property either in person or through another. Nevertheless, for the needs of the sick, and for clothing the other brothers, the ministers and guardians may, as they see that necessity requires, provide through spiritual friends, according to the locality, season, and the degree of cold which may be expected in the region where they live. But, as has been said, they shall never receive money or property.

5. Those brothers to whom the Lord has given the ability to work shall work faithfully and devotedly, so that idleness, which is the enemy of the soul, may be excluded and not extinguish the spirit of prayer and devotion to which all temporal things should be subservient. As the price of their labors they may receive things that are necessary for themselves and the brothers, but not money or property. And they shall humbly receive what is given them, as is becoming to the servants of God and to those who practise the most holy poverty.

6. The brothers shall have nothing of their own, neither house, nor land, nor anything, but as pilgrims and strangers in this world, serving the Lord in poverty and humility, let them confidently go asking alms. Nor let them be ashamed of this, for the Lord made himself poor for us in this world.

10. The ministers and servants shall visit and admonish their brothers and humbly and lovingly correct them. They shall not put any command upon them that would be against their soul and this rule. And the brothers who are subject must remember that for God's sake they have given up their own wills. Wherefore I command them to obey their ministers in all the things which they have promised the Lord to observe and which shall not be contrary to their souls and this rule. . . . I warn and exhort the brothers in the Lord Jesus Christ to guard against all arrogance, pride, envy, avarice, care, and solicitude for this world, detraction, and murmuring. And those who cannot read need not be anxious to learn. But above all things let them desire to have the spirit of the Lord and his holy works, to pray always to God with a pure heart, and to have humility, and patience in persecution and in infirmity, and to love those who persecute us and reproach us and blame us. For the Lord says, "Love your enemies, and pray for those who persecute and speak evil of you" [cf. Matt. 5:44].

Creator and Creatures

Later on many fanciful legends grew up about Francis's love of nature and his empathy with wild creatures. These passages are from Francis's first biographer, Thomas of Celano, *who knew Francis personally. What was new in Francis's attitude to the natural world?*

From *Thomas of Celano*

Francis was filled with the spirit of love. He cared not only for men in need but for dumb animals, reptiles, birds and all other creatures, animate and inanimate. Among all other animals, he loved little lambs with a special affection and regard, because in the sacred scriptures the humility of our Lord Jesus Christ is most often likened to that of a Lamb.

Who can tell the joy he felt when he contemplated in created things the wisdom and power and goodness of the Creator? He was often filled with a wonderful and indescribable rejoicing because of this when he looked at the sun and the moon and gazed on the stars and the heavens.

All the creatures tried to love the saint in return. . . . Near his cell at the Portiuncula a cicada used to perch on a fig tree and chirp all day long. Sometimes the blessed father would hold out his hand and call to it saying, "Sister cicada, come to me." And it flew straight to his hand as if endowed with reason. Then Francis would say, "Sister cicada, sing and praise your Creator with a joyful song."

He told his brothers not to chop down the whole tree when they were cutting wood, so that it could grow again. He told the gardeners not to dig up the border round the garden so that in due season the green grass and beauty of wild flowers would proclaim the beauty of the Father of all things. . . . He picked up worms from the road so that they would not be trampled on, and he ordered that honey and good wine be set out for the bees in the cold of winter lest they perish from want. He called all animals by the name of *brother*, though he cared most of all for the gentle ones.

When he came upon a great field of flowers he preached to them and invited them to praise God as though they could understand him. In the same way he exhorted cornfields and vineyards, stones and woodlands, all the beautiful things of the fields, springs of water and the green plants of gardens, earth and fire, air and wind, to love God and serve him willingly. Finally, he called all creatures *brothers* and in a most excellent manner, unknown to others, he saw into the hidden nature of things with his discerning heart, like one who had already escaped into the glorious freedom of the sons of God.

Often, without moving his lips, he would meditate inwardly and, drawing external things into himself, would raise his spirit on high. Then he directed all his regard and affection to the *one thing he asked of the Lord*, becoming not so much like a man praying as himself a prayer. What sweetness of heart pervaded a man used to such things? He knows; I can only wonder. It is given to one who has experienced such things to know, not to those without experience. And so, his whole soul and his whole appearance melted by a glowing fervor of spirit, he dwelt already in the highest realms of the Kingdom of Heaven.

From *Thomas of Celano* in *Great Issues in Western Civilization*, 3rd ed., Brian Tierney, Donald Kagan, and L. Pearce Williams, eds. (New York: Random House, 1976), pp. 421–422. Copyright © 1967, 1972, 1976 by Random House, Inc. Reprinted by permission of the publisher.

Francis gave vivid expression to his vision of creator and creation in this song.

> *The Canticle of the Sun*
> Most high, omnipotent, good Lord,
>> Praise, glory and honor and benediction all, are Thine.
>> To Thee alone do they belong, most High,
>> And there is no man fit to mention Thee.
> Praise be to Thee, my Lord, with all Thy creatures,
>> Especially to my worshipful brother sun,
>> The which lights up the day, and through him dost Thou brightness give;
>> And beautiful is he and radiant with splendor great;
>> Of Thee, most High, signification gives.
> Praised be my Lord, for sister moon and for the stars,
>> In heaven Thou has formed them clear and precious and fair.
>> Praised be my Lord for brother wind
>> And for the air and clouds and fair and every kind of weather,
>> By the which Thou givest to Thy creatures nourishment.
>> Praised be my Lord for sister water,
>> The which is greatly helpful and humble and precious and pure.
> Praised be my Lord for brother fire,
>> By the which Thou lightest up the dark.
>> And fair is he and gay and mighty and strong.
> Praised be my Lord for our sister, mother earth,
>> The which sustains and keeps us
>> And brings forth diverse fruits with grass and flowers bright.
> Praised be my Lord for those who for Thy love forgive
>> And weakness bear and tribulation.
>> Blessed those who shall in peace endure,
>> For by Thee, most High, shall they be crowned.
> Praised be my Lord for our sister, the bodily death,
>> From the which no living man can flee.
>> Woe to them who die in mortal sin;
>> Blessed those who shall find themselves in Thy most holy will,
>> For the second death shall do them no ill.
> Praise ye and bless ye my Lord, and give Him thanks,
>> And be subject unto Him with great humility.

ON THE MARGIN—HERETICS AND JEWS

Albigensians

The medieval dissidents called Albigensians (from the town of Albi in southern France) believed that only spirit was good and that the material world was intrinsically evil, created by an evil god. Compare this with the views of Augustine (p. 152) and Francis of Assisi.

From *The Writings of Saint Francis of Assisi*, Paschal Robinson, trans. (Philadelphia: Dolphin Press, 1906), pp. 81–86.

From Raynaldus. *Annales*

First it is to be known that the heretics held that there are two Creators; viz. one of invisible things, whom they called the benevolent God, and another of visible things, whom they named the malevolent God. The New Testament they attributed to the benevolent God; but the Old Testament to the malevolent God, and rejected it altogether. . . . They affirmed also, that all the fathers of the Old Testament were damned; that John the Baptist was one of the greater demons. They said also, in their secret doctrine, *(in secreto suo)* that Christ who was born in the visible, and terrestrial Bethlehem, and crucified in Jerusalem, was a bad man, and that Mary Magdalene was his concubine; and that she was the woman taken in adultery, of whom we read in the gospel. For the good Christ, as they said, never ate, nor drank, nor took upon him true flesh, nor ever was in this world, except spiritually in the body of Paul. . . .

They said that almost all the Church of Rome was a den of thieves; and that it was the harlot of which we read in the Apocalypse. They so far annulled the sacraments of the Church, as publicly to teach that the water of holy Baptism was just the same as river water, and that the Host of the most holy body of Christ did not differ from common bread; instilling into the ears of the simple this blasphemy, that the body of Christ, even though it had been as great as the Alps, would have been long ago consumed, and annihilated by those who had eaten of it. Confirmation and Confession, they considered as altogether vain and frivolous. They preached that Holy Matrimony was meretricious, and that none could be saved in it, if they should beget children. Denying also the Resurrection of the flesh, they invented some unheard of notions, saying, that our souls are those of angelic spirits who, being cast down from heaven by the apostasy of pride, left their glorified bodies in the air; and that these souls themselves, after successively inhabiting seven terrene bodies, or one sort or another, having at length fulfilled their penance, return to those deserted bodies.

It is also to be known that some among the heretics were called "perfect" or "good men;" others "believers" of the heretics. Those who were called perfect, wore a black dress, falsely pretended to chastity, abhorred the eating of flesh, eggs and cheese, wished to appear not liars, when they were continually telling lies, chiefly respecting God. They said also that they ought not on any account to swear.

Those were called *believers* of the heretics, who lived after the manner of the world, and who though they did not attain so far as to imitate the life of the perfect, nevertheless hoped to be saved in their faith; and though they differed as to their mode of life, they were one with them in belief and unbelief. Those who were called believers of the heretics were given to usury, rapine, homicide, lust, perjury and every vice; and they, in fact, sinned with more security, and less restraint, because they believed that without restitution, without confession and

From Raynaldus, "Annales," in S. R. Maitland, trans., *History of the Albigenses and Waldenses* (London: C. J. G. and F. Rivington, 1832), pp. 392–394.

penance, they should be saved, if only, when on the point of death, they could say a *Pater noster*, and receive imposition of hands from the teachers.

Heretics were regarded as criminals and as a danger to Christian society. Can you suggest any reason for this?

Decree of Emperor Frederick II (c. 1235)

We decree, in the first place, that the crime of heresy and of reprehensible teaching, of whatever kind, by whatever name its adherents may be known, shall, as provided by the older laws, be included among the recognized crimes. (For should not what is recognized to be an offense against the Divine Majesty be judged more terrible than the crime of leze majesty directed against ourself, although in the eyes of the law one is not graver than the other?) As the crime of treason deprives the guilty of life and property, and even blackens the memory of the dead, so in the aforesaid crimes of which the Patarins[6] are guilty, we wish the same rules to be observed in all respects.

And in order that the wickedness of those who walk in darkness, since they do not follow God, should be thoroughly exterminated, we desire that those who practice this class of crimes should, like other malefactors, be diligently sought for and hunted out by our officers. If such be discovered, even if there be only the slightest suspicion of their guilt, we command that they shall be examined by churchmen and prelates. If they shall be found by these to have deviated from the Catholic faith, even in a single respect, and if, when admonished by such churchmen in their function of pastors, they refuse by leaving the wiles of the devil to recognize the God of light, and stubbornly adhere to their error, we command, by this our present edict, that such condemned Patarins shall suffer the death they court; that, condemned to the sentence of the flames, they shall be burned alive in the sight of the people.

Beguins

Beguins were groups of women who lived together in religious communities without following one of the established monastic rules. Some of them came to believe that Francis of Assisi had come to inaugurate a new age of the world. Do their views resemble those of any modern cults?

From The Inquisitor's Manual of Bernard Gui

They distinguish as it were two churches: the carnal Church, which is the Roman Church, with its reprobate multitude, and the spiritual Church, composed of people whom they call spiritual and evangelical, who follow the life of Christ and the apostles. The latter, they claim, is their Church.

---

[6]The Patarins were an Italian sect accused of holding views like those of the French Albigensians. From W. L. Wakefield and A. P. Evans, *Heresies of the High Middle Ages* (New York: Columbia University Press), pp. 425–426.

Also, they teach that at the end of the sixth era of the Church, the era in which they say we now are, which began with St. Francis, the carnal Church, Babylon, the great harlot, shall be rejected by Christ, just as the synagogue of the Jews was rejected for crucifying Christ. For the carnal Church crucifies and persecutes the life of Christ in those brethren whom they call the Poor and the Spirituals of the order of St. Francis.

Also, they teach that, just as Christ chose from the synagogue of the Jews, after it had been rejected, a few poor men through whom the primitive Church of Christ was founded in the first era of the Church, so, after the rejection and destruction of the carnal Church of Rome in the sixth or present era, there will remain a few chosen men, spiritual, poor, and evangelical. The majority of these, they say, will be drawn from both the orders of St. Francis, the first and the third, and through them will be founded the spiritual Church, which will be humble and good, in the seventh and last era of the Church, which begins with the death of Antichrist. . . .

Also, they teach that the Antichrist is dual; that is, there is one who is spiritual or mystical, and another, the real, greater Antichrist. The first prepares the way for the second. They say, too, that the first Antichrist is that pope under whom will occur and, in their opinion, is now occurring the persecution and condemnation of their sect.

Also, they fix the time within which the greater Antichrist will come, begin to preach, and run his course. This Antichrist, they say, has already been born and will run his course, according to some of them, in the year of our Lord 1325. Others say it will be in the year 1330; while still others put it later, in the year 1335. . . .

Also, drawing further upon their imaginations, they teach that the destruction of the carnal Church will occur amid mighty wars and great destruction of Christian peoples. Large numbers of men will fall in the war they wage in defense of the carnal Church. Then, when almost all the men are dead, the surviving Christian women will embrace trees out of love and longing for men. On this subject they tell a number of other fabulous tales. . . . Then the Church will be reduced to the same number of persons as founded the primitive Church; scarcely twelve shall survive. In them the Church will be established and upon them the Holy Spirit will be poured in equal or greater abundance than when He came upon the apostles in the primitive Church, as is recounted above.

Also, they say that after the death of Antichrist, the said Spirituals will convert the whole world to the faith of Christ and the whole world will be good and merciful, so that there will be no malice or sin in the people of that era, with the possible exception of venial sin in some. Everything will be for use in common and there will be no one to offend another or tempt him to sin, for great love will there be among them. There will then be one flock and one shepherd. This state and condition of men will last, some of them think, for a hundred years. Then, as love wanes, malice will creep in little by little and gradually spread so far that Christ will be forced by the excesses of wickedness, as it were, to come to the universal judgment of all.

Jews

The official policy of the church toward the Jews was one of toleration as expressed in this letter of Pope Innocent III in 1199. What does the letter suggest about abuses commonly inflicted on the Jews?

From *Letter of Innocent III*

We decree that no Christian shall use violence to compel the Jews to accept baptism. But if a Jew, of his own accord, because of a change in his faith, shall have taken refuge with Christians, after his wish has been made known, he may be made a Christian without any opposition. For anyone who has not of his own will sought Christian baptism cannot have the true Christian faith. No Christian shall do the Jews any personal injury, except in executing the judgments of a judge, or deprive them of their possessions, or change the rights and privileges which they have been accustomed to have. During the celebration of their festivals, no one shall disturb them by beating them with clubs or by throwing stones at them. No one shall compel them to render any services except those which they have been accustomed to render. And to prevent the baseness and avarice of wicked men we forbid anyone to deface or damage their cemeteries or to extort money from them by threatening to exhume the bodies of their dead. . . .

Although Judaism was officially tolerated, the Fourth Lateran Council (1216) decreed that Jews should be distinguished from Christians by a different dress. What was the declared purpose of this law?

From *The Fourth Lateran Council*

In some provinces a difference in dress distinguishes the Jews or Saracens from the Christians, but in certain others such a confusion has grown up that they cannot be distinguished by any difference. Thus it happens at times that through error Christians have relations with the women of Jews or Saracens, and Jews and Saracens with Christian women. Therefore, that they may not, under pretext of error of this sort, excuse themselves in the future for the excesses of such prohibited intercourse, we decree that such Jews and Saracens of both sexes in every Christian province and at all times shall be marked off in the eyes of the public from other peoples through the character of their dress. Particularly, since it may be read in the writings of Moses [Numbers 15:37–41], that this very law has been enjoined upon them.

From the twelfth century onward Jews were often accused of the ritual murder of Christian children. Pope Gregory X (1271–1276) rejected the charge.

From O. J. Thatcher and E. H. McNeal, trans., *A Source Book for Mediaeval History* (New York: Charles Scribner's, 1905), pp. 212–213.
From Jacob R. Marcus, *The Jew in the Medieval World* (New York: Atheneum, 1972), pp. 138–139, 152–154. Reprinted through the courtesy of the Hebrew Union College Press.

From *Letter of Gregory X*

Since it happens occasionally that some Christians lose their Christian children, the Jews are accused by their enemies of secretly carrying off and killing these same Christian children and of making sacrifices of the heart and blood of these very children. It happens, too, that the parents of these children or some other Christian enemies of these Jews, secretly hide these very children in order that they may be able to injure these Jews, and in order that they may be able to extort from them a certain amount of money by redeeming them from their straits.

And most falsely do these Christians claim that the Jews have secretly and furtively carried away these children and killed them, and that the Jews offer sacrifice from the heart and blood of these children, since their law in this matter precisely and expressly forbids Jews to sacrifice, eat, or drink the blood, or to eat the flesh of animals having claws. This has been demonstrated many times at our court by Jews converted to the Christian faith: nevertheless very many Jews are often seized and detained unjustly because of this.

We decree, therefore, that Christians need not be obeyed against Jews in a case or situation of this type, and we order that Jews seized under such a silly pretext be freed from imprisonment, and that they shall not be arrested henceforth on such a miserable pretext, unless—which we do not believe—they be caught in the commission of the crime. We decree that no Christian shall stir up anything new against them, but that they should be maintained in that status and position in which they were in the time of our predecessors, from antiquity till now.

The relatively tolerant attitude of the popes did not prevent many outbursts of popular violence against the Jews from the time of the First Crusade onward (p. 211). The English chronicler Roger of Hoveden set down this terse account of a massacre at York in 1189. (The massacre was instigated by a group of knights preparing to leave on the Third Crusade who owed debts to the Jews.)

From Roger of Hoveden. *Annals*

In the same month of March, . . . the Jews of the city of York, in number five hundred men, besides women and children, shut themselves up in the tower of York, with the consent and sanction of the keeper of the tower, and of the sheriff, in consequence of their dread of the Christians; but when the said sheriff and the constable sought to regain possession of it, the Jews refused to deliver it up. In consequence of this, the people of the city, and the strangers who had come within the jurisdiction thereof, at the exhortation of the sheriff and the constable, with one consent made an attack upon the Jews.

After they had made assaults upon the tower, day and night, the Jews offered the people a large sum of money to allow them to depart with their lives; but this the others refused to receive. Upon this, one skilled in their laws arose

From Roger of Hoveden, *Annals*, H. T. Riley trans. 2 vols. (London: Bohn, 1853), 2, pp. 137–138.

and said: "Men of Israel, listen to my advice. It is better that we should kill one another, than fall into the hands of the enemies of our law." Accordingly, all the Jews, both men as well as women, gave their assent to his advice, and each master of a family, beginning with the chief persons of his household, with a sharp knife cut the throats of his wife and sons and daughters, and then of all his servants, and lastly his own. Some of them also threw their slain over the walls among the people; while others shut up their slain in the king's house and burned them, as well as the king's houses. Those who had slain the others were afterwards killed by the people. In the meantime, some of the Christians set fire to the Jews' houses, and plundered them; and thus all the Jews in the city of York were destroyed, and all acknowledgments of debts due to them were burnt.

MEDIEVAL WOMEN

There was no such thing as "the medieval attitude to women." Instead, just as nowadays, there were many attitudes, depending on such things as class, religious outlook, personality, and, of course, gender. In reading this section consider how women were admired, desired, criticized, defended. How was the relationship between husband and wife portrayed by the different authors?

Courtly Love

In the twelfth century a new cult of romantic love grew up among the feudal upper classes. It centered around the novel idea that a noble man should adore a lady and serve her faithfully. Sometimes the lover had no hope that his love would be returned as in this troubadour song of the twelfth century.

Jaufré Rudel. *To His Love Afar*

> When the days lengthen in the month of May,
>> Well pleased am I to hear the birds
>> Sing far away.
> And when from that place I am gone,
> I hang my head and make dull moan,
> Since she my heart is set upon
>> Is far away.

> So far, that song of birds, flower o' the thorn,
>> Please me no more than winter morn,
>> With ice and sleet.
> Ah, would I were a pilgrim over sea,
> With staff and scrip and cloak to cover me,
> That some day I might kneel me on one knee
>> Before her feet.

From Jaufré Rudel, "To His Love Afar," in Helen Waddell, trans., *The Wandering Scholars*, 7th ed. (London: Constable, 1934), pp. 205–206. Reprinted by permission of the publisher.

Most sad, most joyous shall I go away,
 Let me have seen her for a single day,
 My love afar.
 I shall not see her, for her land and mine
 Are sundered, and the ways are hard to find,
 So many ways, and I shall lose my way,
 So wills it God.

Yet shall I know no other love but hers,
 And if not hers, no other love at all.
 She hath surpassed all.
 So fair she is, so noble, I would be
 A captive with the hosts of paynimrie
 In a far land, if so be upon me
 Her eyes might fall.

God, who hath made all things in earth that are,
 That made my love, and set her thus afar,
 Grant me this grace,
 That I may some day come within a room,
 Or in some garden gloom
 Look on her face.

It will not be, for at my birth they said
 That one had set this doom upon my head,
 —God curse him among men!—
 That I should love, and not till I be dead,
 Be loved again.

Some lovers were not content with "love afar." This song was composed by the Countess de Dia (c. 1160).

Countess de Dia. *A Distressed Lover*

I've lately been in great distress
 over a knight who once was mine,
 and I want it known for all eternity
 how I loved him to excess.
 Now I see I've been betrayed
 because I wouldn't sleep with him;
 night and day my mind won't rest
 to think of the mistake I made.

How I wish just once I could caress
 that chevalier with my bare arms,
 for he would be in ecstasy
 if I'd just let him lean his head against my breast.
 I'm sure I'm happier with him

From Meg Bogin, trans. in *The Women Troubadours* (New York: Paddington Press Ltd., 1976), p. 89. Reprinted by permission of the author.

than Blancaflor with Floris.
My heart and love I offer him,
my mind, my eyes, my life.

Handsome friend, charming and kind
when shall I have you in my power?
If only I could lie beside you for an hour
and embrace you lovingly—
know this, that I'd give almost anything
to have you in my husband's place,
but only under the condition
that you swear to do my bidding.

A much debated question was whether true love could exist between a husband and wife. Andreas Capellanus discussed this in a book on courtly love written in c. 1185. What are the arguments against love in marriage? What do you think of the idea that jealousy is a necessary accompaniment of love?

From *The Art of Courtly Love*

What the Effect of Love Is   Now it is the effect of love that a true lover cannot be degraded with any avarice. Love causes a rough and uncouth man to be distinguished for his handsomeness; it can endow a man even of the humblest birth with nobility of character; it blesses the proud with humility; and the man in love becomes accustomed to performing many services gracefully for everyone. O what a wonderful thing is love, which makes a man shine with so many virtues and teaches everyone, no matter who he is, so many good traits of character! There is another thing about love that we should not praise in few words: it adorns a man, so to speak, with the virtue of chastity, because he who shines with the light of one love can hardly think of embracing another woman, even a beautiful one. For when he thinks deeply of his beloved the sight of any other women seems to his mind rough and rude.

A Man of the Higher Nobility Speaks with a Woman of the Simple Nobility   THE WOMAN SAYS: "We are separated by too wide and too rough an expanse of country to be able to offer each other love's solaces or to find proper opportunities for meeting. . . . Besides there is another fact, by no means trivial, which keeps me from loving you. I have a husband who is greatly distinguished by his nobility, his good breeding, and his good character, and it would be wicked for me to violate his bed or submit to the embraces of any other man, since I know that he loves me with his whole heart and I am bound to him with all the devotion of mine. The

From Andreas Capellanus, *The Art of Courtly Love* (Milestone of Thought Series), J. J. Parry, trans., edited and abridged by Frederick W. Locke (New York: Frederick Ungar, 1954), pp. 4, 15–19, 24. Copyright © 1957 by Frederick Ungar Publishing Co. Reprinted by permission of the publisher.

laws themselves bid me refrain from loving another man when I am blessed with such a reward for my love."

THE MAN SAYS: "I admit it is true that your husband is a very worthy man and that he is more blest than any man in the world because he has been worthy to have the joy of embracing Your Highness. But I am greatly surprised that you wish to misapply the term 'love' to that marital affection which husband and wife are expected to feel for each other after marriage, since everybody knows that love can have no place between husband and wife. They may be bound to each other by a great and immoderate affection, but their feeling cannot take the place of love, because it cannot fit under the true definition of love. For what is love but an inordinate desire to receive passionately a furtive and hidden embrace? But what embrace between husband and wife can be furtive, I ask you, since they may be said to belong to each other and may satisfy each other's desires without fear that anybody will object.

"But there is another reason why husband and wife cannot love each other and that is that the very substance of love, without which true love cannot exist—I mean jealousy—is in such a case very much frowned upon and they should avoid it like the pestilence; but lovers should always welcome it as the mother and the nurse of love. From this you may see clearly that love cannot possibly flourish between you and your husband. Therefore, since every woman of character ought to love, prudently, you can without doing yourself any harm accept the prayers of a suppliant and endow your suitor with your love."

THE WOMAN SAYS: "You are trying to take under your protection what all men from early times down have agreed to consider very reprehensible and to reject as hateful. For who can rightly commend envious jealousy or speak in favor of it, since jealousy is nothing but a shameful and evil suspicion of a woman? . . . I ought therefore to choose a man to enjoy my embraces who can be to me both husband and lover, because, no matter what the definition of love may say, love seems to be nothing but a great desire to enjoy carnal pleasure with someone, and nothing prevents this feeling existing between husband and wife."

THE MAN SAYS: "If the theory of love were perfectly clear to you and Love's dart had ever touched you, your own feelings would have shown you that love cannot exist without jealousy, because, as I have already told you in more detail, jealousy between lovers is commended by every man who is experienced in love, while between husband and wife it is condemned throughout the world; the reason for this will be perfectly clear from a description of jealousy. Now jealousy is a true emotion whereby we greatly fear that the substance of our love may be weakened by some defect in serving the desires of our beloved, and it is an anxiety lest our love may not be returned. . . .

According to Andreas Capellanus the parties in the preceding dialogue agreed to submit their problem to Marie, Countess of Champagne for a definitive judgment. This is how she replied.

We have examined carefully the statements of both sides and have in very truth inquired into the matter by every possible means, and we wish to end the case with this decision. We declare and we hold as firmly established that love cannot exert its powers between two people who are married to each other. For lovers give each other everything freely, under no compulsion of necessity, but married people are in duty bound to give in to each other's desires and deny themselves to each other in nothing. Besides, . . . between them there can be no true jealousy, and without it true love may not exist, according to the rule of Love himself, which says, 'He who is not jealous cannot love.'

Therefore let this our verdict, pronounced with great moderation and supported by the opinion of a great many ladies, be to you firm and indubitable truth.

Eve and Mary

The church was torn between the image of Eve, the temptress, and Mary, the virgin mother of the Redeemer. Considering the two, this medieval poet found something fortunate in Eve's sin.

Adam Lay Y-Bounden

> Adam lay y-bounden
> Bounden in a bond;
> Four thousand winter
> Thought he not too long;
> And all was for an apple
> An apple that he took,
> As clerkes finden written
> In theire book.
>
> Ne had the apple taken been,
> The apple taken been,
> Ne hadde never our Lady
> A been heaven's queen.
> Blessed be the time
> That apple taken was!
> Therefore we may singen
> 'Deo Gratias!'

Endless stories were told of Mary's "miracles."

From *Liber Exemplorum*[7]

One more instance of the loving kindness of the glorious Virgin is found in an ancient sermon, and certainly it should not be despised. A certain poor

From Helen Gardner, ed., *The New Oxford Book of English Verse* (Oxford: Oxford University Press, 1972), pp. 12–13.
[7] A *Liber exemplorum* was a book of anecdotes that preachers could use to enliven their sermons. From A. G. Little, ed., *Liber Exemplorum*, G. G. Coulton, trans. in *Life in the Middle Ages* (Cambridge: Cambridge University Press, 1928–1930, Vol. 1, p. 152.)

woman loved the Blessed Virgin, decking her image with roses and lilies and such ornaments as she could find. It befell that her son was taken and hanged. The woman, in the bitterness of her soul, went to the image of the Blessed Virgin and besought her to restore her son; and, seeing that she recovered not her son as soon as she wished, she said: "Is this then the price of service to thee, that thou succorest me not in my need?" Then, as though maddened by the excess of her grief, she said: "If thou restore me not my son, I will take away thy Son." And, as she reached out her hand impetuously to bear away the image of the little Babe, behold! her son stood by her and seized her cloak and cried, "What dost thou, Mother? Hast thou lost thy senses? Behold, the Mother of God hath restored me to thee." So the mother rejoiced to recover her son.

Although Mary, the most perfect of human beings, was a woman, medieval preachers often railed against the frailties of real-life women. What was the cure for vanity in dress according to this thirteenth-century preacher?

From *Sermon of Berthold of Regensburg*

The second snare which the devils set so perilously for us christian folk, they have set specially for women. Women are as well created for the Kingdom of Heaven as men, . . . and many of you would be saved but for this one snare, which is called vain glory and empty honour. In order that ye may compass men's praise ye spend all your labour on your garments—on your veils and your kirtles. Many of you pay as much to the sempstress as the cost of the cloth itself; it must have shields on the shoulders, it must be flounced and tucked all round the hem; it is not enough for you to show your pride in your very buttonholes, but you must also send your feet to hell by special torments, ye trot this way and that way with your fine stitchings; and so many ye make, and with so much pains, that no man may rehearse it all. At the least excuse ye weary yourselves with your garments; all that wherewith ye busy yourselves is nought but vanity. Ye busy yourselves with your veils, ye twitch them hither, ye twitch them thither; ye gild them here and there with gold thread, and spend thereon all your time and trouble. Ye will spend a good six months' work on a single veil, which is sinful great travail,—and all that men may praise thy dress: "Ah, God! How fair! Was ever so fair a garment?" Yea, our Lady was far fairer than thou, yet was she exceeding humble of heart; and St. Margaret, and many other saints. . . . Ye men might put an end to this and fight against it doughtily, first with good words, and if they are still obdurate, then ye should step valiantly in. . . . Take courage, and pluck up heart and tear it from her head, even though four or ten hairs should come away with it, and cast it into the fire! Do thus not thrice or four times only; and presently she will forbear. It is fitting that the man should be the woman's lord and master.

According to the Book of Genesis, *Eve was made from Adam's rib. The story persistently influenced ways of thinking about women. What significance did it have for Thomas Aquinas?*

From *Sermon of Berthod of Regensburg*, G. G. Coulton trans. in *A Medieval Garner* (London: Constable and Co. Ltd., 1910), pp. 361–363.

From Aquinas. *Summa Theologiae*

When all things were first made, it was more suitable for woman to be formed from man than for this to happen in other animals. First, in order thus to give the first man a certain dignity consisting in this, that as God is the principle of the whole universe, so the first man, in likeness to God, was the principle of the whole human race. Hence Paul says that *God made the whole human race from one (Acts* xvii. 26). Secondly, that man might love woman all the more, and cleave to her more closely, knowing her to be fashioned from himself. Hence it is written (*Gen.* ii. 23, 24) : *She was taken out of man, wherefore a man shall leave father and mother, and shall cleave to his wife.* This was most necessary in the human species, in which the male and female live together for life; which is not the case with other animals. Thirdly, because, as the Philosopher says, the human male and female are united, not only for generation, as with other animals, but also for the purpose of domestic life, in which each has his or her particular duty, and in which the man is the head of the woman. Therefore it was suitable for the woman to be made out of man, as out of her principle. Fourthly, there is a sacramental reason for this. For by this is signified that the Church takes her origin from Christ. Therefore the Apostle says (*Ephes.* v. 32) : *This is a great sacrament; but I speak in Christ and in the Church. . . .*

It was right for woman to be made from a rib of man. First, to signify the social union of man and woman, for the woman should neither use authority over man, and so she was not made from his head; nor was it right for her to be subject to man's contempt as his slave, and so she was not made from his feet.

Women's Roles—Two Views

Christine de Pisan (1364–1429), left a widow with three children when she was twenty-five, won the patronage of the French court through her many admired writings. In The City of Ladies, a history of famous women, she rejected the widespread view that women were intellectually inferior to men. How did Christine explain this popular misconception? (In the following dialogue the author speaks with an allegorical Lady Reason.)

From *The City of Ladies*

After hearing these things, I replied to the lady who spoke infallibly [Lady Reason]. "My lady, truly has God revealed great wonders in the strength of these women whom you describe. But please enlighten me again, whether it has ever pleased this God, who has bestowed so many favors on women, to honor the feminine sex with the privilege of the virtue of high understanding and great learning, and whether women ever have a clever enough mind for this. I wish very much to know this because men maintain that the mind of women can learn only a little."

From Aquinas, *Summa Theologiae* in Anton C. Pegis, ed., *Basic Writings of Saint Thomas Aquinas* (New York: Random House, 1945), pp. 881–883.
From Christine de Pisan, *The Book of the City of Ladies*, E. J. Richards, trans. (New York: Persea Books, 1982), pp. 62–63.

She answered, "My daughter, since I told you before, you know quite well that the opposite of their opinion is true, and to show you this even more clearly, I will give you proof through examples. I tell you again—and don't doubt the contrary—if it were customary to send daughters to school like sons, and if they were then taught the natural sciences, they would learn as thoroughly and understand the subtleties of all the arts and sciences as well as sons. And by chance there happen to be such women, for, as I touched on before, just as women have more delicate bodies than men, weaker and less able to perform many tasks, so do they have minds that are freer and sharper whenever they apply themselves."

"My lady, what are you saying? With all due respect, could you dwell longer on this point, please. Certainly men would never admit this answer is true, unless it is explained more plainly, for they believe that one normally sees that men know more than women do."

She answered, "Do you know why women know less?"

"Not unless you tell me, my lady."

"Without the slightest doubt, it is because they are not involved in many different things, but stay at home, where it is enough for them to run the household, and there is nothing which so instructs a reasonable creature as the exercise and experience of many different things."

"My lady, since they have minds skilled in conceptualizing and learning, just like men, why don't women learn more?"

She replied, "Because, my daughter, the public does not require them to get involved in the affairs which men are commissioned to execute, just as I told you before. It is enough for women to perform the usual duties to which they are ordained. . . .

God has given them such beautiful minds to apply themselves, if they want to, in any of the fields where glorious and excellent men are active, which are neither more nor less accessible to them as compared to men if they wished to study them, and they can thereby acquire a lasting name, whose possession is fitting for most excellent men. My dear daughter, you can see how this author Boccaccio testifies to what I have told you and how he praises and approves learning in women."

Christine de Pisan complained about women's "usual duties." Writing at about the same time, an old merchant of Paris explained to his young wife what those duties were. Do you think he gave her good advice?

From *The Goodman of Paris*

Dear sister, if you have another husband after me, be aware that you must take very good care of his person. For generally when a woman has lost her first husband and marriage, it is hard for her, depending on her social status, to find a second who is to her liking, and she remains forsaken and helpless for a long

From *Le menagier de Paris,* Tania Bayard, trans. in *A Medieval Home Companion* (New York: HarperCollins, 1991), pp. 62–64.

time, and even more so when she loses the second. Therefore, cherish your husband's person carefully.

I entreat you to keep his linen clean, for this is up to you. Because the care of outside affairs is men's work, a husband must look after these things, and go and come, run here and there in rain, wind, snow, and hail—sometimes wet, sometimes dry, sometimes sweating, other times shivering, badly fed, badly housed, badly shod, badly bedded—and nothing harms him because he is cheered by the anticipation of the care his wife will take of him on his return—of the pleasures, joys, and comforts she will provide, or have provided for him in her presence: to have his shoes off before a good fire, to have his feet washed, to have clean shoes and hose, to be well fed, provided with good drink, well served, well honored, well bedded in white sheets and white nightcaps, well covered with good furs, and comforted with other joys and amusements, intimacies, affections, and secrets about which I am silent. And on the next day fresh linen and garments.

Indeed, dear sister, these favors cause a man to love and desire the return home and the sight of his good wife, and to be reserved with others. And so I advise you to comfort your second husband on all his homecomings, and persevere in this.

Also keep peace with him. Remember the country proverb that says there are three things that drive a good man from his home: a house with a bad roof, a smoking chimney, and a quarrelsome woman. Dear sister, I beg you, in order to preserve your husband's love and good will, be loving, amiable, and sweet with him. Do for him what the good, simple women of our country claim people have done to their sons when they are enamored elsewhere and they cannot get them back. . . . and who now bray and cry and say that these women have bewitched their children and that they are under a spell, cannot leave them, and are not content if they are not with them. This is not sorcery, no matter what they say. The only enchantment is in the love, kindness, closeness, joy, and pleasures these women show them in all ways. . . . By my soul! I believe doing good is the only enchantment, and one can no better bewitch a man than by giving him what pleases him.

Therefore, dear sister, I pray you to bewitch and bewitch again the husband whom you will have, preserve him from a badly covered house and a smoky chimney, and be not quarrelsome with him, but be sweet, amiable, and peaceful. Mind that in winter he has a good fire without smoke, and that he is well couched and covered between your breasts, and there bewitch him.

PART TEN

AN AGE OF RENAISSANCE— DECLINE AND RENEWAL, 1300–1500

The fourteenth century has been called an "age of adversity." Certainly the people of that time had to endure many disasters—plague, war, peasant rebellions, schism in the church. But society did not disintegrate under all these stresses. Instead people found the resilience to resist them and move on to a new era of expansion and exploration.

In Italy, the generation that survived the great plague of 1347 displayed an extraordinary vitality. Many intellectuals felt a sense of alienation from late medieval culture and a new devotion to the ancient civilizations of Greece and Rome. The rebirth of classical studies led on to an era of brilliant achievement in art and literature. Writers expressed a new sense of the dignity and worth of the human personality; artists found new ways of celebrating natural beauty—especially the beauty of the human body.

The "humanism" of the new age took many forms. Sometimes it stimulated a secularist, skeptical attitude to the traditional teachings of religion and morality. But many leaders of Renaissance thought saw no conflict between the old doctrines of Christianity and their new quest for beauty and truth.

FOURTEENTH-CENTURY CALAMITIES

Pestilence, Persecution, and Flagellants

An epidemic of bubonic plague (the "Black Death") swept through Europe in the 1340s. How did people react to it according to this contemporary chronicler?

From *Jean de Venette's Chronicle*

In A.D. 1348, the people of France and of almost the whole world were struck by a blow other than war. For in addition to the famine which I described in the beginning and to the wars which I described in the course of this narrative, pestilence and its attendant tribulations appeared again in various parts of the world. . . .

All this year and the next, the mortality of men and women, of the young even more than of the old, in Paris and in the kingdom of France, and also, it is said, in other parts of the world, was so great that it was almost impossible to bury the dead. People lay ill little more than two or three days and died suddenly, as it were in full health. He who was well one day was dead the next and being carried to his grave. Swellings appeared suddenly in the armpit or in the groin—in many cases both—and they were infallible signs of death. This sickness or pestilence was called an epidemic by the doctors. Nothing like the great numbers who died in the years 1348 and 1349 has been heard of or seen or read of in times past. This plague and disease came from *ymaginatione* or association and contagion, for if a well man visited the sick he only rarely evaded the risk of death. Wherefore in many towns timid priests withdrew, leaving the exercise of their ministry to such of the religious as were more daring. In many places not two out of twenty remained alive. So high was the mortality at the Hôtel-Dieu in Paris that for a long time, more than five hundred dead were carried daily with great devotion in carts to the cemetery of the Holy Innocents in Paris for burial. A very great number of the saintly sisters of the Hôtel-Dieu who, not fearing to die, nursed the sick in all sweetness and humility, with no thought of honor, a number too often renewed by death, rest in peace with Christ, as we may piously believe.

This plague, it is said, began among the unbelievers, came to Italy, and then crossing the Alps reached Avignon, where it attacked several cardinals and took from them their whole household. Then it spread, unforeseen, to France, through Gascony and Spain, little by little, from town to town, from village to village, from house to house, and finally from person to person. It even crossed over to Germany, though it was not so bad there as with us. . . .

In the year 1349, while the plague was still active and spreading from town to town, men in Germany, Flanders, Hainaut, and Lorraine uprose and began a new sect on their own authority. Stripped to the waist, they gathered

From Richard Newhall, ed., *The Chronicle of Jean de Venette,* Jean Birdsall, trans. (New York: Columbia University Press, 1953), pp. 48–52.

in large groups and bands and marched in procession through the crossroads and squares of cities and good towns. There they formed circles and beat upon their backs with weighted scourges, rejoicing as they did so in loud voices and singing hymns suitable to their rite and newly composed for it. Thus for thirty-three days they marched through many towns doing their penance and affording a great spectacle to the wondering people. They flogged their shoulders and arms with scourges tipped with iron points so zealously as to draw blood. But they did not come to Paris nor to any part of France, for they were forbidden to do so by the king of France, who did not want them. He acted on the advice of the masters of theology of the University of Paris, who said that this new sect had been formed contrary to the will of God, to the rites of Holy Mother Church, and to the salvation of all their souls. That indeed this was and is true appeared shortly. For Pope Clement VI was fully informed concerning this fatuous new rite by the masters of Paris through emissaries reverently sent to him and, on the grounds that it had been damnably formed, contrary to law, he forbade the Flagellants under threat of anathema to practise in the future the public penance which they had so presumptuously undertaken. His prohibition was just, for the Flagellants, supported by certain fatuous priests and monks, were enunciating doctrines and opinions which were beyond measure evil, erroneous, and fallacious. For example, they said that their blood thus drawn by the scourge and poured out was mingled with the blood of Christ. Their many errors showed how little they knew of the Catholic faith. Wherefore, as they had begun fatuously of themselves and not of God, so in a short time they were reduced to nothing. On being warned, they desisted and humbly received absolution and penance at the hands of their prelates as the pope's representatives. Many honorable women and devout matrons, it must be added, had done this penance with scourges marching and singing through towns and churches like the men, but after a little like the others they desisted.

Some said that this pestilence was caused by infection of the air and waters, since there was at this time no famine nor lack of food supplies, but on the contrary great abundance. As a result of this theory of infected water and air as the source of the plague the Jews were suddenly and violently charged with infecting wells and water and corrupting the air. The whole world rose up against them cruelly on this account. In Germany and other parts of the world where Jews lived, they were massacred and slaughtered by Christians, and many thousands were burned everywhere, indiscriminately. The unshaken, if fatuous, constancy of the men and their wives was remarkable. For mothers hurled their children first into the fire that they might not be baptized and then leaped in after them to burn with their husbands and children. It is said that many bad Christians were found who in a like manner put poison into wells. But in truth, such poisonings, granted that they actually were perpetrated, could not have caused so great a plague nor have infected so many people. There were other causes; for example, the will of God and the corrupt humors and evil inherent in air and earth. Perhaps the poisonings, if they actually took place in some localities, reenforced these causes. The plague lasted in France for the greater part of the years 1348 and 1349 and then ceased. Many country villages and many houses in good towns remained empty and deserted. Many houses, including some splendid dwellings, very soon fell into ruins. Even in Paris several houses were thus ruined, though fewer here than elsewhere.

After the cessation of the epidemic, pestilence, or plague, the men and women who survived married each other. There was no sterility among the women, but on the contrary fertility beyond the ordinary. Pregnant women were seen on every side. Many twins were born and even three children at once. . . .

But woe is me! the world was not changed for the better but for the worse by this renewal of population. For men were more avaricious and grasping than before, even though they had far greater possessions. They were more covetous and disturbed each other more frequently with suits, brawls, disputes, and pleas. Nor by the mortality resulting from this terrible plague inflicted by God was peace between kings and lords established. On the contrary, the enemies of the king of France and of the Church were stronger and wickeder than before and stirred up wars on sea and on land. Greater evils than before pullulated everywhere in the world. . . .

The Hundred Years' War

All through the middle years of the fourteenth century the French people suffered from the destructive campaigns of the Hundred Years' War. The most famous events of the war were the great set battles, like Crécy and Poitiers; but this account of an English campaign in 1346 is much more typical of the way in which the war was routinely conducted.

From *Froissart's Chronicle*

Thus the king of England ordered his business, being in the town of Caen. . . .

Then he departed from the town of Caen and rode in the same order as he did before, burning and devastating the country, and took the way to Evreux and so passed by it; and from thence they rode to a great town called Louviers: it was the chief town of all Normandy of drapery, riches, and full of merchandise. The Englishmen soon entered therein, for as then it was not closed; it was overrun, spoiled and robbed without mercy: there was won great riches. Then they entered into the country of Evreux and burnt and pilled all the country except the good towns closed and castles, to the which the king made none assault, because of the sparing of his people and his artillery. . . .

From G. C. Macaulay, ed., *The Chronicle of Froissart*. Lord Berners, trans. (London: MacMillan, 1904), pp. 98–99.

Then the king of England entered into the country of Beauvoisis, burning and devastating the plain country, and lodged at a fair abbey and a rich called Saint-Messien near to Beauvais: there the king tarried a night and in the morning departed. And when he was on his way he looked behind him and saw the abbey a-fire: he caused incontinent twenty of them to be hanged that set the fire there, for he had commanded before on pain of death none to violate any church nor to burn any abbey. Then the king passed by the city of Beauvais without any assault giving, for because he would not trouble his people nor waste his artillery. And so that day he took his lodging betime in a little town called Milly. The two marshals came so near to Beauvais, that they made assault and skirmish at the barriers in three places, the which assault endured a long space; but the town within was so well defended by the means of the bishop, who was there within, that finally the Englishmen departed, and burnt clean hard to the gates all the suburbs, and then at night they came into the king's field.

The next day the king departed, burning and wasting all before him, and at night lodged in a good village called Grandvilliers. The next day the king passed by Dargies: there was none to defend the castle, wherefore it was soon taken and burnt. Then they went forth destroying the country all about, and so came to the castle of Poix, where there was a good town and two castles. There was nobody in them but two fair damosels, daughters to the lord of Poix; they were soon taken, and had been violated, an two English knights had not been, sir John Chandos and sir Basset; they defended them and brought them to the king, who for his honour made them good cheer and demanded of them whither they would fainest go. They said, 'To Corbie,' and the king caused them to be brought thither without peril. That night the king lodged in the town of Poix. They of the town and of the castles spake that night with the marshals of the host, to save them and their town from burning, and they to pay a certain sum of florins the next day as soon as the host was departed. This was granted them, and in the morning the king departed with all his host except a certain that were left there to receive the money that they of the town had promised to pay. When they of the town saw the host depart and but a few left behind, then they said they would pay never a penny, and so ran out and set on the Englishmen, who defended themselves as well as they might and sent after the host for succour. When sir Raynold Cobham and sir Thomas Holland, who had the rule of the rearguard, heard thereof, they returned and cried, 'Treason, treason!' and so came again to Poix-ward and found their companions still fighting with them of the town. Then anon they of the town were nigh all slain, and the town burnt, and the two castles beaten down.

Peasant Rebellion

French peasants, bitterly resentful of the nobility who taxed them and oppressed them but failed to protect them, rose in an inchoate rebellion—soon suppressed—in 1358. (Peasant rebellions occurred in several other countries during the fourteenth century.)

From *Froissart's Chronicle*

Anon after the deliverance of the king of Navarre [1358] there began a marvellous tribulation in the realm of France, as in Beauvoisin, in Brie, on the river of Marne, in Laonnois, and about Soissons. For certain people of the common villages, without any head or ruler, assembled together in Beauvoisin. In the beginning they passed not a hundred in number; they said how the noblemen of the realm of France, knights and squires, shamed the realm, and that it should be a great wealth to destroy them all; and each of them said it was true, and said all with one voice: "Shame have he that doth not his power to destroy all the gentlemen of the realm!"

Thus they gathered together without any other counsel, and without any armour saving with staves and knives, and so went to the house of a knight dwelling thereby, and brake up his house and slew the knight and the lady and all his children great and small and burnt his house. And then they went to another castle, and took the knight thereof and bound him fast to a stake, and then violated his wife and his daughter before his face and then slew the lady and his daughter and all his other children, and then slew the knight by great torment and burnt and beat down the castle. And so they did to divers other castles and good houses; and they multiplied so that they were a six thousand, and ever as they went forward they increased, for such like as they were fell ever to them, so that every gentlemen fled from them and took their wives and children with them, and fled ten or twenty leagues off to be in surety, and left their houses void and their goods therein.

These mischievous people thus assembled without captain or armour robbed, burnt and slew all gentlemen that they could lay hands on, and forced and ravished ladies and damosels, and did such shameful deeds that no human creature ought to think on any such, and he that did most mischief was most praised with them and greatest master. I dare not write the horrible deeds that they did to ladies and damosels: among other they slew a knight and after did put him on a broach and roasted him at the fire in the sight of the lady his wife and his children; and after the lady had been enforced and ravished with a ten or twelve, they made her perforce to eat of her husband and after made her to die an evil death and all her children. They made among them a king, one of Clermont in Beauvoisin: they chose him that was the most ungraciousest of all other and they called him king Jaques Goodman, and so thereby they were called companions of the Jaquery. They destroyed and burnt in the country of Beauvoisin about Corbie, Amiens and Montdidier more than threescore good houses and strong castles. In like manner these unhappy people were in Brie and Artois, so that all the ladies, knights and squires of that country were fain to fly away to Meaux in Brie, as well the duchess of Normandy and the duchess of Orleans as divers other ladies and damosels, or else they had been violated and after murdered. Also there were a certain of the same ungracious people between Paris and Noyon and between Paris and Soissons, and all about the land of Coucy, in the county of Valois, in the bishopric of Laon, Nyon and Soissons.

From G. C. Macaulty, ed., *The Chronicles of Froissart,* Lord Berners, trans. (London: Macmillan, 1904), pp. 136–137.

There were burnt and destroyed more than a hundred castles and good houses of knights and squires in that country.

Joan of Arc

The English attacks inspired a new mood of patriotism in France, focusing on divine-right kingship as the only hope for a restoration of peace and order. This sentiment was strikingly expressed in a letter of Joan of Arc (1412–1431), the French peasant girl who rallied French forces in the final stages of the Hundred Years' War. (Joan was burnt as a witch by the English in 1431.) Compare her view of kingship with the material on Renaissance rulers (pp. 313–319).

Letter of Joan of Arc, 1429

(This letter of Joan was introduced as evidence at her trial.)

JHESUS MARIA

King of England, and you Duke of Bedford, calling yourself regent of France, you William Pole, Count of Suffolk John Talbot, and you Thomas Lord Scales, calling yourselves lieutenants of the said Duke of Bedford, do right in the King of Heaven's sight. Surrender to *The Maid* sent hither by God the King of Heaven, the keys of all the good towns you have taken and laid waste in France. She comes in God's name to establish the Blood Royal, ready to make peace if you agree to abandon France and repay what you have taken. And you, archers, comrades in arms, gentles and others, who are before the town of Orleans, retire in God's name to your own country. If you do not, expect to hear tidings from *The Maid* who will shortly come upon you to your very great hurt. And to you, King of England, if you do not thus, I am a chieftain of war, and whenever I meet your followers in France, I will drive them out; if they will not obey, I will put them all to death. I am sent here in God's name, the King of Heaven, to drive you body for body out of all France. If they obey, I will show them mercy. Do not think otherwise; you will not withhold the kingdom of France from God, the King of Kings, Blessed Mary's Son. The King Charles, the true inheritor, will possess it, for God wills it, and has revealed it to him through *The Maid*, and he will enter Paris with a good company. If you do not believe these tidings from God and *The Maid*, wherever we find you we shall strike you and make a greater tumult than France has heard for a thousand years. Know well that the King of Heaven will send a greater force to *The Maid* and her good people than you in all your assaults can overcome: and by blows shall the favour of the God of Heaven be seen. You Duke of Bedford, *The Maid* prays and beseeches not to bring yourself to destruction. If you obey her, you may join her company, where the French shall do the fairest deed ever done for Christendom. Answer, if you desire peace in the city of Orleans; if not, bethink you of your great hurt soon. Written this Tuesday of Holy Week.

From W. P. Barrett, trans., *The Trial of Jeanne d'Arc* (London: George Routledge, 1931), pp. 165–166. Reprinted by permission of Routledge & Kegan Paul Ltd.

NEW LIGHT IN ITALY

Writers of the early Renaissance sometimes turned away from the troubles of their own world to recover the whole heritage of classical thought and culture.

Ancients and Moderns

Dante Alighieri (1265–1320), the greatest Italian poet, can be regarded as a transitional figure. His vision of heaven, hell, and purgatory in The Divine Comedy *seems essentially medieval. But Dante's treatment of the great figures of ancient Greece and Rome anticipates an aspect of Renaissance culture. In these verses Dante is led by his guide, the Roman poet Vergil, through the first circle of hell where the souls do not suffer actual physical torments. Why are the people that Dante meets there excluded from heaven? What is Dante's attitude toward them?*

From Dante. *The Divine Comedy*

No tortured wailing rose to greet us here
   but sounds of sighing rose from every side,
   sending a tremor through the timeless air.
a grief breathed out of untormented sadness,
   the passive state of those who dwelled apart,
   men, women, children—a dim and endless congress.
And the Master said to me: "You do not question
   what souls these are that suffer here before you?
   I wish you to know before you travel on
that these were sinless. And still their merits fail,
   for they lacked Baptism's grace, which is the door
   of the true faith you were born to. Their birth fell
before the age of the Christian mysteries,
   and so they did not worship God's Trinity
   in fullest duty. I am one of these.
For such defects are we lost, though spared the fire
   and suffering Hell in one affliction only:
   that without hope we live on in desire." . . .
And as he spoke a voice rang on the air:
   "Honor the Prince of Poets; the soul and glory
   that went from us returns. He is here! He is here!"
The cry ceased and the echo passed from hearing;
   I saw four mighty presences come toward us
   with neither joy nor sorrow in their bearing.
"Note well," my Master said as they came on,
   "that soul that leads the rest with sword in hand
   as if he were their captain and champion.

It is Homer, singing master of the earth.
   Next after him is Horace, the satirist,
   Ovid is third, and Lucan is the fourth.
Since all of these have part in the high name
   the voice proclaimed, calling me Prince of Poets,
   the honor that they do me honors them."
So I saw gathered at the edge of light
   the masters of that highest school whose song
   outsoars all others like an eagle's flight.
And after they had talked together a while,
   they turned and welcomed me most graciously,
   at which I saw my approving Master smile.
And they honored me far beyond courtesy,
   for they included me in their own number,
   making me sixth in that high company.
And there directly before me on the green
   the master souls of time were shown to me.
   I glory in the glory I have seen!
Electra stood in a great company
   among whom I saw Hector and Aeneas
   and Caesar in armor with his falcon's eye.
I saw Camilla, and the Queen Amazon
   across the field. I saw the Latian King
   seated there with his daughter by his throne.
And the good Brutus who overthrew the Tarquin:
   Lucrezia, Julia, Marcia, and Cornelia;
   and, by himself apart, the Saladin.
And raising my eyes a little I saw on high
   Aristotle, the master of those who know,
   ringed by the great souls of philosophy.
All wait upon him for their honor and his.
   I saw Socrates and Plato at his side
   before all others there. Democritus
who ascribes the world to chance, Diogenes,
   and with him there Thales, Anaxagoras,
   Zeno, Heraclitus, Empedocles.
And I saw the wise collector and analyst—
   Dioscorides I mean. I saw Orpheus there,
   Tully, Linus, Seneca the moralist,
Eculid the geometer, and Ptolemy,
   Hippocrates, Galen, Avicenna,
   and Averrhoës of the Great Commentary.
I cannot count so much nobility;
   my longer theme pursues me so that often
   the word falls short of the reality.
The company of six is reduced by four.
   My Master leads me by another road
   away from that serenity to the roar
and trembling air of Hell. I pass from light
   into the kingdom of eternal night.

Renaissance scholars studied classical authors both to learn wisdom from them and to cultivate an elegant literary style. (They came to despise medieval Latin with its non-classical usages as "barbaric."). Francesco Petrarch (1304–1374) has been called the first Renaissance humanist. Why did he copy Cicero so assiduously?

From *Petrarch's Letters*

Your Cicero has been in my possession four years and more. There is a good reason, though, for so long a delay; namely, the great scarcity of copyists who understand such work. It is a state of affairs that has resulted in an incredible loss to scholarship. Books that by their nature are a little hard to understand are no longer multiplied, and have ceased to be generally intelligible, and so have sunk into utter neglect, and in the end have perished. This age of ours consequently has let fall, bit by bit, some of the richest and sweetest fruits that the tree of knowledge has yielded; has thrown away the results of the vigils and labours of the most illustrious men of genius, things of more value, I am almost tempted to say, than anything else in the whole world. . . .

But I must return to your Cicero. I could not do without it, and the incompetence of the copyists would not let me possess it. What was left for me but to rely upon my own resources, and press these weary fingers and this worn and ragged pen into the service? The plan that I followed was this. I want you to know it, in case you should ever have to grapple with a similar task. Not a single word did I read except as I wrote. But how is that, I hear someone say; did you write without knowing what it was that you were writing? Ah! but from the very first it was enough for me to know that it was a work of Tullius, and an extremely rare one too. And then as soon as I was fairly started I found at every step so much sweetness and charm, and felt so strong a desire to advance, that the only difficulty which I experienced in reading and writing at the same time came from the fact that my pen could not cover the ground so rapidly as I wanted it to, whereas my expectation had been rather that it would outstrip my eyes, and that my ardour for writing would be chilled by the slowness of my reading. So the pen held back the eye, and the eye drove on the pen, and I covered page after page, delighting in my task, and committing many and many a passage to memory as I wrote. For just in proportion as the writing is slower than the reading does the passage make a deep impression and cling to the mind.

And yet I must confess that I did finally reach a point in my copying where I was overcome by weariness; not mental, for how unlikely that would be where Cicero was concerned, but the sort of fatigue that springs from excessive manual labour. I began to feel doubtful about this plan that I was following, and to regret having undertaken a task for which I had not been trained; when suddenly I came across a place where Cicero tells how he himself copied the orations of— someone or other; just who it was I do not know, but certainly no Tullius, for there is but one such man, one such voice, one such mind. These are his words: "You

From J. H. Robinson and H. W. Rolfe, trans., *Petrarch: The First Modern Scholar and Man of Letters* (New York: Putnam, 1898), pp. 275–278.

say that you have been in the habit of reading the orations of Cassius in your idle moments. But I," he jestingly adds, with his customary disregard of his adversary's feelings, "have made a practice of *copying* them, so that I might *have* no idle moments." As I read this passage I grew hot with shame, like a modest young soldier who hears the voice of his beloved leader rebuking him. I said to myself, "So Cicero copied orations that another wrote, and you are not ready to copy his? What ardour! what scholarly devotion! what reverence for a man of godlike genius!" These thoughts were a spur to me, and I pushed on, with all my doubts dispelled. If ever from my darkness there shall come a single ray that can enhance the splendour of the reputation which his heavenly eloquence has won for him, it will proceed in no slight measure from the fact that I was so captivated by his ineffable sweetness that I did a thing in itself most irksome with such delight and eagerness that I scarcely knew I was doing it at all.

So then at last your Cicero has the happiness of returning to you, bearing you my thanks. And yet he also stays, very willingly, with me; a dear friend, to whom I give the credit of being almost the only man of letters for whose sake I would go to the length of spending my time, when the difficulties of life are pressing on me so sharply and inexorably and the cares pertaining to my literary labours make the longest life seem far too short, in transcribing compositions not my own. I may have done such things in former days, when I thought myself rich in time, and had not learned how stealthily it slips away: but I now know that this is of all our riches the most uncertain and fleeting; the years are closing in upon me now, and there is no longer any room for deviation from the beaten path. I am forced to practice strict economy; I only hope that I have not begun too late. But Cicero! he assuredly is worthy of a part of even the little that I still have left. Farewell.

Petrarch was a skilled Latin scholar but he knew no Greek. Leonardo Bruni (1374–1444) described the enthusiasm with which Greek learning was received in Italy a little later.

From Leonardo Bruni. *Commentarius*

Then first came a knowledge of Greek, which had not been in use among us for seven hundred years. Chrysoloras the Byzantine, a man of noble birth and well versed in Greek letters, brought Greek learning to us. When his country was invaded by the Turks, he came by sea, first to Venice. The report of him soon spread, and he was cordially invited and besought and promised a public stipend, to come to Florence and open his store of riches to the youth. I was then studying Civil Law, but . . . I burned with love of academic studies, and had spent no little pains on dialectic and rhetoric. At the coming of Chrysoloras I was torn in mind, deeming it shameful to desert the law, and yet a crime to lose such a chance of studying Greek literature; and often with youthful impulse I would say to myself: 'Thou, when it is permitted thee to gaze on Homer, Plato and

From H. O. Taylor, *Thought and Expression in the Sixteenth Century* (New York: MacMillan Company, 1920) pp. 36–37.

Demosthenes, and the other poets, philosophers, orators, of whom such glorious things are spread abroad, and speak with them and be instructed in their admirable teaching, wilt thou desert and rob thyself? Wilt thou neglect this opportunity so divinely offered? For seven hundred years, no one in Italy has possessed Greek letters; and yet we confess that all knowledge is derived from them. How great advantage to your knowledge, enhancement of your fame, increase of your pleasure, will come from an understanding of this tongue? There are doctors of civil law everywhere; and the chance of learning will not fail thee. But if this one and only doctor of Greek letters disappears, no one can be found to teach thee. Overcome at length by these reasons, I gave myself to Chrysoloras, with such zeal to learn, that what through the wakeful day I gathered, I followed after in the night, even when asleep.

The Dignity of Man

Some Renaissance scholars derived from their study of classical ideas and from their Christian tradition a new vision of human dignity. It was expressed most eloquently by Pico della Mirandola (1463–1494). How does his outlook differ from modern secular humanism?

From Pico della Mirandola. *Oration on the Dignity of Man*

At last it seems to me I have come to understand why man is the most fortunate of creatures and consequently worthy of all admiration and what precisely is that rank which is his lot in the universal chain of Being—a rank to be envied not only by brutes but even by the stars and by minds beyond this world. It is a matter past faith and a wondrous one. Why should it not be? For it is on this very account that man is rightly called and judged a great miracle and wonderful creature indeed. But hear, Fathers, exactly what this rank is and, as friendly auditors, conformably to your kindness, do me this favor. God the Father, the supreme Architect, had already built this cosmic home we behold, the most sacred temple of His godhead, by the laws of His mysterious wisdom. The region above the heavens He had adorned with Intelligences, the heavenly spheres He had quickened with eternal souls, and the excrementary and filthy parts of the lower world He had filled with a multitude of animals of every kind. But, when the work was finished, the Craftsman kept wishing that there were someone to ponder the plan of so great a work, to love its beauty, and to wonder at its vastness. Therefore, when everything was done (as Moses and Timaeus bear witness), He finally took thought concerning the creation of man. But there was not among His archetypes that from which He could fashion a new offspring, nor was there in His treasurehouses anything which He might bestow on His new son as an inheritance, nor was there in the seats of all the world a place where the latter might sit to contemplate the universe. All was now complete; all things had been assigned to the highest, the middle, and the lowest orders. But in its final creation it was not the part of the Father's power to fail as though exhausted. It was not the part of His wisdom to waver in a needful matter through poverty of counsel. It was not the part of His kindly love that he who was to praise God's divine generosity in regard to others should be compelled to condemn it in regard to himself. At last the best of artisans ordained that the creature to whom He had been able to give nothing proper to himself should have joint possession of whatever had been peculiar to each of the different kinds of being. He therefore took man as a creature of indeterminate nature and, assigning him a place in the middle of the world, addressed him thus: "Neither a fixed abode nor a form that is thine alone nor any function peculiar to thyself have we given thee, Adam, to the end that according to thy longing and according to thy judgment thou mayest have and posses what abode, what form, and what functions thou thyself shalt desire. The nature of all other beings is limited and constrained within the bounds of laws prescribed by Us. Thou, constrained by no limits, in accordance with thine own free will, in whose hand We have placed thee, shalt ordain for thyself the limits of thy nature. We have set thee at the world's center that thou mayest from thence more easily observe whatever is in the world. We have made thee neither of heaven nor of earth, neither mortal nor immortal, so that with freedom of choice and with honor, as though the maker and molder of thyself, thou mayest fashion thyself in whatever shape thou shalt prefer. Thou shalt have the power to degenerate into the lower forms of life, which are brutish. Thou shalt have the power, out of thy soul's judgment, to be reborn into the higher forms, which are divine." O supreme generosity of God the Father, O highest and most marvelous felicity of man! To him it is granted to have whatever he chooses, to be whatever he wills.

RENAISSANCE TYPES—ARTISTS AND COURTIERS

Art and Artists

Giorgio Vasari (1511–1574) described the lives and works of dozens of Renaissance artists in a great history of Italian painting. In his Introduction *Vasari presented, in terms of art history, the common Renaissance theme of a "dark age" following the fall of Rome and a "second birth" of culture centuries later. What did Vasari admire about classical art? What brought about its decline? What was the relationship between art and nature?*

From Giorgio Vasari. *Lives of the Most Eminent Painters* (1550)

We find, then, that the art of sculpture was zealously cultivated by the Greeks, among whom many excellent artists appeared; those great masters, the Athenian Phidias, with Praxiteles and Polycletus, were of the number, while

From Giorgi Vasari, *Lives of the Most Eminent Painters, Sculptors and Architects*, Mrs. J. Foster, trans. (London: H. G. Bohn, 1850), Vol. 1, pp. 12, 15–16, 30–31; Vol. 2, pp. 366–368, 380, 384–385.

Lysippus and Pyrgoteles, worked successfully in intaglio, and Pygmalion produced admirable reliefs in ivory—nay, of him it was affirmed, that his prayers
obtained life and soul for the statue of a virgin which he had formed. Painting
was in like manner honoured, and those who practised it successfully were re-
warded among the ancient Greeks and Romans; this is proved by their according the rights of citizenship, and the most exalted dignities, to such as attained
high distinction in these arts, both of which flourished so greatly in Rome, that
Fabius bequeathed fame to his posterity by subscribing his name to the pictures
so admirably painted by him in the Temple of *Salus*, and calling himself Fabius
Pictor. . . .

   I suggested above that the origin of these arts was Nature herself—the first
image or model, the most beautiful fabric of the world—and the master, that divine light infused into us by special grace, and which has made us not only superior to all other animals, but has exalted us, if it be permitted so to speak, to
the similitude of God Himself. This is my belief, and I think that every man who
shall maturely consider the question, will be of my opinion. And if it has been
seen in our times—as I hope to demonstrate presently by various examples—
that simple children, rudely reared in the woods, have begun to practise the arts
of design with no other model than those beautiful pictures and sculptures furnished by Nature, and no other teaching than their own genius—how much
more easily may we believe that the first of mankind, in whom nature and intellect were all the more perfect in proportion as they were less removed from
their first origin and divine parentage,—that these men, I say, having Nature for
their guide, and the unsullied purity of their fresh intelligence for their master,
with the beautiful model of the world for an exemplar, should have given birth
to these most noble arts, and from a small beginning, ameliorating them by slow
degrees, should have conducted them finally to perfection? . . . neither will I
deny the possibility that one may have assisted another, thus teaching and opening the way to design, to colour, and to relief; for I know that our art is altogether
imitation, of Nature principally, but also, for him who cannot soar so high, of the
works of such as he esteems better masters than himself. . . . But to cease the discussion of this question, which is rendered too obscure by its extreme antiquity,
let us proceed to matters of which we have better knowledge, the perfection of
the arts, namely, their decay and restoration, or rather second birth, of which we
can speak on much better grounds. . . .

   As fortune, when she has raised either persons or things to the summit of
her wheel, very frequently casts them to the lowest point, whether in repentance
or for her sport, so it chanced that, after these things, the barbarous nations of
the world arose, in divers places, in rebellion against the Romans; whence there
ensued, in no long time, not only the decline of that great empire, but the utter
ruin of the whole, and more especially of Rome herself, when all the best artists,
sculptors, painters, and architects, were in like manner totally ruined, being sub-
merged and buried, together with the arts themselves, beneath the miserable
slaughters and ruins of that much renowned city. . . . But infinitely more ruinous
than all other enemies to the arts above named, was the fervent zeal of the new
Christian religion, which, after long and sanguinary combats, had finally over-

come and annihilated the ancient creeds of the pagan world, by the frequency of miracles exhibited, and by the earnest sincerity of the means adopted; and ardently devoted, with all diligence, to the extirpation of error, nay, to the removal of even the slightest temptation to heresy, it not only destroyed all the wondrous statues, paintings, sculptures, mosaics, and other ornaments of the false pagan deities, but at the same time extinguished the very memory, in casting down the honours, of numberless excellent ancients, to whom statues and other monuments had been erected, in public places, for their virtues, by the most virtuous times of antiquity. Nay, more than this, to build the churches of the Christian faith, this zeal not only destroyed the most renowned temples of the heathens, but, for the richer ornament of St. Peter's, and in addition to the many spoils previously bestowed on that building, the tomb of Adrian, now called the castle of St. Angelo, was deprived of its marble columns, to employ them for this church, many other buildings being in like manner despoiled, and which we now see wholly devastated. And although the Christian religion did not effect this from hatred to these works of art, but solely for the purpose of abasing and bringing into contempt the gods of the Gentiles, yet the result of this too ardent zeal did not fail to bring such total ruin over the noble arts, that their very form and existence was lost. . . .

In like manner, the best works in painting and sculpture, remaining buried under the ruins of Italy, were concealed during the same period, and continued wholly unknown to the rude men reared amidst the more modern usages of art, and by whom no other sculptures or pictures were produced, than such as were executed by the remnant of old Greek artists. They formed images of earth and stone, or painted monstrous figures, of which they traced the rude outline only in colour. . . . It was only by slow degrees that those who came after, being aided in some places by the subtlety of the air around them, could begin to raise themselves from these depths; when, towards 1250, Heaven, moved to pity by the noble spirits which the Tuscan soil was producing every day, restored them to their primitive condition. It is true that those who lived in the times succeeding the ruin of Rome, had seen remnants of arches, colossi, statues, pillars, storied columns, and other works of art, not wholly destroyed by the fires and other devastations; yet they had not known how to avail themselves of this aid, nor had they derived any benefit from it, until the time specified above. When the minds then awakened, becoming capable of distinguishing the good from the worthless, and abandoning old methods, returned to the imitation of the antique, with all the force of their genius, and all the power of their industry.

Leonardo da Vinci (1452–1519) was among the many artists described by Vasari. Why is Leonardo often regarded as the most perfect example of the qualities of a Renaissance man? What did Vasari especially admire in him as a man and as an artist?

From Giorgio Vasari. *Lives of the Most Eminent Painters* (1550)

The richest gifts are occasionally seen to be showered, as by celestial influence, on certain human beings, nay, they some times supernaturally and marvellously congregate in one sole person; beauty, grace, and talent being united in such a manner, that to whatever the man thus favoured may turn himself, his every action is so divine as to leave all other men far behind him, and manifestly to prove that he has been specially endowed by the hand of God himself, and has not obtained his pre-eminence by human teaching, or the power of man. This was seen and acknowledged by all men in the case of Leonardo da Vinci, in whom, to say nothing of his beauty of person, which yet was such that it has never been sufficiently extolled, there was a grace beyond expression which was rendered manifest without thought or effort in every act and deed, and who had besides so rare a gift of talent and ability, that to whatever subject he turned his attention, however difficult, he presently made himself absolute master of it. Extraordinary power was in his case conjoined with remarkable facility, a mind of regal boldness and magnanimous daring; his gifts were such that the celebrity of his name extended most widely, and he was held in the highest estimation, not in his own time only, but also, and even to a greater extent, after his death, nay, this he has continued, and will continue to be by all succeeding ages.

Truly admirable, indeed, and divinely endowed was Leonardo da Vinci; this artist was the son of Ser Piero da Vinci; he would without doubt have made great progress in learning and knowledge of the sciences, had he not been so versatile and changeful, but the instability of his character caused him to undertake many things which having commenced he afterwards abandoned. In arithmetic, for example, be made such rapid progress in the short time during which he gave his attention to it, that he often confounded the master who was teaching him, by the perpetual doubts he started, and by the difficulty of the questions he proposed. He also commenced the study of music, and resolved to acquire the art of playing the lute, when, being by nature of an exalted imagination and full of the most graceful vivacity, he sang to that instrument most divinely, improvising at once the verses and the music. . . .

Endowed with such admirable intelligence, and being also an excellent geometrician, Leonardo not only worked in sculpture (having executed certain heads in terra-cotta, of women smiling, even in his first youth, which are now reproduced in gypsum, and also others of children which might be supposed to have proceeded from the hand of a master); but in architecture likewise he prepared various designs for ground-plans, and the construction of entire buildings: he too it was who, though still but a youth, first suggested the formation of a canal from Pisa to Florence, by means of certain changes to be effected on the river Arno. Leonardo likewise made designs for mills, fulling machines, and other engines, which were to be acted on by means of water; but as he had resolved to make painting his profession, he gave the larger portion of time to drawing from nature. . . .

He afterwards gave his attention, and with increased earnestness, to the anatomy of the human frame, a study wherein Messer Marcantonio della Torre, an eminent philosopher, and himself, did mutually assist and encourage each other. Messer Marcantonio was at that time holding lectures in Pavia, and wrote on the same subject; he was one of the first, as I have heard say, who began to apply the doctrines of Galen to the elucidation of medical science, and to diffuse light over the science of anatomy, which, up to that time, had been involved in the almost total darkness of ignorance. In this attempt Marcantonio was wonderfully aided by the genius and labour of Leonardo, who filled a book with drawings in red crayons, outlined with the pen, all copies made with the utmost care from bodies dissected by his own hand. In this book he set forth the entire structure, arrangement, and disposition of the bones, to which he afterwards added all the nerves, in their due order, and next supplied the muscles, of which the first are affixed to the bones, the second give the power of cohesion or holding firmly, and the third impart that of motion. Of each separate part he wrote an explanation in rude characters, written backwards and with the lefthand, so that whoever is not practised in reading cannot understand them, since they are only to be read with a mirror. . . .

For Francesco del Giocondo, Leonardo undertook to paint the portrait of Mona Lisa, his wife, but, after loitering over it for four years, he finally left it unfinished. This work is now in the possession of the King Francis of France, and is at Fontainebleau. Whoever shall desire to see how far art can imitate nature, may do so to perfection in this head, wherein every peculiarity that could be depicted by the utmost subtlety of the pencil has been faithfully reproduced. The eyes have the lustrous brightness and moisture which is seen in life, and around them are those pale, red, and slightly livid circles, also proper to nature, with the lashes, which can only be copied, as these are, with the greatest difficulty: the eyebrows also are represented with the closet exactitude, where fuller and where more thinly set, with the separate hairs delineated as they issue from the skin, every turn being followed, and all the pores exhibited in a manner that could not be more natural than it is: the nose, with its beautiful and delicately roseate nostrils, might be easily believed to be alive; the mouth, admirable in its outline, has the lips uniting the rose-tints of their colour with that of the face, in the utmost perfection, and the carnation of the cheek does not appear to be painted, but truly of flesh and blood: he who looks earnestly at the pit of the throat cannot but believe that he sees the beating of the pulses, and it may be truly said that this work is painted in a manner well calculated to make the boldest master tremble, and astonishes all who behold it, however well accustomed to the marvels of art. Mona Lisa was exceedingly beautiful, and while Leonardo was painting her portrait, he took the precaution of keeping some one constantly near her, to sing or play on instruments, or to jest and otherwise amuse her, to the end that she might continue cheerful, and so that her face might not exhibit the melancholy expression often imparted by painters to the likenesses they take. In this portrait of Leonardo's, on the contrary, there is so pleasing an expression, and a smile so sweet, that while looking at it one thinks it rather divine than human, and it has ever been esteemed a wonderful work, since life itself could exhibit no other appearance.

Courtier and Prince

Baldassare Castiglione (1478–1529) described another type of Renaissance figure, the courtier who sought to advance himself by winning the favor of a powerful prince. Do you think Castiglione's advice would be useful to a person in the service of a modern ruler—a White House aide for instance?

From Baldassare Castiglione. *The Book of the Courtier (1528)*

"I think that the conversation which the Courtier ought most to try in every way to make acceptable, is that which he holds with his prince; and although this word 'conversation' implies a certain equality that seems impossible between a lord and his inferior, yet we will call it so for the present. Therefore, besides daily showing everyone that he possesses the worth we have already described, I would have the Courtier strive, with all the thoughts and forces of his mind, to love and almost to adore the prince whom he serves, above every other thing, and mould his wishes, habits and all his ways to his prince's liking."

Without waiting for more, Pietro da Napoli here said:

"We already have enough Courtiers of this kind, for methinks you have in a few words described for us a noble flatterer."

"You are much in errour," replied messer Federico; "for flatterers love neither their prince nor their friends, which I tell you I wish chiefly in our Courtier.

"Moreover it is possible without flattery to obey and further the wishes of him we serve, for I am speaking of those wishes that are reasonable and right, or of those that in themselves are neither good nor evil, such as would be a liking for play or a devotion to one kind of exercise above another. And I would have the Courtier bend himself to this even if he be by nature alien to it, so that on seeing him his lord shall always feel that he will have something agreeable to say; which will come about if he has the good judgment to perceive what his prince likes, and the wit and prudence to bend himself thereto, and a deliberate purpose to like that which perhaps he by nature dislikes. And adopting these precautions, he will never be out of humour or melancholy before his prince, nor so taciturn as many are who seem to bear a grudge against their patrons, which is a truly odious thing. He will not be given to evil speaking, especially against his own lords; which often happens, for in courts there seems to rage a fury of such sort that those who have been most favoured by their lord and have been raised to eminence from the lowest state, are always complaining and speaking ill of him; which is unseemly not only in such as these, but even in those who chance to have been ill used.

"Our Courtier will show no foolish presumption; he will not be a bearer of evil tidings; he will not be thoughtless in sometimes saying things that offend instead of pleasing as he intends. He will not be obstinate and disputatious, as some are who seem to delight in nothing but to be troublesome and disagreeable like flies, and who make a point of spitefully contradicting everyone without discrimination. He will not be an idle or untruthful tattler, nor a boaster nor pointless flatterer, but modest and reserved, always and especially in public showing that reverence and respect which befit the servant towards the master. . . .

"He will not seek to intrude unasked into his master's chamber or private retreats, even though he be of great consequence; for when great lords are in private, they often like a little liberty to say and do what they please, and do not

From Baldassare Castiglione, *The Book of the Courtier*, L. E. Opdycke, trans. (New York: Charles Scribner's Sons, 1903), pp. 93–95, 98–100.

wish to be seen or heard by any who may criticise them; and it is very proper. Hence I think those men do ill who blame great lords for consorting privately with persons who are of little worth save in matters of personal service, for I do not see why lords should not have the same freedom to relax their minds that we fain would have to relax ours. But if a Courtier accustomed to deal with important matters, chances to find himself in private with his lord, he must put on another face, postpone grave concerns to another place and time, and give the conversation a cast that shall amuse and please his lord, so as not to disturb that repose of mind of which I speak.

"Again, there are also some men who are so reserved that they shun human company beyond reason, and so far exceed a certain limit of moderation that they come to be regarded as either too timid or too proud. For these I have no praise, nor would I have modesty so dry and arid as to become clownishness; but let the Courtier be fluent on occasion, and prudent and sagacious in discussing statecraft, and let him have the good sense to adapt himself to the customs of the nations where he finds himself; then in lesser matters let him be agreeable and speak well about everything.

"But above all, he should make for right; not envious, not evil-tongued: nor let him ever bring himself to seek grace or favour by foul ways or dishonourable means.". . .

Then my lord Ludovico Pio said:

"I should like to have you clear a doubt that is in my mind; that is, whether a gentleman in the service of a prince is bound to obey him in all things that he commands, even if they be dishonourable and infamous."

"In dishonourable things we are not bound to obey any man," replied messer Federico.

"And how," returned my lord Ludovico, "if I am in the service of a prince who uses me well and trusts to my doing for him all that can be done, commanding me to go kill a man or do anything else you please,—ought I to refuse to do it?"

"You ought," replied messer Federico, "to obey your lord in all things that are advantageous and honourable to him, not in those that bring him injury and disgrace. Therefore if he were to command you to commit an act of treachery, not only would you not be bound to do it, but you would be bound not to do it,—both for your own sake and for the sake of not being a minister to your lord's disgrace. True it is that many things which are evil seem at first sight good, and many seem evil and yet are good. Hence in our lords' service it is sometimes permitted to kill not one man but ten thousand, and to do many other things that would seem evil to a man who did not rightly consider them, and yet are not evil."

Then my lord Gaspar Pallavicino replied:

"On your faith, I pray you discuss this a little, and teach us how the really good can be distinguished from that which only seems so."

"Pardon me," said messer Federico; "I am unwilling to enter upon that, for there would be too much to say; but let the whole matter be left to your own wisdom."

RENAISSANCE FAMILIES

Family and Fortune

Leon Battisto Alberti, distinguished both as an artist and a writer, lived in Florence from 1404 to 1472. His book illustrates the central importance of the family as the basic unit of Florentine society. Why were Florentine young men reluctant to marry? Why ought they to do so? What qualities should a man look for in seeking a wife? You could compare Alberti's views with those of Xenophon (p. 81), whose work he knew, and with those of Christine de Pisan (p. 282).

From Alberti. *I Libri Della Famiglia*

In our discussion we may establish four general precepts as sound and firm foundation for all the other points to be developed or added. I shall name them. In the family the number of men must not diminish but augment; possessions must not grow less, but more; all forms of disgrace are to be shunned—a good name and fine reputation is precious and worth pursuing; hatreds, enmities, rancor must be carefully avoided, while good will, numerous acquaintances, and friendships are something to look for, augment, and cultivate. . . .

Families increase in population no differently than do countries, regions, and the whole world. As anyone who uses his imagination will quickly realize, the number of mortal men has grown from a small number to the present almost infinite multitude through the procreation and rearing of children. And, for the procreation of children, no one can deny that man requires woman. Since a child comes into the world as a tender and delicate creature, he needs someone to whose care and devotion he comes as a cherished trust. This person must nourish him with diligence and love and must defend him from harm. Too much cold or too much sun, rain, and the wild blowing of a storm are harmful to children. Woman, therefore, did first find a roof under which to nourish and protect herself and her offspring. There she remained, busy in the shadow, nourishing and caring for her children. And since woman was busy guarding and taking care of the heir, she was not in a position to go out and find what she and her children required for the maintenance of their life. Man, however, was by nature more energetic and industrious, and he went out to find things and bring what seemed to him necessary.

Nature showed, further, that this relationship could not be permitted with more than one wife at a time, since man was by no means able to provide and bring home more than was needed for himself and one wife and children. . . . To satisfy nature, then, a man need only choose a woman with whom he can dwell in tranquility under one roof all his life.

Young people, however, very often do not cherish the good of the family enough to do this. Marriage, perhaps, seems to them to take away their present liberty and freedom. It may be, as the comic poets like to tell us, that they are held back and dissuaded by some mistress. Sometimes, too, young men find it hard enough to manage one life, and fear as an excessive and undesirable burden the task of supporting a wife and children besides. They may doubt their capacity to maintain in honorable estate a family which grows in needs from day to day. Viewing the conjugal bed as a troublesome responsibility, they then avoid the legitimate and honorable path to the increase of a family.

If a family is not to fall for these reasons into what we have described as the most unfortunate condition of decline, but is to grow, instead, in fame and in the prosperous multitude of its youth, we must persuade our young men to take wives. We must use every argument for this purpose, offer incentive, promise reward, employ all our wit, persistence, and cunning. A most appropriate reason for taking a wife may be found in what we were saying before, about the evil of sensual indulgence, for the condemnation of such things may lead young men to desire honorable satisfactions. As other incentives, we may also speak to them of the delights of this primary and natural companionship of marriage. Children act as pledges and securities of marital love and kindness. At the same time they offer a focus for all a man's hopes and desires. Sad, indeed, is the man who has labored to get wealth and power and lands, and then has no true heir and perpetuator of his memory. No one can be more suited than a man's true and legitimate sons to gain advantages by virtue of his character, position, and authority, and to enjoy the fruits and rewards of his labor. If a man leaves such heirs, furthermore, he need not consider himself wholly dead and gone. His children keep his own position and his true image in the family. . . .

When, by the urging and counsel of their elders and of the whole family, young men have arrived at the point of marriage, their mothers and other female relatives and friends, who have known the virgins of the neighborhood from earliest childhood and know the way their upbringing has formed them, should select all the well-born and well-brought-up girls and present that list to the new groom-to-be. He can then choose the one who suits him best. The elders of the house and all of the family shall reject no daughter-in-law unless she is tainted with the breath of scandal or bad reputation. Aside from that, let the man who will have to satisfy her satisfy himself. He should act as do wise heads of families before they acquire some property—they like to look it over several times before they actually sign a contract. . . . The man who has decided to marry must be still more cautious. I recommend that he examine and anticipate in every way, and consider for many days, what sort of person it is he is to live with for all his years as husband and companion. Let him be minded to marry for two purposes: first to perpetuate himself in his children, and second to have a steady and constant companion all his life. A woman is needed, therefore, who is likely to bear children and who is desirable as a perpetual mate.

They say that in choosing a wife one looks for beauty, parentage, and riches. . . . Among the most essential criteria of beauty in a woman is an honorable manner. Even a wild, prodigal, greasy, drunken woman may be beautiful of feature, but no one would call her a beautiful wife. A woman worthy of praise must show first of all in her conduct, modesty, and purity. Marius, the illustrious Roman, said in that first speech of his to the Roman people: "Of women we require purity, of men labor." And I certainly agree. There is nothing more disgusting than a coarse and dirty woman. Who is stupid enough not to see clearly that a woman who does not care for neatness and cleanliness in her appearance, not only in her dress and body but in all her behavior and language, is by no means well mannered? How can it be anything but obvious that a bad mannered woman is also rarely virtuous? We shall consider elsewhere the harm that comes to a family from women who lack virtue, for I myself do not know which is the worse fate for a family, total celibacy or a single dishonored woman. In a bride, therefore, a man must first seek beauty of mind, that is, good conduct and virtue.

In her body he must seek not only loveliness, grace, and charm but must also choose a woman who is well made for bearing children, with the kind of constitution that promises to make them strong and big. There's an old proverb, "When you pick your wife, you choose your children." All her virtues will in fact shine brighter still in beautiful children. It is a well-known saying among poets: "Beautiful character dwells in a beautiful body." The natural philosophers require that a woman be neither thin nor very fat. Those laden with fat are subject to coldness and constipation and slow to conceive. They say that a woman should have a joyful nature, fresh and lively in her blood and her whole being. They have no objections to a dark girl. They do reject girls with a frowning black visage, however. They have no liking for either the undersized or the overlarge and lean. They find that a woman is most suited to bear children if she is fairly big and has limbs of ample length. They always have a preference for youth, based on a number of arguments which I need not expound here, but particularly on the point that a young girl has a more adaptable mind. Young girls are pure by virtue of their age and have not developed any spitefulness. They are by nature modest and free of vice. They quickly learn to accept affectionately and unresistingly the habits and wishes of their husbands. . . .

The matter of dowry is next, which I would like to see middling in size, certain and prompt rather than large, vague, or promised for an indefinite future. I know not why everyone, as if corrupted by a common vice, takes advantage of delay to grow lazy in paying debts. Sometimes, in cases of marriage, people are further tempted because they hope to evade payment altogether. As your wife spends her first year in your house, it seems impossible not to reinforce the new bonds of kinship by frequent visiting and parties. But it will be thought rude if, in the middle of a gathering of kinsmen, you put yourself forward to insist and complain. If, as new husbands usually do, you don't want to lose their still precarious favor, you may ask your in-laws in restrained and casual words. Then you are forced to accept any little excuse they may offer. If you make a more forthright demand for what is your own, they will explain to you their many obligations, will complain of fortune, blame the conditions of the time, complain of other men, and say that they hope to be able to ask much of you in greater difficulties. As long as they can, in fact, they will promise you bounteous repayment at an ever-receding date. . . . This is why the dowry should be precisely set, promptly paid, and not too high. The larger the payments are to be and the longer they are to be carried, the more discussion you will be forced into, the more reluctantly you will be paid, and the more obliged you will feel to spend inordinate sums for all sorts of things. There will be indescribable bitterness and often totally ruinous results in setting dowries very high. . . .

When you have chosen your wife and decided on the girl you like best, when you have received the advice and permission of all your elders, and when she is highly pleasing to you and to your family for her ways and her beauty, then the first thing you ought to do is as Xenophon has the good husband say to Socrates: pray to God that he graciously grant that your bride will be fertile, and that you may always have peace and honor in your house. Address God with abundant piety, for these are the things essential to a wife and without which suffering abounds. With them, on the other hand, a man is happy and grateful for what are truly the gifts of God. Not every man who seeks finds a good wife. Not every man who would like a faithful wife has one, though some perhaps think they have. On the contrary, it has always been a rare and singular favor of God to settle a man with a wholly peaceable wife whose character is above reproach. One may consider oneself lucky if one's wife never gives rise to scandal or disgrace. Blessed is he who is not afflicted with grief through having a bad wife. Many should be the prayers addressed to God, therefore, that he may grant the young husband a wife who will prove good, peaceful, honorable, and, as we have said, prolific. This I repeat: one should never cease praying to God that he may keep one's wife faithful, tranquil, and loving.

A Florentine Family—Fact

Gregorio Dati, a Florentine merchant, left this brief account of his marriages in a diary that he kept over many years.

From *Diary of Gregorio Dati*

In the name of God and the Virgin Mary, of Blessed Michael the Archangel, of SS. John the Baptist and John the Evangelist, of SS. Peter and Paul, of the holy scholars, SS. Gregory and Jerome, and of St. Mary Magdalene and St. Elisabeth and all the blessed saints in heaven—may they ever intercede for us—I shall record here how I married my second wife, Isabetta, known as Betta, the daughter of Mari di Lorenzo Vilanuzzi and of Monna Veronica, daughter of Pagolo d'Arrigo Guglielmi, and I shall also record the promises which were made to me. May God and his Saints grant by their grace that they be kept.

From *The Diary of Gregorio Dati*, trans. J. Martines in *Two Memoirs of Renaissanc(* Brucker (New York: Harper and Row, 1967), pp. 113–115.

On March 31, 1393, I was betrothed to her and on Easter Monday, April 7, I gave her a ring. On June 22, a Sunday, I became her husband in the name of God and good fortune. Her first cousins, Giovanni and Lionardo di Domenico Arrighi, promised that she should have a dowry of 900 gold florins and that, apart from the dowry, she should have the income from a farm in S. Fiore a Elsa which had been left her as a legacy by her mother, Monna Veronica. It was not stated at the time how much this amounted to but it was understood, that she would receive the accounts. We arranged our match very simply indeed and with scarcely any discussion. God grant that nothing but good may come of it. On the 26th of that same June, I received a payment of 800 gold florins from the bank of Giacomino and Company. This was the dowry. I invested in the shop of Buonaccorso Berardi and his partners. At the same time I received the trousseau which my wife's cousins valued at 106 florins, in the light of which they deducted 6 florins from another account, leaving me the equivalent of 100 florins. But from what I heard from her, and what I saw myself, they had overestimated it by 30 florins or more. However, from politeness, I said nothing about this. . . . Our Lord God was pleased to call to Himself the blessed soul of . . . Betta, on Monday, October 2 [1402] . . . and the next day, Tuesday, at three in the afternoon she was buried in our grave in S. Spirito. May God receive her soul in his glory. Amen. . . .

I record that on May 8, 1403, I was betrothed to Ginevra, daughter of Antonio di Piero Piuvichese Brancacci, in the church of S. Maria sopra Porta. The dowry was 1,000 florins: 700 in cash and 300 in a farm at Campi. On . . . May 20, we were married, but we held no festivities or wedding celebrations as we were in mourning for Manetto Dati [Gregorio's son], who had died the week before. God grant us a good life together. Ginevra had been married before for four years to Tommaso Brancacci, by whom she had an eight-month-old son. She is now in her twenty-first year.

After that [1411] it was God's will to recall to Himself the blessed soul of my wife Ginevra. She died in childbirth after lengthy suffering, which she bore with remarkable strength and patience. She was perfectly lucid at the time of her death, when she received all the sacraments: confession, communion, extreme unction, and a papal indulgence granting absolution for all her sins. . . . It comforted her greatly, and she returned her soul to her Creator on September 7. . . . On Friday the 8th she was honorably buried and on the 9th, masses were said for her soul.

Memo that on Tuesday, January 28, 1421, I made an agreement with Niccolò d'Andrea del Benino to take his niece Caterina for my lawful wife. She is the daughter of the late Dardano di Niccolò Guicciardini and of Monna Tita, Andrea del Benino's daughter. We were betrothed on the morning of Monday, February 3, the Eve of Carnival. I met Piero and Giovanni di Messer Luigi [Guicciardini] in the church of S. Maria sopra Porta, and Niccolò d'Andrea del Benino was our mediator. The dowry promised me was 600 florins, and the notary was Ser Niccolò di Ser Verdiano. I went to dine with her that evening in Piero's house and the Saturday after Easter . . . I gave her the ring and then on Sunday evening, ʼarch 30, she came to live in our house simply and without ceremony. . . .

A Florentine Family—Fiction

From Machiavelli. *La Mandragola*

Nowadays Machiavelli (1464–1527) is remembered mainly for his political writings. In his own day he was famous as the author of a play, La Mandragola *(The Mandrake).*

The plot goes like this. Young Callimaco wants to seduce Lucrezia, who is married to Nicia, a foolish, rich old man. Lucrezia is beautiful, virtuous, and intelligent; her only failing as a wife is that she has no children. Callimaco presents himself as a doctor and assures Nicia that a potion made from the mandrake plant will cure Lucrezia's infertility. The only problem, Callimaco says, is that, when a lady has taken the mandrake potion, the first man who sleeps with her afterwards will inevitably die within eight days. Callimaco suggests that Nicia give his wife the potion, then kidnap some youth off the streets and send him to bed with Lucrezia. The youth will naturally make love to Lucrezia and then conveniently die. The problem is to persuade Lucrezia to go along with the plan. Callimaco achieves this by bribing Lucrezia's confessor, Friar Timoteo. . . .

SCENE IX

(Timoteo *alone*)

. . . Messer Nicia and Callimaco are both rich and each for diverse reasons can be well plucked. The thing must be kept dark, that's as important to them as it is to me. Be it as they wish, I'll not repent me of it. Forsooth I doubt not we shall find it hard, for Donna Lucrezia is sensible and good. But I'll work on her kindness, all women have little brains, and if one of them knows enough to say two words, there must be a sermon about it: for in the realm of the blind the one-eyed is king. And here she is with her mother, who is a very beast and will be of great use in bringing her around to my wishes.

SCENE X

(Sostrata *and* Lucrezia)

Sostrata. I'm sure you believe, daughter, that I set as much store by your honor as anybody in the world, and that I should never advise you to do anything that was not good. I have told you and I tell you again that if Brother Timoteo says that there's nothing in it to trouble your conscience, you may do it without another thought.

Lucrezia. I have never had a doubt that the longing Messer Nicia has for children would sooner or later make us do something foolish; and just on this ac-

From Niccolo Machiavelli, *La Mandragola,* Stark Young, trans. (New York: Macaulay Company, 1927), pp. 149–155. Reprinted by permission of the Estate of Stark Young.

count, whenever he has come to me with some notion, have I been jealous and suspicious of it. But of all the things that we have tried, this last seems to me the strangest; to have to submit my body to this outrage, and to cause a man to die for outraging me; I'd never have believed, no not if I were the last woman left in the world and the human race had to start all over again from me, that such a thing could have fallen to my lot.

Sostrata.   I can't explain such matters, daughter; you'll talk to the friar and you'll see what he tells you, and then do as you are advised by him, by us and by those who wish you well.

Lucrezia.   I'm sweating with rage.

SCENE XI

(Timoteo, Lucrezia *and* Sostrata)

Timoteo.   You are welcome both. I know what you wish to know from me, Messer Nicia has told me. Truly I have been in my books more than two hours studying this case; and after much question, I find many things both in general and in particular that are in our favor.

Lucrezia.   Are you serious or jesting?

Timoteo.   Ah! Donna Lucrezia, are these matters for jesting? Is that what you think of me?

Lucrezia.   Father, no; but this seems to me the strangest business I ever heard of.

Timoteo.   Madam, I believe you: but I would not have you say any more in this vein. There are many things which seen at a distance appear terrible, unbearable, strange; but when you come nearer to them they prove to be human, bearable, familiar; wherefore it is said that the fear is worse than the evil. And this is one of them.

Lucrezia.   It's the will of God.

Timoteo.   I'll go back to what I was saying at first. For the sake of your conscience you must go on this general principle: where there is a certain good and an uncertain evil, we must not forsake that good for fear of that evil. Here is a certain good, you will be with child. You will donate a soul to the Lord God. The uncertain evil is that he who lies with you after you've taken the potion, dies: but he will also find himself among those who will never die. But since the thing is dubious, it's right that Messer Nicia should run no risk. And if the act is sinful, it's only in a manner of speaking so after all, for the will is what sins, not the body: it's a sin on the grounds that it displeases your husband, and you please him: it's a sin on the grounds of taking pleasure in it, and you take no pleasure in it. Moreover the end is what you must consider in every case. Your end is to fill a seat in Paradise, to make your husband happy. The Bible says that the daughters of Lot, believing that they alone were left in the world, consorted with their father; and since their intention was good they did not sin.

Lucrezia.	What would you persuade me to?
Sostrata.	Let yourself be persuaded, daughter. Don't you see that a woman who has no children has no home? When her husband is dead she remains, like a beast, deserted by everyone.
Timoteo.	I swear to you, Madam, by the holy sacrament, that your duty in this case is to obey your husband, though it were to eat meat on Wednesdays; which is a sin that no holy water can wash away.
Lucrezia.	Where are you pushing me, father?
Timoteo.	I'm urging you to things that you'll ask God to bless me for, and that next year you'll value more than now.
Sostrata.	She'll do what you wish. I'll put her to bed myself to-night. What are you afraid of, idiot? There are fifty women in this land who would lift their hands to heaven for this that you'll be getting.
Lucrezia.	I consent; but I don't expect to be alive tomorrow morning.
Timoteo.	Have no fear, my daughter: I will pray God for you; I will say a prayer to the angel Rafael to be at your side. Go quickly and prepare for this mystery that the night will bring.
Sostrata.	Rest in peace, father.
Lucrezia.	God and Our Lady keep me from harm.

Everything ends happily for everyone. Callimaco arranges that he is the young man who is kidnapped and put to bed with Lucrezia. He suffers no ill effect from the mandrake, and he pleases Lucrezia so much that she decides to take him as a permanent lover. Nicia remains contentedly ignorant of the affair. One is left with a reasonable hope that Lucrezia's infertility will be overcome.

RENAISSANCE STATECRAFT

Machiavelli (1469–1527) presented a new science of politics—the end proposed was simply to win and hold power by any effective means. What was Machiavelli's view of human nature? How did this affect his advice to rulers? Was his work essentially immoral?

Italy: Prince and State

From Machiavelli. *The Prince*

    Having spoken particularly of all the various kinds of Princedom whereof at the outset I proposed to treat, considered in some measure what are the causes

From Niccolo Machiavelli, *The Prince*, N. Thompson, trans. (Oxford: Oxford University Press, 1897), pp. 83–84, 109–110, 113–115, 118–119, 120–121, 125–130.

of their strengths and weaknesses, and pointed out the methods by which men commonly seek to acquire them, it now remains that I should discourse generally concerning the means for attack and defence of which each of these different kinds of Princedom may make use. . . .

I say then that the arms wherewith a Prince defends his State are either his own subjects, or they are mercenaries, or they are auxiliaries, or they are partly one and partly another. Mercenaries and auxiliaries are at once useless and dangerous, and he who holds his State by means of mercenary troops can never be solidly or securely seated. For such troops are disunited, ambitious, insubordinate, treacherous, insolent among friends, cowardly before foes, and without fear of God or faith with man. Whenever they are attacked defeat follows; so that in peace you are plundered by them, in war by your enemies. And this because they have no tie or motive to keep them in the field beyond their paltry pay, in return for which it would be too much to expect them to give their lives. . . .

It now remains for us to consider what ought to be the conduct and bearing of a Prince in relation to his subjects and friends. And since I know that many have written on this subject, I fear it may be thought presumptuous in me to write of it also: the more so, because in my treatment of it I depart from the views that others have taken.

But since it is my object to write what shall be useful to whosoever understands it, it seems to me better to follow the real truth of things than an imaginary view of them. For many Republics and Princedoms have been imagined that were never seen or known to exist in reality. And the manner in which we live, and that in which we ought to live, are things so wide asunder, that he who quits the one to betake himself to the other is more likely to destroy than to save himself; since any one who would act up to a perfect standard of goodness in everything, must be ruined among so many who are not good. It is essential, therefore, for a Prince who desires to maintain his position, to have learned how to be other than good, and to use or not to use his goodness as necessity requires.

Beginning, then, with the first of the qualities above noticed, I say that it may be a good thing to be reputed liberal, but, nevertheless, that liberality without the reputation of it is harmful; because, though it be worthily and rightly used, still if it be not known, you escape not the reproach of its opposite vice. Hence, to have credit for liberality with the world at large, you must neglect no circumstance of sumptuous display; the result being, that a Prince of a liberal disposition will consume his whole substance in things of this sort, and, after all, be obliged, if he would maintain his reputation for liberality, to burden his subjects with extraordinary taxes, and to resort to confiscations and all the other shifts whereby money is raised. But in this way he becomes hateful to his subjects, and growing impoverished is held in little esteem by any. So that in the end, having by his liberality offended many and obliged few, he is worse off than when he began, and is exposed to all his original dangers. Recognizing this, and endeavouring to retrace his steps, he at once incurs the infamy of miserliness.

A Prince, therefore, since he cannot without injury to himself practise the virtue of liberality so that it may be known, will not, if he be wise, greatly concern himself though he be called miserly. Because in time he will come to be regarded as more and more liberal, when it is seen that through his parsimony his revenues are sufficient; that he is able to defend himself against any who make war on him; that he can engage in enterprises against others without burdening his subjects; and thus exercise liberality towards all from whom he does not take, whose number is infinite, while he is miserly in respect of those only to whom he does not give, whose number is few.

Passing to the other qualities above referred to, I say that every Prince should desire to be accounted merciful and not cruel. Nevertheless, he should be on his guard against the abuse of this quality of mercy. Casare Borgia was reputed cruel, yet his cruelty restored Romagna, united it, and brought it to order and obedience; so that if we look at things in their true light, it will be seen that he was in reality far more merciful than the people of Florence, who, to avoid the imputation of cruelty, suffered Pistoja to be torn to pieces by factions.

A Prince should therefore disregard the reproach of being thought cruel where it enables him to keep his subjects united and obedient. For he who quells disorder by a very few signal examples will in the end be more merciful than he who from too great leniency permits things to take their course and so to result in rapine and bloodshed; for these hurt the whole State, whereas the severities of the Prince injure individuals only.

And here comes in the question whether it is better to be loved rather than feared, or feared rather than loved. It might perhaps be answered that we should wish to be both; but since love and fear can hardly exist together, if we must choose between them, it is far safer to be feared than loved. For of men it may generally be affirmed that they are thankless, fickle, false, studious to avoid danger, greedy of gain, devoted to you while you are able to confer benefits upon them, and ready, as I said before, while danger is distant, to shed their blood, and sacrifice their property, their lives, and their children for you; but in the hour of need they turn against you.

Nevertheless a Prince should inspire fear in such a fashion that if he do not win love he may escape hate. For a man may very well be feared and yet not hated, and this will be the case so long as he does not meddle with the property or with the women of his citizens and subjects. And if constrained to put any to death, he should do so only when there is manifest cause or reasonable justification. But, above all, he must abstain from the property of others. For men will sooner forget the death of their father than the loss of their patrimony. . . .

A Prince should, therefore, understand how to use well both the man and the beast. And this lesson has been covertly taught by the ancient writers, who relate how Achilles and many others of these old Princes were given over to be brought up and trained by Chiron the Centaur; since the only meaning of their having for instructor one who was half man and half beast is, that it is necessary for a Prince to know how to use both natures, and that the one without the other has no stability.

But since a Prince should know how to use the beast's nature wisely, he ought of beasts to choose both the lion and the fox; for the lion cannot guard himself from the toils, nor the fox from wolves. He must therefore be a fox to discern toils, and a lion to drive off wolves.

To rely wholly on the lion is unwise; and for this reason a prudent Prince neither can nor ought to keep his word when to keep it is hurtful to him and the causes which led him to pledge it are removed. If all men were good, this would not be good advice, but since they are dishonest, and do not keep faith with you, you, in return, need not keep faith with them; and no Prince was ever at a loss for plausible reasons to cloak a breach of faith. Of this numberless recent instances could be given, and it might be shown how many solemn treaties and engagements have been rendered inoperative and idle through want of faith in Princes, and that he who has best known to play the fox has had the best success.

It is necessary, indeed, to put a good colour on this nature, and to be skilful in simulating and dissembling. But men are so simple, and governed so absolutely by their present needs, that he who wishes to deceive will never fail in finding willing dupes. One recent example I will not omit. Pope Alexander VI had no care or thought but how to deceive, and always found material to work on. No man ever had a more effective manner of asseverating, or made promises with more solemn protestations, or observed them less. And yet, because he understood this side of human nature, his frauds always succeeded.

It is not essential, then, that a Prince should have all the good qualities which I have enumerated above, but it is most essential that he should seem to have them; I will even venture to affirm that if he has and invariably practises them all, they are hurtful, whereas the appearance of having them is useful. Thus, it is well to seem merciful, faithful, humane, religious, and upright, and also to be so; but the mind should remain so balanced that were it needful not to be so, you should be able and know how to change to the contrary.

And you are to understand that a Prince, and most of all a new Prince, cannot observe all those rules of conduct in respect whereof men are accounted good, being often forced, in order to preserve his Princedom, to act in opposition to good faith, charity, humanity, and religion. He must therefore keep his mind ready to shift as the winds and tides of Fortune turn, and, as I have already said, he ought not to quit good courses if he can help it, but should know how to follow evil courses if he must.

A Prince should therefore be very careful that nothing ever escapes his lips which is not replete with the five qualities above named, so that to see and hear him, one would think him the embodiment of mercy, good faith, integrity, humanity, and religion. And there is no virtue which it is more necessary for him to seem to possess than this last; because men in general judge rather by the eye than by the hand, for every one can see but few can touch. Every one sees what you seem, but few know what you are, and these few dare not oppose themselves to the opinion of the many who have the majesty of the State to back them up.

Moreover, in the actions of all men, and most of all of Princes, where there is no tribunal to which we can appeal, we look to results. Wherefore if a prince succeeds in establishing and maintaining his authority, the means will always be judged honourable and be approved by every one. For the vulgar are always taken by appearances and by results, and the world is made up of the vulgar, the few only finding room when the many have no longer ground to stand on.

Toward 1500, "new monarchs" in various parts of Europe, including France and England, suc-
ceeded in repressing aristocratic rebellions and imposing stronger centralized governments on

their realms. Would Machiavelli have approved of their ways of ruling? Consider, for example, Machiavelli's views on mercenary armies and the fear or love that a monarch might inspire.

France: Louis XI

Louis XI of France reigned from 1461 to 1483. This account is by Philip de Commynes, who knew the king personally.

From *Memoirs of Commynes*

He did many odd things, which made some believe his senses were impaired: but they knew not his character. As to his suspicion, all princes are prone to it: especially those who are wise, and who have many enemies, and have offended many people, as our master had done. Besides, he knew he was not beloved by the nobility of the kingdom, nor by many of the commons; for he had taxed them more than any of his predecessors, though he now had some thoughts of easing their burdens, as I said before; but he should have begun sooner. . . .

Had this king lived long, and kept with him those who were then of his council, without dispute he would by this time have enlarged his dominions very considerably; but, considering what has already occurred, and what is likely to follow upon it, he has laid a great load both upon his own soul, and the souls of his successors, and has given his kingdom a cruel wound, which will bleed a long time; namely, by establishing a terrible band of paid soldiers, in imitation of the princes of Italy. King Charles at his death had laid taxes upon all things in his kingdom, amounting to one million eight hundred thousand francs, and maintained about one thousand seven hundred men at arms, constantly in pay, and in the nature of guards, to preserve the peace, and secure the provinces of the kingdom; by which means, for a long while before his death, there was no free quarter, nor riding up and down the country, which was a great ease to the people. At the death of our master, he raised annually four million seven hundred thousand francs; and had about four or five thousand men at arms, and above twenty-five thousand foot soldiers; so that it is no wonder if he entertained such jealousies and fears of his subjects, and fancied he was not beloved by them. . . .

He inflicted very severe punishments to inspire dread, and for fear of losing his authority, as he told me himself. He removed officers, disbanded soldiers, retrenched pensions, and sometimes took them away altogether; so that, as he told me not many days before his death, he passed his time in making and ruining men. . . . It may be urged that other princes have been more given to suspicion than he, but it was not in our time; and, perhaps, their wisdom was not so eminent, nor were their subjects so good. They might too, probably, have been tyrants, and bloody-minded; but our king never did any person a mischief who had not offended him first, though I do not say all who offended him deserved death. I have not recorded these things merely to represent our master as a suspicious and

From A. R. Scoble, ed., *The Memoirs of Philip de Commynes* (London: Henry G. Bohn, 1856), pp. 43–44, 57, 79–82.

mistrustful prince; but . . . that those princes who may be his successors, may learn by his example to be more tender and indulgent to their subjects, and less severe in their punishments than our master had been: although I will not censure him, or say I ever saw a better prince; for though he oppressed his subjects himself, he would never see them injured by anybody else. . . .

I knew him, and was entertained in his service in the flower of his age, and at the height of his prosperity, yet I never saw him free from labour and care. Of all diversions he loved hunting and hawking in their seasons; but his chief delight was in dogs. As for ladies, he never meddled with any in my time; for about the time of my coming to his court he lost a son, at whose death he was extremely afflicted, and he made a vow to God in my presence never to have intercourse with any other woman but the queen; and though this was no more than what he was bound to do by the canons of the church, yet it was much that his self-command should be so great, that he should be able to persevere in his resolution so firmly, considering that the queen (though an excellent princess in other respects) was not a person in whom a man could take any great delight. . . .

When his body was at rest his mind was at work, for he had affairs in several places at once, and would concern himself as much in those of his neighbours as in his own, putting officers of his own over all the great families, and endeavouring to divide their authority as much as possible. When he was at war he laboured for a peace or a truce, and when he had obtained it, he was impatient for war again. He troubled himself with many trifles in his government, which he had better have let alone: but it was his temper, and he could not help it; besides, he had a prodigious memory, and he forgot nothing, but knew everybody, as well in other countries as in his own.

And, in truth, he seemed better fitted to rule a world than to govern a single kingdom.

England: Henry VII

Henry VII, founder of the Tudor dynasty in England, ruled from 1485 to 1509. This description was written by Francis Bacon in 1622.

From *Bacon's Life of Henry VII*

With his justice, he was also a merciful prince: as in whose time, there were but three of the nobility that suffered; the earl of Warwick, the lord chamberlain, and the lord Audley: . . . there were never so great rebellions, expiated with so little blood, drawn by the hand of justice, as the two rebellions of Blackheath and Exeter. As for the severity used upon those which were taken in Kent, it was but upon a scum of people. His pardons went ever both before and after his sword. But then he had withal a strange kind of interchanging of large and inexpected pardons, with severe executions: which, his wisdom considered, could not be imputed to

From J. R. Lumby, ed., *Bacon's Life of Henry VII* (Cambridge: Cambridge University Press, 1889), pp. 213–218.

any inconstancy or inequality; but either to some reason which we do not now know, or to a principle he had set unto himself, that he would vary, and try both ways in turn. But the less blood he drew, the more he took of treasure. And, as some construed it, he was the more sparing in the one, that he might be the more pressing in the other; for both would have been intolerable. Of nature assuredly he coveted to accumulate treasure. . . . This excess of his had at that time many glosses and interpretations. Some thought the continual rebellions wherewith he had been vexed, had made him grow to hate his people: some thought it was done to pull down their stomachs, and to keep them low: some, for that he would leave his son a golden fleece: some suspected he had some high design upon foreign parts: but those perhaps shall come nearest the truth, that fetch not their reasons so far off; but rather impute it to nature, age, peace, and a mind fixed upon no other ambition or pursuit. Whereunto I should add, that having every day occasion to take notice of the necessities and shifts for money of other great Princes abroad, it did the better, by comparison, set off to him the felicity of full coffers. As to his expending of treasure, he never spared charge which his affairs required; and in his buildings was magnificent, but his rewards were very limited: so that his liberality was rather upon his own state and memory than upon the deserts of others.

He was of an high mind, and loved his own will and his own way: as one that revered himself and would reign indeed. Had he been a private man, he would have been termed proud. But in a wise Prince, it was but keeping of distance, which indeed he did towards all; not admitting any near or full approach, either to his power, or to his secrets: for he was governed by none. His Queen, notwithstanding she had presented him with divers children, and with a crown also, though he would not acknowledge it, could do nothing with him. His mother he reverenced much, heard little. . . .

To his council he did refer much, and sat oft in person; knowing it to be the way to assist his power, and inform his judgment. In which respect also he was fairly patient of liberty, both of advice, and of vote, till himself were declared. He kept a strait hand on his nobility, and chose rather to advance clergymen and lawyers, which were more obsequious to him, but had less interest in the people; which made for his absoluteness, but not for his safety. Insomuch as, I am persuaded, it was one of the causes of his troublesome reign; for that his nobles, though they were loyal and obedient, yet did not co-operate with him, but let every man go his own way. He was not afraid of an able man, as Lewis the eleventh was: but contrariwise, he was served by the ablest men that were to be found; without which his affairs could not have prospered as they did. . . . Neither did he care how cunning they were that he did employ; for he thought himself to have the masterreach. And as he chose well, so he held them up well; for it is a strange thing, that though he were a dark prince, and infinitely suspicious, and his times full of secret conspiracies and troubles; yet in twenty-four years' reign, he never put down, or discomposed counsellor, or near servant, save only Stanley the lord chamberlain. As for the disposition of his subjects in general towards him, it stood thus with him; that of the three affections which naturally tie the hearts of the subjects to their sovereigns, love, fear, and reverence; he had the last in height, the second in good measure, and so little of the first, as he was beholden to the other two.

PART ELEVEN

REFORMATIONS— PROTESTANT AND CATHOLIC

Many elements contributed to the religious upheavals of the sixteenth century. As the peoples of Europe grew into self-conscious nations, it became more difficult for them to remain united in a single religious organization. Resentment against Rome's taxation and jurisdiction increased. The papacy itself became worldly and corrupt.

Perhaps a reform movement would have arisen in any case. But the particular kind of "Reformation" that occurred was shaped by the religious experience of a particular individual, a German monk, Martin Luther (1483–1546). Luther strove to be a good monk but he became convinced that he could not find salvation through his own "good works." After a period of near-despair he came to believe that he was saved, not through any merit of his own, but through the freely given grace of Christ. On the basis of this insight Luther built a whole structure of Lutheran theology, opposed at many points to Catholic doctrine (which emphasized the mediating role of priests and sacraments in human salvation). Other Protestant reformers assimilated elements of Luther's teaching into their own systems of thought.

The Protestant Reformation in the north was matched by a surge of religious vitality in the Catholic lands of central and southern Europe. The Council of Trent (1545–1563) reformed long-standing abuses; Ignatius Loyola founded the immensely influential new order of Jesuits; great saints like Teresa of Avila led reform movements in the old monastic orders. Although all the reformers intended to revitalize the church, not to divide it, one effect of their work was to create permanent religious cleavages that profoundly influenced the subsequent cultural and political history of Europe.

NORTHERN HUMANISTS

Papal Failings

Many writers who never chose to become Protestants criticized the state of the church on the eve of the Reformation. Among them was the great Dutch humanist scholar, Desiderius Erasmus (1461–1536). What was wrong with the papacy according to Erasmus?

From Erasmus. *In Praise of Folly*

Now as to the popes of Rome, who pretend themselves Christ's vicars, if they would but imitate his exemplary life, in the being employed in an unintermitted course of preaching; in the being attended with poverty, nakedness, hunger, and a contempt of this world; if they did but consider the import of the word pope, which signifies a father; or if they did but practice their surname of most holy, what order or degrees of men would be in a worse condition? There would be then no such vigorous making of parties, and buying of votes, in the conclave upon a vacancy of that see: and those who by bribery, or other indirect courses, should get themselves elected, would never secure their sitting firm in the chair by pistol, poison, force, and violence.

How much of their pleasure would be abated if they were but endowed with one dram of wisdom? Wisdom, did I say? Nay, with one grain of that salt which our Saviour bid them not lose the savour of. All their riches, all their honour, their jurisdictions, their Peter's patrimony, their offices, their dispensations, their licences, their indulgences, their long train and attendants (see in how short a compass I have abbreviated all their marketing of religion); in a word, all their perquisites would be forfeited and lost; and in their room would succeed watchings, fastings, tears, prayers, sermons, hard studies, repenting sighs, and a thousand such like severe penalties: nay, what's yet more deplorable, it would then follow, that all their clerks, amanuenses, notaries, advocates, proctors, secretaries, the offices of grooms, ostlers, serving-men, pimps (and somewhat else, which for modesty's sake I shall not mention); in short, all these troops of attendants, which depend on his holiness, would all lose their several employments. This indeed would be hard, but what yet remains would be more dreadful: the very Head of the Church, the spiritual prince, would then be brought from all his splendour to the poor equipage of a scrip and staff. But all this is upon the supposition only that they understood what circumstances they are placed in; whereas now, by a wholesome neglect of thinking, they live as well as heart can wish. . . .

They think to satisfy that Master they pretend to serve, our Lord and Saviour, with their great state and magnificence, with the ceremonies of installments, with the titles of reverence and holiness, and with exercising their episcopal function only in blessing and cursing. The working of miracles is old and out-dated; to teach the people is too laborious; to interpret scripture is to invade

From Erasmus, *In Praise of Folly* (London: Reeves and Turner, 1876), pp. 156–160.

the prerogative of the schoolmen; to pray is too idle; to shed tears is cowardly and unmanly; to fast is too mean and sordid; to be easy and familiar is beneath the grandeur of him, who, without being sued to and intreated, will scarce give princes the honour of kissing his toe; finally, to die for religion is too self-denying; and to be crucified as their Lord of Life, is base and ignominious.

[They claim as Peter's] inheritance, fields, towns, treasures, and large dominions; for the defending whereof, inflamed with a holy zeal, they fight with fire and sword, to the great loss and effusion of Christian blood, thinking they are apostolical maintainers of Christ's spouse, the church, when they have murdered all such as they call her enemies; though indeed the church has no enemies more bloody and tyrannical than such impious popes, who give dispensations for the not preaching of Christ; evacuate the main effect and design of our redemption by their pecuniary bribes and sales; adulterate the gospel by their forced interpretations, and undermining traditions; and lastly, by their lusts and wickedness grieve the Holy Spirit, and make their Saviour's wounds to bleed anew.

Thomas More was another renowned humanist and a friend of Erasmus. A convinced Catholic, he was executed for treason when he refused to accept Henry VIII's breach with the church of Rome. But, in writing about the imaginary land of Utopia ("Nowhere"), More envisaged a state of religion very different from that upheld by the Catholic church of his day. How were religious affairs ordered in Utopia?

Religion in Utopia

From Thomas More. *Utopia*

There are several sorts of religions, not only in different parts of the island, but even in every town; some worshipping the sun, others the moon, or one of the planets: some worship such men as have been eminent in former times for virtue, or glory, not only as ordinary deities, but as the supreme God: Yet the greater and wiser sort of them worship none of these, but adore one eternal, invisible, infinite, and incomprehensible Deity; as a Being that is far above all our apprehensions, that is spread over the whole universe, not by his bulk, but by his power and virtue: him they call the Father of all, and acknowledge that the beginnings, the encrease, the progress, the vicissitudes, and the end of all things come only from him; nor do they offer divine honors to any but to him alone. And indeed, though they differ concerning other things, yet all agree in this; that they think there is one Supreme Being that made and governs the world, whom they call in the language of their country, Mithras. They differ in this, that one thinks the God whom he worships is this Supreme Being, and another thinks that his idol is that God; but they all agree in one principle that whoever is this Supreme Being, he is also that great essence, to whose glory and majesty all honors are ascribed by the consent of all nations. . . .

From Thomas More, *Utopia*, Gilbert Burnett, trans. (London: R. Chiswell, 1684).

After they had heard from us, an account of the doctrine, the course of life, and the miracles of Christ, and of the wonderful constancy of so many martyrs, whose blood, so willingly offered up by them, was the chief occasion of spreading their religion over a vast number of nations, it is not to be imagined how inclined they were to receive it. I shall not determine whether this proceeded from any secret inspiration of God, or whether it was because it seemed so favorable to that community of goods, which is an opinion so particular, as well as so dear to them; since they perceived that Christ and his followers lived by that rule: and that it was still kept up in some communities among the sincerest sort of Christians. From whichsoever of these motives it might be, true it is that many of them came over to our religion, and were initiated into it by baptism. But as two of our number were dead, so none of the four that survived, were in priests orders; we therefore could only baptize them; so that to our great regret, they could not partake of the other sacraments, that can only be administered by priests: But they are instructed concerning them, and long most vehemently for them. They have had great disputes among themselves, whether one chosen by them to be a priest would not be thereby qualified to do all the things that belong to that character, even though he had no authority derived from the pope; and they seemed to be resolved to choose some for that employment, but they had not done it when I left them.

Those among them that have not received our religion, do not fright any from it, and use none ill that goes over to it; so that all the while I was there, one man was only punished on this occasion. He being newly baptized, did, notwithstanding all that we could say to the contrary, dispute publickly concerning the Christian religion, with more zeal than discretion; and with so much heat, that he not only preferred our worship to theirs, but condemned all their rites as profane; and cried out against all that adhered to them, as impious and sacrilegious persons, that were to be damned to everlasting burnings. Upon his having frequently preached in this manner, he was seized, and after trial, he was condemned to banishment, not for having disparaged their religion, but for his inflaming the people to sedition: for this is one of their most ancient laws, that no man ought to be punished for his religion. At the first constitution of their government, Utopus having understood that, before his coming among them, the old inhabitants had been engaged in great quarrels concerning religion, by which they were so divided among themselves that he found it an easy thing to conquer them, since instead of uniting their forces against him, every different party in religion fought by themselves: after he had subdued them, he made a law that every man might be of what religion he pleased, and might endeavor to draw others to it by the force of argument, and by amicable and modest ways, but without bitterness against those of other opinions; but that he ought to use no other force but that of persuasion; and was neither to mix with it reproaches nor violence; and such as did otherwise were to be condemned to banishment or slavery.

This law was made by Utopus, not only for preserving the public peace, which he saw suffered much by daily contentions and irreconcilable heats, but because he thought the interest of religion itself required it. He judged it not fit to determine any thing rashly; and seemed to doubt whether those different forms of religion might not all come from God, who might inspire men in a different manner, and be pleased with this variety; he therefore thought it indecent and foolish for any man to threaten and terrify another to make him believe what did not appear to him to be true. And supposing that only one religion was really true, and the rest false, he imagined that the native force of truth would at last break forth and shine bright, if supported only by the strength of argument, and attended to with a gentle and unprejudiced mind; while, on the other hand, if such debates were carried on with violence and tumults, as the most wicked are always the most obstinate, so the best and most holy religion, might be choked with superstition, as corn is with briars and thorns; he therefore left men wholly to their liberty, that they might be free to believe as they should see cause. . . .

Germany and Rome

In 1515, Jacob Wimpheling, a German humanist, wrote this "Response" to a treatise on Germany by Enea Silvio Piccolomini (who became Pope Pius II). What were the particular complaints of the German people against the papacy?

From *Wimpheling's Response*

Enea makes much of the fact that we Germans received our Christian faith from his compatriots. "Rome," he writes, "preached Christ to you; it was faith in Christ, received from Rome, that extinguished barbarism in you." We concede, of course, that missionaries from Rome brought the saving message of Christ to our land. But by the same token Rome herself was, like Germany, converted to the Christian faith, and Rome should therefore show no less gratitude than Germany for the reception of her faith. For was it not Peter, a Jew from Palestine, who preached the Gospel of Christ in Rome? If Enea's argument were applied to the Romans themselves, they would now be obliged to send annual tributes of gold and silver to Syria. . . .

It is not that we deny our debt to Rome. But we ask: Is Rome not also indebted to us? Have not two of our compatriots, clever and skillful men hailing from Strassburg and Mainz, invented the noble art of printing, which makes it possible to propagate the correct doctrines of faith and morals throughout the world and in all languages? . . . Do we, who have been true and industrious in our service to religion and to the Holy Roman Church, who are steadfast in our faith and even—as Enea admits—prepared to shed our blood for it, who willingly obey orders, buy indulgences, travel to Rome, and send money—do we who perform all these duties deserve to be called barbarians? . . . Despite this slanderous label, Enea speaks with lavish praise of our fatherland, of our cities and buildings. For what purpose? For one only: to

From: Gerald Strauss, trans., *Manifestations of Discontent in Germany on the Eve of the Reformation* (Bloomington, Ind.: Indiana University Press, 1971), pp. 42–43. Reprinted by permission.

make our ears more receptive to the demands coming from Rome dressed in Christian garb but serving Italian interests; in other words, to put us in the mood for wasting our fortunes on foreigners. . . . As it is, our compatriots crowd the road to Rome. They pay for papal reservations and dispensations. They appear before papal courts—and not always because they have appealed a case to Rome, but rather because their cases have been arbitrarily transferred there. Is there a nation more patient and willing to receive indulgences, though we well know that the income from them is divided between the Holy See and its officialdom? Have we not paid dearly for the confirmation of every bishop and abbot? . . .

Thus we are done out of fortune, and for no purpose other than to support the innumerable retainers and hangers-on that populate the papal court. Enea himself gives us a list of these papal lackeys, the number of which increases daily. True, if the pope must furnish court rooms for all the legal business in Christendom, he requires a huge staff. But there is no need for this. Apart from imperial courts, there exist in our German cities learned and honorable judges to whom appeals from lower episcopal courts could be directed. It is in the highest degree objectionable that Rome bypasses courts of higher resort—often on trivial pretexts or out of pique—and compels our compatriots, laymen included, to appear in Rome.

MARTIN LUTHER

Luther as Monk

In casual conversations—recorded by his friends—Luther often referred to the stages of his religious development. How did his experiences as a monk influence his attitude to traditional religious practices?

From *Luther's Table Talk*

I, Martin Luther, entered the monastery against the will of my father and lost favor with him, for he saw through the knavery of the monks very well. On the day on which I sang my first mass he said to me, "Son, don't you know that you ought to honor your father?" . . . Later when I stood there during the mass and began the canon, I was so frightened that I would have fled if I hadn't been admonished by the prior. For when I read the words, "Thee, therefore, most merciful Father," etc., and thought I had to speak to God without a Mediator, I felt like fleeing from the world like Judas. Who can bear the majesty of God without Christ as Mediator? In short, as a monk I experienced such horrors; I had to experience them before I could fight them.

From *Luther's Works*, J. Pelikan and H. T. Lehmann, eds. (Philadelphia: Fortress Press, 1967), Vol. 54, pp. 85, 193–194, 234, 264–265, 339–340. Copyright © 1967 by Fortress Press. Reprinted by permission of Fortress Press.

When I was a monk I was unwilling to omit any of the prayers, but when I was busy with public lecturing and writing I often accumulated my appointed prayers for a whole week, or even two or three weeks. Then I would take a Saturday off, or shut myself in for as long as three days without food and drink, until I had said the prescribed prayers. This made my head split, and as a consequence I couldn't close my eyes for five nights, lay sick unto death, and went out of my senses. Even after I had quickly recovered and I tried again to read, my head went 'round and 'round. Thus our Lord God drew me, as if by force, from that torment of prayers. . . .

I almost fasted myself to death, for again and again I went for three days without taking a drop of water or a morsel of food. I was very serious about it. I really crucified the Lord Christ. I wasn't simply an observer but helped to carry him and pierce [his hands and feet]. God forgive me for it, for I have confessed it openly! This is the truth: the most pious monk is the worst scoundrel. He denies that Christ is the mediator and highpriest and turns him into a judge.

The words "righteous" and "righteousness of God" struck my conscience like lightning. When I heard them I was exceedingly terrified. If God is righteous [I thought], he must punish. But when by God's grace I pondered, in the tower and heated room of this building, over the words, "He who through faith is righteous shall live" [Rom. 1:17] and "the righteousness of God" [Rom. 3:21], I soon came to the conclusion that if we, as righteous men, ought to live from faith and if the righteousness of God should contribute to the salvation of all who believe, then salvation won't be our merit but God's mercy. My spirit was thereby cheered. For it's by the righteousness of God that we're justified and saved through Christ. These words [which had before terrified me] now became more pleasing to me. The Holy Spirit unveiled the Scriptures for me in this tower.

God led us away from all this in a wonderful way; without my quite being aware of it he took me away from that game more than twenty years ago. How difficult it was at first when we journeyed toward Kemberg after All Saints' Day in the year 1517, when I first made up my mind to write against the crass errors of indulgences! Dr. Jerome Schurff advised against this: "You wish to write against the pope? What are you trying to do? It won't be tolerated!" I replied, "And if they have to tolerate it?" Presently Sylvester, master of the sacred palace, entered the arena, fulminating against me with this syllogism: "Whoever questions what the Roman church says and does is heretical. Luther questions what the Roman church says and does, and therefore [he is a heretic]." So it all began.

The Break With Rome

Luther was outraged by the preaching of the Dominican friar Tetzel, who was selling papal indulgences in Germany. (The indulgences were supposed to release sinners from the penalties they would otherwise suffer in purgatory.)

From *Tetzel's Sermon*

You may obtain letters of safe conduct from the vicar of our Lord Jesus Christ, by means of which you are able to liberate your soul from the hands of the enemy, and convey it by means of contrition and confession, safe and secure from all pains of Purgatory, into the happy kingdom. For know that in these letters are stamped and engraven all the merits of Christ's passion there laid bare. Consider, that for each and every mortal sin it is necessary to undergo seven years of penitence after confession and contrition, either in this life or in Purgatory.

How many mortal sins are committed in a day, how many in a week, how many in a month, how many in a year, how many in the whole course of life! They are well-nigh numberless, and those that commit them must needs suffer endless punishment in the burning pains of Purgatory.

But with these confessional letters you will be able at any time in life to obtain full indulgence for all penalties imposed upon you, in all cases except the four reserved to the Apostolic See. Therefore throughout your whole life, whenever you wish to make confession, you may receive the same remission, except in cases reserved to the Pope, and afterwards, at the hour of death, a full indulgence as to all penalties and sins, and your share of all spiritual blessings that exist in the church militant and all its members.

Do you not know that when it is necessary for anyone to go to Rome or undertake any other dangerous journey, he takes his money to a broker and gives a certain per cent—five or six or ten—in order that at Rome or elsewhere he may receive again his funds intact, by means of the letter of this same broker? Are you not willing, then, for the fourth part of a florin, to obtain these letters, by virtue of which you may bring, not your money, but your divine and immortal soul safe and sound into the land of Paradise?

Luther's first attack on indulgences came in these theses, presented as topics that Luther would defend in a public debate.

From *The Ninety-Five Theses (1517)*

Out of love and zeal for truth and the desire to bring it to light, the following theses will be publicly discussed at Wittenberg under the chairmanship of the reverend father Martin Luther, Master of Arts and Sacred Theology and regularly appointed Lecturer on these subjects at that place. He requests that those who cannot be present to debate orally with us will do so by letter.

In the Name of Our Lord Jesus Christ. Amen.

1. When our Lord and Master Jesus Christ said, "Repent" [Matt. 4:17], he willed the entire life of believers to be one of repentance.

From J. H. Robinson and M. Whitcomb, eds., *University of Pennsylvania Translations and Reprints* (Philadelphia: University of Pennsylvania Press, 1902), Vol. 2, No. 6, pp. 9–10.
From *Luther's Works*, J. Pelikan and H. T. Lehmann, eds. (Philadelphia: Fortress Press, 1957), Vol. 31, pp. 25–33. Copyright © 1957 by Fortress Press. Reprinted by permission of Fortress Press.

2. This word cannot be understood as referring to the sacrament of penance, that is, confession and satisfaction, as administered by the clergy.

5. The pope neither desires nor is able to remit any penalties except those imposed by his own authority or that of the canons.

20. Therefore the pope, when he uses the words "plenary remission of all penalties," does not actually mean "all penalties," but only those imposed by himself.

21. Thus those indulgence preachers are in error who say that a man is absolved from every penalty and saved by papal indulgences.

27. They preach only human doctrines who say that as soon as the money clinks into the money chest, the soul flies out of purgatory.

50. Christians are to be taught that if the pope knew the exactions of the indulgence preachers, he would rather that the basilica of St. Peter were burned to ashes than built up with the skin, flesh, and bones of his sheep.

81. This unbridled preaching of indulgences makes it difficult even for learned men to rescue the reverence which is due the pope from slander or from the shrewd questions of the laity.

82. Such as: "Why does not the pope empty purgatory for the sake of holy love and the dire need of the souls that are there if he redeems an infinite number of souls for the sake of miserable money with which to build a church? The former reasons would be most just; the latter is most trivial."

94. Christians should be exhorted to be diligent in following Christ, their head, through penalties, death, and hell;

95. And thus be confident of entering into heaven through many tribulations rather than through the false security of peace.

At first Luther hoped that the papacy would support his reform efforts. By 1520 he was moving toward an open break with Rome.

From *Address to the Christian Nobility of the German Nation*

The Romanists have very cleverly built three walls around themselves. Hitherto they have protected themselves by these walls in such a way that no one has been able to reform them. As a result, the whole of Christendom has fallen abominably.

In the first place, when pressed by the temporal power they have made decrees and declared that the temporal power had no jurisdiction over them, but that, on the contrary, the spiritual power is above the temporal. In the second

From *Luther's Works*, J. Pelikan and H. T. Lehmann, eds. (Philadelphia: Fortress Press, 1966), Vol. 44, pp. 126–127, 129–130, 133–134, 136. Copyright © 1966 by Fortress Press. Reprinted by permission of Fortress Press.

place, when the attempt is made to reprove them with the Scriptures, they raise the objection that only the pope may interpret the Scriptures. In the third place, if threatened with a council, their story is that no one may summon a council but the pope. . . .

May God help us, and give us just one of those trumpets with which the walls of Jericho were overthrown to blast down these walls of straw and paper in the same way and set free the Christian rods for the punishment of sin, [and] bring to light the craft and deceit of the devil, to the end that through punishment we may reform ourselves and once more attain God's favor.

Let us begin by attacking the first wall. It is pure invention that pope, bishop, priests, and monks are called the spiritual estate while princes, lords, artisans, and farmers are called the temporal estate. This is indeed a piece of deceit and hypocrisy. Yet no one need be intimidated by it, and for this reason: all Christians are truly of the spiritual estate, and there is no difference among them except that of office. Paul says in I Corinthians 12 [:12–13] that we are all one body, yet every member has its own work by which it serves the others. This is because we all have one baptism, one gospel, one faith, and are all Christians alike; for baptism, gospel, and faith alone make us spiritual and a Christian people. . . .

It follows from this argument that there is no true, basic difference between laymen and priests, princes and bishops, between religious and secular, except for the sake of office and work, but not for the sake of status. They are all of the spiritual estate, all are truly priests, bishops, and popes. But they do not all have the same work to do. Just as all priests and monks do not have the same work. This is the teaching of St. Paul in Romans 12 [:4–5] and I Corinthians 12 [:12] and in I Peter 2 [:9], as I have said above, namely, that we are all one body of Christ the Head, and all members one of another. Christ does not have two different bodies, one temporal, the other spiritual. There is but one Head and one body. . . .

The second wall is still more loosely built and less substantial. The Romanists want to be the only masters of Holy Scripture, although they never learn a thing from the Bible all their life long. They assume the sole authority for themselves, and, quite unashamed, they play about with words before our very eyes, trying to persuade us that the pope cannot err in matters of faith, regardless of whether he is righteous or wicked. Yet they cannot point to a single letter.[1] This is why so many heretical and un-Christian, even unnatural, ordinances stand in the canon law. But there is no need to talk about these ordinances at present. Since these Romanists think the Holy Spirit never leaves them, no matter how ignorant and wicked they are, they become bold and decree only what they want. And if what they claim were true, why have Holy Scripture at all? Of what use is Scripture? Let us burn the Scripture and be satisfied with the unlearned gentlemen at Rome who possess the Holy Spirit! And yet the Holy Spirit can be possessed only by pious hearts. If I had not read the words with my own

[1] i.e., a single letter of Scripture to support their claim.

eyes, I would not have believed it possible for the devil to have made such stupid claims at Rome, and to have won supporters for them. . . .

The third wall falls of itself when the first two are down. When the pope acts contrary to the Scriptures, it is our duty to stand by the Scriptures, to reprove him and to constrain him, according to the word of Christ, Matthew 18 [:15–17], "If your brother sins against you, go and tell it to him, between you and him alone; if he does not listen to you, then take one or two others with you; if he does not listen to them, tell it to the church; if he does not listen to the church, consider him a heathen." Here every member is commanded to care for every other. How much more should we do this when the member that does evil is responsible for the government of the church, and by his evil-doing is the cause of much harm and offense to the rest! But if I am to accuse him before the church, I must naturally call the church together.

The Romanists have no basis in Scripture for their claim that the pope alone has the right to call or confirm a council. This is just their own ruling, and it is only valid as long as it is not harmful to Christendom or contrary to the laws of God. Now when the pope deserves punishment, this ruling no longer obtains, for not to punish him by authority of a council is harmful to Christendom.

After the initial attack on indulgences, Luther developed his own doctrine of salvation. He presented it in this sermon delivered on his way to the Council of Worms (1521). How could humans be saved according to Luther? Why did he reject the teachings of the ancient Greek philosophers?

From *Luther's Sermon, April 7, 1521*

Now, it is clear and manifest that every person likes to think that he will be saved and attain to eternal salvation. This is what I propose to discuss now.

You also know that all philosophers, doctors and writers have studiously endeavored to teach and write what attitude man should take to piety. They have gone to great trouble, but, as is evident, to little avail. Now genuine and true piety consists of two kinds of works: those done for others, which are the right kind, and those done for ourselves, which are unimportant. In order to find a foundation, one man builds churches; another goes on a pilgrimage to St. James' or St. Peter's; a third fasts or prays, wears a cowl, goes barefoot, or does something else of the kind. Such works are nothing whatever and must be completely destroyed. Mark these words: none of our works have any power whatsoever. For God has chosen a man, the Lord Christ Jesus, to crush death, destroy sin, and shatter hell, since there was no one before he came who did not inevitably belong to the devil. The devil therefore thought he would get a hold upon the Lord when he hung between two thieves and was suffering the most contemptible and disgraceful of

From *Luther's Works*, J. Pelikan and H. T. Lehmann, eds. (Philadelphia: Fortress Press, 1959), Vol. 51, pp. 61–64.

deaths, which was cursed both by God and by men [cf. Deut. 21:23; Gal. 3:13]. But the Godhead was so strong that death, sin, and even hell were destroyed.

Therefore you should note well the words which Paul writes to the Romans [Rom. 5:12–21]. Our sins have their source in Adam, and because Adam ate the apple, we have inherited sin from him. But Christ has shattered death for our sake, in order that we might be saved by his works, which are alien to us, and not by our works.

But the papal dominion treats us altogether differently. It makes rules about fasting, praying, and butter-eating, so that whoever keeps the commandments of the pope will be saved and whoever does not keep them belongs to the devil. It thus seduces the people with the delusion that goodness and salvation lies in their own works. But I say that none of the saints, no matter how holy they were, attained salvation by their works. Even the holy mother of God did not become good, was not saved, by her virginity or her motherhood, but rather by the will of faith and the works of God, and not by her purity, or her own works. Therefore, mark me well: this is the reason why salvation does not lie in our own works, no matter what they are; it cannot and will not be effected without faith. . . .

Therefore, I say again: Alien works, these make us good! Our Lord Christ says: I am your justification. I have destroyed the sins you have upon you. Therefore only believe in me; believe that I am he who has done this; then you will be justified. For it is written, *Justicia est fides*, righteousness is identical with faith and comes through faith. Therefore, if we want to have faith, we should believe the gospel, Paul, etc., and not the papal breves, or the decretals, but rather guard ourselves against them as against fire. For everything that comes from the pope cries out: Give, give; and if you refuse, you are of the devil. It would be a small matter if they were only exploiting the people. But, unfortunately, it is the greatest evil in the world to lead the people to believe that outward works can save or make a man good. . . .

The reason why the world is so utterly perverted and in error is that for a long time there have been no genuine preachers. There are perhaps three thousand priests, among whom one cannot find four good ones—God have mercy on us in this crying shame! And when you do get a good preacher, he runs through the gospel superficially and then follows it up with a fable about the old ass or a story about Dietrich of Berne, or he mixes in something of the pagan teachers, Aristotle, Plato, Socrates, and others, who are all quite contrary to the gospel, and also contrary to God, for they did not have the knowledge of the light which we possess. Aye, if you come to me and say: The Philosopher says: Do many good works, then you will acquire the habit, and finally you will become godly; then I say to you: Do not perform good works in order to become godly; but if you are already godly, then do good works, though without affectation and with faith. There you see how contrary these two points of view are.

At the Council of Worms, held in the presence of Emperor Charles V, Luther was ordered to renounce his "heresies." How did he respond?

From *Luther's Speech at Worms, April 18, 1521*

"... Because I am a man and not God, I am not able to shield my books with any other protection than that which my Lord Jesus Christ himself offered for his teaching. When questioned before Annas about his teaching and struck by a servant, he said: 'If I have spoken wrongly, bear witness to the wrong' [John 18:19–23]. If the Lord himself, who knew that he could not err, did not refuse to hear testimony against his teaching, even from the lowliest servant, how much more ought I, who am the lowest scum and able to do nothing except err, desire and expect that somebody should want to offer testimony against my teaching! Therefore, I ask by the mercy of God, may your most serene majesty, most illustrious lordships, or anyone at all who is able, either high or low, bear witness, expose my errors, overthrowing them by the writings of the prophets and the evangelists. Once I have been taught I shall be quite ready to renounce every error, and I shall be the first to cast my books into the fire.

"From these remarks I think it is clear that I have sufficiently considered and weighed the hazards and dangers, as well as the excitement and dissensions aroused in the world as a result of my teachings, things about which I was gravely and forcefully warned yesterday. .... And concern must be shown lest the reign of this most noble youth, Prince Charles (in whom after God is our great hope), become unhappy and inauspicious. .... Therefore we must fear God. I do not say these things because there is a need of either my teachings or my warnings for such leaders as you, but because I must not withhold the allegiance which I owe my Germany. With these words I commend myself to your most serene majesty and to your lordships, humbly asking that I not be allowed through the agitation of my enemies, without cause, to be made hateful to you. I have finished."

When I had finished, the speaker for the emperor said, as if in reproach, that I had not answered the question, that I ought not call into question those things which had been condemned and defined in councils; therefore what was sought from me was not a horned response, but a simple one, whether or not I wished to retract.

Here I answered:

"Since then your serene majesty and your lordships seek a simple answer, I will give it in this manner, neither horned nor toothed: Unless I am convinced by the testimony of the Scriptures or by clear reason (for I do not trust either in the pope or in councils alone, since it is well known that they have often erred and contradicted themselves), I am bound by the Scriptures I have quoted and my conscience is captive to the Word of God. I cannot and I will not retract anything, since it is neither safe nor right to go against conscience.

"I cannot do otherwise, here I stand, may God help me, Amen."

From *Luther's Works*, J. Pelikan and H. T. Lehmann, eds. (Philadelphia: Fortress Press, 1958), Vol. 32, pp. 111–113. Copyright © 1958 by Fortress Press. Reprinted by permission of Fortress Press.

Celibacy and Marriage

Luther married a former nun who left her convent to become a Protestant. Why did he condemn the Catholic doctrine of celibacy for priests? How did he think husbands should treat their wives?

From *What Luther Says*

First, not every priest can do without a woman, not only on account of the weakness of the flesh but much more because of the needs of the household. If, then, he is to keep a woman, and the pope grants him permission to do so, but he may not have her in marriage, what is this but leaving a man and a woman alone and forbidding them to fall? It is like putting fire and straw together and commanding that there shall be neither smoke nor fire. Secondly, the pope has as little power to give this command as he has to forbid eating, drinking, the natural process of bodily elimination, or becoming fat. No one, therefore, is in duty bound to keep this commandment, and the pope is responsible for all the sins that are committed against this ordinance, for all the souls lost thereby, and for all the consciences thereby confused and tortured. Consequently, he undoubtedly has deserved long ago that someone should drive him out of the world, so many souls has he strangled with this devilish snare; although I hope that God has been more gracious to many of them at their end than the pope had been during their life. Nothing good has ever come out of the papacy and its laws, nor ever will.

Listen! In all my days I have not heard the confession of a nun, but in the light of Scripture I shall hit upon how matters fare with her and know I shall not be lying. If a girl is not sustained by great and exceptional grace, she can live without a man as little as she can without eating, drinking, sleeping, and other natural necessities. Nor, on the other hand, can a man dispense with a wife. The reason for this is that procreating children is an urge planted as deeply in human nature as eating and drinking. That is why God has given and put into the body the organs, arteries, fluxes, and everything that serves it. Therefore what is he doing who would check this process and keep nature from running its desired and intended course? He is attempting to keep nature from being nature, fire from burning, water from wetting, and a man from eating, drinking, and sleeping.

Conjugal love excels all other love. The love toward one's spouse burns like a fire and seeks nothing but the person of the spouse. It says: I do not desire what is yours; I desire neither silver nor gold, neither this nor that; I desire you yourself; I want you entirely or not at all. All other love seeks something else than the person of the loved one. Conjugal love alone wants the entire person of the loved one himself. And if Adam had not fallen, the relation between bride and bridegroom would have been the loveliest. But now love, too, is not pure. For though one spouse desires to have the other, each is, after all, seeking his own pleasure in the other; and this adulterates the love.

The husband should take the initiative and contribute toward keeping unity and love in the marriage relation. But he does this by using reason and not force and by letting things pass without reproving his wife. This he should do because woman is a frail creature and does not have the courage and the stout heart of a man. They are easily disturbed, take something to heart quickly, and are moved to joy and sorrow sooner than men. A man should bear this in mind and not be hard on his wife for it; at times he should overlook what she does and says, help and indulge her with a kind word. But the world considers this discretion an effeminate attitude and rather imagines that it befits a man to be angry and use his fists. Come now! Holy St. Peter well sees what best befits a man and what he should most diligently strive to do. He does not enjoin the use of fists. Use reason, he says. And what is more, he asks a husband to give honor to his wife, that is, to indulge her and make concessions because she is a weaker vessel, with a small, weak, sensitive heart, letting herself be moved and stirred to anger by one word. Learn this and be indulgent. By so doing you will not only keep unity but will also win her heart. For in dealing with people who are what they ought to be one always accomplishes more with kind words than with blows.

My wife can persuade me to do whatever she pleases, for she has the entire household in her hand. And indeed I gladly grant her the complete control of domestic affairs, but despite this I intend to preserve my right intact. The rule of women has never done any good.

God made Adam the lord of all creatures; but when Eve persuaded him to become lord also over God, she spoiled everything. For this we must thank you women who lure men on by cunning and tricks.

DEVELOPMENTS OF PROTESTANT THOUGHT

Switzerland and France

Although they differed among themselves, all the Protestant reformers rejected the Catholic doctrine of transubstantiation in the Eucharist. The Swiss reformer Zwingli (1484–1531) was especially concerned with this question.

Zwingli on the Eucharist

I believe that in the holy Eucharist—i.e., the supper of thanksgiving—the true body of Christ is present by the contemplation of faith; i.e., that they who thank the Lord for the kindness conferred on us in His Son acknowledge that He assumed true flesh, in it truly suffered, truly washed away our sins in His own blood; and thus everything done by Christ becomes present to them by the contemplation of faith. But that the body of Christ in essence and really—i.e., the natural body itself—is either present in the supper or masticated with our

From S. M. Jackson, *Huldreich Zwingli* (New York: G. P. Putnam's Sons, 1900), p. 471.

mouth or teeth, as the Papists and some who long for the flesh-pots of Egypt assert, we not only deny, but firmly maintain is an error opposed to God's Word.

The reformed theology of John Calvin attracted many followers in France and Switzerland. What did Calvin teach about predestination and church discipline?

From John Calvin. *Institutes of the Christian Religion*

If it be evidently the result of the Divine will, that salvation is freely offered to some, and others are prevented from attaining it; this immediately gives rise to important and difficult questions, which are incapable of any other explication, than by the establishment of pious minds in what ought to be received concerning election and predestination:—a question, in the opinion of many, full of perplexity; for they consider nothing more unreasonable, than that of the common mass of mankind some should be predestinated to salvation, and others to destruction. But how unreasonably they perplex themselves will afterwards appear from the sequel of our discourse. Besides, the very obscurity which excites such dread, not only displays the utility of this doctrine, but shews it to be productive of the most delightful benefit. We shall never be clearly convinced as we ought to be, that our salvation flows from the fountain of God's free mercy, till we are acquainted with his eternal election, which illustrates the grace of God by this comparison, that he adopts not all promiscuously to the hope of salvation, but gives to some what he refuses to others. Ignorance of this principle evidently detracts from the Divine glory, and diminishes real humility. But according to Paul, what is so necessary to be known, never can be known, unless God, without any regard to works, chooses those whom he has decreed. "At this present time also, there is a remnant according to the election of grace. And if by grace, then it is no more of works: otherwise, grace is no more grace. . . ." [Romans 11:5–6]

In conformity, therefore, to the clear doctrine of the Scripture, we assert, that by an eternal and immutable counsel, God hath once for all determined, both whom he would admit to salvation, and whom he would condemn to destruction. We affirm that this counsel, as far as concerns the elect, is founded on his gratuitous mercy, totally irrespective of human merit: but that to those whom he devotes to condemnation, the gate of life is closed by a just and irreprehensible, but incomprehensible, judgment. In the elect, we consider calling as an evidence of election, and justification as another token of its manifestation, till they arrive in glory, which constitutes its completion. As God seals his elect by vocation and justification, so by excluding the reprobate from the knowledge of his name and the sanctification of his Spirit, he affords an indication of the judgment that awaits them. Here I shall pass over many fictions fabricated by foolish men to overthrow predestination. It is unnecessary to refute things which, as soon as they are advanced, sufficiently prove the falsehood.

From John Calvin, *Institutes of the Christian Religion*, J. Allen, trans. (London: T. Tegg and Son, 1838), Vol. 2, pp. 120–121, 128–129, 154–155, 365.

But, in order to a further elucidation of the subject, it is necessary to treat of the calling of the elect, and of the blinding and hardening of the impious. On the former I have already made a few observations, with a view to refute the error of those who suppose the generality of the promises to belong equally to all mankind. But the discriminating election of God, which is otherwise concealed within himself, he manifests only by his calling, which may therefore with propriety be termed the testification or evidence of it. "For whom he did foreknow, he also did predestinate to the image of his Son. Moreover, whom he did predestinate, them he also called: and whom he called, them he also justified," in order to their essential glorification. [Romans 8:29–30] Though by choosing his people, the Lord hath adopted them as his children, yet we see that they enter not on the possession of so great a blessing till they are called; on the other hand, as soon as they are called, they immediately enjoy some communication of his election. On this account Paul calls the Spirit received by them both "the Spirit of adoption, and the seal and earnest of the future inheritance;" [Romans 8:15–16] because, by his testimony, he confirms and seals to their hearts the certainty of their future adoption. . . . Those whom God hath chosen, therefore, he designates as his children, and determines himself to be their Father. By calling, he introduces them into his family, and unites them to himself, that they may be one. By connecting calling with election, the Scripture evidently suggests, that nothing is requisite to it but the free mercy of God. For if we inquire whom he calls, and for what reason, the answer is, those whom he had elected. But when we come to election, we see nothing but mercy on every side.

If no society, and even no house, though containing only a small family, can be preserved in a proper state without discipline, this is far more necessary in the Church, the state of which ought to be the most orderly of all. As the saving doctrine of Christ is the soul of the Church, so discipline forms the ligaments which connect the members together, and keep each in its proper place. Whoever, therefore, either desire the abolition of all discipline, or obstruct its restoration, whether they act from design or inadvertency, they certainly promote the entire dissolution of the Church. For what will be the consequence, if every man be at liberty to follow his own inclinations? But such would be the case, unless the preaching of the doctrine were accompanied with private admonitions, reproofs, and other means to enforce the doctrine, and prevent it from being altogether ineffectual. Discipline, therefore, serves as a bridle to curb and restrain the refractory, who resist the doctrine of Christ; or as a spur to stimulate the inactive; and sometimes as a father's rod, with which those who have grievously fallen may be chastised in mercy with the gentleness of the Spirit of Christ.

Scotland and England

John Knox described the practice of church discipline in the Calvinist churches of Scotland.

From John Knox. *The Book of Discipline*

First, if the offence be secret and known to few, and rather stands in suspicion than in manifest probation, the offender ought to be privately admonished to abstain from all appearance of evil; which, if he promises to do, and to declare himself sober, honest, and one that feareth God, and feareth to offend his brethren, then may the secret admonition suffice for his correction. But if he either contemn the admonition, or, after promise made, do show himself no more circumspect than he was before, then must the Minister admonish him; to whom if he be found inobedient, they must proceed according to the rule of Christ, as after shall be declared.

If the crime be public, and such as is heinous, as fornication, drunkenness, fighting, common swearing, or execration, then ought the offender to be called in the presence of the Minister, Elders, and Deacons, where his sin and offence ought to be declared and agredged, so that his conscience may feel how far he hath offended God, and what slander he hath raised in the Church. If signs of unfeigned repentance appear to him, and if he require to be admitted to public repentance, the Ministry may appoint unto him a day when the whole Church conveneth together, that in presence of all he may testify the repentance which before them he professed. Which, if he accept, and with reverence do, confessing his sin, and damning the same, and earnestly desiring the Congregation to pray to God with him for mercy, and to accept him in their society, notwithstanding his former offence, then the Church may, and ought [to] receive him as a penitent. [If the sinner did not repent he was to be excommunicated.]

After which sentence may no person (his wife and family only excepted) have any kind of conversation with him, be it in eating and drinking, buying or selling, yea, in saluting or talking with him, except that it be at the commandment or licence of the Ministry for his conversion; that he by such means confounded, seeing himself abhorred of the faithful and godly, may have occasion to repent and be so saved. The sentence of his Excommunication must be published universally throughout the Realm, lest that any man should pretend ignorance.

His children begotten or born after that sentence and before his repentance, may not be admitted to baptism, till either they be of age to require the same, or else that the mother, or some of his especial friends, members of the Church, offer and present the child, abhorring and damning the iniquity and obstinate contempt of the impenitent. If any think it severe that the child should be punished for the iniquity of the father, let them understand that the sacraments appertain only to the faithful and to their seed: But such as stubbornly contemn all godly admonition, and obstinately remain in their iniquity, cannot be accounted amongst the faithful.

From John Knox, *History of the Reformation in Scotland* (London: Thomas Nelson and Sons, 1949), Vol. 2, pp. 306–308. Reprinted courtesy of Thomas Nelson and Sons Ltd.

The Reformation in England did not begin with a religious uprising as in Germany. King Henry VIII first quarreled with Rome because the pope refused to grant an annulment of his marriage to Catherine of Aragon. The final breach came in this Act of Supremacy.

Act of Supremacy, 1534

Albeit the King's Majesty justly and rightfully is and ought to be the Supreme Head of the Church of England, and so is recognised by the clergy of this realm in their Convocations; yet nevertheless for corroboration and confirmation thereof, and for increase of virtue in Christ's religion within this realm of England, and to repress and extirp all errors, heresies, and other enormities and abuses heretofore used in the same, Be it enacted by authority of this present Parliament that the King our Sovereign Lord, his heirs and successors kings of this realm, shall be taken, accepted, and reputed the only Supreme Head in earth of the Church of England called *Anglicana Ecclesia*, and shall have and enjoy annexed and united to the imperial Crown of this realm as well the title and style thereof, as all honours, dignities, preeminences, jurisdictions, privileges, authorities, immunities, profits, and commodities, to the said dignity of Supreme Head of the same Church belonging and appertaining: And that our said Sovereign Lord, his heirs and successors kings of this realm, shall have full power and authority from time to time to visit, repress, redress, reform, order, correct, restrain, and amend all such errors, heresies, abuses, offences, contempts, and enormities, whatsoever they be, which by any manner spiritual authority or jurisdiction ought or may lawfully be reformed, repressed, ordered, redressed, corrected, restrained, or amended, most to the pleasure of Almighty God, the increase of virtue in Christ's religion, and for the conservation of the peace, unity, and tranquillity of this realm: any usage, custom, foreign laws, foreign authority, prescription, or any other thing or things to the contrary hereof notwithstanding.

The Church of England, although it adopted some central Protestant doctrines, retained more Catholic usages than the other reformed churches. The doctrine of the church was defined in The Thirty-Nine Articles, *promulgated under Queen Elizabeth I in 1562. What authority did the articles attribute to scripture, to national churches, to the queen?*

From *The Thirty-Nine Articles*

Of the Authority of the Church

The Church hath power to decree Rites or Ceremonies, and authority in Controversies of Faith: And yet it is not lawful for the Church to ordain any thing that is contrary to God's Word written, neither may it so expound one

From *Tudor Constitutional Documents,* J. R. Tanner, ed. (Cambridge: Cambridge University Press, 1951), pp. 47–48.
From *Articles Agreed Upon by the Archbishops and Bishops, 1562* (London: R. Barker, 1631).

place of Scripture, that it be repugnant to another. Wherefore, although the Church be a witness and a keeper of holy Writ, yet, as it ought not to decree any thing against the same, so besides the same ought it not to enforce any thing to be believed for necessity of Salvation.

Of the Traditions of the Church

It is not necessary that Traditions and Ceremonies be in all places one, or utterly like; for at all times they have been divers, and may be changed according to the diversities of countries, times, and men's manners, so that nothing be ordained against God's Word. Whosoever through his private judgment, willingly and purposely, doth openly break the traditions and ceremonies of the Church, which be not repugnant to the Word of God, and be ordained and approved by common authority, ought to be rebuked openly (that others may fear to do the like) as he that offendeth against the common order of the Church, and hurteth the authority of the Magistrate, and woundeth the consciences of the weak brethren.

Every particular or national Church hath authority to ordain, change, and abolish, ceremonies or rites of the Church ordained only by man's authority, so that all things be done to edifying.

Of the Civil Magistrates

The Queen's Majesty hath the chief power in this Realm of England, and other her Dominious, unto whom the chief Government of all Estates of this Realm, whether they be Ecclesiastical or Civil, in all causes doth appertain, and is not, nor ought to be, subject to any foreign Jurisdiction.

Where we attribute to the Queen's Majesty the chief government, by which Titles we understand the minds of some slanderous folks to be offended; we give not to our Princes the ministering either of God's Word, or of the Sacraments, the which thing the Injunctions also lately set forth by Elizabeth our Queen do most plainly testify; but that only prerogative, which we see to have been given always to all godly Princes in holy Scriptures, by God himself; that is, that they should rule all estates and degrees committed to their charge by God, whether they be Ecclesiastical or Temporal, and restrain with the civil sword the stubborn and evildoers.

The Bishop of Rome hath no jurisdiction in this Realm of England.

The Laws of the Realm may punish Christian men with death, for heinous and grievous offences.

It is lawful for Christian men, at the commandment of the Magistrate, to wear weapons, and serve in the wars.

THE CATHOLIC REFORMATION

Doctrine Reaffirmed

The Council of Trent that met at intervals between 1545 and 1563 enacted much reform legislation and also responded to Protestant attacks on Catholic doctrine and practices. What particular Protestant teachings were rejected in this profession of faith?

From *Decrees of the Council of Trent*

Profession of Faith

I, *N*, with steadfast faith believe and profess each and all the things contained in the Symbol of faith which the holy Roman Church uses namely "I believe in One God," etc. [The Nicene Creed].

I most firmly acknowledge and embrace the Apostolical and ecclesiastical traditions and other observances and constitutions of the same Church. I acknowledge the sacred Scripture according to that sense which Holy Mother Church has held and holds, to whom it belongs to decide upon the true sense and interpretation of the holy Scriptures, nor will I ever receive and interpret the Scripture except according to the unanimous consent of the Fathers.

I profess likewise that true God is offered in the Mass, a proper and propitiatory sacrifice for the living and the dead, and that in the most Holy Eucharist there are truly, really and substantially the body and blood, together with the soul and divinity of Our Lord Jesus Christ, and that a conversion is made of the whole substance of bread into his body and of the whole substance of wine into his blood, which conversion the Catholic Church calls transubstantiation. I also confess that the whole and entire Christ and the true sacrament is taken under the one species alone.

I hold unswervingly that there is a purgatory and that the souls there detained are helped by the intercessions of the faithful; likewise also that the Saints who reign with Christ are to be venerated and invoked; that they offer prayers to God for us and that their relics are to be venerated. I firmly assert that the images of Christ and of the ever-Virgin Mother of God, as also those of other Saints, are to be kept and retained, and that due honour and veneration is to be accorded them; and I affirm that the power of indulgences has been left by Christ in the Church, and that their use is very salutary for Christian people.

I recognize the Holy Catholic and Apostolic Roman Church as the Mother and mistress of all churches; and I vow and swear true obedience to the Roman Pontiff, the successor of blessed Peter, the chief of the Apostles and the representative [*vicarius*] of Jesus Christ.

I accept and profess, without doubting the traditions, definitions and declarations of the sacred Canons and Oecumenical Councils and especially those of the holy Council of Trent; and at the same time I condemn, reject and anathematize all things contrary thereto, and all heresies condemned, rejected and anathematized by the Church. This true Catholic Faith (without which no one can be in a state of salvation), which at this time I of my own will profess and truly hold, I, *N*, vow and swear, God helping me, most constantly to keep and confess entire and undefiled to my life's last breath, and that I will endeavour, as far as in me shall lie, that it be held, taught and preached by my subordinates

From Henry Bettenson, ed., *Documents of the Christian Church*, 2nd ed. (London: Oxford University Press, 1963), pp. 375–377. Copyright © 1963 by Oxford University Press. Reprinted by permission of Oxford University Press.

or by those who shall be placed under my care: so help me God and these Holy Gospels of God.

On Justification

[The following propositions were condemned.]

1. That man can be justified before God by his own works, which are done either in the strength of human nature or through the teaching of the law, apart from the divine grace through Jesus Christ.

3. That without the prevenient inspiration of the Holy Spirit and his aid a man can believe, hope and love, or can repent, as he should, so that on him the grace of justification may be conferred.

4. That the free will of man, moved and aroused by God, does not cooperate at all by responding to the awakening call of God, so as to dispose and prepare itself for the acquisition of the grace of justification, nor can it refuse that grace, if it so will, but it does nothing at all, like some inanimate thing, and is completely passive.

5. That man's free will has been wholly lost and destroyed after Adam's sin.

6. That it is not in the power of man to make his ways evil, but that evil works as well as good are wrought by God, not just by ways of permission but even by his own personal activity; so that the betrayal of Judas is no less his work than the calling of Paul.

7. That all works before justification, for whatever reason they were done, are in truth sins and deserve the hatred of God, or that the more strongly a man strives to dispose himself to receive Grace, the more grievously he sins.

9. That the impious is justified by faith alone—if this means that nothing else is required by way of co-operation in the acquisition of the grace of justification, and that it is in no way necessary for a man to be prepared and disposed by the motion of his own will.

15. That a man reborn and justified is bound by faith to believe that he is assuredly in the number of the predestinate.

24. That justification once received is not preserved and even increased in the sight of God through good works; but that these same works are only fruits and signs of justification, not causes of its increase.

Religious Reformers

Ignatius Loyola (1491–1556) founded the Jesuit order that championed the cause of a reinvigorated Catholicism. His "Exercises," designed for the spiritual formation of his followers, emphasized personal devotion to Christ and loyalty to the institutions of the Catholic church.

From Ignatius Loyola. *The Spiritual Exercises*

The Nativity
The usual preparatory prayer.

First Preliminary. The story. Our Lady, in the ninth month of her pregnancy, sets out for Nazareth riding, as we may devoutly picture her, on a donkey, accompanied by Joseph and a servant-girl, leading an ox. They are going to Bethlehem to pay the tax which Caesar had levied on all this territory.

Second Preliminary. The picture. Represent to yourself in imagination the road from Bethlehem, in its length and breadth. Is it level or through valleys or over hillsides?
In the same way, study the place of the Nativity. Is the cave spacious or cramped, low or high? How is it furnished?

Third Preliminary. The same as in the preceding contemplation and in the same form.

First Heading. Look at the persons, our Lady, St Joseph, the servant-girl and, after He is born, the Infant Jesus. I must see myself as an impoverished attendant, not fit to be there, but watching and studying them, looking after all their wants as if I were actually present, in a spirit of complete and respectful subservience.
Then I should think of myself to derive some benefit.

Second Heading. See, observe and study what they are saying. Then think of myself, to derive some benefit.

Third Heading. See and reflect on what they are doing. Here it is the journey they have to make, the hardships they have to put up with, before our Lord is born in utter destitution. After all His labours, after suffering from hunger and thirst, heat and cold, being treated with injustice and insulted, He is to die on the Cross—and all for me. Thinking of all this, I will derive some benefit for my soul.
End with a colloquy as in the preceding contemplation, and with an *Our Father.*

The King
The Call of the Earthly King Helps in the Contemplation of the Life of the Eternal King

From *The Spiritual Exercises of Saint Ignatius,* Thomas Corbishley, trans. (New York: P. J. Kennedy and Sons, 1963), pp. 42–44, 47–48, 120–122. Reprinted by permission of Burns & Oates Ltd.

The preparatory prayer will be as usual.

First Preliminary. A picture of the scene. Here it will be to see in imagination the synagogues, towns and hamlets through which Christ our Lord went preaching.

Second Preliminary. To ask the grace I want. Here I ask our Lord the grace not to be deaf to His summons, but ready and enthusiastic to carry out His holy purpose.

First Heading. I imagine a temporal king, chosen by our Lord God, revered and obeyed by the rulers and all the common men of Christendom.

Second Heading. See how this king addresses all his followers, saying: I am determined to bring under my control the entire land of the unbeliever. Anyone, then, who wishes to join me must be satisfied to eat the food I eat, to drink what I drink, to dress as I dress; by day he will have to work alongside me, and take his turn with me at keeping a look-out by night; there will be other things. But his share in my triumph will be proportionate to his share in my hardships.

Third Heading. Think what response loyal subjects must make to a king so generous and so understanding: equally, were one to refuse the appeal of such a king, how he would incur the reprobation of all mankind and be regarded as a disgraceful coward.

The second part of this exercise consists in relating this illustration of the earthly king to Christ our Lord, point for point.

First Heading. If we cannot ignore such a challenge, issued to his followers by an earthly king, how much more worthy of our attention is that of Christ our Lord, the Eternal King, as He confronts the whole world: to each and all He issues His summons in these words: I am determined to bring under my control the whole world and all my enemies, and so to come to the glory of my Father. To anyone, then, who chooses to join me, I offer nothing but a share in my hardships; but if he follows me in suffering he will assuredly follow me in glory.

Second Heading. We realize that anyone possessed of right reason will offer himself totally for the task.

Third Heading. Those who are anxious to show greater enthusiasm still and distinguish themselves in unstinted service of their eternal King and Lord of the universe, will not be content to offer themselves without reservation for the enterprise. Going against their natural weakness and their love of the world and of the flesh, they will make their dedication of themselves still more valuable and worthwhile, in these terms:

Eternal Lord of the Universe, in the presence of Your own infinite goodness, of Your glorious Mother and all the saints of Heaven's court, by Your grace and help, I make this my offering: I intend and desire, and it is my deliberate resolve, granted it be for the more perfect service and greater praise of Your Majesty, to imitate You in putting up with all injustice, all abuse, all poverty in reality no less than in the spirit, should Your Most Sacred Majesty be willing to choose and admit me to this state of life.

The Mind of the Church

The following rules are to be observed in order that we may hold the opinions we should hold in the Church militant.

1. We should put away completely our own opinion and keep our minds ready and eager to give our entire obedience to our holy Mother the hierarchical Church, Christ our Lord's undoubted Spouse.

2. We should speak with approval of confession to a priest, of the reception of Holy Communion once a year, still more once a month, most of all once a week, the requisite conditions being duly fulfilled.

3. We should openly approve of the frequent hearing of Mass, and also of hymns, psalms and lengthy prayers both inside and outside the church, as well as the set times for the divine office as a whole, for prayer in general and for all the canonical hours.

4. We should speak with particular approval of religious orders, and the states of virginity and celibacy, not rating matrimony as high as any of these.

6. We should approve of relics of the saints, showing reverence for them and praying to the saints themselves; visits to Station churches, pilgrimages, indulgences, jubilees, Crusade bulls, the lighting of candles in churches should all be commended.

7. We should approve of the laws of fasting and abstinence in Lent, on Ember Days, vigils, Fridays and Saturdays, as well as mortifications both interior and exterior.

8. We should praise church decoration and architecture, as well as statues, which we should venerate in view of what they portray.

9. Finally, all the Church's commandments should be spoken of favourably, our minds being always eager to find arguments in her defence, never in criticism.

13. To arrive at complete certainty, this is the attitude of mind we should maintain: I will believe that the white object I see is black if that should be the decision of the hierarchical Church, for I believe that linking Christ our Lord the Bridegroom and His Bride the Church, there is one and the same Spirit, ruling and guiding us for our souls' good. For our Holy Mother the Church is guided and ruled by the same Spirit, the Lord who gave the Ten Commandments.

*Teresa of Avila (1515–1582), a great writer on the spiritual life, was also a practical church re-
former. Here she reflects on the role of women in religious orders and their relationship to God.
What was her attitude to the Protestant Reformation?*

From Teresa of Avila. *The Way of Perfection*

This convent was founded for the reasons already given in the work above
mentioned, also on account of certain favours that God showed me, in which He
revealed that He would be served with great fervour in this house. I did not at
first intend that such rigorous bodily mortifications should be practised in it, nor
that it should possess no income; on the contrary, I wished it to have sufficient
means to prevent the possibility of want, though weak and wicked as I am, I
meant rather to do what was right than to seek for self-indulgence.

Just at this time I heard of the miseries France was suffering, of the havoc the
Lutherans were making there, and how this wretched sect was increasing. It
grieved me bitterly, and as if I could have done anything, or have been of any consequence, I cried to God and begged Him to cure this terrible evil. I felt that I
would have laid down a thousand lives to save one of the many souls perishing
there. Yet, as I am but a woman, feeble and faulty, it was impossible for me to serve
God in the way I wished—indeed, all I cared for then, as I do now, was that, as the
enemies of God are so many and His friends so few, these latter might at least be
good ones. Therefore I determined to do what little was in my power, which was
to follow the Evangelical counsels as perfectly as I could and to see that the few
nuns here should do the same. Trusting in the great mercy of God which never
fails those who resolve to leave all things for His sake, I hoped that, as my sisters
here are all that I ever wished them to be, their virtues would be strong enough to
resist the influence of my defects and that I might be able to bring some comfort
to our Lord. Thus, being all of us employed in interceding for the champions of
the Church, and the preachers and theologians who defend her, we might, to our
utmost, aid this Lord of mine who is attacked with such cruelty by those on whom
He has conferred great benefits that it seems as though they would fasten Him to
the Cross again leaving Him no place to lay His head. . . .

It seems presumption in me to imagine that I have any power to obtain
this—I place all my confidence, O my God, in these servants of Thine, who are
with me and who, I know, neither desire nor seek to do aught but please Thee.
For Thee they left the little they possessed, only wishing they owned more to offer Thee. Thou art not ungrateful, O my Creator, that I need think Thou wilt refuse them what they ask, nor, O Lord of my soul, didst Thou hate women whilst
Thou wert in the world, but didst ever favour them and show them tender love
and pitiful compassion! Thou didst put greater trust in them than in men, for
among them was Thy most holy Mother whose merits we share, and whose
habit we wear, unworthy as we are by reason of our sins. We can do nothing for

From Teresa of Avila, *The Way of Perfection,* "A Benedictine of Stanbrook," trans., B. Zimmerman,
ed. (London: Burns & Oates, 1961), pp. 4–5, 17–19. Reprinted by permission of Search Press/Burns
& Oates Ltd.

Thee in public, nor do we dare to tell the truths over which we weep in secret, lest Thou shouldst not hear our most right petition. Just and good as Thou art, O Lord, I will not believe that Thou wilt reject us. Thou art a just Judge, not like earthly judges who, being sons of Adam and stern men, have no faith in women's virtue. The day will come, my King, when all will be known. I speak not for myself, for all men know of my wickedness and I rejoice that it is made public, but seeing in what manner of times we are living, it is not right to repulse the good and valiant though they are but women. When we beg of Thee honours, income, riches, any wordly things, do not listen to us, but how shouldst Thou not hear us when we ask for what concerns the honour of Thy Son? Why, O Eternal Father, shouldst Thou refuse those who would forfeit a thousand honours and a thousand lives for Thee? Not for our sakes, O God, for we deserve it not, but for the sake of Thy Son and of His merits! O Eternal Father, such stripes and insults and such bitter torments should not be forgotten! How can a heart so loving as Thine, my Creator, endure that what was instituted with such ardent love by Thy Son for the sake of pleasing Thee (for Thou didst bid Him love us) should be held of so little value as is the Blessed Sacrament in these days by heretics? For they drive It from Its dwelling-place when they destroy the churches. It is not as if He had left undone aught that could please Thee. No, He consummated everything! Was it not enough, O Eternal Father, for Him to have no place in which to lay His head whilst He lived amid incessant toils, that now they must deprive Him of the place to which He invites His friends, seeing that they are fainting and knowing that those who labour need to be supported by such meat? Has He not paid in overwhelming excess for the sin of Adam? Must this most meek and loving Lamb atone anew for every fresh sin we commit? Do not suffer it, my Sovereign King; let Thy Majesty be appeased; look not on our faults but on Thy most holy Son who has redeemed us; reflect on His merits, on those of His glorious Mother and on how many Saints and Martyrs have died for Thee! But alas, O my God, who am I who have dared to offer Thee this petition in the name of all? My daughters, what a wretched advocate you have to gain a hearing and to present your petition for you! What if my presumption should anger this supreme Judge, as would be only right and just? But remember, O my Sovereign and my Lord, that Thou art the God of mercy; do Thou prove it to this poor sinner and worm who is thus bold with Thee! Look, O my God, upon my desires and on the tears with which I beg this of Thee, and forgetting my evil actions for Thine own sake, take pity on the many perishing souls and have mercy on Thy Church! Do not permit these evils to increase in Christendom, O Lord, but illuminate its darkness!

REFORMATION AND POLITICS

Germany

Economic and religious grievances inspired the great Peasants' Rebellion (1524) in Germany. Some of the peasants' demands apparently echoed Lutheran principles.

From *Twelve Articles of the Peasants*

The First Article. First, it is our humble petition and desire, as also our will and resolution, that in the future we should have power and authority so that each community should choose and appoint a pastor, and that we should have the right to depose him should he conduct himself improperly. The pastor thus chosen should teach us the Gospel pure and simple, without any addition, doctrine or ordinance of man.

The Second Article. According as the just tithe is established by the Old Testament and fulfilled in the New, we are ready and willing to pay the fair tithe of grain.

The Third Article. It has been the custom hitherto for men to hold us as their own property, which is pitiable enough, considering that Christ has delivered and redeemed us all, without exception by the shedding of his precious blood, the lowly as well as the great. Accordingly, it is consistent with Scripture that we should be free and wish to be so. Not that we would wish to be absolutely free and under no authority. . . . We are thus ready to yield obedience according to God's law to our elected and regular authorities in all proper things becoming to a Christian. We, therefore, take it for granted that you will release us from serfdom, as true Christians, unless it should be shown us from the Gospel that we are serfs.

The Fourth Article. In the fourth place it has been the custom heretofore, that no poor man should be allowed to touch venison or wild fowl, or fish in flowing water, which seems to us quite unseemly and unbrotherly, as well as selfish and not agreeable to the word of God.

The Fifth Article. In the fifth place we are aggrieved in the matter of wood-cutting, for the noble folk have appropriated all the woods to themselves alone.

The Sixth Article. Our sixth complaint is in regard to the excessive services demanded of us, which are increased from day to day. We ask that this matter be properly looked into so that we shall not continue to be oppressed in this way, and that some gracious consideration be given us, since our forefathers were required only to serve according to the word of God.

The Seventh Article. Seventh, we will not hereafter allow ourselves to be farther oppressed by our lords, but will let them demand only what is just and proper according to the word of the agreement between the lord and the peasant.

From J. H. Robinson, trans., *Readings in European History* (Boston, Mass.: Ginn and Co., 1906), Vol. 2, pp. 95–99.

The Eighth Article. In the eighth place, we are greatly burdened by holdings which cannot support the rent exacted from them. The peasants suffer loss in this way and are ruined; and we ask that the lords may appoint persons of honor to inspect these holdings, and fix a rent in accordance with justice, so that the peasant shall not work for nothing, since the laborer is worthy of his hire.

The Ninth Article. In the ninth place, we are burdened with a great evil in the constant making of new laws. We are not judged according to the offence, but sometimes with great ill will, and sometimes much too leniently. In our opinion we should be judged according to the old written law, so that the case shall be decided according to its merits, and not with partiality.

The Tenth Article. In the tenth place, we are aggrieved by the appropriation by individuals of meadows and fields which at one time belonged to a community. These we will take again into our own hands.

The Eleventh Article. In the eleventh place we will entirely abolish the due called *Todfall* [i.e., heriot], and will no longer endure it, nor allow widows and orphans to be thus shamefully robbed against God's will, and in violation of justice and right, as has been done in many places, and by those who should shield and protect them. These have disgraced and despoiled us, and although they had little authority they assumed it. God will suffer this no more, but it shall be wholly done away with, and for the future no man shall be bound to give little or much.

Conclusion. In the twelfth place it is our conclusion and final resolution, that if one or more of the articles here set forth should not be in agreement with the word of God, as we think they are, such article we will willingly recede from, when it is proved really to be against the word of God by a clear explanation of the Scripture.

Luther regarded the peasants' demand for freedom as a distortion of his spiritual teaching. When the peasants rose in rebellion he called on the German princes to suppress them mercilessly.

From *Luther's Letter, 1524*

In my preceding pamphlet [on the "Twelve Articles"]. I had no occasion to condemn the peasants, because they promised to yield to law and better instruction, as Christ also demands (Matt. vii. I). But before I can turn around, they go out and appeal to force, in spite of their promises, and rob and pillage and act like mad dogs. From this it is quite apparent what they had in their false minds, and that what they put forth under the name of the gospel in the "Twelve Articles" was all vain pretense. . . .

From J. H. Robinson, *Readings in European History* (Boston: Ginn and Company, 1905), Vol. 2, pp. 106–107.

It is right and lawful to slay at the first opportunity a rebellious person, who is known as such, for he is already under God's and the emperor's ban. Every man is at once judge and executioner of a public rebel; just as, when a fire starts, he who can extinguish it first is the best fellow. Rebellion is not simply vile murder, but is like a great fire that kindles and devastates a country; it fills the land with murder and bloodshed, makes widows and orphans, and destroys everything, like the greatest calamity. Therefore, whosoever can, should smite, strangle, and stab, secretly or publicly, and should remember that there is nothing more poisonous, pernicious, and devilish than a rebellious man. Just as one must slay a mad dog, so, if you do not fight the rebels, they will fight you, and the whole country with you.

A civil war between Protestant and Catholic princes of Germany ended with an acceptance of a permanent religious division of the country. (The agreement did not prevent the outbreak of further savage religious wars in the next century.)

Peace of Augsburg (1555)

In order to bring peace into the holy empire of the Germanic Nation, between the Roman Imperial Majesty and the Electors, Princes, and Estates: let neither his Imperial Majesty nor the Electors, Princes, etc., do any violence or harm to any estate of the Empire on account of the Augsburg Confession,[2] but let them enjoy their religious belief, liturgy and ceremonies as well as their estates and other rights and privileges in peace; and complete religious peace shall be obtained only by Christian means of amity, or under threat of the punishment of the imperial ban.

Likewise the Estates espousing the Augsburg Confession shall let all the Estates and Princes who cling to the old religion live in absolute peace and in the enjoyment of all their estates, rights and privileges.

However all such as do not belong to the two above-mentioned religions shall not be included in the present peace but be totally excluded from it. . . .

In case our subjects, whether belonging to the old religion or to the Augsburg Confession, should intend leaving their homes, with their wives and children, in order to settle in another place, they shall neither be hindered in the sale of their estates after due payment of the local taxes nor injured in their honour.

France

In France Calvin won many influential converts (Huguenots). They prospered until the royal government launched a savage persecution in 1572. This account is by an eyewitness who later became the chief minister of King Henry IV.

From Henry Bettenson, ed., *Documents of the Christian Church*, 2nd ed. (London: Oxford University Press, 1963), pp. 301–302. Copyright © 1963 by Oxford University Press. Reprinted by permission of Oxford University Press.
[2] A statement of Lutheran doctrines.

St. Bartholomew's Day Massacre

If I were inclined to increase the general horror inspired by an action so barbarous as that perpetrated on the 24th of August, 1572, and too well known by the name of the *massacre of St. Bartholomew*, I should in this place enlarge upon the number, the rank, the virtues, and great talents of those who were inhumanly murdered on that horrible day, as well in Paris as in every other part of the kingdom; I should mention at least the ignominious treatment, the fiend-like cruelty, and savage insults these miserable victims suffered from their butchers, whose conduct was a thousand times more terrible than death itself. I have writings still in my hands which would confirm the report, of the court of France having made the most pressing solicitations to the courts of England and Germany, to the Swiss and the Genoese, to refuse an asylum to those Huguenots who might fly from France; but I prefer the honour of the nation to the satisfying a malignant pleasure, which many persons would take, in lengthening out a recital wherein might be found the names of those who were so lost to humanity as to dip their hands in the blood of their fellow-citizens, and even of their own relations. I would, were it in my power, for ever obliterate the memory of a day that Divine vengeance made France groan for, by a continual succession of miseries, blood, and horror, during six-and-twenty years; for it is impossible to judge otherwise, when one reflects on all that happened from that fatal moment till the peace of 1598. It is even with regret that I cannot omit what happened upon this occasion to the prince who is the subject of these Memoirs, and to myself.

Intending on that day to wait upon the king my master,[3] I went to bed early on the preceding evening; about three in the morning I was awakened by the cries of people, and the alarm-bells, which were everywhere ringing. M. de Saint Julian, my tutor, and my valet, who had also been roused by the noise, ran out of my apartments to learn the cause of it, but never returned, nor did I ever after hear what became of them. Being thus left alone in my room, my landlord, who was a Protestant, urged me to accompany him to mass in order to save his life, and his house from being pillaged; but I determined to endeavour to escape to the College de Bourgogne, and to effect this I put on my scholar's gown, and taking a book under my arm, I set out. In the streets I met three parties of the Life-guards; the first of these, after handling me very roughly, seized my book, and, most fortunately for me, seeing it was a Roman Catholic prayer-book, suffered me to proceed, and this served me as a passport with the two other parties. As I went along I saw the houses broken open and plundered, and men, women, and children butchered, while a constant cry was kept up of, "Kill! Kill! O you Huguenots! O you Huguenots!" This made me very impatient to gain the college, where, through God's assistance, I at length arrived, without suffering

From *Memoirs of the Duke of Sully* (London: G. Bell, 1877), Vol. 1, pp. 85–87.
[3]King Henry of Navarre, a Huguenot who later converted to Catholicism and became King Henry IV of France.

any other injury than a most dreadful fright. The porter twice refused me entrance, but at last, by means of a few pieces of money, I prevailed on him to inform M. La Faye, the principal of the college and my particular friend, that I was at the gate, who, moved with pity, brought me in, though he was at a loss where to put me, on account of two priests who were in his room, and who said it was determined to put all the Huguenots to death, even the infants at the breast, as was done in the Sicilian vespers. However, my friend conveyed me to a secret apartment, where no one entered except his valet, who brought me food during three successive days, at the end of which the king's proclamation prohibiting any further plunder or slaughter, was issued. . . .

The massacre of 1572 was followed by years of civil war until in 1598 King Henry IV granted a measure of toleration to the Huguenots. (As in Germany, the settlement did not prove permanent and further religious persecutions occurred in the seventeenth century.)

Edict of Nantes

We ordain that the Catholic, Apostolic and Roman faith be restored and re-established in all those districts and places of this our Realm . . . in which its exercise has been interrupted, there to be freely and peaceably exercised. . . .

And to leave no occasion for trouble or difference among our subjects: We permit those of the so-called Reformed Religion to live and abide in all the towns and districts of this our Realm . . . free from inquisition, molestation or compulsion to do anything in the way of Religion, against their conscience . . . provided that they observe the provisions of this Edict. . . .

We also permit those of the aforesaid Religion to practise it in all the towns and districts of our dominion, in which it had been established and publicly observed by them on several distinct occasions during the year 1596 and the year 1597 up to the end of August, all decrees and judgements to the contrary notwithstanding.

We most expressly forbid to those of this religion the practice thereof, in respect of ministry, organization, discipline or the public instruction of children, or in any respect, in our realm and dominion, save in the places permitted and granted by this edict.

The practice of this religion is forbidden in our court and suite, in our domains beyond the mountains, in our city of Paris, or within five leagues thereof.

PART TWELVE

NEW WORLDS FOR OLD— EXPLORATION, SCIENCE, AND SUPERSTITION

The sixteenth and seventeenth centuries were an age of vastly broadening horizons for the peoples of Western Europe.

Explorers discovered a New World across the Atlantic and a new sea route to the fabulously wealthy East Indies. After the first voyages of discovery, later adventurers— part merchants, part pirates, part conquerors—quickly established the foundations of the great European overseas empires. (The Spanish and Portuguese were first; then English, Dutch, and French soon followed.)

During the same period, major advances occurred in many fields of natural science. The most striking of all were those in astronomy, discoveries that changed the whole picture of the universe and humanity's place in it. Copernicus proposed a heliocentric theory—that the sun, not the earth, was at the center of the universe. Galileo turned his newly invented telescope on the heavens and found evidence to support Copernicus. Bacon and Descartes wrote on scientific method. All the new knowledge flowed together in the great synthesis presented by Isaac Newton in his Principia (1687).

But the new ideas penetrated only slowly among the masses of the people. Most of them clung to a prescientific, magical view of the world that found expression in the prevalent "witchcraft delusion" of the early modern period. The persecution of witches was not a mere eccentricity of the age. It expressed the fears and tensions of a time when old, taken-for-granted certainties about religious truth and the natural order of things were everywhere being called into question. Sometimes we can see the tension in a particular individual, as in the readings from Jean Bodin. Bodin, nowadays remembered mainly as a great political theorist, was conscious that he lived in a "golden age" of scientific achievement; but he was also obsessed by the study of demonology and wrote extensively on the evils of witchcraft.

NEW FOUND LANDS

First Encounters

Columbus encountered the natives of Cuba and Hispaniola during his first voyage across the Atlantic in 1492. How did they differ from Europeans according to his account?

From *Letter of Columbus*

All these islands are very beautiful, and distinguished by a diversity of scenery; they are filled with a great variety of trees of immense height, and which I believe to retain their foliage in all seasons; for when I saw them they were as verdant and luxuriant as they usually are in Spain in the month of May,—some of them were blossoming, some bearing fruit, and all flourishing in the greatest perfection, according to their respective stages of growth, and the nature and quality of each: yet the islands are not so thickly wooded as to be impassable. The nightingale and various birds were singing in countless numbers, and that in November, the month in which I arrived there. There are besides in the same island of Juana [Cuba] seven or eight kinds of palm trees, which, like all the other trees, herbs, and fruits, considerably surpass ours in height and beauty. The pines also are very handsome, and there are very extensive fields and meadows, a variety of birds, different kinds of honey, and many sorts of metals, but no iron. In that island also which I have before said we named Española [Hispaniola], there are mountains of very great size and beauty, vast plains, groves, and very fruitful fields, admirably adapted for tillage, pasture, and habitation. The convenience and excellence of the harbours in this island, and the abundance of the rivers, so indispensable to the health of man, surpass anything that would be believed by one who had not seen it. The trees, herbage, and fruits of Española are very different from those of Juana, and moreover it abounds in various kinds of spices, gold, and other metals. The inhabitants of both sexes in this island, and in all the others which I have seen, or of which I have received information, go always naked as they were born, with the exception of some of the women, who use the covering of a leaf, or small bough, or an apron of cotton which they prepare for that purpose. None of them, as I have already said, are possessed of any iron, neither have they weapons, being unacquainted with, and indeed incompetent to use them, not from any deformity of body (for they are well-formed), but because they are timid and full of fear. They carry however in lieu of arms, canes dried in the sun, on the ends of which they fix heads of dried wood sharpened to a point, and even these they dare not use habitually; for it has often occurred when I have sent two or three of my men to any of the villages to speak with the natives, that they have come out in a disorderly troop, and have fled in such haste at the approach of our men, that the fathers forsook their children

From *Select Letters of Christopher Columbus*, R. H. Major, ed. (London: The Hakluyt Society, 1847), pp. 5–9.

and the children their fathers. This timidity did not arise from any loss or injury that they had received from us; for, on the contrary, I gave to all I approached whatever articles I had about me, such as cloth and many other things, taking nothing of theirs in return: but they are naturally timid and fearful. As soon however as they see that they are safe, and have laid aside all fear, they are very simple and honest, and exceedingly liberal with all they have; none of them refusing any thing he may possess when he is asked for it, but on the contrary inviting us to ask them. They exhibit great love towards all others in preference to themselves: they also give objects of great value for trifles, and content themselves with very little or nothing in return. I however forbad that these trifles and articles of no value (such as pieces of dishes, plates, and glass, keys, and leather straps) should be given to them, although if they could obtain them, they imagined themselves to be possessed of the most beautiful trinkets in the world. It even happened that a sailor received for a leather strap as much gold as was worth three golden nobles, and for things of more trifling value offered by our men, especially-newly coined blancas, or any gold coins, the Indians would give whatever the seller required; as, for instance, an ounce and a half or two ounces of gold, or thirty or forty pounds of cotton, with which commodity they were already acquainted. Thus they bartered, like idiots, cotton and gold for fragments of bows, glasses, bottles, and jars; which I forbad as being unjust, and myself gave them many beautiful and acceptable articles which I had brought with me, taking nothing from them in return; I did this in order that I might the more easily conciliate them, that they might be led to become Christians, and be inclined to entertain a regard for the King and Queen, our Princes and all Spaniards, and that I might induce them to take an interest in seeking out, and collecting, and delivering to us such things as they possessed in abundance, but which we greatly needed. They practise no kind of idolatry, but have a firm belief that all strength and power, and indeed all good things, are in heaven, and that I had descended from thence with these ships and sailors, and under this impression was I received after they had thrown aside their fears. Nor are they slow or stupid, but of very clear understanding; and those men who have crossed to the neighbouring islands give an admirable description of everything they observed; but they never saw any people clothed, nor any ships like ours. On my arrival at that sea, I had taken some Indians by force from the first island that I came to, in order that they might learn our language, and communicate to us what they knew respecting the country; which plan succeeded excellently, and was a great advantage to us, for in a short time, either by gestures and signs, or by words, we were enabled to understand each other. These men are still travelling with me, and although they have been with us now a long time, they continue to entertain the idea that I have descended from heaven; and on our arrival at any new place they published this, crying out immediately with a loud voice to the other Indians, "Come, come and look upon beings of a celestial race": upon which both women and men, children and adults, young men and old, when they got rid of the fear they at first entertained, would come out in throngs, crowding the roads to see us.

Columbus always believed that he had discovered a new westward route to the East Indies. It was the Portuguese Vasco da Gama, however, who really found a new way to the East by sailing round the Cape of Good Hope in 1497. From the beginning, contacts between Europeans and non-European peoples involved bloody clashes as well as peaceful trading. The following incident occurred in 1502 after a party of Portuguese had been killed at Calicut in India.

From *Journal of Gaspar Correa*

The captain-major [Vasco da Gama], on arriving at Calecut, was in a passion because he found the port cleared, and in it there was nothing to which he could do harm, because the Moors, knowing of his coming, had all fled, and hid their vessels and sambuks in the rivers. . . . The King of Calecut thought that he might gain time, so that the captain-major should not do him harm; and when his fleet arrived he sent him a Brahman of his in a boat with a white cloth fastened to a pole, as a sign of peace. This Brahman came dressed in the habit of a friar, one of those who had been killed in the country; and on reaching the ship, he asked for a safe conduct to enter. When it was known that he was not a friar,—for the captain-major and everyone had been joyful, thinking that he was one of our friars,— seeing that he was not, the captain-major gave him a safe conduct, and bade him enter the ship. . . . He then ordered all the fleet to draw in close to the shore, and all day, till night, he bombarded the city, by which he made a great destruction. . . .

Whilst they were doing this business, there came in from the offing two large ships, and twenty-two sambuks and Malabar vessels, which came from Coromandel laden with rice, which the Moors of Calecut had ordered to be laden there, as its price there was very cheap, and they gained much by it; and they came to fetch the port, thinking that our ships, if they had come, would already be at Cochym, and not at Calecut; but our fleet having sighted them, the caravels went to them, and the Moors could not fly, as they were laden, and the caravels brought them to the captain-major, and all struck their sails. Six nakhodas of the sambuks then came to the captain-major, saying they were from Cananor, and mentioned the names of the factor and of Ruy de Mendanha, and other Portuguese, at which the captain-major was pleased. He then ordered the boats to go and plunder the small vessels, which were sixteen, and the two ships, in which they found rice, and many jars of butter, and many bales of stuffs. They then gathered all this together into the ships, with the crews of the two large ships, and he ordered the boats to get as much rice as they wanted, and they took that of four of the small vessels, which they emptied, for they did not want more. Then the captain-major commanded them to cut off the hands and ears and noses of all the crews, and put all that into one of the small vessels, into which he ordered them to put the friar, also without ears, or nose, or hands, which he ordered to be strung round his neck, with a palm-leaf for the King, on which he told him to have a curry made to eat of what his friar brought him. When all the Indians had been thus executed, he ordered their feet to be tied together, as they had no hands with which to untie them: and in order that they

From *The Three Voyages of Vasco de Gama,* H. E. J. Stanley, ed. (London: The Hakluyt Society, 1869), pp. 328–332.

should not untie them with their teeth, he ordered them to strike upon their teeth with staves, and they knocked them down their throats; and they were thus put on board, heaped up upon the top of each other, mixed up with the blood which streamed from them; and he ordered mats and dry leaves to be spread over them, and the sails to be set for the shore, and the vessel set on fire: and there were more than eight hundred Moors; and the small vessel with the friar, with all the hands and ears, was also sent on shore under sail, without being fired. These vessels went at once on shore, where many people flocked together to put out the fire, and draw out those whom they found alive, upon which they made great lamentations.

The New World

The conquest of Mexico and Peru gave rise to a prolonged debate in Spain about the morality of Spanish colonialism. Two of the principal antagonists were Juan Gines de Sepulveda (1490–1573), a Renaissance humanist scholar, and Bartolomé de las Casas (1474–1566), a Dominican friar who spent much of his life as a missionary among the Indians. How did Sepulveda justify the Spanish conquests? How did Las Casas defend the Indians? What abuses of Spanish power did Las Casas attack?

From Sepulveda. *Democrates Alter*

The Spanish have a perfect right to rule these barbarians of the New World and the adjacent islands, who in prudence, skill, virtues, and humanity are as inferior to the Spanish as children to adults, or women to men, for there exists between the two as great a difference as between savage and cruel races and the most merciful, between the most intemperate and the moderate and temperate and, I might even say, between apes and men.

You surely do not expect me to recall at length the prudence and talents of the Spanish. . . . Compare, then, these gifts of prudence, talent, magnanimity, temperance, humanity, and religion with those possessed by these half-men (*homunculi*), in whom you will barely find the vestiges of humanity, who not only do not possess any learning at all, but are not even literate or in possession of any monument to their history except for some obscure and vague reminiscences of several things put down in various paintings; nor do they have written laws, but barbarian institutions and customs. Well, then, if we are dealing with virtue, what temperance or mercy can you expect from men who are committed to all types of intemperance and base frivolity, and eat human flesh? And do not believe that before the arrival of the Christians they lived in that pacific kingdom of Saturn which the poets have invented; for, on the contrary, they waged continual and ferocious war upon one another with such fierceness that they did not consider a victory at all worthwhile unless they sated their monstrous hunger with the flesh of their enemies . . . and since furthermore these

Indians were otherwise so cowardly and timid that they could barely endure the presence of our soldiers, and many times thousands upon thousands of them scattered in flight like women before Spaniards so few that they did not even number one hundred. . . . Although some of them show a certain ingenuity for various works of artisanship, this is no proof of human cleverness, for we can observe animals, birds, and spiders making certain structures which no human accomplishment can competently imitate. And as for the way of life of the inhabitants of New Spain and the province of Mexico, I have already said that these people are considered the most civilized of all, and they themselves take pride in their public institutions, because they have cities erected in a rational manner and kings who are not hereditary but elected by popular vote, and among themselves they carry on commercial activities in the manner of civilized peoples. But see how they deceive themselves, and how much I dissent from such an opinion, seeing, on the contrary, in these very institutions a proof of the crudity, the barbarity, and the natural slavery of these people . . . for everything belongs to their masters whom, with improper nomenclature, they call kings, and by whose whims they live, more than by their own, ready to do the bidding and desire of these rulers and possessing no liberty. . . . And if this type of servile and barbarous nation had not been to their liking and nature, it would have been easy for them, as it was not a hereditary monarchy, to take advantage of the death of a king in order to obtain a freer state and one more favorable to their interests; by not doing so, they have stated quite clearly that they have been born to slavery and not to civic and liberal life. Therefore, if you wish to reduce them, I do not say to our domination, but to a servitude a little less harsh, it will not be difficult for them to change their masters, and instead of the ones they had, who were barbarous and impious and inhuman, to accept the Christians, cultivators of human virtues and the true faith. . . .

Those who surpass the rest in prudence and talent, although not in physical strength, are by nature the masters. Those, on the other hand, who are retarded or slow to understand, although they may have the physical strength necessary for the fulfilment of all their necessary obligations, are by nature slaves, and it is proper and useful that they be so. . . . Aristotle said, "It seems that war arises in a certain sense from nature, since a part of it is the art of the hunt, which is properly used not only against animals, but also against those men who, having been born to obey, reject servitude: such a war is just according to nature. . . ."

From Las Casas. *Apologetic History*

It has been written that these peoples of the Indies, lacking human governance and ordered nations, did not have the power of reason to govern themselves—which was inferred only from their having been found to be gentle, patient and humble. It has been implied that God became careless in creating so immense a number of rational souls and let human nature, which He so largely determined and provided for, go astray in the almost infinitesimal part of the human lineage which they comprise. From this it follows that they have all proven themselves unsocial and therefore monstrous, contrary to the natural bent of all peoples of the world. . . . In order to demonstrate the truth, which is the opposite, this book brings together and compiles [certain natural, special and accidental causes]. . . . Not only have [the Indians] shown themselves to be very wise peoples and possessed of lively and marked understanding, prudently governing and providing for their nations (as much as they can be nations, without faith in or knowledge of the true God) and making them prosper in justice; but they have equalled many diverse nations of the world, past and present, that have been praised for their governance, politics and customs, and exceed by no small measure the wisest of all these, such as the Greeks and Romans, in adherence to the rules of natural reason.

From Las Casas. *Thirty Propositions*

Proposition XXIII: To subject them first by warlike means is a form and procedure contrary to the law, gentle yoke, easy burden and gentleness of Jesus Christ. It was the same method used by Mahomet and the Romans to upset and despoil the world. It is that used today by the Turks and the Moors and which the Sherif is beginning to use. Therefore it is most evil, tyrannical, libelous of the sweet name of Christ, and the cause of infinite new blasphemies against the true God and the Christian religion. We have had very extensive experience with what has been done and is being done today in the Indies; because of it, the Indians consider God to be the most cruel, unjust and pitiless of gods, and consequently it impedes the conversion of many unfaithful, giving rise to the impossibility of infinite people in the new world ever to become Christians. This is, moreover, most clearly the infernal path to all the irreparable and distressing evils and damages set forth in *Proposition XI.*

Proposition XXVIII: Satan could not have invented any more effective pestilence with which to destroy the whole new world, to consume and kill off all its people and to depopulate it as such large and populous lands have been depopulated, than the inventions of the *repartimiento* and *encomiendas,*[1] by which those peoples were divided and assigned to Spaniards as if to all the devils put together, or like herds of cattle delivered to hungry wolves. (This means would have sufficed to depopulate the whole world.) By the *encomienda* or *repartimiento,* which was the cruelest form of tyranny and the one most worthy of hell-fire that could have been invented, all those peoples are prevented from receiving the Christian faith and religion, being held night and day by their wretched and tyrannical overlords, the Spaniards, in the mines, at personal

[1][A *repartimiento* was an allocation of forced Indian labor. An *encomienda* was a conferred right to Indian tribute or labor; the grantee was responsible, though often only in theory, for the Indians' catechization and welfare.]

labors and under incredible tributes; forced to carry loads one and two hundred leagues as if they were beasts or worse; and with clerics who preach the faith and give the Indians instruction and a knowledge of God persecuted and driven out of the Indian villages, leaving no witnesses to the acts of violence, cruelties and continual robberies and murders. Because of the *encomiendas* and *repartimiento* the Indians have suffered and still suffer continual tortures, thefts and injustices to their persons and to their children, women and worldly goods. Because of the *encomiendas* and *repartimiento* there have perished in the space of forty-six years (and I was present) more than fifteen million souls without faith or sacraments, and more than three thousand leagues of land have been depopulated. I have been present, as I say, and as long as these *encomiendas* last, I ask that God be a witness and judge of what I say: the power of the monarchs, even were they on the scene, will not suffice to keep all the Indians from perishing, dying off and being consumed; and in this way a thousand worlds might end, without any remedy.

From the earliest days after the discovery of the New World, women as well as men emigrated to America—as wives, daughters, servants, prostitutes, nuns. The following excerpts are from petitions to the viceroy of Mexico in the years 1540 to 1550. Evidently not all the Spanish conquerors acquired great wealth.

From *Index of Conquistadores*

The wife of Pedro Valenciano, deceased discoverer—he left a daughter—says:

That she was the wife of Pedro Garao Valenciano, deceased, conquistador of this New Spain, and that she came over to this New Spain with Pánfilo de Narváez, married to Bartolomé de Porras, who died, and she married said Pedro Valenciano; and that she has the use of one-third of the town which her husband had, which is very little, because she is poor and has her house and family and two married granddaughters, and she is sick and aged; and that she is a native of Ecija, and the daughter of Pero Núñez Mancheño and Catalina de Cerrana. (1: 103)

Isabel de Ojeda does not say

Where she comes from nor whose daughter she is, and says that she was the wife of Antonio de Villaroel, who came over with Pedrarias to the Mainland, and from there he came to Cuba with Diego Valázquez, and from there he came over to New Spain, with the Marquis, with whom he took part in all the conquests of it and of Michoacán and Panuco and Jalisco, for which he was never compensated; and that she was left with a twenty-thousand-peso debt, and that she has in her house nieces and poor maidens yet to be married, and not having the means, has not married them; and out of the need to provide for them, she is in want, and that he was a gentleman and alderman of this city. (1: 106–07)

Ana de Segura, the wife of Jerónimo Tría; he has gone to Spain and left a son in this land, married to a daughter of Montaño, the conquistador; she says

From J. F. Maura, *Women in the Conquest of the Americas*, J. F. Deredita, trans. (New York: Peter Lang, 1997), pp. 206–207.

That she is a resident of this city, and a native of Seville, and the legitimate daughter of Francisco de Segura, notary public of said city, and of Antonia Maldonada, and that she is the wife of Jerónimo Tría, and first she was the wife of Diego Remón, who died, and she married Juan Catalán, one of the first conquistadores of this New Spain, for which he was given half of the town of Taualilpa in encomienda, and on the death of her said husband, it was taken from her, for which the Marquis [Cortés], seeing that she was poor, gave her the Tlamaco farm, a very small thing, the warrant for which she says she is presenting; and that later she married Jerónimo Tría, and that she is laden down with sons and daughters, and is in want, and has had and has her house full of her family, and she is presenting the copy of the warrant which she has for the town. (1: 108–09)

Exploration and Anthropology

Europeans were fascinated by the discovery of new peoples whose lifestyles were so sharply different from their own. Sometimes comments on exotic customs led on to ironical reflections on contrasting European practices. Here the French essayist Michel Montaigne (1533–1592) writes about the Indians of South America.

From Montaigne. *Of Cannibals*

These nations, then, seem to me barbarous in this sense, that they have been fashioned very little by the human mind, and are still very close to their original naturalness. The laws of nature still rule them, very little corrupted by ours; and they are in such a state of purity that I am sometimes vexed that they were unknown earlier, in the days when there were men able to judge them better than we. I am sorry that Lycurgus and Plato did not know of them; for it seems to me that what we actually see in these nations surpasses not only all the pictures in which poets have idealized the golden age and all their inventions in imagining a happy state of man, but also the conceptions and the very desire of philosophy. . . .

For the rest, they live in a country with a very pleasant and temperate climate, so that according to my witnesses it is rare to see a sick man there; and they have assured me that they never saw one palsied, bleary-eyed, toothless, or bent with age. They are settled along the sea and shut in on the land side by great high mountains, with a stretch about a hundred leagues wide in between. They have a great abundance of fish and flesh which bear no resemblance to ours, and they eat them with no other artifice than cooking.

They have their wars with the nations beyond the mountains, further inland, to which they go quite naked, with no other arms than bows or wooden swords

Excerpted from *The Complete Essays of Montaigne*, translated by Donald M. Frame with the permission of the publishers, Stanford University Press. © 1958 by the Board of Trustees of the Leland Stanford Junior University.

ending in a sharp point, in the manner of the tongues of our boar spears. It is astonishing what firmness they show in their combats, which never end but in slaughter and bloodshed; for as to routs and terror, they know nothing of either.

Each man brings back as his trophy the head of the enemy he has killed, and sets it up at the entrance to his dwelling. After they have treated their prisoners well for a long time with all the hospitality they can think of, each man who has a prisoner calls a great assembly of his acquaintances. He ties a rope to one of the prisoner's arms by the end of which he holds him, a few steps away, for fear of being hurt, and gives his dearest friend the other arm to hold in the same way; and these two, in the presence of the whole assembly, kill him with their swords. This done, they roast him and eat him in common and send some pieces to their absent friends. This is not, as people think, for nourishment, as of old the Scythians used to do; it is to betoken an extreme revenge. And the proof of this came when they saw the Portuguese, who had joined forces with their adversaries, inflict a different kind of death on them when they took them prisoner, which was to bury them up to the waist, shoot the rest of their body full of arrows, and afterward hang them. They thought that these people from the other world, being men who had sown the knowledge of many vices among their neighbors and were much greater masters than themselves in every sort of wickedness, did not adopt this sort of vengeance without some reason, and that it must be more painful than their own; so they began to give up their old method and to follow this one.

I am not sorry that we notice the barbarous horror of such acts, but I am heartily sorry that, judging their faults rightly, we should be so blind to our own. I think there is more barbarity in eating a man alive than in eating him dead; and in tearing by tortures and the rack a body still full of feeling, in roasting a man bit by bit, in having him bitten and mangled by dogs and swine (as we have not only read but seen within fresh memory, not among ancient enemies, but among neighbors and fellow citizens, and what is worse, on the pretext of piety and religion), than in roasting and eating him after he is dead. . . .

So we may well call these people barbarians, in respect to the rules of reason, but not in respect to ourselves, who surpass them in every kind of barbarity.

Their warfare is wholly noble and generous, and as excusable and beautiful as this human disease can be; its only basis among them is their rivalry in valor. They are not fighting for the conquest of new lands, for they still enjoy that natural abundance that provides them without toil and trouble with all necessary things in such profusion that they have no wish to enlarge their boundaries. They are still in that happy state of desiring only as much as their natural needs demand; anything beyond that is superfluous to them. . . . Truly here are real savages by our standards; for either they must be thoroughly so, or we must be; there is an amazing distance between their character and ours.

The men there have several wives, and the higher their reputation for valor the more wives they have. It is a remarkably beautiful thing about their marriages that the same jealousy our wives have to keep us from the affection and kindness of other women, theirs have to win this for them. Being more concerned for their husbands' honor than for anything else, they strive and scheme to have as many companions as they can, since that is a sign of their husbands' valor.

Our wives will cry "Miracle!" but it is no miracle. It is a properly matrimonial virtue, but one of the highest order. In the Bible, Leah, Rachel, Sarah, and Jacob's wives gave their beautiful handmaids to their husbands; and Livia seconded the appetites of Augustus, to her own disadvantage; and Stratonice, the wife of King Deiotarus, not only lent her husband for his use a very beautiful young chambermaid in her service, but carefully brought up her children, and backed them up to succeed to their father's estates. . . .

Three of these men, ignorant of the price they will pay some day, in loss of repose and happiness, for gaining knowledge of the corruptions of this side of the ocean; ignorant also of the fact that of this intercourse will come their ruin (which I suppose is already well advanced: poor wretches, to let themselves be tricked by the desire for new things, and to have left the serenity of their own sky to come and see ours!)—three of these men were at Rouen, at the time the late King Charles IX was there. The king talked to them for a long time; they were shown our ways, our splendor, the aspect of a fine city. After that, someone asked their opinion, and wanted to know what they had found most amazing. They mentioned three things, of which I have forgotten the third, and I am very sorry for it; but I still remember two of them. They said that in the first place they thought it very strange that so many grown men, bearded, strong, and armed, who were around the king (it is likely that they were talking about the Swiss of his guard) should submit to obey a child, and that one of them was not chosen to command instead. Second (they have a way in their language of speaking of men as halves of one another), they had noticed that there were among us men full and gorged with all sorts of good things, and that their other halves were beggars at their doors, emaciated with hunger and poverty; and they thought it strange that these needy halves could endure such an injustice, and did not take the others by the throat, or set fire to their houses. . . .

All this is not too bad—but what's the use? They don't wear breeches.

SCIENTIFIC METHOD

Bacon on Empiricism

Francis Bacon (1561–1626) called for a new approach to scientific discovery. What method did he advocate?

From *The Great Instauration*

There is none who has dwelt upon experience and the facts of nature as long as is necessary. . . . For all those who before me have applied themselves to the invention of arts have but cast a glance or two upon facts and examples and ex-

From *The Great Instauration* in *The Works of Francis Bacon*, J. Spedding, R. L. Ellis, and D. D. Heath, eds. (Boston, Mass.: Taggard and Thompson, 1863), Vol. 8, pp. 31–34, 44–47, 53.

perience, and straightway proceeded, as if invention were nothing more than an exercise of thought, to invoke their own spirits to give them oracles. I, on the contrary, dwelling purely and constantly among the facts of nature, withdraw my intellect from them no further than may suffice to let the images and rays of natural objects meet in a point, as they do in the sense of vision. . . . And by these means I suppose that I have established for ever a true and lawful marriage between the empirical and the rational faculty, the unkind and ill-starred divorce and separation of which has thrown into confusion all the affairs of the human family. . . . I have sought on all sides diligently and faithfully to provide helps for the sense—substitutes to supply its failures, rectifications to correct its errors; and this I endeavour to accomplish not so much by instruments as by experiments. For the subtlety of experiments is far greater than that of the sense itself, even when assisted by exquisite instruments; such experiments, I mean, as are skilfully and artificially devised for the express purpose of determining the point in question. To the immediate and proper perception of the sense therefore I do not give much weight; but I contrive that the office of the sense shall be only to judge of the experiment, and that the experiment itself shall judge of the thing.

But I design not only to indicate and mark out the ways, but also to enter them. And therefore the third part of the work embraces the Phenomena of the Universe; that is to say, experience of every kind, and such a natural history as may serve for a foundation to build philosophy upon. For a good method of demonstration or form of interpreting nature may keep the mind from going astray or stumbling, but it is not any excellence of method that can supply it with the material of knowledge. Those however who aspire not to guess and divine, but to discover and know; who propose not to devise mimic and fabulous worlds of their own, but to examine and dissect the nature of this very world itself; must go to facts themselves for everything. Nor can the place of this labour and search and worldwide perambulation be supplied by any genius or meditation or argumentation; no, not if all men's wits could meet in one. This therefore we must have, or the business must be for ever abandoned. But up to this day such has been the condition of men in this matter, that it is no wonder if nature will not give herself into their hands. . . .

I have made a beginning of the work—a beginning, as I hope, not unimportant:—the fortune of the human race will give the issue;—such an issue, it may be, as in the present condition of things and men's minds cannot easily be conceived or imagined. For the matter in hand is no mere felicity of speculation, but the real business and fortunes of the human race, and all power of operation. For man is but the servant and interpreter of nature: what he does and what he knows is only what he has observed of nature's order in fact or in thought; beyond this he knows nothing and can do nothing. For the chain of causes cannot by any force be loosed or broken, nor can nature be commanded except by being obeyed. And so those twin objects, human Knowledge and human Power, do really meet in one; and it is from ignorance of causes that operation fails.

Descartes on Deduction

René Descartes (1596–1650) was troubled by a revival in his own day of ancient Greek skepticism, the idea that the human mind could not attain any true knowledge of reality. So Descartes sought for a first principle that was absolutely irrefutable as the starting point of his philosophy. What principle did he discover? How did his methodology differ from Bacon's?

From *Discourse on Method*

As a multitude of laws often only hampers justice, so that a state is best governed when, with few laws, these are rigidly administered; in like manner, instead of the great number of precepts of which Logic is composed, I believed that the four following would prove perfectly sufficient for me, provided I took the firm and unwavering resolution never in a single instance to fail in observing them.

The *first* was never to accept anything for true which I did not clearly know to be such; that is to say, carefully to avoid precipitancy and prejudice, and to comprise nothing more in my judgment than what was presented to my mind so clearly and distinctly as to exclude all ground of doubt.

The *second*, to divide each of the difficulties under examination into as many parts as possible, and as might be necessary for its adequate solution.

The *third*, to conduct my thoughts in such order that, by commencing with objects the simplest and easiest to know, I might ascend by little and little, and, as it were, step by step, to the knowledge of the more complex; assigning in thought a certain order even to those objects which in their own nature do not stand in a relation of antecedence and sequence.

And the *last*, in every case to make enumerations so complete, and reviews so general, that I might be assured that nothing was omitted.

The long chains of simple and easy reasonings by means of which geometers are accustomed to reach the conclusions of their most difficult demonstrations, had led me to imagine that all things, to the knowledge of which man is competent, are mutually connected in the same way, and that there is nothing so far removed from us as to be beyond our reach, or so hidden that we cannot discover it, provided only we abstain from accepting the false for the true, and always preserve in our thoughts the order necessary for the deduction of one truth from another.

I had long before remarked that, in (relation to) practice, it is sometimes necessary to adopt, as if above doubt, opinions which we discern to be highly uncertain, as has been already said; but as I then desired to give my attention solely to the search after truth, I thought that a procedure exactly the opposite was called for, and that I ought to reject as absolutely false all opinions in regard to which I could suppose the least ground for doubt, in order to ascertain whether

From René Descartes, *Discourse on Method,* John Veich, trans. (Edinburgh: William Blackwod and Sons, 1873), pp. 61–62, 74–77, 83–87.

after that there remained aught in my belief that was wholly indubitable. Accordingly, seeing that our senses sometimes deceive us, I was willing to suppose that there existed nothing really such as they presented to us; and because some men err in reasoning, and fall into paralogisms, even on the simplest matters of Geometry, I, convinced that I was as open to error as any other, rejected as false all the reasonings I had hitherto taken for demonstrations; and finally, when I considered that the very same thoughts (presentations) which we experience when awake may also be experienced when we are asleep, while there is at that time not one of them true, I supposed that all the objects (presentations) that had ever entered into my mind when awake, had in them no more truth than the illusions of my dreams. But immediately upon this I observed that, whilst I thus wished to think that all was false, it was absolutely necessary that I, who thus thought, should be somewhat; and as I observed that this truth, *I think, hence I am,* was so certain and of such evidence, that no ground of doubt, however extravagant, could be alleged by the Sceptics capable of shaking it, I concluded that I might, without scruple, accept it as the first principle of the Philosophy of which I was in search.

In the next place, I attentively examined what I was, and as I observed that I could suppose that I had no body, and that there was no world nor any place in which I might be; but that I could not therefore suppose that I was not; and that, on the contrary, from the very circumstance that I thought to doubt of the truth of other things, it most clearly and certainly followed that I was; while, on the other hand, if I had only ceased to think, although all the other objects which I had ever imagined had been in reality existent, I would have had no reason to believe that I existed; I thence concluded that I was a substance whose whole essence or nature consists only in thinking, and which, that it may exist, has need of no place, nor is dependent on any material thing; so that "I," that is to say, the mind by which I am what I am, is wholly distinct from the body, and is even more easily known than the latter, and is such, that although the latter were not, it would still continue to be all that it is.

After this I inquired in general into what is essential to the truth and certainty of a proposition; for since I had discovered one which I knew to be true, I thought that I must likewise be able to discover the ground of this certitude. And as I observed that in the words *I think, hence I am,* there is nothing at all which gives me assurance of their truth beyond this, that I see very clearly that in order to think it is necessary to exist, I concluded that I might take, as a general rule, the principle, that all the things which we very clearly and distinctly conceive are true, only observing, however, that there is some difficulty in rightly determining the objects which we distinctly conceive.

In the next place, from reflecting on the circumstance that I doubted, and that consequently my being was not wholly perfect (for I clearly saw that it was a greater perfection to know than to doubt,) I was led to inquire whence I had learned to think of something more perfect than myself; and I clearly recognised that I must hold this notion from some Nature which in reality was more perfect. . . . for to receive it from nothing was a thing manifestly impossible; and, because it is not less repugnant that the more perfect should be an effect of, and dependence on the less perfect, than that something should proceed from nothing, it was equally impossible that I could hold it from myself: accordingly, it but remained that it had been placed in me by a Nature which was in reality more perfect than mine, and which even possessed within itself all the perfections of which I could form any idea; that is to say, in a single word, which was God.

SCIENTIFIC ACHIEVEMENT

Astronomy

Nicolaus Copernicus (1473–1533) noted a "defect" in the cosmologies handed down from the ancient world. The assumption that the earth was the center of the universe made it impossible to provide a wholly adequate mathematical explanation of the observed movements of the planets. This led Copernicus to formulate a radically different hypothesis.

From Copernicus. *Commentariolus*

Having become aware of these defects, I often considered whether there could perhaps be found a more reasonable arrangement of circles, from which every apparent inequality would be derived and in which everything would move uniformly about its proper center, as the rule of absolute motion requires. After I had addressed myself to this very difficult and almost insoluble problem, the suggestion at length came to me how it could be solved with fewer and much simpler constructions than were formly used, if some assumptions (which are called axioms) were granted me. They follow in this order.

Assumptions

1. There is no one center of all the celestial circles or spheres.

2. The center of the earth is not the center of the universe, but only of gravity and of the lunar sphere.

3. All the spheres revolve about the sun as their mid-point, and therefore the sun is the center of the universe.

4. The ratio of the earth's distance from the sun to the height of the firmament is so much smaller than the ratio of the earth's radius to its distance from the sun that the distance from the earth to the sun is imperceptible in comparison with the height of the firmament.

5. Whatever motion appears in the firmament arises not from any motion of the firmament but from the earth's motion. The earth together with its circumjacent elements performs a complete rotation on its fixed poles in a daily motion, while the firmament and highest heaven abide unchanged.

From "Commentariolus" in *Three Copernican Treatises*, Edward Rosen, trans. (New York: Columbia University Press, 1939), pp. 57–60.

6. What appears to us as motions of the sun arise not from its motion but from the motion of the earth and our sphere, with which we revolve about the sun like any other planet. The earth has, then, more than one motion.

7. The apparent retrograde and direct motion of the planets arises not from their motion but from the earth's. The motion of the earth alone, therefore, suffices to explain so many apparent inequalities in the heavens.

Having set forth these assumptions, I shall endeavor briefly to show how uniformity of the motions can be saved in a systematic way. However, I have thought it well, for the sake of brevity, to omit from this sketch mathematical demonstrations, reserving these for my larger work. But in the explanation of the circles I shall set down here the lengths of the radii; and from these the reader who is not unacquainted with mathematics will readily perceive how closely this arrangement of circles agrees with the numerical data and observations.

Accordingly, let no one suppose that I have gratuitously asserted, with the Pythagoreans, the motion of the earth; strong proof will be found in my exposition of the circles. For the principal arguments by which the natural philosophers attempt to establish the immobility of the earth rest for the most part on the appearances; it is particularly such arguments that collapse here, since I treat the earth's immobility as due to an appearance.

The Order of the Spheres

The celestial spheres are arranged in the following order. The highest is the immovable sphere of the fixed stars, which contains and gives position to all things. Beneath it is Saturn, which Jupiter follows, then Mars. Below Mars is the sphere on which we revolve; then Venus; last is Mercury. The lunar sphere revolves about the center of the earth and moves with the earth like an epicycle. In the same order also one planet surpasses another in speed of revolution, according as they trace greater or smaller circles. Thus Saturn completes its revolution in thirty years, Jupiter in twelve, Mars in two and one half, and the earth in one year, Venus in nine months, Mercury in three.

In ancient and medieval cosmologies the heavenly bodies were regarded as perfect spheres, made of a finer substance than the earth—more pure, more perfect, not subject to change or decay. Galileo (1564–1642) turned a telescope on the heavens and saw a different picture. What astronomical discoveries were made possible by his telescope?

From Galileo. *The Starry Messenger*

Great indeed are the things which in this brief treatise I propose for observation and consideration by all students of nature. I say great, because of the excellence of the subject itself, the entirely unexpected and novel character of these things, and finally because of the instrument by means of which they have been revealed to our senses.

Surely it is a great thing to increase the numerous host of fixed stars previously visible to the unaided vision, adding countless more which have never before been seen, exposing these plainly to the eye in numbers ten times exceeding the old and familiar stars.

It is a very beautiful thing, and most gratifying to the sight, to behold the body of the moon, distant from us almost sixty earthly radii, as if it were no farther away than two such measures—so that its diameter appears almost thirty times larger, its surface nearly nine hundred times, and its volume twenty-seven thousand times as large as when viewed with the naked eye. In this way one may learn with all the certainty of sense evidence that the moon is not robed in a smooth and polished surface but is in fact rough and uneven, covered everywhere, just like the earth's surface, with huge prominences, deep valleys, and chasms.

Again, it seems to me a matter of no small importance to have ended the dispute about the Milky Way by making its nature manifest to the very senses as well as to the intellect. Similarly it will be a pleasant and elegant thing to demonstrate that the nature of those stars which astronomers have previously called "nebulous" is far different from what has been believed hitherto.

I have observed the nature and the material of the Milky Way. With the aid of the telescope this has been scrutinized so directly and with such ocular certainty that all the disputes which have vexed philosophers through so many ages have been resolved, and we are at last freed from wordy debates about it. The galaxy is, in fact, nothing but a congeries of innumerable stars grouped together in clusters. Upon whatever part of it the telescope is directed, a vast crowd of stars is immediately presented to view. Many of them are rather large and quite bright, while the number of smaller ones is quite beyond calculation.

But it is not only in the Milky Way that whitish clouds are seen; several patches of similar aspect shine with faint light here and there throughout the aether, and if the telescope is turned upon any of these it confronts us with a tight mass of stars. And what is even more remarkable, the stars which have been called "nebulous" by every astronomer up to this time turn out to be groups of very small stars arranged in a wonderful manner. Although each star separately escapes our sight on account of its smallness or the immense distance from us, the mingling of their rays gives rise to that gleam which was formerly believed to be some denser part of the aether that was capable of reflecting rays from stars or from the sun.

But what surpasses all wonders by far, and what particularly moves us to seek the attention of all astronomers and philosophers, is the discovery of four wandering stars not known or observed by any man before us. Like Venus and Mercury, which have their own periods about the sun, these have theirs about a certain star that is conspicuous among those already known, which they sometimes precede and sometimes follow, without ever departing from it beyond certain limits.[2] All these facts were discovered and observed by me not many days ago with the aid of a spyglass which I devised, after first being illuminated by

---

[2]Galileo refers here to his discovery of the four moons of Jupiter.

divine grace. Perhaps other things, still more remarkable, will in time be discovered by me or by other observers with the aid of such an instrument. . . .

Galileo's observations convinced him that Copernicus's heliocentric theory was true, not just as a mathematical hypothesis but as a description of actual physical reality. His assertion of this position led to a conflict with the church. Why were Galileo's views considered heretical? How did he seek to refute his critics?

From Galileo. *Letter to the Grand Duchess Christina*

Some years ago, as Your Serene Highness well knows, I discovered in the heavens many things that had not been seen before our own age. The novelty of these things, as well as some consequences which followed from them in contradiction to the physical notions commonly held among academic philosophers, stirred up against me no small number of professors—as if I had placed these things in the sky with my own hands in order to upset nature and overturn the sciences. They seemed to forget that the increase of known truths stimulates the investigation, establishment, and growth of the arts; not their diminution or destruction.

Showing a greater fondness for their own opinions than for truth, they sought to deny and disprove the new things which, if they had cared to look for themselves, their own senses would have demonstrated to them. To this end they hurled various charges and published numerous writings filled with vain arguments, and they made the grave mistake of sprinkling these with passages taken from places in the Bible which they had failed to understand properly, and which were ill suited to their purposes. . . .

The reason produced for condemning the opinion that the earth moves and the sun stands still is that in many places in the Bible one may read that the sun moves and the earth stands still. Since the Bible cannot err, it follows as a necessary consequence that anyone takes an erroneous and heretical position who maintains that the sun is inherently motionless and the earth movable.

With regard to this argument, I think in the first place that it is very pious to say and prudent to affirm that the holy Bible can never speak untruth—whenever its true meaning is understood. But I believe nobody will deny that it is often very abstruse, and may say things which are quite different from what its bare words signify. Hence in expounding the Bible if one were always to confine oneself to the unadorned grammatical meaning, one might fall into error. Not only contradictions and propositions far from true might thus be made to appear in the Bible, but even grave heresies and follies. Thus it would be necessary to assign to God feet, hands, and eyes, as well as corporeal and human affections, such as anger, repentance, hatred, and sometimes even the forgetting of things past and ignorance of those to come. These propositions uttered by the

Holy Ghost were set down in that manner by the sacred scribes in order to accommodate them to the capacities of the common people, who are rude and unlearned. . . .

Hence I think that I may reasonably conclude that whenever the Bible has occasion to speak of any physical conclusion (especially those which are very abstruse and hard to understand), the rule has been observed of avoiding confusion in the minds of the common people. . . . Who, then, would positively declare that this principle has been set aside, and the Bible has confined itself rigorously to the bare and restricted sense of its words, when speaking but casually of the earth, of water, of the sun, or of any other created thing? Especially in view of the fact that these things in no way concern the primary purpose of the sacred writings, which is the service of God and the salvation of souls—matters infinitely beyond the comprehension of the common people.

This being granted, I think that in discussions of physical problems we ought to begin not from the authority of scriptural passages, but from sense-experiences and necessary demonstrations; for the holy Bible and the phenomena of nature proceed alike from the divine Word. . . . For that reason it appears that nothing physical which sense-experience sets before our eyes, or which necessary demonstrations prove to us, ought to be called in question (much less condemned) upon the testimony of biblical passages which may have some different meaning beneath their words. . . .

Let us grant then that theology is conversant with the loftiest divine contemplation, and occupies the regal throne among sciences by dignity. But acquiring the highest authority in this way, if she does not descend to the lower and humbler speculations of the subordinate sciences and has no regard for them because they are not concerned with blessedness, then her professors should not arrogate to themselves the authority to decide on controversies in professions which they have neither studied not practiced. Why, this would be as if an absolute despot, being neither a physician nor an architect but knowing himself free to command, should undertake to administer medicines and erect buildings according to his whim—at grave peril of his poor patients' lives, and the speedy collapse of his edifices.

Synthesis

Isaac Newton (1642–1727) succeeded in explaining a great mass of observed phenomena by postulating a few simple laws. (A contemporary poet, Alexander Pope, wrote, "Nature and nature's laws lay hid in night/God said 'Let Newton be' and all was light.")

From *Newton's Principia*

We offer this work as the mathematical principles of philosophy; for all the difficulty of philosophy seems to consist in this—from the phænomena of motions to investigate the forces of nature, and then from these forces to demonstrate the other phænomena; and to this end the general propositions in the first and second book are directed. In the third book we give an example of this in the explication of the System of the World; for by the propositions mathematically demonstrated in the former books, we in the third derive from the celestial phænomena the forces of gravity with which bodies tend to the sun and the several planets. Then from these forces, by other propositions which are also mathematical, we deduce the motions of the planets, the comets, the moon, and the sea. I wish we could derive the rest of the phænomena of nature by the same kind of reasoning from mechanical principles; for I am induced by many reasons to suspect that they may all depend upon certain forces by which the particles of bodies, by some causes hitherto unknown, are either mutually impelled towards each other, and cohere in regular figures, or are repelled and recede from each other; which forces being unknown, philosophers have hitherto attempted the search of nature in vain; but I hope the principles here laid down will afford some light either to this or some truer method of philosophy. . . .

Rules of Reasoning in Philosophy

Rule I. *We are to admit no more causes of natural things than such as are both true and sufficient to explain their appearances.*

To this purpose the philosophers say that Nature does nothing in vain, and more is in vain when less will serve; for Nature is pleased with simplicity, and affects not the pomp of superfluous causes.

Rule II. *Therefore to the same natural effects we must, as far as possible, assign the same causes.*

As to respiration in a man and in a beast; the descent of stones in Europe and in America; the light of our culinary fire and of the sun; the reflection of light in the earth, and in the planets.

Rule III. *The qualities of bodies, which admit neither intension nor remission of degrees, and which are found to belong to all bodies within the reach of our experiments, are to be esteemed the universal qualities of all bodies whatsoever.*

For since the qualities of bodies are only known to us by experiments, we are to hold for universal all such as universally agree with experiments and such as are not liable to diminution can never be quite taken away. We are certainly not to relinquish the evidence of experiments for the sake of dreams and vain fictions of our own devising; nor are we to recede from the analogy of Nature, which uses to be simple, and always consonant to itself. We no other way know the extension of bodies than by our senses, nor do these reach it in all bodies; but because we perceive extension in all that are sensible, therefore we ascribe it universally to all others also. That abundance of bodies are hard, we learn by experience; and because the hardness of the whole arises from the hardness of the parts, we therefore justly infer the hardness of the undivided particles not only of the bodies we feel but of all others. That all bodies are impenetrable, we gather not from reason, but from sensation. The bodies which we handle we find

From *Sir Issac Newton's Mathematical Principles of Natural Science*, Andrew Motte, trans., revised by Florence Cajori (Berkeley, CA: University of California Press, 1934), pp 398–400, 13–14. Reprinted by permission.

impenetrable, and thence conclude impenetrability to be an universal property of all bodies whatsoever.

Lastly, if it universally appears, by experiments and astronomical observations, that all bodies about the earth gravitate towards the earth, and that in proportion to the quantity of matter which they severally contain; that the moon likewise, according to the quantity of its matter, gravitates towards the earth; that, on the other hand, our sea gravitates towards the moon; and all the planets mutually one towards another; and the comets in like manner towards the sun; we must, in consequence of this rule, universally allow that all bodies whatsoever are endowed with a principle of mutual gravitation. For the argument from the appearances concludes with more force for the universal gravitation of all bodies than for their impenetrability; of which, among those in the celestial regions, we have no experiments, nor any manner of observation. Not that I affirm gravity to be essential to bodies: by their *vis insita* [inherent force] I mean nothing but their *vis inertiæ* [force of inertia]. This is immutable. Their gravity is diminished as they recede from the earth.

Rule IV. *In experimental philosophy we are to look upon propositions collected by general induction from phænomena as accurately or very nearly true, notwithstanding any contrary hypotheses that may be imagined, till such time as other phænomena occur, by which they may either be made more accurate, or liable to exceptions.*

This rule must follow, that the argument of induction may not be evaded by hypotheses.

The Laws of Motion

Law I: *Every body continues in its state of rest, or of uniform motion, in a right line, unless it is compelled to change that state by forces impressed upon it.*

Projectiles continue in their motions, so far as they are not retarded by the resistance of the air, or impelled downwards by the force of gravity. A top, whose parts by their cohesion are continually drawn aside from rectilinear motions, does not cease its rotation, otherwise than as it is retarded by the air. The greater bodies of the planets and comets, meeting with less resistance in freer spaces, preserve their motions both progressive and circular for a much longer time.

Law II: The change of motion is proportional to the motive force impressed; and is made in the direction of the right line in which that force is impressed.

If any force generates a motion, a double force will generate double the motion, a triple force triple the motion, whether that force be impressed altogether and at once or gradually and successively. And this motion (being always directed the same way with the generating force), if the body moved before, is added to or subtracted from the former motion, according as they directly conspire with or are directly contrary to each other; or obliquely joined, when they are oblique, so as to produce a new motion compounded from the determination of both.

Law III: *To every action there is always opposed an equal reaction: or, the mutual actions of two bodies upon each other are always equal, and directed to contrary parts.*

Whatever draws or presses another is as much drawn or pressed by that other. If you press a stone with your finger, the finger is also pressed by the stone. If a horse draws a stone tied to a rope, the horse (if I may say so) will be equally drawn back towards the stone; for the distended rope, by the same endeavor to relax or unbend itself, will draw the horse as much towards the stone as it does the stone towards the horse, and will obstruct the progress of the one as much as it advances that of the other. If a body impinge upon another, and by its force change the motion of the other, that body also (because of the equality of the mutual pressure) will undergo an equal change, in its own motion, towards the contrary part. The changes made by these actions are equal, not in the velocities but in the motions of the bodies; that is to say, if the bodies are not hindered by any other impediments. For, because the motions are equally changed, the changes of the velocities made toward contrary parts are inversely proportional to the bodies.

Advances in the sciences led Jean Bodin (1530–1596) to a new comparison of ancient and modern achievements. How did he evaluate them?

From *Bodin's Methodus*

Once there was a golden age, afterwards a silver, then a bronze, and then an iron. At length clay followed. But this opinion must be adjusted, for if anyone examines the meaning of historians, not of poets, certainly he will decide that there is a change in human affairs similar to that in the nature of all things; nor is there anything new under the sun, as that sage master of wisdom says. The age which they call "golden," if it be compared with ours, would seem but iron. . . .

Some one will say, however, that the ancients were inventors of the arts and to them the glory ought to go. They certainly did discover many things—especially the power of the celestial bodies, the calculated courses of many stars—but yet not all—the wonderful trajections of fixed stars and of those called "planets." Then they noted carefully the obscurities of nature and explained many things accurately, and yet they left incomplete many of these things which have been completed and handed down to posterity by men of our time. No one, looking closely into this matter, can doubt that the discoveries of our men ought to be compared with the discoveries of our elders; many ought to be placed first. Although nothing is more remarkable in the whole nature of things than the magnet, yet the ancients were not aware of its use, clearly divine, and whereas they lived entirely within the Mediterranean basin, our men, on the other hand, traverse the whole earth every year in frequent voyages and lead colonies into another world, as I might say, in order to open up the farthest recesses of India. Not only has this discovery developed an abundant and profitable commerce (which formerly was insignificant or not well known) but also all men surprisingly work together in a world state, as if in one and the same city-state. Indeed, in geography, one of the most excellent arts, one may understand how much advance has been made from the fact that information about

From John Bodin, *Method for the Easy Comprehension of History,* Beatrice Reynolds, trans. (New York: Columbia University Press, 1945), pp. 296, 301–302.

India which used to seem fabulous to many (for Lactantius and Augustine said that men who believed in the antipodes were crazy) have been verified by us, as well as the motion of the fixed stars and the trepidation of the great sphere. Moreover, what is more remarkable than that abstraction and separation of forms from matter (if I may speak thus)? From this the hidden secrets of nature are revealed; hence healthful medicines are daily brought forward. I pass over the method of investigating celestial-longitude from equal hours, which could not be calculated by the ancients from the normal to the ecliptic without great error. I will not dwell upon the catapults of our ancestors and the ancient engines of war, which, of course, seem like some boyish toy if compared with our [instruments]. I omit finally countless arts, both handicraft and weaving, with which the life of man has been aided in a remarkable way. Printing alone can easily vie with all the discoveries of all the ancients.

So they who say that all things were understood by the ancients err not less than do those who deny them the early conquest of many arts. Nature has countless treasures of knowledge which cannot be exhausted in any age. Since these things are so and since by some eternal law of nature the path of change seems to go in a circle, so that vices press upon virtues, ignorance upon knowledge, base upon honorable, and darkness upon light, they are mistaken who think that the race of men always deteriorates.

WITCHCRAFT—SUPERSTITION AND PERSECUTION

The Prevalence of Witches

Jean Bodin was a sophisticated intellectual, a distinguished political theorist and historian, but—like many of his contemporaries—he was a firm believer in the evil machinations of witches. Why were witches so feared? What were they specifically accused of? Why were most of the accused women? How was their guilt established?

From *Bodin's Demonology*

But those greatly err who think that penalties are established only to punish crime. I hold that this is the least of the fruits which accrue therefrom to the state. For the greatest and the chief is the appeasing of the wrath of God, especially if the crime is directly against the majesty of God, as is this one. . . . Now, if there is any means to appease the wrath of God, to gain his blessing, to strike awe into some by the punishment of others, to preserve some from being infected by others, to diminish the number of evil-doers, to make secure the life of the well-disposed, and to punish the most detestable crimes of which the human mind can conceive, it is to punish with the utmost rigor the witches. . . . Now, it is not within the power of princes to pardon a crime which the law of God punishes with the penalty of death—such as are the crimes of witches. Moreover,

From *De la Démonomanie des Sorciers*, G. L. Burr, trans. in *University of Pennsylvania Translations and Reprints* (Philadelphia: University of Pennsylvania Press, 1897), Vol. 3, No. 4, pp. 5–6.

princes do gravely insult God in pardoning such horrible crimes committed directly against his majesty, seeing that the pettiest prince avenges with death insults against himself. Those too who let the witches escape, or who do not punish them with the utmost rigor, may rest assured that they will be abandoned by God to the mercy of the witches. And the country which shall tolerate this will be scourged with pestilences, famines, and wars; and those which shall take vengeance on the witches will be blessed by him and will make his anger to cease. Therefore it is that one accused of being a witch ought never to be fully acquitted and set free unless the calumny of the accuser is clearer than the sun, inasmuch as the proof of such crimes is so obscure and so difficult that not one witch in a million would be accused or punished if the procedure were governed by the ordinary rules.

The Frailty of Women

In 1486 two Dominicans published the Malleus Maleficiarum, *a sort of handbook for inquisitors of women witches.*

From *The Hammer of Witches*

Why Superstition is Chiefly Found in Women.

As for the first question, why a greater number of witches is found in the fragile feminine sex than among men; it is indeed a fact that it were idle to contradict, since it is accredited by actual experience, apart from the verbal testimony of credible witnesses. And without in any way detracting from a sex in which God has always taken great glory that His might should be spread abroad, let us say that various men have assigned various reasons for this fact, which nevertheless agree in principle. Wherefore it is good for the admonition of women, to speak of this matter; and it has often been proved by experience that they are eager to hear of it, so long as it is set forth with discretion.

For some learned men propound this reason; that there are three things in nature, the Tongue, an Ecclesiastic, and a Woman, which know no moderation in goodness or vice; and when they exceed the bounds of their condition they reach the greatest heights and the lowest depths of goodness and vice. . . .

Others again have propounded other reasons why there are more superstitious women found than men. And the first is, that they are more credulous; and since the chief aim of the devil is to corrupt faith, therefore he rather attacks them. See *Ecclesiasticus* xix: He that is quick to believe is light-minded, and shall be diminished. The second reason is, that women are naturally more impressionable, and more ready to receive the influence of a disembodied spirit; and that when they use this quality well they are very good, but when they use it ill they are very evil.

The third reason is that they have slippery tongues, and are unable to conceal from their fellow-women those things which by evil arts they know, and,

From *Malleus Maleficiarum*, M. Summers, trans. (London: John Rodker, 1928), pp. 41–44.

since they are weak, they find an easy and secret manner of vindicating themselves by witchcraft. See *Ecclesiasticus* as quoted above: I had rather dwell with a lion and a dragon than to keep house with a wicked woman. All wickedness is but little to the wickedness of a woman. And to this may be added that, as they are very impressionable, they act accordingly.

There are also others who bring forward yet other reasons, of which preachers should be very careful how they make use. For it is true that in the Old Testament the Scriptures have much that is evil to say about women, and this because of the first temptress, Eve, and her imitators; yet afterwards in the New Testament we find a change of name, as from Eva to Ave (as S. Jerome says), and the whole sin of Eve taken away by the benediction of Mary. Therefore preachers should always say as much praise of them as possible.

But because in these times this perfidy is more often found in women than in men, as we learn by actual experience, if anyone is curious as to the reason, we may add to what has already been said the following: that since they are feebler both in mind and body, it is not surprising that they should come more under the spell of witchcraft.

During the centuries of persecution many thousands of persons in many parts of Europe—most of them women—confessed to offenses like the following ones. Often the confessions were made under torture; sometimes they were given voluntarily.

Francoise Secretain confessed in 1598 under threat of torture after having been accused by an eight-year-old child, Loyse Maillat. (Françoise was condemned to death by burning but died in prison before the sentence was carried out.)

Confession of Françoise Secretain (1598)

First, that she had wished five devils on Loyse Maillat.

Second, that she had long since given herself to the Devil, who at that time had the likeness of a big black man.

Third, that the Devil had four or five times known her carnally, in the form sometimes of a dog, sometimes of a cat, and sometimes of a fowl; and that his semen was very cold.

Fourth, that she had countless times been to the Sabbat and assembly of witches near the village of Coyrieres in a place called Combes by the water; and that she went there on a white staff which she placed between her legs.

Fifth, that at the Sabbat she had danced, and had beaten water to cause hail.

Sixth, that she and Groz-Jacques Bocquet had caused Loys Monneret to die by making her eat a piece of bread which they had dusted with a powder given to them by the Devil.

Seventh, that she had caused several cows to die, and that she did so by touching them with her hand or with a wand while saying certain words.

Another example comes from sixteenth-century Scotland.

From Henry Boguet, *An Examen of Witches*, M. Summers, ed. (London: John Rodker, 1929), p. 5.

Trial of Geillis Duncane (1591)

Within the towne of Trenent, in the kingdome of Scotland, there dwelleth one David Seaton, who, being deputie bailiffe in the said towne, had a maid called Geillis Duncane, who used secretlie to absent and lie forth of hir maister's house every other night: This Geillis Duncane tooke in hand all such as were troubled or grieved with anie kinde of sicknes or infirmitie, and in short space did perfourme many matters most miraculous; which things, for asmuche as she began to do them upon a sodaine, having never done the like before, made her maister and others to be in great admiration, and wondered thereat: by meanes whereof, the saide David Seaton had his maide in great suspition that shee did not those things by naturall and lawfull waies, but rather supposed it to bee done by some extraordinarie and unlawfull meanes. Whereupon, her maister began to grow verie inquisitive, and examined hir which way and by what meanes shee was able to performe matters of so great importance; whereat shee gave him no aunswere: nevertheless, her maister, to the intent that hee might the better trie and finde out the truth of the same, did with the help of others torment her with the torture of the pilliwinkles[3] upon her fingers, which is a grievous torture; and binding or wrinching her head with a cord or roape, which is a most cruell torment also; yet would she not confess anie thing; whereuppon, they suspecting that she had beene marked by the Devill (as commonly witches are), made diligent search about her, and found the enemies mark to be in her fore crag, or fore part of her throate; which being found, she confessed that al her doings was done by the wicked allurements and entisements of the Devil, and that she did them by witchcraft. After this her confession, she was committed to prison, where shee continued a season, where immediately shee accused these persons following to bee notorious witches, and caused them forthwith to be apprehended, one after another, viz. Agnes Sampson the eldest witche of them all, dwelling in Haddington; Agnes Tompson of Edenbrough; Doctor Fian alias John Cuningham, master of the schoole at Saltpans in Lowthian, of whose life and strange acts you shal heare more largely in the end of this discourse. These were by the saide Geillis Duncane accused, as also George Motts wife, dwelling in Lowthian; Robert Grierson, skipper; and Jannet Blandilands; with the potter's wife of Seaton: the smith at the Brigge Hallis, with innumerable others in those parts, and dwelling in those bounds aforesaid; of whom some are alreadie executed, the rest remaine in prison to receive the doome of judgement at the Kinges Majesties will and pleasure.

From *Pitcairn's Criminal Trials in Scotland* in G. L. Burr, *University of Pennsylvania Translations and Reprints* (Philadelphia: University of Pennsylvania Press, 1897), Vol. 3, No. 4, pp. 19–20.
[3] An instrument of torture similar to the thumbscrews later in use.

PART THIRTEEN

THE SEARCH FOR ORDER—
ABSOLUTISM
AND ARISTOCRACY

The seventeenth century was a time of great intellectual vitality but also of much political instability. Frequent wars caused widespread devastation. A perceptible worsening of climatic conditions, marked by colder and wetter summers, led to a series of bad harvests and recurring famines. The economic expansion of the sixteenth century came to a halt. In many countries peasant uprisings or aristocratic rebellions occurred.

In these circumstances there was a widely felt need for stability and order. One consequence was that theories of royal absolutism became popular among political thinkers. These theories ranged from the severely rationalist arguments of Thomas Hobbes to various religious doctrines of divine right and patriarchal authority. (Modern political philosophers are usually most impressed by the rationalist arguments, but seventeenth-century people usually found the religious ones more simple and satisfying.)

During the reign of Louis XIV (1643–1715), France became the model of a centralized, absolute monarchy. Royal authority was supported by a large army, a loyal church, and a network of local government officials who were closely supervised by the central government. Louis coped with the problem of an unruly aristocracy by inducing many French nobles to take up residence in the great palace he built at Versailles and to pass their days in the intricate ritual of court life that grew up there. The king's great finance minister, Jean Colbert—following the common "mercantilist" doctrine of the seventeenth century—aimed to enhance France's wealth and power by increasing the country's manufactures and reducing dependence on imports from abroad. For a time it seemed that France might dominate all western Europe.

Meanwhile, in eastern Europe, two other absolutist states experienced changing fortunes. The Turks, who throughout the seventeenth century had threatened to invade the Christian lands of the west, were finally defeated at Vienna in 1683. And Russia took the first major steps toward westernization under Peter the Great. These events helped to shape the course of European history in the modern world.

SOCIAL CONDITIONS

Germany

*The combination of crop failures and destructive wars caused severe hardships for peo-
ple in many parts of Europe. Conditions were probably worst of all in Germany during
the Thirty Years' War from 1618 to 1648. Jacob von Grimmelshausen, who served as a
soldier in the war, wrote a picaresque novel about the adventures of a "Simpleton" in
those grim times.*

From *Simplicissimus*

The Fate of a Farm

When these horsemen took over my father's smoky house, the first thing
they did was to bring in their horses; then each one started to destroy everything
and tear everything to pieces. Some were killing the cattle, and broiling or roasting the carcasses; others were going through the house, determined not to miss
any thing good there might be for them to find; even the privy was not safe from
their investigations, as if we had hidden there Jason's Golden Fleece. Others
were making great bundles of linen and clothes and all sorts of stuff, as if they
were going to open a flea market someplace, and what they weren't going to
carry away with them they pulled to pieces. Some shoved their swords through
the piles of straw or hay as if they hadn't had enough pigs to kill; others shook
the feathers out of the mattresses and filled them with bacon and salt meat and
other things as if they expected to sleep on them better that way. Others were
breaking down the stoves and the window panes, as if they thought that summer was going to last forever. They were smashing the tableware and carrying
away with them these useless pieces of copper or pottery or pewter. They burnt
beds, and the tables, and the chairs, and the benches, when they could have
found plenty of dry fire-wood in the yard. Of pots and of pans they shattered
the lot; either because they didn't want to eat anything but roast meat any more,
or because they only planned to stay with us for one single meal. Our maid underwent such treatment in the stables that she could hardly walk coming out. Is
it not shameful to have such things happening? As for the groom, they laid him
on the ground, they put a funnel into his mouth, and they poured in a whole
tubful of foul matter. They called this "a little drink in the Swedish manner"; but
he didn't find it at all to his taste. They also forced him to guide them on another
raid, where they captured both people and cattle whom they brought into our
yard. Among them they got my father, and my mother, and my sister Ursula.

Then they started to take the flints out of the cocks of the pistols in order to
use them as thumbscrews, and to torture the poor beggars as if they were sor-

From Jacob von Grimmelshausen, *Simplicissimus* (1669), trans. Eugen Weber in *The Western
Tradition*, 2nd ed., Vol. II, pp. 392–393, by Eugen Weber. Copyright © 1965 by D. C. Heath and
Company. Reprinted by permission of the publisher.

cerers who needed to be punished before being burnt. As a matter of fact, the soldiers had already shoved one of the captured peasants into the oven and they were trying to keep him warm in there (so he would tell them the hiding place of his little hoard). They had tied a cord around the head of another, and they were tightening the cord with a garrot, so that with every turn they gave it, the blood gushed out of his mouth, his nose and his ears. In short, each man was busy working out some new kind of torture for the peasants and so each victim had his own particular kind of torment.

However it seemed to me at the time that my father was the luckiest of them all, because he admitted with roars of laughter what the others were forced to reveal in the midst of sufferings and fearful plaints.

This kind of honor was his, no doubt, because he was the head of the family. The soldiers put him before a great fire, they tied him so that he couldn't move his arms or his legs, and they rubbed the soles of his feet with damp salt; then they had our old goat lick it off. He was so tickled by this that he nearly died of laughter. It all seemed to me so pleasant and so silly—I had never seen nor heard my father laugh so long—that, either because his laughter was contagious, or else because I couldn't understand what was going on, I had to laugh too. That is how my father told the raiders what they wanted to know, and revealed the hiding place of his treasure which consisted of gold and pearls and jewels; a much richer hoard than one would have expected a peasant to own.

I cannot say anything about the treatment of the women, the maids, and the young girls who had been captured, because the soldiers didn't let me see what they were doing to them. I know only that one heard sighs and groans in various corners, and I thought that my mother and my sister Ursula were probably no better off than the others.

France

From *Letters of the Abbess of Port-Royal*

(*1649*) This poor country is a horrible sight; it is stripped of everything. The soldiers take possession of the farms and have the corn threshed, but will not give a single grain to the owners who beg it as an alms. It is impossible to plough. There are no more horses—all have been carried off. The peasants are reduced to sleeping in the woods and are thankful to have them as a refuge from murderers. And if they only had enough bread to half satisfy their hunger, they would indeed count themselves happy.

(*1652*) People massacre each other daily with every sort of cruelty. . . . The soldiers steal from one another when they have denuded every one else, and as

From the translations in Cecile Augon, *Social France in the XVII Century* (London: Methuen and Co. Ltd., 1911), p. 189.

they spoil more property than they carry off, they are themselves often reduced to starvation, and can find no more to annex. All the armies are equally undisciplined and vie with one another in lawlessness. The authorities in Paris are trying to send back the peasants to gather in the corn; but as soon as it is reaped the marauders come to slay and steal, and disperse all in a general rout.

THEORIES OF ABSOLUTISM

The disorders of the time led to an increased willingness to accept strong centralized governments. Although the constitutional histories of France and England diverged during the seventeenth century—England emerged as a constitutional monarchy, France as a more absolutist state—important theoretical defenses of absolutism were produced in both countries. Compare the various arguments for absolutism in the following readings. Are any of the arguments convincing?

Rationalism

Jean Bodin wrote during the Wars of Religion that troubled France between 1562 and 1598. Why did he think that monarchy was the best form of government? What was the principal attribute of sovereignty? How should a ruler deal with religious dissent?

From Jean Bodin. *Six Books of the Commonwealth*

Because there are none on earth, after God, greater than sovereign princes, whom God establishes as His lieutenants to command the rest of mankind, we must enquire carefully into their estate, that we may respect and revere their majesty in all due obedience, speak and think of them with all due honour. He who contemns his sovereign prince, contemns God whose image he is. . . . We have also pointed out the absurdities that ensue if one makes sovereigns of vassals, since the lord and his subject, the master and his servant, the man who makes the law and the man on whom it is imposed, the man who issues orders and the man who obeys them, are thereby placed on an equal footing. Since this cannot be, it follows that dukes, counts, and all those who hold of another, or are bound by his laws and subject to his commands, whether of right or by constraint, are not sovereign. The same holds good of the highest officers of state, lieutenant-generals of the king, governors, regents, dictators, whatever the extent of their powers. They are not sovereigns since they are subject to the laws and commands of another and may be appealed against.

Before going any further, one must consider what is meant by *law*. The word law signifies the right command of that person, or those persons, who have absolute authority over all the rest without exception, saving only the law-giver himself, whether the command touches all subjects in general or only some in particular. To put it another way, the law is the rightful command of the sover-

Jean Bodin, *Six Books of the Commonwealth*, M. J. Tooley, trans. (Oxford: Basil Blackwell, 1955), pp. 40, 42–44, 141–142, 196–200. Reprinted by permission of the publisher.

eign touching all his subjects in general, or matters of general application . . . As to the commands of the magistrate, they are not properly speaking laws but only edicts. 'An edict', says Varro, 'is an order issued by a magistrate.' Such orders are only binding on those subject to his jurisdiction, and are only in force for his term of office.

The first attribute of the sovereign prince therefore is the power to make law binding on all his subjects in general and on each in particular. But to avoid any ambiguity one must add that he does so without the consent of any superior, equal, or inferior being necessary. If the prince can only make law with the consent of a superior he is a subject; if of an equal he shares his sovereignty; if of an inferior, whether it be a council of magnates or the people, it is not he who is sovereign. The names of the magnates that one finds appended to a royal edict are not there to give force to the law, but as witnesses, and to make it more acceptable . . .

All the other attributes and rights of sovereignty are included in this power of making and unmaking law, so that strictly speaking this is the unique attribute of sovereign power. It includes all other rights of sovereignty, that is to say of making peace and war, of hearing appeals from the sentences of all courts whatsoever, of appointing and dismissing the great officers of state; of taxing, or granting privileges of exemption to all subjects, of appreciating or depreciating the value and weight of the coinage, of receiving oaths of fidelity from subjects and liege-vassals alike, without exception of any other to whom faith is due.

Even atheists agree that nothing so tends to the preservation of commonwealths as religion, since it is the force that at once secures the authority of kings and governors, the execution of the laws, the obedience of subjects, reverence for the magistrates, fear of ill-doing, and knits each and all in the bonds of friendship. Great care must be taken that so sacred a thing should not be brought into doubt or contempt by dispute, for such entails the ruin of the commonwealth.

I am not concerned here with what form of religion is the best. (There is in fact only one religion, one truth, one divine law proceeding from the mouth of God himself.) But if the prince who has assurance of the true religion wishes to convert his subjects, split by sects and factions, he should not, in my opinion, attempt to coerce them. The more one tries to constrain men's wills, the more obstinate they become. But if the prince in his own person follows the true religion without hypocrisy or deceit, without any use of force, or any infliction of punishments, he may turn his subjects' hearts. In doing this, not only does he escape unrest, trouble, and civil strife, but he guides his errant subjects to the gates of salvation. . . .

[There are] dangers inherent in the monarchical form of government. They are great enough. But they are not so great as those which threaten an aristocracy, and even less than those that threaten popular states. Most of these dangers are avoided when the monarchy passes by hereditary succession, as we shall show in its proper place. Sedition, faction, civil war are a perpetual threat to all types of commonwealth, and the struggle for power in aristocracies and popular states is frequently much more bitter than in a monarchy. In a monarchy conflict over office and over political power only breaks out openly on the death of the prince, and then not very often.

The principal mark of a commonwealth, that is to say the existence of a sovereign power, can hardly be established except in a monarchy. There can only be one sovereign in the commonwealth. If there are two, three or more, not one of them is sovereign, since none of them can either impose a law on his companions or submit to one at their instance. Though one can imagine a collective sovereign power, vested in a ruling class, or a whole people, there is no true subject nor true protector if there is not some head of the state in whom sovereign power is vested, who can unite all the rest. . . .

There are many who make the mistake of thinking that an aristocracy is the best kind of state because many heads are better than one in all matters requiring judgement, experience, and good counsel. But there is a great difference between counsel and command. It is better to take the opinion of many than of one in all matters of counsel, for it is said that many understand better than one. But for taking a decision and issuing an order, one is always better than many. He can think over the advice that each has given and then reach a decision without being challenged. Many cannot achieve this so easily. Moreover ambition is unavoidable where there are several rulers sharing power equally, and there are always some who would rather see the commonwealth ruined than recognize that another was wiser than they. Others recognize it well enough, but pride, and fear for their reputation, prevents them from changing their opinions. In fact it is necessary that there should be a sovereign prince with power to make decisions upon the advice of his council. It is impossible that the commonwealth, which is one body, should have many heads, as the Emperor Tiberius pointed out to the Senate. . . . The statesmen, the philosophers, theologians, and historians who have praised monarchy above every other form of state, have not done so to flatter the prince, but to secure the safety and happiness of the subject. But if the authority of the monarch is to be limited, and subjected to the popular estates or to the senate, sovereignty has no sure foundations, and the result is a confused form of popular state, or a wretched condition of anarchy which is the worst possible condition of any commonwealth.

Thomas Hobbes (1588–1679), an outstanding political philosopher, lived through the English Civil War of the 1640s. How was a commonwealth instituted according to his account? How did the sovereign acquire his power? Why did the subjects have no right to resist the sovereign?

From Thomas Hobbes. *Leviathan*

In the first place, I put for a general inclination of all mankind, a perpetual and restless desire of power after power, that ceaseth only in death. And the cause of this, is not always that a man hopes for a more intensive delight, than he has already attained to; or that he cannot be content with a moderate power: but because he cannot assure the power and means to live well, which he hath present, without the acquisition of more.

From Thomas Hobbes, *Leviathan* (London. Andrew Crook, 1651), Chs. 11, 13, 17, 18.

Hereby it is manifest, that during the time men live without a common power to keep them all in awe, they are in that condition which is called war; and such a war, as is of every man, against every man.

Whatsoever therefore is consequent to a time of war, where every man is enemy to every man; the same is consequent to the time, wherein men live without other security, than what their own strength, and their own invention shall furnish them withal. In such condition, there is no place for industry; because the fruit thereof is uncertain: and consequently no culture of the earth; no navigation, nor use of the commodities that may be imported by sea; no commodious building; no instruments of moving, and removing, such things as require much force; no knowledge of the face of the earth; no account of time; no arts; no letters; no society; and which is worst of all, continual fear, and danger of violent death; and the life of man, solitary, poor, nasty, brutish, and short.

The final cause, end, or design of men, who naturally love liberty, and dominion over others, in the introduction of that restraint upon themselves, in which we see them live in commonwealths, is the foresight of their own preservation, and of a more contented life thereby; that is to say, of getting themselves out from that miserable condition of war, which is necessarily consequent, as hath been shown, to the natural passions of men, when there is no visible power to keep them in awe, and tie them by fear of punishment to the performance of their covenants.

The only way to erect such a common power, as may be able to defend them from the invasion of foreigners, and the injuries of one another, and thereby to secure them in such sort, as that by their own industry, and by the fruits of the earth, they may nourish themselves and live contentedly; is, to confer all their power and strength upon one man, or upon one assembly of men, that may reduce all their wills, by plurality of voices, unto one will: which is as much as to say, to appoint one man, or assembly of men, to bear their person; and every one to own, and acknowledge himself to be author of whatsoever he that so beareth their person, shall act, or cause to be acted, in those things which concern the common peace and safety; and therein to submit their wills, every one to his will, and their judgments, to his judgment. This is more than consent, or concord; it is a real unity of them all, in one and the same person, made by covenant of every man with every man, in such manner, as if every man should say to every man, *I authorize and give up my right of governing myself, to this man, or to this assembly of men, on this condition, that thou give up thy right to him, and authorize all his actions in like manner.* This done, the multitude so united in one person, is called a COMMONWEALTH, in Latin CIVITAS. This is the generation of that great LEVIATHAN, or rather, to speak more reverently, of that *mortal god*, to which we owe under the *immortal God*, our peace and defence. For by this authority, given him by every particular man in the commonwealth, he hath the use of so much power and strength conferred on him, that by terror thereof, he is enabled to form the wills of them all, to peace at home, and mutual aid against their enemies abroad. And in him consisteth the essence of the commonwealth; which, to define it, is *one person, of whose acts a great multitude, by mutual covenants one with another, have made themselves every one the author, to the end he may use the strength and means of them all, as he shall think expedient, for their peace and common defence.*

And he that carrieth this person, is called SOVEREIGN, and said to have *sovereign power*; and every one besides, his SUBJECT.

A *commonwealth* is said to be *instituted*, when a *multitude* of men do agree, and *covenant, every one, with every one*, that to whatsoever *man*, or *assembly of men*, shall be given by the major part, the *right* to *present* the person of them all, that is to say, to be their *representative*; every one, as well he that *voted for it*, as he that *voted against it*, shall *authorize* all the actions and judgments, of that man, or assembly of men, in the same manner, as if they were his own, to the end, to live peaceably amongst themselves, and be protected against other men.

From this institution of a commonwealth are derived all the *rights,* and *faculties* of him, or them, on whom the sovereign power is conferred by the consent of the people assembled.

First, because they covenant . . . they that have already instituted a commonwealth, being thereby bound by covenant, to own[1] the actions, and judgments of one, cannot lawfully make a new covenant, amongst themselves, to be obedient to any other, in any thing whatsoever, without his permission. And therefore, they that are subjects to a monarch, cannot without his leave cast off monarchy, and return to the confusion of a disunited multitude; nor transfer their person from him that beareth it, to another man, or other assembly of men: for they are bound, every man to every man, to own, and be reputed author of all, that he that already is their sovereign, shall do, and judge fit to be done.

Secondly, because the right of bearing the person of them all, is given to him they make sovereign, by covenant only of one to another, and not of him to any of them; there can happen no breach of covenant on the part of the sovereign; and consequently none of his subjects, by any pretence of forfeiture, can be freed from his subjection.

Thirdly, because the major part hath by consenting voices declared a sovereign; he that dissented must now consent with the rest; that is, be contented to avow all the actions he shall do, or else justly be destroyed by the rest. For if he voluntarily entered into the congregation of them that were assembled, he sufficiently declared thereby his will, and therefore tacitly covenanted, to stand to what the major part should ordain.

Fourthly, because every subject is by this institution author of all the actions, and judgments of the sovereign instituted; it follows, that whatsoever he doth, it can be no injury to any of his subjects; nor ought he to be by any of them accused of injustice. For he that doth anything by authority from another, doth therein no injury to him by whose authority he acteth: but by this institution of a commonwealth, every particular man is author of all the sovereign doth: and consequently he that complaineth of injury from his sovereign, complaineth of that whereof he himself is author; and therefore ought not to accuse any man but himself; no nor himself of injury; because to do injury to one's self, is impossible. It is true that they that have sovereign power may commit iniquity; but not injustice, or injury in the proper signification.

---

[1]"Own" here means to acknowledge or authorize.

Fifthly, and consequently to that which was said last, no man that hath sovereign power can justly be put to death, or otherwise in any manner by his subjects punished. For seeing every subject is author of the actions of his sovereign; he punisheth another for the actions committed by himself.

Divine Right

Jacques Bossuet (1627–1704), Bishop of Meaux, was a famous theologian and preacher during the reign of Louis XIV. How did his theory of monarchy differ from that of Hobbes?

From Bossuet. *Politics Drawn from the Very Words of Holy Scripture*

There are four characters or qualities essential to royal authority: First, royal authority is sacred; second, it is paternal; third, it is absolute; fourth, it is ruled by reason. . . .

Royal Authority Is Sacred
God established kings as his ministers and rules peoples by them.

We have already seen that all power comes from God. "The prince," St. Paul adds, "is the minister of God to thee for good. But if thou do that which is evil, be afraid; for he beareth not the sword in vain; for he is the minister of God, a revenger to execute wrath upon him that doeth evil." [Rom. 13:4]

Thus princes act as ministers of God, and as his lieutenants on earth. It is by them that he exercises his rule. . . .

Thus we have seen that the royal throne is not the throne of a man, but the throne of God himself. . . .

The person of kings is sacred.

It thus appears that the person of kings is sacred and that to make an attempt on their lives is a sacrilege.

God has had them anointed by his prophets with a sacred unction as he has his pontiffs and his altars anointed.

But without the external application of this unction, they are sacred by their office, as being the representatives of the divine majesty, deputized by his providence to the execution of his designs. . . .

The title of Christ is given to kings; and they are everywhere called christs, or the anointed of the lord.

Royal Authority Is Paternal and Its Proper Character Is Goodness

After what has been said, this truth has no need of proof.

We have seen that kings take the place of God, who is the true father of the human species. We have also seen that the first idea of power which exists among men is that of the paternal power; and that kings are modeled on fathers.

From J. B. Bossuet, *Politics Drawn from the Very Words of Holy Scripture* (1709), in Brian Tierney, Donald Kagan, and L. Pearce Williams, eds., *Great Issues in Western Civilization*, 3rd. ed., Vol II, pp. 613–615 (adapted), trans. L. Pearce Williams. Copyright © 1967, 1972, 1976 by Random House, Inc. Reprinted by permission of the publisher.

Everybody is also in accord, that the obedience which is owed to the public power can be found in the ten commandments only in the precept which obliges him to honor his parents.

Thus it follows from this that the name of king is a name for father and that goodness is the most natural character of kings. . . .

It is a royal right to provide for the needs of the people. He who undertakes it at the expense of the prince undertakes royalty: this is why it has been established. The obligation to care for the people is the foundation of all the rights that sovereigns have over their subjects.

Royal Authority Is Absolute

Without this absolute authority, he cannot do good nor can he repress evil: it is necessary that his power be such that no one can hope to escape him; and finally the only defense of individuals against the public power ought to be their innocence. . . .

Princes, then, must be obeyed in the same way as justice itself; otherwise there can be no order and no finality in men's affairs.

They are gods, and participate in some sense in the divine independence. "I have said, You are gods, and you are all children of the Most High." [Ps. 81:6.]

There is no one save God alone who may judge their decisions and their lives. . . . The prince may himself redress his own errors when he sees that he has committed a wrong; but against his authority there can exist no remedy save in his authority itself.

There Can Be No Coercive Power Opposing the Prince

A "coercive power" is a power to compel and execute that which is legitimately commanded. Legitimate command belongs to the prince alone; to him alone, therefore, belongs the "coercive power."

It is for this reason that St. Paul gives the sword to him only. "If you do not act rightly, be afraid; for it is not for nothing that he has the sword." [Rom. 13:4.] . . .

Thus it is that for the good of the state, all its force has been united in a single person. Let force exist elsewhere, and you divide the state and destroy the public peace; you set up two masters, contrary to this maxim of the Gospel: "No man can serve two masters." [Matt. 6:24.]

The prince is by his office the father of his people; he is placed by his grandeur above all petty interests; even more: all his grandeur and his natural interests are that the people shall be conserved, for once the people fail him he is no longer prince. There is thus nothing better than to give all the power of the state to him who has the greatest interest in the conservation and greatness of the state itself.

Kings Are Not by This Above the Laws

Kings therefore are subject like any others to the equity of the laws both because they must be just and because they owe to the people the example of protecting justice; but they are not subject to the penalties of the laws: or, as theology puts it, they are subject to the laws, not in terms of its coercive power but in terms of its directive power.

Patriarchy

Bossuet observed that royal power was "paternal." The English author, Robert Filmer (1588–1653), built a whole influential political theory around this idea.

From Robert Filmer. *Patriarcha*

As Adam was lord of his children, so his children under him had a command and power over their own children, but still with subordination to the first parent, who is lord-paramount over his children's children to all generations, as being the grandfather of his people.

I see not then how the children of Adam, or of any man else, can be free from subjection to their parents. And this subjection of children being the fountain of all regal authority, by the ordination of God himself; it follows that civil power not only in general is by divine institution, but even the assignment of it specifically to the eldest parents, which quite takes away that new and common distinction which refers only power universal and absolute to God, but power respective in regard of the special form of government to the choice of the people.

This lordship which Adam by command had over the whole world, and by right descending from him the patriarchs did enjoy, was as large and ample as the absolutest dominion of any monarch which hath been since the creation.

It may seem absurd to maintain that kings now are the fathers of their people, since experience shows the contrary. It is true, all kings be not the natural parents of their subjects, yet they all either are, or are to be reputed, the next heirs to those first progenitors who were at first the natural parents of the whole people, and in their right succeed to the exercise of supreme jurisdiction; and such heirs are not only lords of their own children, but also of their brethren, and all others that were subject to their fathers. And therefore we find that God told Cain of his brother Abel, "His desires shall be subject unto thee, and thou shalt rule over him."

If we compare the natural rights of a father with those of a king, we find them all one, without any difference at all but only in the latitude or extent of them: as the father over one family, so the king, as father over many families, extends his care to preserve, feed, clothe, instruct, and defend the whole commonwealth. His war, his peace, his courts of justice, and all his acts of sovereignty, tend only to preserve and distribute to every subordinate and inferior father, and to their children, their rights and privileges, so that all the duties of a king are summed up in an universal fatherly care of his people.

From Robert Filmer, *Patriarcha* (London: Richard Chiswell, 1680), Ch. 1.

THE COURT OF LOUIS XIV

The palace of Versailles was like a great theater in which an elaborate ritual, centering around the person of an absolute monarch, was acted out in daily life.

Life at Versailles

The Duke of Saint-Simon (1675–1755) lived for many years at the court of Versailles and left a detailed, gossipy account of day-to-day life there. Why did Louis XIV create such a court?

From *Memoirs of the Duke of Saint-Simon*

Very early in the reign of Louis XIV the Court was removed from Paris, never to return. The troubles of the minority had given him a dislike to that city; his enforced and surreptitious flight from it still rankled in his memory; he did not consider himself safe there, and thought cabals would be more easily detected if the Court was in the country, where the movements and temporary absences of any of its members would be more easily noticed. . . . No doubt that he was also influenced by the feeling that he would be regarded with greater awe and veneration when no longer exposed every day to the gaze of the multitude.

His love-affair with Mademoiselle de la Vallière, which at first was covered as far as possible with a veil of mystery, was the cause of frequent excursions to Versailles. This was at that time a small country house, built by Louis XIII to avoid the unpleasant necessity, which had sometimes befallen him, of sleeping at a wretched wayside tavern or in a windmill, when benighted out hunting in the forest of St. Leger. . . . The visits of Louis XIV becoming more frequent, he enlarged the *château* by degrees till its immense buildings afforded better accommodation for the Court than was to be found at St. Germain, where most of the courtiers had to put up with uncomfortable lodgings in the town. The Court was therefore removed to Versailles in 1682, not long before the Queen's death. The new building contained an infinite number of rooms for courtiers, and the King liked the grant of these rooms to be regarded as a coveted privilege.

He availed himself of the frequent festivities at Versailles, and his excursions to other places, as a means of making the courtiers assiduous in their attendance and anxious to please him; for he nominated beforehand those who were to take part in them, and could thus gratify some and inflict a snub on others. He was conscious that the substantial favours he had to bestow were not nearly sufficient to produce a continual effect; he had therefore to invent imaginary ones, and no one was so clever in devising petty distinctions and preferences which aroused jealousy and emulation. The visits to Marly later on were very useful to him in this way; also those to Trianon, where certain ladies, chosen beforehand, were admitted to his table. It was another distinction to hold his candlestick at his *coucher*; as soon as he had finished his prayers he used to name

From *The Memoirs of the Duke de Saint-Simon,* ed. F. Arkwright (New York: Brentano's, n.d.), Vol. V, pp. 271–274, 276–278.

the courtier to whom it was to be handed, always choosing one of the highest rank among those present. . . .

Not only did he expect all persons of distinction to be in continual attendance at Court, but he was quick to notice the absence of those of inferior degree; at his *lever,* his *coucher,* his meals, in the gardens of Versailles (the only place where the courtiers in general were allowed to follow him), he used to cast his eyes to right and left; nothing escaped him, he saw everybody. If any one habitually living at Court absented himself he insisted on knowing the reason; those who came there only for flying visits had also to give a satisfactory explanation; any one who seldom or never appeared there was certain to incur his displeasure. If asked to bestow a favour on such persons he would reply haughtily: "I do not know him"; of such as rarely presented themselves he would say, "He is a man I never see"; and from these judgements there was no appeal.

He always took great pains to find out what was going on in public places, in society, in private houses, even family secrets, and maintained an immense number of spies and tale-bearers. These were of all sorts; some did not know that their reports were carried to him; others did know it; there were others, again, who used to write to him directly, through channels which he prescribed; others who were admitted by the backstairs and saw him in his private room. Many a man in all ranks of life was ruined by these methods, often very unjustly, without ever being able to discover the reason; and when the King had once taken a prejudice against a man, he hardly ever got over it. . . .

No one understood better than Louis XIV the art of enhancing the value of a favour by his manner of bestowing it; he knew how to make the most of a word, a smile, even of a glance. If he addressed any one, were it but to ask a trifling question or make some commonplace remark, all eyes were turned on the person so honored; it was a mark of favour which always gave rise to comment. . . .

He loved splendour, magnificence, and profusion in all things, and encouraged similar tastes in his Court; to spend money freely on equipages and buildings, on feasting and at cards, was a sure way to gain his favour, perhaps to obtain the honour of a word from him. Motives of policy had something to do with this; by making expensive habits the fashion, and, for people in a certain position, a necessity, he compelled his courtiers to live beyond their income, and gradually reduced them to depend on his bounty for the means of subsistence. This was a plague which, once introduced, became a scourge to the whole country, for it did not take long to spread to Paris, and thence to the armies and the provinces; so that a man of any position is now estimated entirely according to his expenditure on his table and other luxuries. This folly, sustained by pride and ostentation, has already produced widespread confusion; it threatens to end in nothing short of ruin and a general overthrow.

Portrait of a Monarch

Saint-Simon belonged to the old nobility whose power was reduced under Louis XIV. How could this affect his portrayal of the king?

From *Memoirs of the Duke of Saint-Simon*

His natural talents were below mediocrity; but he had a mind capable of improvement, of receiving polish, of assimilating what was best in the minds of others without slavish imitation; and he profited greatly throughout his life from having associated with the ablest and wittiest persons, of both sexes, and of various stations. He entered the world (if I may use such an expression in speaking of a King who had already completed his twenty-third year), at a fortunate moment, for men of distinction abounded. His Ministers and Generals at this time, with their successors trained in their schools, are universally acknowledged to have been the ablest in Europe; for the domestic troubles and foreign wars under which France had suffered ever since the death of Louis XIII had brought to the front a number of brilliant names, and the Court was made up of capable and illustrious personages. . . . Glory was his passion, but he also liked order and regularity in all things; he was naturally prudent, moderate, and reserved; always master of his tongue and his emotions. Will it be believed? he was also naturally kind-hearted and just. God had given him all that was necessary for him to be a good King, perhaps also to be a fairly great one. All his faults were produced by his surroundings. In his childhood he was so much neglected that no one dared go near his rooms. He was often heard to speak of those times with great bitterness; he used to relate how, through the carelessness of his attendants, he was found one evening in the basin of a fountain in the Palais-Royal gardens. . . .

His Ministers, generals, mistresses, and courtiers soon found out his weak point, namely, his love of hearing his own praises. There was nothing he liked so much as flattery, or, to put it more plainly, adulation; the coarser and clumsier it was, the more he relished it. That was the only way to approach him; if he ever took a liking to a man it was invariably due to some lucky stroke of flattery in the first instance, and to indefatigable perseverance in the same line afterwards. His Ministers owed much of their influence to their frequent opportunities for burning incense before him. . . .

It was this love of praise which made it easy for Louvois to engage him in serious wars, for he persuaded him that he had greater talents for war than any of his Generals, greater both in design and in execution, and the Generals themselves encouraged him in this notion, to keep in favour with him. I mean such Generals as Condé and Turenne; much more, of course, those who came after them. He took to himself the credit of their successes with admirable complacency, and honestly believed that he was all his flatterers told him. Hence arose his fondness for reviews, which he carried so far that his enemies called him, in derision, "the King of reviews"; hence also his liking for sieges, where he could make a cheap parade of bravery, and exhibit his vigilance, forethought, and endurance of fatigue; for his robust constitution enabled him to bear fatigue marvellously; he cared nothing for hunger, heat, cold, or bad weather. He liked also, as he rode through the lines, to hear people praising his dignified bearing and

From *The Memoirs of the Duke de Saint-Simon*, ed. F. Arkwright (New York: Brentano's, n.d.), Vol. V, pp. 254, 259–263.

fine appearance on horseback. His campaigns were his favourite topic when talking to his mistresses. He talked well, expressed himself clearly in well-chosen language; and no man could tell a story better. His conversation, even on the most ordinary subjects, was always marked by a certain natural dignity.

His mind was occupied with small things rather than with great, and he delighted in all sorts of petty details, such as the dress and drill of his soldiers; and it was just the same with regard to his building operations, his household, and even his cookery. He always thought he could teach something of their own craft even to the most skilful professional men; and they, for their part, used to listen gratefully to lessons which they had long ago learnt by heart. He imagined that all this showed his indefatigable industry; in reality, it was a great waste of time, and his Ministers turned it to good account for their own purposes, as soon as they had learnt the art of managing him; they kept his attention engaged with a mass of details, while they contrived to get their own way in more important matters.

His vanity, which was perpetually nourished—for even preachers used to praise him to his face from the pulpit—was the cause of the aggrandisement of his Ministers. He imagined that they were great only through him, mere mouthpieces through which he expressed his will; consequently he made no objection when they gradually encroached on the privileges of the greatest noblemen. He felt that he could at any moment reduce them to their original obscurity; whereas, in the case of a nobleman, though he could make him feel the weight of his displeasure, he could not deprive him or his family of the advantages due to his birth. For this reason he made it a rule never to admit a *seigneur* to his Councils, to which the Duke de Beauvilliers was the only exception. . . .

But for the fear of the devil, which, by God's grace, never forsook him even in his wildest excesses, he would have caused himself to be worshipped as a deity. He would not have lacked worshippers. . . .

Saint-Simon's description of Louis XIV can be compared with the king's own account of how he took over the reins of power after a long minority.

From Louis XIV. *Letter to His Heir*

Inasmuch as my chief hope in these reforms was based on my will, their foundation at the outstart rested on making absolute my will by conduct which should impose submission and respect : by rendering scrupulous justice to all to whom I owed it; but in the bestowing of favours, giving them freely and without constraint to whomsoever I would, and when it should please me, provided that my subsequent action should let others know that while giving reasons to no one for my conduct I ruled myself none the less by reason, and that in my view the remembrance of services rendered, the favouring and promoting of merit—in a word, doing the right thing—should not only be the greatest concern but the greatest pleasure of a prince.

From J. Longnon, ed. *A King's Lessons in Statecraft* H. Wilson, trans. (New York: Albert and Charles Boni, 1925), pp. 48, 51–53, 57–58, 169–170.

Two things without doubt were absolutely necessary: very hard work on my part, and a wise choice of persons capable of seconding it. . . .

I gave orders to the four Secretaries of State no longer to sign anything whatsoever without speaking to me; likewise to the Controller, and that he should authorise nothing as regards finance without its being registered in a book which must remain with me, and being noted down in a very abridged abstract form in which at any moment, and at a glance, I could see the state of the funds, and past and future expenditure.

The Chancellor received a like order, that is to say, to sign nothing with the seal except by my command, with the exception only of letters of justice, so called because it would be an injustice to refuse them. . . . and to all my subjects without distinction I gave liberty to present their case to me at all hours, either verbally or by petitions.

At first petitions came in very great numbers, which nevertheless did not discourage me. The disorder in which my affairs had been placed was productive of many; the novelty and expectation, whether vain or unjust, attracted not less. A large number were presented connected with law-suits, which I could not and ought not to take out of the ordinary tribunals in order to have them adjudicated before me. But even in these things, apparently so unprofitable, I found great usefulness. By this means I informed myself in detail as to the state of my people; they saw that I was mindful of them, and nothing won their heart so much. Oppression on the part of the ordinary tribunals might be represented to me in such a way as to make me feel it desirable to gain further information in order to take special measures when they were required. One or two examples of this kind prevented a thousand similar ills. . . .

I also made a resolution on a further matter. With a view the better to unite in myself alone all the authority of a master, although there must be in all affairs a certain amount of detail to which our occupations and also our dignity do not permit us to descend as a rule, I conceived the plan, after I should have made choice of my ministers, of entering sometimes into matters with each one of them, and when they least expected it, in order that they might understand that I could do the same upon other subjects and at any moment. Besides, a knowledge of some small detail acquired only occasionally, and for amusement rather than as a regular rule, is instructive little by little and without fatigue, on a thousand things which are not without their use in general resolutions, and which we ought to know and do ourselves were it possible that a single man could know and do everything.

It is not so easy for me to tell you, my son, what ought to be done in the choice of different ministers. In this matter fortune plays always, in spite of us, as large or a greater part than sagacity; and in the part that sagacity is able to play, intuition can do far more than taking thought. . . .

To lay bare to you all that was in my mind, it was not to my interest to choose subjects of a more eminent quality. Before all else it was needful to establish my own reputation, and to let the public know from the very rank from which I chose them, that it was my intention not to share my authority with them. It was important that they should not conceive hopes of higher things than what it pleased me to give them—a matter which is difficult in the case of people of high birth. And these precautions were so necessary that even on that question the world was a fairly long time in getting to know me thoroughly.

Several were able to persuade themselves that within a short time some one of those who approached me would take possession of my mind and my affairs. The greater number regarded the assiduity of my labours as a fervour which would soon relax, and those willing to judge it more favourably were waiting to form their opinion by results.

Time has shown what to believe, and I have now been pursuing for ten years fairly consistently, as it seems to me, the same course, without relaxing my application; kept well informed of everything; listening to the least of my subjects; at any hour knowing the number and quality of my troops, and the state of my fortified towns; unremitting in issuing my orders for all their requirements; dealing at once with foreign ministers; receiving and reading dispatches; doing myself a portion of the replies and giving to my secretaries the substance of the others; regulating the State receipts and expenditure; requiring those whom I placed in important posts to account directly to me; keeping my affairs to myself as much as any one before me had ever done; distributing my favours as I myself chose, and retaining, if I mistake not, those who served me in a modest position which was far removed from the elevation and power of prime ministers, although loading them with benefits for themselves and their belongings.

Kings are often obliged to act contrary to their inclination in a way that wounds their own natural good instincts. They should like to give pleasure, and they often have to punish and ruin people to whom they are naturally well disposed. The interests of the State must come first. One has to do violence to one's inclinations, and not place oneself in the position of having to reproach oneself as regards any important matter which might have been done better had not certain private interests prevented it and turned aside the views one ought to have in the interests of the greatness, the welfare, and the power of the State. . . .

When one has the State in view, one is working for oneself. The good of the one makes the glory of the other. When the State is happy, eminent, and powerful, he who is the cause thereof is covered with glory, and as a consequence has a right to enjoy all that is most agreeable in life in a greater degree than his subjects, in proportion to his position and theirs.

ABSOLUTISM IN PRACTICE

Religion

The Edict of Nantes (1598) had granted a measure of toleration to French Protestants. Louis XIV, unwilling to tolerate the degree of self-government granted to the Protestant cities, revoked the Edict in 1685. What were the consequences?

From *Revocation of the Edict of Nantes (1685)*

1. Be it known that of our certain knowledge, full power, and royal author-ity, we have, by this present perpetual and irrevocable edict, suppressed and re-voked, and do suppress and revoke, the edict of our said grandfather, given at Nantes in April 1598, in its whole extent. . . .

2. We forbid our subjects of the R.P.R.[2] to meet any more for the exercise of the said religion in any place or private house, under any pretext whatever. . . .

3. We likewise forbid all noblemen, of what condition soever, to hold such religious exercises in their houses or fiefs, under penalty to be inflicted upon all our said subjects who shall engage in the said exercises, of imprisonment and confiscation.

4. We enjoin all ministers of the said R.P.R., who do not choose to become converts and to embrace the Catholic, apostolic, and Roman religion, to leave our kingdom and the territories subject to us within a fortnight of the publica-tion of our present edict, without leave to reside therein beyond that period, or, during the said fortnight, to engage in any preaching, exhortation, or any other function, on pain of being sent to the galleys. . . .

7. We forbid private schools for the instruction of children of the said R.P.R., and in general all things whatever which can be regarded as a concession of any kind in favor of the said religion.

From *Memoirs of the Duke of Saint-Simon*

The first-fruits of this dreadful plot were the wanton revocation of the Edict of Nantes, without a shadow of a pretext, and the proscriptions which followed it; its ultimate results were the depopulation of a fourth part of the kingdom and the ruin of our commerce. For a long time the country was given over to the au-thorised ravages of dragoons, which caused the deaths of, literally, thousands of innocent people of all ages and both sexes. Families were torn asunder; men of all classes, often old and infirm, highly respected for their piety and learning, were sent to toil in the galleys under the lash of the overseer; multitudes were driven penniless from their homes to seek refuge in foreign countries, to which they carried our arts and manufactures, enriching them and causing their cities to flourish at the expense of France.

There were many skilled craftsmen and merchants among the Huguenots who were driven out of France. After Louis XIV's death it was proposed that the Huguenot exiles be recalled. Saint-Simon then took a very different line.

---

[2]"Religion prétendue réformée," i.e., "the so-called reformed religion."
From F. A. Isambert, *Recueil général des anciennes lois françaises* (Paris, 1821–23), trans. in J. H. Robinson, *Readings in European History* (Boston: Ginn and Co., 1906), Vol. II, pp. 289–291.
From *The Memoirs of the Duke de Saint-Simon*, ed. F. Arkwright (New York: Brentano's, n.d.), Vol. V, pp. 296, 437.

I reminded [the Regent] of the disturbances and civil wars caused by the Huguenots from the reign of Henry II to that of Louis XIII; pointing out that even when they were comparatively quiet they had formed a body apart within the State, having their own chiefs, courts of justice specially appointed to deal with their affairs, even when they concerned Catholics, with strong places and garrisons at their disposal; corresponding with foreign Powers; always complaining and ready to take up arms: subjects, in short, merely in name, and yielding just as much or as little allegiance to their Sovereign as they thought fit. I recapitulated the heroic struggles by which his grandfather, Louis XIII, had at last beaten down this Hydra; thereby enabling his successor to get rid of it once for all by the mere expression of his will, without the slightest opposition.

I begged the Regent to reflect that he was now reaping the benefit of these struggles in a profound domestic tranquility; and to consider whether it was worth while, in time of peace when no foreign Power was thinking about the question, to make a concession which the late King had rejected with indignation when reduced to the utmost extremities by a long and disastrous war. I said, in conclusion, that if Louis XIV had made a mistake in revoking the Edict of Nantes it was not so much in the act itself as in the mode of carrying it out.

Throughout his reign Louis XIV commanded the support of the established Catholic church (which, in the past, had often been hostile to the claims of absolute monarchy).

From *Declaration of the Gallican Church*

We, the archbishops and bishops assembled at Paris by order of the King, with other ecclesiastical deputies who represent the Gallican Church, have judged it necessary to make the regulations and the declaration which follows:

That St. Peter and his successors, Vicars of Jesus Christ, and the whole Church herself, have received power of God only in things spiritual, and pertaining to eternal salvation, not in things civil or temporal, the Lord Himself having said, "My kingdom is not of this world," and also "Render unto Caesar the things that be Caesar's, and unto God the things that are God's"; as also firmly declareth the Apostle, "Let every soul be subject unto the higher powers; for there is no power but of God; the powers that be are ordained of God; whosoever therefore resisteth the power, resisteth the ordinance of God."

Therefore kings and princes are in no wise subjected by God's appointment to any ecclesiastical power in temporal things; neither can the authority of the Keys of the Church directly or indirectly depose them, or their subjects be dispensed from the obedience and fidelity of their oaths to the same; and this doctrine we affirm to be necessary for the maintenance of public peace, no less profitable to the Church than to the State, and to be everywhere and every way observed as agreeable to the Word of God, to the tradition of the Fathers and the example of the Saints. . . .

From F. A. Isambert, *Recueil général des anciennes lois françaises* (Paris, 1821–23), trans. in T. C. Mendenhall, B. D. Henning and A. S. Foord, *Ideas and Institutions in European History* (New York: Holt, Rinehart and Winston, 1948), Vol. I, p. 318.

Under Louis XIV the church became virtually a department of government.

From Louis XIV. *Letter to His Heir*

I have never failed, when an occasion has presented itself, to impress upon you the great respect we should have for religion, and the deference we should show to its ministers in matters specially connected with their mission, that is to say, with the celebration of the Sacred Mysteries and the preaching of the doctrine of the Gospels. But because people connected with the Church are liable to presume a little too much on the advantages attaching to their profession, and are willing sometimes to make use of them in order to whittle down their most rightful duties, I feel obliged to explain to you certain points on this question which may be of importance.

The first is that Kings are absolute *seigneurs,* and from their nature have full and free disposal of all property both secular and ecclesiastical, to use it as wise dispensers, that is to say, in accordance with the requirements of their State.

The second is that those mysterious names, the Franchises and Liberties of the Church, with which perhaps people will endeavour to dazzle you, have equal reference to all the faithful whether they be laymen or tonsured, who are all equally sons of this common Mother; but that they exempt neither the one nor the other from subjection to Sovereigns, to whom the Gospel itself precisely enjoins that they should submit themselves.

Military Organization

Voltaire, writing in the mid-eighteenth century, looked back on the reign of Louis XIV as a time of order and grandeur.

From Voltaire. *The Age of Louis XIV*

He was the legislator of his armies as well as of his people as a whole. It is surprising that, before his time, there was no uniform dress among the troops. It was he who, in the first year of his administration, ordered that each regiment should be distinguished by the color of its dress or by different badges; this regulation was soon adopted by all other nations. It was he who instituted brigadiers and who put the household troops on their present footing. He turned Cardinal Mazarin's guards into a company of musketeers and fixed the number of men in the companies at five hundred; moreover, he gave them the uniform which they still wear today.

Under him there were no longer constables, and after the death of the Duke of Epernon, no more colonel generals of infantry; they had become too power-

From J. Longnon, ed., *A King's Lessons in Statecraft,* H. Wilson, trans. (New York: Albert and Charles Boni, 1925), p. 149.
From Voltaire, *The Age of Louis XIV,* trans. J. H. Brumfitt (Boston: Twayne Publishers, 1963), pp. 137–139. Copyright 1963 by Twayne Publishers, Inc. Reprinted by permission of the publishers, a division of G. K. Hall and Company.

ful, and he quite rightly wanted to be sole master. Marshal Grammont, who was only colonel of horse of the French Guards under the Duke of Epernon and who took his orders from this colonel general, now took them only from the King, and was the first to be given the title of Colonel of the Guards. The King himself installed his colonels at the head of the regiments, giving them with his own hand a gilt gorget with a pike, and afterward, when the use of pikes was abolished, a spontoon, or kind of half-pike. In the King's Regiment, which he created himself, he instituted grenadiers, on the scale of four to a company in the first place; then he formed a company of grenadiers in each regiment of infantry. He gave two to the French Guards. Nowadays there is one for each battalion throughout the whole infantry. He greatly enlarged the Corps of Dragoons, and gave them a colonel general. The establishment of studs for breeding horses, in 1667, must not be forgotten, for they had been completely abandoned beforehand and they were of great value in providing mounts for the cavalry, an important resource which has since been too much neglected.

It was he who instituted the use of the bayonet affixed to the end of the musket. Before his time, it was used occasionally, but only a few companies fought with this weapon. There was no uniform practice and no drill; everything was left to the general's discretion. Pikes were then thought of as the most redoubtable weapon. The first regiment to have bayonets and to be trained to use them was that of the Fusiliers, established in 1671.

The manner in which artillery is used today is due entirely to him. He founded artillery schools, first at Douai, then at Metz and Strasbourg; and the Regiment of Artillery was finally staffed with officers who were almost all capable of successfully conducting a siege. All the magazines in the kingdom were well stocked, and they were supplied annually with eight hundred thousand pounds of powder. He created a regiment of bombardiers and one of hussars; before this only his enemies had had hussars.

In 1688 he established thirty regiments of militia, which were provided and equipped by the communes. These militia trained for war but without abandoning the cultivation of their fields.

Companies of cadets were maintained in the majority of frontier towns; there they learned mathematics, drawing and all the drills, and carried out the duties of soldiers. This institution lasted for ten years, but the government finally tired of trying to discipline these difficult young people. The Corps of Engineers, on the other hand, which the King created and to which he gave its present regulations, is an institution which will last forever. During his reign the art of fortifying strongholds was brought to perfection by Marshal Vauban and his pupils, who surpassed Count Pagan. He built or repaired a hundred and fifty fortresses.

To maintain military discipline, the King created inspectors general and later directors, who reported on the state of the troops; from their reports it could be seen whether the war commissioners had carried out their duties.

He instituted the Order of Saint-Louis, an honorable distinction which was often more sought after than wealth. The Hôtel des Invalides put the seal on his efforts to merit loyal service.

It was owing to measures such as these that he had, by 1672, a hundred and eighty thousand regular troops, and that, increasing his forces as the number and strength of his enemies increased, he finished with four hundred and fifty thousand men under arms, including the troops of the navy.

Before his time such powerful armies were unknown. His enemies could scarcely muster comparable forces, and to do so they had to be united. He showed what France, on her own, was capable of, and he always had either great successes or great resources to fall back on.

Economy and Local Administration

Louis XIV's finance minister, Jean Colbert (1619–1683), strove to build up French man-ufactures and commerce. Following the common "mercantilist" doctrine of his time, he wanted to augment the wealth of France by maximizing exports and minimizing im-ports. How did he seek to achieve this? What role did the government play in imple-menting the policy?

From *Colbert's Memoranda*

A Memorandum, 1669

The commerce of all Europe is carried on by ships of every size to the num-ber of 20,000, and it is perfectly clear that this number cannot be increased, since the number of people in all the states remains the same and consumption like-wise remains the same. . . .

Commerce is a perpetual and peaceable war of wit and energy among all nations. Each nation works incessantly to have its legitimate share of com-merce or to gain an advantage over another nation. The Dutch fight at present, in this war, with 15,000 to 16,000 ships, a government of merchants, all of whose maxims and power are directed solely toward the preservation and in-crease of their commerce, and much more care, energy, and thrift than any other nation.

The English with 3,000 to 4,000 ships, less energy and care, and more ex-penditures than the Dutch.

The French with 500 to 600.

Those two last cannot improve their commerce save by increasing the num-ber of their vessels, and cannot increase this number save from the 20,000 which carry all the commerce and consequently by making inroads on the 15,000 to 16,000 of the Dutch.

"A Memorandum, 1669": From Charles W. Cole, *Colbert and a Century of French Mercantilism* (New York: Columbia University Press, 1939), p. 320. Copyright 1939 by Columbia University Press. Reprinted by permission.

A Memorandum, 1670

[Formerly] the Dutch, English, Hamburgers, and other nations bringing into the realm a much greater quantity of merchandise than that which they carried away, withdrew the surplus in circulating money, which produced both their abundance and the poverty of the realm, and indisputably resulted in their power and our weakness.

We must next examine the means which were employed to change this destiny.

Firstly, in 1662 Your Majesty maintained his right to 50 sols per ton of freight from foreign vessels, which produced such great results that we have seen the number of French vessels increase yearly; and in seven or eight years the Dutch have been practically excluded from port-to-port commerce, which is carried on by the French. The advantages received by the state through the increase in the number of sailors and seamen, through the money which has remained in the realm by this means and an infinity of others, would be too long to enumerate.

At the same time, Your Majesty ordered work done to abolish all the tolls which had long been established on all the rivers of the kingdom, and he began from then on to have an examination made of the rivers which could be rendered navigable in order to facilitate the descent of commodities and merchandise from inside the realm toward the sea to be transported into foreign lands. Although everything that invites the universal admiration of men was still in disorder in these first years and although the recovery work was a sort of abyss, Your Majesty did not delay in beginning the examination of the tariffs of the *cinq grosses fermes* and scrutinized the fact that the regulation and levying of these sorts of duties concerning commerce had always been done with a great deal of ignorance on the basis of memoranda by tax farmers, who, being solely concerned with their own interests and the increase in the profits from their tax farms while they possessed them, had always overvalued the commodities, merchandise, and manufactured items of the realm which they saw leaving in abundance, and favored the entrance of foreign merchandise and manufactured items, in order to have a greater quantity of them enter, without being concerned about whether money was as a result leaving the realm, for they were indifferent to this as long as their tax farms produced gain for them during the period of their possession.

Finally, after having thoroughly studied this matter, Your Majesty ordered the tariff of 1664, in which the duties are regulated on a completely different principle, that is to say, that all merchandise and manufactured items of the realm were markedly favored and the foreign ones priced out of the market, though not completely; [for] having as yet no established manufacturers in the realm, this increase in duties, had it been excessive, would have been a great burden for the *peuple*, because of their need for the aforesaid foreign merchandise and manufactured

"A Memorandum, 1670": From P. Clement, *Lettres, instructions et mémoires de Colbert* (Paris: Imprimerie Nationale, 1870). Translated excerpts in O. and P. Ranum, *The Century of Louis XIV* (New York: Walker, 1972), pp. 120–123. Reprinted by permission of Walker and Company, Inc.

items; but this change began to provide some means of establishing the same manufactures in the realm; and to this end:

The fabric manufacture of Sedan has been reestablished, and enlarged to 62 from the 12 looms there were then.

The new establishments of Abbeville, Dieppe, Fécamp, and Rouen have been built, in which there are presently more than 200 looms.

The factory for barracan was next established at La Ferré-sous-Jouarre, which is made up of 120 looms;

That of little damasks from Flanders, at Meaux, consisting of 80 looms;

That for carpeting, in the same city, made up of 20 looms . . .

That for tin, in Nivernois;

That for French lace, in 52 cities and towns, in which more than 20,000 workers toil;

The manufacture of brass, or yellow copper, set up in Champagne;

That for camlet of Brussels, in Paris, which will become large and extensive;

Brass wire, in Burgundy;

Gold thread of Milan, at Lyons . . .

[Many other new enterprises were listed.]

And since Your Majesty has wanted to work diligently at reestablishing his naval forces, and since for that it has been necessary to make very great expenditures, since all merchandise, munitions and manufactured items formerly came from Holland and the countries of the North, it has been absolutely necessary to be especially concerned with finding within the realm, or with establishing in it, everything which might be necessary for this great plan.

To this end, the manufacture of tar was established in Médoc, Auvergne, Dauphiné, and Provence;

Iron cannons, in Burgundy, Nivernois, Saintonge, and Périgord;

Large anchors, in Dauphiné, Nivernois, Brittany, and Rochefort;

Sailcloth for the Levant, in Dauphiné;

Coarse muslin, in Auvergne;

All the implements for pilots and others, at Dieppe and La Rochelle;

The cutting of wood suitable for vessels, in Burgundy, Dauphiné, Brittany, Normandy, Poitou, Saintonge, Provence, Guyenne, and the Pyrenees;

Masts, of a sort once unknown in this realm, have been found in Provence, Languedoc, Auvergne, Dauphiné, and in the Pyrenees.

Iron, which was obtained from Sweden and Biscay, is currently manufactured in the realm.

Fine hemp for ropes, which came from Prussia and from Piedmont, is currently obtained in Burgundy, Mâconnais, Bresse, Dauphiné; and markets for it have since been established in Berry and in Auvergne, which always provides money in these provinces and keeps it within the realm.

In a word, everything serving for the construction of vessels is currently established in the realm, so that Your Majesty can get along without foreigners for the navy and will even, in a short time, be able to supply them and gain their money in this fashion. And it is with this same objective of having everything necessary to provide abundantly for his navy and that of his subjects that he is working at the general reform of all the forests in his realm, which, being as carefully preserved as they are at present, will abundantly produce all the wood necessary for this.

A Memorandum, 1672

If the King conquers all the provinces subject to and forming part of the States of the United Provinces of the Netherlands, their commerce becoming commerce of the subjects of the King, there would be nothing more to desire; and if afterwards His Majesty, examining what would be most advantageous to do for the commerce of his old and new subjects, thought it for the good of his service to divide the advantages of this commerce by cutting down a part of that of the Dutch so as to transfer it into the hands of the French, it would be easy to find the necessary expedients to which the new subjects would be obliged to submit.

Much of Colbert's voluminous correspondence was concerned with the supervision of local government officials. What sort of abuses did he have to contend with?

From *Colbert's Correspondence*

To the Count de Grignan, Lieutenant-General of Provence, Paris, 25 December, 1671

I have informed the King of the disorderly conduct in which the Assembly of the Towns of Provence has persisted; and, as His Majesty is not disposed to countenance it longer, he has given the orders necessary to prorogue it and, at the same time, has dispatched ten *lettres-de-cachet*,[3] to commit the ten most discontented deputies to Granville, Cherbourg, Saint-Malo, Morlaix and Concarneau.

To M. de Creil, Intendant of Rouen, Saint-Germain, 3 February 1673

Of all the abuses which come before us from the *généralités*[4], there is none at present which seems more important to the Council than that [practised] by the assistants to the Receivers of the *Tailles*[5], who, under the name of the Receivers, make assessments, in conjunction with the magistrates, to defray the court costs and fees and which they apply to their own profit. As was provided by the order of the Council of 4 July 1664, concerning the regulation of this disorder, pray inform me if it is known or practised in the *généralité* of Rouen, and particularly

[3]*Lettres-de-cachets* were royal letters committing named persons to prison.

[4]Administrative districts.

[5]Land taxes.

"A Memorandum, 1672": From Charles W. Cole, *Colbert and a Century of French Mercantilism* (New York: Columbia University Press, 1939), p. 320. Copyright 1939 by Oxford University Press. Reprinted by permission.

Colbert's Correspondence: From P. Clement, *Lettres, instructions et mémoires de Colbert* (Paris: Imprimerie Nationale, 1870), translated in T. C. Mendenhall, B. D. Henning and A. S. Foord, *Ideas and Institutions in European History* (New York: Holt, Rinehart and Winston, 1948), pp. 315–316, 321.

apply yourself to finding out if any of the Receivers of *Tailles* or Commissioners of Revenue are guilty of this, in order that you may either apply the necessary remedy through your authority or advise me about it.

To M. de Bezons, Intendant of Limoges, 16 November 1680

The King having been advised by M. de Marillac, intendant in the *généralité de Poitiers*, that a man named Baudoin has been guilty of a great many frauds in several parishes of the province of Saintonge, under the pretext of collecting for the *corvées* to repair roads, and on the strength of a commission of the tribunal of the King's lands at Paris giving him permission, His Majesty gave *Sieur* de Marillac verbal powers to institute proceedings against Baudoin; and, this having been done, he has been condemned to the galleys for life and forced to make restitution to those whom he had swindled.

As *Sieur* de Marillac has informed me that in the process of trying Baudoin, he learned that, in the *généralité* of Limoges, there are several other people who have similar commissions and who, under the same pretext, are plaguing the people, I feel free to request that you hunt them down, throughout the entirety of the *généralité* of Limoges, in order to halt their depredations. If you have the facilities there to try them and to make examples of them, the King will, upon your request, send you the authority to try them and to impress the maximum penalties. . . .

To M. d'Herbigny, Intendant of Grenoble, Versailles, 16 November, 1680

I was surprised to learn, by your letter of the 28th last, that you had levied on the *élection* of Vienne an assessment of 4,700 livres, for the construction, subject to my approval, of a bridge to facilitate the transportation of the harvest to Grenoble.

You know as well as I that it is not permissible to make such an assessment on the people without a writ of the King affixed with the Great Seal, and you must take care to do nothing contrary to that general usage of the realm, and never to give so bad an example to the authorities of that province, who are only too much inclined to go beyond the bounds, and to those who will succeed to your position.

To M. Morant, Intendant of Aix, Sceaux, 1 July, 1682

I shall report at the next meeting of the Council on the suggestion which you have sent concerning the public works and the tolls; I am certain that His Majesty will agree with them. You ought afterwards to apply yourself to repairing the roads and to forcing the *seigneurs* to repair and maintain those roads on which they levy the tolls.

As you fully appreciate the importance of these public works to the good of the province, I am sure that you will give them your complete attention. . . .

EASTERN EUROPE

The Turkish Menace

Reason of state influenced relations among the great powers more than ties of religion did. (During the Thirty Years' War, France sided with the Protestant princes of

Germany against Catholic Austria.) An anonymous seventeenth-century observer commented rather cynically on the probable reaction of Louis XIV to an invasion of Germany by Muslim Turks.

From *The Present State of the German and Turkish Empires*

Some perhaps will . . . retort that though Vienna had been taken by the Turk, there was no great fear of his further progress into Germany: Because Louis the King of France surnamed the Great for the things he has done already, would oppose him in such a case with a puissant army, and force him back again to the great loss of the Turks, and his own immortal glory.

This indeed would be great in Louis the Great; and in truth in such a conjuncture of affairs he would be the only prince of Europe in a capacity to stop the progress of such a potent enemy. But first, we may justly question whether he would in such a case be willing, or not, till such time as he were forced to it, for his own defence. For every one knows that knows anything, that clipping the wings of the Austrian eagle (or House of Austria) will extremely add to the splendour of the French monarchy. Whilst then the Turks were invading Germany on the one side, would not both self-preservation, honour and interest invite the French King to be busy on the other? And divide perhaps Germany with the Turks, since in all likelihood he could do no better. . . . The existence of a strong German army occasioned a great change in the affairs of Holland. For then the French thought it no longer secure for them to remain there, and deserted on a sudden the cities they had taken in it partly by force; partly by a free surrender, so that after having caused the citizens to redeem their liberties with great sums of money the French retreated from their new conquests, which they had never done, if the forces of Germany had been diverted by a Turkish invasion.

Out of all this discourse, we may gather that although the French King were able alone to beat the Turks out of Germany, in case they had succeeded in their designs; it's not certain whether he would have been willing to do it, at least till he had been himself possest of the best part of Germany, of Flanders, and Holland likewise. . . .

Peter the Great

Peter the Great (1682–1725) laid the foundations of a centralized Russian state. He combined westernizing reforms with fierce repression of opposition in his rule. Bishop Burnett met the emperor on his visit to England in 1698.

From *Gilbert Burnett's History*

He is a man of a very hot temper, soon inflamed and very brutal in his passion. He raises his natural heat by drinking much brandy, which he rectifies [i.e., distills] himself with great application. He is subject to convulsive motions all

From *The Present State of the German and Turkish Empires* (London, 1684), pp. 38–44.
From J. H. Robinson, *Readings in European History* (Boston: Ginn and Co., 1906), Vol. II, pp. 303–306, 310–312.

over his body, and his head seems to be affected with these. He wants not capacity, and has a larger measure of knowledge than might be expected from his education, which was very indifferent. A want of judgment, with an instability of temper, appear in him too often and too evidently.

He is mechanically turned, and seems designed by nature rather to be a ship carpenter than a great prince. This was his chief study and exercise while he stayed here. He wrought much with his own hands and made all about him work at the models of ships. He told me he designed a great fleet at Azuph [i.e. Azov] and with it to attack the Turkish empire. But he did not seem capable of conducting so great a design, though his conduct in his wars since this has discovered a greater genius in him than appeared at this time.

. . . He was, indeed, resolved to encourage learning and to polish his people by sending some of them to travel in other countries and to draw strangers to come and live among them. He seemed apprehensive still [i.e. ever] of his sister's [i.e. the Princess Sophia's] intrigues. There was a mixture both of passion and severity in his temper. He is resolute, but understands little of war, and seemed not at all inquisitive that way.

After I had seen him often, and had conversed much with him, I could not but adore the depth of the providence of God that had raised up such a furious man to so absolute an authority over so great a part of the world. David, considering the great things God had made for the use of man, broke out into the meditation, "What is man, that thou art so mindful of him?" But here there is an occasion for reversing these words, since man seems a very contemptible thing in the sight of God, while such a person as the tsar has such multitudes put, as it were, under his feet, exposed to his restless jealousy and savage temper.

While Peter was traveling abroad, his sister, Sophia, was involved in a rebellion of the Moscow guard, the Streltsi. *(Von Korb was an Austrian diplomat stationed in Moscow.)*

From *Von Korb's Diary*

How sharp was the pain, how great the indignation, to which the tsar's Majesty was mightily moved, when he knew of the rebellion of the Streltsi, betraying openly a mind panting for vengeance! He was still tarrying at Vienna, quite full of the desire of setting out for Italy; but, fervid as was his curiosity of rambling abroad, it was, nevertheless, speedily extinguished on the announcement of the troubles that had broken out in the bowels of his realm. . . . Nor did he long delay the plan for his justly excited wrath; he took the quick post, as his ambassador suggested, and in four weeks' time he had got over about three hundred miles[6] without accident, and arrived the 4th of September, 1698,—a monarch for the well disposed, but an avenger for the wicked.

His first anxiety after his arrival was about the rebellion,—in what it consisted, what the insurgents meant, who dared to instigate such a crime. And as nobody could answer accurately upon all points, and some pleaded their own ignorance, others the obstinacy of the Streltsi, he began to have suspicions of

---

[6]German miles, each equivalent to about five English.

everybody's loyalty. . . . No day, holy or profane, were the inquisitors idle; every day was deemed fit and lawful for torturing. There were as many scourges as there were accused, and every inquisitor was a butcher. . . . The whole month of October was spent in lacerating the backs of culprits with the knout and with flames; no day were those that were left alive exempt from scourging or scorching; or else they were broken upon the wheel, or driven to the gibbet, or slain with the ax. . . .

To prove to all people how holy and inviolable are those walls of the city which the Streltsi rashly meditated scaling in a sudden assault, beams were run out from all the embrasures in the walls near the gates, in each of which two rebels were hanged. This day beheld about two hundred and fifty die that death. There are few cities fortified with as many palisades as Moscow has given gibbets to her guardian Streltsi.

[In front of the nunnery where Sophia was confined] there were thirty gibbets erected in a quadrangle shape, from which there hung two hundred and thirty Streltsi; the three principal ringleaders, who tendered a petition to Sophia touching the administration of the realm, were hanged close to the windows of that princess, presenting, as it were, the petitions that were placed in their hands, so near that Sophia might with ease touch them.

Peter the Great's enthusiasm for Western practices extended even to fashions in dress. How were his reforms received?

From *De Missy's Life of Peter*

The tsar labored at the reform of fashions, or, more properly speaking, of dress. Until that time the Russians had always worn long beards, which they cherished and preserved with much care, allowing them to hang down on their bosoms, without even cutting the moustache. With these long beards they wore the hair very short, except the ecclesiastics, who, to distinguish themselves, wore it very long. The tsar, in order to reform that custom, ordered that gentlemen, merchants, and other subjects, except priests and peasants, should each pay a tax of one hundred rubles a year if they wished to keep their beard; the commoners had to pay one kopeck each. Officials were stationed at the gates of the towns to collect that tax, which the Russians regarded as an enormous sin on the part of the tsar and as a thing which tended to the abolition of their religion.

These insinuations, which came from the priests, occasioned the publication of many pamphlets in Moscow, where for that reason alone the tsar was regarded as a tyrant and a pagan; and there were many old Russians who, after having their beards shaved off, saved them preciously, in order to have them placed in their coffins, fearing that they would not be allowed to enter heaven without their beards. As for the young men, they followed the new customs with the more readiness as it made them appear more agreeable to the fair sex.

From the reform in beards we may pass to that of clothes. Their garments, like those of the Orientals, were very long, reaching to the heel. The tsar issued an ordinance abolishing that costume, commanding all the boyars (nobles) and all those who had positions at the court to dress after the French fashion, and likewise to adorn their clothes with gold or silver according to their means.

The dress of the women was changed, too. English hairdressing was substituted for the caps and bonnets hitherto worn; bodices, stays, and skirts, for the former undergarment. . . .

The same ordinance also provided that in the future women, as well as men, should be invited to entertainments, such as weddings, banquets, and the like, where both sexes should mingle in the same hall, as in Holland and England. It was likewise added that these entertainments should conclude with concerts and dances, but that only those should be admitted who were dressed in English costumes. His Majesty set the example in all these changes.

PART FOURTEEN

THE SEARCH FOR ORDER— CONSTITUTIONALISM AND OLIGARCHY

W*hile many countries of Europe turned to absolutist governments in the seventeenth century, the English reshaped their medieval institutions into a new kind of constitutional regime.*

England inherited from the late Middle Ages a system of government based on co-operation between king and Parliament. The king conducted affairs of state; Parliament levied taxes and enacted laws. The relative powers of Crown and Parliament were not clearly defined, but the system worked well enough so long as no serious policy differences arose between the king's government and the wealthy, powerful classes represented in the House of Lords and the House of Commons.

Signs of strain began to appear under James I (1603–1625). Under Charles I (1625–1649) the religious and financial policies of the Crown came under attack in the House of Commons from the first years of the reign. When Parliament refused grants of taxes to support policies of which it disapproved, Charles turned to extraparliamentary expedients. But this move only embittered the situation still more. By 1642 the two sides had become so estranged that England drifted into a civil war.

Charles's adversaries entered the conflict with the declared purpose of defending the ancient rights and institutions of England. But during the war, ideas much more radical than those of the parliamentary leaders emerged and found support. The leaders of Parliament soon quarreled with the generals of the army that they had created. The war ended with the execution of the king, the dissolution of Parliament, and the establishment of a military dictatorship under Oliver Cromwell.

When Cromwell died, Charles II (1660–1685) was welcomed back to England with almost universal support. However, the "Restoration" of 1660 was a restoration of Parliament as well as of monarchy, and tensions between Crown and Parliament persisted under Charles II.

The final resolution of the situation came in the next reign. James II (1685–1688) converted to Catholicism and married a Catholic wife. The unwelcome prospect of a

415

permanent Catholic line of succession to the throne united royalist and parliamentary supporters in a common cause. They offered the throne to Prince William of Holland and his wife Mary (a daughter of James II). When William took power he promised to rule in cooperation with Parliament and a Bill of Rights was enacted to define the future pattern of English government.

CROWN AND PARLIAMENT

Earlier Views

Sir John Fortescue described the English system of limited monarchy as it had developed by the end of the Middle Ages. What was the difference between the two kinds of "dominion" that he discussed?

From Fortescue. *The Governance of England (1471)*

There are two kinds of kingdom, of which one is a lordship, called in Latin *dominium regale*, and the other is called *dominium politicum et regale*. And they differ in that the first king may rule his people by such laws as he makes himself. And therefore he may set upon them tallages and other impositions such as he wills himself without their assent. The second king may not rule his people by other laws than those that they assent to. And therefore he may set upon them no impositions without their own assent. . . .

But, blessed be God, this land is ruled under [the] better law; and therefore the people thereof are not in such penury nor thereby hurt in their persons but are wealthy and have all things necessary to the sustenance of nature. Wherefore they are mighty and able to resist the adversaries of this realm and to beat other realms that do or would do them wrong. Lo, this is the fruit of the *ius politicum et regale* under which we live.

Fortescue's account assumed a harmonious relationship between monarch and Parliament. Queen Elizabeth I (1558–1603) did in fact succeed in retaining the support of her Parliaments throughout her long reign. When the queen's last Parliament criticized her grants of commercial monopolies, she won them over with a gracious speech.

From *Elizabeth's "Golden Speech" (1601)*

Mr. Speaker,

You give me thanks; but I doubt me, that I have more cause to thank you all, than you me. And I charge you, to thank them of the lower house from me: for had I not received a knowledge from you, I might have fallen into the lapse of an error, only for lack of true information.

From Sir John Fortescue, *The Governance of England,* ed. C. Plummer (Oxford: Clarendon Press, 1885), pp. 109–114.

From H. Townshend, *Historical Collections* (London, 1680), pp. 264–266.

Since I was queen, yet did I never put my pen unto any grant, but that, upon pretext and semblance made unto me, it was both good and beneficial to the subject in general; though a private profit to some of my ancient servants, who had deserved well at my hands. But the contrary being found by experience, I am exceedingly beholding to such subjects as would move the same at the first. . . . And I take it exceedingly gratefully from them; because it gives us to know that no respects or interests had moved them other than the minds they bear to suffer no diminution of our honour and our subjects' loves unto us. The zeal of which affection, tending to ease my people, and knit their hearts unto me, I embrace with a princely care; for (above all earthly treasure) I esteem my people's love, more than which I desire not to merit.

That my grants should be grievous to my people and oppressions privileged under colour of our patents, our kingly dignity shall not suffer it: yea, when I heard it, I could give no rest unto my thoughts until I had reformed it. . . .

To be a king and wear a crown is a thing more glorious to them that see it than it is pleasing to them that bear it: for myself, I was never so much enticed with the glorious name of a king, or royal authority of a queen, as delighted that God had made me his instrument to maintain his truth and glory and to defend this kingdom (as I said) from peril, dishonour, tyranny, and oppression.

There will never queen sit in my seat with more zeal to my country, care for my subjects, and that sooner with willingness will venture her life for your good and safety, than myself. For it is not my desire to live nor reign longer than my life and reign shall be for your good. And though you have had, and may have many princes, more mighty and wise, sitting in this state; yet you never had, or shall have any that will be more careful and loving.

Elizabeth's successor, James I (1603–1625) adopted a different tone. In 1610 he lectured Parliament about his role as an absolute king.

From James I. *Speech to Parliament (1610)*

The state of Monarchy is the supremest thing upon earth; for kings are not only God's lieutenants upon earth and sit upon God's throne, but even by God himself they are called gods. There be three principal similitudes that illustrate the state of Monarchy: one taken out of the Word of God and the two other out of the grounds of policy and philosophy. In the Scriptures kings are called gods, and so their power after a certain relation compared to the Divine power. Kings are also compared to the fathers of families, for a king is truly *parens patriae* [father of his country], the politic father of his people. And lastly, kings are compared to the head of this microcosm of the body of man.

Kings are justly called gods for that they exercise a manner or resemblance of Divine power upon earth. . . .

As for the father of a family, they had of old under the Law of Nature *patriam potestatem* [paternal power], which was *potestatem vitae et necis* [power of

From *The Works of the Most High and Mighty Prince James* (London: James Montague, 1616), pp. 529–531.

life and death], over their children or family. . . . Now a father may dispose of his inheritance to his children at his pleasure, yea, even disinherit the eldest upon just occasions and prefer the youngest, according to his liking; make them beggars or rich at his pleasure; restrain or banish out of his presence, as he finds them give cause of offence, or restore them in favour again with the penitent sinner. So may the King deal with his subjects.

And lastly, as for the head of the natural body, the head hath the power of directing all the members of the body to that use which the judgment in the head thinks most convenient. . . . It is sedition in subjects to dispute what a king may do in the height of his power; but just kings will ever be willing to declare what they will do, if they will not incur the curse of God. I will not be content that my power be disputed upon, but I shall ever be willing to make the reason appear of all my doings, and rule my actions according to my laws.

The House of Commons responded with complaints about the king's policies. What specifically did they object to?

From *Petition of Grievances (1610)*

The policy and constitution of this your kingdom appropriates unto the Kings of this realm, with the assent of the Parliament, as well the sovereign power of making laws as that of taxing or imposing upon the subjects' goods or merchandises, wherein they have justly such a propriety as may not without their consent be altered or changed. . . .

We therefore, your Majesty's most humble Commons assembled in Parliament, following the example of this worthy care of our ancestors and out of a duty to those for whom we serve, finding that your Majesty, without advice or consent of Parliament, hath lately in time of peace set both greater impositions and far more in number than any your noble ancestors did ever in time of war, have with all humility presumed to present this most just and necessary petition unto your Majesty, That all impositions set without the assent of Parliament may be quite abolished and taken away. . . .

[Also] it is apparent both that proclamations have been of late years much more frequent than heretofore, and that they are extended not only to the liberty but also to the goods, inheritances, and livelihood of men: some of them tending to alter some points of the law and make them new. . . .

By reason whereof there is a general fear conceived and spread amongst your Majesty's people that proclamations will by degrees grow up and increase to the strength and nature of laws; whereby not only that ancient happiness, freedom, will be as much blemished (if not quite taken away) which their ancestors have so long enjoyed, but the same may also (in process of time) bring a new form of arbitrary government upon the realm.

We therefore, your Majesty's humble subjects the Commons in this Parliament assembled . . . have thought it to appertain to our duties, as well towards your Majesty as to those that have trusted and sent us to their service, to

From William Petyt, *Jus Parliamentarum* (London, 1739), p. 321.

present unto your Majesty's view these fears and griefs of your people, and to become humble suitors unto your Majesty that thenceforth no fine or forfeiture of goods or other pecuniary or corporal punishment may be inflicted upon your subjects . . . unless they shall offend against some law or statute of this realm in force at the time of their offence committed.

CIVIL WAR

Charles I. The Break with Parliament

Tensions increased under Charles I (1625–1649). Charles, a devout Anglican, favored for the Church of England an "Arminian,"[1] or high church, policy that retained some elements of Catholic ritual and doctrine. A strong Puritan faction in Parliament wanted a more Calvinist system of doctrine and discipline. Distrusting Charles's policies, Parliament withheld grants of taxes. Charles resorted to forced loans to raise revenue. This action led to a new assertion of the rights of Parliament in 1628. What kind of authorities did the Commons rely on to support their claims?

From *Petition of Right (1628)*

To the King's Most Excellent Majesty

Humbly show unto our Sovereign Lord the King the Lords Spiritual and Temporal and Commons in Parliament assembled, that whereas it is declared and enacted by a statute made in the time of the reign of King Edward the First commonly called Statutum de Tallagio non Concedendo that no tallage or aid should be laid or levied by the King or his heirs in this realm without the good will and assent of the archbishops, bishops, earls, barons, knights, burgesses and other the freemen of the commonalty of this realm; and by authority of Parliament holden in the five and twentieth year of the reign of King Edward the Third it is declared and enacted, that from henceforth no person should be compelled to make any loans to the King against his will because such loans were against reason and the franchise of the land. . . .

Yet, nevertheless of late divers commissions directed to sundry commissioners in several counties with instructions have issued, by means whereof your people have been in divers places assembled and required to lend certain sums of money unto your Majesty. . . .

And where also by the statute called the Great Charter of the Liberties of England it is declared and enacted, that no freeman may be taken or imprisoned or be disseised of his freehold or liberties or his free customs or be outlawed or exiled or in any manner destroyed, but by the lawful judgement of his peers or by the law of the land.

---

[1]The word comes from the name of a contemporary theologian, Arminius.
From S. R. Gardiner, ed., *The Constitutional Documents of the Puritan Revolution*, 2nd ed. (Oxford: Oxford University Press, 1899), pp. 66–69.

And in the eight and twentieth year of the reign of King Edward the Third it was declared and enacted by authority of Parliament, that no man, of what estate or condition that he be, should be put out of his land or tenement, nor taken, nor imprisoned, nor disherited, nor put to death without being brought to answer by due process of law.

Nevertheless against the tenor of the said statutes and other the good laws and statutes of your realm to that end provided, divers of your subjects have of late been imprisoned without any cause shown. . . .

They do therefore humbly pray your most excellent Majesty that no man hereafter be compelled to make or yield any gift, loan, benevolence, tax or such like charge without common consent by Act of Parliament, and that none be called to make answer or take such oath or to give attendance or be confined or otherwise molested or disquieted concerning the same or for refusal thereof. And that no freeman in any such manner as is before mentioned be imprisoned or detained.

Charles accepted the Petition of Right but continued to collect the tax called "tonnage and poundage" without parliamentary consent. There followed a scene of unprecedented protest and turmoil in the House of Commons.

Commons Protestation (1629)

This day, being the last day of the Assembly, as soon as prayers were ended the Speaker went into the Chair, and delivered the Kings command for the adjournment of the House until Tuesday sevennight following.

The House returned him answer, that it was not the office of the Speaker to deliver any such command unto them, but for the adjournment of the House it did properly belong unto themselves, and after they had settled some things they thought fit and convenient to be spoken of they would satisfy the King.

The Speaker told them that he had an express command from the King as soon as he had delivered his message to rise; and upon that he left the Chair, but was by force drawn to it again by Mr. Denzil Holles, son of the Earl of Clare, Mr. Valentine, and others. And Mr. Holles, notwithstanding the endeavour of Sir Thomas Edmondes, Sir Humphrey May, and other Privy Councellors to free the Speaker from the Chair, swore, Gods wounds, he should sit still until they pleased to rise. . . .

Then they required Mr. Holles to read certain Articles as the Protestations of the House, which were jointly, as they were read, allowed with a loud *Yea* by the House. The effect of which Articles are as followeth:

First, Whosoever shall bring in innovation in Religion, or by favour or countenance, seek to extend or introduce Popery or Arminianism or other opinions disagreeing from the true and orthodox Church shall be reputed a capital enemy to this Kingdom and Commonwealth.

From W. Notestein and F. H. Relf, eds., *Commons Debates for 1629* (Minneapolis: University of Minnesota Press, 1921), pp. 101–106.

Secondly, Whosoever shall counsel or advise the taking and levying of the Subsidies of Tonnage and Poundage, not being granted by Parliament, or shall be an actor or instrument therein, shall be likewise reputed an innovator in the government, and a capital enemy to this Kingdom and Commonwealth.

Thirdly, If any merchant or person whatsoever shall voluntarily yield or pay the said subsidies of Tonnage and Poundage, not being granted by Parliament, he shall likewise be reputed a betrayer of the liberties of England and an enemy to the same.

These being read and allowed of, the House rose up after they had sitten down two hours.

The King hearing that the House continued to sit (notwithstanding his command for the adjourning thereof) sent a messenger for the serjeant with the mace, which being taken from the table there can be no further proceeding; but the serjeant was by the House stayed, and the key of the door taken from him, and given to a gentleman of the House to keep.

After this the King sent Maxwell with the black rod for the dissolution of Parliament, but being informed that neither he nor his message would be received by the House, the King grew into much rage and passion, and sent for the Captain of the Pensioners and Guard to force the door, but the rising of the House prevented the bloodshed that might have been spilt.

After this episode Charles ruled as an absolute king, without Parliament, for eleven years. But then a rebellion in Scotland forced him to summon another Parliament. This body enacted statutes outlawing all extraparliamentary taxation and requiring that Parliaments meet at least every three years in future. Charles accepted these measures. But the situation only worsened. A rebellion broke out in Ireland. The leaders of the Commons attacked Charles's religious policies and made more radical demands.

From *Petition Accompanying the Grand Remonstrance* (1641)

We, your most humble and obedient subjects, do with all faithfulness and humility beseech your Majesty,—

1. That you will be graciously pleased to concur with the humble desires of your people in a parliamentary way, for the preserving the peace and safety of the kingdom from the malicious designs of the Popish party:—

For depriving the Bishops of their votes in Parliament, and abridging their immoderate power usurped over the Clergy, and other your good subjects, which they have perniciously abused to the hazard of religion, and great prejudice and oppression of the laws of the kingdom, and just liberty of your people:—

For the taking away such oppressions in religion, Church government and discipline, as have been brought in and fomented by them:—

From S. R. Gardiner, ed., *The Constitutional Documents of the Puritan Revolution*, 2nd ed. (Oxford: Oxford University Press, 1899), pp. 204–205.

For uniting all such your loyal subjects together as join in the same fundamental truths against the Papists, by removing some oppressions and unnecessary ceremonies by which divers weak consciences have been scrupled, and
seem to be divided from the rest, and for the due execution of those good laws
which have been made for securing the liberty of your subjects.

2. That your Majesty will likewise be pleased to remove from your council
all such as persist to favour and promote any of those pressures and corruptions
wherewith your people have been grieved, and that for the future your Majesty
will vouchsafe to employ such persons in your great and public affairs, and to
take such to be near you in places of trust, as your Parliament may have cause
to confide in; that in your princely goodness to your people you will reject and
refuse all mediation and solicitation to the contrary, how powerful and near soever.

*This petition demanded, in effect, that Parliament control church policy and the appointment of
the king's ministers. But it passed by only eleven votes (159 to 148). The king still had substantial support in the House of Commons. But at this point Charles made a tactical blunder. He tried,
unsuccessfully, to arrest five leading members of the House, accusing them of treason.*

Case of the Five Members

And as his Majesty came through Westminster Hall, the Commanders, etc.,
that attended him made a lane on both sides the Hall (through which his
Majesty passed and came up the stairs to the House of Commons) and stood before the guard of Pensioners and Halbedeers (who also attended the king's person) and, the door of the House of Commons being thrown open, his Majesty
entered the House, and as he passed up towards the Chair he cast his eye on the
right hand near the Bar of the House, where Mr. Pym used to sit; but his Majesty
not seeing him there (knowing him well) went up to the Chair, and said, "By
your leave, Mr. Speaker, I must borrow your chair a little." Whereupon the
Speaker came out of the Chair and his Majesty stepped up into it; after he had
stood in the Chair a while, casting his eye upon the members as they stood up
uncovered, but could not discern any of the five members to be there, nor indeed were they easy to be discerned (had they been there) among so many bare
faces all standing up together. Then his Majesty made this speech.

"Gentlemen, I am sorry for this occasion of coming unto you. Yesterday I
sent a Serjeant at Arms upon a very important occasion, to apprehend some that
by my command were accused of high treason; whereunto I did expect obedience and not a message. And I must declare unto you here that, albeit no king
that ever was in England shall be more careful of your privileges, to maintain
them to the uttermost of his power, than I shall be; yet you must know that in
cases of treason no person hath a privilege. And therefore I am come to know if
any of these persons that were accused are here. For I must tell you, Gentlemen,
that so long as these persons that I have accused (for no light crime, but for treason) are here, I cannot expect that this House will be in the right way that I do

From John Rushworth, *Historical Collections* (London, 1721), Vol. 4, pp. 477–478.

heartily wish it. Therefore I am come to tell you that I must have them wheresoever I find them. Well, since I see all the birds are flown, I do expect from you that you shall send them unto me as soon as they return hither. But I assure you, on the word of a king, I never did intend any force, but shall proceed against them in a legal and fair way, for I never did intend any other.

"And now, since I cannot do what I came for, I think this no unfit occasion to repeat what I have said formerly, that whatsoever I have done in favor and to the good of my subjects, I do mean to maintain it.

"I will trouble you no more, but tell you I do expect as soon as they come to the House you will send them to me; otherwise I must take my own course to find them."

After this abortive attempt Parliament raised an army on its own authority, without royal consent, and civil war broke out.

Militia Ordinance

Whereas there hath been of late a most dangerous and desperate design upon the House of Commons, which we have just cause to believe to be an effect of the bloody counsels of Papists and other ill-affected persons, who have already raised a rebellion in the kingdom of Ireland; and by reason of many discoveries we cannot but fear they will proceed not only to stir up the like rebellion and insurrections in this kingdom of England, but also to back them with forces from abroad.

For the safety therefore of His Majesty's person, the Parliament and kingdom in this time of imminent danger.

It is ordained by the Lords and Commons now in Parliament assembled, that Henry Earl of Holland shall be Lieutenant of the County of Berks, Oliver Earl of Bolingbroke shall be Lieutenant of the County of Bedford, &c.

And shall severally and respectively have power to assemble and call together all and singular His Majesty's subjects, within the said several and respective counties and places, as well within liberties as without, that are meet and fit for the wars, and them to train and exercise and put in readiness, and them after their abilities and faculties well and sufficiently from time to time to cause to be arrayed and weaponed, and to take the muster of them in places most fit for that purpose.

A Royal Martyr?

By 1648 Charles was defeated. A majority of Parliament intended to retain him as king, though with limited powers. But the army generals were determined to put Charles on trial and execute him. In December 1648, the generals purged Parliament of all its more moderate members. Only about a hundred members were left, about a fifth of the original membership elected in 1641. This body enacted the following decree. How does it differ from previous parliamentary claims?

From S. R. Gardiner, ed., *The Constitutional Documents of the Puritan Revolution*, 2nd ed. (Oxford: Oxford University Press, 1899), pp. 245–246.

Declaration of Sovereignty

(Resolved) That the commons of England, in parliament assembled, do declare that the people are, under God, the original of all just power. And do also declare, that the commons of England, in parliament assembled, being chosen by and representing the people have the supreme power in this nation. And do also declare, that whatsoever is enacted, or declared for law, by the commons in parliament assembled, hath the force of a law; and all the people of this nation are concluded thereby, although the consent of king, or house of peers, be not had thereunto.

Act Establishing a Court to Try the King

Whereas it is notorious that Charles Stuart, the now King of England, not content with the many encroachments which his predecessors had made upon the people in their rights and freedom, hath had a wicked design totally to subvert the ancient and fundamental laws and liberties of this nation, and in their place to introduce an arbitrary and tyrannical government, and that besides all other evil ways and means to bring his design to pass, he hath prosecuted it with fire and sword, . . . be it enacted and ordained by the [Lords] and Commons in Parliament assembled, and it is hereby enacted and ordained by the authority thereof, that the Earls of Kent, Nottingham, Pembroke, Denbigh and Mulgrave, the Lord Grey of Wark, Lord Chief Justice Rolle of the King's Bench, Lord Chief Justice St. John of the Common Pleas, and Lord Chief Baron Wylde, the Lord Fairfax, Lieutenant-General Cromwell. &c. [in all about 150], shall be and are hereby appointed and required to be Commissioners and Judges for the hearing, trying and judging of the said Charles Stuart.

Charles prepared a speech in his own defense but was not allowed to deliver it at the trial. Both king and Parliament claimed to be defending the "old fundamental laws" of England. Was either claim justified?

Charles's Defense

Having already made my protestations, not only against the illegality of this pretended Court, but also, that no earthly power can justly call me (who am your King) in question as a delinquent, I would not any more open my mouth upon this occasion, more than to refer myself to what I have spoken, were I in this case alone concerned: but the duty I owe to God in the preservation of the true liberty of my people will not suffer me at this time to be silent: for, how can any free-born subject of England call life or anything he possesseth his own, if power without right daily make new, and abrogate the old fundamental laws of the land which I now take to be the present case? . . .

From W. Cobbett, *Parliamentary History of England* (London, 1868), Vol. 3, col. 1257.

From S. R. Gardiner, ed., *The Constitutional Documents of the Puritan Revolution,* 2nd ed. (Oxford: Oxford University Press, 1899), pp. 357–358.

From John Rushworth, *Historical Collections* (London, 1721), Vol. 7, pp. 1403–1404.

And admitting, but not granting, that the people of England's commission could grant your pretended power, I see nothing you can show for that; for certainly you never asked the question of the tenth man in the kingdom, and in this way you manifestly wrong even the poorest ploughman, if you demand not his free consent; nor can you pretend any colour for this your pretended commission, without the consent at least of the major part of every man in England of whatsoever quality or condition, which I am sure you never went about to seek, so far are you from having it. Thus you see that I speak not for my own right alone, as I am your King, but also for the true liberty of all my subjects, which consists, not in the power of government, but in living under such laws, such a government, as may give themselves the best assurance of their lives, and property of their goods; nor in this must or do I forget the privileges of both Houses of Parliament, which this day's proceedings do not only violate, but likewise occasion the greatest breach of their public faith that (I believe) ever was heard of. . . .

This I intended to speak in Westminster Hall on Monday, January 22, but against reason was hindered to show my reasons.

The Sentence

[He is author of the] unnatural, cruel, and bloody wars, and therein guilty of high treason, and of the murders, rapines, burnings, spoils, desolations, damage, and mischief to this nation acted and committed in the said war, and occasioned thereby. For all which treasons and crimes this Court doth adjudge that he, the said Charles Stuart, as a tyrant, traitor, murderer, and public enemy to the good people of this nation, shall be put to death by the severing of his head from his body.

[After the sentence was read], His Majesty then said, Will you hear me a word, Sir?

President of the Court. Sir, you are not to be heard after the sentence.

His Majesty. No, Sir?

President. No, Sir, by your favour, Sir. Guards, withdraw your prisoner.

His Majesty. I may speak after sentence, by your favour, Sir, I may speak after sentence, ever. By your favour, hold—I am not suffered to speak, expect what justice other people may have. . . .

On the scaffold Charles was finally allowed to speak.

Last Words

[As] for the people—truly I desire their liberty and freedom as much as anybody whosoever. But I must tell you that their liberty and freedom consists in

From John Rushworth, *Historical Collections* (London, 1721), Vol. 7, p. 1425.
From *England's Black Tribunal* (London, 1720).

having of government those laws by which their lives and goods may be most their own. It is not for having share in government. That is nothing pertaining to them. A subject and a sovereign are clean different things, and therefore, until they do that—I mean that you do put the people in that liberty as I say—certainly they will never enjoy themselves.

Sirs, it was for this that now I am come here. If I would have given way to an arbitrary way, for to have all laws changed according to the power of the sword, I needed not to have come here. And therefore I tell you (and I pray God it be not laid to your charge) that I am the martyr of the people.

RELIGION AND SOCIAL PROTEST

Radical Dissent

During the civil war period many new religious sects appeared. Sometimes they combined religious dissent with political radicalism. The Levelers argued for egalitarian democracy.

From *The Free-Man's Freedom Vindicated*

Adam . . . and . . . Eve . . . are the earthly original fountain of all and every particular and individual man and woman in the world since, who are, and were, by nature all equal and alike in power, dignity, authority, and majesty, none of them having by nature, dominion or magisterial power one over or above another; neither have they, or can they exercise any, but merely by institution or donation, or assumed by mutual consent and agreement. . . . And unnatural, irrational, sinful, wicked, unjust, devilish, and tyrannical, it is for any man whatsoever, spiritual or temporal, clergyman or layman, to appropriate and assume unto himself a power, authority, and jurisdiction to rule, govern or reign over any sort of man in the world without their free consent, and whosoever doth it . . . do thereby, as much as in them lies, endeavour to appropriate and assume unto themselves the office and sovereignty of God (who alone doth, and is to, rule by his will and pleasure) and to be like the Creator, which was the sin of the devils, not being content with their first station, would be like God, for which sin they were thrown down into Hell. . . .

Parliament claimed to rule in the name of "the people." But in seventeenth-century England only substantial property owners—perhaps ten percent of the male population—had the right to vote in parliamentary elections. The Leveler argument for a more democratic system was put forward in debates among the army leaders in 1647. How did Colonel Rainborough defend democracy? Why did General Ireton oppose it?

From John Lilbourne, *The Free-Mans Freedom Vindicated* (London, 1646).

From *The Army Debates (1647)*

Rainborough: . . . [R]eally I think that the poorest he that is in England hath a life to live, as the greatest he; and therefore truly, sir, I think it's clear, that every man that is to live under a government ought first by his own consent to put himself under that government; and I do think that the poorest man in England is not at all bound in a strict sense to that government that he hath not had a voice to put himself under; and I am confident that, when I have heard the reasons against it, something will be said to answer those reasons, insomuch that I should doubt whether he was an Englishman or no, that should doubt of these things.

Ireton: . . . Give me leave to tell you, that if you make this the rule I think you must fly for refuge to an absolute natural right, and you must deny all civil right; and I am sure it will come to that in the consequence. . . . For my part, I think it is no right at all. I think that no person hath a right to an interest or share in the disposing of the affairs of the kingdom, and in determining or choosing those that shall determine what laws we shall be ruled by here— no person hath a right to this, that hath not a permanent fixed interest in this kingdom, and those persons together are properly the represented of this kingdom, and consequently are [also][2] to make up the representers of this kingdom, who taken together do comprehend whatsoever is of real or per- manent interest in the kingdom. . . . We talk of birthright. Truly [by] birthright there is thus much claim. Men may justly have by birthright, by their very being born in England, that we should not seclude them out of England, that we should not refuse to give them air and place and ground, and the freedom of the highways and other things, to live amongst us. . . . That I think is due to a man by birth. But that by a man's being born here he shall have a share in that power that shall dispose of the lands here, and of all things here, I do not think it a sufficient ground. . . . Those that choose the representers for the making of laws by which this state and kingdom are to be governed, are the persons who, taken together, do comprehend the local interest of this kingdom; that is, the persons in whom all land lies, and those in corporations in whom all trading lies. This is the most fundamental con- stitution of this kingdom and [that] which if you do not allow, you allow none at all. This constitution hath limited and determined it that only those shall have voices in elections.

Rainborough: Truly, sir, I am of the same opinion I was, and am resolved to keep it till I know reason why I should not. . . . I do hear nothing at all that can convince me, why any man that is born in England ought not to have

[2]Words in brackets were supplied by the modern editor where the manuscript record of the de- bates is incomplete.
From A. S. P. Woodhouse, *Puritanism and Liberty. Being the Army Debates* (1647–9) (London: J. M. Dent and Sons Ltd., 1938), pp. 53–58.

his voice in election of burgesses. It is said that if a man have not a permanent interest, he can have no claim; and [that] we must be no freer than the laws will let us be, and that there is no [law in any] chronicle will let us be freer than that we [now] enjoy. Something was said to this yesterday. I do think that the main cause why Almighty God gave men reason, it was that they should make use of that reason, and that they should improve it for that end and purpose that God gave it them. . . . I think there is nothing that God hath given a man that any [one] else can take from him. And therefore I say, that either it must be the Law of God or the law of man that must prohibit the meanest man in the kingdom to have this benefit as well as the greatest. I do not find anything in the Law of God, that a lord shall choose twenty burgesses, and a gentleman but two, or a poor man shall choose none: I find no such thing in the Law of Nature, nor in the Law of Nations. But I do find that all Englishmen must be subject to English laws, and I do verily believe that there is no man but will say that the foundation of all law lies in the people. . . .

Ireton: . . . All the main thing that I speak for, is because I would have an eye to property. I hope we do not come to contend for victory—but let every man consider with himself that he do not go that way to take away all property. For here is the case of the most fundamental part of the constitution of the kingdom. . . . Now I wish we may all consider of what right you will challenge that all the people should have right to elections. Is it by the right of nature? If you will hold forth that as your ground, then I think you must deny all property too, and this is my reason. For thus: by that same right of nature (whatever it be) that you pretend, by which you can say, one man hath an equal right with another to the choosing of him that shall govern him—by the same right of nature, he hath the same [equal] right in any goods he sees—meat, drink, clothes—to take and use them for his sustenance. He hath a freedom to the land, [to take] the ground, to exercise it, till it; he hath the [same] freedom to anything that any one doth account himself to have any propriety in. Why now I say then, if you, against the most fundamental part of [the] civil constitution (which I have now declared), will plead the Law of Nature, that a man should (paramount [to] this, and contrary to this) have a power of choosing those men that shall determine what shall be law in this state, though he himself have no permanent interest in the state, [but] whatever interest he hath he may carry about with him—if this be allowed, [because by the right of nature] we are free, we are equal, one man must have as much voice as another, then show me what step or difference [there is], why [I may not] by the same right [take your property] . . .

Rainborough: . . . For my part, as I think, *you* forgot something that was in *my* speech, and you do not only yourselves believe that [some] men are inclining to anarchy, but you would make all men believe that. And, sir, to say because a man pleads that every man hath a voice [by right of nature], that therefore it destroys [by] the same [argument all property—this is to forget the Law of God]. That there's a property, the Law of God says it; else why [hath] God made that law, *Thou shalt not steal?* I am a poor man, therefore I must be [op]pressed: if I have no interest in the kingdom, I must suffer by all their laws be they right or wrong. . . . And therefore I think that to that it is fully answered: God hath set down that thing as to propriety with this law of his, *Thou shalt not steal.* And for my part I am against any such thought, and, as for yourselves, I wish you would not make the world believe that we are for anarchy.

Often the Levelers' argument was presented in fervid religious rhetoric.

From *A Fiery Flying Roll*

Thus saith the Lord: Be wise now therefore, O ye Rulers, &c. Be instructed, &c. . . . Yea, kisse Beggers, Prisoners, warme them, feed them, cloathe them, money them, relieve them, release them, take them into your houses, don't serve them as dogs without doore, &c.

Owne them, they are flesh of your flesh, your owne brethren, your owne Sisters, every whit as good (and if I should stand in competition with you) in some degrees better than your selves.

Once more, I say, owne them; they are your self, make them one with you, or else go howling into hell; howle for the miseries that are coming upon you, howle.

The very shadow of levelling, sword-levelling, man-levelling, frighted you, (and who, like your selves, can blame you, because it shook your Kingdome?) but now the substantiality of levelling is coming.

The Eternall God, the mightly Leveller is comming, yea come, even at the door; and what will you do in that day. . . .

The Diggers advocated a communistic utopia and began to dig up common lands to put their ideas into practice.

From Winstanley. *Letter to Lord Fairfax*

Our digging and ploughing upon George-hill in Surrey is not unknown to you, since you have seen some of our persons, and heard us speak in defence thereof: and we did receive mildness and moderation from you and your council of war both when some of us were at Whitehall before you and when you came in person to George-hill to view our works: we endeavour to lay open the bottom and intent of our business as much as can be, that none may be troubled with doubtful imaginations about us, but may be satisfied in the sincerity and universal righteousness of the work.

From Abiezer Coppe, *A Fiery Flying Roll* (London, 1649).
From *A Letter to the Lord Fairfax* (London: Giles Calvert, 1649).

We understand that our digging upon that common is the talk of the whole land; some approving, some disowning, some are friends filled with love, and sees the work intends good to the nation, the peace whereof is that which we seek after; others are enemies filled with fury, and falsely report of us that we have intent to fortify ourselves, and afterwards to fight against others and take away their goods from them, which is a thing we abhor: and many other slanders we rejoice over, because we know ourselves clear, our endeavour being no otherwise but to improve the commons, and to cast off that oppression and outward bondage which the creation groans under, as much as in us lies, and to lift up and preserve the purity thereof.

And the truth is, experience shows us that in this work of community in the earth, and in the fruits of the earth, is seen plainly a pitched battle between the lamb and the dragon, between the spirit of love, humility, and righteousness, which is the lamb appearing in flesh; and the power of envy, pride, and unrighteousness, which is the dragon appearing in flesh, the latter power striving to hold the creation under slavery, and to lock and hide the glory thereof from man: the former power labouring to deliver the creation from slavery, to unfold the secrets of it to the sons of men, and so to manifest himself to be the great restorer of all things.

And these two powers strive in the heart of every single man, and make single men to strive in opposition one against the other, and these strivings will be till the dragon be cast out, and his judgment and downfall hastens apace, therefore let the righteous hearts wait with patience upon the Lord, to see what end he makes of all the confused hurley-burleys of the world. . . .

A Digger Song (1649)

> You noble Diggers all, stand up now, stand up now,
> You noble Diggers all, stand up now,
>   The waste land to maintain, seeing Cavaliers by name
>   Your digging do disdain and persons all defame.
> Stand up now, stand up now.
> Your houses they pull down, stand up now, stand up now,
> Your houses they pull down, stand up now;
>   Your houses they pull down to fright poor men in town
>   But the gentry must come down, and the poor shall
>   wear the crown.
> Stand up now, Diggers all! . . .
> To conquer them by love, come in now, come in now,
> To conquer them by love, come in now;
>   To conquer them by love, as it does you behove,
>   For He is King above, no power is like to love.
> Glory *here,* Diggers all.

Parliamentary leaders and army generals had no sympathy with such extreme views. The Leveler and Digger movements were both suppressed.

From C. H. Firth, *Clarke Papers* (London: Camden Society, 1891–1901), Vol. 2, p. 221.

Women's Roles

This view of family structure comes from 1634. In what ways was the traditional role assigned to women challenged in the following years?

From *Domesticall Duties*

But what if a man of lewd and beastly conditions, as a drunkard, a glutton, a profane swaggerer, an impious swearer and blasphemer, be married to a wise, sober, religious matron, must she account him her superior and worthy of an husband's honor?

Surely she must. For the evil quality and disposition of his heart and life doth not deprive a man of that civil honor which God hath given unto him. Though an husband in regard of evil qualities may carry the image of the devil, yet in regard of his place and office, he beareth the Image of God: so do Magistrates in the Commonwealth, Ministers in the Church, Parents and Masters in the Family. Note for our present purpose, the exhortation of St Peter to Christian wives which have infidel husbands, 'Be in subjection to them: let your conversation be in fear'. If Infidels carry not the devil's image and are not, so long as they are Infidels, vassals of Satan, who are? Yet wives must be subject to them.

During the civil war some women were drawn into political activities. The following lines were written in a satirical vein by a Royalist.

From *Hudibras*

> Women, that were our first apostles,
> Without whose aid we'd all been lost else;
> Women, that left no stone unturned
> In which the Cause might be concerned;
> Brought in their children's spoons and whistles,
> To purchase swords, carbines and pistols. . . .
> What have they done, or what left undone,
> That might advance the Cause at London?
> Marched rank and file, with drum and ensign,
> T' entrench the City for defence in;
> Raised ramparts with their own soft hands,
>
> To put the enemy to stands;
> From ladies down to oyster-wenches
> Laboured like pioneers in trenches,
> Fell to their pickaxes and tools
> And helped the men to dig like moles.
> Have not the handmaids of the City

From William Goudge, *Of Domesticall Duties* (London, 1634), p. 274.
From Samuel Butler, *Hudibras*, ed. T. R. Nash (New York: D. Appleton and Company, 1847), pp. 245–247.

Chosen of their members a committee
For raising of a common purse
Out of their wages, to raise horse? . . .

In 1649 the Leveler John Lilbourne and three companions were arrested. A large group of London women petitioned for their release.

Women's Petition (1649)

The Humble Petition of divers well-affected women of the Cities of London and Westminster, etc. Sheweth, that since we are assured of our creation in the image of God, and of an interest in Christ equal unto men, as also of a proportional share in the freedoms of this Commonwealth, we cannot but wonder and grieve that we should appear so despicable in your eyes, as to be thought unworthy to petition or represent our grievances to this honorable House.

Have we not an equal interest with the men of this Nation, in those liberties and securities contained in the Petition of Right, and the other good laws of the land? Are any of our lives, limbs, liberties or goods to be taken from us more than from men, but by due process of law and conviction of twelve sworn men of the neighborhood?

And can you imagine us to be so sottish or stupid, as not to perceive, or not to be sensible when daily those strong defenses of our peace and welfare are broken down, and trod under foot by force and arbitrary power?

Would you have us keep at home in our houses, when men of such faithfulness and integrity as the FOUR PRISONERS our friends in the Tower are fetched out of their beds, and forced from their houses by soldiers, to the affrighting and undoing of themselves, their wives, children and families? Are not our husbands, ourselves, our children and families by the same rule as liable to the like unjust cruelties as they? . . . Doth not the Petition of Right declare that no person ought to be judged by Law Martial (except in time of war). . . ? And are we Christians and shall we sit still and keep at home, while such men as have borne continual testimony against the unjustice of all times, and unrighteousness of men, be picked out and delivered up to the slaughter . . . ?

No. . . . Let it be accounted folly, presumption . . . or whatsoever in us . . . we will never forsake them, nor ever cease to importune you . . . for justice . . . that we, our husbands, children, friends and servants may not be liable to be thus abused, violated and butchered at men's wills and pleasures. . . .

Some radical religious groups held that women could be preachers and ministers. Mary Cary was associated with the "Fifth Monarchy" sect. George Fox was the founder of the Quakers.

From Mary Cary. *The New Jerusalem's Glory*

And if there be very few men that are thus furnished with the gift of the Spirit; how few are the women! Not but that there are many godly women,

From J. O'Faolain and L. Martines, *Not in God's Image* (New York: Harper and Row, 1973), pp. 266–267.
From M. Cary, *The New Jerusalem's Glory* (London, 1656), p. 238.

many who have indeed received the Spirit: but in how small a measure is it? how weak are they? and how unable to prophesie? for it is that that I am speaking of, which this text says they shall do; which yet we see not fulfilled. . . . But the time is coming when this promise shall be fulfilled, and the Saints shall be abundantly filled with the spirit; and not only men, but women shall prophesie; not only aged men, but young men; not only superiours, but inferiours; not only those that have University learning, but those that have it not; even servants and handmaids.

From George Fox. *A Collection of . . . Epistles*

And there are Elder Women in the Truth, as well as Elder Men in the Truth; and these Women are to be teachers of good things; so they have an Office as well as the Men, for they have a Stewardship, and must give account of their Stewardship to the Lord, as well as the Men. Deborah was a judge; Miriam and Huldah were prophetesses; old Anna was a prophetess. . . . Mary Magdalene and the other Mary were the first preachers of Christ's Resurrection to the Disciples . . . they received the Command, and being sent, preached it: So is every Woman and Man to do, that sees him risen, and have the Command and Message. . . . And if the Unbelieving Husband is sanctified by the Believing Wife, then who is the Speaker, and who is the Hearer? Surely such a Woman is permitted to speak and to work the Works of God, and to make a Member in the Church; and then as an Elder, to oversee that they walk according to the Order of the Gospel.

What, are Women Priests? Yes, Women Priests. And can Men and Women offer Sacrifice without they wear the holy Garments? No: What are the holy Garments Men and Women must wear? . . . the Priest's Surplice? Nay. . . . It is the Righteousness of Christ . . . this is the Royal Garment of the Royal Priesthood, which everyone must put on, Men and Women.

The claim of women to play traditionally male roles in church affairs seemed to many people subversive of all established order and deserving of harsh punishment.

From *The Sufferings of the People Called Quakers*

The earliest account of the Sufferings of this People in Cambridgeshire bears Date in the same Month wherein Oliver Cromwell had assumed the Title of Protector, viz. in December, 1653, when Elizabeth Williams and Mary Fisher, the one about fifty and the other about thirty Years of Age, came from the North of England to Cambridge . . . Complaint was forthwith made to William Pickering, then Mayor, that two Women were preaching: He sent a Constable for them and examined them . . . He asked their Names: They replied, their Names were written in the Book of Life. He demanded their Husbands Names: They told him, they had no husband but Jesus Christ, and he sent them. Upon this the Mayor grew angry, called them

From J. O'Faolain and L. Martines, *Not in God's Image* (New York: Harper and Row, 1973), pp. 265–266.
From J. Besse, *A Collection of Sufferings of the People Called Quakers* (London; 1753), Vol. 1, pp. 84–85.

Whores, and issued his Warrant to the Constable to whip them at the Market-Cross until the Blood ran down their Bodies . . . The Executioner commanded them to put off their Clothes, which they refused. Then he stript them naked to the Waste, put their Arms into the Whippingpost, and executed the Mayor's Warrant far more cruelly than is usually done to the worst of malefactors, so that their Flesh was miserably cut and torn . . . and in the midst of their Punishment they sang and rejoiced, saying, "The Lord be blessed, the Lord be praised, who hath thus honoured us, and strengthened us thus to suffer for his Name's sake."

Even in such troubled times many people lived tranquil lives. Most females continued to carry out traditional roles; some young women made happy marriages. The letters of Dorothy Osborne, written from her father's country house, to William Temple, the young man she would eventually marry, remind us of this side of life. What was Dorothy Osborne's attitude to the political crises of the time?

From *Dorothy Osborne's Letters*

You ask me how I pass my time here. . . . I rise in the morning reasonably early, and before I am ready I go round the house till I am weary of that, and then into the garden till it grows too hot for me. About ten o'clock I think of making me ready, and when that's done I go into my father's chamber, from whence to dinner, where my cousin Molle and I sit in great state in a room, and at a table that would hold a great many more. . . . The heat of the day is spent in reading or working, and about six or seven o'clock I walk out into a common that lies hard by the house, where a great many young wenches keep sheep and cows, and sit in the shade singing of ballads. I go to them and compare their voices and beauties to some ancient shepherdesses that I have read of, and find a vast difference there; but, trust me, I think these are as innocent as those could be. I talk to them, and find they want nothing to make them the happiest people in the world but the knowledge that they are so. Most commonly when we are in the midst of our discourse, one looks about her, and spies her cows going into the corn, and then away they all run as if they had wings at their heels. . . . When I have supped, I go into the garden, and so to the side of a small river that runs by it, when I sit down and wish you were with me. . . .

I can assure you we are seldom without news, such as it is; and at this present we do abound with stories of my Lady Sunderland[3] and Mr. Smith; with what reverence he approaches her, and how like a gracious princess she receives him, that they say 'tis worth one's going twenty miles to see it. All our ladies are mightily pleased with the example, but I do not find that the men intend to follow it. . . .

Nothing can alter the resolution I have taken of settling my whole stock of happiness upon the affection of a person that is dear to me, whose kindness I shall infinitely prefer before any other consideration whatsoever, and I shall not blush to tell you that you have made the whole world besides so indifferent to

From E. A. Parry, ed., *Letters from Dorothy Osborne to Sir William Temple 1652–1654*, 3rd ed. (London: Griffith, Farren, Okeden and Welsh, 1888), pp. 37, 61, 80, 91, 100, 170, 290.
[3]Lady Sunderland was the sister of Algernon Sidney, a radical parliamentary leader.

me that, if I cannot be yours, they may dispose of me how they please. Henry Cromwell[4] will be as acceptable to me as any one else. . . .

[*The next letter refers to Oliver Cromwell's seizure of power in 1653 (see p. 438)*]

But, bless me, what will become of us all now? Is not this a strange turn? . . . Tell me what I must think on't; whether it be better or worse, or whether you are at all concern'd in't? For if you are not I am not, only if I had been so wise as to have taken hold of the offer was made me by Henry Cromwell, I might have been in a fair way of preferment, for, sure, they will be greater now than ever. Is it true that Algernon Sydney was so unwilling to leave the House, that the General was fain to take the pains to turn him out himself? Well, 'tis a pleasant world this. If Mr. Pim were alive again, I wonder what he would think of these proceedings, and whether this would appear so great a breach of the Privilege of Parliament as the demanding the 5 members? But I shall talk treason by and by if I do not look to myself. 'Tis safer talking of the orange-flower water you sent me. . . .

The less one knows of State affairs I find it is the better. My poor Lady Vavasour is carried to the Tower, and her great belly could not excuse her, because she was acquainted by somebody that there was a plot against the Protector, and did not discover it. She has told now all that was told her, but vows she will never say from whence she had it. . . .

I have sent you my picture because you wished for it; but, pray, let it not presume to disturb my Lady Sunderland's. Put it in some corner where no eyes may find it out but yours, to whom it is only intended. 'Tis not a very good one, but the best I shall ever have drawn of me; for, as my Lady says, my time for pictures is past, and therefore I have always refused to part with this, because I was sure the next would be a worse. There is a beauty in youth that every one has once in their lives; and I remember my mother used to say there was never anybody (that was not deformed) but were handsome, to some reasonable degree, once between fourteen and twenty. It must hang with the light on the left hand of it; and you may keep it if you please till I bring you the original.

[*Dorothy lived contentedly with her husband for forty years. But she experienced two misfortunes typical of the hazards of seventeenth-century life. Just before her marriage she suffered a severe attack of smallpox which left her face permanently disfigured. Later she had six children, but only one of them lived to maturity.*]

OLIVER CROMWELL AND THE INTERREGNUM

War and Religion

During the civil war Oliver Cromwell emerged as the most brilliant general on the parliamentary side. After the execution of the king he became the effective ruler of the country,

---

[4]Dorothy's father had been a royalist commander, but this did not discourage Henry Cromwell, the second son of Oliver Cromwell, from becoming one of her suitors.

with his power resting on the support of the army. What impressions of his personality and attitudes to religion are conveyed in the following excerpts?

From *Cromwell's Letters and Speeches*

[*On army officers, 1645*]

I had rather have a plain russet-coated captain that knows what he fights for, and loves what he knows, than that which you call a gentleman and is nothing else. I honour a gentleman that is so indeed.

[*On the battle of Naseby, 1645*]

Sir, this is none other but the hand of God; and to Him alone belongs the glory, wherein none are to share with Him. The General [Fairfax] served you with all faithfulness and honour: and the best commendations I can give him is, that I dare say he attributes all to God, and would rather perish than assume to himself. Which is an honest and a thriving way, and yet as much for bravery may be given to him, in this action, as to a man.

[*On tolerance, 1645*]

Presbyterians, Independents, all had here the same spirit of faith and prayer; the same pretence and answer; they agree here, know no names of difference: pity it is it should be otherwise anywhere. All that believe, have the real unity, which is most glorious, because inward and spiritual, in the Body, and to the Head. As for being united in forms, commonly called Uniformity, every Christian will for peace-sake study and do, as far as conscience will permit; and from brethren, in things of the mind we look for no compulsion, but that of light and reason.

[*On Catholics, 1650*]

For that which you mention concerning liberty of conscience, I meddle not with any man's conscience. But if by liberty of conscience, you mean a liberty to exercise the Mass, I judge it best to use plain dealing, and to let you know, Where the Parliament of England have power, that will not be allowed of.

[*On the massacre at Drogheda (Ireland), 1649*]

. . . The enemy retreated, divers of them, into the Mill-Mount: a place very strong and of difficult access, being exceedingly high, having a good graft, and strongly palisadoed. The Governor, Sir Arthur Ashton, and divers considerable Officers being there, our men getting up to them, were ordered by me to put them all to the sword. And indeed, being in the heat of action, I forbade them to spare any that were in arms in the town, and, I think, that night they put to the sword about 2,000 men, divers of the officers and soldiers being fled over the Bridge into the other part of the Town, where about one hundred of them

From Thomas Carlyle, ed., *The Letters and Speeches of Oliver Cromwell,* 3 vols. (New York: G. P. Putnam's Sons, 1904), Vol. 1, pp. 154, 204, 218, 468–469, Vol. 2, p. 15.

possessed St. Peter's church-steeple, some the west gate, and others a strong round tower next the gate called St. Sunday's. These being summoned to yield to mercy, refused, whereupon I ordered the steeple of St. Peter's Church to be fired, where one of them was heard to say in the midst of the flames: "God damn me, God confound me; I burn, I burn."

The next day, the other two towers were summoned, in one of which was about six or seven score; but they refused to yield themselves, and we knowing that hunger must compel them, set only good guards to secure them from running away until their stomachs were come down. From one of the said towers, notwithstanding their condition, they killed and wounded some of our men. When they submitted, their officers were knocked on the head, and every tenth man of the soldiers killed, and the rest shipped for the Barbadoes. The soldiers in the other tower were all spared, as to their lives only, and shipped likewise for the Barbadoes.

I am persuaded that this is a righteous judgment of God upon these barbarous wretches, who have imbrued their hands in so much innocent blood; and that it will tend to prevent the effusion of blood for the future, which are the satisfactory grounds to such actions, which otherwise cannot but work remorse and regret.

Social Legislation

Cromwell's military government enforced a substantial body of Puritan social legislation. What "vices" did the Puritans try to suppress?

From *Acts and Ordinances*

Whereas the Acts of Stage-Plays, Interludes, and common Playes, condemned by ancient Heathens, and much less to be tolerated amongst Professors of the Christian Religion is the occasion of many and sundry great vices and disorders, tending to the high provocation of Gods wrath and displeasure . . . It is ordered and ordained . . . That all Stage-players and Players of Interludes and common Playes, are hereby declared to be, and are, and shall be taken to be Rogues, and punishable, within the Statutes of the thirty ninth year of the Reign of Queen Elizabeth, and the seventh year of the Reign of King James.

And because the prophanation of the Lords-day hath been heretofore greatly occasioned by May-Poles, (a Heathenish vanity, generally abused to superstition and wickedness.) The Lords and Commons do further Order and Ordain, That all and singular May-Poles, that are, or shall be erected, shall be taken down and removed. . . .

And be it further Enacted by the authority aforesaid, That if any man shall from and after the Four and twentieth day of June aforesaid, have the carnal knowledge of the body of any Virgin, unmaried Woman or Widow, every such

From C. H. Firth and R. S. Rait, eds., *Acts and Ordinances of the Interregnum* (London: His Majesty's Stationery Office, 1911), Vol. 1, p. 421, Vol. 2, pp. 385, 388, 861.

man so offending . . . as also every such woman so offending . . . shall for every such offence be committed to the common Gaol, without Bail or Mainprize, there to continue for the space of three Months. . . .

And it is further Enacted and Declared, That every person and persons which upon the said Lords Day, days of Humiliation or Thanksgiving, shall be in any Tavern, Inn, Alehouse, Tobacco-house or Shop, or Victualling-house (unless he lodge there, or be there upon some lawful or necessary occasion) . . . and every person or persons which upon the said days shall be dancing, prophanely singing, drinking, or tipling in any Tavern, Inn, Alehouse, Victualling-house, or Tobacco-house or Shop, or shall harbor or entertain any person or persons so offending; or which shall grinde or cause to be ground in any Mill, any Corn or Grain upon any the said days, except in case of necessity, to be allowed by a Justice of the Peace, every such Offender shall forfeit and pay the sum of ten shillings for every such offence, to be levied as aforesaid.

Whereas the Publique Meetings and Assemblies of People together in divers parts of this Nation, under pretence of Matches for Cock-Fighting, are by experience found to tend many times to the disturbance of the Publique Peace, and are commonly accompanied with Gaming, Drinking, Swearing, Quarreling, and other dissolute Practices, to the Dishonor of God, and do often produce the ruine of Persons and their Families; For prevention thereof, Be it ordained by His Highness the Lord Protector, by and with the Advice and Consent of His Council, That from henceforth there shall be no Publique or Set-meetings or Assemblies of any persons within England or Wales, upon Matches made for Cock-Fighting. . . .

Authority and Consent

Cromwell set out to defend the rights of Parliament against the king. But he could not accept parliamentary control of his policies any more than Charles could. In 1653 Cromwell dismissed the remnant, or "rump," of the Long Parliament and began to rule as a military dictator. Although he later experimented with several types of assemblies, he never created a representative assembly that could legitimize his power.

Dismissal of the Rump Parliament

Calling to Major-General Harrison, who was on the other side of the House, to come to him, he told him, that he judged the Parliament ripe for a dissolution, and this to be the time of doing it. The Major-General answered, as he since told me, "Sir, the work is very great and dangerous, therefore I desire you seriously to consider of it before you engage in it." "You say well," replied the General, and thereupon sat still for about a quarter of an hour; and then the question for passing the Bill being to be put, he said again to Major-General Harrison, "this is the time I must do it"; and suddenly standing up, made a speech, wherein he loaded the Parliament with the vilest reproaches, charging them not to have a

From C. H. Firth, *The Memoirs of Edmund Ludlow* (Oxford: Oxford University Press, 1894), Vol. 1, pp. 352–354.

heart to do any thing for the publick good, to have espoused the corrupt interest of Presbytery and the lawyers, who were the supporters of tyranny and oppression, accusing them of an intention to perpetuate themselves in power, had they not been forced to the passing of this Act, which he affirmed they designed never to observe, and thereupon told them, that the Lord had done with them, and had chosen other instruments for the carrying on his work that were more worthy. This he spoke with so much passion and discomposure of mind, as if he had been distracted. Sir Peter Wentworth stood up to answer him, and said, that this was the first time that ever he had heard such unbecoming language given to the Parliament, and that it was the more horrid in that it came from their servant, and their servant whom they had so highly trusted and obliged: but as he was going on, the General stept into the midst of the House, where continuing his distracted language, he said, "Come, come, I will put an end to your prating"; then walking up and down the House like a madman, and kicking the ground with his feet, he cried out, "You are no Parliament, I say you are no Parliament; I will put an end to your sitting; call them in, call them in": whereupon the serjeant attending the Parliament opened the doors, and Lieutenant-Colonel Worsley with two files of musqueteers entered the House; which Sir Henry Vane observing from his place, said aloud,"This is not honest, yea it is against morality and common honesty." Then Cromwell fell a railing at him, crying out with a loud voice, "O Sir Henry Vane, Sir Henry Vane, the lord deliver me from Sir Henry Vane." Then looking upon one of the members, he said, "There sits a drunkard"; and giving much reviling language to others, he commanded the mace to be taken away, saying, "What shall we do with this bauble? here, take it away." Having brought all into this disorder, Major-General Harrison went to the Speaker as he sat in the chair, and told him, that seeing things were reduced to this pass, it would not be convenient for him to remain there. The Speaker answered, that he would not come down unless he were forced. "Sir," said Harrison, "I will lend you my hand"; and thereupon putting his hand within his, the Speaker came down. Then Cromwell applied himself to the members of the House, who were in number between 80 and 100, and said to them, "It's you that have forced me to this, for I have sought the Lord night and day, that he would rather slay me than put me upon the doing of this work."

The following account concerns a man who refused to pay a tax levied by Cromwell without Parliament's consent.

From *Clarendon's History*

Maynard, who was of counsel with the prisoner, demanded his liberty with great confidence, both upon the illegality of the commitment, and the illegality of the imposition, as being laid without any lawful authority. The judges could not maintain or defend either, but enough declared what their sentence would be; and therefore the Protector's Attorney required a farther day to answer what

From Lord Clarendon, *The History of the Rebellion and Civil Wars in England* (Oxford: Oxford University Press, 1839), Vol. 6, pp. 351–352.

had been urged. Before that day, Maynard was committed to the Tower, for presuming to question or make doubt of his authority; and the judges were sent for, and severely reprehended for suffering that license; and when they with all humility mentioned the law and *Magna Charta*, Cromwell told them, their *magna farta* should not control his actions, which he knew were for the safety of the commonwealth. He asked them who made them judges; [whether] they had any authority to sit there but what he gave them; and that if his authority were at an end, they knew well enough what would become of themselves; and therefore advised them to be more tender of that which could only preserve them; and so dismissed them with caution, that they should not suffer the lawyers to prate what it would not become them to hear.

Ludlow was a parliamentary general who regarded Cromwell as a usurper.

From *Ludlow's Memoirs*

Then I drew near to the council-table, where Cromwell charged me with dispersing treasonable books in Ireland, and with endeavouring to render the officers of the army disaffected, by discoursing to them concerning new models of Government. I acknowledged that I had caused some papers to be dispersed in Ireland, but denied that they justly could be called treasonable. . . .

'You do well,' said he, 'to reflect on our fears . . . I now require you to give assurance not to act against the Government.' I desired to be excused in that particular, reminding him of the reasons I had formerly given him for my refusal, adding, that I was in his power, and that he might use me as he thought fit. 'Pray then,' said he, 'what is it that you would have? May not every man be as good as he will? What can you desire more than you have?' 'It were easy,' said I, 'to tell what we would have.' 'What is that, I pray?' said he. 'That which we fought for,' said I, 'that the nation might be governed by its own consent.' 'I am,' said he, 'as much for a government by consent as any man; but where shall we find that consent? Amongst the Prelatical, Presbyterian, Independent, Anabaptist, or Leveling Parties?' I answered, 'Amongst those of all sorts who had acted with fidelity and affection to the publick.'

Cromwell's Deathbed Prayer

Lord, though I am a miserable and wretched creature, I am in Covenant with Thee through grace. And I may, I will, come to Thee for Thy People. Thou hast made me, though very unworthy, a mean instrument to do them some good, and Thee service; and many of them have set too high a value upon me, though others wish and would be glad of my death. Lord, however Thou do dispose of me, continue and go on to do good for them. Give them consistency of

From C. H. Firth, *The Memoirs of Edmund Ludlow* (Oxford: Oxford University Press, 1894), Vol. 2, pp. 10–11.
From Thomas Carlyle, ed., *The Letters and Speeches of Oliver Cromwell*, 3 vols. (New York: G. P. Putnam's Sons, 1904), Vol. 3, p. 217.

judgment, one heart, and mutual love. And go on to deliver them, and with the work of reformation; and make the Name of Christ glorious in the world. Teach those who look too much on Thy instruments to depend more upon Thyself. Pardon such as desire to trample upon the dust of a poor worm, for they are Thy people too. And pardon the folly of this short Prayer: Even for Jesus Christ's sake. And give us a good night, if it be Thy pleasure. Amen.

A Royalist View

From *Clarendon's History*

He was one of those men, *quos vituperare ne inimici quidem possunt, nisi ut simul laudent;* [whom his very enemies could not condemn without commending him at the same time:] for he could never have done half that mischief without great parts of courage, industry, and judgment. He must have had a wonderful understanding in the natures and humours of men, and as great a dexterity in applying them; who, from a private and obscure birth, (though of a good family,) without interest or estate, alliance or friendship, could raise himself to such a height, and compound and knead such opposite and contradictory tempers, humours, and interests into a consistence, that contributed to his designs, and to their own destruction; whilst himself grew insensibly powerful enough to cut off those by whom he had climbed, in the instant that they projected to demolish their own building. What Velleius Paterculus said of Cinna may very justly be said of him, *ausum eum, quæ nemo auderet bonus; perfecisse, quæ a nullo, nisi fortissimo, perfici possent:* [he attempted those things which no good man durst have ventured on; and achieved those in which none but a valiant and great man could have succeeded.] Without doubt, no man with more wickedness ever attempted any thing, or brought to pass what he desired more wickedly, more in the face and contempt of religion, and moral honesty; yet wickedness as great as his could never have accomplished those trophies, without the assistance of a great spirit, an admirable circumspection and sagacity, and a most magnanimous resolution.

FROM RESTORATION TO REVOLUTION

After the death of Cromwell most English people welcomed a return to the traditional form of government by king and Parliament.

Restoration

John Evelyn (1620–1706), a prominent public servant under Charles II, left a diary that provides many insights into the social and political life of his time.

From Lord Clarendon, *The History of the Rebellion and Civil Wars in England* (Oxford: Oxford University Press, 1839), Vol. 6, pp. 349–350.

From *John Evelyn's Diary*

May 29, 1666   This day, his Majesty, Charles the Second came to London, after a sad and long exile and calamitous suffering both of the King and Church, being seventeen years. This was also his birthday, and with a triumph of above 20,000 horse and foot, brandishing their swords, and shouting with inexpressible joy; the ways strewed with flowers, the bells ringing, the streets hung with tapestry, fountains running with wine; the Mayor, Aldermen, and all the Companies, in their liveries, chains of gold, and banners; Lords and Nobles, clad in cloth of silver, gold, and velvet; the windows and balconies, all set with ladies; trumpets, music, and myriads of people flocking, even so far as from Rochester, so as they were seven hours in passing the city, even from two in the afternoon till nine at night.

The "Glorious Revolution"

How do Evelyn's comments on James II help explain the failure of the king's reign?

From *John Evelyn's Diary*

June 25, 1686   Now his Majesty, beginning with Dr. Sharp and Tully, proceeded to silence and suspend divers excellent divines for preaching against Popery.

November 29, 1686   I went to hear the music of the Italians in the new chapel, now first opened publicly at Whitehall for the Popish Service. . . . The throne where the King and Queen sit is very glorious, in a closet above, just opposite to the altar. Here we saw the Bishop in his mitre and rich copes, with six or seven Jesuits and others in rich copes, sumptuously habited, often taking off and putting on the Bishop's mitre, who sat in a chair with arms pontifically, was adored and censed by three Jesuits in their copes. . . . I could not have believed I should ever have seen such things in the King of England's palace, after it had pleased God to enlighten this nation; but our great sin has, for the present, eclipsed the blessing, which I hope He will in mercy and His good time restore to its purity.

February 3, 1687   Most of the great officers, both in the court and country, Lords and others, were dismissed, as they would not promise his Majesty their consent to the repeal of the test and penal statutes against Popish Recusants.

June 10, 1688   A young Prince born, which will cause disputes.

About two o'clock, we heard the Tower-ordnance discharged, and the bells ring for the birth of a Prince of Wales. This was very surprising, it having been universally given out that her Majesty did not look till the next month.

September 30, 1688   The Court in so extraordinary a consternation, on assurance of the Prince of Orange's intention to land, that the writs sent forth for a Parliament were recalled.

October 7, 1688   In the mean time, [the king] called over 5,000 Irish, and 4,000 Scots, and continued to remove Protestants and put in Papists at Portsmouth and other places of trust, and retained the Jesuits about him, in-

From *Diary of John Evelyn*, ed. W. Bray, 4 vols. (London: Henry G. Bohn, 1862), Vol. 1, p. 365, Vol. 2, pp. 265, 273, 286, 291, 295–297.

creasing the universal discontent. It brought people to so desperate a pass, that they seemed passionately to long for and desire the landing of that Prince, whom they looked on to be their deliverer from Popish tyranny, praying incessantly for an east wind, which was said to be the only hindrance of his expedition with a numerous army ready to make a descent. To such a strange temper, and unheard-of in former times, was this poor nation reduced, and of which I was an eye-witness.

November 5, 1688   I went to London; heard the news of the Prince having landed at Torbay, coming with a fleet of near 700 sail, passing through the Channel with so favourable a wind, that our navy could not intercept, or molest them. . . .

These are the beginnings of sorrow, unless God in His mercy prevent it by some happy reconciliation of all dissensions among us. This, in all likelihood, nothing can effect except a free Parliament; but this we cannot hope to see, whilst there are any forces on either side. I pray God to protect and direct the King for the best and truest interest of his people!

December 18, 1688   I saw the King take barge to Gravesend at twelve o'clock—a sad sight! The Prince comes to St. James's and fills Whitehall with Dutch guards. A Council of Peers meet about an expedient to call a Parliament; adjourn to the House of Lords. The Chancellor, Earl of Peterborough, and divers others taken. . . .

All the world go to see the Prince at St. James's, where there is a great Court. There I saw him, and several of my acquaintance who came over with him. He is very stately, serious, and reserved.

The convention Parliament that transferred power to William and Mary also formulated a Bill of Rights. How would it limit the power of future kings?

From *The Bill of Rights (1689)*

Whereas the said late King James II having abdicated the government, and the throne being thereby vacant, his Highness the prince of Orange (whom it hath pleased Almighty God to make the glorious instrument of delivering this kingdom from popery and arbitrary power) did (by the advice of the lords spiritual and temporal, and diverse principal persons of the Commons) cause letters to be written to the lords spiritual and temporal, being Protestants, and other letters to the several counties, cities, universities, boroughs, and Cinque Ports, for the choosing of such persons to represent them, as were of right to be sent to parliament, to meet and sit at Westminster upon the two and twentieth day of January, in this year 1689, in order to such an establishment as that their religion, laws, and liberties might not again be in danger of being subverted; upon which letters elections have been accordingly made.

And thereupon the said lords spiritual and temporal and Commons, pursuant to their respective letters and elections, being now assembled in a full and free representation of this nation, taking into their most serious consideration

From *The Statutes: Revised Edition* (London: Eyre and Spottiswoode, 1871), Vol. 2, pp. 10–12.

the best means for attaining the ends aforesaid, do in the first place (as their ancestors in like case have usually done), for the vindication and assertion of their ancient rights and liberties, declare:

1. That the pretended power of suspending laws, or the execution of laws, by regal authority, without consent of parliament is illegal.

2. That the pretended power of dispensing with the laws, or the execution of law by regal authority, as it hath been assumed and exercised of late, is illegal.

3. That the commission for erecting the late court of commissioners for ecclesiastical causes, and all other commissions and courts of like nature, are illegal and pernicious.

4. That levying money for or to the use of the crown by pretense of prerogative, without grant of parliament, for longer time or in other manner than the same is or shall be granted, is illegal.

5. That it is the right of the subjects to petition the king, and all commitments and prosecutions for such petitioning are illegal.

6. That the raising or keeping a standing army within the kingdom in time of peace, unless it be with consent of parliament, is against law.

7. That the subjects which are Protestants may have arms for their defense suitable to their conditions, and as allowed by law.

8. That election of members of parliament ought to be free.

9. That the freedom of speech, and debates or proceedings in parliament, ought not to be impeached or questioned in any court or place out of parliament.

10. That excessive bail ought not to be required, nor excessive fines imposed, nor cruel and unusual punishments inflicted.

11. That jurors ought to be duly impaneled and returned, and jurors which pass upon men in trials for high treason ought to be freeholders.

12. That all grants and promises of fines and forfeitures of particular persons before conviction are illegal and void.

13. And that for redress of all grievances, and for the amending, strengthening, and preserving of the laws, parliament ought to be held frequently.

And they do claim, demand, and insist upon all and singular the premises, as their undoubted rights and liberties. . . .

Having therefore an entire confidence that his said Highness the prince of Orange will perfect the deliverance so far advanced by him, and will still preserve them from the violation of their rights, which they have here asserted, and from all other attempt upon their religion, rights, and liberties:

The said lords spiritual and temporal, and commons, assembled at Westminster, do resolve that William and Mary, prince and princess of Orange, be, and be declared, king and queen of England, France, and Ireland. . . .

Upon which their said Majesties did accept the crown and royal dignity of the kingdoms of England, France, and Ireland, and the dominions thereunto belonging, according to the resolution and desire of the said lords and commons contained in the said declaration.

About the Authors

After serving in the Royal Air Force, Brian Tierney received his B.A. and Ph.D. from Cambridge University. He has taught at Catholic University, Washington, D.C., and at Cornell, where he is now Bryce and Edith M. Bowmar Professor in Humanistic Studies Emeritus. He has been the recipient of Guggenheim Fellowships and of fellowships from the American Council of Learned Societies and the National Endowment for the Humanities. Professor Tierney has been awarded the honorary degrees of Doctor of Theology by Uppsala University, Sweden, and Doctor of Humane Letters by Catholic University. A specialist in medieval church history, he has published many articles and several books, among them *Foundations of the Conciliar Theory; Medieval Poor Law;* and *Origins of Papal Infallibility, 1150–1350.* He is coeditor with Donald Kagan and L. Pearce Williams of *Great Issues in Western Civilization.* His most recent work is *The Idea of Natural Rights, 1150–1625.*

Joan W. Scott received her Ph.D. in history from the University of Wisconsin. She has taught at the University of Illinois at Chicago Circle, Northwestern University, the University of North Carolina at Chapel Hill, and Brown University, where she is currently Nancy Duke Lewis University Professor and professor of history. She also is director of Brown's Pembroke Center for Teaching and Research on Women. Professor Scott has held fellowships from the Social Science Research Council, the National Endowment for the Humanities, and the American Council of Learned Societies. She has directed seminars for college teachers sponsored by the National Endowment for the Humanities and has served as a consultant for projects in labor history and women's history. Her fields of research are nineteenth-century French social history and European women's history. She has written numerous articles on both topics and was awarded a prize by the Berkshire Conference of Women Historians for "Women's Work and the Family in Nineteenth Century Europe," coauthored with Louise Tilly. She is author of *The Glassworkers of Carmaux: French Craftsmen and Political Action in a Nineteenth Century City,* which won the American Historical Association's Herbert Baxter Adams prize in 1974. She is coauthor, with Louise Tilly, of *Women, Work and Family.* Her most recent books are *Gender and the Politics of History* (which won the Joan Kelly Prize of The American Historical Association) and *Only Pardoxes to Offer: French Feminists and the Rights of Man.*